Sports Sponsoring

Manfred Bruhn · Peter Rohlmann

Sports Sponsoring

Requirements and Practical Examples for Successful Partnerships

Springer

Manfred Bruhn
Universität Basel
Basel, Switzerland

Peter Rohlmann
PR MARKETING
Rheine, Germany

ISBN 978-3-658-44170-8 ISBN 978-3-658-44171-5 (eBook)
https://doi.org/10.1007/978-3-658-44171-5

This book is a translation of the original German edition "Sportsponsoring" by Manfred Bruhn, published by Springer Fachmedien Wiesbaden GmbH in 2024. The translation was done with the help of an artificial intelligence machine translation tool. A subsequent human revision was done primarily in terms of content, so that the book will read stylistically differently from a conventional translation. Springer Nature works continuously to further the development of tools for the production of books and on the related technologies to support the authors.

Translation from the German language edition: "Sportsponsoring" by Manfred Bruhn and Peter Rohlmann,

This Springer imprint is published by the registered company Springer Fachmedien Wiesbaden GmbH, part of Springer Nature.
The registered company address is: Abraham-Lincoln-Str. 46, 65189 Wiesbaden, Germany

Paper in this product is recyclable.

Preface

In marketing, sponsoring is considered a very successful tool for effectively and efficiently achieving certain marketing and communication goals. This success story has also been significantly shaped by the repeated new editions of the basic work "sponsoring" by Manfred Bruhn, first published in 1987. Already in the last edition of the constantly revised and expanded work on the systematic planning and integrative use of sponsoring, more space was given to its areas of application in sports, culture, the environment, social issues, and the media.

The last edition of the book by

Manfred Bruhn: Sponsoring. Systematic Planning and Integrative Use, 6th Edition, Wiesbaden 2018

will not be continued in its previous form. The areas of application have differentiated so much in sponsoring that it seems necessary to write separate treatises on the different forms. This will begin with the present book on "sports sponsoring" and is intended to continue later with "cultural sponsoring", etc. This, as well as a two-author team, who bring their expertise to the individual special titles, can take into account the peculiarities of the areas of application. As far as "sports sponsoring" is concerned, Manfred Bruhn from the scientific-conceptual side and Peter Rohlmann from the practice-oriented side will jointly address the topic.

Overall, sponsoring has long been established as a fixed component in the communication mix of companies and is indispensable from the communication strategy of many companies. It often no longer functions as a purely supportive communication tool, but is consciously used by companies for profiling in communication competition. In particular, in the conceptual sponsoring work and the integrative linking of sponsoring with other communication tools, there have been far-reaching advances in knowledge recently, which are also taken into account in this book.

However, the sponsoring market is not exclusively characterized by positive developments. Political and economic crises, as well as pandemics, have not spared this industry. While growth can still be expected in some selected sponsoring areas such as sports sponsoring due to attractive sporting events, the future development of socio-environmental sponsoring and culture and media sponsoring depends on global economic and ecological influencing factors and remains to be seen. At the same time, it is becoming increasingly difficult to generally assess where a sponsoring commitment actually promises success. Thus, all forms of sponsoring offer interesting niches and open up opportunities for company-specific sponsoring concepts. The fact that the creativity, innovative strength, and initiative of the companies are more in demand than ever before is beyond doubt. This also applies to sports sponsoring, which makes up the largest share of the entire sponsoring market.

In a modern society, sports, with all its facets, plays a central role. This applies both privately and to the wider public. Similarly, sports as a business platform for entrepreneurial purposes has become increasingly important. From an economic perspective, sports sponsoring offers a unique opportunity to reach a specific target group relatively quickly and effectively, and to use this for the sale of own products and services. In sports sponsoring, providers and demanders of sponsoring rights face each other, with a real competition for exclusive partnerships due to limited availability and sometimes exploding costs in many cases.

While attractive sponsoring offers are a "must" for professional sports operations at all levels, this opportunity for improved revenue situations is also increasingly being used in amateur and mass sports. Especially through the allocation of larger financial resources by the economy, sponsoring combinations occasionally occur from organizations unrelated to the economy (e.g., governmental agencies and state-related institutions), which are partly seen as critical, partly even as dangerous for sports. This can be further potentiated, as the host locations for major sporting events are under strong political influence, which can also have effects on the sponsoring participants.

In-depth knowledge in sports sponsoring enables sports actors to successfully market their sports, their association, their league, their team, their players, their sports venue, or their event, thus creating competitive advantages. In the course of societal and economic development, sports sponsoring has evolved from small beginnings into a highly professional and complex marketing tool that not only affects those directly involved, but also has to include interest groups far from marketing objectives with their own intentions and interests. In addition, societal and general development trends such as digitization and globalization constantly present new challenges to sports sponsoring.

Our book is equally aimed at students and practitioners. For students, it primarily aims to provide an understanding of the classification of sports sponsoring in the marketing and communication mix of companies, and at the same time help to bring them closer to the perspective of those responsible for sponsoring in companies. With this book, we also want to address practitioners, including companies driving sports sponsoring and sponsored parties, as well as agencies and media, and provide assistance in developing successful strategies for sports sponsoring.

The present book delves into the fundamental prerequisites of sports sponsoring and outlines manifestations, initial conditions, targets, and strategy development, as well as concrete implementation measures. Thus, it creates basic knowledge and understanding for successful sports sponsoring. In fifteen chapters, not only is a systematic approach for professional sports sponsoring laid out, it is also clarified with concrete market data and numerous illustrations, and summarized in the form of subject-specific key points. Numerous examples and case studies from practice illustrate what successful sports sponsoring can look like, and provide concrete suggestions for its implementation in everyday life.

The structure of the book is oriented around the individual phases of analysis, planning, implementation, and control of sponsoring concepts. As an introduction to the classification of sponsoring as an element of sports marketing and the different forms of sports sponsoring, the planning process with its individual phases is presented. Building on this, the situation analysis, goal setting, target group planning, strategic orientation, budgeting, selection of sponsorings, integration into the communication and sponsoring mix, design of sponsorings, success control, legal aspects, services of sports agencies, and trends in the use of sports sponsoring are the subject of a detailed treatment. In a concluding chapter, the 2022 Football World Cup is used as an occasion to highlight the critical points of contention in the discussion about sports sponsoring of major events. The question of consequences for upcoming sporting events is also raised. The chapter is intended to contribute to the current discussion of the Football World Cup and will not be represented in future new editions.

In order to not only propagate a noticeable practical relevance, but also to have it substantiated by experts, the authors have agreed on a cooperation with the sponsoring association S20 regarding the inclusion of case studies in the book. The S20—The Sponsors' Voice was founded in 2006 as a registered association and counts notable sports sponsors in Germany among its members. These currently include Adidas, Allianz, Alpecin, Bayer, Hugo Boss, Deutsche Post DHL Group, DKB, Evonik, Henkel, HypoVereinsbank, ING Deutschland, Mercedes-Benz, Rewe Group, ROWE Motor Oil, SAP, Teamviewer, Deutsche Telekom, Viessmann, Warsteiner and Würth.

The S20 pursues the goal of further professionalizing sports sponsoring as an important and successful marketing tool and strengthening its relevance in public perception. The focus is on the topics of sustainability, law, media consumption, entertainment sponsoring, the future of winter sports, and the potential of sponsoring in women's sports.

The authors would like to express their special thanks to the S20 managing director, Jana Bernhard, with whose help it has been possible for nearly half of the members to share their successful sports sponsoring engagements with the readers of this book, thereby providing insights and suggestions for their own sponsoring activities to the interested readership. Three Swiss companies also participated in the case studies. The authors would like to express their sincere thanks to the following companies for their participation:

- Allianz SE
- Bell Food Group AG
- German Credit Bank AG (DKB)
- German Telekom AG
- HypoVereinsbank/UniCredit Bank AG
- ING Germany
- Mercedes-Benz AG
- Novartis International AG
- Penny Markt GmbH (Rewe Group)
- Raiffeisen Switzerland
- Viessmann Climate Solutions SE
- Warsteiner Brewery Haus Cramer KG

Our special thanks go to the many conversation partners and colleagues from the industry who have ultimately contributed to the creation of such a comprehensive work. This is particularly true for the patience and the many hints from our publishing partner, who, in the person of Ms. Barbara Roscher and Ms. Birgit Borstelmann, has shown commendable commitment to the thorough manuscript editing.

Finally, a brief formal note. In the text, we use—for simplification reasons and as is standard in scientific publications—the generic masculine in most cases, without thereby implying discrimination or contempt for any gender or any attitude towards equality. All gender identities are explicitly included, as far as it is necessary for the statement.

We are pleased if this book attracts the interest of many readers and provides suggestions for conceptual and methodological work in the field of scientific and practical sports sponsoring. We also assume that the intensive technical discussion on sponsoring in sports will continue to be pursued vigorously in the future. Therefore, we are grateful for suggestions of all kinds.

Basel, Switzerland — Manfred Bruhn
Rheine, Germany — Peter Rohlmann
November 2023

Acknowledgment

The authors Manfred Bruhn and Peter Rohlmann would like to thank the sponsoring association S20—The Sponsors' Voice e. V. for the excellent collaboration in the creation and integration of case studies into this book. Not only did the managing director Jana Bernhard maintain close contact with us, but many of her members also provided expert conversation partners who superbly accompanied the process of case study creation. This created the best possible conditions to enrich the application of the book in daily use with positive examples and concrete experiences from practice.

Our thanks therefore go to the following member companies and their representatives from S20, as well as to three Swiss companies that have compiled the practical cases:

- Allianz SE: Eike Doerte Bürgel
- Bell Food Group AG: Davide Elia
- German Credit Bank AG (DKB): Marcel Schwarzkopf
- Deutsche Telekom AG: Stephan Althoff
- HypoVereinsbank/UniCredit Bank AG: Raphael Schleiter
- ING Germany: Florian Krenz
- Mercedes-Benz AG: Felix Salzer
- Novartis International AG
- Penny Markt GmbH (Rewe Group): Peter Rack
- Raiffeisen Switzerland: André Stöckli
- Viessmann Climate Solutions SE: Georg van der Vorst
- Warsteiner Brewery Haus Cramer KG: Marcus Bunse

About the S20

The S20—The Sponsors' Voice was founded in 2006 as a registered association and counts notable sports sponsors in Germany among its members. These currently include Adidas, Allianz, Alpecin, Bayer, Hugo Boss, Deutsche Post DHL Group, DKB, Evonik,

Henkel, HypoVereinsbank, ING Germany, Mercedes-Benz, Rewe Group, ROWE Motor Oil, SAP, Teamviewer, Deutsche Telekom, Viessmann, Warsteiner, and Würth.

The S20 pursues the goal of further professionalizing sports sponsoring as an important and successful communication tool and strengthening its relevance in public perception. The focus is on the topics of sustainability, law, media consumption, entertainment sponsoring, the future of winter sports, and the potential of sponsoring in women's sports in general and women's football in particular.

The S20 association, registered as a non-profit organization, is represented in public by a five-member board. The general assembly meets twice a year at different locations in Germany. The association's office was located in Bonn from 2006 to 2019. Since October 1, 2019, S20 has been based in Frankfurt am Main (https://www.s20.de).

Contents

List of Figures

Sponsoring as an Element of Sports Marketing

1

Contents

Abstract

Sponsoring has developed into a significant and above-average growing segment in the communication sector in recent years. While the argumentation with product benefits and additional services often no longer provides sufficient differentiation from the competition, companies are increasingly looking for communication tools that enable experiential benefits and a specific target group approach. Both can be found in sponsoring, which is now often established as a fixed component in the communication mix. This chapter elaborates on the concept and characteristics of sponsoring as well as the development phases in science and practice. The focus is on the description of the structure of the sponsoring market and the importance of sponsoring rights. In addition to a detailed case study on the general sponsoring approach of Raiffeisen Switzerland, there is further practical information on sports sponsoring, including the so-called "shoe dispute" at the DFB.

M. Bruhn and P. Rohlmann, *Sports Sponsoring*,
https://doi.org/10.1007/978-3-658-44171-5_1

1.1 Concept of Sponsoring and Distinctions

Sponsoring has become a common and everyday phenomenon. Companies from various sectors are increasingly using the diverse **opportunities of sponsoring**. In sports, cultural events, as well as in the ecological, social, and media sectors, individuals, institutions, and audiovisual media are specifically supported, and own events are initiated to confront participants and viewers with the communication intentions of companies. This confrontation aims to include events that are in the public interest or of specific target groups and consequently find resonance in the mass media, in the communication work of companies to achieve communicative effects.

The promotion of culture and sports as well as social welfare by companies or entrepreneurs has a long tradition (see Bruhn, 2018). When considering the historical development of the various forms of **corporate sponsoring activities**, a general distinction is made between patronage and donations as specific forms of philanthropy. The Roman Gaius Clinius Maecenas (70–8 BC) is considered the forefather of the promotion of art and culture. As a friend, helper, and advisor to Emperor Augustus, he gathered and supported the significant poets of his time. Even though Maecenas himself did not only promote art for altruistic reasons: The term patronage, derived from his name, characterizes the promotion of culture and the common good by individuals or organizations for altruistic motives.

A **patron** thus promotes individuals or institutions without expecting concrete services in return. The motive for such an action could be the self-commitment of a person, a foundation, or a company to use part of the available budget for the benefit of a specific part of the environment, with artistic, sporting, or socio-political interests in the foreground. However, a closer look at the cultural sponsoring activities of historical patrons (including Maecenas and the Medici) suggests that these cases also had interests of a political, economic, or communicative nature and were therefore not purely altruistic. While it is possible that historical patrons found the motivation for their cultural activities in their love of art and social responsibility, it is also conceivable that they pursued an interest in influencing external images and images with their actions. Nevertheless, the terms patronage and cultural promotion (as opposed to cultural sponsoring) remain associated with positively connoted characteristics to this day, from which companies that describe themselves as patrons or cultural promoters benefit (Rothe, 2001, p. 222).

In the case of classical patronage, the patron would provide support even if his name or that of his company is not associated with the promotion. It is evident that there is therefore hardly a reliable overview of the financial scope of corporate patronage—not only in Germany—as many promotions do not become public. This is all the more true as the tasks of patrons are now partly taken over by **foundations** that fulfill their declared foundation purpose from the proceeds of a foundation's assets.

An evolution of patronage and thus another specific form of philanthropy are activities by companies that are referred to as **Corporate Giving** in the United States and as **donations** in Germany. These are donation campaigns in which companies provide financial or material resources or services free of charge, aware of their socio-political responsibility, with the goal of contributing to the solution of societal problems. In the United States and other Western countries, this systematic promotion is found in health facilities, universities, opera houses, theaters, etc. In Germany, social and confessional associations as well as parties are mainly financed in this way. From a corporate perspective, tax reasons play a major role in the donation; specific services demanded from the beneficiary are rather the exception.

▶ However: Neither **patronage** nor **donations** are to be equated with **sponsoring**.

When considering the etymological meaning of the word "sponsor", the following interpretations are found:

Duden Sponsor: to promote as a sponsor. Sponsor: supporter; financier [in sports]; person, group, who finances radio or television broadcasts [for advertising purposes].

The American Heritage 1. One who assumes responsibility for another person or a group during a period of instruction, apprenticeship, or probation. 2. One who vouches for the suitability of a candidate for admission. 3. A legislator who proposes and urges adoption of a bill. 4. One who presents a candidate for baptism or confirmation; a godparent. 5. One that finances a project or an event carried out by another person or group, especially a business enterprise that pays for radio or television programming in return for advertising time.

Grimm's Dictionary Spons: Fiancé, fiancée, referring to the heavenly bridegroom and → heavenly brides. Spunse: Beloved. Old Spunse: derogatory for an unchaste girl. Sponsieren: 1. to accept as Spons: to engage, to marry, 2. more often: to behave like bride and groom, worldly turned: of sensual courtship: to sponsor, to pimp. Sponsiererin, f. the one who courts, woos, veiled designation of a matchmaker. Sponsierung: Courting.

If one disregards the definition according to the Grimm brothers in the 1830s, "Sponsoring" is primarily associated with terms such as **"guarantee"** and **"partnership"**. In contrast to patronage and donation system, companies that act as sponsors link their commitment to their own communication goals. These are achieved by agreeing on certain services with the sponsored party and making the sponsoring known also with the help of other communication instruments, such as media advertising and sales promotion.

An analysis of the **development of sponsoring understanding** in the scientific field shows a comprehensive discussion of terms, with phase- and event-oriented definitions as well as enumerative-explicative and contract-oriented perspectives being distinguished

(Ahlert et al., 2007, pp. 14 ff.; Bagusat & Marwitz, 2008, pp. 5 ff.; Bruhn, 2018, pp. 3 ff.). For a comprehensive overview of the scientific status of sponsoring in English-language literature, see Cornwell et al. (2005); Walliser (2003).

When looking at developments in practice, it becomes clear that a sometimes very diffuse understanding of the **conceptual content of sponsoring** has emerged among companies, sponsored parties, media representatives, politicians, and the general public in recent years. This has led to almost any form of support, promotion, transaction of business, etc. between individuals, groups, or organizations being erroneously referred to as "sponsoring" in everyday language (examples include the regular provision of pocket money by a mother to her son or the granting of advertising cost subsidies by a manufacturer to its trading partners). This has—in the actual understanding—nothing to do with sponsoring.

The previous consideration shows that the differences between the presented forms of corporate sponsoring activities are primarily based on a diverging focus of the motives for sponsoring. These are supplemented by differing conditions that are placed on the allocation of sponsoring funds by patrons, donors, and sponsors. Fig. 1.1 illustrates the

Form of business support			
Features	Type of funding		
	Patronage	Donations	Sponsoring
Type of donor	Private individuals, Foundations	Private individuals, The company	The company
Motive(s) for promotion	Exclusively promotional motives (altruistic)	Promotional motive dominant, possible tax benefits (public protection)	Promotion motive and achievement of communication goals (self-interest)
Cooperation with sponsored persons	partially (via conveyor areas)	no	yes (implementation of sponsorships)
Media impact	no (rather private)	hardly	yes (public)
Use in the sports sector	very rare	rare	dominant
Use in the area of culture	dominant	frequently	frequently
Social/ecological commitment	frequently	dominant	frequently
Use in the media sector	non-existent	non-existent	dominant
Decision makers In the company	Entrepreneur	Finance, management	Company management, marketing, communication

Fig. 1.1 Forms of corporate sponsoring activities. (*Source*: Bruhn, 2018, p. 4)

differences between the three mentioned **forms of corporate sponsoring activities** based on various characteristics.

Based on these fundamental distinguishing features, the **concept of sponsoring** in its general form is defined as follows (Bruhn, 2018, p. 5):

Sponsoring means the

- Analysis, planning, implementation, and control of all activities,
- that are associated with the provision of money, goods, services, or know-how by companies and institutions
- to promote individuals and/or organizations in the fields of sports, culture, social, environment and/or the media
- under contractual regulation of the performance of the sponsor and the counter-performance of the sponsored,
- in order to simultaneously achieve goals of marketing and corporate communication.

Accordingly, a **Sponsoring** is spoken of when the sponsor and the sponsored party have agreed to carry out a specific project within a specified period under certain conditions.

An analysis regarding the specific characteristics of sponsoring shows that the use of various forms of sponsoring as a tool for marketing and corporate communication is based on partly heterogeneous intentions, taking into account different rules and laws. Regardless of the heterogeneous goals and approaches, the following **characteristics of sponsoring** can be highlighted, which are common to all sponsoring activities:

- Sponsoring is based on the principle of **performance and counter-performance**. The sponsor invests his support funds, such as money, material resources and services, expecting to receive a certain counter-performance from the sponsored party. For example, the sponsored party can offer the effective use of the sponsor's brand or company name for advertising purposes. In addition, it is possible to grant the sponsor the communicative use of the sponsoring, for example within the framework of his public relations.
- Sponsoring does not correspond to the pure purchase of advertising space for a fee. Rather, in sponsoring, the **idea of support** towards the sponsored party is expressed, as the sponsor usually also identifies with the tasks and goals of the sponsored party. Through the character of support and the promotion of activities considered important by society, a sponsor can generate goodwill for himself to an extent that is not possible through media advertising. The extent to which the reputation is positively influenced depends, among other things, on the respective sponsoring activities and how much a company obviously exploits a sponsoring for selfish purposes and suppresses the idea of support.

- For companies, sponsoring is a communication tool. Sponsoring fulfills **communicative functions** for sponsors, which are directly provided by the sponsored party, transported by media, or created by the sponsor himself.
- Sponsoring has to go through a **systematic planning and decision-making process**. It is not enough to provide resources to a sponsored party and wait for the expected effect. Rather, measures need to be planned, organized, implemented and controlled based on a situation analysis and goal formulation. This necessity of carrying out a systematic planning and decision-making process applies equally to sponsors and sponsored parties.
- One of the essential goals of sponsoring is the **image transfer**. The special feature of image transfer in sponsoring lies in the determinants that contribute to a specific brand or corporate image. While in classic communication tools, such as media advertising, the message of an advertising measure and the medium through which it is communicated influence the image transfer independently of each other, in sponsoring, message and medium cannot be separated. The object of a sponsoring commitment embodies both the message and the medium itself. Empirical studies have found that the derived image from a sponsoring largely depends on the form of sponsoring appearance (Christensen, 2006; Huber & Matthes, 2007). Precise image dimensions are derived in a second step from the specific activities within a sponsoring category.
- From a corporate perspective, sponsoring is a component of **Integrated Communication**. This means that companies should not use sponsoring in isolation, but in conjunction with other marketing and communication tools (e.g., public relations, advertising, sales). A clear distinction between sponsoring and other communication tools and forms of corporate promotion is not always given in sponsoring practice based on the mentioned characteristics. Rather, a number of mixed forms have emerged, each of which presupposes the presence of the listed characteristics, but assigns them different levels of importance.
- Sponsoring always requires a **specific public stage or platform**. Therefore, depending on the field of activity and the goals of the sponsor, different commitments can make sense. This means, conversely, that sometimes sports provide the right platform, sometimes culture or social projects, sometimes the top performance category is the right stage, sometimes rather the category in its breadth.

The various forms of sponsoring make it difficult in practice to speak of a uniform concept of "sponsoring". In view of the diverging motives of the sponsors, the diverse possibilities for use and the heterogeneous degree of use of sponsoring for marketing and corporate communication, it is advisable from a company's perspective to typify sponsoring. Fig. 1.2 shows that four **types of sponsoring** can be distinguished with the altruistic as well as the support-oriented and classic sponsoring.

Type 1: Altruistic sponsoring

In altruistic sponsoring by companies, altruistic motives are at the forefront, often anchored in the company's philosophy. A characteristic feature is that the company's

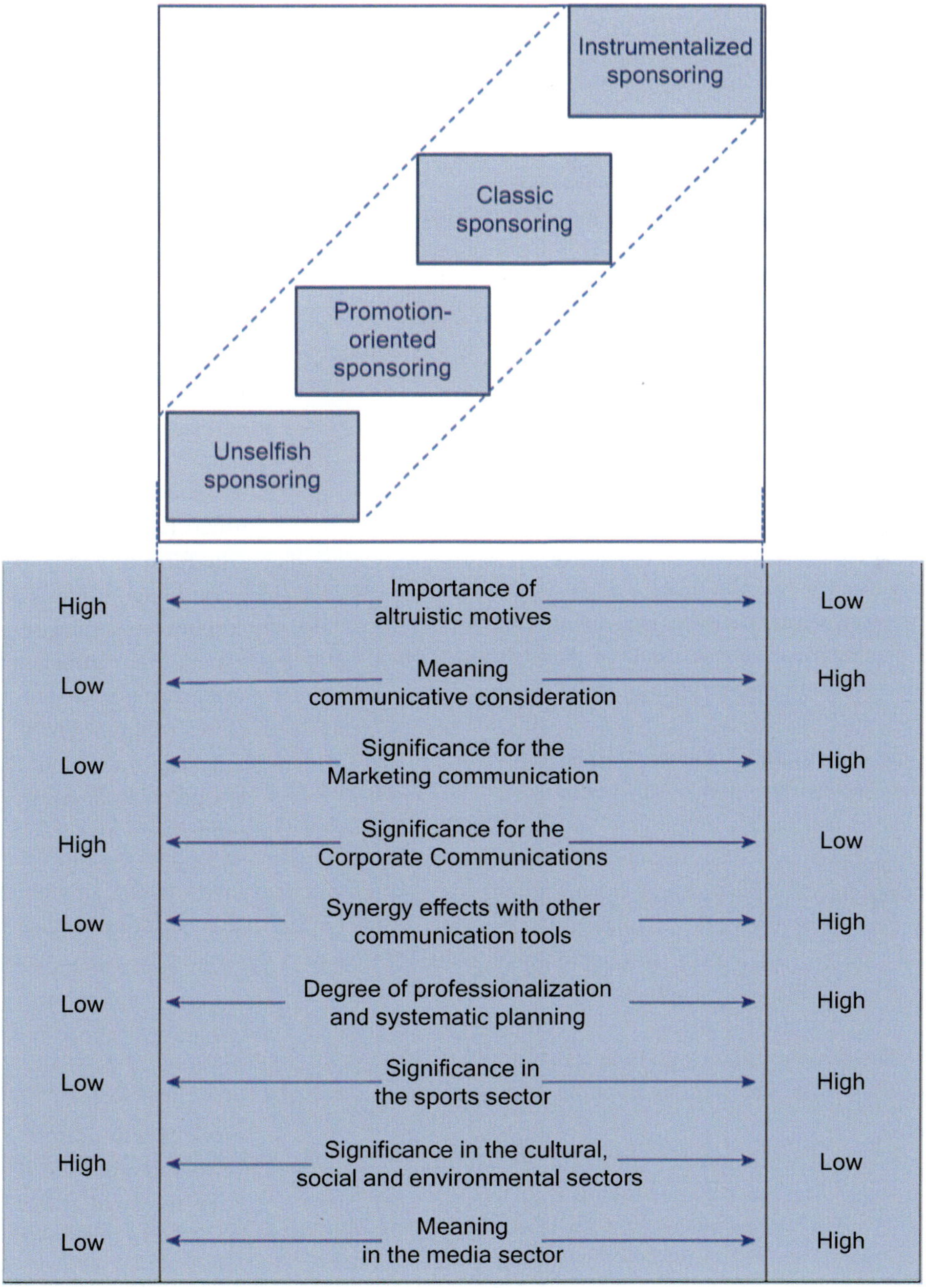

Fig. 1.2 Typology of sponsoring. (*Source*: Based on Bruhn, 2018, p. 8)

commitment is communicated to the public only very cautiously. This form of sponsoring is primarily observed in the support of cultural, social, and other non-commercial institutions. The support is usually provided by the company itself or by company-specific foundations.

Type 2: Promotion-oriented sponsoring
In promotion-oriented sponsoring, the idea of promotion clearly dominates over the desired communicative effect. This form of sponsoring is characterized by the fact that the mention of the promoting company, for example in a specific sponsoring, is not mandatory but desired. The company's commitment is usually brought closer to the public within the framework of public relations work, without a professional and systematic planning. Promotion-oriented sponsoring is primarily used in the socio-environmental and cultural sectors.

Type 3: Classic sponsoring
Classic sponsoring is characterized by the fact that sponsors make it a condition to be mentioned in the sponsorings. The basis of the commitment is the desired communicative effect, while the motive for promotion recedes into the background. The conditions for services and counter-services are intensively negotiated and contractually regulated. A characteristic feature of classic sponsoring is the systematic planning and strategic orientation of the commitment.

Type 4: Instrumentalized sponsoring
Instrumentalized sponsoring is characterized by the fact that sponsors do not actually want to use their commitment for the benefit of the sponsored, but in a partly covert, partly open way only use their often not even directly related commitment to exploit their influence as a political power holder, speculation-oriented investor, etc. In view of the disregard for basic principles of coexistence and human rights, responsible action towards the environment and nature, such behavior is almost equivalent to "sportswashing" and is an abuse of sponsoring.

The typology shows that the transitions between the different types of sponsoring are fluid and the specific classification of a sponsoring has to be made in each individual case.

Looking at the entire market for sponsoring—nationally and internationally—it can be stated that **sports sponsoring** is of greatest importance. According to various estimates, about three quarters of the total sponsoring volume is accounted for by sports sponsoring. This is partly due to tradition, as the first manifestations of sports sponsoring can already be observed in the 1960s. The high **importance of sports in society** is a major motivation for sponsors and underpins the outstanding importance of sports sponsoring for companies.

In 2019, global sponsoring expenditures amounted to approximately 66 billion USD, of which approximately 24.5 billion USD were in the USA, which in 2007 had only spent around 15 billion USD on sponsoring rights. This marked growth was apparently only briefly interrupted by the global pandemic (see Fig. 1.3). Thus, global sponsoring expenditures in 2022 are expected to exceed the 70 billion USD mark. In Europe, sponsoring expenditures in 2019 amounted to approximately 18 billion USD, in 2007 it was only 10.6 billion USD. Investments in Asia were slightly lower at 17 billion USD in 2019 than in Europe, but an above-average growth of sponsoring in Asia is unmistakable and expenditures will continue to be significantly higher than those in Central and South America (just under 5 billion USD in 2019). While the USA has long held the undisputed top position in sponsoring expenditures, it is expected that Europe and especially Asia will reduce the gap to the USA in the future (International Event Group, 2007, 2015a, b; Bagusat & Marwitz, 2008).

Looking at the area of sports sponsoring alone, they were globally before the pandemic at about 70 to 75% of all sponsoring expenditures. However, there are sometimes not insignificant fluctuations regarding the sports-related expenditures by countries and sports.

According to current surveys, the majority of Germans regularly engage in sports activities. The proportion of people who do not engage in sports at all is currently around 40% (Statista, 2022c). In 2021 (Corona times), two-thirds of respondents in a survey stated that they are particularly or somewhat interested in sports (Allensbach Market and Advertising Carrier Analysis, AWA, 2021).

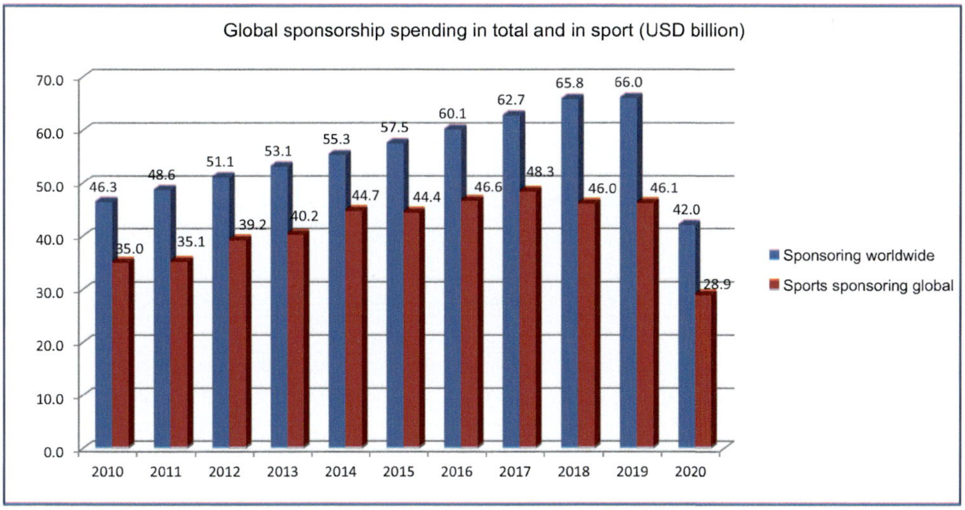

Fig. 1.3 Sponsoring expenditures worldwide and in sports. (*Source*: IEG, 2010–2020)

Much more important for sports sponsoring, however, is the interest in sports events. Surveys have shown that general sports events are popular with just under a quarter of the German population, and broadcasts of the 1st and 2nd Bundesliga are the most popular among Germans with over 27% (see Fig. 1.4). This result is consistent with the record TV ratings for the 2014 World Cup final, which was watched by 34.57 million people on television; this corresponded to a viewing share of 86.2% (Die Welt, 2014).

The interest of companies in getting involved in sports sponsoring has various reasons. Of particular importance are the characteristic **features for the use of sports sponsoring**:

- target groups are addressed in an **emotionally pleasant situation**. The marketing and corporate communication takes place in an environment that is attractive and positively evaluated for certain groups, thus enabling the addressing of target groups, some of which have a rather negative attitude towards traditional media advertising.
- Due to the **broad attention value of sports** in various population groups and the high involvement of the target groups regarding certain sports events, sponsoring is particularly suitable with regard to the contact quality of marketing and corporate communication.
- In this context, sponsors also rely on the **multiplier effect of the media** to deliver messages as efficiently and effectively as possible to target groups.
- The **diversity of possibilities for sponsoring commitments** at different sports events allows a target group-specific orientation of communication as well as differentiation from potential competitors.

Interest in sport	2011	2016	2019	2021
... special and something	69.9 %	68.4 %	68.0 %	66.2 %
... hardly or not at all	30.1 %	31.6 %	32.0 %	33.8 %
Particular interest in soccer	35.1 %	34.8 %	33.6 %	32.1 %
Interest in				
... general sporting events	31.9 %	29.2 %	26.5 %	23.5 %
... 1st + 2nd BL matches	n.a.	28.3 %	28.4 %	27.1 %
Sporting activity				
... never			42.1 %	40.1 %
... regularly			43.3 %	47.3 %

Fig. 1.4 Interest of the German population aged 14 and over in sports. (*Source*: AWA, 2011–2021)

The explained features distinguish sports sponsoring from traditional communication tools. This achieves a communicative **added value through sponsoring**. Regardless of the described characteristics and various forms, the following **concept of sports sponsoring** is assumed:

▶ **Sports sponsoring** sports sponsoring is a form of corporate engagement in the sports sector, in which effects on (internal and external) marketing and corporate communication are intended through the contractually agreed support of individual athletes, sports teams, clubs, sports facilities, (cross-sport) associations, organizations or sports events, among other things.

1.2 Development Phases of Sponsoring in Practice and Science

Sponsoring in general and sports sponsoring in particular can be characterized by a special dynamism and creativity. New forms and sponsoring measures are constantly emerging to increase the benefits for the sponsor and the sponsored. At the same time, it is necessary to keep pace with developments in marketing and digitization. This will also be the case in the future. If one looks at the development of sponsoring, several development phases can be roughly distinguished. This applies equally to practice and science.

Development of sponsoring in practice

The sponsoring commitment of companies has fundamentally changed in the past. While for a long time the negative attitude of sports, cultural and social organizations, associations and individuals as well as restrictive legal conditions stood in the way of a positive development of sponsoring, sponsoring has developed into a central communication tool since the mid-1980s. The **development phases of sponsoring in practice** outlined in Fig. 1.5 can be distinguished.

Phase of "Stealth Advertising" The starting point of sponsoring was the 1960s with a phase of "stealth advertising". This form of conveying advertising messages, particularly at sports events and broadcasts as well as feature films, without the corresponding permission, is characterized by the fact that the advertising recipients do not immediately recognize the purpose of achieving a communicative effect. An intensive discussion has developed about whether this is not a deception of the recipient, and there was a particular call on television for a separation between program and advertising content.

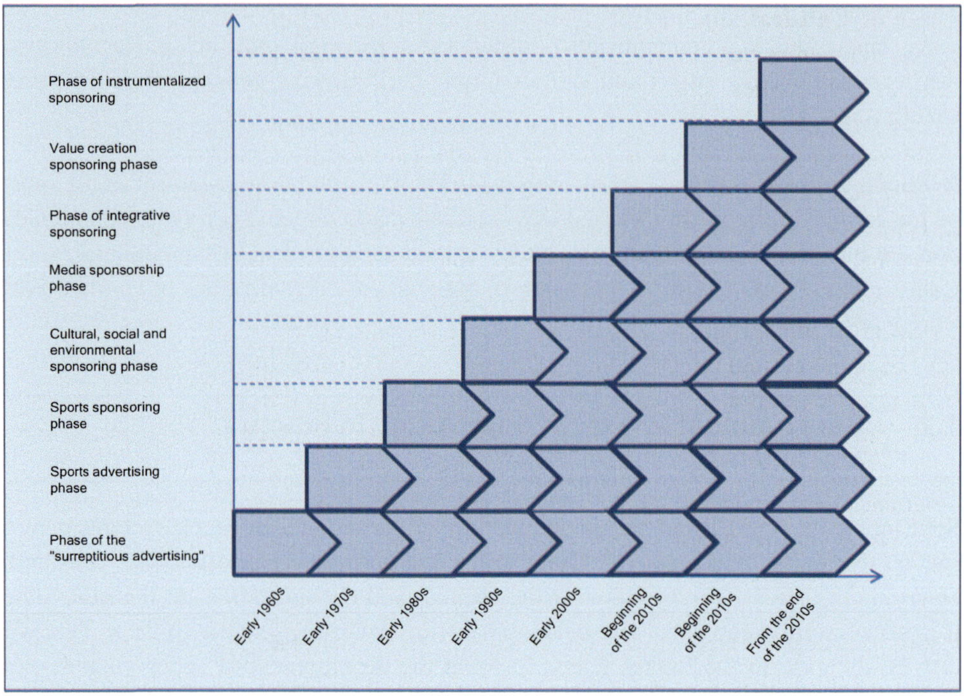

Fig. 1.5 Development phases of sponsoring in practice. (*Source*: Adapted from Bruhn, 2018, p. 9)

Phase of Sports Advertising The subsequent 1970s were characterized by the emergence of a phase of sports advertising. During this time, sports only "tentatively" entered corporate advertising and promotion measures, for example in the form of perimeter and jersey advertising. However, pure perimeter advertising should not be confused with sponsoring, as booking a perimeter at an event is identical to renting an advertising medium and the idea of support is missing. In any case, companies recognized the attractiveness and popularity of sports and considered using them for communicative purposes.

Phase of Sports Sponsoring Only since the 1980s has there been talk of professional sponsoring. During this time, companies, especially in the sports sector, began to systematically plan their commitment and integrate selected sponsorings into their marketing and corporate communication, which is why this period is considered the beginning of a phase of sports sponsoring. This was accompanied by legal regulations through broadcasting agreements, which have made the separation between program, advertising, and sponsoring more liberal. This created more opportunities for sponsors to increase the attention and thus the impact of their commitment through the media.

Phase of Cultural, Social, and Environmental Sponsoring At the beginning of the 1990s, companies began to explore new areas of support outside of sports. The areas of culture, social issues, and the environment gained in importance, so this era is characterized by a phase of cultural, social, and environmental sponsoring. At the beginning of the sponsoring measures in these three areas, sponsoring was rather understood as a kind of patronage, i.e., carried out primarily for altruistic or selfless motives and rarely associated with a specific return service from the sponsored party. This has changed over time.

Phase of Media/Program Sponsoring Since the beginning of the 2000s, companies have been increasingly active in the presentation of television and radio programs, so this period can be referred to for a long time as the beginning of the phase of media sponsoring or program sponsoring. The basis was the again expanded legal possibilities through broadcasting agreements to appear as a sponsor within the framework of audiovisual programs. Meanwhile, sponsoring in other media, such as print and internet, has become widespread, so the term media sponsoring is an apt description for this form. Internet sponsoring can also be included in this.

Phase of Integrative Sponsoring Around the 2010s, the phase of integrative sponsoring developed, which will also continue to gain importance in the future. Companies systematically search for sponsoring opportunities and strive to integrate their various sponsoring activities within the overall communication. According to the results of company surveys, it is 90 to 95% of companies that network their sponsoring measures with other communication instruments, with a large part of the companies realizing networking with five or more instruments (Pilot Checkpoint, 2008). The focus is on public relations work, event marketing, employee communication, and media advertising (Bagusat, 2013). In later years, networking with social media activities also follows. The latter is seen as particularly advantageous as it can extend the duration of a sponsoring commitment. This is reflected, for example, in companies announcing their sponsoring commitment on social media platforms such as Facebook or Twitter or providing a report after the sponsoring event (Cotting, 2011, p. 17). Another advantage is the possibility of emotional interaction with the target groups associated with the integration of social media. Compared to the display of logos or lettering on perimeters or jerseys, more content can be communicated (Panten, 2013, p. 10). Furthermore, the integration of social media activities is associated with the possibility of cost savings compared to costly advertising campaigns (Cotting, 2011, p. 18).

Phase of Value Creation Sponsoring In the further 2010s, the phase of value creation sponsoring intensively formed, which will also be of importance for the future. Companies increasingly pursue economic goals such as customer retention or new customer acquisition within the framework of sponsoring. Furthermore, efficiency measurements are becoming increasingly important. With the increasing efficiency orientation, sponsoring is developing more and more from a pure communication instrument to a value creation instrument, for example in conjunction with sales activities. The goals of sponsoring, such as the pursued image contribution to brand communication, also make it clear that sponsoring is increasingly to be seen as an instrument of strategic brand management (Hermanns & Marwitz, 2008, pp. 41 f.).

Phase of Instrumentalization of Sponsoring Towards the end of the 2010s, there is an increasing instrumentalization of sponsoring for atypical purposes. Investors from Eastern Europe, the Far East, and the Gulf States gain economic and cultural influence in Europe by, for example, taking over traditional football clubs. In addition, state-owned companies and political systems expect a multitude of advantages from hosting major sporting events, especially the major football tournaments and the Olympic Games, in the sense of "sportswashing" (Bruhn & Rohlmann, 2021).

These content descriptions of the phases cannot, of course, always be clearly assigned to individual decades. The assignment of the phases and the transitions between the phases are fluid. The division into development phases aims to highlight the essential beginning of changes in the development of sponsoring, which have then evolved over time.

Development of Sponsoring in Science

Parallel to the outlined development phases of sponsoring in practice, the scientific examination of the communication instrument sponsoring also underwent fundamental changes. The following will show how the research fields in the sponsoring area have developed over time. Such a temporal consideration of sponsoring research shows at which time which topics came up and how these topics have changed over time. The development phases of sponsoring in science are shown in Fig. 1.6.

Initial studies laid the foundation for the scientific sponsoring debate between 1980 and 1984 by dealing with the definition, conceptual boundaries, different perspectives, and characteristics of sponsoring. This research phase is characterized by a high variety of definitions and a lack of consensus. There is only agreement that **sponsoring is understood as an exchange process** (transfer) between sponsor and sponsored to achieve marketing and communication goals. The research in this phase is also characterized by different acceptance of various sponsoring areas (sports, culture, environment). Special features of sponsoring that research has worked out include, among other things, the aspect of performance and counter-performance, the idea of promotion, the communicative function, the basis of a systematic planning and decision-making process, and image transfer (see, among others, Simkins, 1980; Meenaghan, 1983; Hastings, 1984; Townley & Grayson, 1984).

This phase is followed between 1985 and 1989 by research efforts that are dedicated to the strategic orientation and **management of sponsoring**. Topics such as strategy

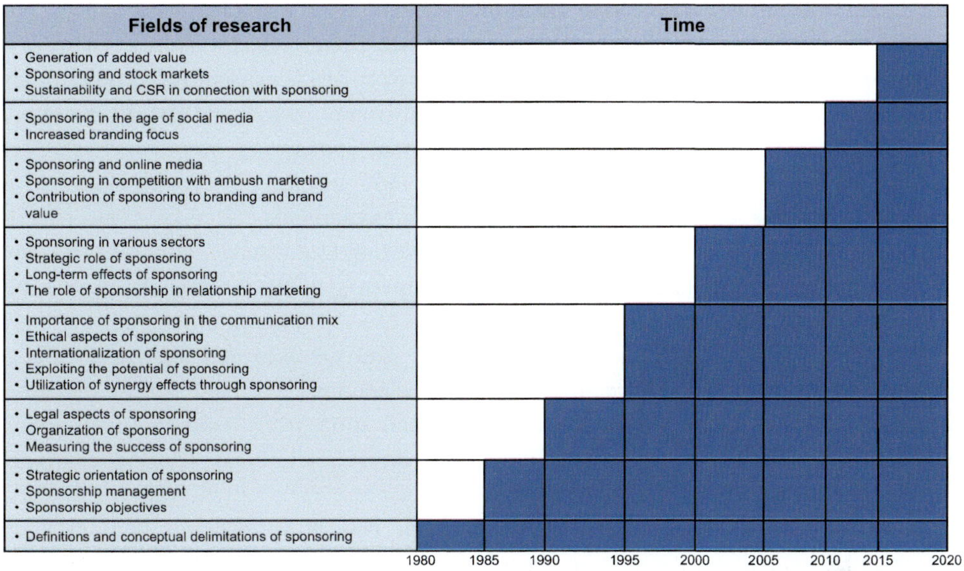

Fig. 1.6 Development phases of sponsoring in science. (*Source*: Based on Bruhn, 2018, p. 12)

determination (Gilbert, 1988) and the positioning of sponsoring in the communication mix are at the center (see, among others, Corkindale & Hastings, 1985; Gardner & Shuman, 1987). The management process and the goals of sponsoring (Abratt et al., 1987) are also the subject of research.

In the context of the research efforts that followed at the beginning of the 1990s, discussions began on **legal, organizational, and success-related aspects**. In legal terms, the focus of research is on the design of sponsoring contracts, tax and media law aspects, and competition law (see, among others, Crawford, 1992; Blackshaw & Hogg, 1993; Townley, 1993; Crompton, 1993; Furlong, 1994). In organizational terms, researchers examine the organizational location of sponsoring in the company and the determination of the responsible instances (see, among others, Witcher et al., 1991; Marshall & Cook, 1992). The measurement of success is characterized by the lack of uniform evaluation standards and thus a lack of comparability. The focus is already, for example, on determining a **Return on Sponsoring Investment (ROSI)** (Crompton, 1994) and determining the awareness, attitude, and image effects of sponsoring using tracking methods (see, among others, McDonald, 1991; Cuneen & Hannan, 1993; Pope & Voges, 1994) and experiments (see, among others, Pham, 1991; Javalgi et al., 1994).

The focus of research efforts in 1995 and 1999 are, on the one hand, questions of the **communication mix**. Here, initial points of integration are analyzed, such as strategic, inter-instrumental, internal, and external integration. On the one hand, sponsoring was discussed as an integration and supplementary instrument (cf. among others Farrelly et al., 1997; Zafer Erdogan & Kitchen, 1998; Bennett & Gabriel, 1999). On the other hand, ethical aspects are also taken into account, such as ethical basic norms, ethical behavior (alibi function of sponsoring, contract violations), the appropriateness of sponsoring and the justifiability of the influence effect of sponsoring (cf. among others Klincewicz, 1998; Nebenzhal & Jaffe, 1998; O'Sullivan & Murphy, 1998). Furthermore, during this phase, the investigation of international sponsoring events increases (cf. among others Stipp & Schiavone, 1996; Vignali, 1997; Easton & Mackie, 1998). Also, research begins to focus on the potential benefits and synergistic effects of sponsoring. In addition to studies on the external effects of sponsoring (e.g., image, attractiveness, and awareness enhancement), initial steps are taken to investigate the internal effects of sponsoring (Grimes & Meenaghan, 1998).

The use of sponsoring in various sectors, its strategic role and long-term effects, as well as its role in the context of relationship marketing, are increasingly discussed between 2000 and 2004. Numerous studies expand sponsoring research to the industrial and non-profit sector (cf. among others Berrett & Slack, 2001; Clark et al., 2003; Farrelly & Quester, 2003).

In addition, some studies attest to the **strategic role of sponsoring**, demonstrating that sponsoring makes a significant contribution to achieving strategic corporate goals (cf. among others Dolphin, 2003; Fahy et al., 2004). The **long-term effects of sponsoring** represent another emerging field of research. Studies show that long-term sponsoring activities are of central importance for the success of a company (cf. among others Cornwell & Relyea, 2000; Cornwell et al., 2001). Further studies dealing with the role of **sponsoring in the context of relationship marketing** show that sponsoring is no longer seen as an element of the more traditional marketing mix management and thus as a tool of mass communication, but rather has become a tool for building relationships (cf. among others Olkkonen et al., 2000; Olkkonen, 2001; Ryan & Fahy, 2003).

Between 2005 and 2009, research efforts increasingly penetrate the areas of **Ambush Marketing, Branding and Online Media**. In the field of ambush marketing, conceptual questions, characteristics, the demarcation to sponsoring, strategies, effects as well as ethical and legal aspects are in the foreground (cf. among others Farrelly et al., 2005; McKelvey & Grady, 2008; Burton & Chadwick, 2009). With regard to branding, the contribution of sponsoring to brand building and to increasing brand value and brand loyalty are particularly examined (cf. among others Cliffe & Motion, 2005; Becker-Olsen & Hill, 2006; Henseler et al., 2007; Sirgy et al., 2008). With regard to sponsoring in the context of online media, research focuses on the potentials, challenges, integration and strategy options as well as the effectiveness (cf. among others Rodgers, 2007; Santomier, 2008; Weeks et al., 2008).

The research trend that began between 2005 and 2009 continues from 2010 onwards. Consequently, research efforts are made regarding the **possible uses** and the **effectiveness of sponsoring** in the age of new media, especially social media (cf. among others Dees, 2011; Meenaghan et al., 2013). Furthermore, since 2010, there has been an increased focus on branding. In this context, studies deal with brand fit constructs, brand image, brand loyalty, and brand value (cf. among others Henseler et al., 2011; Mazodier & Merunka, 2012; Woisetschläger & Michaelis, 2012).

In the years of the second half of the 2010s and from 2020 onwards, it can be observed that questions of **value creation** and the generation of returns are the subject of investigations (see, among others, Eisdorfer & Kohl, 2017; Jensen et al., 2018, 2016; Blake et al., 2018). The **influence of sponsoring on stock markets** is also receiving attention in scientific research (see, among others, Abril Barrie et al., 2018; Abril et al., 2018). In addition, there is an intense discussion about questions of **sustainability and Corporate Social Responsibility (CSR)** in connection with sponsoring (see, among others, Breitbarth, 2016; Sung & Lee, 2016; Djaballah et al., 2017; Miragaia et al., 2017; Demirel, 2020; Sudolska & Lapinska, 2020; Habitzreuter & Koenigstorfer, 2021; Bhuiyan et al., 2022; Harrison et al., 2022).

Overall, it can be expected that **future research** will increasingly deal with current and global crises (e.g., Corona, wars, climate change). Research will also focus more intensively on the negative side effects of sponsoring (e.g., the role of alcohol, negative fan behavior).

The outlined **development phases of sponsoring in practice and science** do not always run in parallel. Lead and lag times can be observed, often depending on societal events and topics as well as the effects of outstanding sporting events.

In addition to the development phases of sponsoring, it is important to also consider the **development of sponsoring as a communication tool**. Every communication tool, due to limited marketing and communication budgets in companies, faces the situation of having to prove itself against other communication tools in the competition for budgets. In this respect, communication tools are conceptually subject to a life cycle. This also applies to sponsoring.

In contrast to other communication tools, whose expenditures are largely stagnating or declining, expenditures for sponsorings continue to rise. For the future, it can be expected that the search for new sponsoring areas by companies will lead to the emergence of new forms of sponsoring and that selected existing areas will gain in importance—albeit with certain restrictions. Fig. 1.7 provides an overview of the previous **market life cycle of sponsoring** in Germany.

The **increasing importance of sponsoring** is reflected not only in steadily increasing sponsoring expenditures, but also in the growing number of companies using sponsoring as a communication tool, and in the increasing share of the sponsoring budget in the total communication budget. This growth is facilitated by the following factors (Bob Bomliz Group, 2008):

- Search for new areas and forms of sponsoring,
- Effectiveness problems of traditional forms of communication and strengths of sponsoring,

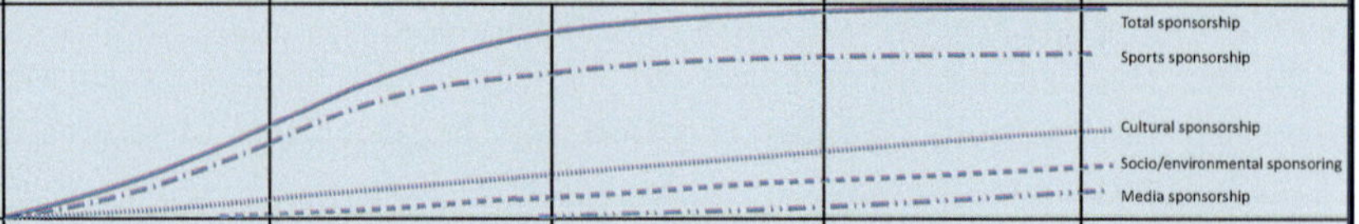

Phases		Origin	Growth		Maturity	Saturation
		1970s	1980s	1990s	2000s	From 2010
Meaning	Sports sponsorship	First beginnings in a few sports	Strong professionalization in selected sports	Development of all Sports and Performance classes	Extensive Dependence of sport on sponsors	Dependence continues to increase, scandals become a problem
	Cultural sponsorship	Minor significance; patronage at best	First beginnings in a few areas of art	Tendency towards Professionalization in selected areas (cutting-edge art)	High importance in attractive art and cultural sectors	Importance increases due to new technologies, even niche art finds sponsors
	Social and environmental sponsoring	Minor importance; at best, support from patrons or donations	First beginnings in a few socio- and Environmental areas	Creation of own sponsorships by companies	Tendency towards professionalization in selected social and environmental areas	Social and environmental sponsoring part of CSR
	Media sponsorship	No significance	First beginnings through surreptitious advertising and product placement	Legal possibility and development for communication	Systematic use by media and companies	Systematic Integration into all online communication measures
Behavior of the parties involved	The company	Initial trials, isolated and sporadic use	Tendency towards Professionalization with positive experiences	Versatile use in various areas	Significant Source of financing in the Framework of the Procurement marketing	Further integration through social media
	Sponsored	First attempts, sporadic interest	High interest, only low professionalization (with exceptions)	Tendency towards professionalization	Significant Source of funding for all media	Sponsoring as a fixed source of income
	Media	Rejecting attitude of the public media	High level of interest from private media providers	Heavy use by private/public media providers	Creation of new rules and protective measures	High importance for all media
	State	Indifferent attitude	Ambivalent attitude of various government agencies	Promotion in selected areas; framework conditions	Promotion in selected areas; framework conditions	Stronger Regulation of certain sponsorships
	Population	Indifferent attitude	Broad acceptance with initial reactions	Stronger reactances in certain areas	Stronger reactances in certain areas	Rejection of overly intensive sponsorships

Fig. 1.7 Market life cycle and diffusion of sponsoring in Germany. (*Source*: Bruhn, 2018, p. 15)

- Interest and acceptance of target groups,
- Increasing media effectiveness and professionalism in the organization of sports events.

Sponsors and sponsored parties are constantly looking for **new areas and forms of sponsoring**. Commitments range from sports sponsoring to investments in the cultural, socio and environmental sectors, to program and online sponsoring. Within these areas, sponsors develop various forms of sponsoring. For example, sports venue sponsoring only took hold in Germany in the 2000s and has experienced an explosive development to this day. The "naming" of first Bundesliga sports venues with sponsor names has now become standard. Sports venue sponsoring has now firmly established itself and has thus become a major form of sponsoring (Stadionwelt INSIDE, 2015).

With increasing **effectiveness problems of traditional forms of communication**, such as media advertising, caused by general information overload and increasing reactance of target groups, the strengths of sponsoring and the added value come increasingly into play. Sponsoring allows for targeted addressing of target groups through leisure activities and the media, creates attention, and conveys special experiential values in an authentic way.

Other promoting factors of sponsoring include the **interest and acceptance of target groups**, which have overall increased significantly, and ultimately also result from the conscious selection of sponsoring objects and areas by the sponsors. Commitments in sports and culture as well as in the socio-environmental area are only successful if there is a pronounced interest in the sponsoring object and the sponsoring area and a certain target group acceptance is achieved. After stagnating expenditures in recent decades, investments in environmental sponsoring increased again in the 2010s. The increasing interest in this area is not least due to the media-effective discussion about environmental protection, resource scarcity, climate change, global warming, and greenhouse gas emissions. Nevertheless, investments in the area of sports sponsoring, especially commitments to extraordinary sports events such as world championships, continue to rise unabated. However, it is also foreseeable and recorded that due to the economic crisis in 2009, numerous sponsoring commitments were not continued or entered into.

Ultimately, the increasing media effectiveness and professionalism with which international sports events such as the Football World Cup or the Olympic Games are organized contribute to a **"sponsoring boom"**. A record for viewing figures in Germany was reached during the broadcast of the Football World Cup final in 2014 in Brazil (Germany against Argentina) on ARD with an average of 34.57 million viewers. With the increasing fascination and popularity of events among certain target groups, the willingness of sponsors to invest also grows.

Looking at **sponsoring in other countries**, sponsoring in Germany has now reached a high level of development. In England and France, higher sponsoring expenditures can be observed in the areas of sports and culture. This is even more true for the United States, where there is also intensive socio-sponsoring (especially in the areas of health and universities) and the sponsoring of television programs (bartering, product placement) has an even higher value. The emergence of specialized sponsoring agencies is seen as an indicator of the spread of sponsoring in individual countries, which have a great importance in the USA, England, France, and now also in Germany.

1.3 Structure of the Sponsoring Market

The **expenditures for sponsoring** have continuously increased in Germany over the past decades. Since the mid-1980s, double-digit growth rates have been observed annually. Only in the year after the 2006 Football World Cup was a decline of 300 million EUR recorded for the first time. While in 1985 about 102 million EUR were spent by companies on sponsoring activities, the expenditures in 2008 by company and agency representatives were 4.6 billion EUR and in 2018 6.0 billion EUR. During the economic crisis from 2009, a decline in sponsoring expenditures to 4.2 billion EUR can be seen until 2011. From 2012, expenditures began to rise again continuously and amounted to 5.5 billion EUR for the year 2016 and even 6.3 billion EUR for 2019 (Statista, 2016a; Rohlmann, 2016; Nielsen Sports, 2021).

The **impact of the Corona crisis on the sponsoring volume** is shown, among other things, by a study by Nielsen Sports. While the German sports sponsoring volume in the year before the pandemic (2019) was still at 4.13 billion EUR, it fell by around 10% to 3.76 billion EUR in 2020. In 2021, expenditures in sports sponsoring in Germany were already approaching the pre-crisis level again with 3.95 billion EUR (see Fig. 1.8). However, the pandemic and the resulting "new normal" have also changed the way companies deal with their acquired rights in sponsoring. While the 1990s and 2000s focused on visibility, the current trend is towards a much deeper look at sponsoring opportunities.

Looking ahead to the coming years, a profound **change in sports sponsoring** can be observed in that the fans and thus the target groups have largely changed from a large location-based real audience to a more distant, partly fragmented, digitally shifted fan base, which affects both new sponsoring models and the type and distribution of content. Owners of sports rights and media owners have to take this change into account with appropriate marketing strategies in order to achieve their goals in the future (ESA, 2022).

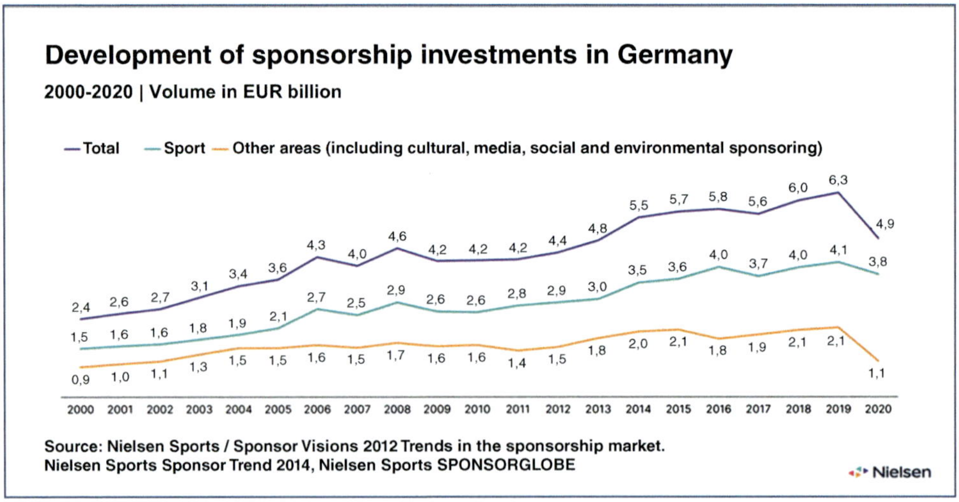

Fig. 1.8 Company expenditures in Germany for total sponsoring and in sports. (*Source*: Nielsen Sports)

The sports sponsoring market essentially divides first into the **direct participants** such as the sponsors (corporate and product brands, industries, government agencies and organizations) and the sponsored (sports, performance levels, reference objects). In addition, the market for sports sponsoring includes the **indirect participants**, which, in addition to sports agencies as intermediaries (e.g., marketers of sponsoring rights) and sports service providers as implementation helpers (e.g., manufacturers of LED boards), also includes the media, which due to the great interest in sports of the public, on the one hand, operate their business model with sports content and on the other hand, act as a multiplier for the communication messages in sponsoring (see Fig. 1.9).

When talking about the structure of the sports sponsoring market, this is most often related to the highest performance level and thus the **elite sports**. Top professional sports attract the most attention of all participants and also have the highest sponsoring amounts. This is associated with a very high degree of professionalism to perfect the sponsoring rights. However, any company that wants to use sports sponsoring as part of its corporate communication is well advised not to follow the so-called "mainstream" exclusively, and only to participate where, in view of many sponsors, a new "player" is hardly noticeable, and this is only achieved with excessively elaborate activations. Therefore, the selection of the right sport and sports partner is particularly important for a successful sponsoring commitment. Sponsoring is also suitable outside of elite sports in **amateur sports**. This applies not only to the number 1 popular sport, football, but

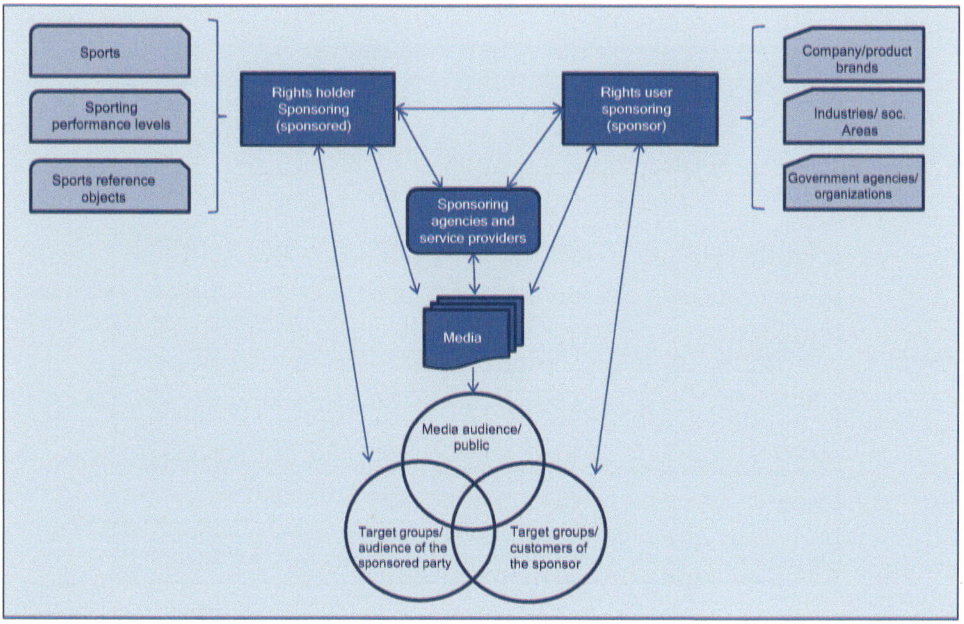

Fig. 1.9 Structure of the sports sponsoring market

also to less dominant sports and new trend sports as well as individual athletes and individual sports events.

With regard to the development of sponsoring in Germany, the following **trends** are evident:

1. The **market volume** for sponsoring grew in all areas until 2005 (see Fig. 1.10). The main reasons for this were price increases of sponsorings, technological developments that opened up new possibilities for sponsoring, the trend towards a leisure and "event society", and the fact that more and more companies are using this instrument of corporate and brand communication (Oschmann, 1997, p. 12; Meenaghan & Shipley, 1999, p. 328). However, since 2005, growth has slowed down, and initial signs of saturation are appearing in some areas (Pilot Checkpoint, 2000, 2002, 2008; ZAW, 2006–2021; Nielsen Sports, 2021). Since 2010, sponsoring expenditures again increased more strongly, but were severely affected by the Corona pandemic in 2020. Nevertheless, the long-term growth trend seems to be unbroken, as the first surveys on sponsoring expenditures after the pandemic show.
2. In an assessment of the **growth potential** of individual sponsoring forms, company and agency forecasts diverge, although the future development in sponsoring overall is generally rated as positive. Experts expect that sponsoring as part of the communication mix will continue to gain importance (Pilot Checkpoint, 2008; Nielsen Sports (formerly Repucom), 2015, 2021). The development in the area of media sponsoring (especially internet and social media) is consistently rated positively. Especially in

Year	Sports sponsoring	Non-sports sponsoring	Total sponsorship
2001	1.6	1.0	2.6
2006	2.7	1.6	4.3
2011	2.8	1.4	4.2
2016	4.0	1.8	5.8
2017	3.7	1.9	5.6
2018	4.0	2.0	6.0
2019	4.1	2.2	6.3
2020	3.8	1.1	4.9
2021	4.1	1.2	5.3

Fig. 1.10 Corporate expenditure in Germany for sponsoring by focus (figures in billion EUR). (*Source*: Nielsen Sports)

sports sponsoring, particularly in football, a majority of experts expect further growth rates. Opinions on cultural, socio and environmental sponsoring, however, are less unanimous and fluctuate between increasing and remaining the same (Nielsen Sports (formerly Repucom), 2015). Fig. 1.11 also shows that the entire sports sponsoring suffered during Corona times, but not as much as the other sponsoring forms.

3. The importance of sponsoring as a communication tool is reflected not only in the absolute investment amounts of companies, but also in the relative amount of sponsoring expenditures. While the **sponsoring share of total advertising expenditures** (media advertising, sales promotion, trade fairs and exhibitions, promotional items, telemarketing, public relations, multimedia and customer media) in Germany was still at 4.6% in 2000, the share of the sponsoring budget in the total communication budget in 2016 was already 18.3% (Statista, 2017) and now more than 20%. Accordingly, there has been a continuous increase in the average communication budget for sponsoring measures since 1998. In Austria, the sponsoring share of total advertising expenditures is 18.7%, and in Switzerland it is 21.5% (ZHAW, 2015). The distribution of these budgets across the various types of sponsoring varies between 62–64% for sports sponsoring, 18–20% for media sponsoring, 11–12% for public sponsoring and 6–8% for cultural sponsoring (see Fig. 1.12).

	2000-2005	2005-2010	2010-2015	2015-2020	1999-2019
Sponsorship - total increase	+ 50 %	+ 17 %	+ 36 %	- 14 %	+ 180 %
Sports sponsorship Rates of change	+ 31 %	+ 24 %	+ 38 %	+ 6 %	+ 179 %

Fig. 1.11 Change rates for sponsoring in certain periods. (*Source*: Nielsen Sports)

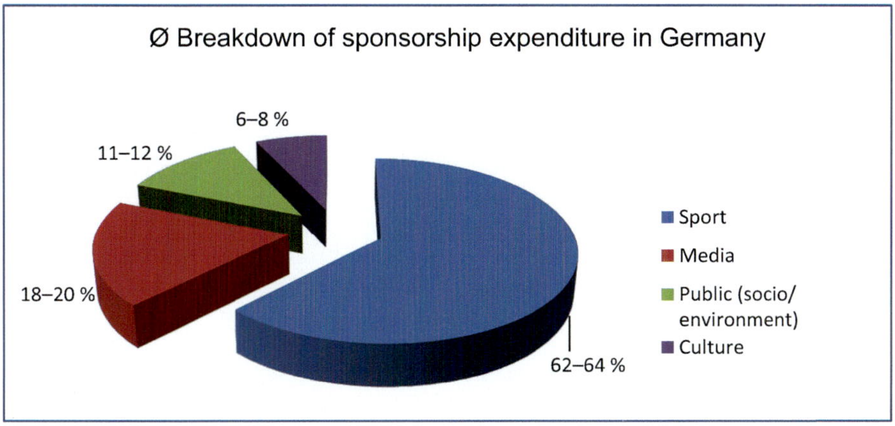

Fig. 1.12 Sponsoring expenditure in Germany by use. (*Source*: Nielsen Sports)

4. The **sports sponsoring,** which accounts for the major share of sponsoring expenditures, has particularly developed into a significant financing instrument in top-level sports. Major top-level sports events, for example in motor sports, athletics, tennis, or during the entire season of national football or ice hockey leagues, are hardly possible today without the involvement of sponsors (Drees, 1989; Freyer, 2018). In contrast, the expenditures of the economy for grassroots sports are significantly lower.
   Relevant sports in terms of sponsoring include football, handball, tennis, motor sports, athletics, basketball, cycling, boxing, golf, equestrian sports, sailing, and winter sports such as biathlon, speed skating, ski jumping, Nordic skiing, alpine skiing, or ice hockey. About two-thirds of all sponsoring investments go into football. The highest endowed individual contracts in Germany are concluded by sponsors with football clubs or associations (see Fig. 1.13).
   How large the sums are in concrete terms was determined by the data service provider Statista for the sports year 2018/2019. According to this, companies worldwide spent 30.87 billion USD on sports sponsoring, with most of the money going to leagues and teams (see Fig. 1.14).
5. When considering **cultural sponsoring**, it becomes apparent that sponsoring expenditures in this area, compared to public subsidies for art and culture, have been relatively low in the past. However, sponsoring has now become a significant source of funding for certain forms of culture, such as art prizes and music festivals. The awarding of numerous cultural prizes would no longer be possible today without corporate sponsoring, and festivals could not take place. Furthermore, the cultural activities of companies are reflected in an increasing number of cultural foundations

Fig. 1.13 Sponsoring by sports. (*Source*: *Nielsen Sports/Repucom, 2015; ** Statista, 2022e)

Sport type	2014/15*	2020/21**	Trend
Soccer	71 %	75 %	↗
Motorsport	18 %	13 %	↘
Golf	2 %	n.a.	→
Athletics	n.a.	1 %	→
Cycling	n.a.	1 %	→
Basketball	2 %	3 %	↗
Winter sports	n.a.	1 %	→
Ice hockey	2 %	2 %	→
Handball	1 %	1 %	→
other	1 %	2 %	

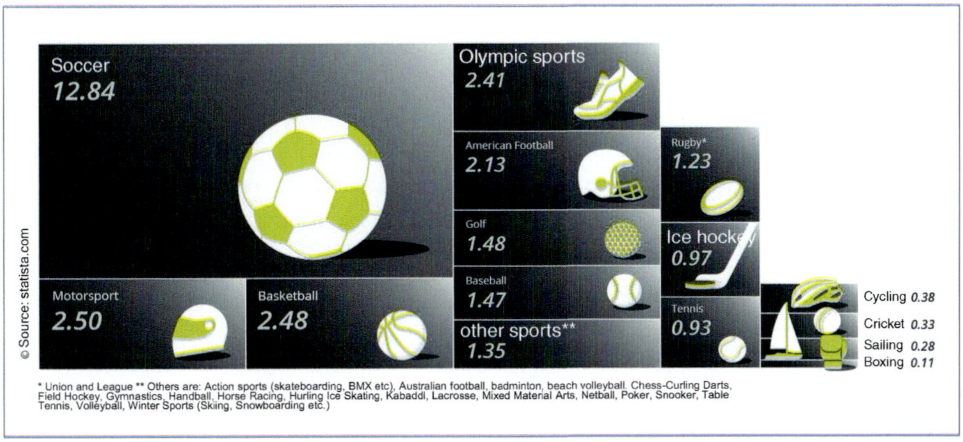

Fig. 1.14 Global expenditure for sponsoring by sports. (*Source*: Statista, 2019)

initiated by businesses. In the future, due to cuts in cultural funding by public budgets, the importance of cultural sponsoring as a financing instrument for cultural institutions is expected to increase further (Bob Bomliz Group, 2008; Nielsen Sports (formerly Repucom), 2015) and, following the model of the USA, there will be more cooperation between the public sector and private companies (Public Private Partnership).

6. The area of public sponsoring with the focus on **social and environmental** issues has only played a supplementary role as a source of funding for non-commercial organizations, measured against public expenditures for social, educational, and ecological tasks, in the past (Bruhn, 1990a, b; Bruhn & Dahlhoff, 1990). Since the mid-1990s, the number of companies that have discovered socio-environmental sponsoring as a communication tool has increased, and companies have increasingly aimed to convey social responsibility through their social or ecological commitment and thus generate image advantages (Zollinger, 1995, p. 122; Busch et al., 2008; Bruhn, 2012). Although the years 2008 to 2011 were characterized by stagnating sponsoring expenditures in the area of socio-environmental sponsoring, mainly due to the financial and economic crisis, a positive trend has been observed in recent years (ZAW, 2006–2021, Nielsen Sports, 2018a). About 50% of the surveyed company and agency representatives (versus 37% in 2007 and 26% in 2006) expect an increasing willingness to invest in this area (Pilot Checkpoint, 2008; W&V, 2012).
7. With the entry into force of the Broadcasting State Treaty on January 1, 1992, it is possible in Germany, under certain conditions, to engage in **program sponsoring** (Bruhn & Mehlinger, 1999, pp. 216 ff.), i.e., to sponsor specific television or radio

programs and be mentioned as a supporting company. Since the beginning of program sponsoring and especially its expansion to other media, high growth rates have been observed for this communication tool, into which companies now invest more money than in cultural, socio, or environmental sponsoring. The current volume is about 1 billion EUR, and further growth is expected in the future (Statista, 2016a). Media sponsoring is particularly important for branded goods, as audiovisual media reach a wide audience and brand manufacturers can achieve communication goals, such as increasing brand awareness.

8. With the increasing and now widespread use of the internet and new media, **internet sponsoring** or **digital sponsoring** as a form of media sponsoring has gained importance. Although the assessment of the increasing importance of the internet has been lower in recent years than in previous years, according to a study, 72% of the surveyed advertisers and agencies still expect growing importance in the coming years (Nielsen Sports (formerly Repucom), 2015). Another study shows that already 57.1% of the surveyed companies are engaged in internet sponsoring (ZHAW, 2015). Thus, internet sponsoring is considered the most used form of media sponsoring before TV-sponsoring (Nielsen Sports (formerly Repucom), 2015, 2018a, b; ZHAW, 2015).

When assessing the future importance of certain forms of sponsoring, the development of the population's interest in various leisure fields as well as the**Acceptance of sponsoring** in different areas should be considered. An analysis of the public's interest in various leisure fields relevant to sponsoring at the beginning of the sponsoring boom showed that the areas of nature/environment, music, and social issues are particularly important to the public (INRA Germany GmbH, 2000). Further acceptance surveys followed. In 2014, the results regarding the acceptance of sponsoring in the areas of sports, culture, environment, and social issues (IPSOS GmbH, 2014) showed that sponsoring in all four areas is widely accepted by the public. Furthermore, it can be observed that in all areas the target group of sports, culture, environment, and social interest is somewhat more open to sponsoring than the general population. A study by the Association of Sports Sponsoring Providers (VSA) from 2019 was finally able to confirm that consumers view sports sponsoring even more than conventional advertising as a contemporary, likeable,and credible communication tool (see Fig. 1.15). Furthermore, a study from the football sector shows that fans, who are often described as being opposed to the commercialization of their sport, actually show more understanding and acceptance for sponsoring than the general population (Nielsen Sports, 2018a, b).

Sports sponsoring benefits from the previously mentioned high acceptance like hardly any other form of communication. This is due to the above-average interest of

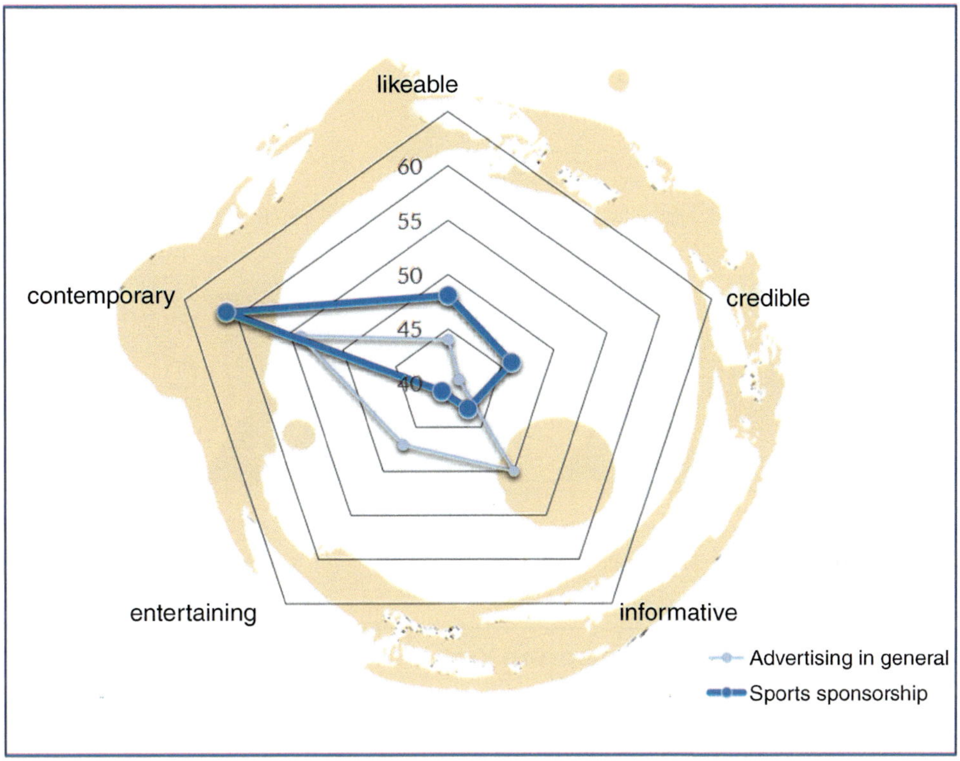

Fig. 1.15 Sports sponsoring as a contemporary communication tool. (*Source*: VSA, 2019)

the population in sports—whether as active or passive participants. In addition, there are other **special features of sports sponsoring** that make it particularly attractive. For example, the sports sector provides a highly emotional platform where people meet, share common experiences and serve as multipliers for their preferred sports and athletes. Another special feature in sports sponsoring is the high frequency of contact. The message is usually present throughout the entire sports event, and media such as TV, print, or the internet, which report on such sports competitions, further enhance the presence and perception of a sponsoring commitment. An important task of the rights holders in sports sponsoring is therefore to credibly and verifiably demonstrate this potential (e.g., through solid impact research), to transform it into suitable rights grants, and thereby to create transparency and trust for sponsor contacts.

The mutual network of relationships among the actors involved in the sports sponsoring market (sponsors, sponsored parties, and media) is therefore aptly referred to as the **"Magic Triangle"** of sports marketing and sponsoring (see Fig. 1.16).

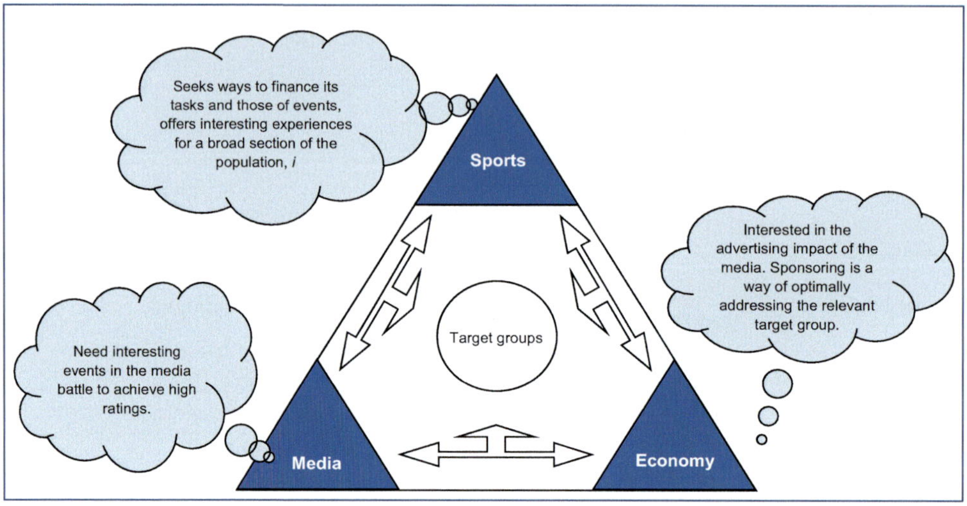

Fig. 1.16 The "Magic Triangle" of sports marketing and sponsoring. (*Source*: Bruhn & Rohlmann, 2022)

1.4 Importance of Sponsoring Rights (incl. Case Study Raiffeisen Switzerland)

In sponsoring, according to common parlance, it is about one partner offering certain services in the form of special advertising rights **(rights provider)** and transferring or assigning their communicative use against certain counter-services, predominantly in the form of money payments—less often as in-kind services—to another **(rights recipient)**. In colloquial language and also in sports, rights are generally spoken of without it always becoming clear which rights are involved in detail and who is the entitled party behind these rights. In the true sense, it is therefore a matter of **rights trading** or sale of rights in sports, which is described by the parties involved, the type of rights, their exclusivity, and the user groups (see Fig. 1.17).

The resulting network of relationships usually has a complex structure and requires the owner of the original rights to clearly **define and delimit** them as well as to provide legally valid protection, which is either undoubtedly present by law or agreement (e.g., property and employment relationships, personal rights, association law) or is ensured by other formats such as copyright, trademark law, house rights, event rights, etc.

It seems sensible to first attempt a clean **classification of different sports rights** in order to then clarify who is the owner of these rights, how this can be recognized, whether these are exclusive or non-exclusive, and who else can participate in sports sponsoring.

- Partners in the rights trade (rights holders, rights brokers, rights users)
- Type of rights (e.g. media, communication, service, etc.)
- Exclusivity of rights
- Usage groups (end users, companies)
- Relationship structure (B2C, B2B)

Fig. 1.17 Rights trading in sports

In sports sponsoring, several **exploitation rights** usually belong to an agreement, with different rights holders being involved again and again without the rights recipient being really aware of this. As part of a basic distinction, **person-related, club- and association-related as well as sports venue- and location-related rights** can be distinguished (see Fig. 1.18).

The sponsored parties can offer the sponsor a multitude of **communicative usage possibilities** either individually or as a package with various rights within a sponsoring partnership (see Fig. 1.19), always ensuring that the sponsored parties actually still own these rights and have not possibly transferred them by contract to the club (team athletes) or as a member of a national team to the belonging sports association.

Examples

The so-called **"Shoe Dispute"** in the German national football team almost escalated after the 2006 World Cup, when some national players even threatened to boycott if their wish for free shoe choice was not met (FAZ, 2006). In other countries, footballers had long had the opportunity to always wear their own shoes through private sponsoring contracts with a sports equipment manufacturer. An agreement was reached

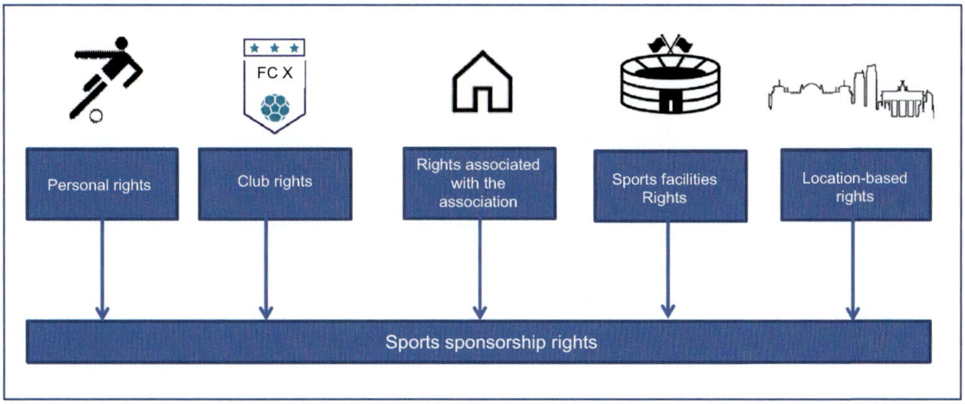

Fig. 1.18 Sponsoring rights in sports

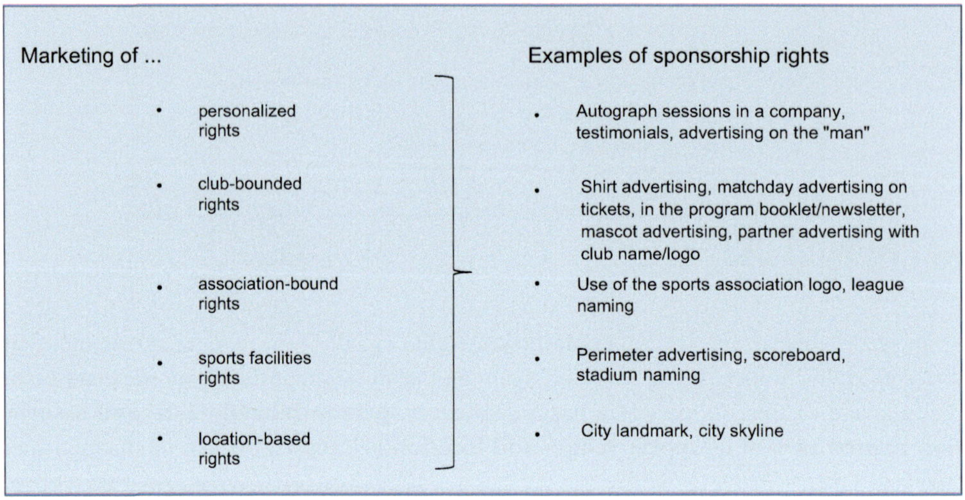

Fig. 1.19 Rights trading as a marketing task

in August 2006. Until then, all national players of the DFB had to appear in Adidas shoes at international matches, despite personal equipment contracts. This particularly affected national goalkeeper Jens Lehmann and the then World Cup and Bundesliga top scorer Miroslav Klose. Both had a contract with Nike.

There was also repeated trouble due to private sponsors on the racing clothing between the most successful German Olympian at winter games, Claudia Pechstein, and the German Speed Skating Association (DESG). ◄

Especially in the sponsoring of individual athletes, **conflict situations** can occur with the sponsoring of sports clubs or sports associations. Such coordination problems between the various sponsored parties, who are connected at different levels in the organizational structure in sports (athlete/sports club/association), can become a risk factor. This applies to both the sponsor in question and the sponsored party, who has to deal with legal problems in addition to his sports (Nagel, 2012). The increase in private equipment contracts with individual athletes has intensified conflicts in recent years. Often such "sponsoring confrontations" are deliberately brought about, so they do not always occur randomly or because of a lack of coordination, increasing density of sponsoring and/or unclear rules for the various sponsored parties, counterproductive or (partially) contradictory contract terms exist. Especially in team sports, where the clubs often have their own jersey and shoe sponsors, there is quickly a competitive relationship with the athlete's sponsor at competitions and official appointments.

Such actions are now also counted as in sports and are recurring actions by companies that either lost in the sponsoring competition or believe they cannot afford or want to avoid official partnerships. In such a case, the club can be "punished" by its own sponsor

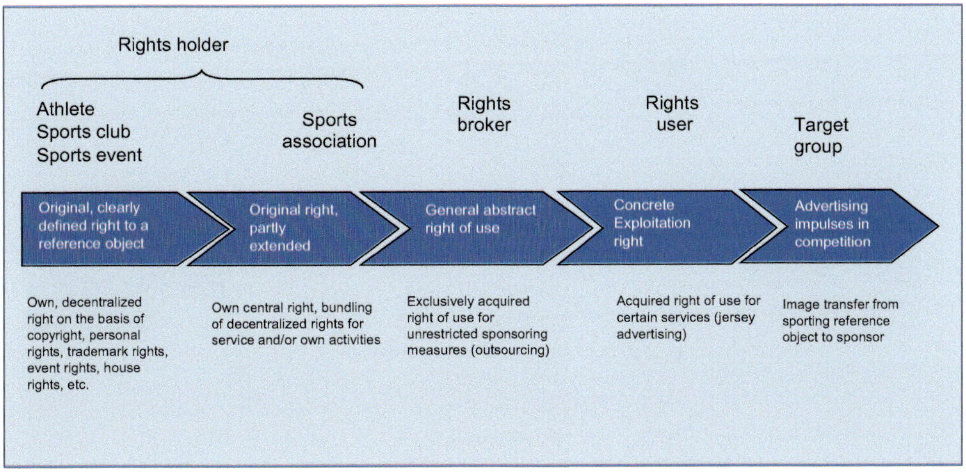

Fig. 1.20 Value creation process in sports sponsoring

because it has violated its contractual obligations. The player will then in turn get into conflicts with the club, which can ultimately even lead to sporting penalties on his part.

The actual rights holders also have to ensure that the involvement of so-called rights brokers in marketing (including sponsoring agencies, marketing offices) does not lead to overlaps or lack of performance fulfillment with the sponsors. This must be observed in the **value creation process in rights trading in sports sponsoring**, especially the relationships between the rights holders, the rights brokers and the rights users (see Fig. 1.20).

Special attention should also be paid to the **ownership of sports facilities** and their advertising exploitation, because in the often long-term lease contracts with municipal facilities or private organizations, short-term sponsoring opportunities often remain unused or are only limitedly implementable. About half of all Bundesliga stadiums are—at least in part—municipally owned (Stadionwelt, 2019), but the operation is usually taken over by private operating companies or external service providers. Most stadiums that are entirely municipally owned are outsourced to municipal companies. This is mainly for legal reasons regarding liability in the event of insolvency. If the issue of stadium sponsoring is not clearly defined by contract in terms of responsibility and financial participation, significant sources of income may be lost to the sports clubs as tenants. In addition to municipal owners, there are private owners and operators as well as public-private partnerships that shape the stadium landscape.

In some cases, a **sponsoring right can also be derived from the location**, if the place is virtually representative or synonymous for a certain sport (e.g., Oberhof for biathlon), its fame surpasses that of the sports actor (e.g., a track and field athlete) or the place basically acts as its own brand (e.g., Eugene—Track Town/USA).

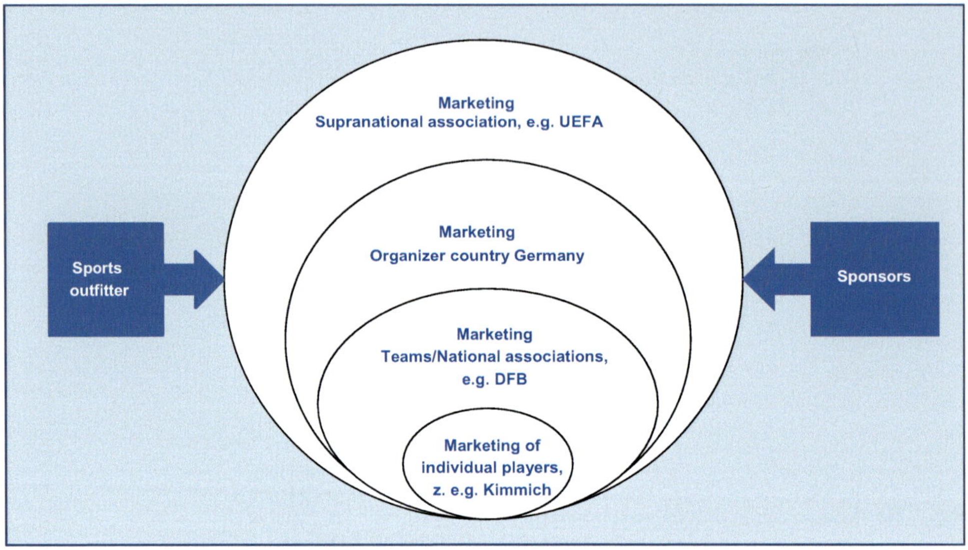

Fig. 1.21 Potential conflicts in sponsoring due to the convergence of various brand rights using the example of UEFA EURO 2024

How strongly major sporting events can be associated with **conflicts due to sponsoring rights** of various rights holders is shown in Fig. 1.21.

The rights of sports actors (athletes, clubs, associations, etc.), which can be used by sponsoring partners, remain the most important factors in sports sponsoring. This is also confirmed by regular surveys on the growth of various **marketing rights in sports** (see Fig. 1.22). A study by PwC shows that despite an already relatively high level, further increases can be expected in the future (PricewaterhouseCoopers, 2020).

The introductory chapter illustrates on the one hand the diversity with which **sponsoring can be used as a communication tool by companies**. On the other hand, it has also become clear that some basic elements must be considered when using sports sponsoring. These are summarized below.

Case Study Raiffeisen Switzerland—digital and sales-oriented sponsoring activation in sports

The following case study was compiled by **André Stöckli**, Head of Sponsoring & Events at Raiffeisen Switzerland, and is made with the kind support and permission of Raiffeisen Switzerland.

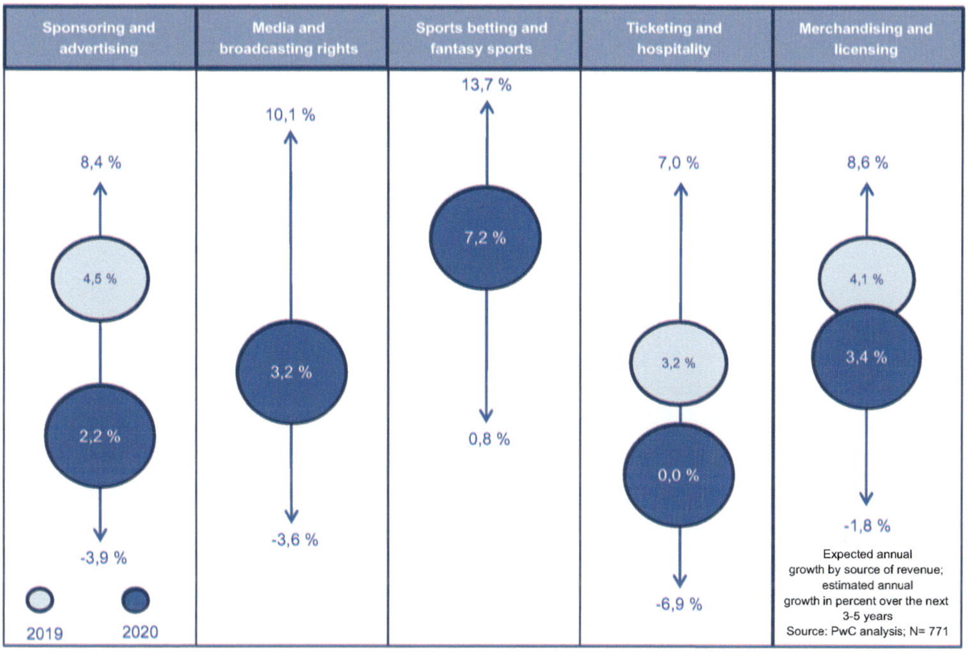

Fig. 1.22 Results on the growth of marketing-relevant offers. (*Source*: PricewaterhouseCoopers, 2020)

Review and Initial Situation

The **Raiffeisen Group** is the leading Swiss retail bank. The third force in the Swiss banking market had a total of 1.96 million cooperative members and 3.6 million customers at the end of 2021. The Raiffeisen Group is present at 820 locations throughout Switzerland. The 219 legally autonomous and cooperatively organized Raiffeisen banks are united in the Raiffeisen Switzerland Cooperative. This has the strategic leadership function of the entire Raiffeisen Group and provides central services for the entire Raiffeisen Group, including in the areas of risk management, products & cooperations, IT, training, as well as marketing and sponsoring.

Until 2004, Raiffeisen had not undertaken any overarching national sponsoring commitments as part of a national sponsoring strategy, except for occasional major events. The management decided in 2004 to initiate a **national sponsoring concept**. The selected sponsoring commitments should achieve various coordinated marketing goals and reach a broad target group, and additionally meet the following **requirements**:

- Three-tier usability of sponsoring activities: local, regional, and national with the goal of generating a concrete benefit for the local market processing of the Raiffeisen banks,

- Coverage of the whole of Switzerland taking into account all language regions,
- Focus on sustainable and long-term sponsorings instead of one-off events,
- Several months of strong media presence,
- Fit of the sponsoring to the image values of Raiffeisen.

Snow Sports Commitment—Swiss-Ski

In 2005, Raiffeisen joined Swiss-Ski as an association partner as part of the initiated national sponsoring strategy and has since successfully occupied the snow sports topic. Detailed information on the snow sports strategy and its implementation is given in the Activation Strategy section.

Football Commitment—Raiffeisen Super League

In addition to the national snow sports commitment, Raiffeisen decided in 2011 to take over the title sponsoring of the top Swiss football league, the "Super League", from the Swiss Football League for the 2012/2013 season, thus nationally occupying the football topic.

The consideration to expand the national sponsoring portfolio with two major platforms was primarily driven by the following four **strategic considerations**:

- **Market:** Raiffeisen had strong market shares in rural regions and therefore aimed for market growth in urban areas of Switzerland. A large number of Swiss cities in all parts of the country are actively involved in Swiss top football with corresponding presence and fan base.
- **Target group:** While in snow sports the reached target group is rather older (45+) and more rural, football could address a more urban and compared to snow sports younger and "more male" target group. The two target groups thus complement each other to a certain extent.
- **Member benefits:** In the Raiffeisen member benefit program "MemberPlus", in which experience benefits are offered for cooperatives, a relevant benefit from the sports sector was sought to complement the existing member benefits from the entertainment (music & events) and tourism sectors. The Raiffeisen Super League, with 180 games per year throughout Switzerland, was perfect for this. Thus, the benefit—50% discount on all Sunday games of the Raiffeisen Super League for Raiffeisen members—was created, which was used more than 30,000 times a year.
- **Seasonality:** A final and absolutely central point was the search for a seasonal complement. Snow sports mainly take place in the media and thus the presence of Raiffeisen from mid-November to mid-March. In the remaining months, the reach and thus brand presence was greatly reduced. The commitment to football proved to be an ideal seasonal complement, allowing the brand presence to be maintained throughout the year.

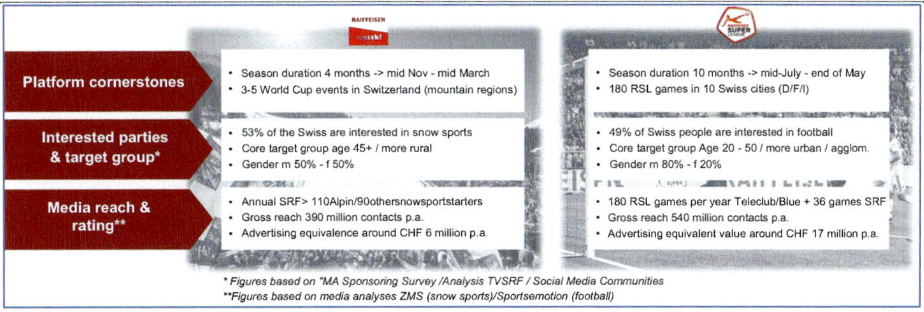

Fig. 1.23 Combination of snow sports and football of the Raiffeisen Group. (*Source*: Raiffeisen)

Ultimately, it can be highlighted that the combination of snow sports and football represented an exciting and well-functioning combination for Raiffeisen from various perspectives, some data are shown in Fig. 1.23.

After nine successful years as title sponsor of the Raiffeisen Super League, in which many of the targeted goals could be achieved, Raiffeisen decided for overarching strategic reasons to end its commitment to football at the end of the 2020/2021 season and to focus, among other things, on strengthening the perception of competence in the investment business in overall marketing.

Crowdfunding platform—lokalhelden.ch

As a complement or alternative to the large number of direct local commitments of the Raiffeisen banks in sports, culture and social projects, Raiffeisen launched its own **crowdfunding platform for non-profit projects** lokalhelden.ch in 2016 to round off and in the sense of digitizing the Raiffeisen cooperative idea of "self-help". As a commitment to society, Raiffeisen provides the platform to project initiators free of charge (the market practice is 8–12% fees of the collected funds) and thus enables many projects a free and alternative way of financing non-profit projects and events. Since its launch in 2016, lokalhelden.ch has grown very successfully and has positioned itself as a relevant and strong platform in the market. The development of the annual projects and funding sums is shown in Fig. 1.24.

Structure of Raiffeisen Group's sponsoring

In summary, the sponsoring structure of the Raiffeisen Group consists of four different elements as well as the commitments for the member benefits of the Raiffeisen cooperatives. This structure is shown in Fig. 1.25.

The foundation of Raiffeisen sponsoring is a large number of local and regional commitments by the approximately 220 independent Raiffeisen banks in sports, culture, and social affairs. Every year, Raiffeisen invests between 12 and 16 million CHF locally and regionally for a vibrant Switzerland. As a strategic, national, and far-reaching platform, Raiffeisen occupies the snow sports theme with the

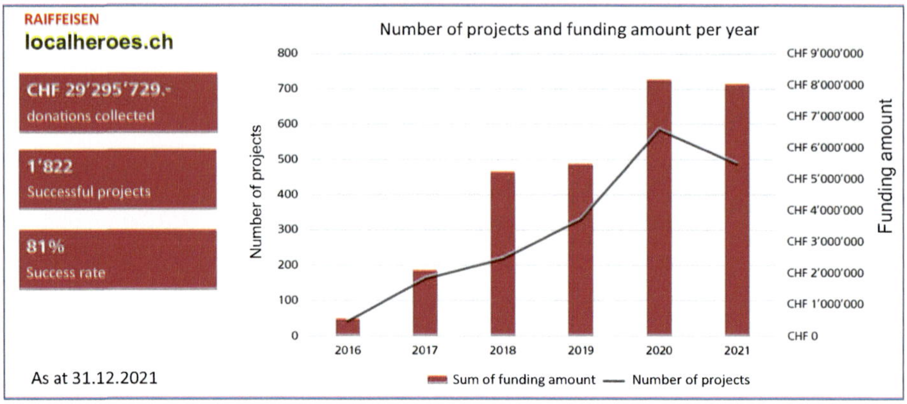

Fig. 1.24 Development of the platform lokalhelden.ch. (*Source*: Raiffeisen)

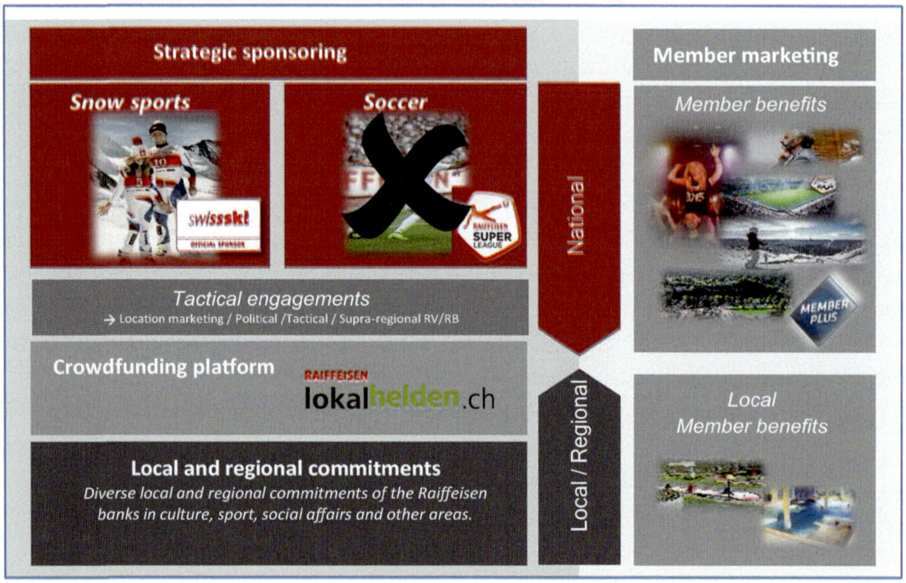

Fig. 1.25 Sponsoring structure of the Raiffeisen Group. (*Source*: Raiffeisen)

main commitment to Swiss-Ski and other snow sports commitments in elite sports, mass sports, youth development, and sports for people with disabilities. In addition to the strategic snow sports commitment, Raiffeisen has a small number of tactical commitments in the area of long-standing testimonials (e.g., Viktor Röthlin), occasional federal events, and regional support in the topic of wrestling. The previously mentioned donation platform lokalhelden.ch serves as an alternative financing option for all projects and events that Raiffeisen cannot directly support.

In addition to the mentioned classic sponsoring commitments of Raiffeisen Switzerland and the Raiffeisen banks, Raiffeisen maintains larger sponsoring partnerships for the purpose of generating experience advantages for its cooperative members, among others in the areas of culture (Swiss Museum Pass → member benefit: free admission to Swiss museums) and concerts & events (Various concert and show organizers → member benefit up to 50% discount on admissions), tourism (over 25 Swiss ski areas → member benefit 40% discount on ski day tickets) and sustainability/mobility (Car Sharing provider Mobility → member benefit free trial subscription/50% discount on the annual subscription).

Core goals of national sponsoring and integration into overall marketing strategy of Raiffeisen Switzerland

In the context and in coordination with the overarching marketing strategy of Raiffeisen Switzerland, the national sponsoring should not only focus on the classic sponsoring goals in the area of brand presence and strength, but also increasingly on sales support and lead generation. In addition, contributions in the areas of loyalty/member benefits and employer branding should be made with the national sponsoring. The core goals of the national sponsoring are shown in Fig. 1.26.

National Snow Sports Strategy

As part of its national sponsoring strategy, Raiffeisen occupies the theme field **snow sports**. A sustainable and effective occupation is achieved on the one hand through various commitments not only in elite sports, but also in mass sports, youth development, and sports for people with disabilities, and on the other hand through a combination of national and regional commitments. An overview is provided in Fig. 1.27.

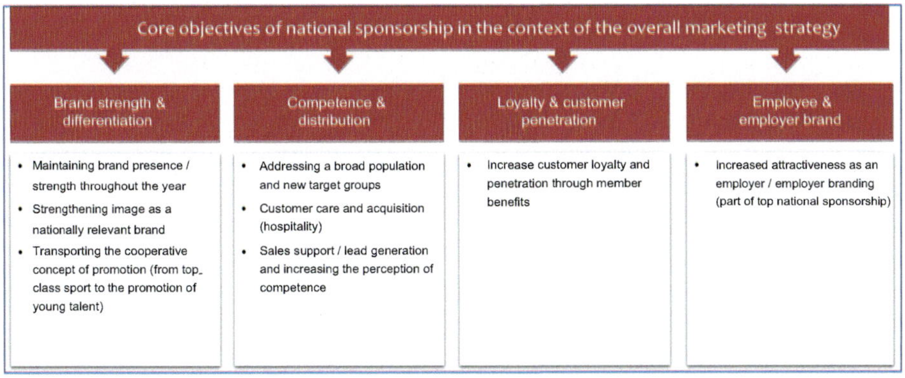

Fig. 1.26 Goals of the national sponsoring of Raiffeisen Switzerland. (*Source*: Raiffeisen)

Fig. 1.27 Snow sports strategy. (*Source*: Raiffeisen)

The holistic occupation of the topic allows Raiffeisen a consistently strong perception and activation. The local commitments as well as the commitments in the area of youth, mass sports, and sports for people with disabilities reflect the cooperative idea and thus fit the DNA of Raiffeisen.

Activation Strategy Raiffeisen Snow Sports Commitment

The activation strategy of Raiffeisen's snow sports commitment comprises four **core pillars:** The improvement of brand presence, brand awareness and image, the creation of hospitality platforms, local anchoring and promotion, and the generation of member benefits.

Brand Presence, Brand Awareness and Image

To strengthen the brand awareness and brand image of Raiffeisen, both classic media visibility activations and on-site appearances and content productions are used, such as:

- Swiss-Ski-Sponsor → Logo presence on all athletes/in all disciplines,
- SRF TV-sponsoring → 250 races in various disciplines, around 300 million gross contacts,
- Partner Swiss World Cup races → Band logo presence in the finish area,
- Ski World Cup races Adelboden/Wengen/Crans Montana → on-site appearances with own activation zone (e.g. fondue chalet/photo actions/hat sales),
- 16 Raiffeisen athletes → Content & campaigns.

Hospitality Platforms

Especially in the financial services sector, where complex products are in use and where it is about the personal financial affairs of customers, trust is an elemental factor. Hospitality invitations serve to build trust with the personal advisor and are therefore a central activation element for customer retention and acquisition. As part of the snow sports commitment, Raiffeisen Switzerland provides various types of hospitality platforms for booking to the Raiffeisen banks, such as:

- Official VIP platforms Swiss World Cup races → 600+ customer invitations per year,
- Raiffeisen-exclusive platform at the Lauberhorn race → own chalet at the Minschkante including slope inspection after the race,
- Care of Raiffeisen guests by the Raiffeisen ambassadors Pirmin and Silvan Zurbriggen.

Local Anchoring and Promotion

As previously described, regional commitments and targeted promotion of grassroots sports, young talent and sports for people with impairments are both a central element for Raiffeisen in the sense of their cooperative idea and also important for the comprehensive occupation of the snow sports theme field. To achieve this, Raiffeisen has launched the following commitments and activations over time:

- Support of all eleven ski regional associations and the three national performance centers,
- Raiffeisen hat action → Sale of 400,000+ ski hats for the young talent with donation proceeds of over 2 million CHF since the launch of the action,
- Young talent donation pot on lokalhelden.ch (https://www.lokalhelden.ch/rb/nachwuchs) → Support of over 80 young talent athletes/projects,
- Support of a large number of local ski clubs and regional squads by the regional Raiffeisen banks,
- Initiation and title sponsor Raiffeisen Snow Camps with MS Sports → nationwide 10 full-week snow sports camps for children,
- Main partner Snow Sports Initiative Switzerland → The platform GoSnow.ch offers schools and teachers ready-organized snow sports camps and days at attractive prices to animate especially children and teenagers to snow sports again,
- Partnerships Special Olympics Switzerland and Swiss Paralympics → Promotion and support of people with impairments in snow sports.

Member Benefits—Winter Sports Benefits for Raiffeisen Members

As a fourth activation pillar, targeted winter sports benefits are offered as part of the member benefits program "MemberPlus" for the Raiffeisen cooperators. These include:

- 50% member benefits on admission to selected Swiss World Cup races (e.g. Adelboden/Wengen),
- 40% member benefit on ski day tickets in over 25 ski areas in Switzerland.

Expansion of a digital and sales-oriented activation strategy in snow sports engagement

As a general conclusion, it can be stated that the four described activation pillars guarantee a solid and functioning activation. Due to changing framework conditions (e.g., media usage behavior, social media, advertising overload, etc.) and the adjustment of the target focus, with the desire for a stronger sales orientation of the sponsoring, the following questions and challenges arose for the sports sponsoring of the Raiffeisen Group:

- Do we still reach the fans via the traditional channels?
- How can we actively interact with the fans?
- How can the snow sports platform be played 365 days a year?
- How can sponsoring be used to support sales?

The strategy of the future: welovesnow.ch—editorial owned media content platform

The initial core question of the realignment of the sponsoring was how to continuously reach the target group envisaged with the snow sports engagement and actively interact with it.

Traditional and at first glance also well-functioning are classic live marketing appearances on site at the Ski World Cup races, which Raiffeisen has been successfully using in their activation strategy for years. However, this form of activation also has some significant disadvantages and limitations. As early as 2017, Raiffeisen therefore additionally considered playing and interacting with the snow sports target group using content marketing. This then visionary approach, not yet implemented by any sponsor in this consequence, seemed to bring along some exciting and potential advantages besides a few known and unknown challenges. The tension between live marketing and content marketing is shown in Fig. 1.28.

Against the background of this initial situation and findings, Raiffeisen launched their digital owned media content platform named **welovesnow.ch** in 2017. In return, the use of traditional paid media campaigns (print/online) was waived and the financial resources were reallocated for the construction and operation of the platform.

The construction of the platform and the implementation of the **digital content strategy** were carried out over a longer period and in four main phases. Together with their cooperation partner Sportal Media (integrated into Ringier Sports AG since 2020), the technical framework of the platform was developed in a first step

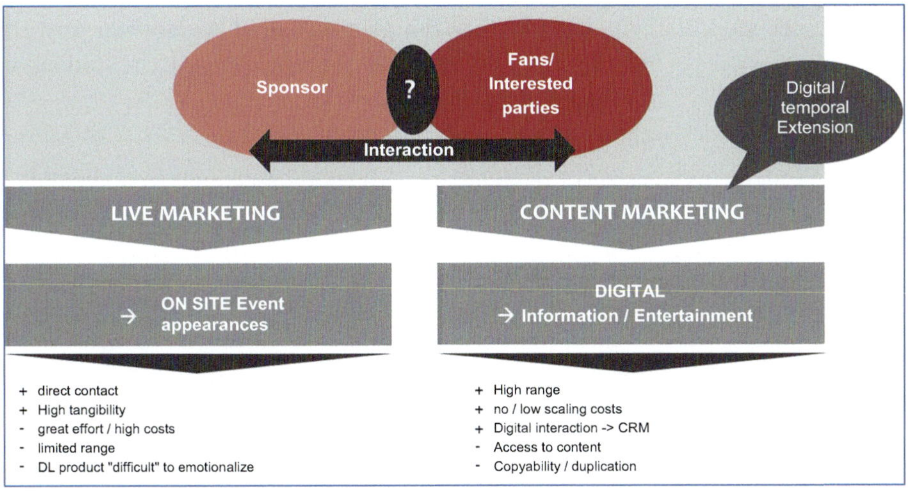

Fig. 1.28 Live Marketing vs. Content Marketing

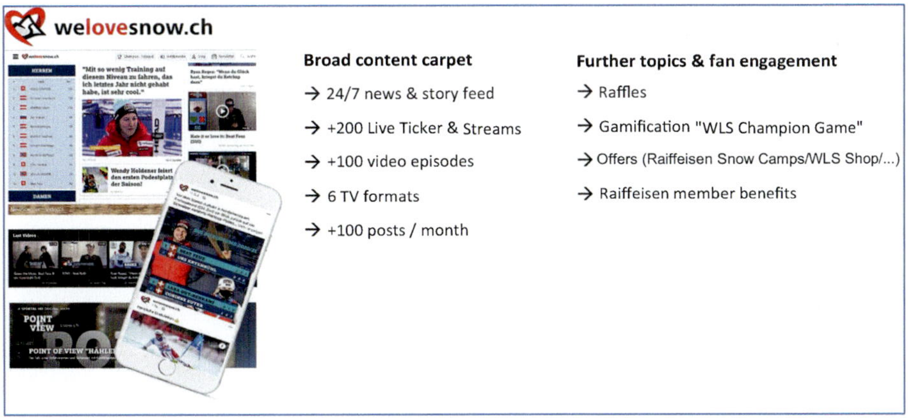

Fig. 1.29 welovesnow.ch—Content carpet and contents. (*Source*: Raiffeisen)

and in a second phase the content carpet was produced and continuously expanded (see in detail Fig. 1.29). The third phase was focused on building digital communities via social media and directing traffic to the platform. The fourth phase focused on the backward implementation of marketing automation/CRM tools for playing and converting the target group.

The decision to launch the **platform detached from the brand and CI/CD** of Raiffeisen was very consciously chosen. This step was central for the positioning as an editorial topic platform and for the acceptance among snow sports fans. Raiffeisen's presence on the platform is native through the content, where Raiffeisen as a sponsor of Swiss-Ski with the included logo visibility is automatically present, and through accompanying content and offers on the platform.

The **core goal of the platform from the perspective of sponsoring** was not primarily to increase the visibility of Raiffeisen, but rather to build its own **snow sports community**, in which Raiffeisen has data sovereignty. This should then be played with exciting and relevant snow sports and Raiffeisen offers, and existing Raiffeisen members should be more closely tied or new Raiffeisen members should be acquired.

Basic model of a sales-supported activation

The operation of an editorial owned media platform does not yet produce a direct sales-supporting effect. Rather, from this perspective, the platform is a means to an end and forms the basis for playing the snow sports-affine users in a segmented, automated and event-based manner. This relationship is shown in Fig. 1.30.

Users interested in snow sports are primarily targeted via social media (Facebook/Instagram) with teaser content of interest to them and are directed to the platform welovesnow.ch via link posts, where the complete content is visible. After reading or viewing the sought-after content on the platform, the following further **goals** are in the foreground:

- Consumption of further content → Increase in usage and loyalty,
- Generation of user data (name/first name/address/email/age/gender) via competitions, raffles, prediction games, etc. → Building and expanding the community,
- Continuation to current business campaign → Jump-off interested party to www.raiffeisen.ch.

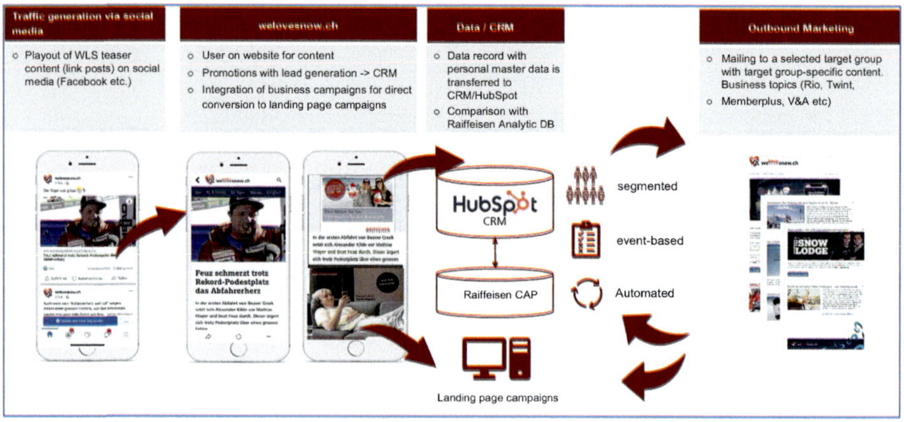

Fig. 1.30 Process sales-oriented activation. (*Source*: Raiffeisen)

The collected user data is managed in a CRM and continuously updated with user event data. The community is then **segmented, automated, and event-based** played with relevant content in the form of newsletter marketing. In addition to editorial snow sports content, Raiffeisen business content and offers are also specifically transported. The promotion of member benefits (e.g., 40% discount on ski day tickets, up to 50% discount on concerts & events, etc.) is particularly suitable as exciting content. Users who are not yet Raiffeisen members can test the benefits using a promo code and attempts are made to convert them from prospects to customers in the classic sales funnel.

Development of welovesnow.ch

The question arises whether such an approach can generate corresponding reach, whether a relevant community size can be built up and whether snow sports as a sponsoring platform can really be played 365 days a year.

Against this background, here are a few figures and key data: At the launch of the platform in 2017, just over 200,000 visits to welovesnow.ch were registered.

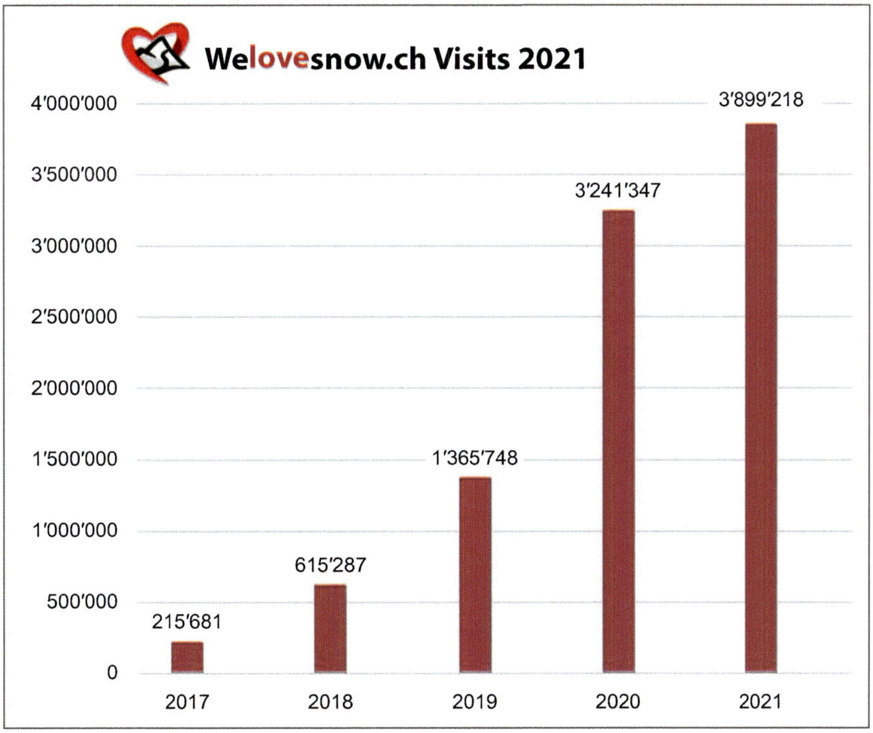

Fig. 1.31 Development of visits to welovesnow.ch since 2017. (*Source*: Raiffeisen)

In 2021, this number was already close to 4 million (see the development of visits in Fig. 1.31), which is a substantial size. In comparison, the Raiffeisen stock exchange page generates less traffic than welovesnow.ch. The platform has around 300,000 unique visitors per month or around 800,000 unique visitors per year. This means that Raiffeisen has at least one contact with around 800,000 snow sports fans per year, as a comparison to the alternative of live marketing through appearances on site: The spectator record at the Lauberhorn races in 2019 was 67,200 spectators, spread over three race days. It goes without saying that not all of these spectators can be reached with on-site measures.

The 365-day activation also works very well. The snow and racing months from December to March are clearly the strongest, but even in the intermediate months, the platform regularly records well over 200,000 visits per month, as shown in Fig. 1.32.

From the generated traffic—without the newsletter marketing that is central from a sales perspective—more than 50,000 business jumps to raiffeisen.ch are generated each year solely through the promotion of business campaigns on the welovesnow.ch page.

Building the welovesnow.ch community

Over time, a homogeneous **snow sports community** of over 50,000 people has been built up on social channels, which consists almost exactly half of men and women. The age distribution is certainly interesting, with the largest group on Facebook being the 65+ segment, clearly refuting the idea that only young people can be reached via digital and social channels. This is also documented in Fig. 1.33. Based on this community, a reach of over 50 million people is achieved through the daily welovesnow.ch social media posts, of which over 80% are organic.

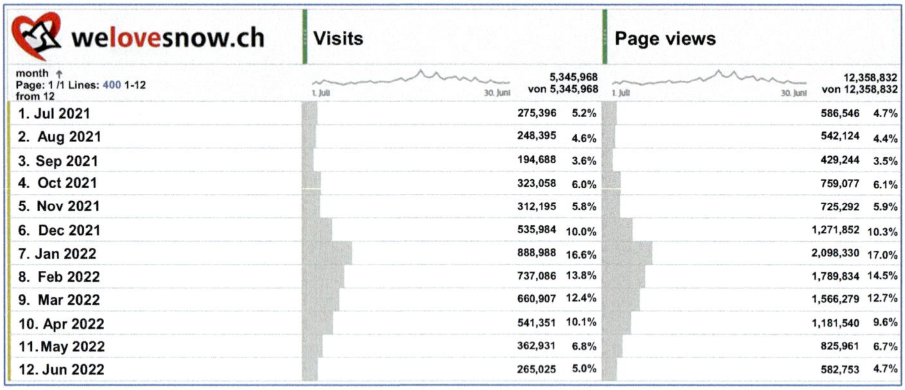

welovesnow.ch	Visits		Page views	
month ↑ Page: 1 /1 Lines: 400 1-12 from 12	5,345,968 von 5,345,968		12,358,832 von 12,358,832	
1. Jul 2021	275,396	5.2%	586,546	4.7%
2. Aug 2021	248,395	4.6%	542,124	4.4%
3. Sep 2021	194,688	3.6%	429,244	3.5%
4. Oct 2021	323,058	6.0%	759,077	6.1%
5. Nov 2021	312,195	5.8%	725,292	5.9%
6. Dec 2021	535,984	10.0%	1,271,852	10.3%
7. Jan 2022	888,988	16.6%	2,098,330	17.0%
8. Feb 2022	737,086	13.8%	1,789,834	14.5%
9. Mar 2022	660,907	12.4%	1,566,279	12.7%
10. Apr 2022	541,351	10.1%	1,181,540	9.6%
11. May 2022	362,931	6.8%	825,961	6.7%
12. Jun 2022	265,025	5.0%	582,753	4.7%

Fig. 1.32 Visits to welovesnow.ch per month. (*Source*: Raiffeisen)

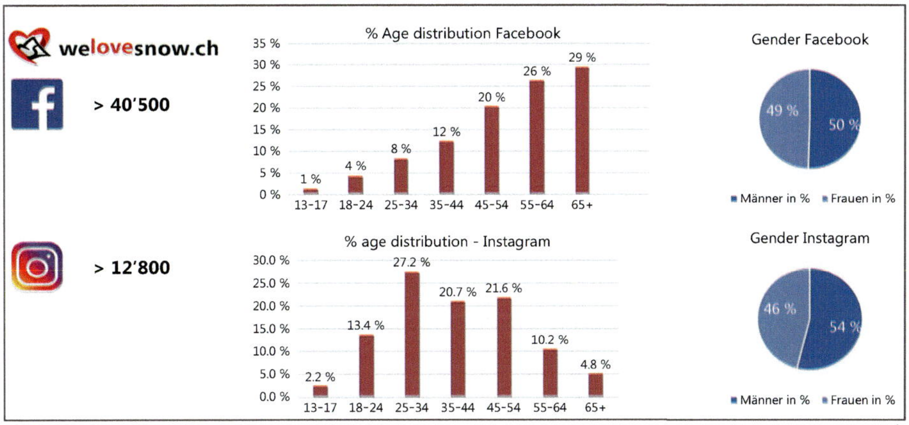

Fig. 1.33 Social Media Community of welovesnow.ch (as of December 2021). (*Source*: Raiffeisen)

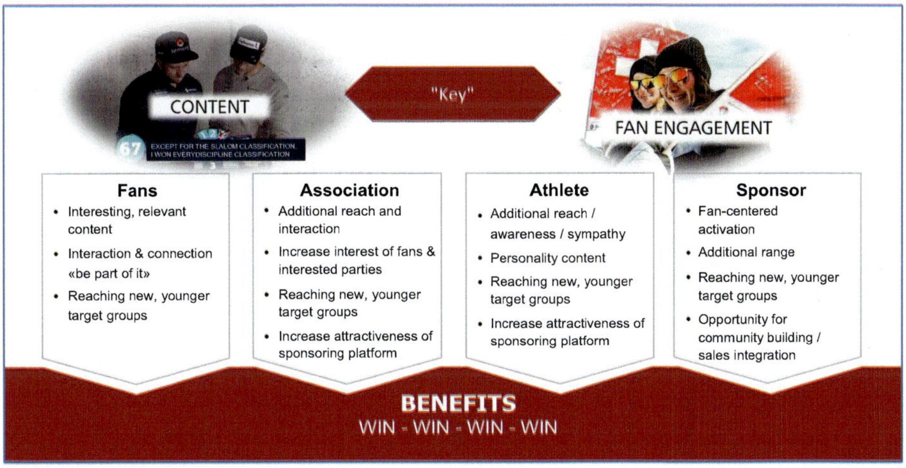

Fig. 1.34 Benefits of a content strategy for various stakeholders

In addition to the social media community, which is primarily relevant for generating traffic, the newsletter community, which is central to sales-oriented activation, has been expanded to over 150,000 welovesnow.ch subscribers over time. This means that Raiffeisen has over 150,000 snow sports-affine 1st party data addresses that it can play with any content at any time.

Fan Engagement and Sales-Oriented Activation

Such an owned media activation approach is not only exciting from a sponsoring and sales perspective, but also offers relevant **added value** to other stakeholders such as the association, the athletes, and of course, especially the fans, which can be described as a win-win-win-win situation. Different benefit components for various stakeholders are shown in Fig. 1.34.

Adjustment and Use of Athletes and Ambassador Strategy

The shift in strategic focus away from pure brand visibility towards a stronger sales orientation of the sponsoring has also led to Raiffeisen adjusting its individual sponsoring strategy and aligning it with the **content theme**. While the focus until 2018 was on 2–3 selected head sponsorings (main sponsor) of athletes (including Beat Feuz), the strategy was adjusted for the 2019/2020 season and a broad portfolio was built on the second sponsoring level without direct visibility with 14 alpine, 1 freeski, 1 Paralympics athletes and 2 ambassadors. The Raiffeisen athletes and the ambassador portfolio are shown in Fig. 1.35.

Fig. 1.35 Raiffeisen Athlete and Ambassador Portfolio. (*Source*: Raiffeisen)

Fig. 1.36 Campaign use of athletes. (*Source*: Raiffeisen)

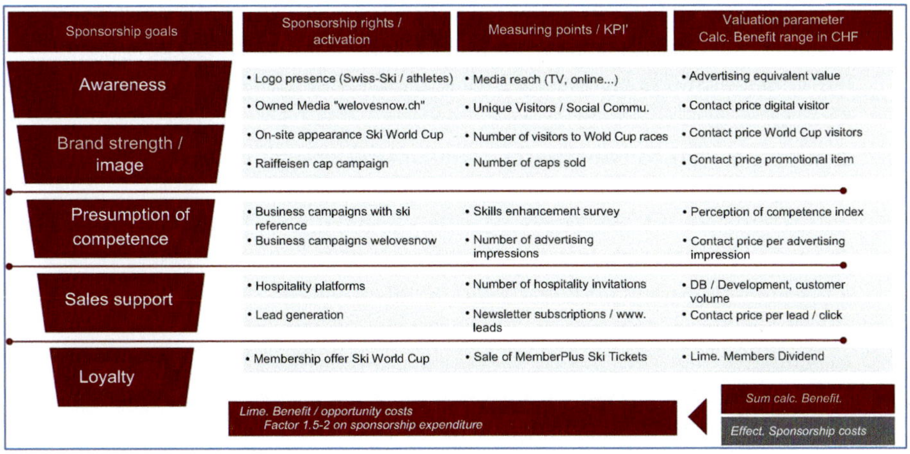

Fig. 1.37 Calculatory cost-benefit model of Raiffeisen sponsoring. (*Source*: Raiffeisen)

Through these partnerships, rights were secured for use in campaigns, which works perfectly even without head sponsoring (see the examples in Fig. 1.36), as well as for content production, social media extensions, and traditionally for events or guest care.

Cost-Benefit Evaluation Model for Snow Sports Sponsoring

As explained in this case study, a sponsoring activation strategy consists of many different elements. In addition to the individual assessment of individual measures based on specific KPIs, an indicative evaluation model along the marketing funnel was developed for a holistic cost-benefit consideration of the sponsoring or the measures taken, which allows a rough statement about the calculatory benefit compared to the sponsoring expenses. This is in the range of factor 1.5–2.0 for Raiffeisen's snow sports commitment, which means that the snow sports strategy and the chosen activation are successful and cost-efficient. The elements of the calculatory cost-benefit model of Raiffeisen sponsoring are shown in Fig. 1.37.

1.5 Key Points

To classify sponsoring as an element of sports marketing and sports sponsoring, it is helpful to pay particular attention to the following aspects:

Key Points

1. Sponsoring in sports is a special **form of promotion and communication** by a company or organization that wants to achieve certain effects.

2. Sponsoring is ultimately an **agreement between sponsors and those sponsored.** In the context of sponsoring, the achievement of marketing and corporate communication goals should be paramount.
3. **New areas and forms of sponsoring**: Sponsoring often offers more communicative competitive advantages through new possibilities and technological solutions than with traditional communication tools.
4. When assessing the **development of the importance of types of sponsoring**, the increasing interest in leisure fields and the acceptance of the population for different leisure activities should be taken into account. Sports sponsoring has gained increasing importance due to the growing importance of sports in society.
5. **Sports is the main area of application** for sponsoring as part of marketing and corporate communication and claims the most funds. Within this category, popular team sports, especially football, account for the largest budget share. Other sports are less crowded and therefore sometimes offer better opportunities.
6. After a modest start in the 1970s, sports sponsoring is in a **phase of value creation and instrumentalization**. This is associated with new challenges. sponsoring is also noticeably influenced by megatrends such as digitization and sustainability.
7. **Sponsoring rights**, which a holder grants to interested users, can be person-related, club and association-related, as well as sports venue and location-related. The individual opportunities and risks must be carefully weighed.
8. The strengths of sponsoring commitments can be optimally utilized if a **expansion of sponsoring into a comprehensive communication platform** is carried out and placed at the center of a company's communication policy. It must be checked individually for each company whether and to what extent sports as a focus or a spread is sensible.
9. The use of sponsoring should be based on a **systematic planning and decision-making process** with careful analysis, planning, implementation, and control. In addition, the implementation or activation of sponsoring requires further resources and expertise.
10. In the **Ecosystem sports sponsoring**, not only the directly involved parties (sponsor and sponsored party) participate, but also other actors such as rights brokers and intermediaries (e.g., agencies) as well as service providers (e.g., advertising board or content service).

References

A

Abratt, R., Clayton, B. C., & Pitt, L. F. (1987). Corporate objectives in sports sponsoring. *International Journal of Advertising, 6*(4), 299–312. https://doi.org/10.1080/02650487.1987.11107030.

Abril Barrie, C., Sánchez Herrera, J., & Recio Naranjo, T. (2018). Does Wall Street love sports sponsoring? Stock market reactions to the announcement of global official sponsorings. *Journal of Advertising Research, 58*(3), 297–310. https://doi.org/10.2501/jar-2017-016.

Abril, C., Sanchez, J., & Recio, T. (2018). How does Wall Street react to global sports sponsoring announcements?: An analysis of the effect on sponsoring companies' stock market prices. *Journal of Advertising Research, 58*(3), 297–310. https://doi.org/10.2501/jar-2017-016.

Ahlert, D., Vogel, V., & Woisetschläger, D. (2007). Ist Sponsoring der Zaubertrank einer starken Marke? In D. Ahlert, D. Woisetschläger, & Vogel, V. (Hrsg.), *Exzellentes Sponsoring. Innovative Ansätze und Best Practices für das Markenmanagement* (2. Aufl., S. 3–32). https://doi.org/10.1007/978-3-8350-9639-4_1.

Allensbacher Markt- und Werbeträgeranalyse (AWA 2011–2021). Allensbacher Markt- und Werbeträgeranalyse Codebuch.

B

Bagusat, A. (2013). *Sponsoring trends 2012*. https://www.ostfalia.de/export/sites/default/de/ispm/Blickpunkt_Sportmanagement/Sponsoring_Trends_2012.pdf. Zugegriffen: 17. Febr. 2016.

Bagusat, A., & Marwitz, C. (2008). Sponsoring. Faszinierendes Instrument der Marketingkommunikation. In A. Bagusat, C. Marwitz, & M. Vogl (Hrsg.), *Handbuch Sponsoring. Erfolgreiche Marketing- und Markenkommunikation* (S. 3–15). Erich Schmidt.

Becker-Olsen, K. L., & Hill, R. P. (2006). The impact of sponsor fit on brand equity. The case of nonprofit service providers. *Journal of Service Research, 9*(1), 73–83. https://doi.org/10.1177/1094670506289532.

Bennett, R., & Gabriel, H. (1999). Schools sponsoring: Corporate philanthropy or integrated marketing communications weapon? *Journal of Communication Management, 4*(2), 135–158. https://doi.org/10.1108/eb023514.

Berrett, T., & Slack, T. (2001). A framework for the analysis of strategic approaches employed by non-profit sport organisations in seeking corporate sponsoring. *Sport Management Review, 4*(1), 21–45. https://doi.org/10.1016/s1441-3523(01)70068-x.

Bhuiyan, M. A. H., Darda, M. A., & Hossain, M. B. (2022). Corporate social responsibility (CSR) practices in Islamic banks of Bangladesh. *Social Responsibility Journal, 18*(5), 968–983. https://doi.org/10.1108/srj-07-2020-0280.

Blackshaw, I. S., & Hogg, G. (1993). *Sports marketing Europe: The legal and tax aspects*. Kluwer Law International.

Blake, J., Fourie, S., & Goldman, M. (2018). The relationship between sports sponsorings and corporate financial returns in South Africa. *International Journal of Sports Marketing and Sponsoring, 20*(1), 2–25. https://doi.org/10.1108/IJSMS-12-2016-0088.

Bob Bomliz Group. (2008). Sponsoring Trends 2008, Studie in Zusammenarbeit mit dem Institut für Marketing, Universität der Bundeswehr München, Bonn.

Breitbarth, T. (2016). Unternehmerischer Nutzen von Sponsoring und sozialem Engagement im Sport-Im olympischen Rio wie in der heimischen Region. *Industrieanzeiger, 17*(6), 24–26.

Bruhn, M. (1990a). *Sozio- und Umweltsponsoring. Engagements von Unternehmen für soziale und ökologische Aufgaben*. F. Vahlen.

Bruhn, M. (1990b). Sponsoring als Instrument der Unternehmenskommunikation. Erscheinungsformen, Planungskonzepte und Integrationsaspekte, in: Meffert, H. & Wagner, H. (Hrsg.), *Arbeitspapier Nr. 55 der Wissenschaftlichen Gesellschaft für Marketing und Unternehmensführung e. V.* (S. 3–14)..

Bruhn, M. (2012). *Marketing für Nonprofit-Organisationen. Grundlagen, Konzepte, Instrumente* (2. Aufl.). W. Kohlhammer GmbH.

Bruhn, M. (2018). *Sponsoring. Systematische Planung und integrativer Einsatz* (6. Aufl.). https://doi.org/10.1007/978-3-658-13313-9.

Bruhn, M., & Dahlhoff, H. D. (Hrsg.). (1990). *Sponsoring für Umwelt und Gesellschaft. Neue Instrumente der Unternehmenskommunikation*. BDW Service- und Verlagsgesellschaft Kommunikation GmbH.

Bruhn, M., & Mehlinger, R. (1999). *Rechtliche Gestaltung des Sponsoring. Sport-, Kultur-, Sozial-, Umwelt- und Programmsponsoring* (Bd. II, Spezieller Teil, 2. Aufl.). C.H. Beck.

Bruhn, M., & Rohlmann, P. (2021). Instrumentalisierung im Fußball und Auswirkungen auf die Stakeholder. *Absatzwirtschaft online, 64*(11). Zugegriffen: 15. Nov. 2021.

Bruhn, M., & Rohlmann, P. (2022). *Sportmarketing. Grundlagen—Strategien—Instrumente*. Springer Gabler. https://doi.org/10.1007/978-3-658-37176-0.

Burton, N., & Chadwick, S. (2009). Ambush marketing in sport: An analysis of sponsoring protection means and counter-ambush measures. *Journal of Sponsoring, 2*(4), 303–315.

Busch, R., Dögl, R., & Unger, F. (2008). *Integriertes Marketing. Strategie, Organisation, Instrumente* (4. Aufl.). Gabler Verlag.

C

Christensen, S. R. (2006). Measuring consumer reactions to sponsoring partnerships based upon emotional and attitudinal responses. *International Journal of Market Research, 48*(1), 61–80. https://doi.org/10.1177/147078530604800105.

Clark, J., Lachowetz, T., Irwin, R. L., & Schimmel, K. (2003). Business-to-business relationships and sport: Using sponsoring as a critical sales event. *International Journal of Sports Marketing and Sponsoring, 5*(2), 38–53. https://doi.org/10.1108/ijsms-05-02-2003-b004.

Cliffe, S. J., & Motion, J. (2005). Building contemporary brands: A sponsoring-based strategy. *Journal of Business Research, 58*(8), 1068–1077. https://doi.org/10.1016/j.jbusres.2004.03.004.

Corkindale, D., & Hastings, G. B. (1985). The role of sponsoring for marketing. *International Journal of Advertising, 4*(4), 371–372. https://doi.org/10.1080/02650487.1985.11106945.

Cornwell, B. T., Clinton, S. W., & Donald, P. R. (2005). Sponsoring-linked marketing: Opening the black box. *Journal of Advertising, 34*(2), 21–42. https://doi.org/10.1080/00913367.2005.10639194.

Cornwell, T. B., & Relyea, G. E. (2000). Understanding long-term effects of sports sponsoring: Role of experience, involvement, enthusiasm and clutter. *International Journal of Sports Marketing and Sponsoring, 2*(2), 39–55. https://doi.org/10.1108/ijsms-02-02-2000-b005.

Cornwell, T. B., Roy, D. P., & Steinard, E. A., II. (2001). Exploring managers' perceptions of the impact of sponsoring on brand equity. *Journal of Advertising, 30*(2), 41–51. https://doi.org/10.1080/00913367.2001.10673636.

Cotting, P. (2011). Interview Medien. http://www.sponsoringextra.ch/file/archiv/Interview_Medien/Social%20Media%20im%20Sponsoring-06-2011.pdf. Zugegriffen: 02. Febr. 2016.

Crawford, C. T. (1992). IRS attacks exempt organization income from corporate sponsoring fees. *The Journal of Taxation, 76*(4), 230–234.

Crompton, J. L. (1993). Sponsoring of sport by tobacco and alcohol companies: A review of the issues. *Journal of Sport & Social Issues, 17*(2), 148–167. https://doi.org/10.1177/019372359301700210.

Crompton, J. L. (1994). Measuring the return on sponsoring investments at major recreation events. *Journal of Park and Recreation Administration, 12*, 73–73.

Cuneen, J., & Hannan, M. J. (1993). Intermediate measures and recognition testing of sponsoring advertisIng at an LPGA tournament. *Sport Marketing Quarterly, 2*(1), 47–56.

D

Dees, W. (2011). New media and technology use in corporate sport sponsoring: Performing activational leverage from an exchange perspective. *International Journal of Sport Management and Marketing, 10*(3–4), 272–285. https://doi.org/10.1504/ijsmm.2011.044795.

Demirel, A. (2020). CSR in sport sponsoring consumers' perceptions of a sponsoring brand's CSR. *International Journal of Sports Marketing and Sponsoring, 21*(2), 371–388.

Djaballah, M., Hautbois, C., & Desbordes, M. (2017). Sponsors' CSR strategies in sport: A sensemaking approach of corporations established in France. *Sport Management Review, 20*(2), 211–225. https://doi.org/10.1016/j.smr.2016.07.002.

Dolphin, R. R. (2003). Sponsoring: Perspectives on its strategic role. *Corporate Communications: An International Journal, 8*(3), 173–186. https://doi.org/10.1108/13563280310487630.

Drees, N. (1989). *Sportsponsoring*. https://doi.org/10.1007/978-3-663-06737-5.

E

Easton, S., & Mackie, P. (1998). When football came home: A case history of the sponsoring activity at Euro'96. *International Journal of Advertising, 17*(1), 99–114. https://doi.org/10.1080/02650487.1998.11104708.

Eisdorfer, A., & Kohl, E. (2017). Corporate sport sponsoring and stock returns: Evidence from the NFL. *Critical Finance Review, 6*, 179–209. https://doi.org/10.1561/104.00000041.

ESA. (2022). *The 2022 ESA sponsoring market overview*. ESA.

F

Fahy, J., Farrelly, F., & Quester, P. (2004). Competitive advantage through sponsoring: A conceptual model and research propositions. *European Journal of Marketing, 38*(8), 1013–1030. https://doi.org/10.1108/03090560410539140.

Farrelly, F., & Quester, P. (2003). The effects of market orientation on trust and commitment: The case of the sponsoring business-to-business relationship. *European Journal of Marketing, 37*(3/4), 530–553. https://doi.org/10.1108/03090560310459078.

Farrelly, F., Quester, P., & Greyser, S. A. (2005). Defending the co-branding benefits of sponsoring B2B partnerships: The case of ambush marketing. *Journal of Advertising Research, 45*(3), 339–348. https://doi.org/10.1017/s0021849905050348.

Farrelly, F. J., Quester, P. G., & Burton, R. (1997). Integrating sports sponsoring into the corporate marketing function: An international comparative study. *International Marketing Review, 14*(3), 170–182. https://doi.org/10.1108/02651339710170249.

FAZ. (2006). Von nun an herrscht freie Schuhwahl. Beitrag vom 31.08.2006. https://www.faz.net/aktuell/sport/fussball/nationalmannschaft-von-nun-an-herrscht-freie-schuhwahl-1358153.html.

Freyer, W. (2018). *Sportmarketing—Modernes Marketingmanagement für die Sportwirtschaft* (5. Aufl). Erich Schmidt.

Furlong, R. (1994). Tobacco advertising legislation and the sponsoring of sport. *Australian Business Law Review, 22*(3), 159–189.

G

Gardner, M. P., & Shuman, P. J. (1987). Sponsoring: An important component of the promotions mix. *Journal of Advertising, 16*(1), 11–17. https://doi.org/10.1080/00913367.1987.10673055.

Gilbert, D. (1988). Sponsoring strategy is a drift. *The Quarterly Review of Marketing, 14*(1), 6–9.

Grimes, E., & Meenaghan, T. (1998). Focusing commercial sponsoring on the internal corporate audience. *International Journal of Advertising, 17*(1), 51–74. https://doi.org/10.1080/02650487.1998.11104705.

H

Habitzreuter, A. M., & Koenigstorfer, J. (2021). The impact of environmental CSR-linked sport sponsoring on attitude toward the sponsor depending on regulatory fit. *Journal of Business Research, 124*, 720–730. https://doi.org/10.1016/j.jbusres.2018.11.040.

Harrison, V. S., Vafeiadis, M., & Bober, J. (2022). Greening professional sport: How communicating the fit, proximity, and impact of sustainability efforts affects fan perceptions and supportive intentions. *Sustainability (Switzerland), 14*(6). https://doi.org/10.3390/su14063139.

Hastings, G. B. (1984). Sponsoring works differently from advertising. *International Journal of Advertising, 3*(2), 171–176. https://doi.org/10.1080/02650487.1984.11105012.

Henseler, J., Wilson, B., Götz, O., & Hautvast, C. (2007). Investigating the moderating role of fit on sports sponsoring and brand equity. *International Journal of Sports Marketing and Sponsoring, 8*(4), 34–42. https://doi.org/10.1108/ijsms-08-04-2007-b005.

Henseler, J., Wilson, B., & Westberg, K. (2011). Managers' perceptions of the impact of sport sponsoring on brand equity: Which aspects of the sponsoring matter most? *Sport Marketing Quarterly, 20*(1), 7–21.

Hermanns, A., & Marwitz, C. (2008). *Sponsoring. Grundlagen, Wirkungen, Management, Markenführung* (3. Aufl.). Vahlen.

Huber, F., & Matthes, I. (2007). Sponsoringwirkung auf Einstellung und Kaufabsicht. Theoretische Grundlagen und Ergebnisse einer empirischen Studie. *Marketing ZFP, 29*(2), 90–104. https://doi.org/10.15358/0344-1369-2007-2-90.

I

INRA Deutschland GmbH. (2000). Grundlagenuntersuchung Sponsoring XIII, Mölln.

International Event Group (IEG). (2007). http://www.sponsoring.com/About-IEG/Press-Room/Sponsoring-Spending-To-Total-$14.93-Billion-In-20.aspx. Zugegriffen: 17. Febr. 2016.

International Event Group (IEG). (2015a). http://www.sponsoring.com/About-IEG/Press-Room/IEG-Projects-North-American-Sponsoring-Spending-t.aspx. Zugegriffen: 17. Febr. 2016.

International Event Group (IEG). (2015b). *Sponsoring spending report 2015*. http://www.sponsoring.com/IEG/files/4e/4e525456-b2b1-4049-bd51-03d9c35ac507.pdf. Zugegriffen: 17. Febr. 2016.

International Event Group (IEG). (2010–2020). *IEG sponsoring report*. https://sponsoring.com.

Ipsos GmbH. (2014). Grundlagenstudie Sponsoring 2014, Hamburg.

J

Javalgi, R. G., Traylor, M. B., Gross, A. C., & Lampman, E. (1994). Awareness of sponsoring and corporate image: An empirical investigation. *Journal of Advertising, 23*(4), 47–58. https://doi.org/10.1080/00913367.1943.10673458.

Jensen, J. A., Cobbs, J. B., & Turner, B. A. (2016). Evaluating sponsoring through the lens of the resource-based view: The potential for sustained competitive advantage. *Business Horizons, 59*(2), 163–173. https://doi.org/10.1016/j.bushor.2015.11.001.

K

Klincewicz, K. (1998). Ethical aspects of sponsoring. *Journal of Business Ethics, 17*(9/10), 1103–1110. https://doi.org/10.1023/a:1006027601493.

M

Marshall, D. W., & Cook, G. (1992). The corporate (Sports) sponsor. *International Journal of Advertising, 11*(4), 307–324. https://doi.org/10.1080/02650487.1992.11104507.

Mazodier, M., & Merunka, D. (2012). Achieving brand loyalty through sponsoring: The role of fit and self-congruity. *Journal of the Academy of Marketing Science, 40*(6), 807–820. https://doi.org/10.1007/s11747-011-0285-y.

McDonald, C. (1991). Sponsoring and the image of the sponsor. *European Journal of Marketing, 25*(11), 31–38. https://doi.org/10.1108/eum0000000000630.

McKelvey, S., & Grady, J. (2008). Sponsoring program protection strategies for special sport events: Are event organizers outmaneuvering ambush marketers. *Journal of Sport Management, 22*(5), 550–586. https://doi.org/10.1123/jsm.22.5.550.

Meenaghan, T. (1983). Commercial sponsoring. *European Journal of Marketing, 17*(2), 5–73. https://doi.org/10.1108/eum0000000004825.

Meenaghan, T., & Shipley, D. (1999). Media effect in commercial sponsoring. *European Journal of Marketing, 33*(3/4), 328–347. https://doi.org/10.1108/03090569910253170.

Meenaghan, T., McLoughlin, D., & McCormack, A. (2013). New challenges in sponsoring evaluation actors, new media, and the context of praxis. *Psychology & Marketing, 30*(5), 444–460. https://doi.org/10.1002/mar.20618.

Miragaia, D. A. M., Ferreira, J., & Ratten, V. (2017). Corporate social responsibility and social entrepreneurship: Drivers of sports sponsoring policy. *International Journal of Sport Policy, 9*(4), 613–623. https://doi.org/10.1080/19406940.2017.1374297.

N

Nagel, S. (2012). Sponsoring und Vermarktungsrechte der Sportler und der Verbände. *Causa Sport, 1*, 55–63.

Nebenzhal, I. D., & Jaffe, E. D. (1998). Ethical dimensioins of advertising executions. *Journal of Business Ethics, 17*(7), 805–815. https://doi.org/10.1023/a:1005850812845.

Nielsen Sports. (2015). Sponsor-Trend 2015: Status und Trends im Sponsoringmarkt in Deutschland, Österreich und Schweiz. http://www.marketing.ch/Portals/0/Wissen/Allgemein/Repucom%20Insights_Sponsor-Trend%202015_DACH_SFS.pdf. Zugegriffen: 17. Febr. 2016.

Nielsen Sports. (2018a). Sponsor-Trend 2018: Status und Trends im Sponsoringmarkt in Deutschland, Österreich und Schweiz.

Nielsen Sports. (2018b). *World football report 2018.*

Nielsen Sports. (2021). Sportsponsoren in Deutschland 2020/21. https://nielsensports.com/sportsponsoren-in-deutschland-2020-2021. Zugegriffen: 01. Mai. 2022.

Nielsen Sports/Repucom. (2015). Sportsponsoren in Deutschland 2014/15, Köln.

O

O'Sullivan, P., & Murphy, P. (1998). Ambush marketing: The ethical issues. *Psychology & Marketing, 15*(4), 349–366. https://doi.org/10.1002/(sici)1520-6793(199807)15:4<349::aid-mar5>3.0.co.2-8.

Olkkonen, R. (2001). Case study: The network approach to international sport sponsoring arrangement. *Journal of Business & Industrial Marketing, 16*(4), 309–329. https://doi.org/10.1108/eum0000000005503.

Olkkonen, R., Tikkanen, H., & Alajoutsijärvi, K. (2000). Sponsoring as relationships and networks: Implications for research. *Corporate Communications: An International Journal, 5*(1), 12–19. https://doi.org/10.1108/13563280010317532.

Oschmann, A. (1997). Viel Image für gutes Geld. *Der Handel, 26*(4), 12–14.

P

Panten, D. (2013). Sponsoring goes Social Media—Aktivierung von Zielgruppen im digitalen Zeitalter. *Media 41—Journal für Media & Marketing, 41*(5), 6–10.

Pham, M. T. (1991). The evaluation of sponsoring effectiveness: A model and some methodological considerations. *Gestion 2000, 7*(4), 47–65.

Pilot Checkpoint. (2000). *Sponsor visions 2000.*

Pilot Checkpoint. (2002). *Sponsor visions 2002.*

Pilot Checkpoint. (2008). *Sponsor visions 2008.*

Pope, N. K. L., & Voges, K. E. (1994). Sponsoring evaluation: Does it match the motive and the mechanism? *Sport Marketing Quarterly, 3*(4), 37–45.

PricewaterhouseCoopers. (2020). Studie PwC's Sports Survey 2020—Deutsche Ausgabe.

R

Rodgers, S. (2007). Effects of sponsoring congruity on e-sponsors and e-newspapers. *Journalism & Mass Communication Quarterly, 84*(1), 24–39. https://doi.org/10.1177/107769900708400103.

Rohlmann, P. (2016). Sportsponsoring—Wachstum ohne Grenzen? Sponsoring als unverzichtbarer Bestandteil der Sportvermarktung. *Stadionwelt INSIDE*, Sonderheft Sponsoring, S. 79.

Rothe, C. (2001). Kultursponsoring und Image-Konstruktion. Interdisziplinäre Analyse der rezeptionsspezifischen Faktoren des Kultursponsoring und Entwicklung eines kommunikationswissenschaftlichen Imageapproaches, Bochum.

Ryan, A., & Fahy, J. (2003). A relationship marketing perspective on the sponsoring of the arts in Ireland: A Galway arts festival-nortel networks case study. *Irish Marketing Review, 16*(1), 31–42.

S

Santomier, J. (2008). New media, branding and global sports sponsoring. *International Journal of Sports Marketing and Sponsoring, 10*(1), 9–22. https://doi.org/10.1108/ijsms-10-01-2008-b005.

Simkins, J. (1980). Sponsoring 1980/81, Rockville.

Sirgy, M. J., Lee, D. J., Johar, J. S., & Tidwell, J. (2008). Effect of self-congruity with sponsoring on brand loyalty. *Journal of Business Research, 61*(10), 1091–1097.

Stadionwelt. (2019). Besitzverhältnisse der Bundesligastadien, Beitrag vom 20.11.2019. https://www.stadionwelt.de/news/19697/besitzverhaeltnisse-der-bundesligastadien.

Stadionwelt INSIDE. (2015). Naming Right für Stadien und Arenen: intensive Beziehung mit hohem Potenzial, Ausgabe Mai, S. 44–51.

Statista. (2016a). Investitionsvolumen auf dem deutschen Sponsoringmarkt im Jahr 2014 und Prognosen für 2015 und 2016 (in Milliarden Euro). http://de.statista.com/statistik/daten/studie/4789/umfrage/investitionsvolumen-fuer-sponsoring-prognose/. Zugegriffen: 17. Febr. 2016.

Statista. (2017). Anteil des Sponsoring am Kommunikationsbudget von deutschen Unternehmen im Jahresvergleich 2013 und 2016. https://de.statista.com/statistik/daten/studie/302340/umfrage/anteil-des-kommunikationsbudget-von-unternehmen/. Zugegriffen: 01. Mai. 2022.

Statista. (2019). In diese Sportarten fließt das Geld (Werte in Milliarden US-Dollar pro Jahr). https://www.horizont.net/marketing/nachrichten/statista-studie-30-milliarden-dollar-fuer-sport-sponsoring%2D%2D-und-so-wenig-fliesst-in-den-frauensport-178891.

Statista. (2022c). Bevölkerung in Deutschland nach Häufigkeit des Sporttreibens in der Freizeit von 2017 bis 2021.

Statista. (2022e). Sportsponsoring-Ausgaben in Deutschland nach Sportarten 2020/2021. https://de.statista.com/statistik/daten/studie/431355/umfrage/formen-des-sport-sponsorings-in-deutschland-oesterreich-und-der-schweiz/.

Stipp, H., & Schiavone, N. P. (1996). Modeling the impact of Olympic sponsoring on corporate image. *Journal of Advertising Research, 36*(4), 22–28.

Sudolska, A., & Łapińska, J. (2020). Implementation of the CSR concept through sport sponsoring: The case of the polish chemical capital group. *Journal of Physical Education and Sport, 20*, 1100–1105.

Sung, M., & Lee, W. Y. (2016). What makes an effective CSR program? An analysis of the constructs of a cause-related participant sport sponsoring event. *International Journal of Sports Marketing and Sponsoring, 17*(1), 56–77. https://doi.org/10.1108/ijsms-02-2016-004.

T

Townley, S., & Grayson, E. (1984). *Sponsoring of sport, arts and leisure: Law, tax and business relationships*. Sweet & Maxwell.

Townley, S. E. (1993). Some legal issues associated with international sports marketing. *Sport Marketing Quarterly, 2*(2), 31–42.

V

Vignali, C. (1997). The MIXMAP-model for international sport sponsoring. *European Business Review, 97*(4), 187–193. https://doi.org/10.1108/09555349710175315.

VSA. (2019). Sportsponsoring: Volltreffer mit gezielter Wirkung, Berlin. Zugegriffen: 01. Mai. 2022.

W

W&V (Verlag Werben und Verkaufen GmbH). (2012). Sponsor Visions 2012: Sport-Sponsoring boomt. http://www.wuv.de/medien/sponsor_visions_2012_sport_sponsoring_boomt. Zugegriffen: 17. Febr. 2016.

Walliser, B. (2003). An international review of sponsoring research. Extension and update. *International Journal of Advertising, 22*(1), 5–40. https://doi.org/10.1080/02650487.2003.11072838.

Weeks, C. S., Cornwell, T. B., & Drennan, J. C. (2008). Leveraging sponsorings on the internet: Activation, congruence, and articulation. *Psychology & Marketing, 25*(7), 637–654. https://doi.org/10.1002/mar.20229.

Die Welt. (2014). *Die Nationalmannschaft sprengt alle TV-Rekorde.* http://www.welt.de/sport/article135215406/Die-Nationalmannschaft-sprengt-alle-TVRekorde.html. Zugegriffen: 05. Apr. 2016.

Witcher, B. J., Craigen, G., Culligan, D., & Harvey, A. (1991). The links between objectives and function in organizational sponsoring. *International Journal of Aduertising, 10*(1), 13–21. https://doi.org/10.1080/02650487.1991.11104431.

Woisetschläger, D. M., & Michaelis, M. (2012). Sponsoring congruence and brand image: A pre-post event analysis. *European Journal of Marketing, 46*(3/4), 509–523. https://doi.org/10.1108/03090561211202585.

Z

Zafer Erdogan, B., & Kitchen, P. J. (1998). Managerial mindsets and the symbiotic relationship between sponsoring and advertising. *Marketing Intelligence & Planning, 16*(6), 369–374. https://doi.org/10.1108/02634509810237578.

ZAW (Zentralverband der Deutschen Werbewirtschaft). (2006–2021). Werbung in Deutschland, Bonn.

ZHAW. (2015). (Zentrum für Kulturmanagement, School of Management and Law, Zürcher Hochschule für Angewandte Wissenschaften. "Sponsor-Visions 2014/15"- Eine empirische Studie zum Sponsoringmarkt Schweiz. http://www.swa-asa.ch/de-wAssets/docs/artikel-print-medien/2015/Studie_Sponsor_Visions_Schweiz_2014-15.pdf. Zugegriffen: 17. Febr. 2016.

Zollinger, H. (1995). In T. Tomczak, F. Müller, & R. Müller (Hrsg.), *Die Nicht-Klassiker der Unternehmenskommunikation* (S. 118–124). THEXIS.

Further Reading

Jensen, J. A., Walsh, P., & Cobbs, J. (2018). The moderating effect of identification on return on investment from sponsor brand integration. *International Journal of Sports Marketing and Sponsoring, 19*(1), 41–57. https://doi.org/10.1108/IJSMS-10-2016-0077.

Forms of Sports Sponsoring

2

Contents

Abstract

Sports is an event that is associated with a multitude of emotions for both active athletes and spectators of sporting events. Companies try to use this emotional environment to achieve communication policy targets through a sponsoring appearance. The focus of these efforts is the transfer of various image components of sports to the company or a brand and the achievement of specific target groups. In addition, more and more companies are using their activities in sports sponsoring to carry out targeted customer care, promote customer loyalty, and create additional value. In addition to the detailed case study of ING Bank and Allianz, there are further practical examples of the German Olympic Sports Confederation, Football World Cups, the Football Bundesliga and Olympic Games, various clubs (e.g. Bayern Munich, Borussia Dortmund, VfL Bochum, Hertha BSC, Schalke 04, VfB Stuttgart), some individual athletes (including Roger Federer, Lionel Messi, Dirk Nowitzki) and other sponsoring actors such as Adidas, Audi, Hugo Boss, Deutsche Bahn, DKB, Mercedes-Benz and others.

M. Bruhn and P. Rohlmann, *Sports Sponsoring*,
https://doi.org/10.1007/978-3-658-44171-5_2

2.1 Overview of Classifications

Considering the of **the importance of sports sponsoring**, it is the oldest and—measured by the share of investment volume—the most significant type of sponsoring. The connection to sports can already be traced back to the 1928 Olympic Games in Amsterdam. Coca-Cola supplied the US Olympic team with the eponymous soft drink and used this sponsoring commitment in marketing and corporate communication in the context of corresponding advertisements and posters. Since this time, the commitment to sports sponsoring has gradually established itself in companies as an integral part of communication (Hermanns & Marwitz, 2008, p. 7 f.).

The **manifestations of sports sponsoring** have accordingly evolved continuously. As mentioned, sports sponsoring has gone through various phases, such as "stealth advertising", sports advertising, etc., up to value creation sponsoring. In the following, various classifications are presented in the sense of an inventory, reflecting the diversity of manifestations. Different **criteria for classification** are in the foreground:

- Classification by recipients (sponsored parties) and donors (sponsors) in sports sponsoring,
- Classification by the extent of the sponsoring commitment,
- Classification by the measures of a sponsoring,
- Classification by the sponsoring object,
- Classification by organizational units.

Classification by Recipients (sponsored parties) and Givers (sponsors) in Sports Sponsoring

Insight into the basic principles of sponsoring is facilitated by considering the different perspectives of sponsors and sponsored parties from a marketing perspective. From the perspective of the sponsored parties, sports marketing is operated in the sense of marketing with sports—with a professional approach. Agencies, service providers, and media also help to improve their services. These include, for example, the planning of target group-oriented measures, the development of event concepts, the search for media resonance, and the offer of innovative communication platforms. From the **perspective of the sponsored parties**, sponsoring represents an opportunity to tap into additional sources of funding (see again Fig. 1.9).

After football, as a pioneer in European sports sponsoring, has dynamically and extensively driven the development, numerous other sports actors (including other team sports, racing and winter sports, and individual athletes) have started to increasingly apply marketing principles to achieve their own goals. In sports marketing, this also applies to the most important national and international sports associations (Hermanns &

Riedmüller, 2008; Freyer, 2018), which are responsible for the marketing of many sports events in addition to association marketing.

From the **sponsor's perspective**, the use of sponsoring as an additional instrument of marketing and corporate communication primarily pursues the goal of ensuring individual target group communication. Based on the given communication situation, it is becoming increasingly important for companies to identify target group-appropriate areas of activity, such as media-effective topics and events as well as individuals, groups, or actions. A sponsoring comes about when the cooperation results in advantages for both sides.

In recent years, there has been an increasing interest in sponsoring from the business sector. The reasons for this change in importance can be seen both in the development of the media market and in the leisure behavior of the population. It is primarily increased costs for traditional advertising media, the possibility of addressing target groups in non-commercial situations, the increased leisure needs of the population, advertising restrictions for tobacco and alcohol, and increasing reactances of the population towards media advertising that are cited as reasons for the popularity of sponsoring (Nieschlag et al., 2002, p. 586; Bruhn, 2012).

Classification According to the Scope of the Sponsoring Commitment

The question of the scope of a sponsoring commitment primarily arises in the sponsoring of individual sports events, but is also fundamentally conceivable for other sponsoring objects. On the sponsor's side, the type and scope of the resources provided are determined, and on the sponsored party's side, the different possibilities for communicative use are determined accordingly. The following **forms of sponsoring** can be distinguished according to the type of scope:

- Full sponsoring,
- Main sponsoring,
- Co sponsoring.

With **Full sponsoring**, a sponsor creates the best possible conditions for achieving communicative goals, as all resources to support the sponsored party are provided by one sponsor alone, and in return, all rights regarding measures for communicative use are attributed to him as a counter-performance. In contrast to main and co sponsoring, no other sponsors are associated with the sponsored object in full sponsoring. Thus, the risk of interference factors in the form of additional sponsors and different communicative messages is minimized.

Financing larger sports events, such as the Football World Cup or the Four Hills Tournament, requires investments from several sponsors. If several sponsors are involved in an event, a team or an individual athlete, this is referred to as either main or co-sponsoring. In **Main sponsoring**, there are usually few larger sponsors who receive exclusive rights, such as the labeling of sports clothing or parts of the sports venue with the company logo. Main sponsors usually carry the title "Official Sponsor". Within this form of sponsoring, there is an increasing trend from major or main sponsor to investor. This trend sometimes goes so far that sponsors in some countries buy entire sports units or take a capital stake. An example of this is the capital participation of the main sponsor Allianz SE in the German record champion FC Bayern Munich: On February 11, 2014, the Munich insurance group acquired 8.33% of FC Bayern Munich AG worth 110 million EUR. In previous years, Adidas and Audi had also acquired shares in FC Bayern Munich AG. As a result of this capital participation, Allianz became the third strategic partner of the club (FC Bayern Munich AG, 2014).

A co sponsor invests less resources in relation to the main sponsors and therefore receives usage rights to a lesser extent. The opportunities to present oneself as a sponsor are limited in **Co sponsoring**. In co sponsoring, sponsors usually receive exclusive rights for a certain product area, but not necessarily further rights for separate communication measures. The presence of several co sponsors and possibly main sponsors results in sometimes very strong distraction effects for individual sponsors with limited rights. The more extensive a sponsor's usage rights are, the greater the prospect of reaching a desired target group with a specific message.

Sports actors who want to use certain sponsoring rights for their marketing have a wide range of measures available, the suitability of which for sponsoring-seeking companies must be evaluated and selected individually, and which are often bundled into a coherent sponsoring package (see Fig. 2.1).

Classification according to the measures of a sponsoring

Sponsors use different measures for the communicative use of a sponsoring commitment. These are largely dependent on the sponsoring object and the respective sports. Basically, the following **core measures** can be distinguished:

- Marking of objects,
- Presence at sports events,
- Use of predicates,
- Naming of sponsoring objects,
- Use of sports personalities.

The **marking of equipment** implies the labeling of sports clothing, sports equipment and equipment of the sponsored as well as printed matter and other promotional items with the logo, product or company name of the sponsor. Depending on the sports, this form of sponsoring is subject to certain restrictions and varies considerably in terms of

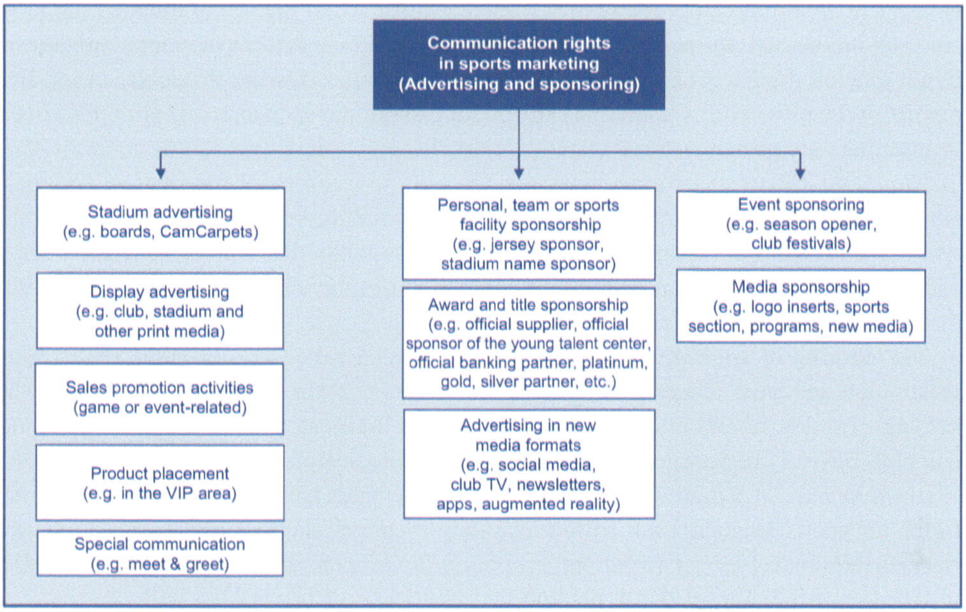

Fig. 2.1 Advertising and sponsoring rights in sports

scope. For example, clothing in professional boxing and swimming offers a rather limited advertising space compared to football or handball.

Another measure of sponsoring is the **presence in the pre- and surrounding area of sports events**. With announcement posters, press information, road shows, invitation letters and tickets, sponsors pursue communicative goals before the start of a sports event and integrate themselves into sports events. Well-known and popular measures at events are perimeter and flag advertising. Technical developments, such as the rotating and changing perimeter system or LED perimeter advertising, increase the communication quality for sponsors at certain points, as only one or a few messages are visible at the same time, but these are alternately displayed for certain intervals. With the rotating and changing perimeter technology, sponsors have larger advertising spaces in the sense of exclusive perimeter sponsoring for a limited period of time. Also in the area of flag advertising, attention is achieved with the help of new advertising forms, such as flying banners.

Further **presence measures at sports events** are available to sponsors in the form of playing field advertising (e.g. in ice hockey or handball), product offers (e.g. official substitution display), services (e.g. presentation or bringing in of the game ball) and various organizational means (e.g. corner flags in football), which are important for the course of an event. This also includes, for example, video boards, coach and player benches, start and finish tapes or victory podiums. Sponsors communicate with their target groups via different communication concepts such as promotion actions, information stands, halftime actions and autograph sessions. Increasingly, social media communication tools are used before and during sports events. For example, a sports event can be announced in advance on the Facebook page or via Twitter messages. During the sports event, live reports or the provision of additional information about the sponsored event on Facebook or Instagram are possible.

Numerous sponsoring contracts include the right to use **official predicates**. The most well-known predicates are "Official Sponsor", "Official Supplier", "Partner of". In addition to the official title, sponsors usually receive an emblem that indicates the sponsoring and can be used by the sponsor for a certain period of time, detached from the event, for marketing and corporate communication.

The **naming of sponsoring objects** ranges from so-called title or name sponsoring, where club and team names as well as sports events contain the sponsor's name, to the naming of sports venues by a sponsor. The most well-known examples include the football club Bayer Leverkusen, the former team T-Mobile in Road cycling, the Audi FIS Ski World Cup and the Allianz Arena in Munich. On the other hand, the awarding of naming rights for sports leagues, such as the renaming of the Basketball Bundesliga to "Beko Basketball Bundesliga", is rather the exception in Germany (Drees & Trautwein, 2008, p. 107; Pommer & Kaiser, 2014, pp. 466 ff.).

Among the versatile measures in the context of marketing and corporate communication is the use of sports personalities as **testimonials**. Sponsored athletes are used both in traditional advertising and for sales promotion and PR activities.

Classification according to the sponsoring object

Every sports sponsoring commitment of a company can be classified, as shown in Fig. 2.2, based on the dimensions "performance level", "sports" and "organizational unit" and accordingly arranged in a three-dimensional space (Drees & Trautwein, 2008).

When considering the **performance levels** of a possible commitment, it becomes clear that sports sponsoring has developed into a significant financing instrument, particularly in the field of elite or competitive sports (Ahlert et al., 2007, p. 7 f.; Hermanns & Marwitz, 2008, pp. 65 ff.). The financing of major events in **elite sports**, such as international tennis or golf tournaments, is no longer conceivable without the involvement of sponsors. Furthermore, there has been a trend for some time now for companies to increasingly support young athletes.

Example: sponsoring in elite sports

The car manufacturer Mercedes organizes the "Mercedes-Benz Junior Cup", which took place for the 30th time in 2020 with the support of various top football clubs from Europe and around the world. This indoor tournament, which is one of the best in the world, involves young people from various U-19 teams (Mercedes-Benz Group AG, 2020). Due to Corona, the next event could not take place until January 2023. ◄

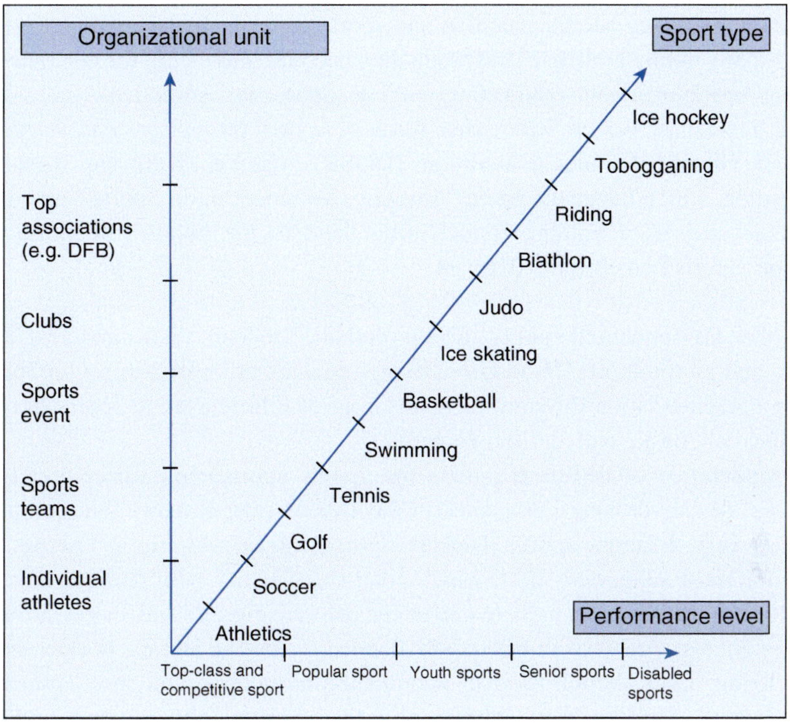

Fig. 2.2 Decision dimensions of a sports sponsoring commitment. (*Source*: Based on Drees & Trautwein, 2008, p. 100 f.)

In addition, numerous companies are active as sponsors in **mass sports** (Drees, 2003, p. 55). Often, this is deliberately used to create a counterpoint to competitors who are dedicated to the sponsoring of elite and professional sports. Sponsoring activities in mass sports have the advantage of targeting a mass audience and allowing companies to build a specific image. In particular, location- and region-specific sponsoring in amateur sports can ensure that not only economic and communicative goals are better achieved, but also a significant contribution is made to the recruitment of young talent and employees.

Example: sponsoring in mass sports

The "Trimm-Aktion" of the German Sports Federation (today "German Olympic Sports Federation") is to be mentioned as a broad and large-scale campaign for (national) mass sports. In this campaign, which has been in existence since 1970, around 3000 events are organized annually by the various sports clubs. The financing of the action is covered 90% by funds from sponsors, promoters and free advertising services (German Olympic Sports Federation, 2016). Even after 50 years, the campaign continues because running and sports apps on smartphones are indispensable for many hobby athletes. Thus, such data become interesting for insurance companies and health insurance companies, making sponsorings attractive.

An interesting, so far little used form of sports promotion was started by the German Olympic Sports Federation (DOSB) together with the Robert Bosch Foundation, which under the name "Attractive Volunteering in Sports" aimed to honor the achievements of volunteers and bring them to the public's attention (German Olympic Sports Federation, 2016). ◀

The most heavily sponsored **sports** include football, handball, tennis and golf, as well as horse, ski and motor sports. In addition, many sponsors are now aiming for specific target group communication through the sponsoring of different trend sports (for example beach volleyball, basketball and snowboarding).

The **importance of different sports for sports sponsoring** varies greatly. A survey of over 200 advertising companies in the DACH region shows that companies are involved in very different sports (Nielsen Sports, 2018a). As Fig. 2.3 shows, football is by far the most supported sport, which companies justify with its high effectiveness, good value for money and high reach in the advertising-relevant target group. Many companies are also involved in basketball, handball, running and ice hockey, but also in golf and tennis. Even though football remains the most important sport from the sponsors' perspective, fortunately the gap between the world's number 1 sport and the other sports in the ranking is closing a little (40 percentage points last year, 28 percentage points currently). Basketball and running were able to make significant gains compared to the previous year's study.

Furthermore, the company survey showed that decision-makers increasingly highlighted the future importance of **E-sports** in the sponsoring environment. While the value for its importance in 2017 was 49% (i.e., relatively high in the ranking), it has increased significantly and now stands at 56%. This could be due to the fact that a number of providers and sponsors entered the E-sports sector in 2016/2017 and have now gathered initial (positive) experiences (see Fig. 2.4).

Classification by Organizational Units

Another dimension for systematizing sports sponsoring commitments is the organizational units that receive support from companies. According to this, the sponsoring of **individual athletes, sports teams, sports events, clubs or sports organizations** can be distinguished. Analyses of companies' sports sponsoring commitments in terms of the supported organizational units show that primarily teams and clubs, but also individual athletes and events are sponsored. Sponsoring of sports associations is less common (Bagusat, 2013; ZHAW, 2015). Cross-sport commitments, such as the partnership

	Leagues	2018/19	Leagues share	Athletes and event shares
Soccer	10.12	12.84	78.8 %	21.2 %
Racing		2.50		
Basketball	1.39	2.48	56.0 %	44.0 %
Olympics		2.41		
American Football	1.45	2.13	68.1 %	31.9 %
Golf		1.48		
Baseball	1.43	1.47	97.3 %	2.7 %
else. Team sports		1.35		
Rugby	0.86	1.23	69.9 %	30.1 %
Ice field hockey	0.94	0.97	96.9 %	3.1 %
Tennis		0.93		
Cycling		0.38		
Cricket		0.33		
Sailing		0.28		
Boxing		0.11		
US college sports	0.86			
Total	**17.05**	**30.89**		
of which women's sport		7 %		
of which leagues and teams		63 %		
of which individual athletes		5 %		
thereof events		25 %		

Fig. 2.3 Sponsoring in sports worldwide in billion USD. (*Source*: Statista, 2019)

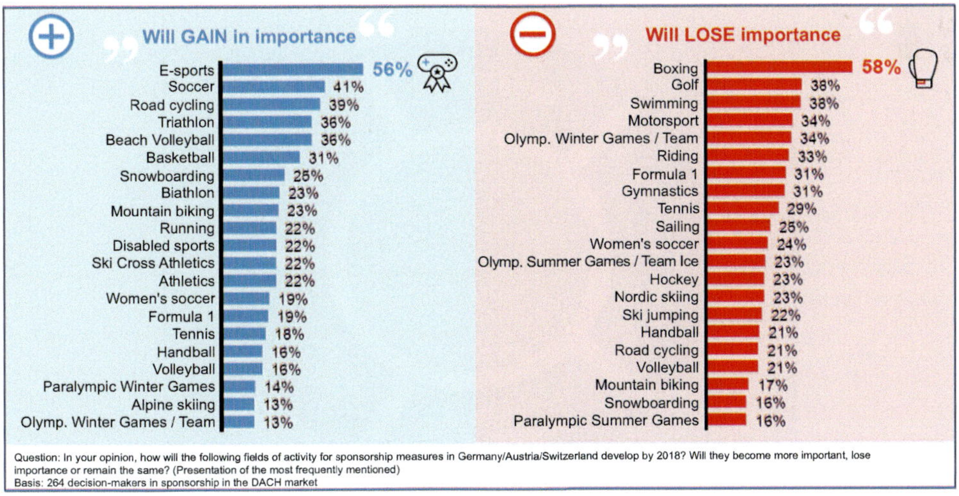

Fig. 2.4 Development of various sponsoring forms in the DACH region. (*Source*: Nielsen Sports, 2018a, p. 22)

between Coca-Cola and the IOC that has existed since the 1928 Olympic Games, are rather the exception (IOC, 2016).

By classifying various sponsoring commitments based on the explained dimensions of sports, object (performance level, organizational unit), sponsoring status, scope/measures, and geographical validity, a clear classification or characterization is possible (see Fig. 2.5). At the same time, a specific approach to different target groups with different preference structures becomes more easily recognizable. The consideration of selected organizational units for which a sponsor is committed is particularly relevant and will be further discussed.

2.2 Sponsoring of Individual Athletes (incl. Case Study ING)

In the case of **sponsoring of individuals**, active or former athletes (e.g., sports stars, individual athletes, coaches) receive financial or material donations and in return take on communicative tasks for the sponsor. From the perspective of the sponsored individuals, these tasks consist either of actively appearing as product presenters or passively tolerating the sponsor's advertising measures with their person. Typically, the sponsored individual athletes are the respective top athletes in their sports. Well-known German sports personalities like Dirk Nowitzki, Felix Neureuther, Magdalena Neuner, Lukas Podolski or Thomas Müller are sponsored by several companies at the same time and integrated into the marketing and corporate communication in various ways. Frequently used options are the advertising of sports and/or leisure clothing as well as the integration of

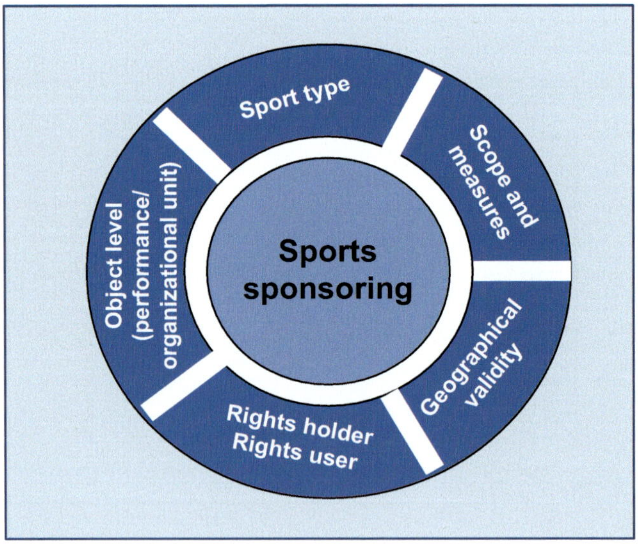

Fig. 2.5 Classification criteria in sports sponsoring

the athletes into the media advertising, sales promotion or personal communication of the companies.

In the context of **sponsoring of top athletes**, which can be observed in both individual sports (e.g., tennis, golf, skiing, horse riding) and team sports (e.g., football, handball), the following **requirements for the selection of athletes** must be met:

- Fame and athletic performance,
- Sympathy,
- Image profile,
- Credibility and industry affinity.

To select suitable individual athletes based on the listed criteria, it is essential to refer to current market research data. If no useful or up-to-date information is available, sponsors usually work with market research agencies to collect data. The following will examine the mentioned selection criteria in more detail.

Fame and Athletic Performance of the Athlete

The **fame of the athlete** is a necessary prerequisite for achieving a high attention effect of the sponsoring commitment. It is generally true that an athlete is more firmly anchored in the consciousness of consumers the more successful he or she is.

Athlete's Sympathy

In addition to fame and athletic performance, the **sympathy values of the athlete** among consumers are another important decision criterion. Companies use well-known and successful athletes to emotionalize their brand and participate in the popularity and popularity of the athletes. Market research provides insights into the image and fame of selected athletes through analyses, thereby creating a basis for evaluation for companies. Exemplarily, the supported fame and sympathy of selected Olympians after the Olympic Winter Games in Sochi 2014 are shown in Fig. 2.6 (Ipsos GmbH, 2014).

Athlete's Image Profile

The decision of a company to establish a connection with an individual athlete also depends on the extent to which the existing **image profile of the athlete** among consumers matches the desired company image. For example, the sports equipment manufacturer Nike maintains a sponsoring contract with professional golfer Tiger Woods, to transfer his personality traits (including determination, perfection, continuity) to the company (Business Insider, 2013; Nike, 2016). However, this commitment also shows the risks associated with the behavior of top athletes.

Athlete's Credibility and Industry Affinity

Another important decision criterion is the **credibility of the athlete**. Credibility refers both to the personality of the athlete himself and to his **industry affinity**. The connection between the athlete and his sponsor or the advertised service must be understandable and credible for consumers. Therefore, before making a commitment, companies must carefully examine to what extent the athlete fits the company. In general, the more different products an athlete promotes, the more unbelievable the commitment becomes.

The **sponsoring of active individual athletes** offers many opportunities, but from a corporate perspective, it is also associated with dangers. The following **risks** are associated with the sponsoring of individual athletes:

- The level and **sustainability of the athlete's performance**. Since the athletic performance of individual athletes is usually unpredictable, sponsoring commitments represent a high investment risk. For example, in the event of an athlete's early

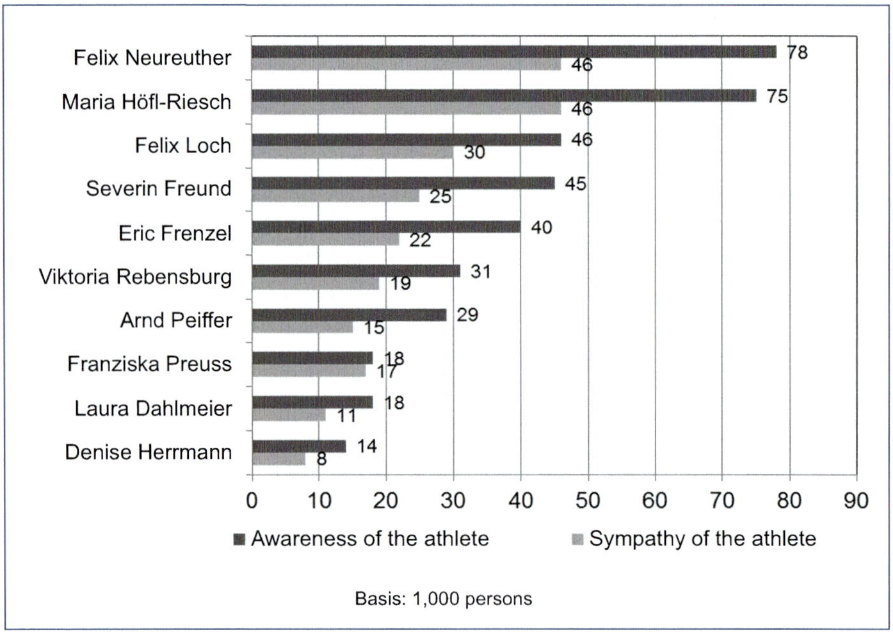

Fig. 2.6 Supported fame and sympathy of selected Olympians. (*Source*: Ipsos GmbH, 2014)

elimination from important competitions or a permanent drop in performance, the sponsoring funds invested in him usually do not lead to the desired communication success.

- **Violations of societal and sporting norms** have an extremely negative impact on the image profile of the individual athlete. The athlete is perceived correspondingly negatively in public (Schaub, 2008, p. 7 f.). Ultimately, there is a risk that this negative perception will also transfer to the sponsor. For example, the issue of doping not only has serious implications for sponsored parties and sponsors, but also for entire sports. A well-known example is the doping cases in cycling, which led to sponsors such as T-Mobile, Adidas, and Audi withdrawing from cycling sponsoring in 2007 and the entire sport losing public interest. Similarly, more and more doping scandals were uncovered in athletics, with the result that one of the most important sponsors of the Athletics Association, Adidas, considered ending its commitment prematurely (Spiegel, 2016).
- The safety or the athlete's **behavior in dealing with the media** is seen as another risk. If individual athletes appear extremely insecure in the media over a longer period of time or do not behave in public according to societal norms, there is a possibility of a negative image impact.
- Many individual athletes advertise for different products and manufacturers over the course of their careers, which sometimes leads to **wear and tear** of previous advertising measures. If advertising appearances for competing products and manufacturers occur, there is also the risk of losing the credibility of product recommendations. The credibility of athletes decreases faster the more advertising appearances and thus an "overload" for different brands occur in the same or almost the same period.
- Risks associated with the **private lives of athletes** should also be considered. Incidents that inhibit acceptance, even within the privacy of a sponsored individual in the public interest, often affect their sponsoring commitments. Thus, private faux pas by athletes can have negative effects and lead to companies terminating sponsoring contracts. An example was Tiger Woods with his private affairs many years ago. He had to accept sponsoring losses worth 25 to 30 million USD due to the termination of sponsorings by General Motors, Accenture, and AT&T as sponsors. Other sponsors like Tag Heuer or Nike remained with him, as for them only the athletic performance and not the private matters were decisive (Perform Media Deutschland GmbH, 2010; Business Insider, 2013).

Overall, there has been a tendency in recent years for German companies to become more cautious in dealing with the sponsoring of top athletes due to the existing risks.

Examples: Sponsorings with top athletes

- The sports equipment manufacturer **Adidas** sponsors, among others, the footballers Lionel Messi and Thomas Müller, the boxer Arthur Abraham as well as the tennis player Alexander Zverev.

- The fashion manufacturer **Hugo Boss** sponsors various individual athletes, such as the former Formula 1 world champion Nico Rosberg, as well as several young professional golfers, such as Henrik Stenson. In addition, Hugo Boss has been the official fashion outfitter of the most successful German football club Bayern Munich since 2017.
- The **Deutsche Kreditbank AG**has been supporting German top athletes, sports clubs, and sports associations since 2002, e.g. in handball, biathlon, e-sports, and equestrian sports. The sporting appearance is often combined with social projects, such as the initiative for diversity and community HandbALL TOGETHER and the FC St. Pauli blind football team.
- The tennis professional **Roger Federer** currently has 14 advertising contracts, among others, with the car manufacturer Mercedes-Benz, the bank Credit Suisse, the sports equipment manufacturers Uniqlo, On and Wilson, the watch manufacturer Rolex, among others. ◀

The commitments usually focus on individual athletes with a high level of recognition and popularity among the population or on promising talents in sports. Meanwhile, the sponsoring share already outweighs the share of salary, prize money, or other sports-related earnings in the **total income of well-known athletes**. Estimates of the highest-paid athletes in individual or private sponsoring suggest that the billion-dollar mark has now been exceeded (see Fig. 2.7).

Top athletes are in certain sports, such as athletics, not only in a sporting performance competition but also in the competition for sponsoring money, with a connection between the two. The winning of significant sports competitions immediately changes the market price of the respective athlete. This is particularly true for winning world championships and Olympic medals. The question of what a top athlete is worth plays a central role, especially in transfer and transfer sums, but also in equipment and advertising contracts. These amounts are often based on the so-called **market value of the athletes**. The market value strongly depends on the current sporting performance and the future potential of the respective player. The market values of the currently most expensive Bundesliga football professionals are shown in Fig. 2.8.

The **market value** is thus almost exclusively based on sporting performances and represents a financial forecast. It therefore only provides an indication of a top athlete's market position. In this context, the **brand value** is becoming increasingly important, which is increasingly making its way into sports. The brand value indicates the conscious and unconscious perception of a top athlete as a brand. Consequently, athletes are no longer just athletes, but actors who combine sporting performances with a special personality and a unique appearance in sports. Well-known athletes serve as role models for how to do something for oneself (e.g., appearance, health) with sports. Active and successful people with good looks have a role model character for young people through their sporting and non-sporting behavior.

Athletes		2014/15	2016/17	2017/18	2018/19	2019/20	2020/21
Roger Federer	Tennis	0.058	0.058	0.065	0.086	0.086	0.085
Tiger Woods	Golf	0.050	0.037	0.042	0.054	0.054	0.054
James LeBron	Basketball	0.044	0.055	0.052	0.053	0.053	0.054
Crist. Ronaldo	Soccer	0.027	0.035	0.047	0.044	0.045	0.055
Stephen Curry	Basketball	n.a.	0.035	0.042	0.042	0.042	0.042
Phil Michelson	Golf	0.044	0.040	0.037	0.036	0.036	0.036
Lionel Messi	Soccer	0.022	0.027	0.030	0.035	0.035	0.037
Kevin Durant	Basketball	0.035	0.034	0.033	0.035	0.035	0.034
Key Nishikori	Tennis	n.a.	n.a.	0.032	0.033	0.033	0.033
Rory McIlroy	Golf	0.032	0.034	0.034	0.031	0.031	0.034
Novak Djokovic	Tennis	0.031	0.028	0.029	0.031	0.031	0.030
Neymar Jr.	Soccer	0.017	0.022	0.024	0.030	0.030	0.030
Usain Bolt	Athletics	0.021	0.032	0.030	End of career		
Jordan Spieth	Golf	n.a.	0.029	0.030	0.029	0.029	0.026
Rafael Nadal	Tennis	0.028	0.026	0.029	0.026	0.026	0.026
Subtotal		**0.409**	**0.492**	**0.527**	**0.510**	**0.511**	**0.576**
Other prominent athletes							
Total athlete sponsorship		**0.800**	**0.900**	**1.000**	**1.000**	**1.000**	**1.200**

Fig. 2.7 Estimated sponsoring income of well-known top athletes in billion USD. (*Sources*: Forbes/Statista/Industry estimates)

Soccer player	Origin	Club	Market value in EUR million
Jude Bellingham	England	Borussia Dortmund	80.0
Joshua Kimmich	Germany	FC Bayern Munich	80.0
Christopher Nkunku	France	RB Leipzig	80.0
Alphonso Davies	Canada	FC Bayern Munich	70.0
Matthijs de Ligt	Netherlands	FC Bayern Munich	70.0
Florian Wirtz	Germany	Bayer 04 Leverkusen	70.0
Sadio Mané	Senegal	FC Bayern Munich	70.0
Jamal Musiala	Germany	FC Bayern Munich	65.0
Leon Goretzka	Germany	FC Bayern Munich	65.0
Serge Gnabry	Germany	FC Bayern Munich	65.0

Fig. 2.8 Market values of the ten most expensive footballers of the Bundesliga in the 2022/2023 season. (*Source*: Statista, 2022b and www.Transfermarkt.de)

In sports, it is of particular importance to win outstanding athletes and athletes for a sports event or a team in order to make one's own appearance even more attractive to the target groups and to increase the **marketing opportunities**. Thus, certain sports events will use the participation of world champions and prominent athletes for the rest of the marketing as "workhorses" just like team sports clubs, which such athletes provide so much more attention and approval that their costs (e.g., appearance premiums, transfer sums, and salaries) quickly amortize.

Example: Marketing Opportunities in Football Transfers

A much-noticed football transfer in the summer of 2021 was the change of Lionel Messi (FC Barcelona) to Paris St. Germain (PSG), who were reportedly promised around 35 million EUR as net salary. According to media reports, the attractiveness of the top club PSG, already equipped with Kylian Mbappé and Neymar, could be increased once again with Lionel Messi and took the Parisian football club to a new level on many levels, including the Lionel Messi transfer brought the club PSG ten new sponsoring deals and led to a 13% increase in revenues in this area alone: from 290.2 million EUR in 2020/2021 to 327.9 million EUR in 2021/2022. PSG achieved further additional income through jersey and merchandise sales, partially increased broadcasting sums abroad, and higher appearance fees at friendly matches. ◄

Case Study ING—Long-term focused sponsoring on a sports

The following case study was compiled by **Florian Krenz**, Head of Sponsoring & Events at ING Germany, and is made with the kind support and permission of ING Germany (ING).

The **ING Germany** is part of the global ING Group. With over 9 million customers, ING Germany is the third-largest bank in Germany. Their core products in the private customer business are current accounts, building finance, savings, consumer loans, and securities. In the business customer segment Business Banking, ING grants loans to small and medium-sized enterprises. In the area of Wholesale Banking, it offers banking services for large, international companies. With over 6000 colleagues, ING is represented in Frankfurt am Main (headquarters), Berlin, Hanover, and Nuremberg.

Initial Situation

In 2001, DiBa started as a direct bank brand, with a focus on performance to differentiate and distinguish the bank in the market. Since 2003, the bank has increasingly supported and **basketball,** which Klaus Oskar Schmidt, then ING-DiBa board member, believed in 2009 stood for dynamism, fairness, and team performance. These terms described then and still describe important success factors of ING Germany today. Therefore, this sport fits very well with the bank. In the course of further considerations, it turned out that mainstream football was not an option for ING. Instead, they chose basketball because the bank saw it as a fresh, very young, very dynamic sport of the future. ING Germany now sponsors basketball at all levels, from elite sports to grassroots sports and wheelchair sports, for both women and men. Dirk Nowitzki, Germany's most successful basketball player of all time, acts as a testimonial and brand ambassador.

The **sponsoring of ING** involves engagements in the areas of sports, music/festivals, and art/culture. Fig. 2.9 illustrates that the DBB sponsoring plays a central role in this.

The guiding principle has been and remains to pursue a consistent sports sponsoring strategy and to comprehensively occupy the sport of basketball. Since 2003, ING has been the **main sponsor of the German Basketball Federation** and Dirk Nowitzki, supporting not only the national teams but also the youth work. Since June 2005, it has also been the main sponsor of the German Wheelchair Basketball National Team. With the ING 3×3 Tour, based on the basketball variant streetball, the DBB and ING have been bringing the sport from the hall to public squares in German cities since 2017.

Since 2003, sponsorings in basketball have been a fixed and permanent part of ING Germany's communication—and not just during sporting highlights. Basketball is a daily part of ING culture.

Goals and Target Groups

sponsorings are generally used at ING Germany to achieve economic and psychological goals and are initiated by individual departments (e.g., HR: Employer Branding, Public Affairs: Network, Wholesale Banking Business Customers: Acquisition & Customer Retention, Executive Board: Cultural Promotion at the locations, etc.).

In sports sponsoring at ING Germany, the following are the most important **target metrics**:

Fig. 2.9 ING sponsoring. (*Source*: ING; Photo: Sven Kuczera)

- **Psychological:**
  - Recognition as a sponsor,
  - Sympathy (as the most important driver for economic goals),
  - Relevant set and recommendation.
- **Economic:**
  - Customer retention,
  - Customer acquisition,
  - Financial support for the sponsoring partner.
- **Social Commitment:**
  - Corporate Citizenship,
  - Promotion of sports,
  - Promotion of social participation through sports.

With regard to the **target groups**, two levels are distinguished in sports sponsoring at ING Germany:

- **External target groups:**
  - Freedom Mindset: For ING, the strategic target group of the "Freedom Mindset" is of particular importance. This mindset is the point of connection, the correspondence of the brand orientation of 'do your thing' and answers the question, for whom is ING there.
  - The Freedom Mindset (FM) is not a sociodemographic target group in the traditional sense, but the FM encompasses a set of attitude characteristics. The guiding principle of the FM is "freedom". The freedom to live freely, to experiment, to express oneself and to be the person one wants to be. The freedom to do more of the things that are important to one. The main characteristics of the FM are openness, tolerance, and flexibility. About a third of society can identify with almost all attributes of the FM. The core of the FM is curious, sociable, and loves to have new experiences, which is why the FM is also fascinated by different lifestyles and cultures. People with an FM are cosmopolitan and tolerant. They have a modern attitude towards life and society. This means they are liberal and open to new things, other cultures, and any forms of thought and lifestyle. They love diversity and live it. This segment can also be seen as a pioneer in adapting to new technologies and activities. Their view is forward and not backward. They are future-oriented and pursue their goals.
- **Internal target groups:**
  - Employees at all locations: Frankfurt, Nuremberg, Hanover, and Berlin.

Strategic Orientation and Criteria for Selecting Sponsorings

Global **sponsoring guidelines** are used as guidelines for the selection and implementation of appropriate sponsoring commitments, which contain specifications on topics/platforms to standardize the ING sponsoring in all countries of the banking group. In addition, national sponsoring guidelines are applied. They contain additional specifications on the regulatory processes as a bank "ABC" (Anti Bribery & Corruption) and exclude certain sponsoring relationships.

In the course of evaluating sponsorings, ING applies the following **criteria**:

- Compliance with specifications and guidelines,
- Fit with the extensive brand specifications and objectives,
- Reach and visibility of the brand,
- Opportunity for ING to act as an "enabler" (facilitator, enabler, pathfinder),
- Price of the collaboration.

In search of a dynamic team sport that positively endorses the image attribute "performance", basketball was identified in 2003 and the DBB was chosen as a partner to support the sports as an "enabler" and to polarize less than with a usual team sponsoring. The **partnership with Dirk Nowitzki** (see Fig. 2.10), the best German basketball player, was the logical addition and aimed at using his personality for advertising to increase the popularity of the brand. In addition, wheelchair basketball is also an important part of the ING sports sponsoring (see Fig. 2.11).

Fig. 2.10 Dirk Nowitzki as sports testimonial of ING. (*Source*: ING; Photo: PHILIPPREINHARD.COM)

ING Germany has a decades-long partnership with the DBB, which is also documented by the fact that the sponsoring contract was last extended until 2024. With Dirk Nowitzki, there is a very special kind of sponsoring, because it is a lifetime partnership, i.e., a collaboration that continues indefinitely even beyond his active career. Dirk Nowitzki is thus the face of ING and has been used extensively in TV spots and increasingly for digital advertising media over the last 20 years.

Activation of Sponsorings

For the **implementation of sponsorings**, a variety of rights were agreed in the sponsoring contract. As far as team support is concerned, in addition to the usual logo presence on jerseys and pants as well as on competition and leisure clothing, perimeter and floor advertising as well as "On-the-Ground" areas are used, as well as special title designations and their logos. Other advertising elements are also included, e.g., logo prints on tickets, content production with the team as well as Media Days, a fan bench at the edge of the field, "Courtside Seats", use of the Game-Worn-Shirts, promotion in/outside the halls, use of the mascot, PR appointments with the teams, advertisements, logos on all sponsor areas of the DBB, presence in digital media and on social channels with logos and content, sweepstakes (including Meet&Greet), youth camps, merchandise with ING logo and presence at the Albert Schweitzer Tournament (worldwide basketball tournament for male U18 national teams).

Fig. 2.11 Wheelchair basketball as part of the ING sports sponsoring. (*Source*: ING)

Fig. 2.12 Charity football match Champions 4 Charity 2022. (Photo: PHILIPPREINHARD.COM)

Fig. 2.13 The "BasKIDball" project with patron Dirk Nowitzki. (Photo: Sven Kuczera)

In the context of the **collaboration with Dirk Nowitzki**, the production of TV and social media spots as well as the execution of PR appointments, content production, usage rights as well as joint events with the Dirk Nowitzki Foundation such as BasKIDball (a joint initiative of iSo—Innovative Social Work and ING) and Champions for Charity (regular charity football match) are at the center (see Fig. 2.12 for a charity match and Fig. 2.13 for the "BasKIDball" project).

Depending on the reference object of the ING sports sponsoring, a different **activation** is pursued:

DBB Partnership

The rights package around the DBB is extensively activated by ING at every international match and its own presence is continuously further developed. Since 2022, ING has been using an innovative video/photo tool on site. The Jump Challenge and a 3×3 Fan Court round off the basketball experience with ING. Best tickets for "Courtside Seats" are regularly raffled off via social media channels.

Dirk Nowitzki

The media coverage of the partnership with Dirk Nowitzki is the core of the sponsoring. The athlete and personality of Dirk Nowitzki are activated intensively and permanently as previously described. Since 2003, he has been the protagonist in ING's TV commercials and has become the face of the brand. Increasingly, content topics for social media are also produced with him to make the campaigns visible on all channels. He is also used internally for various measures and actions. In the earlier advertising measures, the focus was still on the athlete, the later spots staged Dirk Nowitzki as a person and a figure of sympathy. The hype around Dirk Nowitzki made the campaign even more interesting. The sporting success as NBA champion with the Dallas Mavericks and the award of the NBA Finals MVP Award for the most valuable player of the final series was an absolute highlight.

Youth

A youth promotion project is the initiative "Talents with Perspective" launched in 2008. For the first time, the DBB, with the support of ING-DiBa, sought young talents under 14 years of age in nationwide tournaments. The national coaches of the German Basketball Federation acted as talent scouts and nominated U14 perspective squads.

Children & Adolescents

The non-profit project "BasKIDball" is a free leisure offer for young people and combines afternoon homework supervision with an open basketball meeting. The idea was developed by Holger Geschwindner, mentor and coach of Dirk Nowitzki, together with the youth welfare organization Innovative Social Work e. V. and successfully established "BasKIDball" in Bamberg. ING-DiBa has been supporting "BasKIDball" since 2007.

ING 3×3 Tour

As part of the cooperation with the DBB, the accompanying naming right to the ING 3x3 Tour has emerged. With the nationwide tour to the "ING 3×3 German Championship", DBB and ING have been bringing basketball from the hall to public places in German cities since 2017.

EuroBasket 2022

ING Germany appeared as a sponsor of the Basketball European Championship for the second time in 2022 and presented the EuroBasket to fans all over Germany both on site at both venues and on many channels. As a national sponsor, ING was active at the two German venues Berlin and Cologne with branding areas and LED bands at the edge of the field as well as many smart participatory actions and raffles for the audience on site. Dirk Nowitzki was also integrated into the actions as EuroBasket ambassador and Lifetime Partner of ING. For all fans, ING presented ten podcast special editions of "LAUSCHANGRIFF—Finally something with sports!". In these, the sports commentators Frank Buschmann and Florian Schmidt-Sommerfeld reported on the daily tournament events with guests. The hybrid sponsoring commitment was rounded off with social media actions, Instagram stickers and ticket competitions for basketball fans and ING employees.

Involved Departments and Agencies

The sponsorings are managed internally by ING, with agencies used for support on a point-by-point basis. The management of the sponsorings, the activation and implementation of the rights packages, and the media campaigns are primarily carried out by the sponsoring & Events and Advertising & Media departments, with networking with other events and activities almost inevitable. The partnership with Dirk Nowitzki, for example, also includes the BasKIDball project, which promotes children and young people. The Champions for Charity event also originated from the partnership with Dirk Nowitzki.

Success Measurement, Selected Insights and Parameters

With its broad commitment, ING has managed to cover all areas of German basketball and achieve its essential **goals**:

- ING is THE basketball sponsor in Germany,
- TV spots with Dirk achieve the best values in market research. As soon as Dirk is visible, the viewer knows: It's an advertisement from ING.

The values regularly determined by market research and media analyses confirm the correctness of the decision made about 20 years ago. Thus, ING achieved better perception values at the Basketball European Championship than the global FIBA sponsors (with more presence) among the spectators on site. Basketball enthusiasts find ING even more likable than the general population. This effect increases even more among those who have explicitly perceived ING as a sponsor.

The sponsoring in basketball is very efficient from ING's point of view. The advertising values are above the industry-standard benchmarks (ratio of advertising value to budgets). The initial contract with the DBB from 2003 was endowed with 600,000 EUR per year and had a term of five years. This was followed by numerous extensions, which have been adjusted in the endowment according to the services. The current contract runs for four years and was concluded in 2020.

If one wants to draw a **conclusion** about ING's sports sponsoring, it is important to note:

- Being a sponsor for 20 years is something very special, only a few partnerships last that long, and above all, all participants and their cooperation have evolved.
- All participants have benefited from the partnership, Dirk Nowitzki on a sporting and human level, the DBB and ING from an economic point of view. Everyone has managed to bring their own changes into the partnerships, to develop together and to remain a "dream team".
- Continuity is an important success factor for ING, whether in customer service and product portfolio or in cooperation with the testimonial Dirk Nowitzki and the basketball association.

Of course, there were also special **challenges** in such a long partnership. For example, the geographical distance to Dirk Nowitzki in the USA. Coupled with the tight NBA schedule (more than 80 games per season) and his regular participation in international tournaments with the DBB team, it was always a challenging task to find suitable dates. With his retirement, this has now become somewhat easier. Dirk Nowitzki himself also comments on the long-term sponsoring with ING: "It is a stroke of luck to have a partner like ING for such a long time, a partner who not only pursues short-term goals, but who also supports our sustainable and important projects for children and sports with enthusiasm. Over the years, the cooperation has become a real and personal partnership."

2.3 Sponsoring of Sports Teams

In the Sponsoring of sports teams, entire teams are generally supported. The **sponsoring of club teams** is most common, especially in the German football leagues and other sports. Such a sponsoring commitment is often associated with a multitude of communication measures. These include, for example, kit and perimeter advertising, loudspeaker announcements, advertising in program booklets and on tickets, etc. Other exemplary measures are the use of honor boxes or VIP rooms for special guests as well as the implementation of halftime actions and the design of the team bus.

In addition to club teams, **national or association teams** are the contract partners for sponsoring activities. For example, sports teams that appear at tournaments, Olympic Games, World and European Championships, or international matches are supported.

The subsequent **renaming of a club team** in connection with the sponsoring company is more or less pronounced in Germany—depending on the sport and league. While the majority of teams in the first basketball league have a name sponsor, this is rather rare in leagues of other sports. In the Football Bundesliga, the **naming sponsoring of club teams** is even excluded. This was already prohibited in 1973 for the Jägermeister manufacturer Günter Mast at the football club Eintracht Braunschweig. The media impact associated with the public discussion is not further discussed here. The decision to reject was less about the name connection (see, for example, the traditional clubs Bayer Leverkusen, Salamander Kornwestheim, Quelle Fürth), but rather the target of a subsequent renaming of the club name for commercial reasons. Due to a procedural error, the negative decision was lifted in 1973, but entrepreneur Mast refrained from reapplying for a name change.

Examples: Sponsorings of Sports Teams

- Numerous companies are active as jersey sponsors or equipment suppliers for the football teams of the Bundesliga. For example, since 2002, the **Deutsche Telekom** has sponsored the FC Bayern Munich club as a jersey sponsor with an estimated 45 million EUR annually, the **Mercedes-Benz-Bank** sponsors VfB Stuttgart with a rumored 10 million since 2012/2013, and the online used goods dealer **Autohero** sponsors Hertha BSC Berlin with about 8 million EUR since 2022. Equipment suppliers include Adidas, Nike, Puma, Jako and several other companies.
- Others see the opportunity in the sleeve sponsoring, which has been allowed in Germany since 2017, to be present on the official match clothing of a well-known Bundesliga club for more or less manageable effort. For example, at the Bundesliga club VfL Bochum, the company **Viactiv** pays "only" 0.5 million EUR in 2022/2023, while **Q atar Airways** spends 13 million EUR at FC Bayern Munich in the same season.
- Discount store **Penny** has been the main sponsor of the German ice hockey national team since 2020 and is involved as a jersey sponsor. In addition, the company has taken over the naming sponsoring of the ice hockey league.
- The **Sparkasse Leverkusen** has been supporting the activities of the disabled sports department of TSV Bayer 04 Leverkusen for many years.
- At the beginning of the Bundesliga season 2020/2021, Borussia Dortmund and the telecommunications company **1&1** started a new partnership. The company 1&1 became the main and jersey sponsor. The special thing: The logo of 1&1 is actually white lettering on a blue background. Since blue and white are the club colors of the "arch-rival" Schalke 04, the color on the Borussia Dortmund jersey was changed from blue to black.
- The **Volksbank** has been a partner of the football Bundesliga club Schalke 04 since 2005 and offers the club's fans the opportunity to open a so-called "Schalke

checking account", with which they can participate in the Schalke bonus program to collect fan miles. In addition, the bank offers exclusive fan events such as raffles, autograph sessions, and other promotions. ◀

The sponsoring of club or association teams is associated with lower **risks** than a partnership with individual athletes. When selecting sports teams, a company will primarily focus on the team's level of recognition, its environment, the image of the sport, and its importance to the target group. Another selection criterion is the fan potential. In the Bundesliga, FC Bayern Munich has a fan potential of about 9-10 million people in Germany and has also already secured a clear lead in global reach on the most important social media platforms compared to German competition. The club is also considered the most popular club in Germany, followed by Borussia Dortmund and Borussia Mönchengladbach (SLC, 2021).

In particular, when it comes to **sponsoring of association teams**, it is important that the attributes of the respective sports are in some relation to the performance of the advertised products or services. It is increasingly observed that sports clubs and associations enter into medium to long-term commitments with companies to secure lasting (financial and communicative) benefits for both sides. As can be seen in Figs. 2.14 and 2.15, the **team sponsoring of various sports** receives different levels of support. Football absolutely dominates. However, in terms of the importance for total revenue, the so-called smaller team sports are much more dependent on sponsoring.

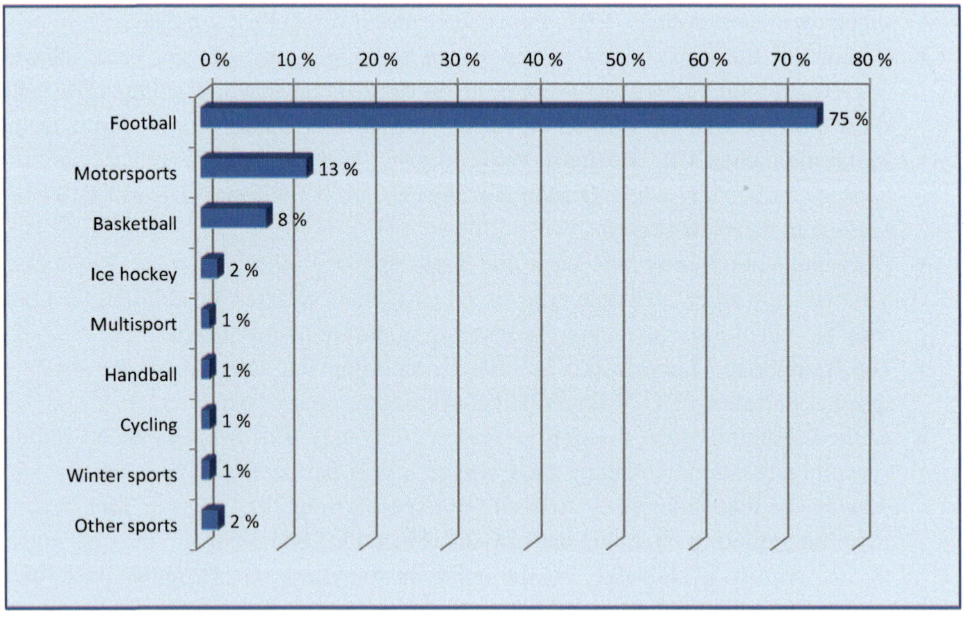

Fig. 2.14 Sponsoring in sports in Germany 2020/2021. (*Source*: Statista, 2021a)

Amount of revenue in EUR million							Spectators
Season 18/19	Matchday	TV money	Sponsoring	Merchandising	Otherwise	Total	Average
Soccer	520	1483	845	220	276	3344	42.738
Handball	27	3	70	2	4	105	4806
Basketball	26	4	92	2	12	132	4189
Ice hockey	42	5	69	3	12	130	6341
Volleyball	2	0	11	0	3	16	1100
Top Teamsport	617	1495	1088	226	307	3727	

Share of revenue sources						
Saison 18/19	Matchday	TV money	Sponsoring	Merchandising	Otherwise.	Total
Soccer	16 %	44 %	25 %	7 %	8 %	100 %
Handball	26 %	3 %	67 %	1 %	4 %	100 %
Basketball	20 %	3 %	70 %	1 %	7 %	100 %
Ice hockey	32 %	3 %	53 %	2 %	9 %	100 %
Volleyball	12 %	0 %	69 %	0 %	19 %	100 %
Top Teamsport	**16.6 %**	**40.1 %**	**29.2 %**	**6.1 %**	**8.2 %**	**100 %**

Fig. 2.15 Sponsoring in team sports in Germany. (*Source*: Association information)

Fig. 2.16 Sponsoring in team sports figures in million USD worldwide. (*Source*: Statista, 2019 and PR MARKETING)

Team sports leagues	2018/19
Premier League	1,860
NFL	1,390
NBA	1,120
LaLiga	1,050
Bundesliga	0,960
MLB	0,890
Ligue 1	0,730
NHL	0,560
Serie A	0,457
Other leagues	10,293
Sum of all leagues and teams	**19,310**
Top 5 soccer leagues in Europe only	**5,057**

Internationally, football also leads the ranking of sports best supported in terms of sponsoring. According to market surveys in 2018/2019, the **sponsoring volume for football** in league sports was over 10 billion USD (see Fig. 2.16).

Even in football, where sponsoring moves the largest amounts of money, there are large differences among the top clubs and within the leagues. The **appropriation of sponsoring money** for specific purposes also varies from club to club, but a look at the different types of sponsoring in the Bundesliga repeatedly shows where and to what extent changes are taking place. A quarter of the income is currently generated by the clubs through kit sponsoring, a sixth through equipment contracts, and slightly more than a twentieth through the relatively new sleeve sponsoring.

2.4 Sponsoring of sports events (incl. Allianz case study)

In the case of **sponsoring of sports events**, sports events are financially supported with the goal of using the event for the company's advertising purposes. This type of sponsoring has gained significantly in importance in recent years. The reasons lie in the increasing demand of companies for a presence in a sporting environment and in the increasing costs of conducting national and international championships, tournaments, Olympic Games, etc. Such events can no longer be covered by spectator revenues and broadcasting fees alone, and they rely on being financially secured by sponsors.

International Sporting Events

A great dependency on sponsoring money exists especially in international high-performance sports events. Most events in various sports would no longer be financially viable and feasible without sponsors. This applies, for example, to the following events:

- Motor racing,
- Equestrian tournaments,
- Golf tournaments,
- Olympic Games,
- Tennis tournaments,
- Football and other team sports events.

Example: Event Sponsoring

The 2014 Football World Cup in Brazil would not have been possible without sponsors. FIFA concluded the World Cup in Brazil with a record revenue of 4.8 billion USD, thus increasing the turnover compared to South Africa four years ago by about 1.17 billion USD. However, with 1.3 billion USD, over 25% of the revenue came from the commitment of sponsors. The sale of around 3 million tickets contributed only 527 million USD, a comparatively small contribution of 11% to FIFA's revenue (FIFA, 2011, 2015). Over the past six World Cups, FIFA's sponsoring revenues at World Cups have ranged between a quarter and a third of all revenues (see Fig. 2.17). ◀

Example: Event Sponsoring (Olympic Games)

Similarly, at the Olympic Games, sponsoring money plays a significant role in financing. The International Olympic Committee concluded the 2012 London Summer Games with revenues of around 5.2 billion USD. In total, about 2.2 billion USD was transferred by television stations for broadcasting rights. The sale of tickets brought the IOC only about 800 million USD. Approximately 1.1 billion USD was paid by domestic sponsors of the Games. The sum is completed by the commitments of the 12 TOP sponsors, for example Coca-Cola, General Electric, McDonalds, Panasonic and VISA (IOC, 2012).

	2002	2006	2010	2014	2018	2022
Total World Cup revenue	1,685	2,325	3,655	4,826	5,357	5,650
Sponsoring	512	562	1,072	1,629	1,660	1,700
Number of sponsors	15	21	19	20	21	20
Sponsoring share	30.4%	24.2%	29.3%	33.8%	31.0%	30.1%
Ø Amount per sponsor	34.1	26.8	56.4	81.5	79.0	85.0

Fig. 2.17 FIFA revenues and sponsoring at Football World Cups (figures in million USD). (*Source*: FIFA Annual Reports)

	1993-1996	1997-2000	2001-2004	2005-2008	2009-2012	2013-2016	2017-2020	2021-2024
Total revenues	2,224	3,770	4,189	5,676	8,053	7,790	11,390	12,200
TOP sponsors worldwide	279	579	663	866	957	1,003	1,368	3,200
Sponsors Host country	534	655	796	1,555	1,838	2,037	4,194	3,000
Total sponsorship	813	1,234	1,459	2,421	2,795	3,040	5,562	6,200
Share of sponsorship	37%	33%	35%	43%	35%	39%	49%	51%

Fig. 2.18 Total revenues and sponsoring at Olympic Games in the respective cycle (figures in million USD). (*Sources*: IOC Reports and PR MARKETING)

IOC TOP partner	2001-2004	2005-2008	2009-2012	2013-2016	2017-2020	2021-2024
Europe	2	2	2	2	2	3
North America	7	7	6	6	7	4
Africa/Middle East	0	0	0	0	0	0
Asia	2	3	3	3	5	4
Total amount	11	12	11	11	14	11

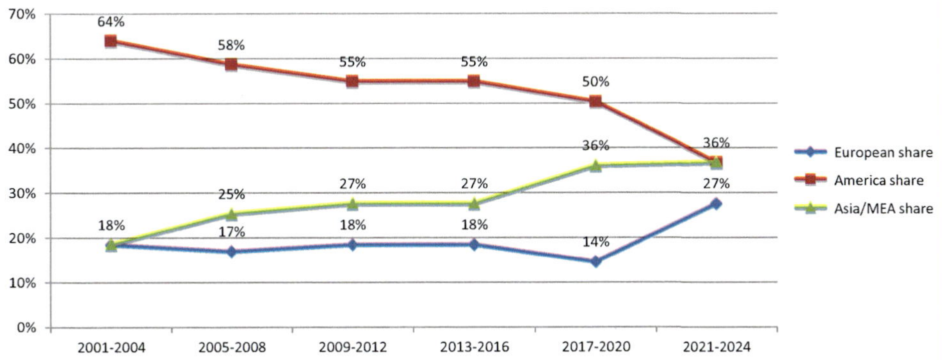

Fig. 2.19 TOP partners by number and origin at Olympic Games in the respective cycle. (*Sources*: IOC Reports and PR MARKETING)

At the Olympic Games, sponsoring is even more important for economically successful implementation than in football, as Figs. 2.18 and 2.19 show. Up to half of all revenues come from the IOC's sponsoring (global TOP program) and the (regionally limited) sponsoring activities of the host country. The increasingly refined TOP program of the IOC is mainly responsible for this growth. There is also a clear shift and change in the origin of sponsors (Fig. 2.20). ◄

Selection Criteria for Sporting Events

The sponsoring of sports events has become increasingly attractive for German companies in recent years due to the growing transparency regarding the possibilities of corporate involvement and a well-founded conception of the events. As the risks of potential negative image effects are often highly estimated in sponsoring commitments with individual athletes and sports teams, many companies tend to increasingly engage in **sports events** (Hermanns & Marwitz, 2008, p. 76 f.). In such an engagement, there is no risk that a sporting failure or misconduct of athletes in other areas will be directly associated with the company.

Another reason for the increasing interest of companies in sports events is the fact that the **use of event marketing** has gained importance in recent years. By staging events as a platform for an experience- and dialogue-oriented presentation of a company's services, the primary aim is to trigger activation processes with regard to the services offered and to maintain contact with important individuals for the company (Bruhn, 2019, pp. 443 ff.). This applies to both externally initiated sports events and company-specific sports events.

Golf	Pferdesport	Tennis	Trendsportarten	Sonstige Sportarten
• John Deere Classic • Mercedes-Benz Trophy • The Honda Classic • The Barclays • BMW Asian Open • Sony Open • Rolex Series • Omega European Masters	• Sarasin Swiss Open • Henkel Rennen • The Land Rover America`s Polo Cup • Nürnberger Burg-Pokal • Mercedes CSI • IVG-Preis von Europa • Samsung Super League • Grand Prix Credit Suisse • Rolex FEI World Cup • VR Classics	• BNP Paribas Open Indian Wells • Davidoff Swiss Indoors Basel • Porsche Grand Prix Stuttgart • Crédit Agricole Suisse Open Gstaad • BMW Open München • Qatar Exxon Mobil Open • Terra Wortmann Open Halle • Zürich Open	• Red Bull Air Race • Audi FIS Ski Cross World Cup • BMW Beachvolleyball Cup München • Land Rover Kite-Surf World Cup • Mercedes Benz Windsurf World Cup Sylt • A1 Beach Volleyball Grand Slam • Helvetia Nordic Trophy • LG Action Sports	• Volvo Ocean Race • HASPA Marathon Hamburg • Mainova Frankfurt Marathon • BMW Berlin Marathon • Louis Vuitton America's Cup Chicago • Bitburger Läufercup • BASF Triathlon-Cup • BMW IBU Weltcup • Bemer Cyclassics Hamburg

Fig. 2.20 Examples of title sponsoring at sporting events. (*Source*: Based on Bruhn, 2018, p. 127)

If we consider in a further step central **selection criteria for an engagement at a sports event**, the following points are particularly worth mentioning:

- Level of awareness,
- Public interest/fascination,
- Media impact,
- Acceptance of sponsoring,
- Degree of exclusivity as a sponsor,
- Implementation and marketing rights.

A crucial criterion in the selection of a sports event is its **level of awareness** among the relevant target groups. It turns out that the most important sports events already have a very high level of awareness. For example, the level of awareness of the Football World Cup, the Olympic Games, the 1st Football Bundesliga, the UEFA Champions League and Formula 1 has been extremely high for years (almost 100%). However, it should be noted in such surveys that the levels of awareness of individual events strongly depend on the time of the survey and that better ratings can usually be expected for events close to the survey.

In addition to the level of awareness of the event, the **public interest** should also be considered when selecting a sports event. Another criterion for the attractiveness of a sports event for sponsors is the **fascination** of a sports event, which also allows conclusions to be drawn about the public interest and the involvement of the spectators. The greatest enthusiasm is usually triggered by the Football World Cup, followed by the Olympic Games.

Of crucial importance for the sponsor in the selection of the sports event is also the **media impact**, which is particularly given in official competitions. This forms the basis for achieving high reach of the communication measures used and for mentioning the company in press and television reports.

Another decision criterion regarding the engagement at a sports event, which will gain in importance, is the development of the **acceptance of sponsoring** among individual organizers and sports associations and especially among the spectators (Walzel & Schubert, 2018; Streppelhoff & Pohlmann, 2020).

The potential sponsor will also pay attention to his **position in relation to the co-sponsors**, as the degree of exclusivity as a main or secondary sponsor determines both the advertising opportunities (e.g. position and number of boards in the stadium or frequency of announcements) and the communication impact of the sponsoring commitment.

In the case of larger national and international sports events, various forms of **implementation and marketing rights** for the events must also be examined when awarding sponsorings. This initially concerns the rights to the implementation of the event and the associated rights to the allocation of advertising opportunities. In addition, it must be clarified who has been granted the television rights to broadcast the sports event.

Examples: Sponsorings of Selected Events and Competitions

- The automotive company Audi has been one of the main sponsors of the **Kieler Woche** since 2010, with a two-year interruption. The company not only finances the broadcaster "Kieler Woche TV powered by Audi", but also offers an exclusive regatta ride with a sailing professional on board for Audi customers and celebrities. In this way, exclusive guests can experience the competition up close.
- The **Football World Cup** 2014 was sponsored by six global official FIFA partners, including the companies Adidas, Hyundai/Kia, Coca-Cola, Sony, VISA and Emirates counted. Only they had the right to advertise with the official FIFA logo and were assured that none of their competitors could do the same. However, each Football World Cup also has national sponsors, such as Apex Brasilia or Garoto.
- The sport of Trends **Beach volleyball** is becoming increasingly popular and well-known. Particularly popular events are the Beach Volleyball World and European Championships, which attract renowned Sponsors such as Swatch, Sony, Mikasa and others.
- The Czech car manufacturer Škoda is in 2022 the main sponsor of the **Ice Hockey World Championship** for the 30th time and is one of the companies with the longestofficial sponsoring of a World Championship.
- As the official main sponsor of the **Tour de France**, Škoda provides more than 200 support vehicles to the world's most famous bicycle race every year. In 2022, Škoda was the official main partner of the Tour for the 19th time. ◄

Marketing Rights for Sporting Events

The allocation of sponsorings at events is not only done directly by the clubs or associations. In Germany, both **marketing companies** and **sports agencies** are commissioned to handle the allocation of sponsorings in whole or in part. An example is the German sports-Marketing GmbH, the marketing company of the German Olympic Sports Confederation (DOSB) and the German Disabled Sports Association (DBS) mentioned. In some disciplines, sponsoring agencies are also involved, which market the event rights (e.g., title rights, broadcasting rights) and other sponsoring-relevant measures on behalf of the organizer.

Example of Event Marketing

An example of professional marketing of an event in the international arena is the **Olympic Games**. The responsibility for their management lies with the International Olympic Committee (IOC) as the owner of the Olympic Games and the Olympic brands. The marketing of the Olympic Games is organized by the IOC's marketing department, founded in 1989 and based in Lausanne (Switzerland). ◀

In addition to the interests of the official organizers, the **rights of sports venue operators** must also be taken into account when implementing sponsorings. This is particularly relevant given that the question of sponsoring rights to the event is not clearly defined for certain sporting events. These rights lie with clubs, associations, marketing companies, and sports venues. Often, sports venues, many of which are municipally owned (e.g., city halls, football stadiums, exhibition halls), have their own advertising contracts with local companies for perimeter advertising, but these do not extend to larger sporting events.

Sporting Events and Television Rights
In addition to an analysis of the owners of the marketing rights of a sporting event, it is necessary to check which institution holds the television rights to an event. Depending on which broadcasting station has the broadcasting rights for a sporting event, it is more or less appropriate for a company to enter into program sponsoring due to the varying degrees of alignment of the broadcaster's and the sponsoring company's target groups and the differing reach.

The general trend in the cost of acquiring sports broadcasting rights, triggered by increasing competition between television companies in recent years, is characterized by significant growth rates both nationally and internationally.

Situation in the German Sports Rights Market
The costs of acquiring sports broadcasting rights in Germany have risen disproportionately since the mid-1980s. Central causes are the start of private television programs, which triggered competition for sports broadcasting rights, and the acquisition of broadcasting licenses by sports rights agencies.

The establishment of a joint sports rights and marketing agency (SportA) in 1995 enables ARD and ZDF to increase competitiveness in the sports rights market and to reduce dependence on agencies when acquiring sports rights. SportA, as a 100 percent subsidiary of both broadcasters, purchases the majority of sports broadcasting rights for ARD and ZDF, thus becoming the "rights holder". Only in exceptional cases does a broadcaster purchase the rights directly.

Use of Event Rights

With the organization of events, an organizer has rights that can be purchased and used by sponsors. These primarily include titles, predicates, and licenses, for example, for the use of mascots, emblems, and signs.

A sponsor primarily obtains a dominant position (or exclusivity) through title sponsoring. **title sponsoring** characterizes the renaming of an event or group of active participants in the interest and at the behest of a sponsor; the company or product name is incorporated into the event title or team name and announced accordingly. Some examples of title sponsoring at events in various sports are listed in Fig. 2.20.

In addition to title sponsoring, opportunities for licensing are used in the sponsoring of sporting events. **Licensing** denotes the promotional use of mascots, emblems, and other signs for which a sponsored party can grant the necessary licenses. These licenses for emblems, mascots, etc. are primarily granted in the course of significant sporting events or by associations. For example, the Bitburger Brewery was a partner of the German Football Association until 2017 in the DFB nutrition pool and had the DFB equipment license for all DFB events for the Bitburger Drive alcohol-free brand. Another example is the use of emblems and mascots of the Olympic Games. The Olympic Rings are one of the most well-known and respected symbols worldwide, and the mascots of the Olympic Games are often used by companies for various products or in media advertising.

In Germany, too, **sports venue sponsoring** is becoming increasingly widespread, where companies contribute to the costs of, for example, a new football stadium and in return, the stadium is named after the sponsor (Grass & Backhaus, 2007, pp. 141 ff.). From a legal perspective, when naming a stadium or sports arena, the initial consideration is who has the **right to name** it. The owner of the stadium or the tenant or organizer are primarily considered. For instance, the football team Bayer Leverkusen, as the title sponsor of the BayArena in Leverkusen, is also the sole shareholder of Bayer Leverkusen GmbH, so the name giver is not an external sponsor. However, there is also the possibility of transferring the naming rights to a third party, with two different arrangements conceivable. If the naming rights are transferred to a third party for marketing, the marketer ultimately determines the name, leaving the sports club with no control options. If, on the other hand, the sports club directly transfers the right to name to a specific company, it retains some influence over the naming (Wichert & Leda, 2001). Most clubs use the sale of naming rights as a lucrative source of income.

However, the legal situation is often not clearly defined and the **renaming of existing stadiums** does not always proceed without conflict.

Examples: Renaming of Sports Stadiums

As an example of the difficulties in renaming stadiums, the debate over the sale of the naming rights to the **Fritz-Walter-Stadion** of 1. FC Kaiserslautern to a sponsor or the renaming of the **Hamburger Volksparkstadion** to "AOL Arena" at the beginning of 2001 can be mentioned. Until 2007, the Internet provider paid Hamburger SV 15.3

million EUR. However, the stadium has since been renamed twice: In 2007 to HSH Nordbank Arena and from 2010 to 2015 to Imtech Arena. In 2015, German entrepreneur Klaus-Michael Kühne acquired the naming rights and returned its original title "Volksparkstadion", much to the delight of tradition-conscious fans, and finally secured the naming rights until summer 2023 (Handelsblatt, 2015; Zeit, 2022a).

Other clubs, however, are actively seeking financial supporters for their stadiums. For example, in 2005, the insurance group Allianz acquired the naming rights to the new **football arena in Munich** (Allianz Arena) and eventually extended the contracts until 2041 (Allianz Arena, 2014). Between 2010 and 2015 alone, several more naming rights agreements for football stadiums were concluded, including the Audi-Sportpark of FC Ingolstadt, the C \oface Arena (then Opel Arena, now MEWA Arena) of 1. FSV Mainz05 and the WWK Arena of FC Augsburg. Most recently, VfB Stuttgart has re-marketed its stadium name. ◀

The development of sports venue sponsoring can be illustrated by the proportion of sports venues named after sponsors in the first football Bundesliga. While there were no naming rights agreements with sponsors until 1990 (Grass & Backhaus, 2007, p. 143), by 2016 almost all clubs in the 1st Bundesliga were using sports venue sponsoring as a source of income (Statista, 2016b). The top five football leagues in Europe and the five North American Major Leagues have currently earned approximately 823 million USD

Soccer clubs from 1. and Bundesliga 2	Former stadium name or former venue	New stadium name or sponsor	Since...	Investment in EUR million	Term until
VfB Stuttgart	Gottlieb Daimler Stadium	Mercedes-Benz Arena	2008	20.0 as a one-off amount	2023
Borussia Dortmund	Westfalenstadion	Signal Iduna Park	2005	5.8	2026
FC Bayern Munich	Olympic Stadium	Allianz Arena	2005	6.0	2041
FC Schalke 04	Arena in Berger Feld	Veltins-Arena	2005	6.0	2027
Eintracht Frankfurt	Commerzbank Arena	Deutsche Bank Park	2020	5.5	2027
1.FSV Mainz 05	Opel Arena	MEWA Arena	2021	2.0	2026
FC Augsburg	SGL Arena	WWK Arena	2015	1.4	2025
Hamburger SV	Imtech Arena	Volksparkstadion	2015	4.0	2023
Hannover 96	HDI Arena	Heinz von Heiden Arena	2022	1.5	2027
SV Darmstadt 98	Böllenfalltor stadium	Merck Stadium at Böllenfalltor	2014	0.4	2024 (+ option 2. J.)

Fig. 2.21 Examples of naming rights agreements in German football leagues. (*Source*: PR MARKETING)

through a total of 147 naming rights agreements. Of this, 730 million USD comes from North America alone, with only 11% contributed by the Bundesliga, Ligue 1, Serie A, LaLiga, and the Premier League (see Figs. 2.21 and 2.22).

Sponsoring with Predicates

Another form of sponsoring is sponsoring with so-called predicates. These are promotional predicates or special titles with an exclusive character. **Predicate sponsoring** encompasses the advertising-communicative use of attributes (e.g., club logo, club names) that are granted by a sponsored party for a certain period of time. This type of sponsoring is often closely linked with other rights in close connection, because such a title alone cannot demonstrate the partnership attentively enough. The right to use predicates can be acquired independently, unlike most other rights in sponsoring. Accordingly, it is also suitable for isolated use in communication work and can also provide smaller interested companies with a first entry into sponsoring (e.g., official partner of the training start in a certain season).

The use of the following **predicates** is often found:

- Official outfitter,
- Official leisure or fashion outfitter,
- Official supplier,

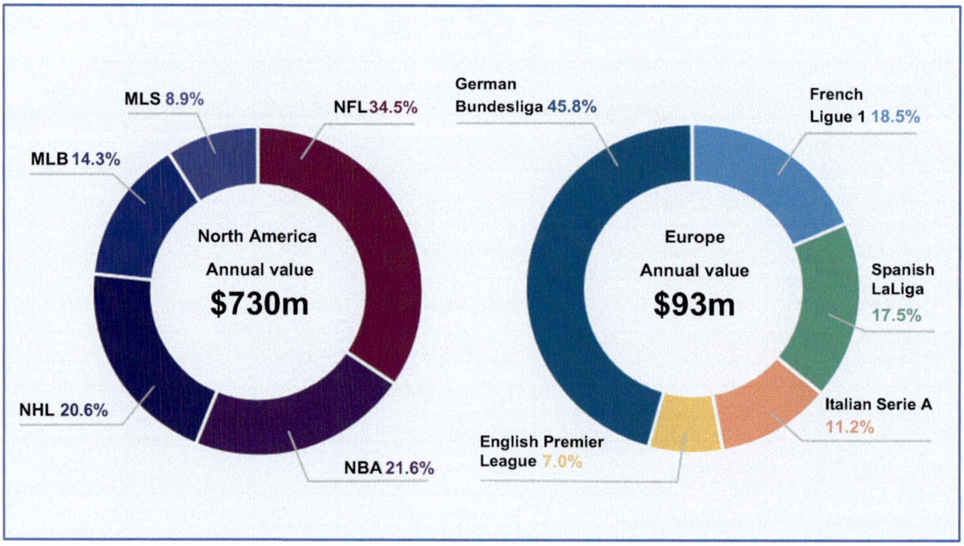

Fig. 2.22 Scope and distribution of naming rights agreements in the USA and Europe. (*Source*: SportBusiness Stadium Naming Rights Report, 2021; Kottke, 2022)

- Official promoter,
- Official partner,
- Official sponsor.

The predicate is a frequently chosen form of sponsoring by sports associations (e.g., German Football Association), sports events (e.g., Football World Cup, Olympic Games and other international major events) and sports teams (e.g., national handball team), but it is also often used by non-profit organizations.

Case Study Allianz—Olympic and Paralympic Commitment

The following case study was compiled by **Eike Doerte Bürgel**, Global Head of Olympic & Paralympic Program, and is made with the kind support and permission of Allianz.

The Allianz Group is one of the world's leading insurers and asset managers and serves more than 126 million private and corporate customers in more than 70 countries. Allianz insurance customers use a wide range of services from property, life and health insurance to assistance services and credit insurance to industrial insurance. Allianz is one of the world's largest investors and manages an investment portfolio of about 706 billion EUR on behalf of its insurance customers. In addition, the asset managers PIMCO and Allianz Global Investors manage 1.7 trillion EUR for third parties. With the systematic integration of ecological and social criteria into business processes and investment decisions, Allianz is one of the leading insurers in the Dow Jones Sustainability Index. In 2022, over 159,000 employees generated a turnover of 152.7 billion EUR for the group.

Initial Situation

Sports and cultural sponsoring—in a holistic sense—is a central component of brand management for Allianz. However, we do not speak of sponsoring, but of partnerships or platforms. The partnerships and commitments help to positively charge the brand in an emotional environment and to convey messages. In addition to the targets of sponsoring known from literature, there are various aspects and **criteria** for the company to bring a partnership to life:

- Support of the business and sales,
- Influence on brand building such as brand awareness, brand sympathy, willingness to buy,
- Employee engagement and increasing the attractiveness of the company for potential employees.

Often, strategic and tactical questions in combination with local, regional or global orientations are the starting point for deciding on a particular partnership. However, it is crucial that the partnership aligns with the company's values and provides a positive economic added value.

It is important for Allianz not to reduce sports sponsoring to a single sport such as football. Sports and cultural platforms such as those of the Olympic and Paralympic movements, Formula E, MOMA or locally relevant commitments shape the portfolio. Therefore, Allianz has deliberately broadened its approach to sponsoring. As far as the Olympic and Paralympic movement is concerned, Allianz relies on a brand triad with the rings and the Paralympics (Fig. 2.23).

Goals and Target Groups

As a globally operating company, we serve various target groups with different targets in various regions. For the first time, an approach was chosen in the Olympic and Paralympic partnership that goes far beyond the "usual" marketing targets. In the partnership with the International Olympic and Paralympic Committee, our declared goal is to generate added value globally in various business areas:

- **People:** Internal awareness of the commitment and positive sentiment of the partnership for the external attractiveness of Allianz as a potential employer for new talents,
- **Business:** Increase of new business (Gross Written Premiums) through and with the partnership in a defined sports ecosystem,
- **Brand:** Increase in brand awareness and sympathy and thus the willingness to buy.

Fig. 2.23 Brand triad of Allianz/Olympic Rings/Paralympic Agitos. (*Source*: Allianz)

With regard to the target groups in connection with sports sponsoring, the company takes a rather broad, pragmatic approach. The reason for this is the diversity of the insurance business and offer, as well as that of the target groups and the questions to be solved in the 70 countries where Allianz is active. The program for the Olympic and Paralympic partnership addresses target groups from young to old. Depending on the target, the marketing and sales measures can be designed.

In general, Allianz also distinguishes between internal and external segments in the context of general **target group approach**:

Internal

- All employees of Allianz in general,
- Sales staff.

External

- Consumers and potential future customers,
- Existing customers,
- Recruitment of new employees (talents),
- Various stakeholders.

Strategic Orientation and Selection

Sports sponsoring is a central component of Allianz's brand management. It contributes to achieving the coordinated corporate and marketing goals. Global sponsoring or global partnerships are located in the Group Strategy, Marketing, Distribution department. Observing universally valid principles, there is a global partner strategy, including with regard to overarching and local partnerships. Behind each partnership lies both a decision-making process with certain criteria that must be met, and a business case that justifies the partnership. The underlying selection criteria can also vary. Depending on the target group and target for a partnership, there are different reasons such as brand building, positioning and emotionalizing the brand, employee engagement, sales support, business expansion, etc.

The **sponsoring portfolio** of Allianz has always been internationally oriented. The partnership with the Olympic Movement has been built on the long-standing partnership with the Paralympic Movement (since 2006)—unlike most other TOP partners. The mission of the Olympic Movement "Building a better world through sports" in combination with the positive radiance of the Olympic Rings (over 90% recognition value worldwide) speaks for itself and holds great potential for the partners. It should not be forgotten that the Olympic and Paralympic Games are the largest and third largest multi-sport event in the world. Almost every person has a positive memory of the Olympic or Paralympic Games. All these criteria—in addition to a business case—have flowed into the decision-making process for a partnership, which has led to an eight-year global partnership with the Olympic and Paralympic Movements. Allianz is a partner of the Olympic and Paralympic Movements alongside 14 other companies.

In January 2021, the worldwide Olympic and Paralympic partnership with Allianz began. Even though the Olympic and Paralympic sponsoring occupies a prominent position in Allianz's sports sponsoring, an attempt is made—also from the understanding formulated at the beginning—to network the other sports partnerships with it. This has already happened specifically in the areas of golf, basketball, and football.

Implementation and Results

Since the announcement of the partnership with the Olympic and Paralympic Movements in September 2018, the focus has initially been on building the basis and infrastructure for a successful partnership and testing some measures in the pilot markets (China, France, Australia, and Spain). This is especially important when considering the size and complexity of the Olympic and Paralympic ecosystems.

Exemplary are the following of **measures** to mention:

- How do you measure success? What market research and tracking systems need to be established?
- Building the team with the appropriate structures and processes. It also needs to be regulated how to work with the Allianz markets in 70 countries around the world and how to involve and further educate colleagues worldwide so that the partnership is used to its maximum extent.
- Collaborating with colleagues from the International Olympic and Paralympic Committees to understand correlations and structures, but also to define projects and create win-win situations, e.g., by developing a joint digital strategy or the athlete program. By both sides of the partnership bringing in their expertise, a maximum result can be created for both.

In the strategic development of all measures, we focus on the **three pillars**: people, business, and brand. Some examples include:

- **People:** This is primarily about informing colleagues and employees and engaging them with the partnership. A best practice example is the "Buddy Program"—a kind of mentorship program in which an Olympic or Paralympic athlete reflects on topics such as motivation, resilience, teamwork, etc. with 5 to 8 Allianz colleagues. More than 20 countries worldwide have participated in the program with very positive feedback from athletes and employees. Another example from the French market: Allianz France is working with the Organizing Committee of the 2024 Olympic Games in Paris to encourage people to run for the "Club Paris 2024"; an initiative to inspire sports and movement. In this way, citizens become part of the games.

- **Business:** Collaboration with the Olympic and Paralympic Committees, International and National Associations is particularly important in relation to Allianz's insurance expertise, for example when it comes to insuring events, teams and athletes or risks around the Olympic and Paralympic Games. At the same time, various initiatives have been launched to support sales with point-of-sale activities and product promotions.
- **Brand:** The top priority here is the topic of "Olympising". This means that the Olympic and Paralympic logo is carried on all communication measures, thus increasing the awareness of Allianz as a partner of the movements. This applies from the envelope to digital formats to product and brand campaigns. An example of successful campaigns is #sparkconfidence: Both athletes and employees tell their stories and the respective moment that gave them the confidence to participate in the games and win a medal, but also to be part of a sports event in the amateur sector (see Fig. 2.24).

Fig. 2.24 Allianz and #SparkConfidence. (*Source*: Allianz)

In addition, there are two more **initiatives** that are very important for Allianz:

- **Athlete Program:**Athletes are the heart of every sports competition—and of course also of the Olympic and Paralympic Games. Allianz has developed a program to accompany athletes both on their journey from amateur to professional athlete and on their life path after their sports career. Examples here can include further education programs, career conferences, and scholarships.
- **Move Now:** Allianz is convinced of the impact of sports on the social and professional development of children and young people. Statistically, many young people stopped being physically active during Corona. 66% of children between 5 and 15 years and 51% of young people from 16 to 24 years were less physically active. Under the umbrella of "Move Now", Allianz wants to bring children and young people back to sports. Various initiatives have already been carried out. In the Allianz Sports Camps, young people are playfully taught the philosophy and values of the movements by trying out different sports, making friends, and learning from athletes (see Fig. 2.25).

Of course, there are many more measures. Each activity has its KPIs and contributes to the set targets. In doing so, Allianz follows the principle "If you can't measure it don't do it".

That's why **success control** is particularly important, also to see whether a measure was successful or what can be done better in the future. Allianz, for example, relies on Quarterly Performance Measurement & Research, Logo Research, Campaign tracking, A-B Testing, and Qualitive Research. In terms of media

Fig. 2.25 Allianz and Move Now. (*Source*: Allianz)

impact, measurement criteria such as partnership and brand awareness, brand likeability, and consideration (purchase consideration) are used.

Additional **success criteria** may include:

- Mood in media and social media channels,
- Number of employees involved,
- Number of markets/countries utilizing the partnership,
- Number of submissions of communication media (requests for approval).

KPIs are collected and reviewed at both global and local levels. This has been and continues to be carried out at the employee, business, and brand level to ensure the success of the partnership.

This most challenging sports sponsoring in terms of scope and structure worldwide will never be completely without one or another difficulty, despite good preparation. Various problems from operations, risk management, communication issues to organizational structure can arise. A partnership like this must be embraced by the company.

As initially emphasized, sports sponsoring is a central **component of brand management** for Allianz. This in turn means that all areas and communication tools are integrated and networked in such a way that a consistent appearance is created. The partnership with the Olympic movement is lived in many areas of the company. Almost all areas of the company are involved, from legal and compliance to communication, sales, HR, and market management. The aim here is to live the partnership and make the most or best of the partnership with the expertise of various departments. For Allianz, it is important to live this partnership from within and thus achieve an external impact.

If one draws a first **balance** after almost two years of Olympic sponsoring and two Olympic and Paralympic Games (Summer Games Tokyo 2021 and Winter Games Beijing 2022), all goals as set out in the business plan for brand, employee engagement, and insurance business have been achieved. There is also a positive influence on the brand funnel (customer perception behavior), employee engagement, and talent attraction.

2.5 Virtual sponsoring

Looking at the history of sports promotion by third parties, there is an increasing shift towards brands as sponsors and an expansion and refinement of technical possibilities. In this respect, **virtual sponsoring** is a phenomenon that no longer takes place in real space-time dimensions, but in artificial spaces that can be produced and/or animated by digital techniques. It is in a certain sense a kind of "illusionary world" because the

Time	Motivation	Tool	
Greek and Roman times	Demonstrate cities' prestige and standing	Investment in events such as Olympics, gladiator fights or chariot races	The Olympic Games of antiquity were held between 776 BC and 393 AD in the Sacred Grove of Olympia. During the games, weapons were laid to rest. It was all about glory and honor.
Early 20th century	Product placement	Provision of free equipment to athletes	Examples: 1902 Wimbledon tennis tournament 1936 Jesse Owens and adidas
Mid and late 20th century	Brand visibility	Logo placement in stadiums and on athletes' equipment	Examples: 1950/60 Broadcast of major sporting events on TV 1970/80 Sports boom and commercialization
21st century	Fan engagement and relationship	Storytelling via digital media	Examples: 2004 Facebook 2010 Instagram 2015 Digital Overlays

Fig. 2.26 Sports sponsoring—past, present, and future. (*Source*: Deloitte, 2020a)

audiovisual signals suggest that there is something that is only electronically simulated (Vogelsang, 2019). The terms are largely used synonymously in the following. Fig. 2.26 illustrates the technical development of sports sponsoring phenomena.

The digital boom (advancing technology, new media formats) often means higher effort for rights holders in sponsoring, but also many **opportunities for higher revenues**, for rights users new creative presentation possibilities with comparatively low activation effort. There are many new integration possibilities for sponsors in the digital channels, which were not only enormously important for bridging the Corona crisis, but also hold additional opportunities for both partners in the future.

▶ **Virtual sponsoring** In **virtual sponsoring**, as usual in sponsoring, activities involve a partnership of reciprocity with a specific reference object, but these do not take place in the analog space, but in the digital space and/or using digital technology. Therefore, virtual sponsoring is only perceptible for people/viewers in the digital space.

As a rule, brand logos and advertising messages are presented on digital channels or inserted into existing analog formats. In sports broadcasts, for example, this technology can replace the existing advertising banners in the stadium with other advertising or display a logo on the field. In addition, the sports event is "extended and expanded" because it does not only take place in the sports venue and at a certain time, but enables new and also time-stretched interactions with the fans.

For virtual sponsoring, it is important to distinguish between the **forms** of (see also Fig. 2.27):

- sponsoring at virtual events,
- Use of virtual tools for the presentation of companies and products,
- Virtual implementation of sponsoring.

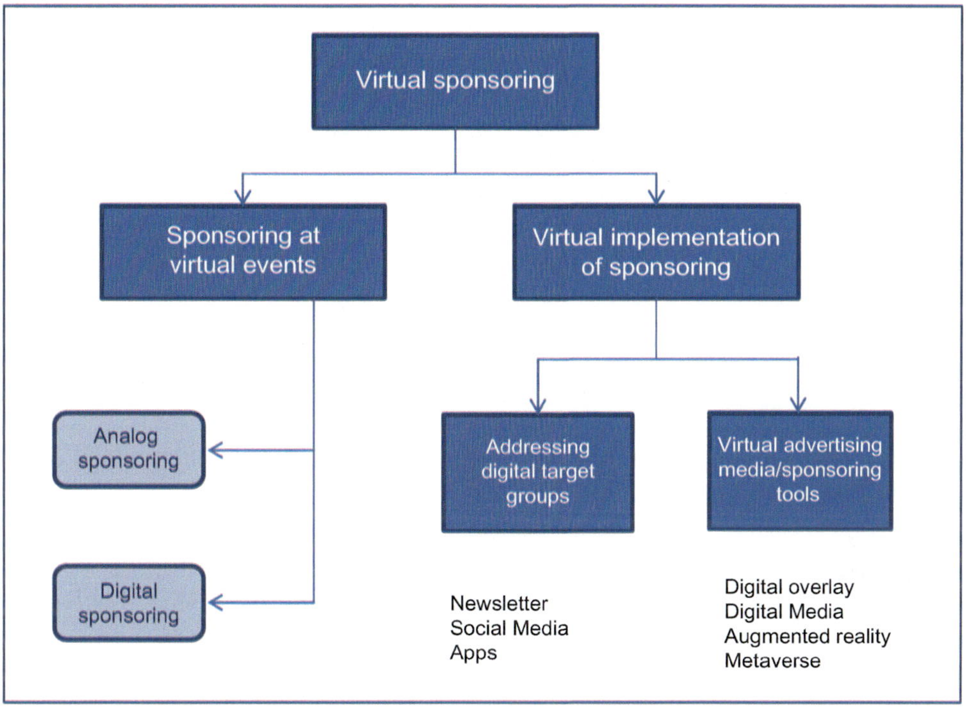

Fig. 2.27 Forms of virtual sports sponsoring

Sponsoring at virtual events

Numerous virtual events take place via live stream. There are many opportunities to offer sponsors an interesting platform, using both analog and digital tools. Banners, logos, and pop-up ads can be easily integrated, and breaks and other pauses between event processes can be bridged with commercials. Various advertising inserts can be used, for example, to point out the websites and products of the event's sponsors. The biggest challenges of virtual events are the lack of personal interactions and the lack of uncomplicated and direct networking. Sponsored parties' contact activations may serve as a stimulus, allowing participants to get to know each other and familiarize themselves with the format. Such activities can be carried out by a sponsor or in their name. Ideas such as surveys, competitions, challenges, and quiz formats have proven successful.

Use of virtual tools for the presentation of companies and products

Virtual sponsoring means that almost all sponsoring measures are digitized—both in development and implementation as well as in use by the target groups. Digital channels are ideally suited to contact participants and/or potential customers before the sports event and afterwards. Visitors to a sports event no longer receive tickets/vouchers/info in paper form as with classic sponsoring, but these means are transmitted on a digital platform, e.g. in the case of a voucher as a "digital goodie bag". Digital sponsoring is ideally suited as an additional medium to classic sponsoring. The fact that the trend is often towards digital sponsoring and the use of digital media does not mean, however, that the means of classic sponsoring have become obsolete.

Virtual implementation of sponsoring

There are numerous **possibilities** for the virtual implementation of sponsoring (Walzel & Schubert, 2018; Gundacker, 2021):

- Digital communication: customer approach via online (e.g. newsletter), social media (Schröder, 2019), apps,
- Virtual advertising, sometimes also called Digital Overlay: With virtual advertising, real existing surfaces are overlaid with virtual sponsor logos and lettering or advertising spaces are created that are not actually present. Thus, virtual overlays become tailor-made communication for sponsors.
- Augmented Reality is at the same time an integrative Experience Technology in the Metaverse and creates Experiences at the interface between virtual and real world—a so-called Digital Reality Experience (short: DRX),
- Social Media-sponsoring,
- E-sports-sponsoring,
- Smart Stadium (application of networked technology in sports venues),
- Virtual perimeter advertising.

Studies on the **effects of virtual sports advertising** show quite positive effects, in detail the following results can be highlighted (Walzel & Schubert, 2018, p. 328):

- On the cognitive level, virtual advertising can lead to significantly better results, depending in particular on the implementation (e.g. design, positioning).
- On the affective level, predominantly positive attitudes towards virtual advertising were determined, although the risk of too intrusive use is always mentioned.
- The networking with classic advertising is promising in terms of higher effects in sports sponsoring.

Example: Virtual Perimeter Advertising in the Bundesliga

According to research by the magazine SPONSORs (Sponsors, 2022b), virtual perimeter advertising has been used in just over 120 games in the first four years (2017/2018–2021/2022), i.e., only about 10% of all matches and in about half of the Bundesliga stadiums. This form of advertising has regularly been used in home games of FC Bayern Munich, and especially in matches of Bundesliga clubs that cooperate with the sports agency Sportfive. In addition to all home games of Borussia Dortmund, selected home games of Hertha BSC, the FC Augsburg and Borussia Mönchengladbach were covered with virtual advertising. According to SPONSORs, all participating clubs have generated additional sponsoring revenues of over 30 million EUR over the past four seasons with 70 to 80 virtually integrated partners.

Sponsoring experts estimate the potential value of possible additional revenues for the current Bundesliga season, in which the use of games with virtual advertising is to be doubled, at 100 million EUR. This is likely to be contributed to by the fact that transmission costs will fall to at least half due to new technologies, from almost 100,000 EUR per game—depending on factors such as the number of signals and the total number of games implemented.

Whether and how intensively individual Bundesliga clubs deal with the topic of virtual advertising apparently depends primarily on two criteria: firstly, on the state of their own internationalization, i.e., in particular the demand from international fans and international sponsors for a club, and secondly, on the international network and the technical know-how of the service providers and marketers with whom a club cooperates. ◀

Not only in the acquisition of new sponsors, e.g., companies that have not yet had contact with a sports club and initially only see the opportunities of a virtual additional appearance in a certain foreign market as classic media bookers, can the use of digital sponsoring help. The bond with existing sponsors can also be significantly strengthened through virtual sponsoring.

Most companies use the **digital form as a supplement to traditional sponsoring**, others also rely on supporting a sports actor or a sports event virtually by sponsoring virtual sports events or offering their own online formats for this purpose (Fig. 2.28). Further sponsoring tools are advertising formats in virtual club or third-party portals, through which the events are streamed live and on-demand, others prefer blockchain tickets or virtual advertising spaces (VSA, 2021).

Applications \ Virtual Share	Partial	Complete
Existing sponsor	**Type I** (Additional offers such as social media advertising or presence on e-ticket)	**Type II** (complete switch from analog to digital forms of sponsorship)
New sponsor	**Type III** (restriction to focussed areas, e.g. foreign TV signal for stadium bands)	**Type IV** (comprehensive use of all digital sponsoring platforms)

Fig. 2.28 Scope and areas of application of virtual sports sponsoring

Just like in the analog world, sponsoring for the virtual space also needs to be planned consistently. This includes appropriate offers for the sponsoring of online events, how to compile these into sponsoring packages and above all, how to offer these to sponsors. Experience examples and expert knowledge can help with the first steps (Davey, 2021).

An excerpt from the Delphi study of the Association of Sports Sponsoring Providers (VSA, 2021) shows the **benefit potentials of virtual sponsoring** for rights holders. The fact that emotions and technology do not have to exclude each other, but can rather condition each other, is shown by the approval rate for the forecast "sports sponsoring will disproportionately benefit from the improved transmission of emotions (using digital technologies)". The probability of occurrence is rated by the respondents at 71%, making this projection the second most likely in the entire study. Key technologies here are virtual reality, augmented reality, advanced camera and transmission techniques or holograms. Ultimately, traditional offline measures such as perimeter or kit sponsoring also benefit from this. The probability of occurrence of the statement "New distribution channels will increase the impact of offline sponsoring" achieves the fourth highest value (66%) of all given projections. The experts recognize a benefit in new technologies for sponsoring, however, the successful expansion of the advertising space over a period of ten years is rather viewed skeptically.

The **digital sports sponsoring in German professional football** has so far had a rather low significance. On average, each club from the Bundesliga has generated 5% of its sponsoring revenues through digital formats. Forecasts suggest that the average potential for revenues from digital rights packages is 20% of total sponsoring revenues. The American sports marketing agency Two Circles estimates the potential at up to 36%. With the exception of the record football champions FC Bayern Munich, which took in a total of 196 million EUR through sponsoring in the 2018/2019 season, the average sponsoring volume in the Bundesliga was around 37 million EUR per club. If the forecasts are applied to the revenues from the 2018/2019 season, then according to the calculation by Two Circles, average revenues of up to 13.5 million EUR per team from digital sponsorings would be possible. With the calculated 20%, the median value would be just under 7.5 million EUR (Sponsors, 2020a).

2.6 Equipment Sponsoring as a Special Case of Sports Sponsoring

Sporting goods companies play a very important role as **equipment providers in professional sports**, because they not only provide the necessary equipment for good performance, but also contribute significant financial contributions to the revenue of sports actors. Likewise, the sponsoring manufacturer benefits from the exclusivity of such a partnership, which gives them competitive advantages over other market participants.

In addition, other forms of collaboration (e.g., merchandising) often follow, because sports actors like to take advantage of the (often international) distribution power of the manufacturers. Therefore, it is understandable that sports units and their equipment

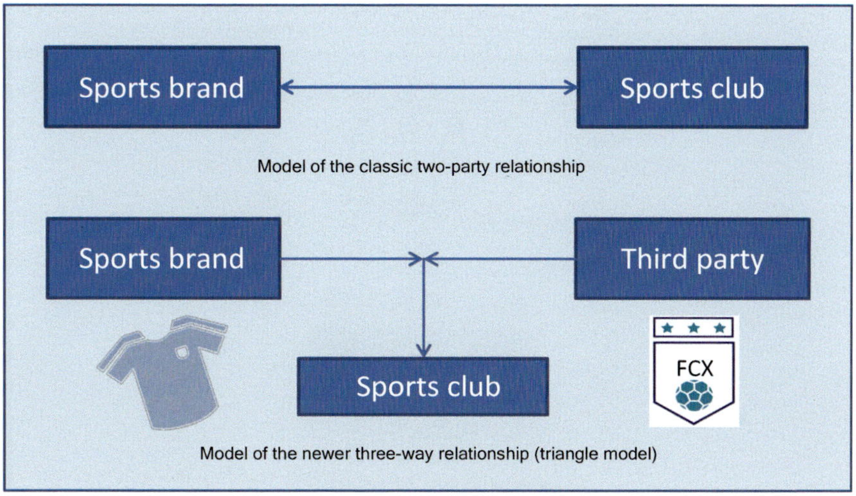

Fig. 2.29 Classic and newer model of equipment-club relationships

providers find themselves in a kind of **community of fate**, which hardly anyone wants to give up in case of success (Rohlmann, 2022a).

In this respect, **sporting goods companies have a special position** among sponsoring companies—also because they view the equipment of a sports unit almost like a sponsoring commitment that arises naturally or can also be seen as inevitable.

While before 1995 most professional clubs had to procure or buy their playing clothes themselves, this changed with the **emergence of merchandising** and the further professionalization of club marketing relatively quickly (Rohlmann, 2023). Before the turn of the millennium, the major sports brands felt among themselves and the equipment sponsoring was still in its infancy in terms of amount (e.g., under 20 million EUR for all 18 Bundesliga football clubs). But afterwards and with increasing speed, the demands and claims of successful sports clubs became ever larger, so that even renowned manufacturers reached their limits and made considerations regarding the relevance or importance and cost of equipment sponsoring. The **traditional equipment models**, in which direct relationships exist between the sports club and the sponsoring equipment provider, began to wobble, were changed and partly reinvented. So-called **triangle models** were developed, in which the previous two-way relationship became a three-way relationship (see Fig. 2.29).

At present, both the classic and the newer equipment models are proven practice, and these do not only concern smaller clubs. In the context of such a collaboration, the parties involved will make their decision based on various criteria (see Fig. 2.30), so that from the individual **cost-benefit analysis** in the best case a win-win-win situation for all parties involved will result.

If one also takes into account certain **planning and implementation times in equipment-club relationships**, which can last up to 1.5-2 years, for example, in terms of the development and design of individual jersey designs, it becomes clear that careful and anticipatory action is required in the event of a partner change.

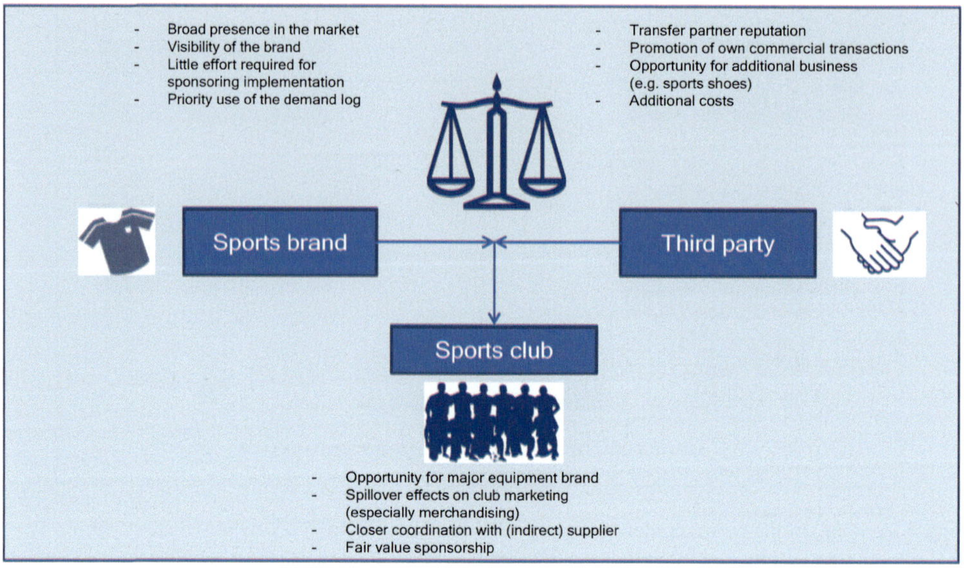

Fig. 2.30 Cost-benefit considerations among the participants

Top 3 sporting goods brands	2014	2015	2016	2017	2018	2019	2020	2021
Marketing expenditure	5,981	6,813	7,230	6,924	7,552	7,907	7,215	6,970
Sponsorship expenditure	2,209	2,401	2,544	2,698	3,134	3,241	3,157	3,124
Sponsorship as a % of marketing	37 %	35 %	35 %	39 %	42 %	41 %	44 %	45 %
Sponsorship as a soccer supplier	1,065	1,058	1,245	1,215	1,500	1,618	1,893	2,032
Kit sponsorship as % of total sponsorship	48 %	44 %	49 %	45 %	48 %	50 %	60 %	65 %
Sponsorship as a soccer supplier as a percentage of marketing	18 %	16 %	17 %	18 %	20 %	20 %	26 %	29 %

Fig. 2.31 Sponsoring of the top 3 brands (Nike, Adidas, Puma) among sporting goods manufacturers (figures in million EUR, exchange rates as of 30.6. of the year). (*Source*: PR MARKETING)

Often these companies spend disproportionately more on individual sponsoring rights as well as within the entire marketing for it. Thus, the **sponsoring share of the marketing costs** of the three largest sporting goods brands (Nike, Adidas, Puma) is now almost half and football sponsoring alone almost 30% of the marketing costs (see Fig. 2.31).

Over the past decades, a significant **dynamics in the market of equipment sponsoring**, especially in football, has emerged. This is not only due to the fact that the economic data and facts in professional football have developed in a way that was hardly thought possible before (e.g., with regard to three-digit million amounts for player

	2018/19	2019/20	2020/21
Sponsorship of the two top leagues in Europe's TOP 5 countries (GB, ESP, GER, ITA, FRA)	904	1,180	1,296
Share of first division clubs	92.4%	94.5%	94.8%
Share of second division	7.6%	5.5%	5.2%
Research basis (number of clubs in 1st and 2nd division of Europe's TOP 5 countries)	202	202	202
Sponsorship of first division clubs in other European countries			286
Number of clubs in other European leagues except TOP 5 countries			53
Supplier sponsorship in 10 or 15 (2020/21) European leagues			1,582
Research basis (number of clubs)			255

Fig. 2.32 Equipment sponsoring by sports equipment manufacturers in Europe's football leagues in million USD. (*Source*: Sportcal, 2020; Rohlmann, 2018)

transfers and equipment sponsorings), but also to the fact that the major sports equipment manufacturers increasingly have to pay attention to their cost-benefit ratios and are increasingly being pushed by creative and financially strong manufacturers with new ambitions (New Balance, Under Armour, Castore), with great past (e.g., Umbro, Le Coq Sportif) or with focused sports equipment program (e.g., Hummel, Jako, Joma, Macron) bedrängt are.

At the same time, especially **well-known and successful football clubs** are a kind of "accelerator" for sports equipment companies acting as sponsors in terms of reach, reputation, sales opportunities, and competitive advantages. This became increasingly clear to the sponsored clubs, and therefore they were able to continuously raise their demands and expectations regarding the value of a collaboration.

In this respect, the extremely grown **market for equipment sponsoring** has primarily benefited the already financially and fan-strong major clubs in football: Around 95% are attributable to the 98 clubs of the five top European leagues (ENG, ESP, FRA, GER, ITA). The study results (Sportcal, 2020; Rohlmann, 2018) also show that sports equipment manufacturers spend well over 1.5 billion USD on football sponsoring alone in Europe (see Fig. 2.32).

A time series comparison of the clubs from Deloitte's Football Money League over 20 years (annual analysis of the 20 highest-grossing football clubs worldwide) clearly

Top 20 clubs	2000/01	2005/06	2010/11	2015/16	2020/21
Total revenue	2,423.8	3,345.3	4,402.7	7,417.6	8,186.9
Commerce. Revenue				3,190.0	3,532.0
Comm. Share of revenue				43.0 %	43.1 %
Kit Sponsorship	**131.0**	**184.1**	**230.0**	**503.3**	**872.2**
Kit Spons. share of revenue	5.4 %	5.5 %	5.2 %	6.8 %	10.7 %
Kit spons. share of comm. in.				15.8 %	24.7 %
Jersey sales in units	3,700,000	8,995,000	9,502,500	13,065,000	13,785,000

Fig. 2.33 Economic data, especially kit sponsoring of the top 20 clubs in worldwide football (figures in million EUR). (*Sources*: Deloitte; PR MARKETING)

Sponsorship commitments	2019	2020	2021
adidas (financial year ending Dec. 31)	6,808	5,948	5,712
Nike (financial year ending May 31)	9,238	9,342	8,392
Puma (financial year ending Dec. 31)	1,228	1,148	1,157
Total of the BIG 3 together	17,274	16,438	15,261

Fig. 2.34 Sponsoring and advertising contractual obligations of the major sports goods brands (figures in million EUR). (*Sources*: Manufacturers' annual reports)

shows how equipment sponsoring has developed among the major professional clubs and their relationship with each other. The **revenue share of kit sponsoring** among these clubs has increased from 131 to almost 900 million EUR in two decades and currently has twice the revenue share of the total revenues of the top 20 clubs than two decades ago (see Fig. 2.33).

In the same way, the sponsors were also able to profit because **merchandising** and especially jersey sales have also increased significantly. The sale of club jerseys (replicas) alone has grown by over 10 million pieces. This is not only due to the growing popularity of sports and their representatives, but also to the fact that sportswear is becoming more fashionable and stylish and is therefore worn by fans in their leisure time and everyday life in some countries. In addition, the release of new and additional jersey designs per season has increased as well as the regularly newly raised jersey prices, so that first critical voices are now being heard, demanding from their clubs and the sponsors to think more about the fans and the environment in this "flood of offers", and to demand a reduction in the number of new jerseys and their prices.

However, it is not just football that is driving the sponsoring of sports goods companies ever higher, but all sports, including individual athletes, are making ever higher demands. The three major brands in the sports goods industry report on their ongoing sports and sponsoring commitments to clubs, athletes, universities, associations and organisers in their annual financial statements at the end of each respective financial year. Accordingly, financial support from the "big three" for sports amounting to around 16 billion EUR is pledged for the coming years. The annual financial reports of the sports goods manufacturers also show how important sponsoring is for their business activities: about 40% of all marketing funds are invested by the sports goods industry into sports sponsoring, with the vast majority going into athlete and team sponsoring (see Fig. 2.34).

2.7 Ambush Marketing in Sports Sponsoring

For many years, a large number of companies have been using sports sponsoring to achieve specific goals of marketing- and corporate communication. However, more and more companies are trying to benefit from the advantages of sports sponsoring without taking on the obligations of an official sponsor. This necessarily weakens the (communicative) effect of the official sponsoring activities (Bruhn & Ahlers, 2003, p. 271; Nufer & Bühler, 2014). This use of foreign-staged events is referred to as **Ambush Marketing** (to ambush = to attack from ambush) and is particularly noticeable in sports sponsoring. The offence is committed when an advertising company undertakes activities in connection with or in close relation to a sporting reference object in order to benefit from the successes of a **"pseudo-sponsoring"**, i.e. without taking on the obligations of an official sponsor. Ambushers therefore have no marketing rights, but nevertheless build a supposed proximity to a sports actor through their marketing.

Many examples illustrate that it is not only the official sponsors who benefit from their commitments in sports, but increasingly other companies that do not have an official sponsoring position.

Examples of Ambush Marketing

Warsteiner raffled off ten "VIP football trips" to Brazil for the 2014 Football World Cup and established a connection to this event without having to make sponsoring payments to the DFB like Bitburger, for example.

The **German Railway** also succeeded in a successful ambush marketing action at this major sporting event. In reference to the octopus Paul, who became famous as a World Cup oracle, the German Railway launched a TV campaign that advertises the "Winner's BahnCard" with a whole series of quirky oracles such as a cow oracle, pug oracle and office oracle. In this way, the German Railway made use of the 2014 World

Cup for its marketing without, however, being an official sponsor of this major event (Kuske, 2014).

The campaign launched by sports goods manufacturer **Nike** during the 2012 Summer Olympics in London is considered a particularly successful example of ambush marketing. The "Find Your Greatness" campaign, which started in 32 countries at the opening of the games, is a prime example of talking about something without naming it directly. The campaign shows amateur athletes in London. The special thing about it is that these are not the British capital, but smaller towns and villages in the USA, Canada or Jamaica, all of which bear the name "London". Thus, the film neither explicitly points out that the athletes shown live in a place called London, nor does it draw a comparison with sports in the British capital (Horizont, 2012; The Wall Street Journal, 2012). ◀

In each of the cases presented, a large number of viewers assumed a connection between the companies and the respective event. Ambush marketing has existed as a **side effect of sports sponsoring** for as long as companies have been sponsoring. Opinions on ambush marketing range from a serious threat to both sponsors and organisers of major sports events to a new, innovative communication tool (Drees & Trautwein, 2008; Handelsblatt, 2014).

Ambush marketing has many forms and is characterized by constantly new creative manifestations. Some constitutive **characteristics of ambush marketing** can be mentioned (Bruhn & Ahlers, 2003; Nufer, 2010):

- Ambush marketing represents activities of a company that serve to be associated with a particular sports event or an athlete without taking on an official sponsoring. The ambusher and sponsor usually come from the same industry and are considered competing companies or brands.
- Ambush marketing is not exclusively seen as a competition-oriented strategy, but is fundamentally aimed at the positive use of events, mainly in the sports sector.
- Ambush marketing achieves an effect on the viewers of a sports event in terms of the connection between the sponsoring object (sports event, team or athlete) and the ambusher.
- Practices of ambush marketing cause a shift of attention between the official sponsor and the ambusher—with the consequence that the official sponsoring loses its communicative effect.

▶ **Ambush Marketing** Referring to the constitutive characteristics, **ambush marketing** is the alignment of communication and marketing measures of companies to a sports reference object in order to achieve a communicative effect with certain target groups without having an official sponsor position and providing a consideration.

Companies can use different measures in the direct and indirect environment of a sports event to practice ambush marketing (Bruhn & Ahlers, 2004). However, the range between legal and illegal action is relatively large (see Fig. 2.35):

- Ambush marketing within a "subcategory" of a sports event,
- Ambush marketing through outdoor advertising,
- Ambush marketing through television advertising,
- Ambush marketing by obscuring communicative measures of sponsors,
- Ambush marketing through program sponsoring.

Ambush Marketing within a "Subcategory" of a Sports Event

Due to the strong differentiation of sponsoring, a multitude of different sponsoring levels or categories have emerged in recent years. For example, a distinction is made between main sponsors and national promoters. The latter in turn differ from licensees and public outfitters. The resulting complexity of sponsoring measures allows companies to gain the attention of certain target groups through the sponsoring of a "subcategory" and to bear relatively low costs. For example, the delivery company UPS, which has been one of the TOP partners of the Olympic Games for years, was powerless in Sydney when the tickets were distributed by the competitor TNT. As a result, a large part of the audience associated TNT with the Olympic Games (Pechtl, 2007).

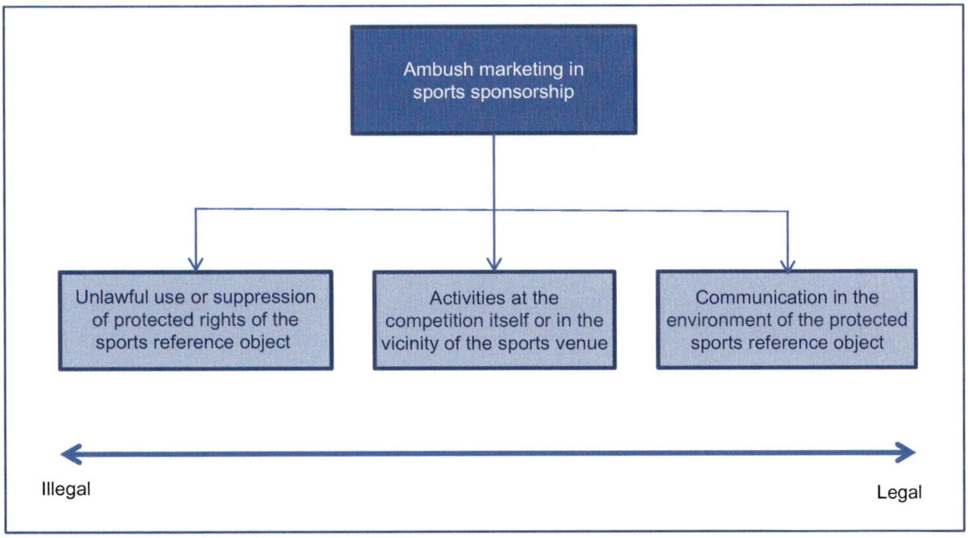

Fig. 2.35 Ambush marketing in sports sponsoring

Ambush Marketing through Outdoor Advertising

Existing campaigns, however, make it clear that ambush marketing measures are by no means limited to the event site, but also come into play in the context of outdoor advertising. In addition to the installation of posters and the distribution of flyers, more cost-intensive communication measures such as the staging of aerial advertising or similar belong to outdoor advertising. For example, during the 2006 Football World Cup, the sports equipment manufacturer Puma arranged for the company's predator logo to be attached to 27 planes of the airline Deutsche BA (Eschenbach, 2011, p. 33).

Ambush Marketing through Television Advertising

The broadcasting of major sports events on television allows companies to obtain advertising slots in a sports-affine environment and to create an association with the respective event through event- or sports-related design of their TV spots. In principle, it is legitimate for a company to place TV spots in the commercial breaks of a sports event without being the owner of an official sponsoring position. If the advertising content has a direct or indirect reference to the sports event, it is referred to as ambush marketing from a close perspective. For example, Samsung, VW and Nike—they were not official partners of FIFA—placed numerous TV spots during the 2014 Football World Cup that referred to the topic of football (n-tv, 2014).

Ambush Marketing by Concealing Sponsors' Communicative Measures

Instead of putting their own brand in the spotlight, ambushers sometimes "block" the trademarks of official sponsors. At the Olympic Games in Barcelona, the players sponsored by Nike, Charles Barkley and Michael Jordan, covered the logos of the official sponsor of the American basketball team, Reebok, on their tracksuits with a US flag during the award ceremony. Both players admitted afterwards that they had deliberately acted in favor of their individual sponsor Nike with this action (Lyberger & McCarthy, 2001, p. 132; McDonald & Davidson, 2002, p. 23; Nufer, 2005, p. 216). Similarly, the Hyundai, official sponsor of the 2006 Football World Cup, was no longer clearly identifiable as a sponsor at a press conference of the German national players, as Mercedes stars were visible in the room (Liebetrau, 2007, p. 15).

Ambush Marketing through Program Sponsoring

Taking over the program sponsoring of a televised sports event is a legitimate form of sponsoring that can be interpreted as ambush marketing if the program sponsor is not an official sponsor of the event. This is especially true if the official sponsor is a direct competitor or a company from the same industry. Compared to the event sponsor, the program sponsor usually reaches a much larger audience with a higher attention effect. A particularly impressive example is the program sponsoring of Bitburger on German public television during the 1998 Football World Cup. The company managed to achieve a higher unaided recall value than two-thirds of the official main sponsors of the event through program sponsoring (Nufer & Bühler, 2014, p. 153).

Since ambush marketing occurs as a side effect of sports sponsoring, the **consequences and dangers of ambush marketing** primarily affect the main participants of the sponsoring. Therefore, primarily three groups, which were also referred to as the "magic triangle" of sponsoring, are affected. Consequences arise for the official sponsors, the sports organizations or organizers of sports events, as well as for the media.

The "ambush marketers" (often also referred to as "free riders") aim to confuse consumers about the actual or official **sponsors of an event** through different—often extremely innovative—measures. This deception carries the risk that a large part of the attention is directed towards the ambusher and the desired image dimensions are not transferred to the sponsor, but to the ambusher. This ultimately results in a weakening of the communicative effect and a loss of value of the sponsoring for official sponsors. Especially in economically tense times, this often leads to a reevaluation of the sponsoring within the communication mix.

For the **organizers**, the most attractive possible marketing of the organized sports events is one of the central targets. Since international events have a huge financing need, organizers depend on the acquisition of financially strong external sponsors. These receive in return a direct or indirect advertising for their company or a brand, in order to establish a positive association with the sports event among their target groups. If the unique association, or the communicative success of the sponsoring commitment, is no longer guaranteed due to ambush marketing, the sponsorings inevitably lose value. Companies withdraw from the sponsorings as a consequence or demand a reduction of the sponsoring fees, so that the sources of income of the organizers are burdened.

The uncertainty regarding the financing of sports events also poses dangers for the **media**. For many media, sports broadcasts have become an essential program component and a profiling tool against media competition. Significant sports events achieve high viewing figures, which in turn are the prerequisite for the realization of high advertising revenues for the media. Uncertainties on the part of the organizers therefore also affect the financial situation of the TV stations.

The **network of relationships in ambush marketing** between the main participants in sponsoring shows that the consequences of ambush marketing do not only relate to individual groups, but lead to uncertainties in the entire (sports) sponsoring market, which ultimately represent a threat to sponsoring growth (Pechtl, 2007, pp. 43 ff.). These relationships are schematically represented in Fig. 2.36. As soon as sponsors withdraw from their commitments on a large scale, a large number of organizers lack the financial basis for carrying out the events. The organization of significant and popular events such as the Olympic Games, football championships, tennis tournaments and motor races, which are financed between 70 and 100% by external funds, are at risk in the medium term (Bruhn & Ahlers, 2004, p. 49).

The following will examine starting points for **measures against ambush marketing** for organizers and sponsors. The measures primarily relate to the prevention of ambush marketing.

Ambush marketing often occurs as a result of the increasing complexity of sponsoring rights. A fundamental prerequisite for avoiding ambush marketing is an even clearer **structuring and control of sponsoring rights** on the part of rights holders. Furthermore, it is important to precisely define in sponsoring contracts which rights are exclusively granted to the affected sponsor and which rights are acquired by other sponsors. This also requires clear contracts with the participating athletes and

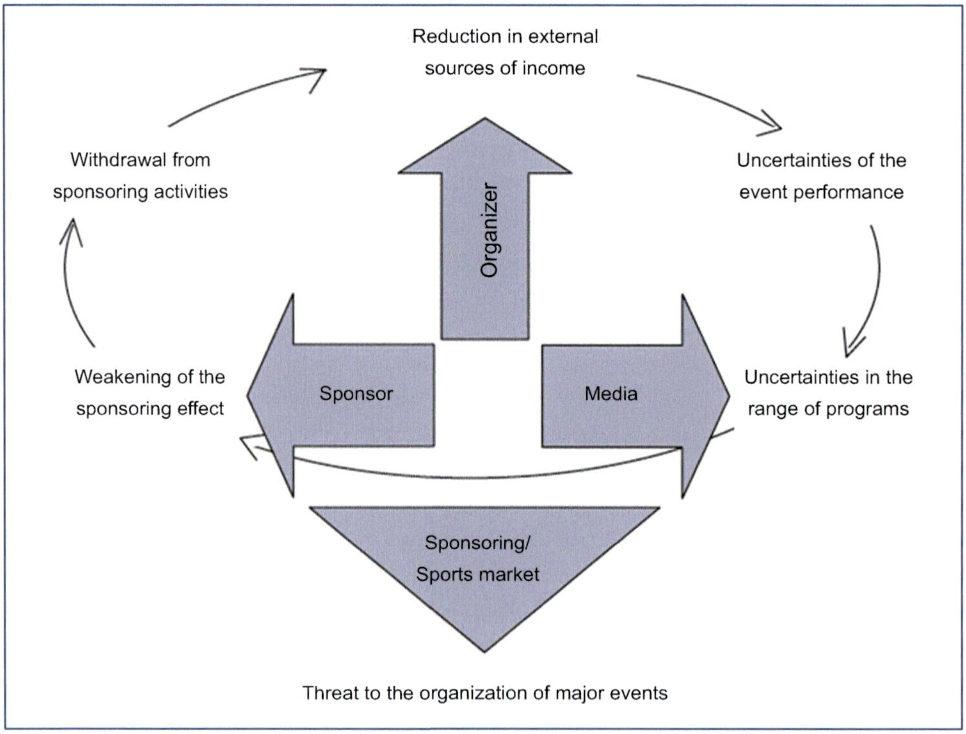

Fig. 2.36 Network of consequences of ambush marketing. (*Source*: Bruhn & Ahlers, 2004)

their associations in the relationship between the organizer and the sponsored parties (Mitschke, 2007, p. 127 f.).

Particular importance is attached to the **protection of the intellectual property** of the sponsors by the organizer. This serves to prevent the unauthorized use of logos, slogans, mascots, etc., which are associated with a sports event (Kalamadi, 2012). In addition to defining the respective "trademarks", this includes precise specifications for the use and representation of the respective brands. For example, FIFA has established its own program to protect FIFA trademark rights, which includes aspects such as intellectual property, protection of the rights of sponsors, and protection of the World Cup brand (FIFA, 2016).

Companies place a high value on a "clean" environment in sponsorings within the framework of an event, which is not distracted by the communicative activities of the sponsors. Numerous examples of ambush marketing show that the **control of the event location** involves both the immediate surroundings of a sports event, such as VIP lounges and boards, as well as the wider environment. The latter in particular poses a huge challenge for large-scale events, such as marathons or sailing races.

Even though sponsoring has now established itself as an essential element of the communication mix, there is often a lack of professionalism in the planning and implementation on the part of sponsors. Therefore, the defense against ambush marketing requires an even more intensive **examination of the legal situation** in sponsorings.

In order to estimate the **potential for ambush marketing** in advance, in addition to critically examining existing sponsoring contracts, the identification of potential access points for ambushers is becoming increasingly important, especially when not all sponsoring rights are granted and controlled by the organizer himself. For financially strong companies, the risk of ambush marketing can be significantly reduced by acquiring as comprehensive sponsoring packages as possible.

In addition to the **control of program sponsoring**, product or industry exclusivity in TV advertising during the sports event is a preventive measure. This includes both the advertising ban for direct competitors of official sponsors and the ban for non-sponsors to deliberately create associations with a specific sports event in TV spots.

An effective defense against ambush marketing lies primarily in the **design of the sponsorings**. In an increasingly competitive competitive environment, it will be increasingly important for companies in the future to communicate their position as a sponsor unmistakably and to create an immediate association with a specific event through verbal and visual communication tools. The implementation of the sponsorings is supported by the use of creative communication tools and by accompanying measures within the framework of a pre- and post-sponsoring (Bruhn & Ahlers, 2003).

Central importance is attached to the consistent **integration of sponsoring into the communication mix**. With the help of linking the sponsoring with other communication tools (**inter-instrumental integration**), a synergistic reinforcement of the overall effect of communication is achieved. This solidifies the connection between a company and the sponsored event or athlete in the consciousness of consumers, reducing the attack surface for ambush marketers (Bruhn & Ahlers, 2003).

In addition to inter-instrumental integration, the **intra-instrumental integration** of a company's individual sponsorings is significant for defending against ambush marketing. Often, companies do not only sponsor one event, but are active at different events and in different sports. A content, formal, and temporal integration of the individual communicative measures of the sponsoring in the sense of a superordinate guiding idea increases the credibility of the sponsoring and strengthens the desired image transfer (Bruhn & Ahlers, 2003).

2.8 Key Points

To better understand sports sponsoring in its various forms, the following central aspects are particularly emphasized:

Key Points

1. **Sponsoring has different perspectives for the participants**. For the sponsored, it represents an opportunity to tap into additional sources of funding. From the sponsor's perspective, the use of sponsoring is an additional tool for marketing and corporate communication.
2. Sports sponsoring can be practiced in different **scope** (e.g., main, co-, secondary and partial sponsoring) or with completely different **references**(e.g., performance level, sports, organizational unit).
3. **Sports sponsoring for teams** (clubs/associations) is usually well-planned and hardly susceptible to disruptive factors, because the commitment is spread across many actors and the team as a whole.
4. **Famous athletes** are usually not just "advertising figures", but serve as role models for the benefits one can derive from sports for oneself (e.g., appearance, health). Especially for young people, successful athletes have a role model character through their athletic and extracurricular behavior, but slumps, injuries or other disruptive factors (e.g., doping, private life) can also occur.
5. The **sponsoring of major sporting events** gives partners particularly quick and concentrated attention. This is especially true when sponsors can present themselves through the geographical reach of the event where they plan to expand or enter the market.

6. Also, **stadium sponsoring** is becoming more and more widespread, as particularly well-known stadiums and halls radiate a constant high presence throughout the year. In return, the stadium can be named after the sponsor.
7. **Virtual sponsoring** is a relatively new phenomenon that no longer takes place in real space-time dimensions, but in somewhat artificial spaces that can be produced and/or animated by digital techniques. For many, the digital form is a welcome addition to traditional sponsoring.
8. **Equipment suppliers in professional sports** play a very important role in sports sponsoring, as they not only provide the necessary equipment for good performance, but also contribute significant financial contributions to the sports actors' revenues. Of course, the sponsoring manufacturer also benefits from the exclusivity of such a partnership.
9. The **traditional equipment supplier models**, where direct relationships exist between the sports club and the sponsoring equipment supplier, have been partially changed and reinvented. So-called **Triangle models** have been developed, in which the previous two-way relationship has become a three-way relationship.
10. Some advertising companies undertake activities in connection or in close relation with a sports reference object to benefit from the successes of a "pseudo-sponsoring", i.e., without taking on the obligations of an official sponsor. This so-called **Ambush Marketing** takes place without official marketing rights and can lead to damage for the official sponsors.

References

A

Ahlert, D., Vogel, V., & Woisetschläger, D. (2007). Ist Sponsoring der Zaubertrank einer starken Marke? In D. Ahlert, D. Woisetschläger, & Vogel, V. (Hrsg.), *Exzellentes Sponsoring. Innovative Ansätze und Best Practices für das Markenmanagement* (2. Aufl., S. 3–32). https://doi.org/10.1007/978-3-8350-9639-4_1.

Allianz Arena. (2014). Allianz stellt Kooperation mit FC Bayern München auf langfristige Basis, Beitrag vom 13.02.2014. https://allianz-arena.com/de/news/2014/02/allianz-steigt-beim-fc-bayern-munchen-ein.

B

Bagusat, A. (2013). *Sponsoring trends 2012*. https://www.ostfalia.de/export/sites/default/de/ispm/Blickpunkt_Sportmanagement/Sponsoring_Trends_2012.pdf . Zugegriffen am 17.02.2016.

Bruhn, M. (2012). *Marketing für Nonprofit-Organisationen. Grundlagen, Konzepte, Instrumente* (2. Aufl.). W. Kohlhammer GmbH.

Bruhn, M. (2018). *Sponsoring. Systematische Planung und integrativer Einsatz* (6. Aufl.). https://doi.org/10.1007/978-3-658-13313-9.

Bruhn, M. (2019). *Kommunikationspolitik. Systematischer Einsatz der Kommunikation für Unternehmen* (9. Aufl.). https://doi.org/10.15358/9783800648924.

Bruhn, M., & Ahlers, G. M. (2003). Ambush Marketing. "Angriff aus dem Hinterhalt" oder intelligentes Marketing? *Jahrbuch der Absatz- und Verbrauchsforschung, 49*(3), 271–294.

Bruhn, M., & Ahlers, G. M. (2004). Ambush marketing. "Attack from behind". *Yearbook of Marketing and Consumer Research, 2*(1), 40–61.

Business Insider. (2013). *Why brands like Nike stuck with Tiger Woods through his scandal*. https://www.businessinsider.com/tiger-woods-a-tale-of-two-images-2013-4?IR=T.

D

Davey, T. (2021). Wie Sie attraktive Sponsoring-Pakete für Ihre Online-Veranstaltungen erstellen, Beitrag vom 17.12.2021. https://www.eventtia.com/de/blog/wie-sie-attraktive-sponsoring-pakete-fur-ihre-online-veranstaltungen-erstellen.

Deloitte. (2020a). *Sponsoring sports in today's digital age*. Deloitte. https://www2.deloitte.com/content/dam/Deloitte/lu/Documents/sports-consulting/lu-sponsoring-sports-today-digital-age.pdf.

Deutscher Olympischer Sportbund. (2016). Attraktives Erhrenamt im Sport. https://ehrenamt.dosb.de/attraktives-ehrenamt#akkordeon-11739.

Drees, N. (2003). Bedeutung und Erscheinungsformen des Sportsponsoring. In A. Hermanns & F. Riedmüller (Hrsg.), *Sponsoring und Events im Sport* (S. 47–66). Vahlen.

Drees, N., & Trautwein, S. (2008). Erscheinungsformen des Sponsoring. In A. Bagusat, C. Marwitz, & M. Vogl (Hrsg.), *Handbuch Sponsoring. Erfolgreiche Marketing- und Markenkommunikation* (S. 89–112). Erich Schmidt.

E

Eschenbach, F. (2011). Erfolgsfaktoren des Ambush-Marketing. Eine theoretische und empirische Analyse am Beispiel der Fußball-Europameisterschaft 2008. Wiesbaden. https://doi.org/10.1007/978-3-8349-6624-7.

F

FC Bayern München AG. (2014). Allianz beteiligt sich an FC Bayern München AG, Pressemitteilung vom 11.02.2014. https://fcbayern.com/de/news/2014/02/allianz-beteiligt-sich-an-fc-bayern-munchen-ag.

FIFA. (2011). FIFA-Finanzbericht 2010, Zürich.

FIFA. (2015). FIFA-Finanzbericht 2014, Zürich.

FIFA. (2016). Programm zum Schutz der Fifa-Markenrechte. http://de.fifa.com/about-fifa/marketing/brand-protection/index.html.

Freyer, W. (2018). *Sportmarketing—Modernes Marketingmanagement für die Sportwirtschaft* (5. Aufl). Erich Schmidt.

G

Grass, A., & Backhaus, C. (2007). Theorie und Praxis des Sportstättensponsorings am Beispiel der Allianz Arena. In D. Ahlert, D. Woisetschläger, & V. Vogel (Hrsg.), *Exzellentes Sponsoring. Innovative Ansätze und Best Practices für das Markenmanagement* (2. Aufl., S. 141–157). Deutscher Universitätsverlag. https://doi.org/10.1007/978-3-8350-9639-4_7.

Gundacker, L. (2021). Sportsponsoring im Zeitalter der Digitalisierung Erfolgsfaktoren für Vereine im deutschen Profifußball, Bachelorarbeit der Hochschule Mittweida.

H

Handelsblatt. (2014). Die Weltmeister der inoffiziellen Werbung. http://www.handelsblatt.com/unternehmen/handel-konsumgueter/fussball-wm-in-brasilien-nur-fussball-und-brasilien-reicht-nicht-fuer-gute-werbung/9816614-3.html.

Handelsblatt. (2015). Aus der Imtech-Arena wird wieder das Volksparkstadion. http://www.handelsblatt.com/sport/fussball/fussball-tempel-aus-der-imtech-arena-wird-wieder-das-volksparkstadion/10272992.html.

Hermanns, A., & Marwitz, C. (2008). *Sponsoring. Grundlagen, Wirkungen, Management, Markenführung* (3. Aufl.). Vahlen.

Hermanns, A., & Riedmüller, F. (2008). *Management Handbuch Sportmarketing* (2. Aufl.). Vahlen.

Horizont. (2012). Nike liefert zum Olympiastart Geniestreich im Ambush-Marketing. http://www.horizont.net/marketing/nachrichten/-Nike-liefert-zum-Olympiastart-Geniestreich-im-Ambush-Marketing%2D%2D109033.

I

International Olympic Committee (IOC). (2012). *London 2012—Report and accounts*.

International Olympic Committee (IOC). (2016). *Olympic marketing*. http://www.olympic.org/sponsors/coca-cola . Zugegriffen am 23.02.2016.

Ipsos GmbH. (2014). Grundlagenstudie Sponsoring 2014, Hamburg.

K

Kalamadi, S. (2012). Intellectual property and the business of sports management. *Journal of Intellectual Property Rights, 17*(5), 437–442.

Kottke, M. (2022). Mehr als nur ein Name: Naming Rights Sponsoring, Beyond the match – Insights von Sportfive 09.03.2022. https://beyond-the-match.com/insights/mehr-als-nur-ein-name-naming-rights-sponsoring/ . Zugegriffen am 01.05.2022.

Kuske, T. (2014). Deutsche Bahn mit Ambush-Kampagne zur WM vom 13.05.2014. http://www.tobiaskuske.de/2014/05/13/deutsche-bahn-ueberzeugt-mit-wm-kampagne/.

L

Liebetrau, M. (2007). Ambush Marketing—eine qualitative Analyse am Beispiel der FIFA Fußballweltmeisterschaft 2006. *Erfurter Hefte zum angewandten Marketing, 15*, 13–23.

Lyberger, M. R., & McCarthy, L. (2001). An assessment of consumer knowledge of, interest in, and perceptions of ambush marketing strategies. *Sport Marketing Quarterly, 10*(2), 130–137.

M

McDonald, J., & Davidson, J. (2002). Avoiding surprise results at the olympic games. *Managing Intellectual Property, 115*, 22–27.

Mercedes-Benz. (2020). *Mercedes-Benz junior cup*. https://group-media.mercedes-benz.com/mars-MediaSite/de/instance/ko/Mercedes-Benz-Junior-Cup.xhtml?oid=9265680.

Mitschke, M. (2007). Rechtliche Grenzen des Sponsoring. Ahlert, D., Woisetschläger, D., & Vogel, V. (Hrsg.), *Exzellentes Sponsoring. Innovative Ansätze und Best Practices für das Markenmanagement* (2. Aufl., S. 119–135). https://doi.org/10.1007/978-3-8350-9639-4_6.

N

Nielsen Sports. (2018a). Sponsor-Trend 2018: Status und Trends im Sponsoringmarkt in Deutschland, Österreich und Schweiz.

Nieschlag, R., Dichtl, E., & Hörschgen, H. (2002). *Marketing* (19. Aufl.). Duncker & Humblot.

Nike. (2016). *Tiger Woods*. http://news.nike.com/tiger-woods . Zugegriffen am 23.02.2016.

n-tv. (2014). Trittbrett-Werbung bei der WM. Wenn Neymars Schlüpfer die Fifa empört. http://www.ntv.de/sport/fussball_wm_2014/Wenn-Neymars-Schluepfer-die-Fifa-empoert-article13173361.html . Zugegriffen am 27.05.2016.

Nufer, G. (2005). Ambush Marketing. Angriff aus dem Hinterhalt oder eine Alternative zum Sportsponsoring? In H. D. Horch, G. Hovemann, S. Kaiser, & K. Viebahn (Hrsg.), *Perspektiven des Sportmarketing. Besonderheiten, Herausforderungen, Tendenzen* (S. 209–227). Institut für Sportökonomie und Sportmanagement Köln.

Nufer, G. (2010). *Ambush Marketing im Sport: Grundlagen—Strategien—Wirkungen*. Erich Schmidt.

Nufer, G., & Bühler, A. (2014). Ambush Marketing im Sport—Wie Nicht-Sponsoren Sportveranstaltungen zur Markenkommunikation nutzen. In H. Preuss, F. Huber, H. Schunk, & T. Könecke (Hrsg.), *Marken und Sport* (S. 145–164). Gabler.

P

Pechtl, H. (2007). Trittbrettfahren bei Sportevents: Das Ambush-Marketing. Wirtschaftswissenschaftliche Diskussionspapiere, (1), Rechts- und Staatswissenschaftliche Fakultät, Universität Greifswald.

Perform Media Deutschland GmbH. (2010). Woods: Verlust von 50 Millionen Dollar. http://www.spox.com/de/sport/golf/1004/News/tiger-woods-verliert-durch-eskapaden-50-millionen-dollar-skandal-affaere-verlust-sponsoren.html . Zugegriffen am 23.02.2016.

Pommer, J., & Kaiser, D. (2014). Beko Basketball Bundesliga—die Schaffung und Positionierung einer neuen Marke. In H. Preuß, F. Huber, H. Schunk, & T. Könecke (Hrsg.), *Marken und Sport—Aktuelle Aspekte der Markenführung im Sport und mit Sport* (S. 465–483). Gabler.

R

Rohlmann, P. (2018). Ausrüsterverträge im Fußball gestern—heute—morgen. Marktdaten, Akteure, Strategien, Nutznießer und Trikotabsatz aus den TOP 5-Ligen Europas sowie einem Ausblick in die Zukunft des Fußballartikelmarktes, Rheine/St. Gallen.

Rohlmann, P. (2022a). Sportklubs und Sportartikelhersteller—eine Schicksalsgemeinschaft besonderer Art, Rheine/St. Gallen.

Rohlmann, P. (2023). *Sportmerchandising—Konzeptionelle Grundlagen, Marktdaten und Trends*. ESV-Verlag.

S

Schaub, R. (2008). *Sponsoring und Doping. Beendigung von Sponsoringverträgen wegen Verfehlungen des Gesponserten, insbesondere in Dopingfällen, Göttingen*. Universitätsverlag Göttingen. https://doi.org/10.17875/gup2008-175.

Schröder, S. (2019). Sportsponsoring und Social Media—die neue Herausforderung für die Erfolgskontrolle, Beitrag vom 29.01.2019. https://www.marktforschung.de/marktforschung/a/sportsponsoring-und-social-media-die-neue-herausforderung-fuer-die-erfolgskontrolle/.

SLC. (2021). Beliebtheitsstudie zur Fußball Bundesliga 2021, 7. Erhebung, Nürnberg.

Spiegel. (2016). Korruptionsskandal: Adidas zieht sich offenbar als Sponsor aus der Leichtathletik zurück, Beitrag vom 25.01.2016. http://www.spiegel.de/sport/sonst/adidas-zieht-sich-laut-bbc-als-sponsor-aus-leichtathletik-zurueck-a-1073684.html.

Sponsors. (2020a). Warum Clubs ihren Fokus mehr auf digitales Sponsoring legen sollten, Beitrag vom 30.06.2020. https://www.sponsors.de/news/themen/clubs-digitales-sponsoring?active=1.

Sponsors. (2022b). Virtuelle Werbung: Zusatzerlöse von 100 Millionen Euro für die Bundesliga? Beirag vom 15.09.2022. https://www.sponsors.de/news/themen/virtuelle-werbung-zusatzerloese-von-100-millionen-euro-fuer-die-bundesliga.

Sportbusiness Consulting. (2021). *Stadium naming rights report*. https://www.sportbusiness.com/stadium-naming-rights-report/.

Sportcal. (2020). *The 2020–21 European club Soccer kit supply report*.

Statista. (2016b). Welche Sportarten schauen Sie gerne im Fernsehen? https://de.statista.com/statistik/daten/studie/235067/umfrage/die-beliebtesten-sportarten-im-tv/.

Statista. (2019). In diese Sportarten fließt das Geld (Werte in Milliarden US-Dollar pro Jahr). https://www.horizont.net/marketing/nachrichten/statista-studie-30-milliarden-dollar-fuer-sport-sponsoring%2D%2D-und-so-wenig-fliesst-in-den-frauensport-178891.

Statista. (2021a). Anteil der Sportarten an den Sportsponsoring-Investitionen der Top-100-Sponsoren in Deutschland in der Saison 2020/2021. Zugegriffen am 09.09.2022.

Statista. (2021b). Bevölkerung in Deutschland nach Häufigkeit des Sporttreibens in der Freizeit von 2017 bis 2021. https://de.statista.com/statistik/daten/studie/171911/umfrage/haeufigkeit-sport-treiben-in-der-freizeit/.

Statista. (2021c). Das Milliardengeschäft mit dem digitalen Sport. https://de.statista.com/infografik/8643/esport-umsatz-und-zuschauer-weltweit/.

Statista. (2021d). E-Sport-Sponsoring widersteht Coronakrise, Beitrag vom 25.01.2021. https://de.statista.com/infografik/26671/prognostizierter-jahresumsatz-mit-e-sports-nach-quelle/.

Statista. (2022b). Marktwert der teuersten Fußball-Bundesligaprofis in der Saison 2022/2023 (Quelle: transfermarkt.de). https://de.statista.com/statistik/daten/studie/1454/umfrage/marktwert-der-teuersten-bundesligaprofis/.

Streppelhoff, R., & Pohlmann, A. (2020). *Sportgroßveranstaltungen in Deutschland. Band 1: Bewegende Momente*. Sonderpublikation des Bundesinstituts für Sportwissenschaft.

V

Vogelsang, F. (2019). Das Virtuelle digitaler Medien ist nie nur virtuell. Es ist Teil der menschlichen Realität. https://frank-vogelsang.de/2019/03/28/ist-die-kommunikation-in-digitalen-medien-nur-virtuell-was-ist-dann-real/.

VSA. (2021). Delphi-Studie: Zukunft 2030—Sportsponsoring im Wandel, WHU—Otto Beisheim School of Management, Center for Sports and Management, Düsseldorf.

W

Wall Street Journal. (2012). Ambush Marketing: Die Raubritter bei Olympia. http://www.wsj.de/nachrichten/SB10001424052702304181204579368573188797410.

Walzel, S., & Schubert, M. (2018). Sportsponsoring—Grundlagen, Konzeption und Wirkungen, Wiesbaden, Springer Gabler Verlag. https://doi.org/10.1007/978-3-662-55246-9.

Wichert, J., & Leda, L. (2001). Namensrechte an Stadien und Arenen. *Sponsors, 6*(Ausgabe März), 45–46.

Z

Zeit. (2022a). Investor Kühne erwirbt Namensrechte am Volksparkstadion, Beitrag vom 31.03.2022. https://www.zeit.de/news/2022-03/31/investor-kuehne-erwirbt-namensrechte-am-volksparkstadion.

ZHAW. (2015). (Zentrum für Kulturmanagement, School of Management and Law, Zürcher Hochschule für Angewandte Wissenschaften. „Sponsor-Visions 2014/15"- Eine empirische Studie zum Sponsoringmarkt Schweiz. http://www.swa-asa.ch/de-wAssets/docs/artikel-print-medien/2015/Studie_Sponsor_Visions_Schweiz_2014-15.pdf . Zugegriffen am 17.02.2016.

Planning Process of Sports Sponsoring

3

Contents

Abstract

Sports sponsoring has developed since the 1980s into a communication tool that has increasingly emancipated itself compared to other tools of corporate and marketing communication and has become a significant economic factor in the sports market. The demonstrated forms of sports sponsoring illustrate that there is also an increasing differentiation in sponsorings, which are increasingly undergoing a systematic decision-making process. An extensive case study of Novartis vividly illustrates the associated processes and procedures.

3.1 Task Definition

Regardless of the form of sports sponsoring, it is necessary to base the use of sponsoring on a systematic **planning and decision-making process**. As a first step, it is advisable to adopt the known thought patterns of market communication for the systematization of task definitions within the planning of Sportssponsoring.

M. Bruhn and P. Rohlmann, *Sports Sponsoring*,
https://doi.org/10.1007/978-3-658-44171-5_3

The **thought pattern of sponsoring** can be established by the following question formulations (W-questions) (Bruhn, 2018, p. 43):

Paradigm of sponsoring

Who says	Sponsor
What and promotes	Communication message
Whom under	Sponsored party
What conditions over	Situational circumstances
Which channels with	Media, communication carriers
Which measures to	Sponsoring mix
Whom in	Target groups of the sponsoring
Which area by	Catchment area
What cost by	Sponsoring expenditure
What consequences?	Sponsoring effects

These memorable question formulations simplify the problem dimensions of sponsoring. However, for a systematic analysis of the individual components of sponsoring planning from a company's perspective, it is advisable to base it on a targeted planning and decision-making process. This is capable of analyzing the decision-making facts relevant to the company when using sponsoring.

The planning process of sponsoring is ideally divided into several phases, in which specific information is used to make partial decisions about the sponsoring. Generally, four **phases of the management process** are distinguished:

- **Analysis phase** (especially the situation analysis of the sponsor and sponsored party),
- **Planning phase** (especially the definition of objectives, identification of target groups, determination of the sponsoring strategy and philosophy),
- **Implementation phase**(especially the calculation of the sponsoring budget, selection of sponsorings, development and design of individual measures),
- **Control phase** (especially the impact and success control of the sponsoring).

These phases of the management process are to be converted into a specific process for sports sponsoring (Bruhn, 2018, pp. 137 ff.). Fig. 3.1 shows the **planning process of sports sponsoring from a company's perspective**.

The planning process is based on the ideal-typical process of management with the classic phases of analysis, planning, implementation, and control. These are presented in their basic structure with their decision-making facts and methods. For a professional use of sponsoring, this planning process is indispensable. In a similar

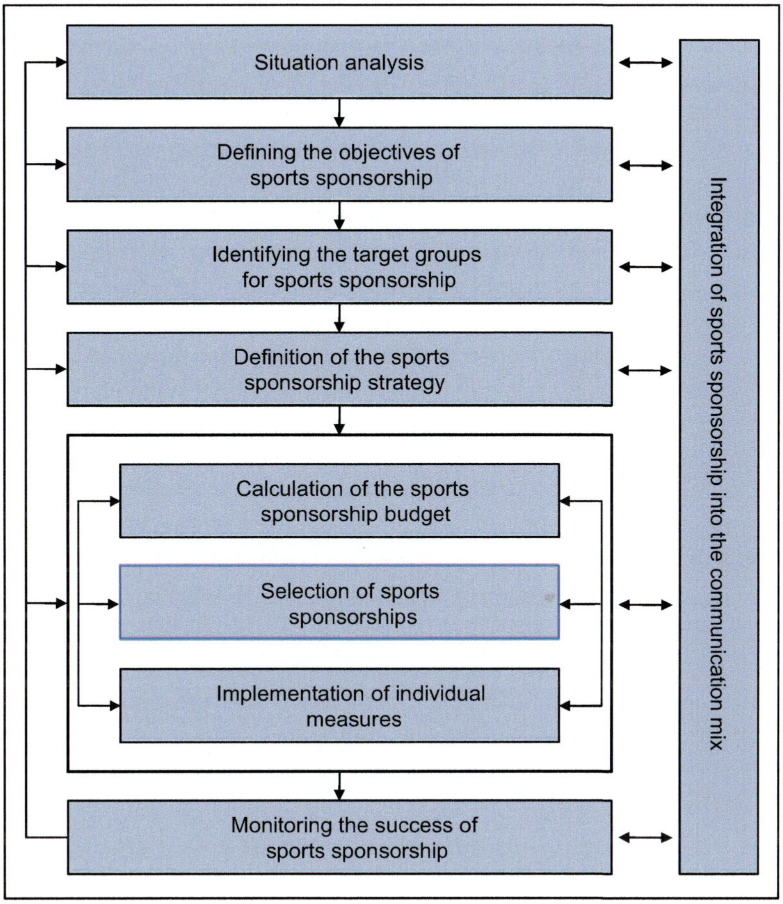

Fig. 3.1 Planning process of sports sponsoring from a company's perspective. (*Source*: Bruhn, 2018, p. 138)

way, the other instruments of corporate and marketing communication are systematically planned within the communication mix. This means an intensive examination of the decision-making facts of analysis, planning, implementation, and control for sports sponsoring.

3.2 Analysis Phase of Sports Sponsoring

The starting point of every effective marketing decision of a company is the **analysis of the specific marketing and communication situation** of a company (cf. Bruhn, 2018, pp. 44 ff.). In order not to leave the effect of sponsoring to chance, sponsoring planning must build on a systematic and structured data basis to create market-oriented communication concepts. As a result, the situation analysis, i.e., the collection, analysis, and processing of necessary information and data, is at the beginning of the systematic sponsoring-related planning process (see also Chap. 4). However, the situation analysis should not only be limited to the sponsoring activities carried out so far. Rather, many different aspects in the entire environment of the sponsored and the sponsor must also be taken into account, which have an influence on the specific sponsoring project.

In practice, the situation analysis is often carried out only very sporadically and not systematically due to insufficiently compiled information and data and usually time restrictions. However, the intensity, the degree of differentiation, and a systematic approach to conducting the situation analysis are crucial for the quality of the analysis results. The more elaborate, systematic, and differentiated the situation analysis in sports sponsoring is designed, the more detailed and transparent the scope for improving previous activities becomes. The company receives a multitude of starting points for using sponsoring commitments more effectively and efficiently.

In order for a situation analysis not to be carried out hastily and arbitrarily, it is necessary to base it on an analytical, i.e., systematic and structured approach. The current and future situation of a company is specified in the respective internal and external conditions, which need to be recorded and analyzed in the situation analysis. While the internal conditions concern the company itself, the external conditions are specified in the macro and micro environment of a company. These two areas provide the information basis for a goal-oriented communication policy within the framework of sports sponsoring.

As part of the **actual analysis** of the sponsoring situation, it is therefore necessary to use specific analysis tools that measure the achieved level of target variables and their dependencies on influencing factors. For example, in the case of the main target group of customers in sponsoring-related activities, the relationships are to be determined through image, positioning, and other market studies. These methods are also used for partial publics, possibly supported by expert surveys or special surveys of opinion leaders. At the employee level, the relevant information on the perception of sponsoring activities can be obtained, for example, through employee surveys. It is advisable not only to use individual study-oriented forms of market research, but also to proceed in a holistic manner, i.e., to develop a comprehensive understanding of the structure and regularity of the sponsoring market.

One of the most important and most frequently used analysis methods in practice is the **SWOT analysis** (Strengths-Weaknesses-Opportunities-Threats), which can be used to depict the actual situation at the time of information gathering. The SWOT analysis represents a comprehensive and integrative methodology, as it aims to condense the multitude of collected individual information from the internal and external analysis to the essentials and present it in a structured manner. Before strengths, weaknesses, opportunities, and risks can be derived, it is first necessary to obtain the required information through internal and external analyses. For this purpose, numerous area-specific analysis tools exist that focus on specific questions or areas and can be used independently of a SWOT analysis depending on the communicative question. These include market segment analyses, customer structure analyses, competitor analyses, image analyses, etc.

As a consequence of evaluating the identified strengths and weaknesses of the company or the opportunities and risks in the market, the **communicative problem of the company** for a sponsoring commitment in sports can be identified, which serves as a starting point for further planning steps, especially the formulation of sponsoring goals and the determination of the sponsoring strategy. For example, the communicative problem may turn out to be that a company is perceived by the public as primarily conservative and "dusty" and primarily arouses the interest of an older clientele, although the company sees itself as modern, innovative, and dynamic and also wants to appeal to young target groups. With the goal of correcting this image and reaching the desired target groups, a corresponding sponsoring strategy in sports can be developed for the future.

In the analysis phase of sports sponsoring, the primary task is to work out whether sports sponsoring can contribute to solving the company's communicative problem. This requires an intensive examination of the sports, communication, and media market. The specific advantages of sports sponsoring are that they take place in the leisure area of the target groups and can convey emotional content.

For a detailed presentation of the content and methods of the analysis phase of sports sponsoring, see Chap. 4 (Situation analysis in sports sponsoring) of this book.

3.3 Planning Phase of Sports Sponsoring

The elaboration of the communicative problem (e.g., low level of awareness, weaknesses in selected image dimensions, customer care with key accounts in an attractive environment, attractive offers for employees) is the basis for further planning considerations (see Bruhn, 2018, pp. 44 ff., 137 ff.). In the **planning phase** of sports sponsoring, the following decision-making aspects are in the foreground during the planning phase:

- Determination of the goals of the sponsoring,
- Identification and selection of the target groups of the sponsoring,
- Determination of the sponsoring strategy.

The basic considerations for the individual planning processes of the decision-making aspects will be presented in the following. A concretization and specification will take place in the following chapters.

Determination of the goals of the sponsoring

Starting from the overarching goals of marketing and corporate communication as well as the communicative positioning of the company or individual brands, the formulation of sponsoring goals is the next step (see also Chap. 5). This is a first starting point in which direction and with which contents the commitment in sports sponsoring is aimed at.

With the realization of an increasing importance of the customer relationship as a starting point of the sponsoring activities, a **success chain of the sponsoring** can be used as a basis for these basic considerations for the formulation of sponsoring goals, which reflects the development from a transaction-oriented to a relationship-oriented marketing. The aim of the success chain is to enable the planning, control and monitoring of the influences by including the relevant aspects of the demand and supply view and to achieve the desired goals (e.g., Bruhn, 2016).

The underlying idea is the content combination of factors that are in an inner context and causal relationship. Within the chain, the effects between the factors are depicted, thus enabling a structured analysis and derivation of measures. The basic structure of a success chain is divided into four **links of the success chain**:

- Company activities as input of the company (e.g., sponsoring in football),
- Psychological effects on the customer as a result of the sponsoring activities (e.g., increase in awareness),
- Behavioral effects on the customer (e.g., creation of purchase preferences),
- Economic success as output of the company (e.g., increase in sales).

The success chain of the sponsoring is simplified in Fig. 3.2. In the context of sports sponsoring, goals for sports sponsoring can be derived—referring to the individual links of the chain. These are to be operationalized according to content, extent, time and target group reference.

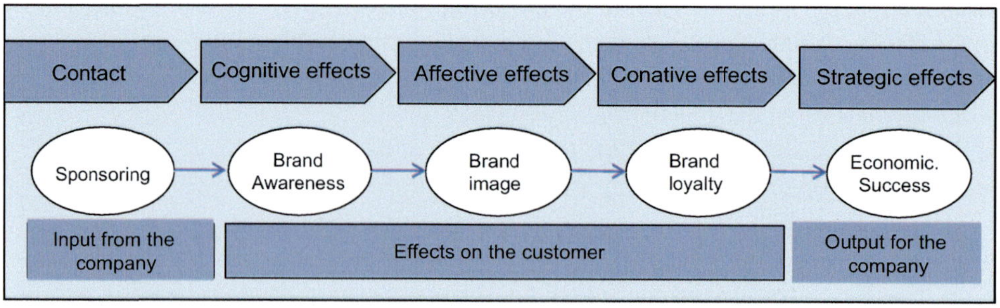

Fig. 3.2 Exemplary success chain of the sponsoring. (*Source*: Bruhn, 2018, p. 49)

The success chain can be used to make a certain **logic in sponsoring** clear. This sponsoring logic is characterized by the connection of customer-related and company-related variables. While on the one hand the use of corporate activities (sports sponsoring as input) is considered, psychological effects on customers are to be identified, which cause behavioral influences, and ultimately lead to economic success (output) via these pre-economic variables. These ideal-typical considerations of the success chain assume a **cause-effect relationship between the links of the chain.**

The **relationships within a success chain**are not always clear. Thus, an independent factor does not completely influence the dependent factor. In addition, the relationships vary greatly depending on the industry, customers, etc. These influencing variables are moderating factors or a kind of **"disturbing factors"** that influence the links of the chain and their ideal-typical effect relationships. In sports sponsoring, these could be, for example, the athletic performances of athletes or teams, poor organization of sponsoring events, activities of ambush marketing, etc. These "disturbing factors" can significantly affect the impact of the sponsoring commitment.

For the systematic derivation and tracking of sponsoring goals, a **structuring of these sponsoring goals** is useful. There are different structural and categorization approaches. Based on the concept of the success chain, company-related economic and psychological goals can be derived from the customer-related economic, behavioral, and psychological goals of the customer-related success chain:

- The company-related **economic goals** correspond to the overall goals of a company. These are achieved through strategic impact, as the last link in the success chain.
- The company-related **psychological goals** either directly or indirectly influence the economic goals at the company level through the customer-related success chain. The psychological goals can in turn be subdivided into cognitive (knowledge-related), affective (emotion-related), and conative (behavior-related) goals according to the impact categories at the recipient level.

Economic goals

Economic goals are usually pursued when the company's products or services are closely related to the sponsoring commitment. They include monetary economic variables, such as sales or turnover. They represent the original goals of all instruments within the communication mix and also form the overall goal of the success chain of sponsoring. The advantage of economic goals is that they can be clearly measured or quantified by monetary or economic variables. However, the exclusive specification of goals assignable to this category is not sufficient due to the lack of action impulses for the sale of products or services of the company. In individual cases, however, this can very well be the case. For example, in the context of equipment sponsoring for sports goods manufacturers, there is not only the desire for an image transfer through the sponsored party, but also for a sale of team jerseys and other co-branded merchandise items that partially refinances the sponsoring.

Psychological goals

Especially in the consumer goods and services sector, economic overall goals can only be achieved in the long term through the specification of psychological goals such as customer loyalty and satisfaction—or at a higher level, awareness and image. Like most other communication tools, sports sponsoring primarily pursues psychological target sizes or communication effects with the target groups. In contrast to economic goals, a quantitative operationalization of psychological goals is much more problematic. The reason is that the implementation of the goals into valid measurement sizes is hardly possible due to the influence of other instruments that cannot be ruled out. In the long term, the pursuit of psychological sponsoring goals supports the implementation of economic goals.

The totality of psychological goals of sponsoring can be further specified into **cognitive, affective, and conative goals** (see Fig. 3.3).

At the level of **cognitive goals**, sports sponsoring primarily pursues the stabilization or increase of awareness of companies, products, services, or brands. The stabilization or improvement of a company's or brand's awareness are central communicative goals of sponsoring measures (Walraven et al., 2014). This is especially true for those forms of sports sponsoring that can expect broad media resonance (e.g., through television broadcasts). If the company already has a high level of awareness domestically, there is also the possibility, as with Deutsche Telekom, for example, to formulate an increase in international awareness as a sponsoring goal (Althoff, 2007, pp. 90 ff.). In a multitude of studies, the positive effect of sponsoring on brand awareness has been empirically proven (see, for example, Rowley & Williams, 2008; Walraven et al., 2014). Other cognitive goals of sponsoring are the transmission of knowledge about new services and the creation of attention for innovations.

Since sponsoring is one of the experience-oriented communication tools, **affective goals** are of particular importance. Often, companies pursue the goal of building,

Cognitive-oriented goals	Affective-oriented goals	Conative-oriented goals
• Stabilizing and increasing awareness of companies, products, services and brands • Creating awareness of new products • Publicizing international brands • Imparting knowledge about new services • Creating awareness through innovations, etc.	• Emotional experience of companies and brands • Creation of goodwill • Building trust • Creating acceptance among customers • Improving employee motivation and more. • Development, maintenance or modification of the corporate or brand image	• Strengthening customer loyalty • Increase in purchase intention and repurchase • Promotion of cross-buying of services • Creating incentives for referrals • Customer care and customer support and more.

Fig. 3.3 Target figures of sponsoring. (*Source*: Bruhn, 2018, p. 50)

maintaining, or modifying the image of a company or brand through their sponsoring activities. The influence of sponsoring on brand image has been empirically proven several times (Grohs et al., 2004; Grohs & Reisinger, 2014; Lobo et al., 2014). The aim is to influence the attitudes of the target groups towards the company, its products or brands.

The basis is the **principle of image transfer**, according to which, in a long-term connection of a company or a brand to a sport (or also to a cultural/social commitment or certain (programs in) media), the image dimensions of the respective sponsoring object are transferred to the company or the brand. At the center of the image transfer is therefore the transfer of the image of a sponsored party to the sponsor through the joint appearance of the two parties within the framework of sponsoring measures. The sponsored parties, whose image the sponsor wants to benefit from, acts as the transfer subject, representing a combination of sponsored area, organizational unit, and performance level. The role of the transfer object is most often taken on by a brand or, in the case of a company brand, the company or the sponsor itself. The transfer content finally appears in the form of certain associations connected with the sponsored party. The main aim is to improve individual image dimensions (e.g., dynamism, performance, technology). The sponsor uses the transfer to build a desired image, to communicate existing image features more accentuated, or to reposition itself.

The **target of image transfer** is particularly important in sports sponsoring due to the now low distinguishability of products and services. Under these circumstances, corporate communication must focus more on providing the relevant target groups with an **"emotional added value"** that influences their purchasing decision. The sympathy value of a product, the design, and the image of the entire company or a brand are becoming increasingly important for successful market communication. Sponsoring commitments offer the opportunity to benefit from the public, positive image of the sponsored party (Lang & Haunert, 1995; Grohs & Reisinger, 2014). Sponsoring is particularly capable of conveying emotional experiences to the target groups. Therefore, the brand policy use of sponsoring primarily focuses on the "experience profile" of the brand.

In addition to an improved image, companies strive for other affective goals such as generating goodwill, trust, and acceptance among the target groups and documenting social responsibility. In this context, the sustainability of sponsoring commitments is of particular importance. Sponsoring is also aimed at improving the relationship with its own employees by supporting activities or areas that reflect their interests. Positive effects on the leisure behavior of its own employees, especially in the sports sector, in turn contribute to improving employee motivation, which is reflected in increased commitment to the company.

In addition to cognitive and affective goals, companies also pursue **conative goals** with their sponsoring commitment, which include behavior and behavioral intentions. Thus, sponsoring contributes to strengthening customer loyalty as well as increasing purchase intention and repeat purchase by consumers (Mazodier & Merunka, 2012; Koronios et al., 2016). In connection with the conative target sizes, **contact maintenance and customer care**, i.e., the dialogue with selected customers, opinion leaders, and media representatives, are at the center of numerous sponsoring activities. The organization of hospitality measures within the framework of sponsoring activities offers various possibilities for targeted contact maintenance with company-relevant persons.

As the **subject of hospitality measures**, any activities of a sponsor related to sports sponsoring are understood, which are based on their right of disposal over a fixed quota of tickets and offer the possibility to use boxes, other rooms within the sports venue, or tents or other mobile or fixed rooms in the vicinity of the sports event for personal care of invited target persons (Bassenge, 2000, p. 141). This can also be transferred to other areas of sponsoring. In sponsoring practice, hospitality measures have now gained significant importance, and often the actual occasion of the staged event, the advertising, and the sales policy goals take a back seat (Lang & Haunert, 1995, p. 36). In contrast, building and maintaining relationships is becoming increasingly important. This plays a special role for certain sports (e.g., football, golf, tennis) and sports events (e.g., international matches, tournaments).

Advantages are seen in the fact that companies have the opportunity to make it clear that they share and financially or materially support the interests and leisure activities of their target groups. In addition, personal contact offers the opportunity to build trust with the target groups and thus positively influence the **quality of the relationship**. Especially for service providers, whose services are often in need of explanation and immaterial, this type of sponsoring offers a way to inform about the range of services, to personify the service provider, and in this way to gain both rational and emotional acceptance from customers. In this case, the influence on the company image is no longer determined solely by the transfer of image characteristics of the sponsored party to the company, but is also determined by the dialogue possibilities between the sponsor and invited guests. It is also considered advantageous that visitors to sporting (also cultural) events are usually in a favorable relaxed mood and receive advertising messages under the influence of enthusiasm, excitement, and pleasure with less reactance (Bennett, 1999, p. 94; Nicholls et al., 1999, p. 369).

The empirical results of various studies regarding the importance of sponsoring goals show that **image stabilization** and **improving brand awareness** are the central goals in sports sponsoring. Companies primarily see comparative advantages of sponsoring over other communication tools in addressing specific target groups and thus minimizing scatter loss in communication work. Sponsoring is also considered superior in making products or brands tangible, promoting employee motivation, transferring desired image dimensions, and emotionally binding target groups.

A concrete example of **goals of sponsors** in general and in sports is shown in Fig. 3.4. Image and brand awareness goals remain the primary motives for a sponsoring commitment in general and in sports, with a rising trend. Behind this is the increasing trend to emotionalize the brand through sponsoring and to communicate brand messages. In general, the linking of sponsoring investments with tangible corporate goals is increasing significantly.

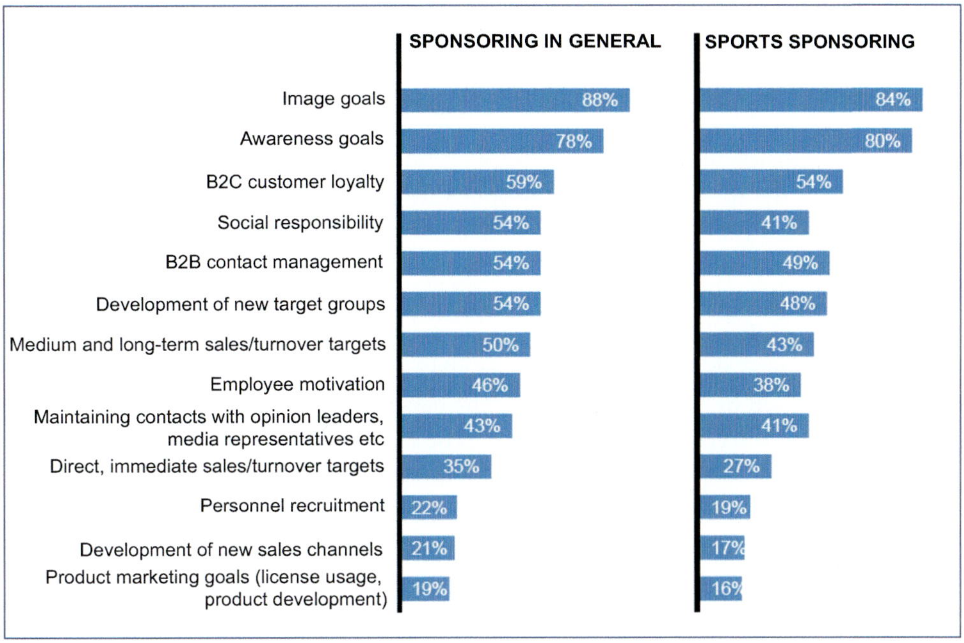

Fig. 3.4 Current goals of sponsors in general and in sports sponsoring. (*Source*: Nielsen Sports, 2018a, p. 7)

The **control of the effects** of sponsoring measures requires precise goal planning. The sponsor has the task of specifying his expectations towards the sponsored party. This means in detail that companies have to consider what improvement in awareness among the target groups is possible, which image is to be transferred to the brand name, or to what extent the sponsoring serves to maintain contact with selected target groups when a concrete sponsoring offer is presented. The goals pursued with the sponsoring are to be formulated clearly, realistically, and operationally. In sports sponsoring, extensive data material is available for this purpose (e.g., media data such as viewing figures and reach, members and fan club information, visitor and follower numbers, image characteristics).

Identification and selection of the target groups of sports sponsoring

Following the determination of the goals of the sponsoring, the company needs to specify which target groups are to be addressed with the commitment in sports (see also Chap. 5). A consistent **target group orientation** is indispensable against the background of increasing opportunities for sponsorings and rising costs per commitment, in order to ensure an efficient use of the sponsoring activity. By determining the target groups and characterizing them in terms of their attitudes and behaviors, it is ensured that the company's appearance as a sponsor is aligned with the needs of the targeted target group and primarily addresses those segments where a high degree of goal achievement can be realized.

In principle, the **identification of the sponsoring target groups** must be carried out from two different perspectives. A distinction must be made between the **target groups of the sponsor and the sponsored**:

Target groups of the sponsor

The target groups of the sponsor are the so-called "basic target groups" of the company. They are addressed by using various communication tools. From a company's perspective, a **variety of different target groups** can be distinguished, with which communication relationships are to be maintained. The following target groups are to be mentioned in particular:

- Consumers,
- Trade partners,
- Capital providers,
- Suppliers,
- Politicians (local and national),
- Association representatives,
- Executives and employees in the company,
- Opinion multipliers,
- Media representatives, etc.

It goes without saying that the **selection of target groups** by the sponsor in sports depends on the goals and the type of sponsorings. At mass sports events, goals of awareness and image are often in the foreground, where consumers as a target group usually have a special significance. However, if contact maintenance and customer care are in the foreground, occasions in the environment of attractive sports will be suitable, for example, to get in touch with key customers or opinion leaders.

Target groups of the sponsored

The target groups of the sponsored include the circle of those who are reached by his respective activities, for example in sports. It must be checked to what extent these are of interest to the sponsor. In general, the following groups of people can be distinguished as **target groups of the sponsored** and thus **user groups for the sponsors**: active participants in sports, visitors to sports events, and media users of sports broadcasts.

The ideal **approach to target group planning** of a company can be described as follows, which applies equally to sports sponsoring and other forms of sponsoring. In a first step, the basic target groups of the company are identified and described according to various characteristics. These core target groups are compared with those target groups that are reached by a sponsoring commitment. The goal of this approach is an analysis of the extent to which there are overlaps between the target groups of the company and the target groups addressed by the potential sponsoring. Only if there is a high target group affinity (with correspondingly low scatter losses) is the sponsoring worthwhile for a company.

Defining the Sponsoring Strategy

Starting from the results of the situation analysis as well as the determination of the target system and the target groups of the sponsoring, the strategy to be pursued in sports sponsoring must be defined (see also Chap. 6). While the determination of goals and target groups is considered a future-oriented guideline for the company, strategies represent structured measures or channels within which the determination of sponsoring measures takes place as an operational planning process. A **sponsoring strategy** is therefore understood as the conscious and binding determination of the focal points in a company's sponsoring activities over a longer period of time in order to achieve the desired sponsoring goals.

In the planning phase of the sponsoring, one focus is on defining the sponsoring strategy. The use of the various forms of sponsoring is fixed and justified. This is of particular importance for the sponsor in order to bundle resources and thus increase the degree of effectiveness. Various **decision-making aspects of the sports sponsoring strategy** can be distinguished:

- **Elements of a sports sponsoring strategy**
  Here, a strategic determination of the sponsoring subject, the sponsoring target groups, the sponsoring message, the sponsored parties, the sponsoring measures, the sponsoring area, and the sponsoring timing must be made.
- **Strategy types in sports sponsoring**
  The communicative focal points and thus the strategy focus could be publicity, target group development, customer retention, image profiling, etc.
- **Guidelines of a sponsoring philosophy**
  The essential elements of a sponsoring strategy are written down in the form of a philosophy or also in the form of principles or guidelines and declared binding—as a guideline for the selection of sports sponsorings.

There is agreement that sports sponsoring—like other communication tools—must be aligned with **superordinate strategy components of the company**. These include, for example, the focal points in the company, marketing, brand, and communication strategy. The result of these conceptual considerations is the binding formulation of a sports sponsoring strategy that defines the content focal points of the commitments.

For a detailed presentation of the content and methods of the **planning phase of sports sponsoring**, see Chap. 5 (goals and target groups of sports sponsoring), Chap. 6 (Strategic orientation of sports sponsoring), Chap. 9 (Integration of sports sponsoring into marketing and corporate communication) and Chap. 10 (Operational design of sports sponsoring) of this book.

3.4 Implementation Phase of Sports Sponsoring

In addition to the analysis and planning of sports sponsoring, the implementation phase of sports sponsoring plays a special role (see Bruhn, 2018, pp. 63 ff.). In the implementation and execution of sports sponsoring, the prerequisites for the degree of effectiveness and the success of a sponsor's commitment are ultimately created. The following **decision-making aspects of implementation** are of central importance:

- Calculation of the budget for sports sponsoring,
- Selection of sponsorings in sports sponsoring,
- Implementation of individual measures in sports sponsoring,
- Collaboration with agencies in sports sponsoring.

The basic considerations and procedures for the individual decision-making aspects will be explained in the following.

Calculation of the Budget for Sports Sponsoring

The decision for a sponsoring commitment in sports is not only dependent on the pursued sponsoring goals and strategic considerations, but especially on economic considerations and calculations. From a company's perspective, sports sponsoring is a communication tool that is considered an investment to achieve effects with the relevant target groups. To this end, the total costs of the sponsoring commitment must first be determined before the available sponsoring budget can be drawn up and distributed.

Costs of sponsoring The costs or prices for sponsoring measures in sports vary depending on the sponsoring area, the respective sponsoring activity, and the importance or "market value" of the athletes, sports teams, sports events, sports associations, etc. to be sponsored. Factors such as performance level, the sponsored party's counter-performance, the importance of the event, media impact, and the use of various advertising opportunities are also significant in cost calculation.

Only very rough, general indications can be given for the amount of cost components. So far, no fixed prices for sponsorings have been established and there are hardly any special price lists for sponsors. Rather, an independent calculation of cost components by the companies and sponsored parties dominates, which forms the basis for determining the sponsor contributions. Contrary to expectations, the proportion of expenditures made directly to the sponsored party has been steadily increasing for decades, while the proportion invested in communication and implementation of the measures has decreased.

Budgeting of Sponsoring The calculation of cost components in sports sponsoring is the basis for budgeting the sponsoring (see also Chap. 7). Budgeting of sponsoring includes the calculation of the total sponsoring budget and the allocation to individual sponsoring measures. To this end, all costs of the company's sponsoring activities must be determined. Ideally, the budget is set at the same time as the planning of individual measures, as the amount of costs largely depends on the chosen sponsorings. Similar to budgeting for traditional media advertising, it is necessary in sponsoring to budget all expenses associated with the measures for a planning period.

As part of the budgeting process, it is also necessary to clarify from which company budgets the sponsorings are funded. A study in this context shows that sponsoring is organizationally most often part of the marketing department (50.8%) or the PR department (20.5%). Only 1.7% of the companies surveyed have their own sponsoring department (BBDO Live, 2010, p. 21). Accordingly, sponsoring expenses are mostly borne by the marketing and public relations departments.

Selection of Sponsorings in Sports Sponsoring

The selection of sponsorings in sports is fundamentally to be interpreted as a step-by-step process that takes place on two levels (see also Chap. 8):

On the first level, a **rough selection** is made regarding the areas of support suitable for the company (selection of sponsoring areas), i.e., levels of sports (athletes, teams, institutions). In addition, there is a specification and focus on individual sports that are particularly suitable for the targeted goals.

On the second level, a **fine selection** takes place, i.e., an analysis and evaluation of various alternatives within the defined sponsoring areas. Suitable decision criteria for the selection of types of sponsoring and individual sponsorings are necessary, for example, to determine the form of support in the respective area (i.e., the sponsoring of individuals, groups, institutions, projects, or events).

Rough Selection

As part of the rough selection, a **selection of sponsoring areas in sports** is made, i.e., decisions regarding the sports suitable for the company. The identification of potential sponsoring projects is particularly important for successful strategic company or brand management. Therefore, it is necessary to search for those thematic connections that exist between the company, or the brand, and the sponsoring areas. This relationship pattern—or the so-called "fit"—is determined by various connecting lines ("links") between the sponsor and the sponsored parties.

Fine Selection

The fine selection of sponsorings in sports includes the analysis and **selection of various sponsoring alternatives** within the defined sports and support areas available to a company willing to sponsor. Depending on the support of individual athletes, teams, sports projects, or sports events, specific decision criteria must be used, e.g., previous performances and successes of the sponsored party, expected visitor numbers and anticipated media presence of an event, or activities of competitors in the respective sponsoring area. When selecting sponsorings, it is particularly important to ensure the highest possible affinity between the company's target groups and the target groups that can be reached by the sponsoring event.

Implementation of Individual Measures in Sports Sponsoring

Once the decision for a specific sponsoring has been made, a detailed action plan for the sponsoring in sports must be drawn up, which includes all the **individual measures required** for the implementation of the sponsoring commitment (see also Chap. 10). This includes, in addition to the definition of services and counter-services, the legal design of the sponsoring, the calculation of individual costs, and possibly the selection of agencies to support the sponsoring planning and implementation. A systematic approach is also recommended for the planning and selection of individual measures of engagement in sports sponsoring (see also Chap. 10). Various influencing factors must be taken into account. Thus, the decision for measures depends on the size of the sponsorings, their relative importance, the legally agreed possibilities (see also Chap. 12) as well as the available budgets.

Collaboration with Agencies in Sports Sponsoring

The professionalization in sponsoring is largely responsible for the fact that companies and sponsored parties regularly involve **specialized agencies** in the planning and implementation of sponsorings (see also Chap. 13). This is particularly true for sports sponsoring.

In the implementation phase of sports sponsoring, the entire implementation and enforcement of sports sponsoring takes place. Here, the conditions must be created for the strategy of sports sponsoring to achieve its effect.

For a detailed presentation of the contents and methods in the **implementation phase of sports sponsoring**, see Chap. 7 (Budgeting of sports sponsoring), Chap. 8 (Selection of Sponsoring in Sports), Chap. 10 (Operational Design of Sports Sponsoring), Chap. 12

(Legal Aspects in Sports Sponsoring) and Chap. 13 (Services of Sports Agencies) of this book.

3.5 Control Phase of Sports Sponsoring (incl. Novartis Case Study)

The **control of sponsoring success** concludes the ideal-typical planning process of sponsoring (see also Chap. 11). The subject of success control is both the examination of the communicative effect through the sponsoring on the target groups (effectiveness control) and the examination of whether the financial effort has "paid off" (efficiency control). Depending on the results of the impact control, more or less strong adjustments of the conception must be made with regard to sponsorings to be carried out in later periods. With the dynamics in sports sponsoring, the control phase takes on a special significance (Limbach, 2020).

With regard to the application of **success control in practice**, divergent results are available.

Thus, the results of two studies conducted in Germany show that in 2012, just under 32% of companies did not carry out any success control. This represents a significant increase in the implementation of sponsoring controls. In 2004, only 12.1% refrained from doing so (BBDO Live, 2010, p. 47; Bagusat, 2013, p. 31). Those companies that control the success of their sponsoring commitments most frequently carry out media and reach analyses. Some companies also measure efficiency and recall effect with the help of recall and recognition tests. But event checks and social media monitoring are also used. Impact tracking, day-after recalls, and tracking are also carried out, albeit less frequently (Bagusat, 2013, p. 34; ZHAW, 2015). Another result emerges from surveys of companies in Switzerland and Austria. The study conducted in Switzerland reveals that 75% of companies control the achievement of their sponsoring goals. The examination of awareness and image goals is of central importance here (ZHAW, 2015, p. 21). For Austrian companies, a proportion of only 4% of companies is reported that do not carry out any success control. Just over a third of companies (37%) always check their sponsoring activities (sports + Markt AG, 2013, p. 44).

The success control in corporate and marketing communication, as well as in sports sponsoring, is characterized by the use of various content and methods of control (see Bruhn, 2018, pp. 75 ff., 182 ff.). Simplified, three **forms of success control** can be distinguished:

- **Process controls:** Control of the progress of sports sponsoring projects,
- **Effectiveness controls:** Control of the impact on the target groups due to sports sponsoring,
- **Efficiency controls:** Control of the cost-effectiveness of an engagement in sports sponsoring in terms of a cost-benefit comparison.

Process Controls
Process controls deal with the verification of the implementation of sports sponsorings, such as monitoring all necessary activities to prepare a company's appearance at a sponsored sports event. The focus is on checking organizational and personnel processes in connection with the implementation of sponsoring commitments.

Effectiveness Controls
Effectiveness controls refer to the realization of the desired communicative effects on the target groups of sports sponsoring. This involves measuring the degree of target achievement (response) realized due to certain communication measures (stimuli), i.e., the degree of achieving the communicative goals. They must be oriented towards the goals defined at the beginning of the planning process and control their achievement. For sports sponsoring, the aim is generally to achieve higher degrees of impact on the recipients through the integrated use of sports sponsoring with other communication tools than through the isolated use of various communication measures in sponsoring. The impact measurement can be carried out both at the level of sports sponsoring and at the level of overall communication, i.e., the entire communication mix of companies.

Efficiency Controls
The primary goal of efficiency controls is to obtain indications of the cost-effectiveness of sports sponsoring. For this purpose, cost-benefit comparisons are set up to assess the sponsoring activities within the framework of efficiency controls, i.e., the costs incurred for all sponsoring activities are compared with the realized benefits. The comparison of the two elements forms the basis of a cost-benefit comparison.

The success control of sponsoring still faces numerous methodological and content-related challenges. Therefore, the **problems of success control in sports sponsoring** also need to be addressed. The biggest problem is the interdependencies of effects and, depending on this, the attribution of effects. The available methods of sponsoring control only partially solve these problems. Thus, the existing procedures are sometimes only used to reveal starting points and indicators for determining the success of sponsorings. Despite or precisely because of the difficulties that success control in sponsoring entails, science and business practice are increasingly called upon in the future to further develop existing approaches to process, effectiveness, and efficiency controls in sponsoring and to research and implement new approaches.

In the future, there will be a need for the sponsoring control to develop **new approaches to success measurement**. These need to be worked out and empirically tested. Despite the increasing growth rates in the last decade, which can largely be explained by the innovativeness of the communication tool and its specific advantages over media advertising, the cost-effectiveness of different sponsoring measures will be the focus in the future. This development requires professional controlling tools to subject the company's sponsoring portfolio to a systematic effectiveness and efficiency analysis. Consequently, the importance of efficiency control of sports sponsoring will continue to increase.

For a detailed presentation of the content and methods of the **control phase of sports sponsoring**, see Chap. 11of this book.

Case Study: Sports Sponsoring by Novartis

The following case study was commissioned by Novartis and is published with the kind support and permission of Novartis.

Initial Situation

For many years, Novartis has dominated the list of the world's largest pharmaceutical companies and ranks high in Fortune's "World's Most Admired Companies" in the pharma sector. Novartis looks back on a company history of over 150 years and reaches almost a billion people with its products available in more than 180 countries. As a globally operating health company, Novartis achieved a net turnover of 45.6 billion USD in 2021 and employs 110,000 people worldwide with 144 nationalities, of which about 11,900 employees are based in Switzerland alone, most of them at the headquarters in Basel. Accordingly, Novartis' commitment to its locations is also large in sports, culture, social concerns, and the promotion of science, as it is also one of the largest companies originating from Switzerland. In addition to its headquarters in Northwestern Switzerland, Novartis also established itself in the Zug region, in Central Switzerland, in 2013.

Role of Sponsoring

Novartis' funding focus is on activities that have a connection to its business activities or a geographical proximity to Novartis' company locations. Such a connection therefore exists in the areas of health & medicine, research & science, and neighborhood & employees. Novartis' sponsoring is primarily focused on Switzerland, to signal a clear commitment to the origin of the globally active company. In addition, it aims to generate sympathy among the population and make a significant contribution for the employees to experience the corporate culture as lively and attractive. Sports sponsoring therefore offers Novartis an ideal platform to convey these values, and so the company invests about 35% of its total sponsoring budget in this area. In addition to commitments with smaller sports clubs and running events in the region, the focus is primarily on the partnership with FC Basel 1893, and the Swiss National League club in ice hockey, EV Zug. These, as well as all other commitments on the part of sponsoring & donations in the areas of sports, social and culture, are regularly reviewed and adjusted if necessary to strategic realignments or changed framework conditions.

Targets

Since a pharmaceutical company like Novartis is subject to strict regulations, it is hardly possible to pursue economic goals through sports sponsoring. Novartis therefore primarily focuses on achieving **psychological goals**:

- **Cognitive goals**
  - Increasing brand awareness
- **Affective goals**
  - Brand image maintenance and experience profile
  - Gaining sympathy (social commitment)
  - Goodwill and acceptance
  - Employee motivation
  - Employee identification
- **Conative goals**
  - Improving the quality of relationships with the public and employees

In summary, the target of Novartis' sports sponsoring is to promote a positive image and to gain goodwill, acceptance, and a positive reputation among the public and its own workforce. The emphasis on the local reference is paramount to strengthen the identification and motivation of the employees in Switzerland.

Criteria for awarding sponsorings

In selecting its partners, the healthcare company uses various criteria to assess a potential commitment:

- **Effectiveness**
  What exactly is achieved with the project? What changes as a result of the project?
- **Sustainability of the project**
  Can the project continue successfully after the funding has ended? Are there declarations of intent to continue?
- **Social relevance**
  How relevant is the respective project for society and individual groups?
- **Transparency and verifiability**
  Does the organization have transparent structures and finances?
- **Professionalism**
  Do the project managers have the appropriate training and experience to successfully manage the project?
- **Cultural affinity**
  Novartis is an international company. Values such as dialogue, openness, and encounter are central values in the corporate culture. Projects that embody similar cultural values are preferably supported by Novartis.

- **Image affinity**
  As one of the leading health companies worldwide, values such as innovation, excellence, and sustainability are associated with Novartis. This corporate philosophy is reflected in the support of projects that embody similar values.
- **Know-how reference/Possibility for know-how transfer**
  A continuous exchange of information and knowledge is crucial for Novartis' success. Projects that have a potential for know-how transfer are preferably supported.

Novartis as Leading Partner of FC Basel 1893

With a total of 20 Swiss championship titles won, FC Basel 1893 is one of the most successful football clubs in Switzerland. In the Northwest Switzerland region, it is considered a major source of sympathy in sports and has over 600,000 fans in total. Novartis and FC Basel 1893 look back on a long partnership: Novartis has been sponsoring the junior teams since 1996 and has been the main sponsor of the first team since 2004. The aspect of long-term commitment plays a major role in Novartis' engagements, as this is the only way a sustainable partnership can be lived, from which both partners can mutually benefit and acceptance can be created in society. Since Novartis' sponsoring is purely location-based and primarily intended to serve the surrounding population and employees, FC Basel 1893 offers an ideal platform. In contrast to the sponsoring of individual sports events, FC Basel 1893 is present all year round and allows Novartis to gain attention outside of Switzerland through international appearances, such as in the Conference League. This also visually underlines Novartis' origin in an emotional environment abroad.

Integration Measures

Successful networking of sports sponsoring within the partnership of FC Basel 1893 and Novartis is achieved through various measures. On the one hand, Novartis achieves a high level of visibility through the kit sponsoring. The logo placement is in the center of the players' jerseys (see Figs. 3.5 and 3.6). The team bus is also adorned with the Novartis logo. During home games, the logo in the form of perimeter advertising ensures appropriate attention. In addition, advertisements are placed on flyers or accompanying booklets on the occasion of each game (see Fig. 3.7). As a leading partner, a 30-second advertising trailer is broadcast on the screen/in-house TV before the start of each game. The Novartis logo can also be found on various smaller LED screens in the stadium, in the hospitality lounges, and on the FC Basel 1893 website.

Fig. 3.5 Novartis logo. (*Source*: Novartis)

NOVARTIS

Fig. 3.6 Advertisement of Novartis as Leading Partner of FC Basel 1893 in the 2016/2017 season. (*Source*: Novartis)

Fig. 3.7 Advertisement of Novartis as Leading Partner of FC Basel 1893 in the 2016/2017 season. (*Source*: Novartis)

As the main sponsor, Novartis has the right to a certain ticket quota for the home games of the first team. The pharmaceutical company uses this contractual component for its internal communication and raffles off tickets to its employees for each game via the company's intranet. In addition, Novartis organizes two "free games" per season for its employees. On these specific match days, employees can obtain 2 free adult tickets and tickets for their own children and experience a home game of FC Basel 1893 in the stadium up close. In addition, some players from the first team are invited to the Novartis campus for an autograph session on the occasion of periodically held family days. These actions offer enormous potential for strengthening the identification and increasing the motivation of Novartis employees.

Success Control

The success control of the partnership with FC Basel 1893 is carried out in counter-cyclical surveys among the spectators in order to determine recall and recognition values as well as image profiles in this way.

Fig. 3.8 Advertisement by Novartis as main sponsor and Official Health Care Partner of EV Zug in the 2021/2022 season. (*Source*: Novartis)

Novartis as Main Sponsor and Official Health Care Partner of EV Zug

Similar to FC Basel 1893 in Northwestern Switzerland, EV Zug enjoys high esteem in Central Switzerland in ice hockey and became Swiss Champion in 2021 and 2022. Moreover, ice hockey is one of the most popular sports in sponsoring in Switzerland. With the partnership around EV Zug, Novartis once again signals its local connection to the branch in Rotkreuz and in this way also offers the local population and the approximately 230 employees a platform for identification (see Fig. 3.8). In this partnership too, sustainable talent promotion plays a major role and Novartis is committed as a platinum sponsor of the new Zug training concept "The Hockey Academy". The aim here is to promote the professional training of the sporting, professional, academic, and social skills of young Swiss ice hockey top talents.

Integration Measures

At the center of activities in the Zug area is again the promotion of employee motivation and awareness within society. This is achieved through appropriate branding presence in the ice hockey stadium on the face-off circle, the LED boards, and the equipment of the physio team. With a diameter of 9 meters, the Novartis logo on the ice surface in the face-off circle receives an exclusive presence. The Novartis logo and a 40-second trailer about the location in Rotkreuz are presented at every home game on the 224-meter-long arena LED board, various video screens, and an LED ring in the middle of the stadium. In addition, Novartis receives board presence on the home player bench, and the clothing and bags of the physiotherapists are adorned with the logo of the pharmaceutical company. Furthermore, advertisements are placed in game accompanying flyers and in magazines on the subject of ice hockey (see Fig. 3.8). With this commitment, Novartis also has a certain ticket quota per season available, which is distributed to the employees at the Rotkreuz location.

Success Measurements

The success control is carried out in the same way as with the partnership to FC Basel 1893. Thus, the success of the sponsoring activities in relation to EV Zug is measured using counter-cyclical surveys—carried out externally.

Key Learnings

Novartis provides an example with its sports sponsoring of how a globally active multinational corporation can harmonize internationality and a sense of home. The pharmaceutical company succeeds in expressing its roots in Switzerland and thus signals security and tradition to the population as well as its own workforce. With its two major, long-term commitments in the field of football and ice hockey, Novartis meets the current trend in the Swiss sponsoring market, achieves high acceptance and identification within society, and increases the motivation of its employees.

3.6 Key Points

The planning process in sports sponsoring aims to maximize the probability of success of a corresponding commitment through a systematic approach:

Key Points

1. Regardless of the form of sports sponsoring, it is necessary to base the use of sponsoring on a systematic planning and decision-making process. The **paradigm of sponsoring** provides a good basis.
2. At the beginning of the sponsoring-related planning process is the **situational analysis**, i.e., the collection, analysis, and preparation of necessary information and data on the decision-relevant topic.
3. As part of the current analysis of the sponsoring situation, it is also necessary to use specific **analysis tools** that measure the achieved level of target variables and their dependencies on influencing factors, e.g., image, positioning, and other market studies and SWOT analyses.
4. In the **planning phase** of sports sponsoring, the following decision-making situations are in the foreground, such as setting the goals of the sponsoring, identifying and selecting the target groups of the sponsoring, and defining the sponsoring strategy.
5. **Economic and psychological goals** need to be operationalized: A professional sports sponsoring requires that both economic and psychological goals be operationalized and differentiated according to content, extent, timing, and target group relevance.
6. **Target groups of sports sponsoring** need to be identified. Parallel to goal formulation, the target groups to be addressed by the sponsoring need to be selected and their attitudes and behaviors precisely characterized.
7. When **defining the sponsoring strategy**, the focus is on justifying and fixing the priorities in the use of the various forms of sponsoring. It is particularly important to clarify the elements of a sports sponsoring strategy, the types of strategies in sports sponsoring, and the creation of principles and guidelines for the sponsoring strategy.
8. In the **implementation** of sports sponsoring, the prerequisites for the effectiveness and success of a sponsor's commitment are ultimately created. Central to this are the calculation of the budget for sports sponsoring, the selection of one or more sponsorings in sports, the implementation of individual measures in sports sponsoring, and the possible cooperation with agencies to support sports sponsoring.
9. **Integration of sports sponsoring into the communication mix**, i.e., the use of sports sponsoring needs to be networked with other instruments of marketing and corporate communication to achieve a synergistic amplification of the overall effect of communication.

10. The **control** of sponsoring success concludes the ideal-typical planning process of sponsoring. The subject of success control is both the examination of the communicative effect of the sponsoring on the target groups (effectiveness control) and the examination of the cost-benefit ratio of sports sponsorings (efficiency control).

References

A

Althoff, S. (2007). Das Sportsponsoring der Telekom—und was dahinter steckt. In D. Ahlert, D. Woisetschläger, & Vogel, V. (Hrsg.), *Exzellentes Sponsoring. Innovative Ansätze und Best Practices für das Markenmanagement* (2. Aufl., S. 77–100). https://doi.org/10.1007/978-3-8350-9639-4_4.

B

Bagusat, A. (2013). *Sponsoring trends 2012*. https://www.ostfalia.de/export/sites/default/de/ispm/Blickpunkt_Sportmanagement/Sponsoring_Trends_2012.pdf. Zugegriffen am 17.02.2016.

Bassenge, C. (2000). *Dienstleister als Sponsoren. Imageprofilierung durch kommunikatives Engagement im Sport*. https://doi.org/10.1007/978-3-322-89616-2.

BBDO Live GmbH. (2010). Sponsoring Trends 2010, Studie in Zusammenarbeit mit dem Institut für Marketing, Universität der Bundeswehr München, Bonn.

Bennett, R. (1999). Sport sponsorings. *European Journal of Marketing, 33*(3/4), 291–313. https://doi.org/10.1108/03090569910253071.

Bruhn, M. (2016). *Relationship Marketing. Das Management von Kundenbeziehungen* (5. Aufl.). https://doi.org/10.15358/9783800651849.

Bruhn, M. (2018). *Sponsoring. Systematische Planung und integrativer Einsatz* (6. Aufl.). https://doi.org/10.1007/978-3-658-13313-9.

G

Grohs, R., & Reisinger, H. (2014). Sponsoring effects on brand image: The role of exposure and activity involvement. *Journal of Business Research, 67*(5), 1018–1025. https://doi.org/10.1016/j.jbusres.2013.08.008.

Grohs, R., Wagner, U., & Vsetecka, S. (2004). Assessing the effectiveness of sport sponsorings. An empirical examination. *Schmalenbach Business Review, 56*(2), 119–138. https://doi.org/10.1007/bf03396689.

K

Koronios, K., Psiloutsikou, M., Kriemadis, A., Zervoulakos, P., & Leivaditi, E. (2016). Sport sponsoring: The impact of sponsor image on purchase intention of fans. *Journal of Promotion Management, 22*(2), 238–250. https://doi.org/10.1080/10496491.2016.1121739.

L

Lang, R., & Haunert, F. (1995). *Handbuch Sozial-Sponsoring. Grundlagen, Praxisbeispiele, Handungsempfehlungen*. Beltz.

Lobo, A., Meyer, D., & Chester, Y. (2014). Evaluating consumer response associated with sponsoring of major sporting events in Australia. *Sport, Business and Management: An International Journal, 4*(1), 52–70. https://doi.org/10.1108/sbm-05-2011-0043.

M

Mazodier, M., & Merunka, D. (2012). Achieving brand loyalty through sponsoring: The role of fit and self-congruity. *Journal of the Academy of Marketing Science, 40*(6), 807–820. https://doi.org/10.1007/s11747-011-0285-y.

N

Nicholls, J. A. F., Roslow, S., & Dublish, S. (1999). Spectator recall and brand preference at sponsored Golf and Tennis tournaments. *European Journal of Marketing, 33*(3/4), 365–386. https://doi.org/10.1108/03090569910253198.

Nielsen Sports. (2018a). Sponsor-Trend 2018: Status und Trends im Sponsoringmarkt in Deutschland, Österreich und Schweiz.

Nielsen Sports. (2018b). *World football report 2018*.

R

Rowley, J., & Williams, C. (2008). The impact of brand sponsoring of music festivals. *Marketing Intelligence & Planning, 26*(7), 781–792. https://doi.org/10.1108/02634500810916717.

S

Sport + Markt AG. (2013). Sponsoring Barometer Österreich 2012/2013, Köln.

W

Walraven, M., Bijmolt, T. H., & Koning, R. H. (2014). Dynamic effects of sponsoring: How sponsoring awareness develops over time. *Journal of Advertising, 43*(2), 142–154. https://doi.org/10.1080/00913367.2013.835754.

Z

ZHAW. (2015). (Zentrum für Kulturmanagement, School of Management and Law, Zürcher Hochschule für Angewandte Wissenschaften. "Sponsor-Visions 2014/15"- Eine empirische Studie zum Sponsoringmarkt Schweiz. http://www.swa-asa.ch/de-wAssets/docs/artikel-print-medien/2015/Studie_Sponsor_Visions_Schweiz_2014-15.pdf. Zugegriffen am 17.02.2016.

Further Reading

Limbach, M. (2020). Erfassung der Effektivität von Sportsponsoring als Marketingkommunikationsinstrument auf der impliziten und expliziten Verarbeitungsebene von Konsumenten als Handlungsgrundlage für operative und strategische Managemententscheidungen Hannover: Institutionelles Repositorium der Leibniz Universität Hannover.

Situation Analysis in Sports Sponsoring

4

Contents

Abstract

The starting point for engagement in sports sponsoring is a systematic situation analysis on various levels. This includes the level of relevant markets, the position of marketing and the company's brand in the industry, the company's appearance in communication and in sponsoring—this requires thorough analyses. In order to create the best conditions for success for all participants in a sports sponsoring project, a compilation of a number of information is necessary. Internal variables of the sponsoring partners are just as important as external factors, i.e. those from the environment of the participants. In order to capture the diverse situation variables that influence the strategic sponsoring orientation and the use of individual sponsoring instruments in as much detail as possible, a structured approach is recommended.

M. Bruhn and P. Rohlmann, *Sports Sponsoring*,
https://doi.org/10.1007/978-3-658-44171-5_4

4.1 Necessity of a Systematic Situation Analysis

An overview of the relevant **areas and levels for the situation analysis** is provided by Fig. 4.1. Engagement in a sports sponsoring project requires both the perspective of the sponsor (company) and the perspective of the sponsored party.

The analysis of a company's marketing situation forms the starting point of every effective marketing decision. This also applies to sports sponsoring. As a result, at the beginning of the systematic sponsoring-related planning process, there is an analysis of the communicative, especially sponsoring-specific situation of the involved partners (Bruhn, 2019).

Planning in sports sponsoring only benefits sponsors and sponsored parties if the planning activities are based on an informative foundation of data and insights appropriate to the relevance of the partnership. In order not to leave the impact of sports sponsoring to chance, planning for the creation of market-oriented and promising sponsoring concepts must be based on a systematic and structured data basis. The collection, analysis, and processing of the necessary information and data take place within the framework of the **sponsoring-related situation analysis**. The situation analysis should not only focus on activities carried out so far and their success. Rather, many other aspects in the entire environment of the participants must be taken into account, which influence the awarding and use of the sponsoring commitment. For example, legal framework conditions or qualitative and quantitative developments on the demand side have an impact

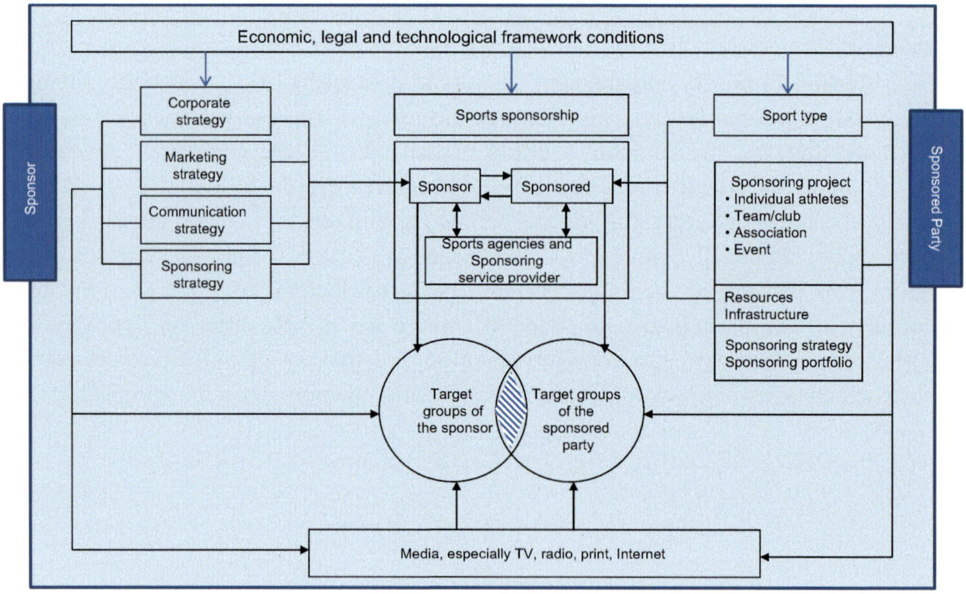

Fig. 4.1 Areas of an inventory in sports sponsoring

on the offer of rights holders and the use of sponsoring rights by corporate communication. The assessment of the market, competitors, customers, and the company's own situation, as well as all relevant environmental variables for a specific decision situation, such as society, economy, technology, law, and politics, is to be considered as the starting point of every marketing decision.

The **result of the situation analysis** in sports sponsoring is the description and evaluation of the internal and external sponsoring-related situation of the participants. Based on the thus recorded current state, the sponsor planner can derive which target state (sponsoring goals) should be aimed for and which related sponsoring rights are relevant, i.e., which individual measure(s) with which contents are to be directed at which target group. The framework conditions for the formulation of sports sponsoring strategies are thus composed of the results of a corresponding situation analysis and, building on this, the results of the goal planning. The formulation of sports sponsoring strategies, in turn, creates the framework of action through which the operational use of the individual instruments can be channeled towards achieving the goals.

With the help of a systematic situation analysis, specific questions can be worked out that relate, for example, to the following **topic areas**:

- Awareness of one's own opportunities through sports sponsoring,
- Recognition of the sponsoring behavior of the main competitors (possibly innovative campaigns of important competitors),
- Awareness of the efficiency of one's own behavior in sports sponsoring in the past (analysis of so-called critical success factors in sports sponsoring),
- Recognition of behavioral tendencies and changes in the market (e.g., concentration processes in trade),
- Anticipation of trends, interests, and reactions of the target group(s),
- Localization of new communicative possibilities, e.g., through digital sponsoring,
- Specification of competitive advantages with sports sponsoring,
- Recognition of unused communicative resources among rights holders and rights takers,
- Determination of internal barriers and reactances of employees, among others.

Such an approach will not completely eliminate the risk of sponsoring-related wrong decisions, but it will contribute to minimizing it or maximizing planning security (Huth & Pflaum, 2005). For these reasons, the situation analysis is at the beginning of the planning process in sports sponsoring and serves as a basis for the development of successful sponsoring strategies.

The situation analysis in the context presented here is based on the following definition:

▶ **Situation Analysis** A **situation analysis** in sports sponsoring includes the inventory of communication-relevant facts with the goal of revealing sponsoring-specific opportunities and risks as well as strengths and weaknesses. It includes processes of information needs determination, information procurement, and the analysis and processing of internal and external data. The result of a situation analysis is the development of the sponsoring-relevant problem situation of the involved partners (rights holders and rights takers in sports sponsoring).

4.2 Analysis Fields and Methods of a Sponsoring-Related Situation Analysis

In order for a situational analysis to not be arbitrary, it is necessary to apply an analytical, i.e., systematic and structured approach. The current and future situation of a market participant is specified in the respective internal and external conditions, which need to be captured and analyzed in the context of the situational analysis. While the internal conditions concern the participants themselves, the external conditions are specified in the macro and micro environment of the sponsoring partners. These two areas, as general fields of analysis, provide the information basis for a goal-oriented communication policy.

To obtain information in the individual fields of analysis, the sponsoring participants or their agency have various methods of situational analysis at their disposal, with the help of which the multitude of possible internal and/or external influencing factors can be systematically and detailedly recorded. The analysis tools refer to economic and psychological facts, can be carried out as ex-post or ex-ante analyses, and have various objects and market participants (e.g., products, services, brands, customers, competitors, etc.) as their subject.

The identification of strengths, weaknesses, opportunities, and risks requires obtaining the necessary information through internal and external analyses (see Bruhn, 2019, p. 113 ff.). For this purpose, numerous special, i.e., area-specific, non-integrative analysis tools exist, which focus on specific questions or areas. The area-specific analysis methods are to be used depending on the question relevant to sponsoring. Fig. 4.2 provides an overview of **fields of analysis and selected methods of a communication-related situational analysis**. In addition to the integrative SWOT analysis, some of these area-specific analysis methods, which are often used in the context of a communicative situational analysis, will be discussed.

Among the most important and most frequently used analysis methods in practice is the **SWOT analysis** (Strengths—**W**eaknesses—**O**pportunities—**T**hreats), whose goal is to work out the sponsoring-specific problem of the actors. The SWOT analysis can depict the current situation at the time of information gathering. The SWOT analysis

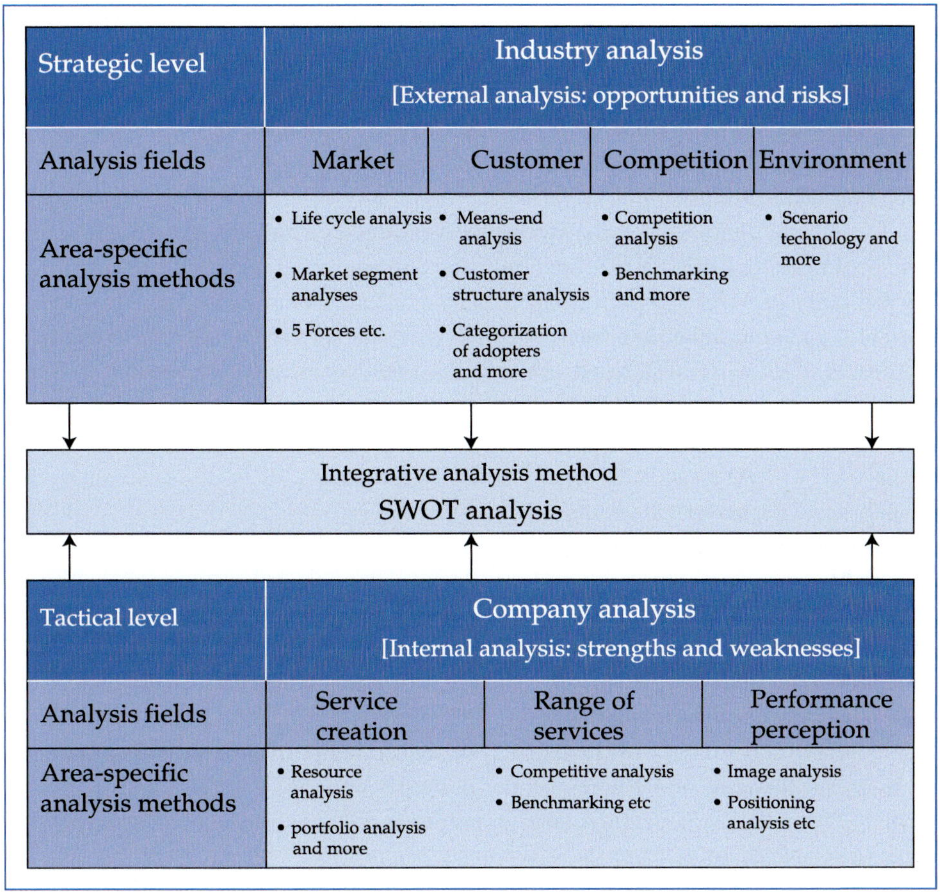

Fig. 4.2 Overview of fields of analysis and selected methods of the communication-related situational analysis. (*Source*: Bruhn, 2019, p. 118)

represents a comprehensive and integrative methodology, as it aims to condense the multitude of collected individual information from the internal and external analysis to the essentials and present it in a structured manner. The following **knowledge goals** can be derived from the SWOT analysis or the following benefits can be generated:

- Presentation of strengths and weaknesses in sports sponsoring, reflected in the opportunities and risks in the market, each related to the specific partner,
- Focus on significant sponsoring activities,
- Identification of need for action in the context of sports sponsoring,
- Development of a basis for the determination of goals and measures in sports sponsoring, etc.

The results of the SWOT analysis are of particular relevance in the context of sponsoring planning. The critical reflection of past activities and the identification of resulting strengths and weaknesses form the basis for efficient and effective sponsoring in the future. In particular, the critical examination of the effects achieved with past activities regarding important goals of the actors provides new impulses for an effective future sponsoring relationship.

In the internal analysis, i.e., the **strengths-weaknesses analysis**, the specific sponsoring-related resources of a partner are compared and evaluated with those of competitors. This primarily involves the performance analysis of a sponsoring partner. To conduct a systematic and comprehensive internal analysis of the sponsoring-related strengths and weaknesses of an actor, a strengths-weaknesses analysis must be carried out in the following three categories:

- Analysis of performance creation,
- Analysis of the performance offer,
- Analysis of performance perception.

In the analysis of **performance creation**, the available internal resources of a company for creating communicative activities are determined. This includes, for example, the resource analysis, the portfolio analysis, and process management. The analysis of the **performance offer** represents the evaluation of the services from the perspective of the respective sponsoring partner, which he offers in comparison to the competition in the market. The analysis of the entire product/service portfolio, the positioning analysis of its services, and studies on the price-performance ratio are assigned to this point. The analysis of **performance perception** reflects the subjective perception of the performance offer from the customer's perspective. This involves, for example, determining a Unique Communication Proposition, image analysis, etc.

To capture the strengths and weaknesses of a company, checklists or scoring models are generally used. A checklist, for example, contains those criteria that have special significance for the success or failure of a company. These criteria are each evaluated as to whether they represent a strength or a weakness for the company, each in reference to the performance of the strongest competitors. However, the graphical representation of the information obtained using a **strengths-weaknesses profile** is clearer. Compared to the checklist, the scoring model also takes into account the degree of strength or weakness and individual weighting factors (Scharf et al., 2015).

While the strengths-weaknesses analysis refers to internal factors, the perspective in the **opportunities-risks analysis** is directed at the environment of the sponsoring partners. The task is to examine the external environment of the participants for signs of threats and opportunities for current sponsoring activities and the various sports and reference objects of the sponsoring. Thus, as part of the opportunities-risks analysis, the market-relevant and general environmental factors relevant to communication success must be identified and evaluated in terms of the opportunities and risks for a sponsoring relationship. To do this, developments in the macro and micro environment of the partners must be analyzed. For the assessment of the external sponsoring situation, it is recommended to carry out an analysis in the following **environmental areas**:

- Market situation (e.g., relevant market, market segments, market structure, market participants),
- Customer situation (e.g., current and potential customers),
- Competitive situation (e.g., competitors in the industry and in sports),
- Environmental situation (e.g., general or global).

In individual cases, it must be checked whether additional areas need to be included and how the individual areas are to be weighted in the situational analysis. For a detailed analysis of the individual situation categories, different methods or tools are used (see again Fig. 4.2).

The evaluation of the **presentation of opportunities and risks** of a company can be done using a point evaluation procedure or semantic differential. Furthermore, opportunities and risks arising from the external analysis can be represented and evaluated in the form of a matrix. Opportunities in sports sponsoring, for example, are to be arranged in terms of their attractiveness and probability of success.

As mentioned, the SWOT analysis combines the results of a strengths-weaknesses analysis and an opportunities-threats analysis by juxtaposing them in a so-called **SWOT matrix** (see Fig. 4.3). When merging the two areas, the SWOT analysis ensures that all relevant factors are systematically recorded and the information is condensed and structured. The SWOT analysis thus contributes to the reduction of complexity. Based on the juxtaposition of the results of the internal and external analyses, a structured development of strategies in sports sponsoring can take place.

The core of a SWOT matrix lies in the **elaboration of the sponsoring-relevant problem**. This is done in reference to one of the four fields of the matrix (S = Strengths, W = Weaknesses, O = Opportunities, T = Threats) and can be based on the so-called SO field (utilization of opportunities through strengths), the ST field (use of strengths to meet risks), the WO field (reduction of weaknesses to utilize opportunities) or the WT field (reduction of weaknesses and utilization of opportunities in niches). Accordingly, the sponsoring-relevant problem can vary greatly. Here are some examples of **sponsoring-relevant problems** of potential sponsors:

- A brewery has spread itself thin with its sponsoring activities in sports. It sponsors dance events in the region, jersey advertising for football clubs, perimeter advertising on tennis courts, chess championships, and more. On the national level, the brewery is present at football broadcasts on television, perimeter advertising in the Bundesliga for handball and ice hockey clubs, partner with the ski association, and more. The sponsoring-relevant problem lies in focusing on a few sports suitable for

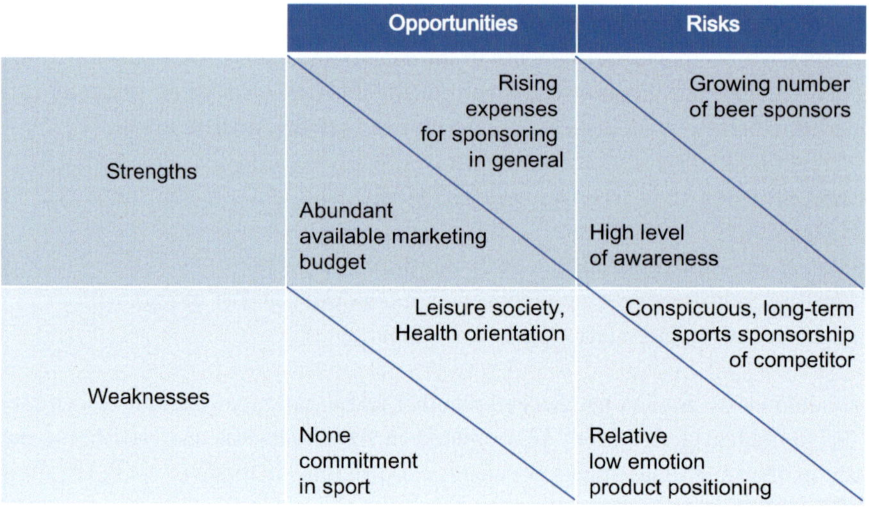

Fig. 4.3 Example of a sponsoring-related SWOT matrix for a brewery. (*Source*: adapted from Bruhn, 2019, p. 121)

the company's sponsoring goals and concentrating on effective forms of appearance within sports.

- A manufacturer of nationally distributed DIY tools has been a non-exclusive sponsor of national team sports clubs for years, once in handball, once in basketball. Prompted by the shortage of skilled workers, the company's board of directors is reconsidering its previous commitments and now wants to put the topic of employer branding at the center of its sports sponsoring. Therefore, the marketing department is commissioned to link a concept in this regard with regional sports sponsoring.

The **goal of the external analysis** is a systematic presentation of the opportunities and risks of a sponsoring partner in the market. Opportunities are sponsor-specific actions where an actor can generate competitive advantages. In contrast, market risks are environmental hazards that threaten the company's existence (Kotler & Keller, 2016). The external analysis serves, for example, to recognize or determine the following **developments in the macro environment**:

- Identification of new technological developments,
- Recognition of a changed communication behavior of the target group,
- Recognition of increased communication pressure.

In addition to the analysis of the general or global (macro-) environment of a sponsoring partner, which is generally difficult to influence or control, the **analysis of the market-relevant micro-environment** within the situation analysis is of central importance, as the alignment of sponsoring decisions to the requirements of the market is essential for success-oriented sports sponsoring. The goal of the analysis of the market-relevant environment is to obtain information about those market elements that, in addition to the participants, determine the sponsoring events on the market.

In detail, this means examining, in addition to the market itself, the competitors, the customers, and the public (state, media, consumer protection) with regard to sponsoring-relevant questions. The sponsoring partners and their closer market environment also operate in a global environment. The goal of the analysis of the global environment is to recognize and respond to **opportunities and risks** arising from the general environment for a partner in a timely manner. The global environment includes the economic, ecological, socio-cultural, political-legal, and technological environment.

4.3 Internal Situation Analysis in Practice

In the context of an **internal analysis** (or also: **self-analysis**) it is necessary to check whether the prerequisites for the upcoming sponsoring are given at all, i.e. whether the necessary services and counter-services can be provided in a sufficient and timely manner. In this respect, a self-analysis of the sponsored party and a self-analysis of the sponsor is required.

Self-analysis of the Sponsored Party

As part of the self-analysis, the structures relevant to the sponsored party for the sponsoring must be identified and their suitability for the upcoming sponsoring project must be checked. This is essentially a **strengths and weaknesses analysis**, to what extent the granting of sponsoring rights also allows the corresponding performance promises. All services to be offered to a sponsor or of interest to him must be tested for their feasibility.

In addition, the sports actor will have to answer the question of what special and unique characteristics distinguish him from other sponsoring providers (**"unique sponsoring proposition"**) and how his values, sports activities and his fan base match the ideas of companies willing to sponsor.

The **development of a "unique sponsoring proposition"** must always be done in relation to the potential sponsored parties in the sports category. Here too, there is competition among the sponsored parties for attractive sponsors. In this context, the party to be sponsored will ask numerous questions, here are a few examples of **general questions**:

- Do we have a clear brand image? How are we perceived from the outside?
- What image does our sports have? To what extent do we deviate positively from it?
- What sponsoring activities have been carried out so far? Which of these have been particularly successful, which were problematic or in need of improvement?
- What performance offers can we as a sports actor offer seriously and reliably? Do we have the personnel and material resources as well as the appropriate infrastructure for such a promise or are investments necessary here?
- In what and at which points can this offer differ from others in the market?
- What benefits does my potential sponsor expect from a commitment? How can I express this in the offer?
- etc.

Surveys on the image of sports can be found at numerous market research institutes. Individual sports actors can gather insights about their appearance and image through surveys among members, at events or in public spaces.

In addition, the party to be sponsored has to deal with the **potential sponsors**. In this context, considerations about the desired sponsoring relationship must also be made from the sponsor's point of view. This results in a variety of questions, such as the following **case-specific questions**:

- How does the upcoming sponsoring commitment fit into my other sponsoring strategy as a sports actor?
- How do I collect information about possible sponsors that fit my specific offer, and how do I create a kind of sponsor profile?
- How many sponsors are appropriate? Should there be an equal pool of sponsors or a tiered sponsoring offer? Are standard packages suitable or are individual offers necessary?
- What prices are customary or possible for certain sponsoring services? Are there already experiences with the specific sponsoring offer?
- Which potential sponsors/companies are even suitable? It is advisable to prepare a list of possible partner addresses with contact person and contact priority in advance.
- Which companies have already been contacted regarding the specific sponsoring project? What was the result, what was positive, what was negative?
- How has the contact with the sponsor been made so far? What are the responsibilities? What was positive, what was negative?
- Are suitable employees available internally or is external help needed? If no adequate responsibility can be found in a manageable period of time through quality and competence improvement, it makes sense to contact a sports agency.
- How can the (personal) contact be maintained continuously and professionally after a conclusion, and possibly even expanded?
- etc.

The self-analysis of the party to be sponsored requires—as with the sponsor—a **professional approach**. This requires specific expertise, which can be covered by own employees with the corresponding know-how, or the support of external consultants.

Sponsor's Self-Analysis

The **internal analysis of the potential sponsor** should not only be limited to the sponsoring activities carried out so far and their success. Rather, additional aspects in the entire environment of the company willing to sponsor, which influence the communication situation in the company's sports sponsoring, must also be taken into account.

In other words, as part of the situation analysis, both the **communication situation** for the entire company and the various market and environmental factors that the sponsor faces depending on his sponsoring commitments are analyzed. This requires that both the individual communication departments and the company management are involved in the situation analysis through the targeted use of market research methods. The goal is to capture the current situation of communication or specifically to filter out how the communicative appearance of the company as an overall impression of the sponsoring measures used is perceived by the various recipients, and which factors influence this communication situation.

Internally, the potential sponsor also has to ask numerous questions. This concerns questions of communication, but also of organization, personnel, etc. The following **questions** are mentioned as examples:

- What role should or can sports sponsoring play in marketing and corporate communication?
- What can the new sponsoring commitment bring for our own goals? What and why can it do better than previous partnerships? Does it possibly replace a previous sponsoring relationship?
- What specific added value can I expect as a potential sponsor? Can a requirement profile for a sponsoring relationship be created?
- Are the sponsoring partner and his offer fair and serious? Can I as a sponsor finance and maintain the overall package of rights acquisition and activation? Is the review of the financial and other consequences positive?
- Is the sports actor competent and credible? What references can he provide?
- What reasons speak for him compared to competitor offers?
- Are there clear responsibilities in the company for the upcoming sponsoring project?
- What is the sponsor's plan B in case of problems or failure?
- How should contact take place (active or passive)?
- etc.

A central question of a future commitment in sports sponsoring is the position of the individual instruments of marketing and corporate communication. This can possibly be answered by a **communication-related portfolio analysis**, in such a way that, for example, the effectiveness in reaching the target group is compared to the saturation level in the use of instruments. Fig. 4.4 shows an example of a communication-related portfolio analysis.

4.4 External Situation Analysis in Practice

In the **external analysis**, from the perspective of the sponsored and the sponsor, the framework conditions in which the future commitment in sports sponsoring will take place are particularly important. This concerns developments in the areas of politics, economy, society, technology, ecology, and law alike. In principle, this is a

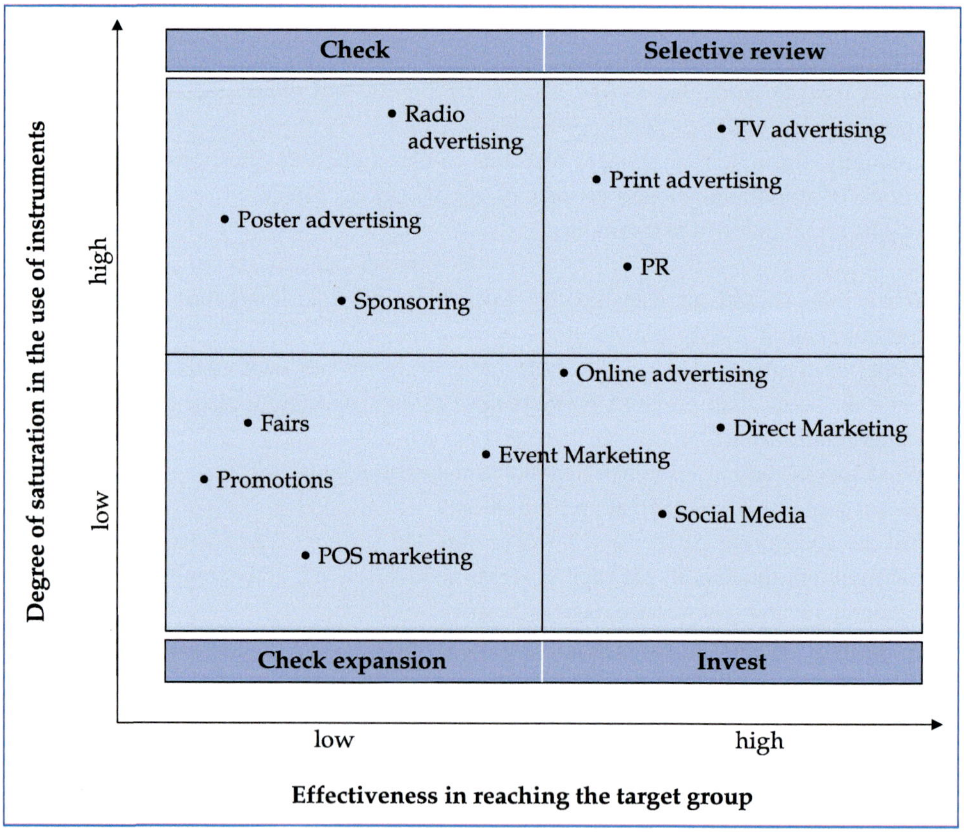

Fig. 4.4 Example of a communication-related portfolio analysis from the sponsor's perspective. (*Source*: Bruhn, 2019, p. 144)

sponsoring-related PESTEL analysis (PESTEL = **P**olitical, **E**conomic, **S**ocial, **T**echnological, **E**nvironmental, **L**egal). Here too, an external analysis of the sponsored and the sponsor is required.

External Analysis of the Sponsored

The sponsored parties grant sponsoring rights and thus communication services for interested companies. They have to deal with the special circumstances and the **development trends of the relevant sponsoring area**. This also includes the specific characteristics and customs of the market environment that are important for the sponsored party or the rights holder, such as:

- The **sports and the sponsoring options**. Each sport has its peculiarities, both in terms of possible forms of sponsoring and the breadth of individual measures. The sports actor operates within a certain range of services, which allows for special offers primarily through creative additions and intelligent networking. Points of clarification include, among others, the previous performances or successes of the sponsored party, the assessment and acceptance by the target groups, the management qualifications in the organization and association, the public relations work by the sports organization, the participation of certain individuals in sports events, the expected media presence, the type of predicates, licenses and titles in connection with the sports team or sports event, the position of the sponsor compared to other sponsors, the use of advertising opportunities before, during or after the sponsoring, the costs for the sponsoring including preparation and follow-up, and the activation of the commitment.
- The **competing sports actors**. Each rights holder is in competition for sponsors with the same interests in his league or competition. Therefore, it goes without saying that every sports actor must know his competitors and their sponsoring offers, especially if he has certain unique advantages.
- The **influence of sports agencies**. In some submarkets of sports sponsoring (e.g., foreign markets), little can be achieved without the support of experienced agencies. Therefore, it should also be checked whether and to what extent the involvement of an agency can help achieve the sponsoring goals of the sponsored party more easily and quickly.
- **Economic conditions**. In view of economic trends (e.g., economic or energy crisis), which also affect the individual scope of action of companies willing to sponsor, the willingness to engage in sponsoring may generally decrease or decrease in scope. This can also change sponsoring preferences, so that in the specific case, openness and flexibility on the part of the sponsored party can improve the chances of cooperation.
- **Legal conditions**. If general legal bases, such as the general ban on tobacco advertising in sports, the ban on gambling advertising or the limits for virtual advertising, are

in flux or become fact, the rights holder must take this into account early on. There may also be guidelines from national and international sports associations, which are responsible for the organization of sports competitions, regarding certain types of advertising that are allowed in one sport but prohibited in another. In football, for example, the pitch may not be used as an advertising space, while this is possible in sports such as handball or ice hockey.

- **Technological conditions**. Especially with the development of the internet and particularly in new media, sponsoring opportunities are opening up that were unthinkable a few years ago. It is expected that digitization will not only expand traditional sponsoring relationships (e.g., expansion of perimeter advertising in the stadium) through virtual additional forms, but also create different types of collaboration in the course of e-sports.
- **Access to target groups of the potential sponsor**. It is a considerable advantage if sponsored parties make even more effort to know the needs and wishes of their potential sponsors as well as possible. The more specifically the sponsoring services meet the goals of potential partners, the more likely a deal will be concluded. This includes knowledge about the partner's target groups as well as arguments as to why these can be reached precisely with the help of the sponsored party.

External Analysis of the Sponsor

In the external analysis of the sponsor, the **development trends** play an important role. Here, it is necessary to observe the situation and development of various markets, the customers and sales intermediaries, the competitors and the environment:

- **Market-related influencing factors**. First, it is the market-related influencing factors of sports sponsoring that need to be analyzed. The **sports market** shows the opportunities to acquire rights and to engage as a sponsor. Here, the current sponsoring developments in the sub-markets, the penetration of new sponsoring forms and also saturation phenomena and misdevelopments in sports are to be analyzed. The **communication market** is characterized by the various opportunities for companies to transport their messages through diverse channels. Here, sports sponsoring competes with the impact of traditional media advertising, public relations, trade fairs and exhibitions, event marketing, social media activities, etc. Sports sponsoring has to put its specific advantages (e.g., emotionalization) compared to other communication instruments to the test. The **media market** is also an important partner in sports sponsoring. Here, the interest of individual auditory, visual, audiovisual and digital media in broadcasts and reports about sporting events is to be observed.

- **Customer-related influencing factors**. In the context of customer-related influencing factors, for example, the leisure behavior of customers, the sports behavior and sports interest, the information needs of the target groups, the emotional perception of brands, expectations of products or services, customer satisfaction and the degree of information overload by communication media are to be examined.
- **Sales intermediary-related influencing factors**. The sales intermediary-related influencing factors include, for example, the demands of sports venues, sports intermediaries, sports agencies, manufacturers of merchandising articles, etc. They can increase the effectiveness of sports sponsoring through creative solutions.
- **Competition-related influencing factors**. The competition-related influencing factors include, for example, the communication and sponsoring strategies as well as the communication effort of the main competitors, the implemented sponsoring measures and the positioning of the competitors. As part of the competition analysis, the company has to examine which sports sponsoring activities are carried out by direct competitors, in which situations, with what intensity and with what success.
- **Environment-related influencing factors**. As environment-related influencing factors of sponsoring, for example, the development of technology, the legal framework, the societal discussion about sports as well as topics such as sustainability, digitalization, instrumentalization, etc. in sports are to be considered.

The listed situation variables do not occur in isolation, but are **interdependent influence relationships**. For each company, the task is to determine the relevant influencing factors of sponsoring and the relationships between the variables. For example, the sponsoring goals and instruments determined in previous planning periods influence the current actual situation of the sponsoring. Accordingly, the already achieved goals and their influencing factors must also be examined in the actual analysis.

The **result of the situation analysis** is finally the description and evaluation of the internal and external sponsoring-related communication situation. Based on the thus recorded actual state, the sponsoring planner derives which target state (sponsoring goals) is to be aimed for and which communication policy activities are to be taken, i.e., which message is to be directed to which target group with the help of which communication tools and media. The framework conditions for the formulation of sponsoring strategies are thus composed of the results of the sponsoring-related situation analysis and, building on this, the results of the sponsoring goal planning.

When potential sponsors decide to commit, **decision criteria by in the selection of sponsoring** such as the target groups-fit and the emotional radiance of the sponsored, in addition to reach and exclusivity in the given sponsoring portfolio, are of outstanding importance. This is shown by the results of a company survey, which are reproduced in Fig. 4.5.

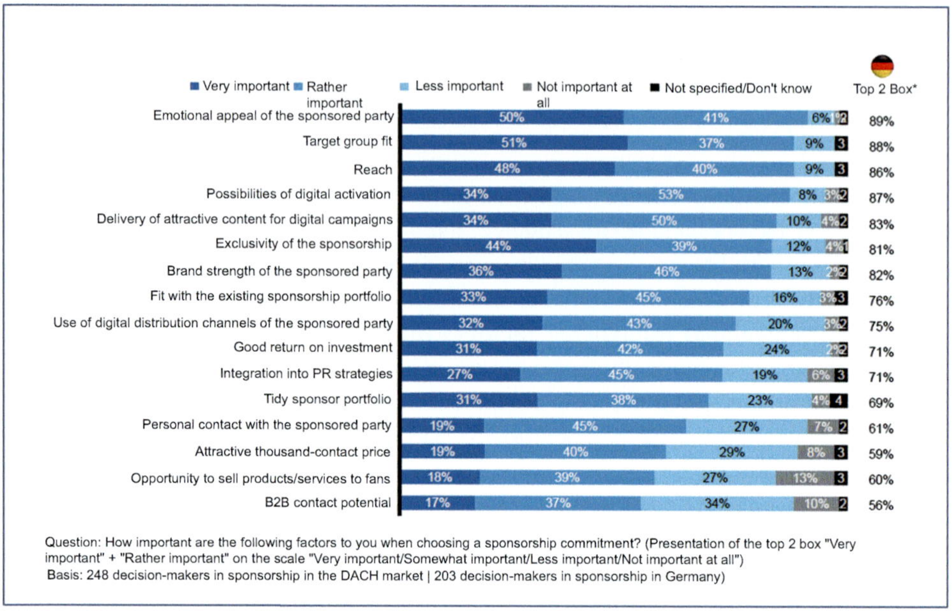

Fig. 4.5 Decision criteria in the selection of sponsoring. (*Source*: Nielsen Sports, 2018a, p. 16)

4.5 Interdependencies in External and Internal Situation Analysis

The explanations illustrate that both internal and external analyses and their individual analysis fields or categories cannot be considered independently of each other. Rather, there are numerous interdependencies between internal and external as well as market-, customer-, competition- and environment-related situation analysis, and also within these categories. For example, the sponsoring potential, i.e., the sponsoring-specific know-how of a participant, is closely related to the chosen sponsoring strategy **(Interdependencies within the category)**. Depending on the sponsoring-specific know-how of a partner, the corresponding argumentation also varies, which is reflected in both the sponsoring concept and its implementation.

A comprehensive and at the same time differentiated situation analysis in sports sponsoring also requires consideration of relationships between the situation variables **(Interdependencies between the categories)**. For example, it can be assumed that the (internal) sponsoring potential is closely related to the market situation, which is examined in the context of the market-related situation analysis. If it is a monopoly, a low sponsoring potential is usually diagnosed. In a monopoly, products or services "sell themselves" and rely only on minimal—if any—communicative support through communication and sponsoring. In contested markets, on the other hand, products and services often require high communicative support, including through sports sponsoring, to stand out from the multitude of offers and ensure good conditions for sales.

In summary, it becomes clear that the **sponsoring-related situation analysis** is determined by a multitude of different influencing factors. The increasing number of influencing factors and the resulting increasing mutual dependencies between the situation factors lead to companies driving sponsoring facing an increasingly complex business environment. However, it should be noted that as the situation analysis becomes more detailed and differentiated, the cost increases. This may be a reason why many sponsoring partners forego a differentiated and detailed situation analysis. However, such a situation analysis should not only be considered from a cost perspective, but also as an investment in a successful sponsoring concept and thus in the success of a company willing to sponsor.

4.6 Key Points

The situation analysis has outstanding importance within the analysis phase because it provides the fundamental information needed for the subsequent phases of decision-making. The following points should be particularly noted.

Key Points

1. The marketing situation of a company forms the **starting point of every effective marketing decision**. This also applies to sports sponsoring and an analysis of the communicative, especially sponsoring-specific situation of the involved partners.
2. Planning for the creation of market-oriented and promising sponsoring concepts must be based on a **systematic and structured data basis**. The acquisition, analysis, and processing of the necessary information and data takes place within the framework of a situation analysis that relates to communication and sponsoring.
3. The result of the situation analysis in sports sponsoring is the **description and evaluation of the internal and external sponsoring-related situation** of the participants. Based on the thus recorded current state, the sponsoring planner can derive which sponsoring goals to pursue and which related sponsoring rights are relevant.
4. In order for a situation analysis not to be arbitrary, it is necessary to apply an analytical, i.e., **systematic and structured approach**. The current and future situation of a market participant is specified in the respective internal and external conditions.
5. The sponsoring participants have various **methods of situation analysis** available. Among the most important and most frequently used analysis

methods in practice is the SWOT analysis as a comprehensive and integrative methodology.

6. In the **internal analysis**, i.e., the strengths-weaknesses analysis, the specific sponsoring-related resources of a partner are compared and evaluated with those of the competitors.
7. In the opportunities-risks analysis, the perspective is directed towards the environment of the sponsoring partners. The task is to examine the **external environment** of the participants for signs of a threat to the current sponsoring activities and for new opportunities.
8. The **sports actor or the one to be sponsored** must ask himself whether he has a **"unique sponsoring proposition"**, i.e., what special and preferably unique characteristics distinguish him from other sponsoring providers and how his values, sports activities, and fan base match the expectations of the companies willing to sponsor.
9. In the **external view**, from the perspective of the sponsored and the sponsor, the other market participants are to be considered in terms of the extent and how the upcoming sponsoring commitment could have an impact.
10. Internal and external analyses as well as their individual analysis fields or categories are not to be considered independently of each other. Rather, there are numerous **interdependencies** between internal and external as well as market, customer, competition, and environment-related situation analysis, as well as within these categories.

References

B

Bruhn, M. (2019). *Kommunikationspolitik. Systematischer Einsatz der Kommunikation für Unternehmen* (9. Aufl.). https://doi.org/10.15358/9783800648924.

H

Huth, R., & Pflaum, D. (2005). *Einführung in die Werbelehre* (7. Aufl.). Kohlhammer.

K

Kotler, P., & Keller, K. L. (2016). *Marketing management*. https://doi.org/10.1556/9789630597784.

N

Nielsen Sports. (2018a). Sponsor-Trend 2018: Status und Trends im Sponsoringmarkt in Deutschland, Österreich und Schweiz.
Nielsen Sports. (2018b). *World football report 2018*.

S

Scharf, A., Schubert, B., & Hehn, P. (2015). Marketing. Einführung in Theorie und Praxis, 7. Aufl., Stuttgart. https://doi.org/10.34156/9783799269506.

Goals and Target Groups of Sports Sponsoring

5

Contents

Abstract

The situation analysis in sports sponsoring serves to identify the economic and non-economic problems for the involved parties. From the **sponsor's perspective**, the question arises as to what specific contribution sports sponsoring can make to solve the particularly communicative problem. The specific **competitive advantages of sports sponsoring** over other communication tools include, among other things, that involvement in sports can convey attractive and emotional image dimensions (e.g., performance, competence, dynamism), the media can contribute to the multiplication of reach for message transmission, and the sporting environment can offer opportunities for contact maintenance in a pleasant leisure atmosphere. The case study of Hypovereinsbank clearly shows a stringent orientation towards sales targets.

M. Bruhn and P. Rohlmann, *Sports Sponsoring*,
https://doi.org/10.1007/978-3-658-44171-5_5

5.1 Setting the Goals and Motives of Sports Sponsoring

From the **perspective of the sponsored**, the primary focus is on generating revenue from the granting of sponsoring rights, which can help improve the practice and quality of athletic performance. While prestigious sponsoring partnerships can also make further sponsor acquisitions more attractive and thus easier, the economic goals are clearly in the foreground (see Fig. 5.1).

When deciding to engage in sports sponsoring from a corporate perspective, systematic planning will require clarity about two central elements of sports sponsoring in the next steps:

- Setting the **sponsoring goals**,
- Identification and description of the **sponsoring target groups**.

Both the sponsoring goals and the sponsoring target groups are essential prerequisites for being able to carry out a success control after the implementation of the sports sponsorings. Therefore, it is necessary to work out goals and target groups as concretely and operationally as possible (see Bruhn, 2018, pp. 54 ff., 143 ff.).

The starting point of any goal formulation in sports sponsoring are the existing **marketing and communication goals** of a company or its product brands, as well as the insights from the previous situation analysis. The goals of sports sponsoring should be formulated in such a way that the various sponsoring activities of the company in sports contribute to achieving the existing overall goals of marketing and corporate

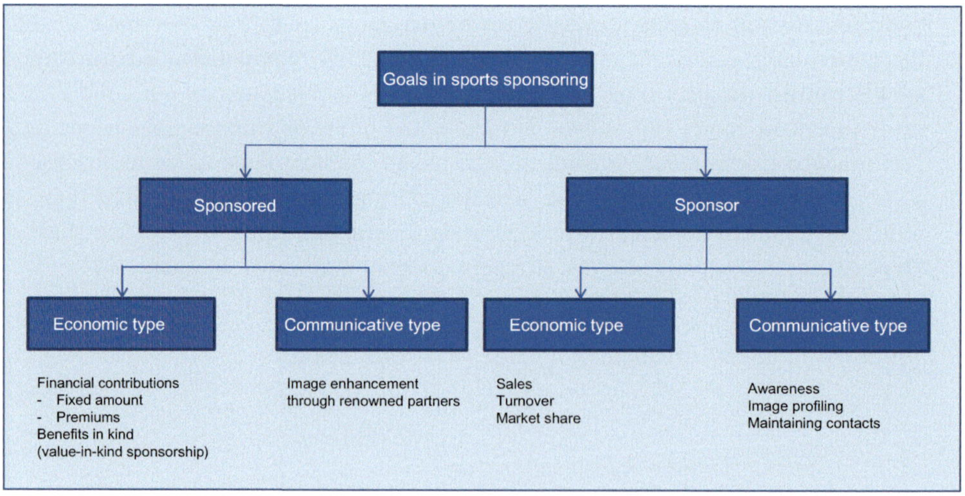

Fig. 5.1 Targets in sports sponsoring from the perspective of the involved parties

communication (e.g., brand positioning, improvement of image dimensions, increase or stabilization of awareness).

In formulating the goals of sports sponsoring, a further subdivision into **economic and psychological goals** can be made, similar to other communication tools.

Economic Goals of Sports Sponsoring

Direct economic goals are rather rare in corporate and marketing communication, as there is often a lack of a direct cause-effect relationship between the use of communication tools and sales data. Nevertheless, in certain industries, the classical **economic marketing goals**, such as profit or sales, turnover or profit, also play a role for sports sponsoring.

On the one hand, the economic goals for selected **industries with a sports connection** have a special significance, i.e., especially for manufacturers of products that are directly or indirectly related to the relevant sports area. This applies particularly to sports equipment, shoes and clothing that are directly related to the sponsored sports. For example, sales increases of tennis rackets of a certain brand can be achieved after victories of tennis idols, as well as clothing of a textile company after victories of a golf professional. The same applies to brand manufacturers in the areas of soft drinks, chocolate bars, watches, etc., who sponsor top sporting events, have a broad media impact and for whom athletes appear with a sympathetic image. Other examples of the relatively short-term and direct achievement of economic goals via sponsoring are sports event-independent measures such as promotion actions with sponsored athletes in the sales rooms of a retail business (Bassenge, 2000, p. 77).

Furthermore, it should be noted that the **pre-economic goals** (e.g., awareness, image) have a means-end relationship with the economic goals. Ultimately, it is about the psychological goals creating important prerequisites for economic goals to be achieved. This fact was already pointed out in connection with the success chain of sponsoring (see in Chap. 3, Fig. 3.2).

Psychological Goals of Sports Sponsoring

The psychological goals are the upstream, so-called pre-economic goals. These psychological goals generally dominate in corporate and marketing communication and are also of central importance for sports sponsoring. A distinction according to **cognitive, affective and conative goals** has proven to be useful.

Cognitive Sponsoring Goals

Cognitive goals involve the transmission of knowledge to recipients. Due to the usually broad media resonance, measures of sports sponsoring are particularly suitable for large sports events such as World Championships, to achieve an **improvement in the level of awareness** of a company or a brand. However, it is more problematic to make new products known through sports sponsoring, to increase knowledge about certain products, or to demonstrate new uses for products. The reason for this is that in most forms of sports sponsoring, only the brand or company name appears, without the sponsor being able to argue more differentiated or convey specific advertising messages. Therefore, sports sponsoring is particularly suitable for established product brands that already have a certain (minimum) level of awareness.

Furthermore, the **transmission of product knowledge** is also possible to a limited extent, such as hints on new tariffs, new models from providers, etc. Here, Deutsche Telekom can be mentioned, which, due to its high aided awareness, specifically aims to present new products and services through its sponsoring activities (e.g., MagentaSport). In a similar way, energy suppliers as well as banks and insurance companies have taken into account new tariffs/offers in their message transmission (YouGov, 2021).

Affective Sponsoring Goals

Affective goals reflect the evaluations or opinions of recipients. In the context of the affective goals of sports sponsoring, **image profiling** is in the foreground. The basis of image profiling is an image transfer, for example from the image (or the image dimensions) of an athlete's performance, a sports team, or the atmosphere of a competition venue, to the image of the sponsor. The **principle of image transfer** assumes that in a long-term connection of a company to a sport, the image dimensions of the sport or an athlete or a team transfer to the company (Mattmüller & Oettgen, 2008, p. 288). Numerous car manufacturers want to transfer the image of technological competence to their products through their motorsport commitments. For example, Mercedes aims for a winner image through the sponsoring of its own factory team in motorsport in order to be perceived more as a sports brand (Nufer & Bühler, 2015). Another illustrative example of a strong focus on image transfer is provided by the beverage manufacturer Red Bull with its commitment in national and international football (Rohlmann, 2021).

Conative Sponsoring Goals

The conative goals in communication refer to the behavior or behavioral intentions of recipients. Against the background of the relevance of increasing relationship quality, the conative goal of **customer loyalty** in the context of sports sponsoring is also becoming more important for companies. Sports sponsoring is particularly suitable in this context for achieving goals, as visitors to sports events are usually in a favorable, relaxed mood and advertising messages are often positively received against the background of emotions, enthusiasm, excitement, and pleasure.

In various company surveys, the goals associated with the use of sports advertising and sports sponsoring were recorded. Here, reference is made in particular to the following **studies**:

- Study "Sponsoring Trends 2012": The data base consists of the 5000 companies with the highest turnover in Germany (Bagusat, 2013),
- Study "Sponsor Visions Switzerland 2014/15" by the ZHAW School of Management and Law, Association for Sponsoring and Special Advertising Forms (FASPO),
- The studies "Sponsor Trend 2015" and "Sponsor Trend 2016" by Nielsen Sports (formerly Repucom), which look at the sponsoring markets in Germany, Austria and Switzerland. The data base consists of 251 (Sponsor Trend, 2015) and 191 (Sponsor Trend, 2016) sponsors and agencies (Nielsen Sports—formerly Repucom, 2015).
- Study "Sponsor Trend 2018" by Nielsen Sports (Nielsen Sports, 2018a) and Study "Sport Marketing Trends 2022" (Nielsen Sports, 2022).

The results of the existing empirical studies regarding the **importance of different sports sponsoring goals** confirm that image stabilization and improvement of awareness are the two central sponsoring goals in sports. However, awareness is continuously losing its importance as a target of sponsoring—with the exception of industries that are new to a market (for example, energy suppliers)—while the other goals remain the same or increase in importance. Companies see comparative advantages of sponsoring over other communication measures primarily in the **addressing of specific target groups** and thus the minimization of scatter losses. The communication instrument sponsoring is also considered superior in the empirical studies in terms of the **experience of products or brands** and the **promotion of employee motivation**.

The communication objectives of companies are not constants, but change depending on the existing degree of target achievement. Thus, **sponsoring goals over time** will also change. In addition to the short-term goals pursued by the sponsoring company, such as increasing brand awareness, every sponsor will consider which medium and long-term goals can be achieved through sports sponsoring. When considering the significance of economic and psychological goals over time, the relationships shown in Fig. 5.2 emerge. It becomes clear that psychological goals have a means-end relationship with economic goals and that medium to long-term economic goals are pursued, i.e., sports sponsoring contributes to the increase in sales or market share of companies in the long term—at least indirectly.

The result of **goal planning in sports sponsoring** is the clear, realistic, and above all operational formulation of desired goals that can be achieved through sponsoring. The goal planning must be specified by the sponsor with regard to the following four **requirements for operationalization**, which are explained using examples:

- **Goal content**: Increase in active brand awareness through perimeter and jersey advertising in football.

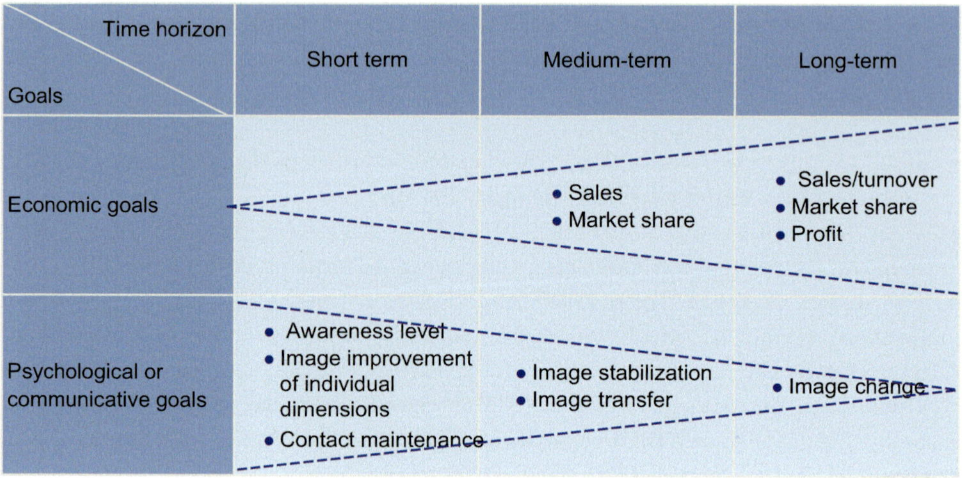

Fig. 5.2 Significance of various goals of sports sponsoring over time

- **Goal extent**: Increase in active brand awareness by 10% or improvement of the image dimensions "dynamics" and "sportiness" by one point on a 7-point scale.
- **Time reference**: Increase in brand awareness through the sponsoring of three tennis tournaments within one year.
- **Target group reference**: Increase in awareness among 30- to 40-year-old male end consumers.

Only precise goal planning enables the sponsor to specify his expectations towards the sponsored parties and to carry out a **control of the degree of achievement of the sponsoring effects** after the implementation of the sponsorings. This means in detail that companies have to decide, when presented with a specific sponsoring offer or before developing their own sports-related sponsorings, to what extent an improvement in awareness is possible in the specific case with the target groups, which image is transferred to the brand name, and to what extent sports sponsoring serves to maintain contact with selected company representatives and customers.

In addition to these classic goals, it is particularly worth mentioning for sports sponsoring that **personal motives** are often the background for sponsoring decisions. Here, personal relationships and interests of decision-makers can be the reason for an engagement in sports sponsoring. This will be less observable in top-level sports, where often very high financial resources are used, but certainly in local and regional sports, where the promotional motive and the personal relationships between the participants are more in the foreground.

5.2 Target Group Planning of Sports Sponsoring

In identifying the target groups in sports sponsoring, a distinction must be made between the **target groups of sponsors and those sponsored**. What for the sponsor are the potential partners from the business world, for the sponsor are the potential partners from the sports sector with the fan base behind them. Especially the consideration of the target groups of the sponsored requires special attention due to various peculiarities in sports sponsoring.

Target Groups of the Sponsors

Firstly, from the sponsor's perspective, the various **target groups of the company** need to be considered. Consumers, companies, dealers, etc. come into question as recipients of company services, in addition, suppliers, opinion leaders, media representatives, politicians, etc. are important for communication. These various target groups are described according to different characteristics (sociodemographic characteristics, psychological characteristics, behavioral characteristics, etc.). On this basis, it is necessary to check whether and in what form sports sponsoring is suitable for target group communication.

For target group planning in sports sponsoring, the psychological characteristics and behavior of consumers are particularly relevant for decision-making. Here, their references to sports need to be examined more closely. The following criteria are relevant in order to be able to assess the **importance of sports for the target groups**:

- **Interest in sports:** Which different sports are the relevant target groups interested in?
- **Active sports behavior:** Which sports are actively pursued, which age groups are particularly involved?
- **Passive sports behavior:** Which sports events are attended and consumed in which media?
- **Sport-specific media behavior:** Which live or re-live broadcasts of sports are followed on which devices?

Information about the sports-oriented leisure and media behavior of the company-relevant target groups can be taken from their own customer analyses, market research studies, statistics, consumer typologies (e.g. from sports associations, publishers or media providers, social media statistics), etc.

Target Groups of the Sponsored

Sponsoring companies also have to deal with the target groups among the sponsored. It is necessary to carry out as precise an analysis and evaluation of sports as possible according to various characteristics. It needs to be checked which **user groups in sports** are present and addressable and whether these sports are suitable for reaching the company's target groups.

Based on this, the following **levels of user groups and target groups** can initially be distinguished for the individual sports and sports sponsoring, which will be discussed in more detail below.

- **Active participants:** Individuals who actively participate in the sporting events themselves (e.g. recreational athletes),
- **Visitors:** passive event participants (e.g. visitors to sports competitions),
- **Media users:** target groups that are indirectly reached via print or electronic media (e.g. newspaper readers, television viewers, radio listeners or internet users).

For the individual target group levels and user groups, there are analyses and **target group data** that are differentiated to varying degrees. In some cases, rough structural data and qualitative information about the target groups to be reached via sports are used. Here too, available information from market research studies by clubs and associations as well as general market research institutes such as the Allensbach advertising carrier analysis can be used. In addition, reports and statistics from various providers are available (including agencies, consulting firms, universities).

Active Participants as a Target Group in Sports Sponsoring

A first important target group of sports sponsoring are the actively **participating athletes**. In particular, the active individuals and groups involved in so-called recreational sports represent a broad target group. The attractiveness of actively participating athletes as a target group arises for sponsors primarily in the context of grassroots sports and the promotion of sports among company employees.

Figures on actively participating individuals are available, for example, in connection with the **membership of sports clubs**. As Fig. 5.3 shows, in 2021 more than 23.3 million people in Germany were members of sports clubs. While men between the ages of 41 and 60 represent the largest group of members in a sports club in absolute terms, the highest percentage is among male adolescents between the ages of 7 and 14.

A further consideration of sports (beyond the organization in clubs and associations), where there is **interest in sports** and where **sports activities** are carried out, shows that jogging, cycling, yoga, and swimming are particularly popular. In general, the variety of sports activities continues to increase. In particular, training in the gym, mountain climbing, and golfing have experienced a tremendous upswing in recent years (see Fig. 5.4).

According to surveys, there are 14.3 million people in Germany who exercise several times a week. Approximately 15.2 million Germans were physically active several times a month. Only 29% of the population do not engage in sports at all (Statista, 2021b). Further insights for companies are provided by studies that segment the sports-interested

After		Number of memberships	How many people are members of a sports club	Proportionate to the population	Population (Stat yearbook, 31.12.2020)
up to 6 years:	m.	615,170	4.61	21.68%	2,837,536
	w.	535,059	5.03	19.88%	2,691,943
7-14 years:	m.	2,293,548	1.33	74.98%	3,058,829
	w.	1,650,833	1.75	57.13%	2,889,492
15-18 years:	m.	998,416	1.57	63.60%	1,569,850
	w.	665,803	2.22	45.13%	1,475,333
19-26 years:	m.	1,498,359	2.54	39.39%	3,803,507
	w.	858,416	4.04	24.73%	3,471,212
27 - 40 years:	m.	2,297,713	3.34	29.97%	7,666,921
	w.	1,277,251	5.71	17.52%	7,290,533
41 - 60 years:	m.	3,666,674	3.23	31.00%	11,826,137
	w.	2,337,645	5.02	19.90%	11,745,900
over 60 years:	m.	2,772,957	3.70	27.02%	10,263,739
	w.	1,910,44	6.58	15.20%	12,564,099
Overall:	m.	14,142,837	2.90	34.47%	41,026,519
	w.	9,235,051	4.56	21.92%	42,128,512
Total		23,377,888	3.56	28.11%	83,155,031

Fig. 5.3 Members in sports clubs and degree of organization by gender and age groups. (*Source:* Deutscher Olympischer Sportbund, 2021, p. 12)

Strong or some interest in...	Change 2021 to 2019	Relative	Corona influence	And. 2019 to 2011	Relative	Trend in 8 yrs.	Change 2021 to 2011	Relative	Trend in 10 yrs.
Soccer	-2.52	-5.6 %	strongly negative	-1.23	-2.7 %	sinking	-3.75	-8.2 %	noticeably
Handball	0.55	2.0 %	positive	1.5	5.9 %	rising	2.05	8.0 %	rising
Basketball	-0.06	-0.4 %	stable	0.75	4.9 %	rising	0.69	4.5 %	rising
Ice hockey	-0.67	-3.3 %	negative	-0.16	-0.8 %	Almost stable	-0.83	-4.1 %	sinking
Car racing	-0.92	-3.8 %	negative	-7.6	-24.1 %	falling sharply	-8.52	-27.0%	falling sharply
Cycling	-0.25	-1.2 %	slightly negative	-1.58	-7.2 %	noticeably decreasing	-1.83	-8.4 %	noticeably decreasing
Athletics	-1.62	-5.3 %	strongly negative	-0.23	-0.7 %	Almost stable	-1.85	-6.0 %	sinking
Golf	-0.59	-8.8 %	strongly negative	-0.14	-2.0 %	sinking	-0.73	-10.7%	noticeably
Swimming	-1.93	-8.1 %	strongly negative	-4.49	-15.8 %	falling sharply	-6.42	-22.6%	falling sharply
Olympia	-12.67	-32.4 %	Very strongly negative						
Own activity - regularly or occasionally	**And. 2021 to 2019**	**Relative**	**Corona influence**	**And. 2019 to 2011**	**Relative**	**Trend in 8 yrs.**	**And. 2021 to 2011**	**Relative**	**Trend in 10 yrs.**
Playing soccer	-0.35	-2.5 %	negative	-0.54	-3.7 %	sinking	-0.89	-6.1 %	sinking
Hiking	0.09	0.2 %	stable	2.2	5.9 %	rising	2.29	6.2 %	rising
Mountaineering	-0.02	-0.2 %	stable	1.55	21.0 %	strongly	1.53	20.7%	strongly increasing
Golfing	0.25	8.7 %	strongly positive	0.42	17.0 %	strongly	0.67	27.1%	strongly increasing
Jogging	0.54	2.4 %	positive	-0.33	-1.5 %	slightly	0.21	0.9 %	stable
Walking	0.47	2.6 %	positive	1.73	10.4 %	rising	2.2	13.3%	rising
Fitness studio	0.36	1.8 %	positive	2.60	14.8 %	strongly	2.96	16.9%	strongly increasing
Yoga	0.98	10.3 %	strongly positive						
Sauna/steam bath	-0.57	-2.1 %	negative	0.82	3.2 %	rising	0.25	1.0 %	rising
Thermal bath/spa	0.08	0.2 %	stable	2.91	9.9 %	rising	2.99	10.2%	rising
Board games	-0.39	-1.0 %	Relatively stable	-0.42	-1.1 %	Relatively	-0.81	-2.0 %	sinking
Computer games	0.07	0.2 %	stable	0.6	2.1 %	rising	0.67	2.3 %	rising
Handicrafts/Crafts/Pottery	0.18	0.6 %	stable	5.66	24.2 %	strongly	5.84	25.0%	strongly increasing

Fig. 5.4 Changes in interest and personal activity in certain sports and leisure activities in the German-speaking population (age between 14 and 64 years; figures in millions). (*Source:* AWA, 2021)

population according to selected socio-demographic characteristics. Since a general interest in sports is not sufficient for the selection of possible sponsorings due to the heterogeneity of sports, further **differentiations of sports enthusiasts** are offered according to individual sports. Fig. 5.5 shows which sports are particularly enjoyed actively (AWA, 2021). In total, 30.87 million of the German-speaking population aged 14 and over go dancing more or less regularly, and almost 40 million go hiking.

Against the background of the increasing importance of different trend sports for sponsoring, various market and opinion research institutes now regularly conduct studies that specifically deal with the popularity of various trend sports, segment trend sports enthusiasts according to socio-demographic characteristics, and examine their sports activities (Wegner, 2020).

Visitors as a target group for sports sponsoring

If interesting events are held in the sports that are relevant for companies, information about the visitors to the events is of interest. The **attractiveness of visitors as a target group** results from a comparison with the target groups of sponsors. In addition, it is also worth mentioning the usual practice in sponsoring that the sponsor itself specifically invites and looks after people relevant to the company during the event (e.g., in the VIP lounge).

Rank	Sport type	Number of German-speaking people who do this frequently or occasionally (2021)
1	Hiking	39.38 Millionen
2	Dancing	30.87 Millionen
3	Jogging	22.76 Millionen
4	Visit to the gym	20.51 Millionen
5	Walking	18.80 Millionen
6	All-rounder	16.25 Millionen
7	Mountain biking	16.03 Millionen
8	Playing soccer	13.76 Millionen
9	Yoga	10.47 Millionen
10	Mountaineering	9.91 Millionen

Fig. 5.5 Top 10 sports and leisure activities in the German-speaking population (age between 14 and 64 years, figures in millions). (*Source:* AWA, 2021)

Precise descriptions of the characteristics of **event visitors** are rarely available. The information usually only mentions the number of visitors. For larger tournaments and events in the areas of golf, tennis, sailing, alpine skiing, horse riding, motorsport, athletics, etc., depending on the size of the venue and the relative importance of the event, visitor numbers between 5000 and 60,000 people are expected. The visitor potential itself is of lesser importance for the sponsoring of larger sports events; here, the sponsor will primarily calculate with coverage in the mass media. However, good visitor frequencies are a powerful argument for sponsoring commitments below top-level sports. For example, women's football has experienced enormous popularity during the 2022 European Championship and with the start of the new Bundesliga season (spectators on site and on TV), which is also noticeable in increased sponsor interest.

Media users as a target group in sports sponsoring

The media impact achieved is crucial for national and international events and larger sports events. This includes, above all, coverage on television, in print media, on the Internet, and also in the company's own media. The **attractiveness of media users as a target group for sponsors** primarily results from the reach of the media. Here, the commitment of sponsors can particularly come into its own. Social media is also becoming increasingly important in this context.

For the **analysis of media users** in sports, a variety of information is available, both from potential sponsorees and from the media providers themselves. Examples include:

- Reach and market shares of sports broadcasts, radio programs, print and social media,
- Interest in sports in the media,
- Program offerings of media providers,
- Sport-specific viewing habits.

An important basis for the analysis of media users as a target group in sports sponsoring is information about the **reach and market shares of sports broadcasts**, radio programs, print and social media. The data allows conclusions to be drawn about the presence and thus the reach of one's own company in the various media when supporting certain sports or events. Sponsors also have to adapt to changes in the behavior of their target groups. In this respect, the social media activities of the sponsorees are becoming increasingly important.

Not only for the younger target group has the presence of sponsors in social media become an important tool. It helps with improvements in fan interactions, ticket sales, and merchandising. Football still accounts for the most sponsoring money. However, the **fan behavior** and the **media usage of the fans** is changing. Stadium newspapers or perimeter advertising are receiving less and less attention. FC Bayern Munich was the quickest to recognize the potential of social media in football. They founded their own social network and created their own TV channel. The club now serves around 100 million followers through its social media channels (see Fig. 5.6). 80% of all Bundesliga followers focus solely on FC Bayern Munich and Borussia Dortmund (Sponsors, 2022a). These platforms are becoming increasingly interesting for companies because, for example, there are advertising spaces specifically reserved for sponsors on these TV channels.

Furthermore, the **interest in sports** in the media is an indicator of general media behavior during sporting events. It is particularly important to find out which media consumers primarily use to inform themselves about the topic of sports in general. A survey in 2017 already showed the trend that a large part of media users obtain current information about sporting events more via the Internet than via print media or on television (see Fig. 5.7).

The different interest of the population in various sports also influences the program offerings of media providers. The **viewing interest of the population** shows a clear order regarding the sports (see Fig. 5.8). This leads to an increasing number of broadcasts of the most popular sports moving to the (paid) pay-TV scene.

Selection of Target Groups for Sports Sponsoring

Regardless of the distinction in target groups of the sponsor and the sponsored, in the course of strategic sponsoring planning, the target groups to be reached through specific sponsoring activities need to be identified and described according to quantitative and qualitative criteria. For the **description of the target groups** of the sponsoring, demographic, socio-economic, psychographic, and behavioral criteria can be used, just like

2021/22	Facebook	Instagram	Twitter	YouTube	TikTok	Other	Total
Bayern Munich	54.54	30.30	5.80	2.41	7.30	0.09	100.44
Borussia Dortmund	15.10	15.10	3.90	0.97	5.00	0.04	40.11
Bayer 04 Leverkusen	2.85	1.60	0.39	0.05	0.54	0.01	5.43
VfL Wolfsburg	1.52	0.61	0.29	0.05	0.49	0.00	2.95
RB Leipzig	0.66	1.20	0.16	0.05	0.49	0.01	2.57
Bor. M'Gladbach	1.30	0.72	0.16	0.08	-	0.01	2.27
1. FC Cologne	0.77	0.42	0.64	0.07	0.24	0.01	2.16
Eintracht Frankfurt	0.93	0.60	0.06	0.09	0.20	0.02	1.90
VfB Stuttgart	0.54	0.35	0.53	0.05	-	0.01	1.47
Hertha BSC	0.38	0.22	0.39	0.07	0.13	0.01	1.19
All other clubs							< 1.00

Fig. 5.6 Top 10 Bundesliga clubs with the most follower numbers in 2021/2022 (figures in millions). (*Source:* Footgoal, 2022)

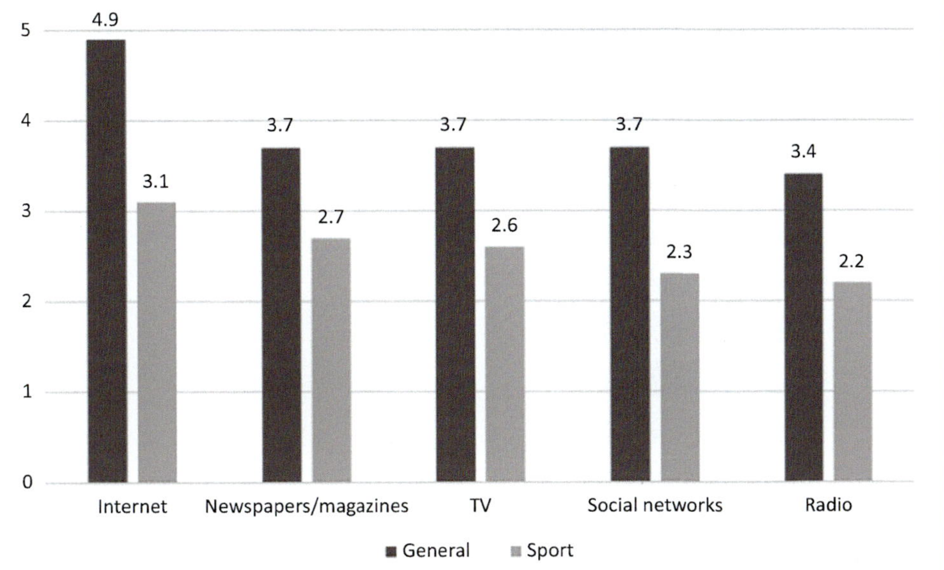

Note: n = 882. Question: "How often do you use the following media in general?", "How often do you specifically use sport in the following media? (never = 1, daily/almost daily = 5)". Mean values.

Fig. 5.7 Media usage in general and in sports. (*Source:* von Berkel, 2017, p. 36)

with other communication tools. For the target groups of sports sponsoring, the criteria that indicate the affinity of individual groups of people towards certain sports areas need to be determined as descriptive features. When looking at consumers, attempts are made to capture them through surveys or other market research methods according to as differentiated **target group characteristics** as possible. The classic criteria of target group analysis are primarily used:

- **Demographic criteria**: gender, age, marital status, household size, place of residence, etc.
- **Socio-economic criteria**: income, profession, education, social class, ownership and equipment characteristics, etc.
- **Psychological criteria**: general personality traits, attitudes, preferences, motives, utility expectations, lifestyles, etc.
- **Behavioral criteria**: brand choice, shopping location choice, purchase intensities, price behavior, usage behavior, service behavior, media usage, etc.

Market research and media agencies regularly deal with empirically examining the fans of certain sports and deriving special **fan typologies** from the data. The media usage and consumer behavior of football fans, for example, is regularly examined by the fan

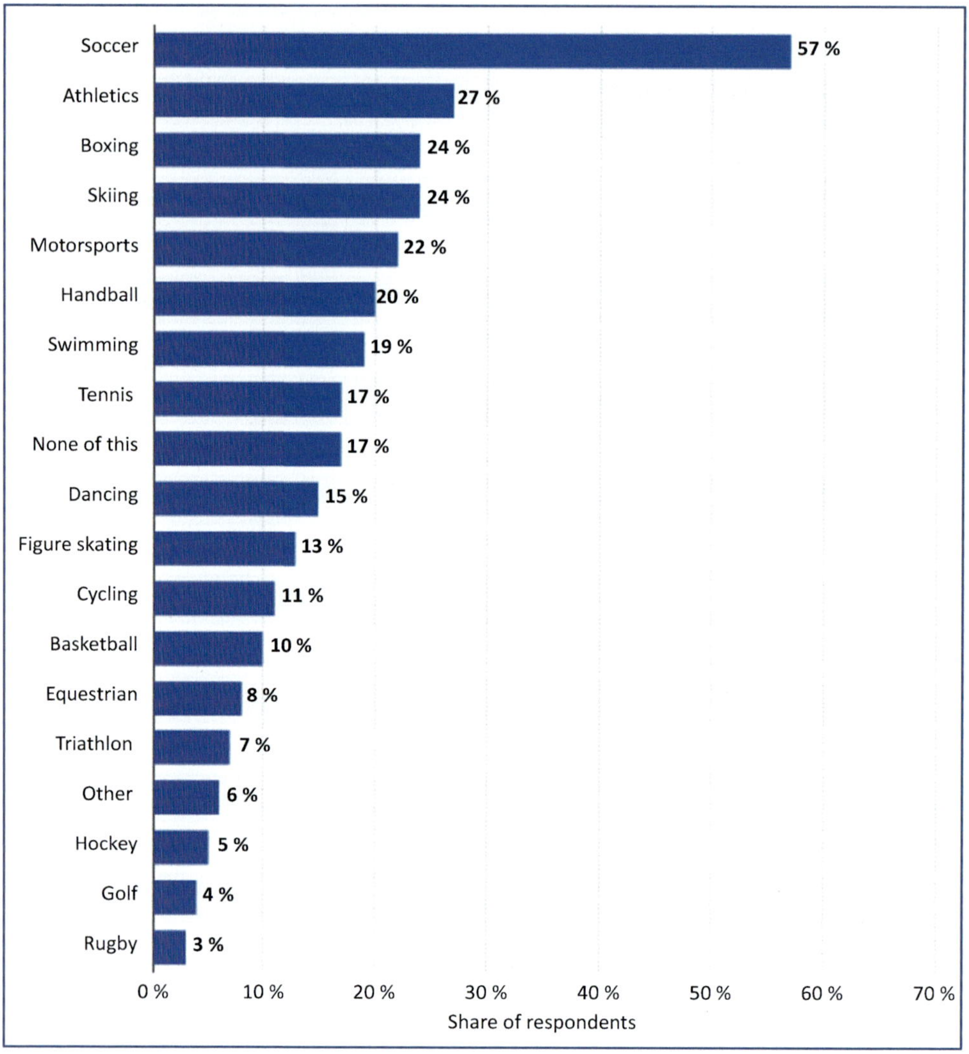

Fig. 5.8 Viewing interest in sports broadcasts on German television. (*Source:* Statista, 2016b)

typology of the communication and media agency Carat in cooperation with the research team from Resolutions from the Dentsu Aegis Network.

The Carat fan typology distinguishes between four different **fan types**, who are represented to varying degrees with their interest in the Bundesliga:

- Manic fan (9%),
- Passionate fan (32%),
- Sympathetic fan (24%),
- Affine fan (15%).

The Manic is the most intensely interested fan. The largest group is made up of the Passionate, followed by the Sympathizers and the Affine, who are only marginally interested (see Fig. 5.9). For these types, various information is available, so a **fan description** can be made, because their media usage, life areas, and product interests, as well as sponsor perceptions, also vary accordingly. 68% of the manic fans notice product advertising with a footballer or other celebrities from one of the Bundesliga clubs more. 51% of these types of fans judge such advertised products as more sympathetic, and 45% would rather buy them. Among the Sympathizers and Affine, prominent faces have a lesser impact on perception. A large majority of the manic fans (80%) notice companies positively that support their favorite club through advertising. In the affine fan group, this perception is shown by 30%, behind passionate fans (65%) and sympathizers (46%). Therefore, the advertising commitment of companies in their favorite club has a positive effect on sympathy, interest, and credibility among all four fan types. The effect of sponsoring on the preferred purchase of products is most promising among the manic fans at 55%. Among the passionate fans, 36% can be encouraged to buy. For the Sympathizers and Affine, the corresponding values are still 21% and 10%. Therefore, it can be stated: sports sponsoring meets with higher acceptance as the enthusiasm of the fans increases (Carat, 2019).

In target group planning in Sport, a specific **target group advantage in sports sponsoring** can be noted. For companies, sports sponsoring provides the opportunity to address specific target groups of the company that are difficult to reach with other communication tools (e.g., teenagers). On the other hand, sports sponsoring takes place in an attractive environment and in the leisure area of the target groups, which allows for a special emotional appeal to the target persons.

After identifying and describing possible target groups, a **target group selection** must be made in sports sponsoring. The necessity of prioritizing and narrowing down

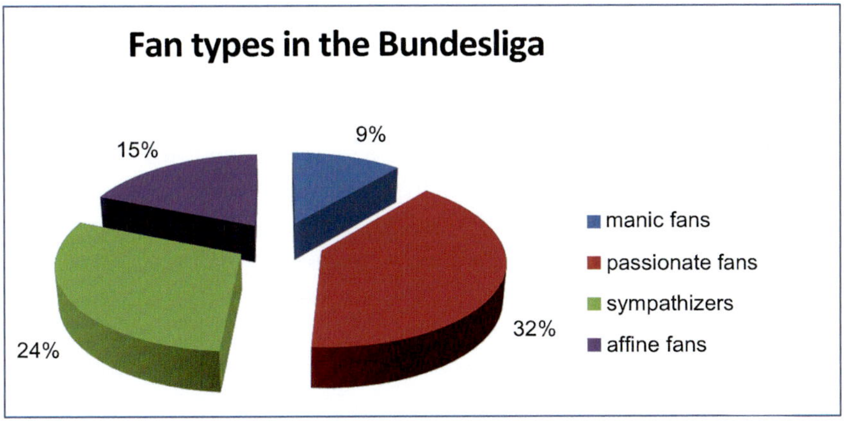

Fig. 5.9 Fan typology in the Bundesliga. (*Source:* Carat, 2019)

the target groups to be addressed with different sponsoring measures inevitably arises for companies due to internal restrictions regarding financial and personnel resources. Therefore a **prioritization of the target groups** must be made. Considerations must be made as to which target groups are to be addressed with which measures, and to what extent the measures are to be used with individual target groups.

For example, from a cost-benefit perspective, it will not be efficient to invite all customers interested in sports to an exclusive hospitality event as part of a sports event. Nor is it to be assumed that particularly significant customers can be reached by advertising in which sponsoring activities are discussed. The compilation of a catalogue that defines central **criteria for target group selection** enables a strategic selection of the target groups to be addressed and thus prevents an arbitrary selection, for example through personal relationships of those responsible.

The following economic and non-economic **criteria for prioritizing target groups** are relevant in this context (Bruhn, 2018, pp. 57 f.):

- **Sponsoring goal-related benefit of the target groups**: The sponsoring goal-related benefit reflects the degree of realization of the sponsoring goals among the various target groups. If a company pursues the increase of its popularity in the population through sports events with its sponsoring activities, a different target group prioritization must be made than when pursuing a relationship maintenance strategy. If the sponsoring primarily aims at promoting the motivation and identification of the employees within the company, internal target groups are of interest.
- **Communication needs of the target groups**: In the sense of a relationship-oriented orientation of the company's communication policy, the prioritization of the target groups requires consideration of the target group-specific communication needs. Of interest, for example, is whether the potential sponsoring target groups primarily consume and experience sports events passively through the perception of media or whether a personal dialogue with company representatives is in the foreground. According to these needs, different sponsorings in sports are suitable for reaching the target groups.
- **Integrative benefit of the target groups**: The integrative benefit results from the degree of affinity of the target group planning. This indicates to what extent the target groups of the sponsoring (e.g., the target group of a football game) simultaneously represent target groups of the company. To minimize the scattering losses of the activities in sponsoring, the highest possible degree of affinity should be aimed for.
- **Relative sales importance of the target groups**: The relative sales importance shows how important a target group is compared to other target groups for the company's sales. The more significant a target group is in terms of "key customers" (Key Accounts), the more "worthwhile" is the use of elaborate sponsoring measures (e.g., VIP events). For less significant target groups, sponsoring measures that are associated with less effort are primarily suitable (e.g., information on the homepage).

- **Importance of customer value**: In the context of relationship marketing, customer value for evaluating customers(-relationships) is of essential importance. This is the evaluated past and future contribution of a customer to achieving the monetary and non-monetary goals of the provider (Bruhn, 2022). Relationship-oriented goals also play a central role in the context of sponsoring activities, so the future customer value is particularly suitable for prioritizing target groups in sports sponsoring.
- **Costs for processing the target groups**: The costs associated with the sponsoring deployment largely depend on the respective measures or on which target groups are targeted with these measures. For example, a relatively high budget is needed for an exclusive hospitality measure or a broadcast of TV spots during attractive sports broadcasts. The target audience of media advertising is much broader than at a VIP event, so the per-person costs need to be put into perspective. Another example is the placement of print ads in different magazine genres (e.g., special interest titles such as sports magazines, leisure titles, entertainment magazines). The broader the range of magazines chosen, the more target groups can be reached with the ads to inform about the sponsoring in sports. At the same time, however, this also increases the costs of target group processing, which are lower the more specific the media selection is.

For the final selection of the target groups or the **prioritization of target groups** and measures, a mix of the criteria presented here must ultimately be used. A challenge often lies in gathering the necessary information. While the collection of the costs of sponsoring proves to be comparatively simple, determining the benefit is fraught with problems. On the one hand, the benefit of the individual sponsoring measures cannot be scaled in the same way as the costs incurred, and on the other hand, comprehensive knowledge about the effects of sponsoring is necessary, which in reality is difficult to ascertain and especially to anticipate. Therefore, indicators for the level of effects on the target groups, such as the reactions of the target groups to previous sponsoring activities, are to be sought. In the case of attractive sports, there are data from the past and other experience values that can be used. Determining the communication needs of the target groups requires the implementation of continuous target group observations and targeted target group surveys. These data are also important for the success control of companies' sports commitments.

Overall, the **information available for target group description** for the purposes of sports sponsoring can still be improved. Some structural data are available through publications by sports associations, statistical offices and television stations, as well as through media analyses of print media and market research agencies (e.g., GfK, TNS Emnid, AWA, Nielsen Sports). They are subjected to a differentiated analysis in individual cases—especially with regard to sociodemographic and psychographic criteria. In the future, it will be the task of the sports associations to collect even more extensive data for their sports, so that better planning data for their target group planning are available for potential sponsors.

5.3 Target Group Planning for the Sponsoring Recipients (Including HypoVereinsbank/Unicredit Case Study)

Just as sponsoring companies, sports actors interested in sponsoring will look for relevant target groups in the context of their sponsor selection and approach. Depending on the level of performance and charisma, several **target groups for the sponsor recipients** can be distinguished. Fig. 5.10 shows, for example, which target groups in the regional area could be potential sponsors.

Sponsors who are committed to life and people or non-profit organizations (including sports clubs) in a **municipality** include, for example, city/county utilities, city/county savings banks, and municipal real estate/construction companies. Contacting companies outside the immediate club environment is particularly suitable for sponsoring projects with a supra-regional (national or international) reach.

When looking for sponsors, a systematic approach is useful that allows the sponsored party to check which industries and which companies suit them based on certain **criteria for selecting sponsors**. Such an approach avoids high scattering losses and costs from the outset, which are usually associated with an unfiltered and unsystematic search for sponsors. This can even lead to a aimless search for sponsors permanently impairing the entire sponsoring success due to the disclosure of wrong contacts and because of the tedious conversations. One approach to making a selection and prioritizing potential

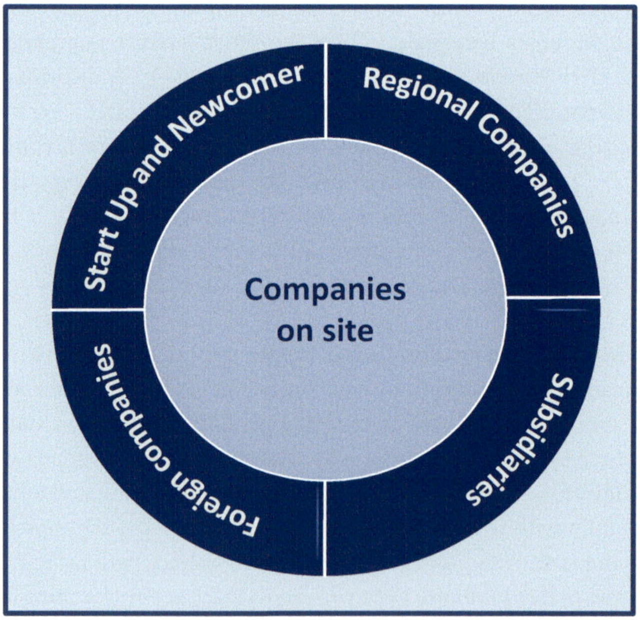

Fig. 5.10 Target groups from the perspective of sports actors interested in sponsoring

sponsors is the application of certain **"affinity criteria"**, i.e., whether the relevant candidates on the part of potential sponsors match the sponsor recipient, such as (Bruhn, 2018, pp. 153 f.):

- Product and service affinity,
- Target group affinity,
- Image affinity,
- Regional affinity.

Product and Service Affinity

Overall, four different degrees can be distinguished that describe the proximity of the products and services offered by the sponsor to the respective sports actor (cf. Drees, 1989, p. 50). The following **categories of product and service affinities** can be identified:

- First degree products/services **(Companies not so close to sport)**
  These include, for example, sports goods companies whose products are used in sports (e.g., sports shirts, tennis rackets, sports shoes, ski boots, handballs).
- Second degree products/services **(Companies close to sports)**
  This category includes companies with products that are not directly used for sports, but are used in almost direct connection with sports (sports drinks, fitness food, care products such as shower gels, medications for injuries, floor coverings, etc.).
- Third degree products/services **(Companies distant from sports)**
  These are companies with products and services that only have an indirect relationship to sports (e.g., car and airplane as means of transport to get to a sports event; bank that manages the club account; hotel where athletes stay).
- Fourth degree products/services **(Companies unrelated to sports)**
  This group includes products and services that have neither direct nor recognizable references to sports, but want to reposition themselves via image transfers.

The most credible is obviously a sponsoring commitment in sports with companies that offer first-degree products. These are mainly sports goods manufacturers, such as Adidas, Nike, Puma, and many others. Approaching such companies is generally associated with the greatest chances of success in sponsor acquisition.

Target Group Affinity

Target group affinity is a second important criterion for a first selection of potential sponsoring providers. If the target group structure of the sponsored party (e.g., the member structure in a sports club or association or the visitor structure at a sports event) matches an important customer target group of a company, this increases the likelihood of cooperation with a company willing to sponsor. These will be very interested in winning new target groups in sports or through sports or in profiling themselves in existing market segments. Therefore, a sponsor needs as detailed information as possible from the sponsored party about its target groups and the communication channels through which they can be reached.

Image Affinity

Another important criterion in the selection of partners from the business world is the image of the sports to be sponsored or the image of the sponsored party itself. This forces the sponsored party to also gain knowledge about the image of their sports and their own image. If, in addition to the appropriate image of the sports, the sponsored parties also have a positive appearance (e.g., successful, professionally managed, innovative, dynamic), this can be an important argument for the sponsor to decide to cooperate with the sponsored party.

Regional Affinity

Another selection criterion for business partners is often the local/regional factor. Not only larger companies want to document their connection with the region through a commitment to a club or a successful athlete from the same city, municipality or surrounding area. If a company addresses and feels connected to the concerns at its company location, this usually results in the development and expansion of a positive image, especially as the aspect of social and economic responsibility (CSR) is increasingly included in sponsoring considerations.

In general, it can be stated that **sponsored parties with a local sphere of influence** have the greatest chances of success with local companies. Contacting large companies that do not have their company headquarters in the same region as the sponsored parties is particularly relevant when the sponsoring project has a supra-regional (e.g., national or international) impact. Especially smaller companies often need to be "picked up" by professionally positioned sponsors. They need to be reassured about sponsoring. It is recommended to actively approach such potential partners, as the companies often do not know what, for example, a small sports club offers, and what forms of support are available in the local and regional area.

In summary, the more affinity criteria a company interested in sponsoring meets, the greater the likelihood that the sponsored party's acquisition efforts will be successful.

Figure 5.11 exemplifies which **types of sponsors** (large companies, SMEs, etc.) and **industries** (sports, beverages, credit cards, etc.) could be considered for the sponsored parties in the individual affinity areas.

Case Study HypoVereinsbank/UniCredit—Sales Driven Sponsoring

The following case study was compiled by **Raphael Schleiter**, head of sports sponsoring, and is carried out with the kind support and permission of UniCredit Bank AG/HypoVereinsbank (HVB) and FC Bayern Munich.

The **HypoVereinsbank** is part of UniCredit, a pan-European commercial bank with a targeted offering in Italy, Germany and Central and Eastern Europe. Their group-wide claim is: Empower Communities to Progress. It includes offering the best to all stakeholders and thereby unfolding the potential of their customers and their employees throughout Europe. The bank serves more than 15 million customers worldwide. They are the focus of action in all markets.

UniCredit is composed of four **core regions** and two **product areas** that offer solutions for corporate and private customers. This way, the bank can be close to its customers and use the range of services of the entire group to supply all markets with the best products. Digitization and a clear commitment to ESG principles are essential prerequisites for their services. They support those responsible in excellently accompanying their stakeholders and shaping a sustainable future for their customers, their communities and their employees.

Initial Situation

For over 20 years, sports sponsoring has been an important and relevant part of the company. HVB recognized the opportunity to generate special attention in relevant target groups through sports sponsoring and developed a **sales- and distribution-oriented sponsoring** over the years. Here, the **FC Bayern Munich** quickly became the preferred partner for Dirk Huefnagels, head of marketing at HVB, as the local proximity and

Affinities	Potential types of sponsors	Examples of typical industries
Product affinity	Well-known and recognized companies for sports equipment	Sporting goods industry (e.g. with regard to certain sports)
Service affinity	Specialist companies for ticketing, catering, transportation, etc.	Full-service companies (e.g. system catering, ticket exchanges)
Target group affinity	Companies with the same target group orientation	Beverage industry (e.g. breweries in soccer)
Image affinity	Companies in the higher quality and price segment	Luxury goods industry (e.g. luxury watches for golf and tennis)
Regional affinity	SMEs in the region, branches of large corporations	Location-related companies (including on the topics of CSR and employer branding)

Fig. 5.11 Types of sports sponsors and industry relationships according to the affinity concept

sporting successes made the two houses a good fit. And so the 2002/2003 season was the starting point of a long and still ongoing cooperation.

In addition to its role as the house bank of FC Bayern Munich, the bank launched corresponding **FC Bayern Munich Banking products** for the first time in 2003. These included account, savings and credit card offers, which are still available as products today.

In the meantime, HVB's commitment to FC Bayern Munich has been extended several times. The decisive criterion for extending the sponsoring is that it is set up as a **business case** with the goal of generating returns. This means that the declared goal is not to increase brand awareness or maximize reach, but to judge based on measurable monetary key figures, and the aforementioned criteria are merely means to an end. In addition, the long-standing good relationship of trust between the two companies also plays a significant role.

Goals and Target Groups

The two business areas **private and corporate customers** are taken into account for achieving the goals in sports sponsoring. Thus, sports sponsoring serves all relevant external customer areas.

The **private customer sector** of HVB is the focus target group of the sponsoring. For this target group, the mentioned special FC Bayern-Banking products have been launched, which are also visually recognizable as FC Bayern Munich fan products in club design, such as with the credit and other bank cards (see Fig. 5.12). The bank regularly receives **customer feedback** that they are proud to present their FC Bayern Munich card when shopping.

With the FC Bayern Munich savings card or FlexSparen, the FC Bayern Munich fan account, the FC Bayern Munich MasterCard and the FC Bayern Munich Visa Debit Card, FC Bayern Munich fans also benefit from further advantages. For example, owners of the FC Bayern Munich credit and debit cards have the opportunity to secure two tickets for a home game of FC Bayern Munich via the specially launched "**Premium Ticket Service**". This is a special customer advantage, as it has often been difficult in the past to purchase available tickets for a home game of FC Bayern Munich (see Fig. 5.13).

Further features concern better or special **conditions**, e.g. with interest rates. All products of "FC Bayern Banking" are specifically used for new customer acquisition as well as customer upselling. The sale of the products is primarily carried out through the **branches**. Taking into account the fact that there are approximately 10 million FC Bayern Munich fans nationwide, these products can also be sold well in customer discussions in regions outside of Bavaria. For example, the fan base of FC Bayern Munich in the Hamburg catchment area is larger than that of the local clubs.

In addition to the private customer sector, the sponsoring also targets **business banking customers**, segments of whom receive invitations to home games of FCB in the HVB box.

Fig. 5.12 Financial products of HVB within the context of the sponsoring with FC Bayern Munich. (*Source:* HVB/Unicredit)

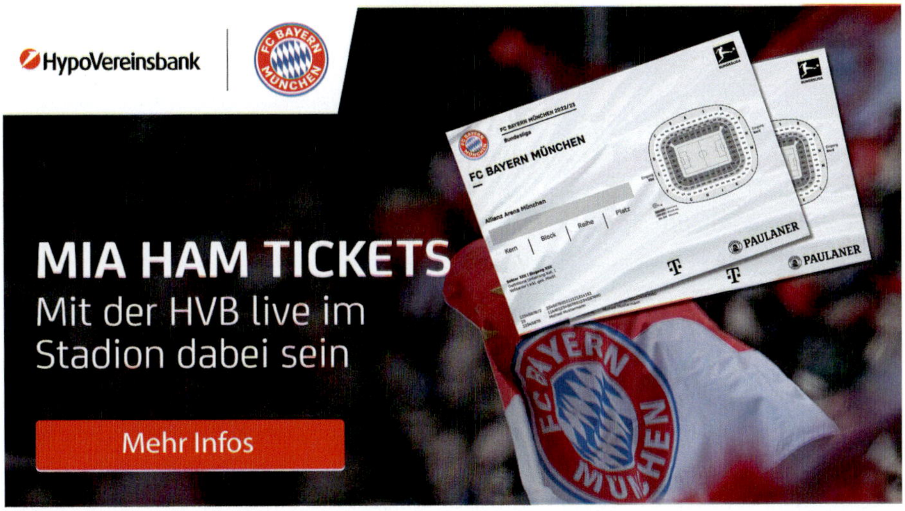

Fig. 5.13 Special advantage of HVB customers within the context of the sponsoring with FC Bayern Munich. (*Source:* HVB/Unicredit)

In addition to these external target groups and the focus on sales and customer retention, the sponsoring is also directed inwards: **Employees** have the opportunity to get the coveted home game tickets in occasional ticket campaigns or can occasionally visit training sessions of FC Bayern Munich. All these factors are important points of identification for employees with their employer. In the **Human Resources** (HR) area, there were exchange programs for young employees as well as joint events and the cooperation also proves to be a major attractiveness factor of HVB as a potential employer in personnel recruitment, e.g. in the marketing area.

Strategic Orientation and Criteria for Selection of Sponsorings

The **sales support** is the main goal of HVB sponsoring with FC Bayern Munich. Various specially developed products and services for different target groups contribute to this goal. At the same time, these are regularly adjusted and reviewed for their contribution. The large **reach of the sponsoring provider** is an important prerequisite for achieving this goal and also positively influences the acquisition of new customers.

Ultimately, however, the **sponsoring provider and own brand** must match each other. Both companies share the fact that they have Bavarian roots and their offers and services must meet the highest standards. With the international orientation that both companies also pursue, the fit is thus given.

Another important aspect of brand building is that **football is associated with emotions** that regularly connect people and create awareness—and thus offer the opportunity to emotionally charge bank products and make them even more interesting.

Activation of Sponsorings

Even though the high **level of recognition** and large **reach of FC Bayern Munich** are a guarantee of success for the declared sales goals of HVB, the bank must consistently work on activating the sponsoring. Specifically, this means that organic reach is not sufficient to activate the appropriate target groups. It is always necessary to find **communicative occasions**, use them and connect them with the appropriate offers. Examples of this are championships and titles, the start of the season or the launch of a new jersey.

In this context, a distinction is made between predictable and unpredictable **"FC Bayern Munich Moments"**. The first group includes, for example, the start of the season or the first Champions League match. These form the basis of the communicative "kick-off chain" which is conceived before the start of a season and supplemented during the season by short-term or sudden events. Each of these events is an opportunity for the bank to specifically play out its offers and services with increased awareness and thus also positively influence the sales figures, with the sponsored parties also being intensively involved (see Fig. 5.14).

Subsequently, all **communication channels (online and offline)** are activated and synchronized. The messages must be on point and the offers must fit, including the appropriate incentives such as Allianz Arena tickets or jersey vouchers.

Fig. 5.14 FC Bayern Munich Banking Promotion in FC Bayern Munich World in Weinstraße/Munich. (*Source:* HVB/Unicredit)

HVB recognized the **opportunities of digital reach** very early on and used them as part of the partnership activation. For many years now, the focus of the sponsoring has been on social media and online presence. HVB operates its own section **"FCB-Banking"** on the FC Bayern Munich website to promote its own products and services. This is complemented by various HVB banners on the fcbayern.com/de.

In addition, the offers can also be found on the **HVB.de website**. For this purpose, a decision was made to set up a shop-in-shop website and deliberately separate FCB-Banking visually from the rest of the corporate identity. The presentations are, for example, emotionally charged with pictures of players etc. and the presentation of the products also deviates from the classic web presence.

In the area of **social media**, relevant channels are consistently played with appropriate offers and suitable products and incentives are presented. Both banners and short clips are used for this purpose.

Specifically for the target group of economically interested individuals, HVB and FC Bayern Munich have set up the **LinkedIn format "Business Forum"**. Its goal is to present common economically relevant aspects of both companies to a highly qualified target group in various formats from infographics to elaborate video production (see Fig. 5.15).

In addition to online communication and online product offers, sales through customer advisors in the branches are still of high relevance. In particular, the **customer retention options** of joint visits to FC Bayern Munich home games are incentives that the advisors on site use to promote customer loyalty.

Fig. 5.15 Activation example of HVB for economically interested fans of FC Bayern Munich. (*Source:* HVB/Unicredit)

The communication of the sponsoring is part of the **overall communication of HVB** and the planning, implementation and monitoring of the activation measures is carried out by the in-house marketing department. The communication of the sponsoring-relevant activations takes place in a partnership-based interaction between HVB and FC Bayern Munich.

Success Measurement, Selected Insights and Parameters

Regular success measurement is the central element of the sponsoring. The focus is on all demonstrably made **sales**, but also **customer development indicators** (e.g., cross-selling index) or **new customer rates**. In addition, the development of reach, such as click numbers or followers, is considered. Essential for sales are also the so-called RoPo effects, i.e., that online searching and comparing, but still offline "purchasing" is done. Moreover, the success of this business case is not significantly due to a single measure, but the sum of the measures and the consistency are the decisive criterion.

HVB sees itself confirmed in the choice and implementation of its sports sponsoring by the long-term cooperation with FC Bayern Munich and the positive target values: With FC Bayern Munich, the bank has a very good sponsoring partner, which among other things also provides many options in the area of digitalization.

Outlook

In the view of HVB, sponsoring will in the future be measured much more by **criteria of social or ecological sustainability** measure. This applies equally to the sponsor, who must be aligned accordingly, and to the sponsoring recipient, who must implement appropriate measures. Accordingly, HVB's sponsoring of FC Bayern Munich will continue to evolve.

As a first initiative, HVB, together with FC Bayern Munich, the Allianz Arena, and the **Fan-Club Rollwagerl 93 e.V.**, has set up a delivery service for wheelchair users at FC Bayern Munich's home games. Here, affected fans can conveniently order their food and drinks via an app and have them delivered to their seats. The initiative has been very positively received by the target group and is to be expanded in the future. In times of tighter budgets, **co-sponsoring measures** are also likely to become more relevant in order to pool resources or achieve greater reach.

Also, from HVB's point of view, further **regulatory and compliance-related restrictions** will make sponsorings more difficult in the future, and the constantly changing behaviors of younger target groups will lead to the activities and measures being constantly further developed.

5.4 Key Points

In the context of goal and target group planning, the question from the perspective of the participants is what specific contribution sports sponsoring can make to solving the particularly communicative problem with their target groups. The following aspects should be particularly considered:

Key Points

1. From the **perspective of the sponsored**, the primary goal is to generate income from the granting of sponsoring rights, which can help improve the performance and quality of the sporting performance.
2. The starting point for the **goal formulation of the sponsors** are the existing marketing and communication goals of a company or its product brands, as well as the insights from the previous situation analysis, in order to achieve the existing overall goals of marketing and corporate communication.
3. Similar to other communication tools, the goals of sports sponsoring should be divided into **economic and psychological goals**. Cognitive, affective, and conative goals have proven to be useful for the latter.
4. In addition to **market-related goals** such as increasing awareness, image profiling, and stronger customer loyalty, **employee-related targets** are also gaining importance in sports sponsoring.
5. Goals in sports sponsoring can change over time. In addition to the short-term goals pursued by the sponsor, every company will consider which **medium and long-term goals can be achieved through sports sponsoring**.

6. Through precise goal planning, a sponsor can specify his expectations towards the sponsored and, after the implementation of the sponsorings, carry out a **control** of the degree of achievement of the sponsoring effects.
7. For **target group planning** in sports sponsoring, the psychological characteristics and behavior of consumers are of particular importance. The sponsor should take a closer look at their connections to sports.
8. Sponsoring companies have to deal with the **target groups of the sponsored**. It is recommended to carry out as precise an analysis and evaluation of the sports according to various characteristics as possible.
9. **Information on the target group description** of the sponsored is relatively easily available. Numerous structural data are available through publications by sports associations, statistical offices and television stations, through media analyses of print media and market research agencies.
10. From the perspective of the sponsored, certain **"affinity criteria"** (product and service affinity, target group affinity, image affinity, regional affinity) can be used to check whether the potential sponsors fit the sponsoring recipient.

References

A

Allensbacher Markt- und Werbeträgeranalyse (AWA 2011–2021). Allensbacher Marktanalyse Werbeträgeranalyse Codebuch.

B

Bagusat, A. (2013). *Sponsoring trends 2012*. https://www.ostfalia.de/export/sites/default/de/ispm/Blickpunkt_Sportmanagement/Sponsoring_Trends_2012.pdf. Accessed: 17. Febr. 2016.

Bassenge, C. (2000). *Dienstleister als Sponsoren. Imageprofilierung durch kommunikatives Engagement im Sport*. https://doi.org/10.1007/978-3-322-89616-2.

Bruhn, M. (2018). *Sponsoring. Systematische Planung und integrativer Einsatz* (6. Aufl.). https://doi.org/10.1007/978-3-658-13313-9.

Bruhn, M. (2022). *Relationship Marketing. Das Management von Kundenbeziehungen* (6. Aufl.). Vahlen.

C

Carat. (2019). Carat Fantypologie 2019 vom 16.08.2019. https://www.dentsu.com/de/de/carat-fantypologie-2019.

D

Deutscher Olympischer Sportbund. (2021). Bestandserhebung 2021, Fassung vom 01.10.2021, Frankfurt am Main.

Drees, N. (1989). *Sportsponsoring*. https://doi.org/10.1007/978-3-663-06737-5.

F

Footgoal. (2022). *Top 10 Bundesliga football clubs with most fans in the world in 2022*. https://footgoal.pro/top-10-bundesliga-football-clubs-with-most-fans-in-the-world-in-2022/

M

Mattmüller, R., & Oettgen, N. (2008). Der Einsatz des Sponsoring im Handelsmarketing. In A. Bagusat, C. Marwitz, & M. Vogl (Hrsg.), *Handbuch Sponsoring. Eine erfolgreiche Marketing- und Markenkommunikation* (S. 287–297). Erich Schmidt.

N

Nielsen Sports. (2015). Sponsor-Trend 2015: Status und Trends im Sponsoringmarkt in Deutschland, Österreich und Schweiz. http://www.marketing.ch/Portals/0/Wissen/Allgemein/Repucom%20Insights_Sponsor-Trend%202015_DACH_SFS.pdf. Accessed: 17. Febr. 2016.

Nielsen Sports. (2016). Sponsor-Trend 2016: Status und Trends im Sponsoringmarkt in Deutschland, Österreich und Schweiz.

Nielsen Sports. (2018a). Sponsor-Trend 2018: Status und Trends im Sponsoringmarkt in Deutschland, Österreich und Schweiz.

Nielsen Sports. (2022). Sportmarketing-Trends 2022: So verändern Fans das Sportbusiness, Köln.

Nufer, G., & Bühler, A. (2015). Wie Erfolg in der Formel 1 die Marke Mercedes pusht. Nachspielzeit – die Schriftenreihe des Deutschen Instituts für Sportmarketing, herausgegeben von Gerd Nufer & André Bühler, Nr. 2015–2.

R

Rohlmann, P. (2021). Red Bull und Fußball – Eine Analyse der Fußballaktivitäten des Red Bull Konzerns (Red Bull Global Soccer), Rheine/St. Gallen.

S

Sponsors. (2022b). Virtuelle Werbung: Zusatzerlöse von 100 Millionen Euro für die Bundesliga? Beirag vom 15.09.2022. https://www.sponsors.de/news/themen/virtuelle-werbung-zusatzerloese-von-100-millionen-euro-fuer-die-bundesliga.

Statista. (2016b). Welche Sportarten schauen Sie gerne im Fernsehen? https://de.statista.com/statistik/daten/studie/235067/umfrage/die-beliebtesten-sportarten-im-tv/.

Statista. (2021b). Bevölkerung in Deutschland nach Häufigkeit des Sporttreibens in der Freizeit von 2017 bis 2021. https://de.statista.com/statistik/daten/studie/171911/umfrage/haeufigkeit-sport-treiben-in-der-freizeit/

V

von Berkel, M. (2017). „The more you know, the more you enjoy“? – Empirische Überprüfung von Netzwerkeffekten in medialen Sportangeboten. *Journal für Sportkommunikation und Mediensport, 2*(1), 31–45. https://doi.org/10.25968/JSkMs.2017.1.31-45

W

Wegner, R. (2020). Zur Genese und Entwicklung von Trendsportarten angesichts wirtschaftlicher Paradigmenwechsel und digitaler Informationsmöglichkeiten, Dissertation der Technischen Universität Kaiserslautern.

Y

YouGov. (2021). Finanzdienstleister-Studie: Sport-Sponsoring zahlt schon nach kurzer Zeit auf das Markenimage ein, Beitrag vom 04.05.2021. https://yougov.de/news/2021/05/04/finanzdienstleister-studie-sport-sponsoring-zahlt-/.

6 Strategic Orientation of Sports Sponsoring

Contents

Abstract

Companies face the challenge of strategically using sponsoring commitments to achieve their communicative targets. The individual elements and types of a sponsoring strategy characterize the communicative problem that the companies face. On the other hand, the specific communication objectives and the target groups to be addressed must be taken into account in strategy development. The chapter presents both the strategy dimensions and the strategy types and forms of sports sponsoring. They form the basis for formulating guidelines for sports sponsoring, in which the cornerstones of the sports sponsoring strategy are written down and bindingly recorded. In addition to the case studies from the Bell Food Group, DKB, Penny and Warsteiner, other sponsoring examples from Rakuten, Homeday, regional banks, Bitburger, BMW, Lotto, Melitta, Roche and the Stadtwerke Tübingen are also discussed.

M. Bruhn and P. Rohlmann, *Sports Sponsoring*,
https://doi.org/10.1007/978-3-658-44171-5_6

6.1 Dimensions of Sports Sponsoring Strategy

A first **strategic fundamental decision** of a company in sports sponsoring is the decision for or against a sponsoring commitment. It must be examined to what extent the communication instrument sponsoring is integrated into the company's, marketing or brand strategy, and whether it is compatible with the image of the company and the products or services, but also with the corporate culture. The strategic fundamental decisions are therefore always to be made on the basis of the brand identity and the content associated with the concepts derived from it. Only on the basis of these conceptual considerations are the product- and brand-specific reasons for a sponsoring commitment in sports given.

The sponsoring strategy targeted by a company includes various content focuses in individual dimensions depending on the communication objectives and numerous situational influencing factors. The content **determination of the sponsoring strategy** represents a complex planning problem in which several decisions have to be made simultaneously. When fixing the content of the sponsoring strategy, the framework conditions for the selection of sponsorings are determined, with orientation towards various elements. The **dimensions of a sponsoring strategy** are illustrated in Fig. 6.1. They include the following seven dimensions (Bruhn, 2018, p. 59):

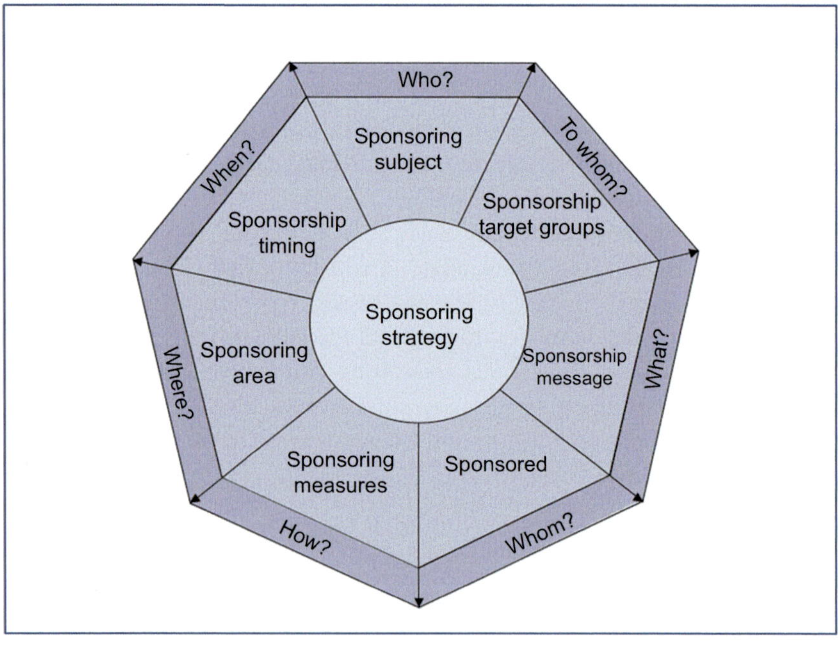

Fig. 6.1 Dimensions of a sponsoring strategy. (*Source:* Bruhn, 2018, p. 59)

- **Sponsoring subject**: In a first step, the subject appearing as a sponsor in public is determined. The sponsoring subject either appears in the form of a whole company, a product line or individual product brands or service programs in the communicative focus of a sponsoring commitment in sports.
- **Sponsoring target groups:** In a further step, the target groups to be addressed by the company are determined (e.g., sports-interested men aged between 30 and 50 years, key customers, opinion leaders). Basically, all target groups of corporate and marketing communication are eligible for sports sponsoring, i.e., both external target groups such as customers, suppliers and investors, as well as employees as an internal target group.
- **Sponsoring message:** Subsequently, the message to be communicated is determined. For example, in the form of a name, logo, slogan or emblem. When determining the sponsoring message, it should be noted that the content and design of the message are not only subject to company-specific restrictions, but also to the framework conditions in sports sponsoring (e.g., advertising on boards and jerseys, restrictions on rights exploitation).
- **sponsored party:** The determination of the sponsored party is made in terms of content, personnel and time (e.g., sponsoring of an athlete, a sports team or sports event for three years).
- **Sponsoring measures:** Finally, the various instruments in the form of advertising media and means of commitment in sports sponsoring are determined (e.g., advertising in the environment, jersey advertising, merchandising items, sales promotion measures such as distribution of product samples, personal invitations to the VIP lounge, etc.).
- **Sponsoring area:** With the decision on the sponsoring area, a company determines whether it primarily aligns its sponsoring activities with local, regional, national or international sports.
- **Sponsoring timing:** Here, a decision has to be made about the temporal allocation of the sponsoring activity. The sponsoring timing, i.e., the determination of the time frame and the intensity of the use of individual measures, is closely linked to the content of the message. For example, a comprehensive image campaign requires a different timing than measures to introduce a new product. The duration of a commitment in sports sponsoring must therefore be contractually fixed.

Example: Sponsoring Strategy of Rakuten

As an example of a successful strategy in sports sponsoring, the Japanese online retailer **Rakuten** can be cited. Rakuten was a no-name in all foreign markets until 2017, before the internet company entered partnerships in sports. The Japanese internet corporation maintains numerous sponsorings in sports, including with the Spanish football club FC Barcelona (2017–2022) as a jersey sponsor, as well as with the Golden State Warriors (2017–2023) from the American National Basketball League (see Fig. 6.2). According to calculations, Rakuten receives twice as much

Fig. 6.2 Successful sponsoring strategy using the example of Rakuten. (*Source:* Rakuten)

advertising performance from the Golden State Warriors as the corporation pays for the kit sponsoring (20 million USD per year). Rakuten's commitment is a vivid example of successful sponsoring on a "large" sports stage. In particular, the consideration of the cost-benefit ratio is important, as this question is at the forefront for potential sponsors.

There are analyses that allow a comparison with other forms of advertising, such as: How much would it cost to transfer the visibility of the brand from sponsoring to advertising on TV or on the internet? This involves logo presence versus spot bookings. According to this, Rakuten's kit sponsoring with the NBA series champion Golden State Warriors is worth 40 million USD per year, determined by the data analysis agency GumGumSports. The amount is composed as follows: 19 million USD annually for the images and videos with the Golden State Warriors on social networks, with the lion's share resulting from postings on external pages in the form of sports news. Approximately 21 million USD is the team's presence on television. According to this evaluation, this would be a doubling of the sponsoring amount that Rakuten pays to the Golden State Warriors to be allowed to attach a (rather small) logo to their game jerseys. For Rakuten, the investment has likely paid off so far. Rakuten recently announced that its brand awareness in the USA has increased by about 47% since the partnership with the Warriors. Similar to the case of FC Barcelona regarding the European markets, Rakuten has high expectations for the sponsoring of the Golden State Warriors in the USA. The commitment has also opened the doors to the NBA for the Japanese. Games of the US basketball league can be seen live on Rakuten TV in Japan—a significant unique selling point for the streaming service. ◄

6.2 Types of Strategies in Sports Sponsoring

The desired sponsoring goals are achieved through coordination with the company's communication strategy. The **strategy of sports sponsoring** must first be aligned with the basic communicative task of the company. It is necessary to analyze which communicative problem the company has to solve in the medium term and to what extent the use of sports sponsoring contributes to the solution of the problem. This can refer to the updating of a brand, the introduction of a new product with certain image dimensions, the differentiated approach to customer segments, profiling against the competition, etc.

According to the **Affinity Concept** (Waite, 1979; Bruhn, 2019), different connection lines are conceivable, which—as shown in Fig. 6.3—can serve as the basis for strategy finding. A rough distinction can be made between the following **types of strategies in sports sponsoring** (Bruhn, 2019, pp. 226 ff.):

- A prerequisite for pursuing a **performance profiling strategy** is the existence of a relationship between the sponsor's performance and the situation of the sponsored party. In sports, such a connection is given, for example, in a partnership between a manufacturer of sports shoes and the sponsoring of a football team. A similar constellation exists when, for example, a credit card company is involved in organizing a global sports event, and its credit card can then be used worldwide as a means of payment.
- An **awareness strategy** aims to increase the awareness and acceptance of products or brands among customers and other market participants. This applies to existing products or brands as well as to new products. Consequently, this strategy focuses

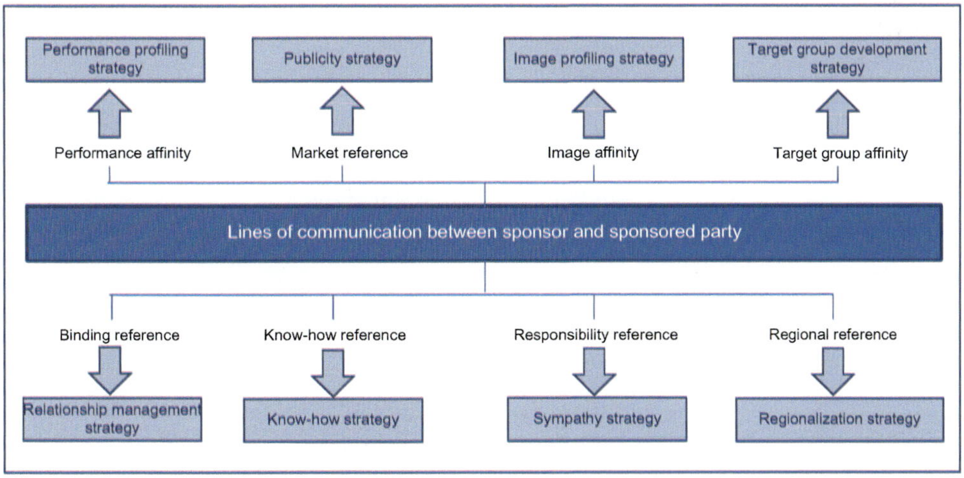

Fig. 6.3 Types of strategies in sports sponsoring based on the Affinity Concept. (*Source:* Adapted from Bruhn, 2019, p. 226)

on the pure penetration of the product, company or brand name. For this, attractive sports such as football, motorsport, tennis, etc. are particularly suitable. This refers, for example, to the updating of a brand, which can be achieved through the combined use of several communication instruments, including sports sponsoring activities.

Example: Awareness strategy of Homeday

The goal of the company **Homeday** in 2020 was to quickly increase its brand awareness. This was the challenge faced by the online real estate agent Homeday from Berlin. As a young company that had not long outgrown its start-up status, Homeday set itself an ambitious goal: The awareness values should increase significantly in as short a time as possible in order to catch up with the industry leaders, e.g. Engel & Völkers. Against this background, the extraordinary sponsoring situation at the football Bundesliga club Hertha BSC at the end of 2020 turned out to be a stroke of luck for all involved: Because the main sponsoring on the jersey was still available due to the pandemic, Homeday had the opportunity to conclude one of the most valuable partnerships in the first league of German football with the club during the already ongoing Bundesliga season 2020/2021. Within just five months, Homeday has significantly reduced the gap to the market-leading competition. This is particularly true among football enthusiasts and Hertha fans (see Fig. 6.4). ◄

- An **image profiling strategy** targets specific image dimensions of a brand or company that are realized or consolidated in the consciousness of the target groups with the help of the sponsored promotion areas. The profiling strategy can refer to various image dimensions of a brand. They are derived from the Unique Selling Proposition (USP) of the brand and can include factors such as sustainability, service, price, quality features, etc. For example, the health insurance company AOK supports the

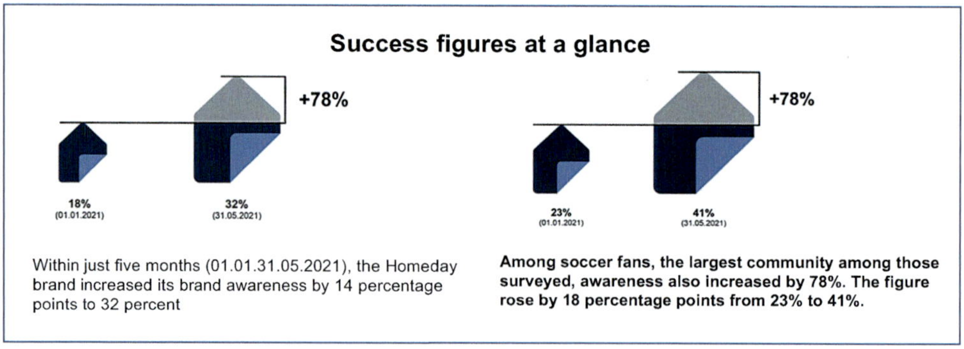

Fig. 6.4 Success example Homeday and Hertha BSC. (*Source:* Angermair, 2021)

German Handball Federation and emphasizes with this partnership the goal of inspiring its insured persons to do more sports and exercise (AOK.de, 2016). Health insurance companies spend a total of 200 million EUR annually on sponsoring, a large part of it for professional sports.

Example: Image strategy of regional banking institutions

Many major banks are not doing as planned because international expansion intentions are not working as designed and many cost-cutting programs are being implemented. Cost reduction through branch closures and staff layoffs are the order of the day and many financial resources are needed for the necessary digitization. This also affects the programs to streamline sports sponsoring.

In return, new sponsor names are appearing in sports, e.g. smaller, more regionally active banks, which support their local sports heroes and thus strengthen their image and position around the location. Especially since the trust in the banking industry was severely shaken during the financial crisis in 2008. Unencumbered banks, as described above, are of course at an advantage. If they show themselves as promoters of sports on site, they strengthen their regional identity and can, if the sponsorings are also well implemented, improve their image and increase their awareness. ◀

Numerous such partnerships have been observed in recent years. For example, the Märkische Bank from the North Rhine-Westphalian Hagen has extended its main sponsoring with the DEL club Iserlohn Roosters tdespite the shock phase caused by Corona. The cooperation has been running for 20 years and is now valid until 2024.

The cooperation includes logos on the shoulder and back of the player jerseys. Similarly, the BB Bank, until 1999 Baden Civil Servants Bank, hopes for a large media presence from summer 2020 thanks to the naming rights to the newly built football stadium in Karlsruhe. Although the Zweitligist Karlsruher SC has been playing in the BB Bank Wildpark since the start of the 2020/2021 season, this is still the old sports facility. The reopening is expected for summer 2023.

- A **target group development strategy** focuses on specific target groups, such as teenagers, whose development for a product or brand is additionally sought. Currently, many companies are trying to reach the predominantly young group of people in e-sports through sponsoring. On average, e-sports viewers are young, well-educated, grew up with digital media, value-oriented, and have a rather high income. It is not the younger Generation Z (16 to 25 years) that is most strongly represented among e-sports viewers, but the Millennials (26 to 40 years) (Deloitte, 2021).

Example: Target group development strategy of BMW

The car manufacturer **BMW** has also made intensive efforts to win over specific target groups through targeted sponsoring strategies. In recent years, BMW has been increasingly committed to running sports. The company is the sponsor of various running marathons and city runs. Studies show that one in four BMW customers is an active runner. With its sponsoring commitment in running sports, the company therefore specifically wants to address those groups who participate in running sports or show interest in running events (Seibert & Wiese, 2013). ◄

- A **relationship maintenance strategy** focuses on building and maintaining contacts and relationships with relevant target groups with the goal of increasing the quality of relationships and customer loyalty. The relationship maintenance strategy can be observed particularly at sports events, where particularly important customers are invited and entertained by the sponsor in VIP rooms.

Example: Relationship maintenance strategy of Bitburger

For this strategy, the brewery **Bitburger** can be used as an example—representative for the brewing industry. From 1992 to 2018, Bitburger was a sponsor of the German Football Association, in order to bind its most important target group, middle-aged men, to itself through this partnership. Regardless of gender, about 65% of 30- to 59-year-olds are interested in this ball sport, with men it is even over 80%. Of those who regularly consume alcoholic beverages, almost 70% are interested in football (Nufer & Rützel, 2016, p. 5). The brewery group traditionally accompanied its commitment with massive advertising campaigns also during the TV broadcasts. In addition, an attractive offer for business customers (especially catering and food companies) ensured that this target group could access the international matches in the form of hospitalities and special ticket programs. ◄

- A **knowledge-based strategy** is based on the fact that some companies, due to their market activities, have special knowledge or unique internal capabilities to promote certain sponsoring areas. Thus, the resources or potentials available in the company, i.e., personnel, products, or services, are used to actively support specific sports-related issues. For example, consider computer companies that provide hardware and software for sports competitions. With their sponsoring commitments, companies demonstrate their special knowledge and skills to the public, making them known to a wider audience and distinguishing themselves from the competition.
- Pursuing a **sympathy strategy** in sponsoring requires a responsibility relationship between a company and the sponsoring object. This is associated with the ethical obligation of the company to address social or ecological problems and contribute to their solution. This can be seen, for example, in sports partnerships of energy companies that produce green electricity, or in connection with environmental service providers who take care of closed-loop recycling in sports. Compared to the strategy options presented so far, the credibility of the company is of particular importance in the sympathy strategy to fulfill an assumed responsibility. For the sponsoring company, it is necessary to credibly demonstrate to the target groups which factual and

personal motives are important for its commitment. As credibility increases, the likelihood that companies can build sympathy with their commitments and thus achieve positive communicative effects increases. However, if there is a lack of "fit" between sponsoring and brand or product or service, reactions may be expected from the public and the company's target groups.

- When pursuing a **regionalization strategy**, the central prerequisite is that a regional connection between the sponsor and the sponsored party is recognizable. For example, a company can support a regional sports club or contribute to solving regional or local issues with its sponsoring commitment, e.g., promoting sports with toddlers or people with disabilities. This approach is particularly interesting for companies that aim to integrate into their geographical-social environment, for example, to strengthen acceptance of their business policy in the region or to improve the conditions for hiring new employees. A regionalization strategy is also of interest to companies that have regional brands and want to anchor them more firmly in consumers' consciousness.

In Fig. 6.5, the different types of strategies are summarized, exemplifying which goals are pursued, how they are designed, and which examples can be used as a reference.

Strategy types	Goals	Design	Examples
Performance profiling	Proof of competence and reputation for the sponsor's performance	Credible performance - accountability for the sponsored party's performance	Sports outfitter
Announcement	Perception, awareness and acceptance	Massive sponsorship with high reach and intensive presence	Homeday
Image profiling	Image enhancement, credibility, positive customer attitude	Sponsorship design more as a sports promoter than as use for commercial purposes	Regional banks
Target group development	Concentration on market participants with certain characteristics, customer acquisition	Concentrated use of funds in the living and sports environment of said groups	BMW
Relationship management	Establishing and expanding contacts, increased customer loyalty	Supporting the target groups in their private environment through presence and consumer offers	Bitburger Brewery
Know-how	Proof of special know-how for sports performance	Advertise the majority of sponsorship as a benefit in kind for sports betting such as timekeeping, result display, etc.	Computer companies/watch manufacturers
Sympathy	Identification and acceptance of fundamental responsibility between sponsor and sponsored party	Sponsorship as a contribution to the better fulfillment of social and climate policy goals of the sponsored party	Energy companies, environmental and climate service providers
Regionalization	Raising awareness of a regional connection between sponsor and sponsored party	Sponsorship contribution to solving regional or local issues through sport (popular, youth, disabled sport)	Companies with a strong local or regional focus such as municipal utilities, savings banks, etc.

Fig. 6.5 Summary presentation of different strategy types in sports sponsoring

6.3 Forms of Strategies in Sports Sponsoring (Incl. Bell Food Group Case Study)

Every company interested in sponsoring will consider, as part of its strategic considerations, what focus it wants to place on sports sponsoring and which commitment comes closest to its targets. This does not always have to be the generally usual path via classic sponsoring in elite sports, but there are also other forms such as niche and regional sponsoring. Such possibilities can be differentiated according to criteria such as scope (e.g., regional, supra-regional, national, international), performance level (hobby sports, mass sports, professional sports, top sports), effort (large or small, over- or under-proportional) as well as restrictions (e.g., legal or health-related) (see Fig. 6.6).

The following will show the possibilities and **forms of appearance** in the following areas:

- Mainstream sponsoring,
- Niche sponsoring,
- Regional sponsoring.

Mainstream Sponsoring

In sports sponsoring, the so-called **mainstream engagement** is usually at the forefront, which refers to the commonand predominantly practiced sponsoring. It mainly refers to professional or media sports and especially to the sports popular among the

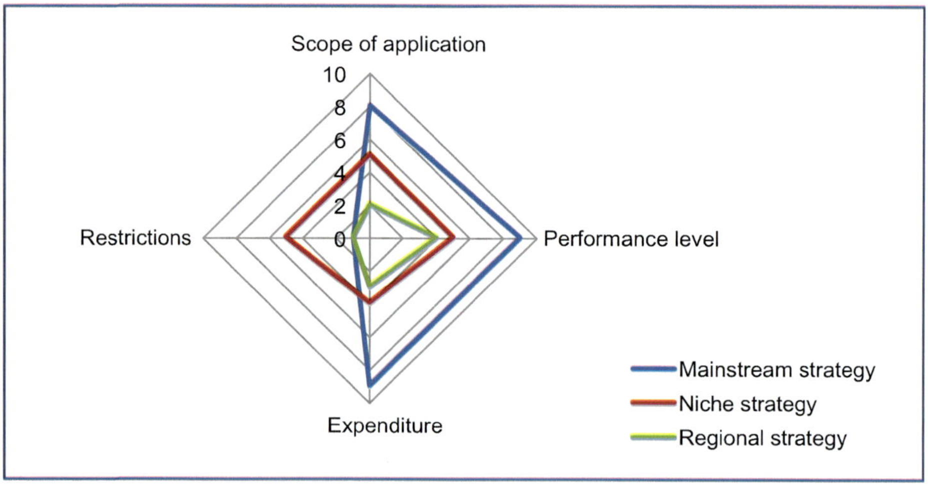

Fig. 6.6 Criteria for describing strategies in sports sponsoring (exemplary representation)

population, such as football, which absorbs more than 70% of the funds from German companies. Such an engagement is generally associated with a considerable amount of time and money and refers to at least regional or national presence. This form of sports sponsoring also includes the so-called top clubs, in which mainly large companies with high communication budgets are involved. These companies often pursue strategies that are oriented across sports and countries and use sports sponsoring as a marketing tool very professionally, as documented in Fig. 6.5. Even in a multi-year comparison, little changes in the particularly active companies in sports sponsoring. Six out of ten companies that were also in the top 10 a few years ago are again among the "big spenders" (Fig. 6.7).

Niche Sponsoring

Sports sponsoring holds an important position in many companies' corporate communication. Meanwhile, over half of the 5000 largest German companies are active in sports sponsoring. A crucial preliminary decision for successful sponsoring is the decision about the sports and the sports sector. In contrast to mainstream sponsoring, **niche sponsoring**can also be considered, which refers to grassroots and youth sports, fringe sports (e.g., table tennis or disabled sports), trend sports, etc. (see Fig. 6.8).

Despite the initially apparent attractiveness in football, sometimes excessively high, sometimes even extreme prices are offered for inferior sponsoring rights or second-rate advertising placements. This is compounded by the enormous **competition on the football sponsoring platform**. In addition to the numerous logo accumulations on second and third bands, sponsors compete with placements in online media and advertising brands on the second screen. The result is logo or advertising graveyards, which are no

rank	2014/15	Sportsponsorships
1	Volkswagen	140.0
2	Sparkassen	91.0
3	Mercedes Benz	85.0
4	adidas	85.0
5	Deutsche Telekom	50.0
6	Bayer AG	39.0
7	BMW	30.0
8	Allianz	21.0
9	Coca-Cola	19.0
10	Nike	19.0
	Top 10	**579.0**

rank	2020/21	Sportsponsorships
1	adidas	160.0
2	Volkswagen	140.0
3	AUDI	120.0
4	Sparkassen	75.0
4	Red Bull	75.0
6	Deutsche Telekom	60.0
7	Puma	42.5
8	Porsche	32.5
8	BMW	32.5
8	Bayer AG	32.5
	Top 10	**770.0**

Fig. 6.7 Top 10 of the major sports sponsors in Germany over time (estimated amounts in million EUR). (*Source:* Nielsen Sports, 2021; Nielsen & Repucom, 2015)

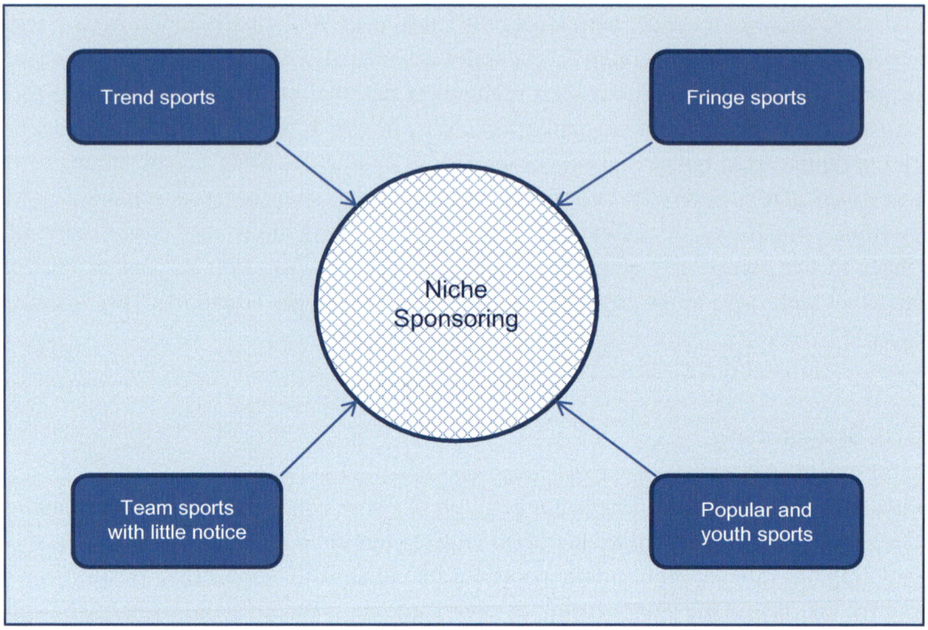

Fig. 6.8 Niche sponsoring in sports

longer to be surpassed in confusion and therefore the benefit for the sponsors is questionable. Nevertheless, companies with an interest in **sponsoring in the niche sector**have numerous opportunities for a promising sports sponsoring with a good price-performance ratio.

High prices in the sponsoring market reflect a high demand for attractive target objects. Precisely for this reason, it is worthwhile for creative and return-oriented sponsors to look at other sports than football, towards **sports in the niche sector**, which are not in the public eye and rather lead a niche existence. This applies equally from large corporations to smaller craft businesses. Here, there is often astonishing advertising potential that is (still) neglected by many potential sponsors. The quantitative reach cannot keep up with that of football. However, if the right products are placed in the right target group with an ideal "fit", a much higher return-on-sponsoring-investment can be expected for a rather low budget, while even with a high reach, as is the case in football, the scatter loss for the rights holder is not always in a reasonable proportion to the sponsoring effort.

Strong commitments to still growing sports and in the immediate vicinity of a company are ideal prerequisites for using sponsoring specifically for one's own communication. This is about the sports-related **presentation of the brand** and not about cheap cost per thousand contact prices. In this way, stories can be created for PR work, which ideally create additional added value through high media coverage.

On various digital platforms, companies interested in sponsoring can identify from an extensive **database** of thousands of athletes or sports clubs those advertising partners that exactly match their profile and fit into their budget (Sponsor-Service, 2022; Sponsors, 2022c).

Niche sponsoring usually deals with narrower target groups. This can be less of a disadvantage and more of an advantage, because with appropriate better information about the scope and type of the target group or fans, hardly any scatter losses occur. After all, a niche sponsor is not one of many, but can get more involved and finds a stronger **co-design and development opportunity** with the sponsored. This often results in decisive competitive advantages for the sponsoring company, as it can benefit from the "first mover" effect in a developing environment and growing market.

The interesting **niche fields** are usually sports of (actual or suspected) limited commercial value, both for the sports units active there and for potential sponsors. However, many examples show how "new sports business markets" can be gradually built up in the interaction of media, sponsors, and sports participants. Several winter sports such as ski jumping (see Milka and Vierschanzentournee) and biathlon (Viessmann has been a sponsor in biathlon for decades, as well as in luge and ski jumping) are included, as are sports like beach volleyball. Other examples of successful niche sponsoring are provided by companies like the insurance giant Allianz (since 2006 National Sponsor of the German Disabled Sports Association and Team Germany Paralympics) or the Barmer Health Insurance (for several years health partner of the first and second basketball Bundesliga). Niche sponsoring generally requires more preliminary considerations and creativity in terms of implementation. However, the sponsor often reaps the return for his commitment more clearly and emphatically.

Regional Sponsoring

In many cases—and this is especially true in the field of Bread and youth sports—the focus is more on **local and regional sports sponsoring**. Sponsors who are committed to the common good, the people or non-profit organizations (including sports clubs) in a municipality, include, for example, city/county utilities, city/county savings banks and municipal real estate/construction companies. Contacting companies outside the immediate environment of a sports actor is instead considered for sponsoring projects with a supra-regional (national or international) reach. A regionally limited sponsoring in sports is capable of placing messages precisely to the target group and minimizing scatter losses. Such commitments are often underestimated. However, their impact can be controlled as precisely as in few other marketing disciplines.

Sponsoring is also established and popular in the **communication mix of small and medium-sized enterprises**. Contacting selected target groups without interference in a manageable emotional environment allows for a usually higher contact quality compared to traditional communication tools. Positive side effects such as national radiation beyond the region are also not excluded and can be consciously included depending on the design of a partnership.

Furthermore, it can be observed that smaller companies, due to their sales market, are more regionally oriented. Especially in sports sponsoring with a regional character, aspects of **local loyalty** and internal **networking with the staff** play a major role. For sponsors who are involved in local or regional sports, the focus of the commitment is less on increasing awareness or image transfer. For locally and regionally active companies, in most cases, it is about **social commitment** and making a contribution to the community for the people at the company's location, i.e., the motive for promotion is primary here. Especially for small and medium-sized enterprises, it is more or less part of social responsibility to contribute to sports or other topics in the region. Broad and youth sports in particular benefit from such commitment and are largely dependent on it. Often, sponsoring is practiced in connection with the current topic of civic or societal commitment of companies—also known as Corporate Social Responsibility (CSR)—, which is why it is occasionally referred to as **Responsible sponsoring** (S20, 2021).

Regional (sports-)sponsoring offers numerous opportunities. The following arguments are particularly worth mentioning as **advantages of regional sponsoring**:

- It is concrete, personally tangible and can be actively influenced by the sponsor.
- It happens in the immediate neighborhood and shows that the company also wants to commit itself as a "good neighbor".
- It takes place in front of the employees, gives them the opportunity to participate and therefore has a strong internal effect.
- It improves the relationship with the people with whom the regional sponsor deals with on a daily basis, be it customers, local media, politicians or representatives of authorities.
- It supports the sponsors in recruiting employees for the company.

From a company's perspective, the **credibility of the sponsoring** is the most important success factor. A collaboration is perceived by the public as credible and positively evaluated, especially when a sports club and its sponsor match well. This is the case, for example, when the target groups and products of the sponsor as well as its image match the sports club, the sponsor can prove a regional reference to the sports club, and a medium to long-term cooperation is agreed.

Example: Füchse Berlin and Lotto Berlin

The partnership with Füchse Berlin is one of the building blocks in the strategy of **Lotto Berlin** to position itself as the number 1 of digital lottery games in the Berlin and Brandenburg region and to keep the nationwide competition at a distance (Dircks, 2022). To achieve this goal, the cooperation with the Handball Bundesliga team was specifically aligned with digital advertising measures for the 2021/2022 season. The target group rooted in the city and the region is to be reached less through TV-relevant measures in the future, but rather directly via the channels of Füchse Berlin. This includes SEO content in the form of a Lotto blog, which was integrated on the club homepage, as well as the digital extension of the content via the social media channels. ◀

Studies on regional sponsoring
Regional sports sponsoring has a positive resonance with the end customer, as the fan base of the "regional sports heroes" is quite comparable to that in "large" sponsoring. This is the conclusion of a **survey on regional sponsoring** by the market research institute Ipsos Germany in cooperation with the European Sponsoring Exchange ESB from 2002 (Ipsos Germany/ESB, 2002). In this survey, 1000 Germans aged 14 and over were asked about their interest in regional sports and their opinion on regional sponsors. The result showed that seven out of ten respondents considered regional sports sponsoring to be a good marketing action by companies, which is "better than any advertising". Moreover, four out of ten Germans say they would prefer a regional sports sponsor over other companies, with this figure even reaching 50% among sports enthusiasts. Last but not least, one in three working people and even 42% of all trainees would like to work for a sponsor.

The study is evidence that traditional advertising is losing acceptance and that **regional sponsoring is gaining importance**. Football, for example, is also the most popular sport among the regional population. According to IPSOS, almost half (44%) of people expressed their interest in football events in their vicinity, a figure that is constantly increasing compared to previous years. Further results show that 84% of medium-sized businesses commit to sponsoring. A total of 74% of these are involved in sports, one in ten (11%) is engaged in cultural sponsoring, and 15% are involved in social, environmental, etc. The multiple nominations also show the broader commitment in medium-sized businesses, which is also an expression of social responsibility on site. As for the use of money for individual sports, 26% went to the then regional football league (now 3rd league), 21% to handball, 20% to equestrian sports, and 17% to trend sports. Regarding the geographical extent, it was determined that 67% of the funds flow into the local environment, but 40% also engage in a larger region around their city.

More recent surveys also confirm the **approval of regional sponsoring commitments** by fans. The companies FanQ and IRIS surveyed nearly 4000 football fans in December 2019 as part of an online study on their perception of the companies driving sponsoring in professional football (FanQ/Intelligent Research in sponsoring, 2020). The study asked about the sympathy values of the respective main, jersey, sleeve, beer, and betting partners as well as the namesakes of the respective Bundesliga stadiums. The results allow, among other things, analyses in the areas of regionality and long-term nature of sponsor partnerships among the fans of the respective clubs. The results show above all that the cross-industry market trend "regionality" is highly valued among football fans. As part of the study, supporters of various football clubs were asked to rate the companies active in the Bundesliga for sympathy (1 = unsympathetic to 5 = very sympathetic). While non-regionally based main sponsors received an average rating of 3.24 from their own fans, the average popularity level of regionally engaged companies is significantly higher at 3.96.

The study results show that in football, particularly regionally based sponsors receive a **positive rating from the fans**. A positive example of a successful partnership from the perspective of the club supporters is Schwarzwaldmilch, the former sponsor of SC Freiburg, the. The locally based main and jersey partner was able to achieve an exceptionally good sympathy value of 4.25 among the local fans. The beer partners of the respective clubs also achieve high popularity values. The popularity values of the partner breweries are usually even significantly above the 3-point mark (average = 3.92). Here too, the factor "regionality" could play a decisive role. A completely different picture, however, is drawn on the side of the betting partners. With an average popularity of 2.98 points, the popularity of this group of sponsors is far below the overall average.

Example: Melitta—Sponsoring on a Small and Large Scale

Sports convey intense emotions and provide very special moments and experiences. Sports stand for motivation and inspiration as well as for dynamism, vitality, and joy of life. In addition, sports convey values that the **Melitta** brand also stands for: team spirit, fairness, passion, tradition, commitment, success. For this reason, Melitta has been very connected to sports for years and supports both grassroots and competitive sports at regional, national, and international levels (see Melitta's commitments in Fig. 6.9; Melitta, 2019).

Sponsored party	Sport type	Duration	Amount
TSV GWD Minden	Handball	1964 – ongoing	0.3
Bessel Rowing Club Minden	Rowing	2009 – ongoing	0.1
Manchester United	Soccer	2017 – ongoing	5.0
Arminia Bielefeld	Soccer	2018 – ongoing	0.4
Borussia Dortmund	Soccer	2019 – ongoing	1.8

Fig. 6.9 Sports sponsoring of the Melitta Group (amounts are estimates in million EUR per year). (*Source:* Melitta)

Melitta maintains an intense **relationship at the regional level** with the handballers of GWD Minden, where in addition to the Bundesliga team, other teams in the men's and youth sectors are also supported, as well as the Besseler Rowing Club, whose women's and men's team start in the Rowing Bundesliga as Melitta Eight. Another partner at the regional level is the football Bundesliga club Arminia Bielefeld. In the **relationship at the national level**, Melitta is committed to the Federalliga club Borussia Dortmund. Since the 2019/2020 season, Melitta has taken over as the official coffee partner the entire coffee supply in the Signal Iduna Park and works together with BVB on various communication and marketing activities. A **relationship at the international level** is the collaboration with Manchester United. Since 2017, Melitta has entered into a comprehensive partnership with the English record champion that goes far beyond a classic sponsoring. ◀

Example: VfL Osnabrück

In German professional football, only the presence in the 1st and 2nd Bundesliga seems to guarantee a permanent opportunity to survive economically—even for so-called smaller professional clubs. The 3rd league, on the other hand, is seen as very critical for numerous ambitious clubs that find themselves in a difficult economic situation. This can be explained using the example of **VfL Osnabrück**. VfL is the club that has spent the most seasons in the 2nd Bundesliga with 23 seasons, without ever having played in the 1st Bundesliga. After eight years in the 3rd league, the club was promoted back to the 2nd Football Bundesliga in 2019, but had to be relegated again in the summer of 2021, but managed to be promoted again in 2023.

Since the spin-off of the KGaA in 2013, the club has not succeeded in activating its fan and member potentials. The separate structures of the club (e. V.) and club (KGaA) did not sufficiently utilize the potential so important for the audience and economic success of a football club. Since 2018 and especially through the promotion in 2019, existing success potentials in the fan and member base have been exploited more efficiently and an increase in fans, members, stadium visitors, and supporters has been generated. After all, the revenues from sponsoring and advertising have been between 3.9 and 5.7 million EUR for many years, only the media revenues in the 2nd Bundesliga were and are higher (see Fig. 6.10). ◀

It has become clear that sports sponsoring, from a strategic perspective, encompasses a wide range of different commitments. Various **examples of strategic focal points** in sports sponsoring are shown in Fig. 6.11. The positioning of this range is served by the dimension of sports (traditional or usual versus modern or unusual) and the dimension of sponsor status (dominant-exclusive versus non-dominant-exclusive). The successful case examples document that strategic focal points must be set by the sponsor in sports sponsoring.

	2015/16	2016/17	2017/18	2018/19	2019/20	2020/21
VfL Osnabrück	3. league	3. league	3. league	3. league	2. BL	2. BL
Spectator fees	1.94	1.97	1.80	2.80	2.87	0.12
Marketing and advertising	**3.94**	**3.88**	**4.30**	**4.70**	**5.74**	**4.41**
TV money	0.92	0.80	0.80	0.80	9.39	9.98
Merchandising	0.26	0.28	0.32	0.43	0.76	0.81
Catering	0.49	0.50	0.48	0.86	0.70	0.01
Total income	7.6	8.0	9.5	11.1	20.2	17.3
Net profit/loss for the year	-0.79	-1.35	+0.46	-0.60	+0.92	-0.30
Audience average	8620	9214	8066	11.907	14.611*	185**
Members	3100	3250	3569	3800	3800	3800
Final place in respective league	5.	6.	17.	1.	13.	16.

Fig. 6.10 Economic key data of VfL Osnabrück as a regional football club (*only 13 out of 17 home games with spectators; **in the following year only a total of 3200 spectators due to Corona-related ghost games). (*Source:* Club information and PR MARKETING)

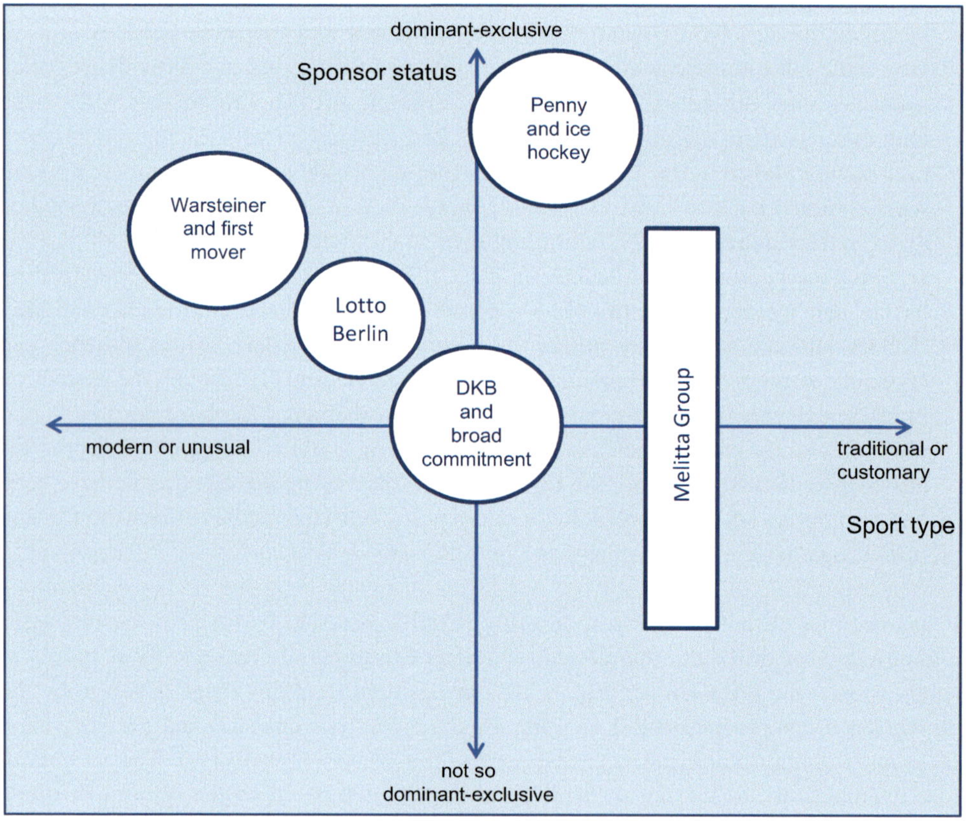

Fig. 6.11 Strategic focal points in sports sponsoring (with examples)

Case Study Bell Group—Regional sponsoring at FC Basel

The following case study was compiled by **Davide Elia**, Head of Corporate Marketing & Communication, and is made with the kind support and permission of the Bell Food Group.

The Bell Food Group is one of the leading European manufacturers of meat and convenience products and is the market leader in Switzerland. The company employs more than 12,500 people in 15 countries. The roots of the traditional company go back to 1869 when Samuel Bell opened his first butcher shop in downtown Basel. Today, the range includes fresh meat, poultry, charcuterie, seafood, and ultra-fresh, fresh, and durable convenience products. The offer is aimed at food service, the food industry, and retail. With the brands Bell, Eisberg, Hilcona, Hügli, and other specialty brands, Bell provides millions of consumers with diverse moments of pleasure and improved quality of life every day.

Initial Situation

As part of a **revision of the brand strategy**, the following considerations were made for the Bell brand, among others:

- Sharpening of positioning,
- Resetting of performance and personality characteristics.

The basis for this revision were the existing **brand values** (DNA of the brand), the perception of the target groups (numerous results from market research were available) as well as the desired future value development.

Due to the **new orientation** of the brand strategy, all marketing instruments were reassessed and adjusted with the goal of supporting the defined brand values and dimensions. In this context, the **sponsoring concept** was also revised. As a result, the main focus of sponsoring is now on anchoring the Swiss Bell production sites in their location regions (location marketing).

It was concluded that **sports sponsoring**is very suitable for this, because when attending sports events (football, ice hockey, tennis), catering is also of high relevance, and in most cases, the main product groups of Bell (sausage, burger, hot dog, etc.) can be at the center. These **basic considerations** can be described in more detail as follows:

- Sports, and football in particular, evoke strong emotions in a broad population, which benefits the emotional charging of the Bell brand values.
- Eating is part of the overall experience of a sports event and thus has a natural connection to the offers and brands of the Bell Food Group.

- Bell will focus on a few commitments, but set these up carefully and comprehensively, not just a logo placement on the sponsor board. Bell already has a supported awareness level of over 90% in Switzerland. Therefore, mainly image dimensions are promoted by developing their own storytelling, various touchpoints, creative ideas, increasing the experience value (Bell enjoyment moment), and making the brand tangible.
- For its own employees, it should also strengthen identification with the company, convey values, and make Bell better perceived as an employer brand overall.

After careful consideration, the management decided to consider **football** because of its great popularity and the local **FC Basel** (FCB), one of the leading Swiss football clubs, known abroad for its sporting successes, as a partner for a sports sponsoring commitment.

Goals and Target Groups

The aforementioned initial conditions led to a clear target for the desired sports sponsoring. The following **communicative and economic goals** were formulated:

- Supporting the regional anchoring of Bell and thereby strengthening the emotional bond,
- Image transfer from the commitment to FC Basel and the St. Jakob-Stadium to the Bell brand,
- Emotionalizing the brand,
- Exploiting sales potential through the supply of stadium caterers,
- Indirect revenue generation through the placement of Bell products in the stadium range, their brand endorsement and integration into additional sales channels such as retail cash & carry markets and food service.
- The Bell Joggeli Sausage—a product specifically designed for the stadium—is to be introduced and established in the stadium as well as in retail (non-exchangeable service).
- 80% of FCB fans who have an annual subscription should know the Bell enjoyment moment (activation in the stadium) and know that Bell is the meat/charcuterie partner of FC Basel. Bell should be perceived as a "symbiotic" partner (similar to, for example, VW and Wolfsburg).
- Bell should be perceived as an attractive and dynamic employer at the various production sites—internally as well as externally.

The Bell Food Group wants to reach and address the following **target groups** with sports sponsoring in general and in particular with the concrete sponsoring:

- Fans of the sports/sporting event (in the case of the concrete sponsoring, the fans of FC Basel) as well as general meat/charcuterie lovers and families with children (high affinity to products and sports), i.e. the broad market,

- Customers and other stakeholders through hospitality programs,
- Employees as an internal target group, especially at the locations, but also spread across the many countries in which the company operates.

Strategic Orientation and Selection

Bell aims to promote social life in its location regions and thereby increase its visibility and be perceived as an attractive company. From this basic understanding, one to two sports sponsorings are defined for each location. **Sports sponsoring projects** that embody a **tradition in Switzerland** and appeal to a broad audience are preferred. In addition, the Bell moment of enjoyment should ideally be staged during local engagement. However, the selection of sponsoring opportunities is sometimes very limited, especially in smaller municipalities/regions where there are not many suitable sponsoring offers. Nevertheless, Bell has managed to find **sponsoring partners** in various areas. These are listed in Fig. 6.12.

The **Bell sponsoring manager** is located in central marketing and looks after the larger commitments; he also coordinates and controls the smaller activities at the decentralized locations. For larger commitments with diverse contact points, overall concepts are created, which are approved by the management.

Because Bell focuses on broad sections of the population, sports like football are favored for sponsoring. This is also popular as a mass sport and has a high reach. Because the Bell Food Group understands its **sponsoring commitment also as location marketing**, it was obvious to connect with a flagship of Swiss and European football on site. The **reasons for the commitment to FC Basel** were in detail:

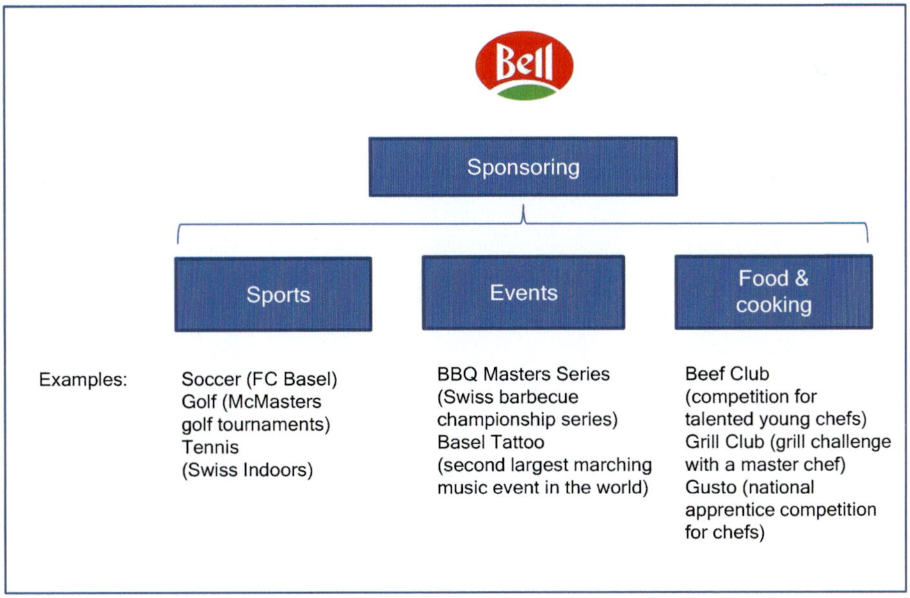

Fig. 6.12 Bell Food Group as a sponsoring partner. (*Source:* Bell Food Group)

- Traditional club from Basel with a large, loyal following across all social classes,
- Popular figure and an important size in the corresponding sports sector,
- Bell had previously had a partnership with FCB and gained a lot of experience during this,
- The Bell brand values fit perfectly with this sponsoring,
- Excellent elaboration of a concept and offer by the club,
- The commitment is planned for the long term (5-year contract).

In addition to advertising and hospitality rights, the **supply rights** are an essential part of the cooperation. Bell was also able to create its own flagship product (Joggeli sausage). In the spring of 2022, FC Basel 1893 then announced the multi-year partnership. Partnerships with local companies that have a national impact are particularly well suited to FC Basel, the club reported. Accordingly, the club was happy to be able to enter into another such cooperation. Bell CEO Lorenz Wyss also said that with the commitment to FCB, Bell underlines its traditional, close connection to Basel. Many employees have a deep passion for the club and the city. Therefore, FCB and Bell fit very well together. As a Rotblau partner of FCB (see Fig. 6.13), Bell has access to numerous rights. The package includes various branding, communication and hospitality services as well as delivery rights for meat, charcuterie, fish and convenience.

Implementation and Results

As special implementation elements, Bell used the **introduction of its new product**, the **Joggeli Sausage**, as well as other new communication measures during the game such as branding in the center circle and of course its hospitality rights (see Fig. 6.14).

Fig. 6.13 Bell as a Rotblau partner of FC Basel. (*Source:* Bell Food Group)

Fig. 6.14 Sponsoring implementation at FC Basel. (*Source:* Bell Food Group)

In particular, the following **activation measures** have been successfully used in the FCB sponsoring:

- Launch of the Joggeli Sausage in the stadium from the start of the 2022/2023 season,
- Launch of the Joggeli Sausage in retail/gastronomy (2023),
- Development of a new suitable halftime game, which is about the enjoyment of Bell products,
- Multiple branding areas such as boards, catering stands, center circle on the field, eating utensils (napkins, sausage plates, etc.),
- Video clips via web and social media about Bell's commitment to FCB,
- Online communication via newsletters and social media,
- Internal and external communication with regular reporting on the commitment,
- Internal and external competitions for FCB match tickets,
- Measures of the sponsoring recipient FCB at the start such as media information at the start of the partnership, storytelling via their own channels (web, social media, newsletter, reports in their own publications),
- Co-branding on Bell transport vehicles.

Due to the length of the commitment, both FC Basel and Bell are motivated and ready to develop **new creative measures** together during this time. Numerous departments are also involved internally: Marketing, Brand Management, Online

Communication, Sales Department for goods delivery, Product Management for the launch of the Joggeli Sausage and of course Communication (internal/external).

Networking with other sports sponsorings is possible, but has not yet been implemented. The commitment to FCB is the largest sponsoring of the Bell Food Group from a financial point of view. In addition, specific marketing activation programs have been adopted.

Given the fact that the partnership was only concluded at the start of the 2022/2023 season, there are only a few **control results** available:

- Initial reactions from fans and media were very positive; the commitment is understood and also perceived. Thanks to good networking in the region, Bell has a lot of feedback.
- The media impact is checked through the evaluation of media clippings, forums and social media interactions.
- Further impact controls relate to sales/turnover of goods deliveries, use and impact of hospitality programs, the use of the catering offer by stadium visitors and the visibility of branding in the media (e.g. air-time on TV).
- The reach of the commitment is evaluated through a tracking of the audience numbers and through the analysis of the media clippings.

Due to the rather extensive sponsoring of Bell with FCB, which also includes the delivery rights, the **replacement of the existing, long-term partner** in the meat/charcuterie area posed a special problem, which does not occur in otherwise usual, purely marketing-oriented commitments. The challenge was therefore to make the change noticeable through better quality, a great brand image, perfect know-how and authentic connection to Basel as well as additional ideas for the target groups. The difficulty was that the largest caterer in the stadium was not a professional provider and was unable to deliver a qualitative and timely performance. This led to long waiting times at the stands and poor food quality, which could indirectly have had a negative impact on Bell's brand image. Therefore, a task force was formed, which was partly supportive on site and also trained the grillers in courses. This problem could be solved by FC Basel: From January 2023, a professional caterer took over the entire catering in the stadium.

6.4 Strategic Principles and Guidelines in Sports Sponsoring (Incl. Case Studies DKB, Penny and Warsteiner)

A Sportsponsoring strategy should always be based on a written and binding **philosophy of sports sponsoring**. Accordingly, this philosophy serves as a frame of reference for determining the individual contents of a sponsoring strategy, such as the determination of sports and the selection of the organizational framework. Precisely formulated goals and binding strategies, which are enshrined in a sports sponsoring philosophy, are still the exception in sponsoring practice. Mainly companies with high sponsoring budgets sometimes proceed in such a way that they establish the philosophy in the form of **principles and guidelines of sponsoring**, which they use as a guide when selecting sponsorings (see Bruhn, 2018, pp. 62 f.; 151 ff.).

In formulating a philosophy, principles or guidelines in sports sponsoring, various central elements can be distinguished as **building blocks**:

- Determination of the sports with justification for the selection (e.g., product or image affinities),
- Decision for or against certain forms of sports sponsoring (e.g., top athletes, teams, organizations, sports events),
- Determination of the level of sports promotion (e.g., elite sports, mass sports, youth development),
- Conditions for a media presence in sports reporting,
- Position of the company compared to other sponsors (e.g., exclusive versus co-sponsoring),
- Conditions for the use of advertising materials (e.g., jersey and perimeter advertising, VIP invitations),
- General conditions (e.g., duration of contracts, use within the company, geographical catchment areas, internal responsibilities).

Example: Pharmaceutical company Roche—Guidelines for the selection of sponsorings

At **Roche AG** then guidelines for the selection of sponsorings were formulated as follows (Roche, 2022):

- Through Roche's commitments, a sustainable business model and an innovative corporate culture are to be expressed.
- The focus is placed on projects that are characterized by innovation, collaboration, quality, and sustainability.
- With projects and partnerships, Roche wants to illustrate the connection to the local community.
- The focus is on sustainable impact, not financial expenditure.
- Roche prefers a limited number of selected projects in order to use the resources available to it as efficiently as possible.
- The focus is on humanitarian and social projects, science and education, art and culture, and community and environment.
- Roche does not support projects with a religious, political, or commercial background and does not launch image campaigns.
- No responses are given to mass mailings, requests without a signature, or collective calls. ◄

Example: Stadtwerke Tübingen—Sponsoring Guidelines of a Public-Law Economic Entity

Not only commercial companies are engaged in sports sponsoring to achieve their specific communication goals, but also non-commercial institutions and public-law economic entities. For example, the **Stadtwerke Tübingen** have formulated their sponsoring guideline as follows (Stadtwerke Tübingen, 2022): sponsoring is an investment in our brand for us. Therefore, all measures must contribute to the formation of the desired brand characteristics.

For this reason, all sponsoring commitments are subject to the following individual concrete **guidelines for the selection of sponsorings**:

- **Appropriateness:** In sponsoring, an appropriate ratio of performance and consideration must be agreed. The contracting parties agree that the funds used contribute to the company's image maintenance.
- **Regional:** As a provider for Tübingen and the region, we only sponsor in our core area Tübingen and its districts as well as in our network concession areas.
- **Attractiveness:** We only sponsor projects and events with public impact. Ideally, there is a high media, participant and spectator presence.
- **Leading Sponsor Role:** We strive for partnerships at the top two sponsoring hierarchy levels as main sponsor or co-sponsor. The other sponsors must not be local, regional or national competitors in one or more markets where we operate.
- **Regular:** We sponsor projects and events that take place regularly or over a longer period of time. One-time projects and events are not sponsored.
- **Sustainability:** Our sponsoring commitments are designed for sustainable, long-term impact. Therefore, we do not sponsor organizations, projects and events that are aimed at short-term, fast-paced success.
- **Quality and Reliability**: We only appear at projects and events that ensure high quality and reliability in the implementation of the sponsoring commitment.
- **Networking:** We can publish and use all measures of the sponsoring commitment in different communication channels to achieve maximum impact and distribution.
- **Dependence—Independence:**The respective supported organization must not be permanently dependent on us or become so. It must be able to continue independently after the sponsoring has ended.
- **Customer of Stadtwerke Tübingen:**We only sponsor clubs and institutions that are electricity and/or natural gas customers of Stadtwerke Tübingen.
- **Taboos**: We do not sponsor individuals (e.g., individual athletes, artists, musicians), no trips, no risk and extreme sports, and no events and sports associated with high CO_2emissions, a high amount of waste and environmental destruction. Furthermore, we do not accept requests from third parties (e.g., marketing and sponsoring agencies). ◄

The strategic orientation of the sponsoring is of particular importance for a commitment. Here, not only the Dimensions of strategy development, but especially the **focuses in the strategic orientation** need to be worked out. This should be documented in writing in sponsoring guidelines in order to document the strategic orientation of the sponsor externally and internally.

Case Study DKB—Sustainable Positioning of DKB

The following case study was compiled by **Marcel Schwarzkopf**, Strategic Marketing Manager, and is made with the kind support and permission of Deutsche Kreditbank AG (DKB).

The **Deutsche Kreditbank AG (DKB)**headquartered in Berlin was founded in 1990 and today serves over 5 million business and private customers with its 5000 employees. DKB is considered one of the most sustainable banks among the top 20 banks in Germany, it is the largest financier of renewable energies in the country and has set itself the goal that by 2030 a total of 85% of its loan portfolio will significantly contribute to the fulfillment of the SDGs (already 79% today). Sustainability is thus part of the DKB DNA, the bank uses the hashtag #geldverbesserer for its brand story and transfers its efforts to external partnerships.

In this way, the bank also succeeds in initiating targeted sustainable changes within the framework of its sports sponsoring appearance and using them communicatively for the DKB brand. The following describes the initial situation, goals, targeted target groups and relevant selection criteria for the sponsorings. Another part of the case study is a description of relevant activation measures and their results.

An overview of the **sponsoring commitments of DKB** is provided in Fig. 6.15. The focus is on national and regional sports as well as arts & culture.

Initial Situation

DKB has been an active supporter of sports in Germany since 2004. It supports associations, clubs, athletes in disciplines such as handball, biathlon, e-sports, and other sports. Since 2022, it has been the presenting partner of the NFL games in Germany. The portfolio is continuously reviewed. In addition to logo presence and hospitality, great importance is placed on diverse activation possibilities. The activation takes place in two pillars:

- **Digital Innovations**
  DKB supports clubs and associations with digital innovations that measurably improve the sports themselves as well as their athletes and optimize the fan experience. An example is the live tracking and analysis with real-time data from KINEXON in the Handball Bundesliga and the development of the Handball Performance Index as a transparent KPI for handball.

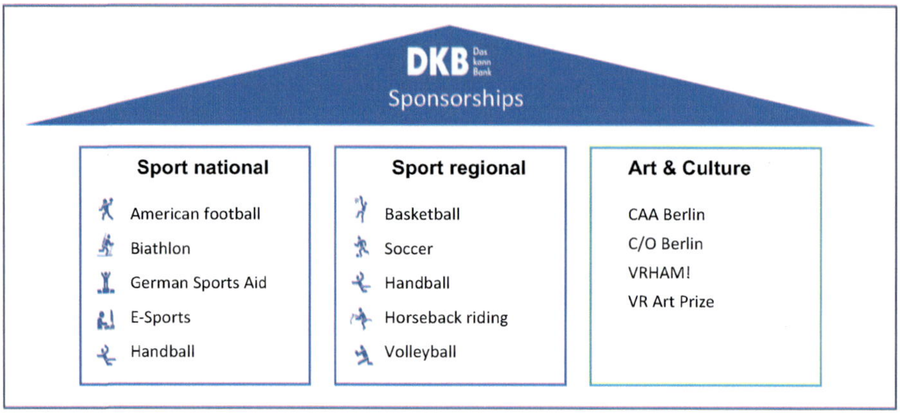

Fig. 6.15 Sponsoring commitments of DKB. (*Source:* DKB)

- **Social Sustainability**
  DKB enables access to top-level sports through sustainable talent promotion and the breaking down of barriers. Examples include handball (HandbALL TOGETHER, an initiative for diversity in handball with the DHB and the 360° support for youth teams ofFüchse Berlin, SC DHfK Leipzig, SC Magdeburg and Thüringer HC), Biathlon (support of the biathlon junior squad "DKB Squad with Perspective"), E-Sports (DKB Diamonds as its own talent team), blind football (sponsoring FC St. Pauli) and the Flag Football Program (NFL Germany).

Goals and Target Groups

For the consideration of goals in sports sponsoring, the two business areas of DKB as a bank for private and business customers must be taken into account. This results in different **priorities in the selection of sponsorings**:

- Implementation of **national sponsorings** for year-round, high-reach media presence with corresponding successful sports (handball, biathlon, e-sports, and NFL games in Germany),
- Implementation of **regional sponsorings** as a dialogue platform (especially with business customers and partners) and access to regional business networks (equestrian, selected clubs of the 1st and 2nd league in football, handball, volleyball, basketball, running events) as well as the lived, societal responsibility in the regions.

Considering these two orientations, the following three **goals of sports sponsoring** for DKB can be formulated:

- **Brand Building**: Increase the awareness of DKB and sharpen the profile of the brand,

- **Relationship Management**: Create moments of appreciation to increase loyalty and willingness to recommend,
- **Social Responsibility**: Contribute to a sustainable and livable community.

With the various commitments in sports sponsoring, DKB naturally wants to address the **target groups** defined by the corporate goals. They can be divided into external and internal groups.

- **External target groups:**
  - Private and business customers (e.g., direct bank customers, municipal utilities, and renewable energy project developers),
  - Business partners and service providers (e.g., intermediaries and sales partners),
  - Politics, supervision, associations, rating agencies,
  - Media, NGOs, and others.
- **Internal target groups:**
  - Shareholders, subsidiaries, and employees,
  - Applicants.

Strategic Orientation and Criteria for the Selection of Sponsorings

Sports sponsoring is an essential part of DKB's strategic marketing and is derived from the company's strategy. The following example illustrates this well: Starting from the goal of rejuvenating the private customer target group, DKB engaged with the area of gaming/e-sports and decided in 2020 to enter the League of Legends Prime League.

Quantitative and qualitative **evaluation criteria for the selection of sponsorings** are included in the decision-making processes:

- Target group fit, among other things, according to the characteristics of socio-demography, media usage behavior, usage and attitude towards financial services,
- Advertising impact and development potentials: sports, rights holders, fan base in Germany, media reach (live/delayed, social), visibility of sponsors, sponsoring environment,
- Understanding and efforts of sustainability (ESG check),
- Design possibilities within the framework of activations.

In this case study, the activations for a total of six sponsoring areas are considered to illustrate the integration of DKB's sustainable positioning in sports sponsoring.

Handball

Handball is the second most popular team sport in Germany (source: Allensbach Market and Advertising Carrier Analysis, 2021). In view of the EM 2024 and WM 2027 in Germany, a "decade of handball" is also being talked about.

For DKB, the **goals in handball**are to increase awareness and image profiling in the target group aged 18–59 years. A nationwide platform for B2C and B2B communication is available and the translation of the #geldverbesserer brand story through suitable activation measures in sports. Also important are the communication campaigns with the German Handball Federation (DHB; premium partner) and the Handball Bundesliga (HBL; league partner) for the transfer of DKB products and services. Measures include logo presence (jersey back, coach sleeve), LED boards and back goal banners, as well as HandbALL TOGETHER as a platform for integration and recruitment of young talent. With the HBL, measures such as an extensive media and ticket package, a technology partnership with KINEXON and various activations are implemented. The focus is on four regional club commitments (Füchse Berlin, SC Magdeburg, SC DHfK Leipzig, Thüringer HC), where measures such as hospitality and 360° promotion of youth teams are also used.

Biathlon
Biathlon is the most popular winter sport in Germany. A total of 35% of the German population aged 16 to 69 years state that they are interested in biathlon. This corresponds to 29 million people (source: Nielsen Sports Fan Insights, 2021).

From DKB's perspective, the primary **goals in biathlon engagement** are to increase awareness and image profiling in the target group aged 18–59 years, TV presence with high viewing figures on German channels such as ARD/ZDF, and networking through events at relevant World Cup locations. As a partner, the International Biathlon Union (IBU) is available at the premium sponsor level and measures such as a broadly based media package with boards, time gallows, start numbers, etc. are implemented. The German Ski Association (DSV) is a team partner and measures such as logo presence on the coach's cap, talent promotion and comprehensive social media activation are used.

E-Sports
League of Legends (LoL) is one of the most played games worldwide and is characterized by a young target group. The LoL Prime League is the highest national league with the best teams from the DACH region and convincing reach.

As **E-Sports goals**, DKB aims to increase awareness and image profiling in the young target group (18–39 years) and to position itself as a sustainable TechBank. This is achieved through digital communication measures, targeted top-level sports promotion, the involvement of employees through their own tournaments, tickets for events and exclusive coaching. Positive effects on the employer brand are also expected. As a partner, the League of Legends Prime League (RIOT) is available at the main partner level and measures such as logo presence and content formats in all Prime League channels are applied, as well as offline activation at final tournaments and trade fairs such as Gamescom. The esports player foundation acts as an enabling partner, implementing measures to further develop e-sports through scholarships and the own talent team DKB Diamonds.

Football
Football has an attractive and growing fan base in Germany. Already over 17 million people are interested in this sport. Football is also the second most popular TV sport in Germany.

DKB associates football **goals**such as increasing awareness and image profiling in the target group 18–39 years via digital and highly individualizable channels, acquiring new customers through exclusive product offers and competitions, customer loyalty and recommendation in the defined B2B sectors through exclusive events within the framework of the NFL Germany games, and promoting young talent with the NFL Flag Program at over 150 schools in Germany. The partner is the National Football League (NFL) as the presenting partner. Measures such as branding and logo presence (Fanfest, stadium, app, etc.), ticket/hospitality package within the framework of the Germany games in Munich and Frankfurt, presenting partner of the NFL Flag Program in Germany are perceived.

FC St. Pauli Blind Football
Blind football is fast, action-packed, and physical. Blind footballers keep the ball close to their foot, so the ball can be constantly perceived tactilely. This sport deserves more attention—and the athletes more support. That's why DKB supports the team from FC St. Pauli as the main sponsor. Measures are taken to support the team with necessary equipment and logo presence on the jersey. In addition, a tactile guidance system is initiated at the Millerntor to improve the stadium experience for people with visual impairments and an extension on the club's social media channels. Fig. 6.16 shows a scene from FC St. Pauli's blind football.

Activation of Sponsorings in the Area of Social Sustainability
DKB is committed to actively shaping the future of sports in Germany. It focuses its activations on two pillars: digital innovation and social sustainability. Together with the sports partners, the bank develops its own programs/initiatives and creates solutions for previous challenges and barriers.

The activation measure **HandbALL TOGETHER**—as an initiative for integration, diversity, and community in handball—includes nationwide various action days including training sessions with children, where they get to know national players and visit a game of the HBL or the national teams. In addition, there are virtual press conferences where the children get the opportunity to ask their idols questions, e.g., shortly before departure to the Handball World Cup 2021 with Uwe Gensheimer and Johannes Golla. With the HandbALL TOGETHER action

Fig. 6.16 DKB and FC St. Pauli Blind Football. (*Source:* DKB)

days, not only children are to be enthused for handball, but clubs are also encouraged to organize and carry out similar projects. The 360° promotion is implemented with regional partner clubs such as Füchse Berlin, SC Magdeburg, DHfK Leipzig, and Thüringer HC. To promote the holistic athlete and make the youth players of the partner clubs fit off the field as well, an educational series on various topics is offered e.g., dealing with social media and digital stress, hate speech, fake news and cyberbullying, digital revenues, money management and security, nutrition. Fig. 6.17 gives an insight into the Handball Action Day 2021.

Activation measures in connection with the **DKB Squad with Perspective** support young biathletes on their way to the top of the world. The problem is that many sporting talents are lost on their individual path to the top of the world due to lack of promotion opportunities. Public funding cannot serve all young talents. To meet this challenge, the DKB Squad with Perspective was created. Together with the DSV, up to twelve athletes are supported annually. The courses for the athletes aim to promote and challenge the talents both athletically and in their personal development. For this, they are trained in all perspectives with coaches and mentors from the A-squad.

Together with the **esports player foundation**, the **DKB Diamonds** are at the forefront of activation in E-Sports: The DKB Diamonds are a free agent League of Legends talent team. The team enables talented players to establish themselves in the scene and draw attention to their skills. The DKB Diamonds do not function as a classic E-Sports team, but as a pathfinder and springboard for young talents. The players should train in a highly professional environment and get used to routines

Fig. 6.17 DKB and Handball Action Day 2021. (*Source:* DKB)

of professional athletes. The players can expect not only in-game coaching, but also important aspects such as fitness, nutrition, and mental health. The commitment is a further development of the 2020 initiated DKB E-Sports scholarships, which were also implemented with the esports player foundation. Already in the first two splits of the 2022 season, the DKB Diamonds were able to move up from Division 5 to Division 3 of the League of Legends Prime League.

The **FC St. Pauli** of 1910 e. V. has had its own **Blind Football Bundesliga Team**since May 2006, in which twelve active players and various coaches, guides and supervisors are involved. The club has been playing continuously in the German Blind Football Bundesliga since 2008. As the main sponsor, DKB invites regional business and network partners to club match days, who can try out the "Experience Blind Football" themselves—and are impressed by the team's athletic achievements. With this, DKB pursues the goal of anchoring blind football more firmly in the middle of society. As part of the partnership, a tactile guidance system was also installed in the Millerntor Stadium of FC St. Pauli to improve the stadium experience for people with visual impairments.

Activation at the **NFL FLAG Program**: DKB presents the NFL FLAG Football school program exclusively in Germany, introduces students to the non-contact variant of American football and supports the participating schools with FLAG Football equipment. The teachers are trained in workshops by experienced football coaches and receive extensive teaching materials. The program promotes creativity and at the same time conveys the values lived by the NFL such as respect, responsibility, integrity and resilience, as well as the importance of a healthy, active lifestyle. The NFL FLAG Program is specifically designed for physical education in schools and is suitable for participants aged 11–14. Fig. 6.18 provides an insight into the NFL FLAG Program Final Munich 2022.

The **implementation of the sponsorings**is carried out in cross-functional teams, consisting of Strategic Marketing Managers from the bank's corporate development, sponsoring, event and graphic specialists from the "in-house agency" DKB Service GmbH and partner managers from the clubs, associations and marketers.

The **communication of the sponsorings**and the activation measures described above primarily takes place on the channels of the respective partners or rights holders. This approach is chosen because the greatest possible overlap with the sports-enthusiastic and receptive target group is expected there.

Highlights from the respective activations are communicated on DKB's channels. Examples include: The DKB squad with perspective was introduced to the DKB community with a kick-off video, and the journey over a season was accompanied in Instagram stories. Uwe Gensheimer, former captain of the German men's handball national team and ambassador of the initiative HandbALL TOGETHER, has already acted as a testimonial and brand ambassador for DKB.

A direct connection to internal stakeholders is created both through intensive accompaniment of the sports commitments on the internal communication channels such as social intranet and through the participation of athletes at DKB events. Furthermore, the DKB Diamonds are available for individual coaching and show matches against DKB employees. The best DKB League of Legends team is determined annually as part of an employee tournament.

Fig. 6.18 DKB and NFL Flag Program Final Munich 2022. (*Source:* DKB)

In 2021, DKB joined the S20 and the **Working Group "Corporate Responsibility"**. The working group has set itself the goal of developing a standard for measuring the sustainability impact of sponsoring commitments. As part of the working group, DKB was able to subject five of the six measures described (HandbALL TOGETHER, 360° promotion, DKB squad with perspective, DKB Diamonds, FC St. Pauli Blind Football) to a sustainability audit in 2022.

The audit was carried out by the strategy and management consultancy concern GmbH. Along the 17 Sustainable Development Goals (SDGs) and 169 sub-goals of the United Nations (UN), the five commitments were evaluated in terms of their impact. As a result, a direct **contribution of the commitments to the following SDGs** was determined:

- SDG 3: Good Health and Well-being,
- SDG 4: Quality Education,
- SDG 5: Gender Equality,
- SDG 8: Decent Work and Economic Growth,
- SDG 10: Reduced Inequalities,
- SDG 11: Sustainable Cities and Communities,
- SDG 16: Peace, Justice and Strong Institutions.

This result supports DKB's sustainable business model also from the sports sponsoring perspective. This should be both an incentive and an ambition. Further measures such as an explicit sustainability evaluation of all sponsorings will follow.

Measurement of Success, Selected Insights and Parameters

For the sponsorings in handball, biathlon, and the NFL Germany games, a **media monitoring** of the specific (live, delayed) and secondary reporting (magazines, news) in Germany (TV and central live streams) as well as on digital platforms (online and social media) takes place. The individual activation measures are not measured separately, but are qualitatively considered at the end of the season and compared to benchmarks. In conducting resonance analyses, the following **results** were achieved for the individual sponsorings:

HandbALL TOGETHER

- More than 250 participating children and adolescents since the start of the measure,
- National unpaid coverage on sports media Sky sports, Ran, Spox, Sportdeutschland.TV.

DKB Squad with Perspective

- Vanessa Voigt already promoted to A-squad one year after the start of the program and fourth place in the individual race at the 2022 Olympic Games,

- DSV channel, Instagram platform: Ø engagement rate of the 2021/2022 season with over 5% above the channel average and comparable values from biathlon.

DKB Diamonds
- Start of e-sports career for five athletes since the start of the promotion through transfer to professional League of Legends teams,
- Show matches against established e-sports teams like BIG and VININE achieve above-average reach on Twitch,
- Sport1 started content creation with DKB Diamonds on its own.

NFL Flag Program
- Over 150 participating schools in the first year of promotion and implementation in 2022,
- National unpaid coverage on sports media such as ran and Spox as well as cross-interest platforms like FAZ, Süddeutsche, Berliner Tageszeitung.

The explanations of the DKB sponsorings in handball, biathlon, e-sports, football, and blind football prove that **modern sponsoring** involves more than just logo placement. The two business areas of DKB as a private and business customer bank require a conscious selection of sports commitments, as goals, target groups and associated activation measures differentiate.

What remains the same is the connecting and emotional power of sports. Combined with creative activation, the active involvement of target groups, and comprehensive communicative support, DKB strengthens its position as a (socially) sustainable bank and at the same time provides added value for society.

Case Study Penny—Dominant Sponsoring

The following case study was compiled by **Peter Rack**, Head of Loyalty, Content & sponsoring, and successfully carried out with the kind support and permission of Penny.

Penny is an internationally active German food discounter, which has branches in Germany and five other European countries and was founded in 1973. The headquarters of the **Penny Markt GmbH** is in Cologne. Since 1989, Penny has been fully owned by the Rewe Group. Currently, Penny has about 2150 markets in Germany.

Initial Situation

Until its entry into ice hockey sponsoring, Penny had limited itself to festival sponsoring with a few short exceptions (Energie Cottbus, 1. FC Köln women's team). After many years of abstinence in sports sponsoring, a sponsoring opportunity was once again brought to Penny's attention when Covestro, the main sponsor of the

German Ice Hockey League (DEL), withdrew at the end of the 2019/2020 season. The offer was thoroughly examined and alternative sports sponsoring opportunities were identified and evaluated. Due to the content fitting of the sports to Penny and the target group affinity, Penny decided to **enter into ice hockey sponsoring,**which, in addition to the naming rights of the DEL (first title sponsor of the highest German ice hockey league), also included a premium partnership with the German Ice Hockey Federation (DEB) as well as an engagement with para-sports (so-called sled hockey) and youth development. Fig. 6.19 shows the sponsoring commitments of Penny.

Goals and Target Groups

The target was and is clearly focused on an **increase in sympathy for the Penny brand** and thus also the probability of shopping among the approximately 20 million ice hockey enthusiasts. In addition, from the very beginning, the goal was defined with the partners to establish ice hockey as the second most popular sport behind football and ahead of handball and basketball. The actual challenge should be that Penny establishes itself as a partner of German ice hockey and, similar to a generic brand, is almost synonymous with the sport. Moreover, Penny decided on the sponsoring at a time when the first wave of Corona and the resulting measures were taking place and there was extreme uncertainty in the markets. However, since Penny is also fundamentally committed to societal issues and has a societal promotion idea, the company consciously took this risk to support the league, clubs, and the sport during this uncertain time.

As a national discounter, Penny naturally has a very **broad target group**. Therefore, it was also important to choose a national sponsoring that also reaches a very broad target group. At Penny, the focus is on the household head (usually female) with a low to medium household income. These people can also be found in the sport of ice hockey. Even though ice hockey appears to be a male sport at

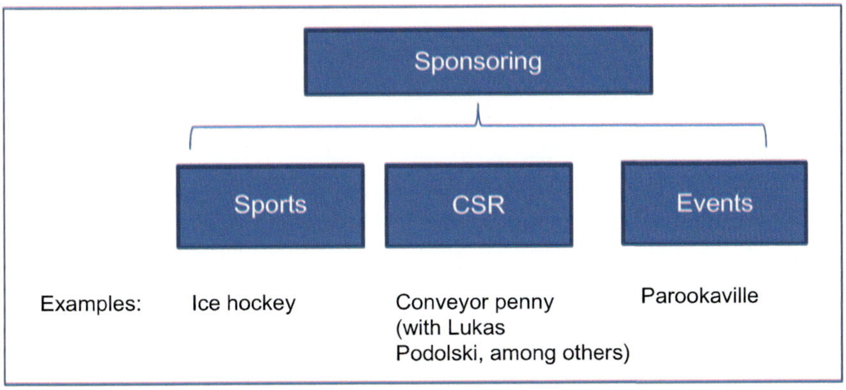

Fig. 6.19 Sponsoring commitments of Penny. (*Source:* Penny)

first glance, the proportion of female fans and interested parties as well as female arena visitors is almost 50%.

The **fit to the brand** was also important for internal marketing. To make the sponsoring noticeable internally, the company raffles off more than 1000 tickets to Penny employees each year.

Strategic Orientation and Selection

The parent company Rewe-Group has issued company-wide **sponsoring guidelines** for the approval, implementation, and evaluation of such activities. Penny relies on a dominance strategy, i.e., the company does not just want to be a sponsor, but wants to be perceived as *THE* partner par excellence, which one associates with a sport. However, this **dominance strategy** can hardly be achieved in a mass sport like football, which is why a niche sponsoring is often the better way. There, one is not just one among many. Visibility and association require dominant presence. This applied and still applies to the commitment in ice hockey. Therefore, from the very beginning, the naming rights (PENNY-DEL) were in focus and the sponsoring was extended to the DEB, para-sports, and the youth. This created a credible basis for the title “Supporter of German Ice Hockey” (see also Fig. 6.20).

In the course of the negotiations, a comprehensive **analysis of the sports sponsoring market** was carried out. The most relevant sports, including football and biathlon, were examined for reach, fit, activation possibility, availability, etc., and a ranking was created that identified ice hockey as the clear number one for Penny. Both the analysis and evaluation of the offer for the basic decision and the contract negotiations were carried out in Penny’s marketing department by the “Loyalty, Content & sponsoring” department.

Implementation and Results

The initial contracts from 2020 had a term of four years. The early extension in 2022 until the end of the 2027/2028 season now results in a total term of eight years and proves that the partners are a good match. Therefore, it was also important to further support women’s ice hockey, which prompted Penny to become the main sponsor there immediately. The long-term DEB partnership continues to provide that Penny will support the “Urmel Badge”, the children’s sports badge in ice hockey named after the national team’s mascot, from 2022 onwards. The cooperation is rounded off by various activation rights that will benefit ice hockey fans. With the signing of the cooperation, Penny ultimately documented a **commitment to ice hockey**in Germany from the professional sector to the youth and recreational sports, which is also reflected in the total budget including activation in the mid-seven-figure range per year.

In addition to comprehensive branding (naming rights, double logo, kick list, referees, boards, etc.), a comprehensive **activation concept** was also created.

Fig. 6.20 PENNY-DEL—first title sponsor of the highest German ice hockey league. (*Source:* Penny)

The goal was to further develop ice hockey in terms of advertising. The company succeeded in doing this with new, innovative content formats (e.g., grill championship, Unsung Hero Award, Supporting 6, among others), large and great competitions (e.g., Ticket Abstauber, Supporting 6, among others) as well as advertising formats (innovative LED boards in 3 arenas, among others). Three own-brand products have also already been launched on the market as PENNY-DEL editions in the form of promotional goods.

In the **integration of the sponsoring**, due to the organizational structure, certain departmental barriers had to be overcome initially, and the sponsoring had to prove its success in the first years. In the future, due to the proven success, which was also internally visible through the early and long-term extension, it is expected that ice hockey will achieve even more integration in campaigns and own channels. However, it should be noted that ice hockey is only relevant for a small part of Penny's customers in the shopping context and must be evaluated depending on the channel or campaign. Especially when occupying their own channels such as the flyer, the ice hockey commitment competes with a multitude of other topics for available spaces, which are becoming increasingly scarce due to raw material prices.

The **efficiency of the ice hockey sponsoring**in the customer market is not only important for the basic commitment, but also for internal acceptance. Nielsen Sports evaluates the achievement of goals in terms of awareness (of the sponsoring), sympathy, and purchase probability twice a year using its own market research. The partners also provide information on the reach of the channels and branding, which is then supplemented and summarized by Nielsen Sports. In total, this results in an ROI for the entire sponsoring, which has already shown the association Penny equals ice hockey and vice versa. Looking back, Penny was in the right place at the right time with its sponsoring in 2020, and at the same time, the cooperation that began during the pandemic has welded the parties together at all levels.

The beginning of the **collaboration between Penny and the partners**, DEB and DEL, was fraught with difficulties that were not the fault of any of the parties. Corona has greatly influenced the first two years of the ice hockey partnership, which has been reflected in the modification of the game operation, the exclusion of spectators in the arenas, and also in the changed media consumption. Nevertheless, the results were so encouraging that an early expansion of the partnership was already made after two years, and in 2022 the food discounter extended its partnership with the DEB prematurely until 2028. The positive feedback from the market has further increased motivation and commitment to establish ice hockey as sports No. 2 among all participants. For Penny, it also showed how useful the support from outside through a competent and committed agency is.

Case Study Warsteiner—First Mover

The following case study was compiled by **Marcus Bunse**, Brand Activation Manager sports & Event, and is made with the kind support and permission of Warsteiner.

The **Warsteiner Brewery** is one of the largest private breweries in Germany. Founded in 1753, it is a family business in its ninth generation. The Warsteiner Group includes the Herforder and Paderborner breweries, the private brewery Frankenheim as well as shares in the König Ludwig Schlossbrauerei Kaltenberg and the Irish Rye River Brewing Company. Warsteiner now actively distributes its products in over 50 countries worldwide.

Initial Situation

From the outset, Warsteiner's approach to sponsoring was to consciously forge new paths and support projects that allowed brand fans to experience the company in refreshingly different ways. Often, these were rather unconventional commitments, such as the Montgolfiade since 1986, where balloonists from all over the world meet. Therefore, when it comes to dealing with sponsoring, the Warsteiner Group always needs specific **occasions** that can make the following possible:

- Increase in buyer reach,
- Increase in sympathy for the Warsteiner brand,
- Creation of awareness for individual products.

The live-streaming portal Twitch, which started as a platform for broadcasting video games and e-sports events, increasingly made a name for itself, and some companies discovered the platform for themselves. Since 2020, **Beach Volleyball** has also been streamed on Twitch—right in the middle of the Corona pandemic. This was an occasion for Warsteiner, who had often seen and recognized sponsoring opportunities first, to get involved here. In addition, at that time, little to nothing else in terms of sports and events was taking place or was allowed to take place. Moreover, it was an exciting experiment for the sport of beach volleyball. After all, German beach volleyball was struggling with the effects of the pandemic and also faced major, self-made challenges.

With Alexander Walkenhorst, brother of Olympic champion Kira Walkenhorst, an active player took matters into his own hands and seized the opportunity: He organized a tournament series under the title "**Beach League**" a, which provided the active players with opportunities to play, gave the sport appropriate presence, and created a completely new type of experience for this sport with Twitch: In addition to streaming, every viewer could and can actively intervene and partly also co-design. Thus, starting from June 13, 2020, for 30 days, the "Beach League" started with a fixed field of 16 teams. Every day, eight games were played on one of two official competition courts in the Arena Sports Park in Düsseldorf. Spectators were not allowed for the first three weeks (afterwards only max. 100), but the games were streamed live, free of access, interactive and free of charge on www.twitch.tv/dieBeach-Liga.

Goals and Target Groups

In this novel environment, the Warsteiner Group saw new and challenging opportunities to get involved as a sponsor. Their goal was to charge the brand sympathetically in an emotional environment. The consumer should consider products from the Warsteiner Brewery when shopping due to the positive experience (e.g., in the aftermath of such a sports event) like the Beach League. The **sponsoring goals** can be concretized as follows:

- **Psychological goals:**In the specific sponsoring, a connection between the sports-affine community on Twitch and the Warsteiner brand should be created through the approachable communication of the streaming hosts with the end consumer. The end consumer could thus come into contact with our brand in a familiar environment.
- **Economic goals:** At the end of the day, Warsteiner wanted to land in the consumer's "Relevant Set" through the cooperation with the Beach League as a brand and thus win new buyers for our products.

Further **advantages for the Warsteiner Group** resulted from the target group fit of the sponsoring occasion. With the various commitments in sports sponsoring, the target group defined by the corporate goals between 18 and 59 years should be addressed. In general, sponsorings are always first and foremost aimed at the external effects and target groups. The external **target groups** can be very well described based on market research data. But inevitably, these are also found among the company's employees, which is why the sponsoring commitment should also be used internally. With the Twitch Beach League sponsoring, we are addressing a target group that is two-thirds between 18 and 34 years old and thus belongs to the core target group of our brand.

Strategic Orientation and Selection

For the Warsteiner Group, it is true that **sports sponsoring is a component of the marketing mix**. It is intended to contribute to achieving the well-known corporate and marketing objectives. One of the most important goals is to increase the buyer's reach and thus gain market shares and sales. The **evaluation criteria for sponsorings** consist of various components. These include reach (both on-site and in the media), the proportion of the target group in the respective environment, and the sales to be achieved.

The **sports sponsoring is organizationally located in marketing** and, along with sales, is part of the company's sales organization. The specialist department is responsible for evaluating sponsoring opportunities and prepares incoming offers from marketing and sales for decision-making.

The diversity of the **sponsoring engagement of the Warsteiner Group** is shown in Fig. 6.21. It becomes clear that sports are in the foreground, but

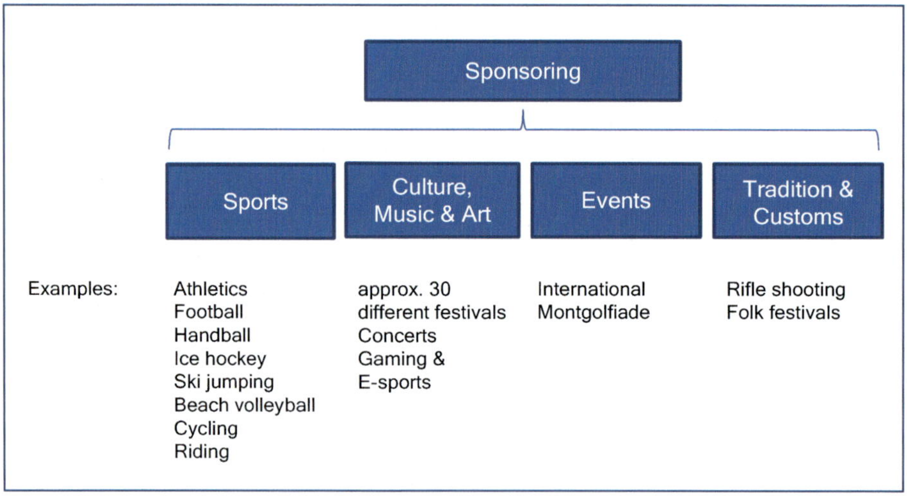

Fig. 6.21 sponsoring of the Warsteiner Group. (*Source:* Warsteiner)

commitments are also made in the areas of culture, music & art, events, tradition & customs.

When selecting the Twitch Beach League sponsoring, there was one main reason. In June 2020, many sports leagues, sports events, and even festivals were canceled or at least suspended due to Corona. With the conclusion of the new sponsoring, the opportunity was seen to reach younger end consumers despite all event cancellations. A main reason for the positive vote was that, based on experience, the reach had to be good due to the commitment to front page placement. Furthermore, budget had become available due to other cancellations. So there were free funds to get involved in this case. Another important criterion for the decision was that the topic of live sports on the Twitch platform had never existed before. The final decision was then made when the Warsteiner Group saw the chance to be a first mover in the brewery sector, just like in the e-sports area.

In the first step, there was a sponsoring contract for the duration of the Beach League, which lasted 30 days. This included classic services such as banners, advertising materials, product placement, and social media integrations. A special feature of the contract was that the sponsoring sum was based on the reach achieved by the streams and did not have to be paid as a fixed sum. In addition, there was no mention of possible sales volumes, as all games took place without spectators and the sponsoring was used exclusively digitally.

Fig. 6.22 Warsteiner and "The Beach League" Sponsoring on Twitch in 2020. (*Source:* Warsteiner. Athlete: Sarah Schulz, Photographer: Florian Treiber)

Fig. 6.23 Warsteiner and "The Beach League" Sponsoring on Twitch in 2020. (*Source:* Warsteiner. Athlete: Alexander Walkenhorst, Photographer: Florian Treiber)

Implementation and Results

In the implementation of the Twitch Beach League Sponsorings, advertising boards were set up in a traditional manner, which were then visible during the broadcasts of the games in the stream. Figures 6.22 and 6.23 provide an insight into the game action. Furthermore, there was a "Warsteiner Content Couch". Here, certain individuals gathered for small talk formats before, during the breaks, and after the games. Other elements were the chat command and a custom emoji.

The rights holder integrated Warsteiner into all of its **social media channels**. These included Twitch and Instagram, as well as TikTok and Discord, in addition to the agreed upon. The company itself also extended the cooperation via its own Instagram channel. The most significant measure was the stream and the format itself. Due to the down-to-earth and approachable communication of the streamers and a previously unprecedented league system in beach volleyball, a community was quickly built up that celebrated all partners who committed themselves to the sport and the format from the beginning. The clear commitment of the community was also demonstrated by positive feedback emails to the brewery.

Due to the pandemic, there was only the possibility to extend the **sponsoring via digital media**, as normal life was very limited and there were neither events nor trade fairs, etc. Internally, other departments such as Media/Digital, Brand Management and Corporate Communications were involved in the Twitch Beach League sponsoring. Media/Digital spread the sponsoring across the company's social media channels. The Brand department supported the implementation of the LED motifs and Corporate Communications ensured internal and external reporting. The sponsoring was later linked with other sponsorings or own events. Here, the commitment with the Saris Rouvy Sauerland cycling team and the Warsteiner Mühlenkopf Kraxler should be mentioned.

During and after the sponsoring engagements of the Warsteiner Group, **success controls** were carried out and a final overall evaluation was made. The **results of the Twitch Beach League sponsoring** can be summarized as follows:

- Warsteiner was able to significantly increase its popularity and reach among buyers.
- For impact and success control, there was an online survey at the end of the Beach League, in which more than 5000 people participated.
- The media effects could also be very well specified and evaluated based on the very detailed information of each viewer during the registration process.

In addition to the very strong reach and the increase in popularity in the community, it should also be emphasized that Warsteiner, as one of the few brands in a time when little to no sports competitions took place, was able to show presence and strongly anchor itself in the community of a sport.

The **conclusion** is: In terms of input to outcome, it was a very efficient sponsoring. A comprehensive view could be taken very well for the Beach League, and it shows that the sponsoring was an absolute success. In terms of the overall case of sports broadcasting on Twitch, however, only initial trends can be derived. Due to the very short duration of this form of live sports broadcasting, an overall evaluation is not yet possible.

The **special feature** and the **risk of this commitment** were that Warsteiner acted as a first mover with one of the most innovative sports broadcasts. The greatest difficulty was the evaluation of the sponsoring before the contract was signed. At that time, there were no experiences for this type of sports broadcast. The commitment of the other sponsors was also an experiment at the beginning with the hope and belief in the success of the Beach League. The commitment of all partners, beyond monetary compensation, was immensely large and the identification with the case was enormous. Organizer Walkenhorst drew a successful balance of the premiere event with "very positive" resonance already after the opening week of the women's games. On average, 128,000 viewers followed the games per day over a longer period of time, 91% of them from Germany, which is understandable given the field of participants (Horizont, 2020). "I knew that beach volleyball works well online," said Walkenhorst, seeing the young audience and interactive features as advantages of Twitch. This is also what Warsteiner had hoped for with this sponsoring engagement, where they even had to do without beer sales on site.

6.5 Key Points

In the context of the strategic orientation of a sports sponsoring, the following points are particularly important to consider and take into account.

Key Points

1. Create clarity about the **goals of marketing and corporate communication**: Check the relevance and use of sports sponsoring against the background of marketing and corporate communication goals, preferably create sponsoring guidelines.
2. Pay detailed attention to all **decision dimensions in sports sponsoring** (subject, target groups, message, sponsored parties, measures, geographical area, time aspect).
3. Look for suitable sponsoring commitments and do not just let yourself be addressed: **New sponsoring areas and forms** can often achieve communicative competitive advantages better than overcrowded usual sponsoring platforms.
4. Observe the importance and **trends of types of sponsoring**: The development of the population's interest in leisure fields as well as the population's acceptance of different areas must be recognized and taken into account.
5. Develop **sponsoring as a central communication platform** and integrate and coordinate it with other communication and sales measures, which can also require its own strategic priorities, oriented towards the company perspective and competition.
6. To get closest to your own corporate and marketing goals, you do not always have to take the generally usual path via classic sponsoring in top-level sports, because other forms such as **niche and regional sponsoring** often offer themselves.
7. A **sports sponsoring philosophy**has quasi the function of a frame of reference for determining the individual contents of a sponsoring strategy, such as the determination of sports and the selection ofwhat the organizational framework should look like.
8. Especially because of limited resources, no sponsoring company can be "all things to all people". The clearer and more precise the own **principles and guidelines of sports sponsoring** are formulated, the less there is a risk of scatter losses or wrong commitments.
9. Sponsoring is also established in the **communication mix of small and medium-sized enterprises** and can be used well. Contacting selected, especially local and regional target groups without interference in a manageable emotional environment often allows for a better effect compared to classic communication instruments.

> 10. Sponsoring must be consistently put to the test: The **assessment of the cost-benefit ratio** of a sponsoring is a constant task and must also be assessed from a strategic perspective if you do not want to miss out on using your main commitments efficiently.

References

A

Allensbacher Markt- und Werbeträgeranalyse (AWA 2011–2021). Allensbacher Markt- und Werbeträgeranalyse Codebuch.

Angermair, T. (2021). Best Case Sponsoring: Der außergewöhnliche Fall HOMEDAY x Hertha BSC. https://beyond-the-match.com/sponsoring/best-case-sponsoring-homeday-x-hertha-bsc/.

AOK.de. (2016). AOK und Deutscher Handballbund: Ein starkes Team. https://www.aok.de/inhalt/starkes-doppel-aok-kooperiert-mit-dem-dhb-1/. Accessed: 20. Dec. 2016.

B

Bruhn, M. (2018). *Sponsoring. Systematische Planung und integrativer Einsatz* (6. Aufl.). https://doi.org/10.1007/978-3-658-13313-9.

Bruhn, M. (2019). *Kommunikationspolitik. Systematischer Einsatz der Kommunikation für Unternehmen* (9. Aufl.). https://doi.org/10.15358/9783800648924.

D

Deloitte. (2021). *Let's Play! 2021. The European esports market*. Deloitte. https://www2.deloitte.com/content/dam/insights/articles/de154437-lets-play-2021/DI_Lets-Play-2021.pdf.

Dircks, M. (2022). Regionales Sportmarketing: Ihr Unternehmen im Fokus der Region. https://beyond-the-match.com/sponsoring/regionales-sportmarketing-ihr-unternehmen-im-fokus-der-region/.

F

Fahy, J., Farrelly, F., & Quester, P. (2004). Competitive advantage through sponsoring: A conceptual model and research propositions. *European Journal of Marketing, 38*(8), 1013–1030. https://doi.org/10.1108/03090560410539140.

FanQ/Intelligent Research in Sponsoring. (2020). *Regionalität liegt auch bei Fußballfans voll im Trend*! (FanQ/IRIS 2020). https://fanq-app.com/wpcontent/uploads/2020/01/pressemitteilung_sponsorenstudie2019_final.pdf. Accessed: 2. Nov. 2021.

H

Horizont. (2020). Beachvolleyball: Liga-Blaupause in Düsseldorf, Beitrag vom 25.06.2020. https://www.horizont.net/media/media/32/2026_Sportbusiness_II.pdf-319324.pdf.

I

Ipsos Deutschland/ESB. (2002). Regionales Sport-Sponsoring. www.esb-online.com/literatur/SportSponsoringRegional2002.pdf.

M

Melitta. (2019). 111 Jahre Melitta Sportsponsoring. Beitrag vom 16.07.2019.

N

Nielsen Sports. (2021). Sportsponsoren in Deutschland 2020/21. https://nielsensports.com/sport-sponsoren-in-deutschland-2020-2021. Accessed: 1. May 2022.

Nielsen Sports/Repucom. (2015). Sportsponsoren in Deutschland 2014/15, Köln.

Nufer, G., & Rützel, F. (2016). Best Practices im Sportsponsoring, Nachspielzeit – die Schriftenreihe des Deutschen Instituts für Sportmarketing, herausgegeben von Gerd Nufer & André Bühler, Nr. 2016–7.

R

Roche. (2022). Spenden und Sponsoring bei Roche in Deutschland. https://www.roche.de/ueber-roche/verantwortung-dialog/gesellschaft-umwelt/sponsoring-roche-deutschland.

S

S20. (2021). Responsible Sport-Sponsoring. Modernes Sportsponsoring – verantwortungsvoll, nachhaltig und relevant. Whitepaper der S20 e.V. Bonn.

Seibert, J., & Wiese, M. (2013). Sponsoring kann die Neukundengewinnung unterstützen. *Marketing Review St. Gallen, 30*(1), 6–10. https://doi.org/10.1365/s11621-013-0184-3.

Sponsor.news. (2022a). Banken. Mit einer Reihe von Neuabschlüssen fallen Regionalbanken in einem ansonsten schwierigen Marktumfeld auf, Ausgabe 2, S. 4–5.

Sponsor.news. (2022b). „Telekom und FC Bayern: „Unser ‚T' kommt über 5.000 Minuten ins Bild", Ausgabe Aug./Sept., S. 4.

Sponsors. (2022c). *Sponsors data.* https://sites.sponsors.de/data/.

Sponsor-Service. (2022). Sponsor-Service, der internationalen Sponsorbörse. http://www.sponsor-service.com/german.htm.

Stadtwerke Tübingen. (2022). Sponsoring-Leitlinien der SWT. https://www.swtue.de/fileadmin/user_upload/4Unternehmen/Verantwortung/GesEngagement/220413_swt-Sponsoring_Leitlinien.pdf.

W

Waite, N. (1979). Sponsoring in Context. Unveröffentlichte PhD-Thesis. Cranefield Institute of Management, Cranefield.

Budgeting of Sports Sponsoring 7

Contents

Abstract

Engagement in sports sponsoring often involves a significant financial commitment. This not only refers to the agreed funds for the sponsored party, but also to the costs that the sponsor has to incur to achieve the desired effects. These are costs that are not always precisely calculated and where the sponsor can quickly face a situation that arises when entering into a planned commitment too carelessly: The budget is not sufficient, savings must be made, success is only partially or difficult to measure, and often other departments such as sales, personnel or production complain about disproportionate marketing costs. Starting the activities without a well-planned sponsoring budget and promising goals does not correspond to professional planning. This chapter provides the necessary guidance for calculating and budgeting sports sponsoring.

M. Bruhn and P. Rohlmann, *Sports Sponsoring*,
https://doi.org/10.1007/978-3-658-44171-5_7

7.1 Criteria for Budgeting

To avoid financial misplanning, it is advisable to develop a kind of **strategic guideline** for the planning, justification, and use of a sponsoring budget. This ensures that not only sufficient resources (money and personnel) are available for a successful sports sponsoring project, but also that the operational (staff) and external (customer base) acceptance is promoted (see Bruhn, 2018, pp. 63 ff., 165 ff.).

The decision for a sponsoring commitment ultimately depends largely on the pursued sponsoring goals and strategic considerations. The economic considerations and the **calculation of the budget** are therefore of high importance in sports sponsoring. To this end, the total costs of the sponsoring commitment must first be determined before the available sponsoring budget can be drawn up and distributed. The costs or prices for externally initiated sponsoring measures vary depending on the sponsoring area, the respective sponsoring activity, and the importance or "market value" of the person, team, or institution to be sponsored. In addition, factors such as the performance level, the services provided by the sponsored party, the significance of the event, the media impact, and the use of various advertising opportunities are significant in cost calculation.

The **marketing budget**—the money that a company or its marketing department has available over the course of a fiscal year for campaigns, measures, advertising materials, lead generation, and target achievement—is one of the cornerstones in the annual planning of marketing. Therefore, the provision of sufficient funds is essential. It is necessary to calculate a sufficient budget for sports sponsoring so that sports sponsoring can effectively and efficiently use sponsorings within the overall marketing strategy of a company. Central reference points for the **criteria for budgeting** are provided by the following key points:

- the sponsoring goals that are to be achieved with the budget,
- the sponsoring strategy, which is aimed at a mass market or a niche,
- the performance level that is to be sponsored,
- the degree of exclusivity aimed for through the sponsorings,
- the target group and their leisure and media behavior,
- the industry/sector in which the respective company operates,
- the company size and the company turnover,
- the degree of networking with other communication tools in the company,
- the number and experience of the employees entrusted with the implementation of sponsoring, among other things.

7.2 Components of the Sponsoring Budget

A crucial task in budgeting is to identify the relevant types of costs and cost centers in the company for the planned sponsoring activities. Basically, at least the following seven **cost components of a sponsoring budget** can be distinguished:

1. The actual **sponsoring amount** includes cash amounts, in-kind contributions, or other considerations that the sponsored parties directly receive for their services.
2. The **action budget** in the company includes the financial resources for designing all further sponsoring measures such as banners, stands, or sales promotion actions.
3. The **personnel costs** include the expenses for the use of internal or external employees who are entrusted with the planning and implementation of the sponsorings as part of a full-time or part-time employment or as a contract mandate (e.g., sponsoring agency).
4. In addition, possible **follow-up costs** for further communicative measures, for example in the context of public relations, sales promotion, or employee communication, should be taken into account.
5. Various management processes accompany a sponsoring, in particular **control and follow-up costs** for the sponsorings include, among other things, the costs for conducting impact studies and sending press releases.
6. In the event that sponsoring agencies, intermediaries, or consultants have also been involved, their **commissions or fees** should be taken into account.
7. Even in the event of an impending termination of the sponsoring relationship, certain expenses usually occur, especially when a non-harmonious or dissonance-laden end occurs. In this case, **termination costs** need to be calculated, which necessitates transparency in the public through communication campaigns to accompany the termination of the sponsoring relationship (Dreisbach, 2018, p. 131; Salzer, 2022).

In Fig. 7.1, the different budgets in sports sponsoring are listed to determine the total budget. It is particularly important not only to calculate the externally caused costs but also to allocate the internal (calculatory) costs according to their cause.

In Fig. 7.2, a fictitious **example of calculating a sponsoring** is shown, which refers to the individual partial costs. The example makes it clear that when considering the total budget, in addition to acquiring the actual sponsoring rights, at least the same amount should be expected for the implementation of a sponsoring.

However, in practice, only very rough and general indications can be observed for the amount of individual cost components. There will rarely be fixed prices for sponsorings, nor are there any special price lists for sponsors. Rather, a primarily independent **calculation of cost components** by the companies and sponsored parties based on past experience values, which form a basis for setting the sponsor contributions, dominates. Contrary to expectations, the proportion of expenses that were paid directly to the

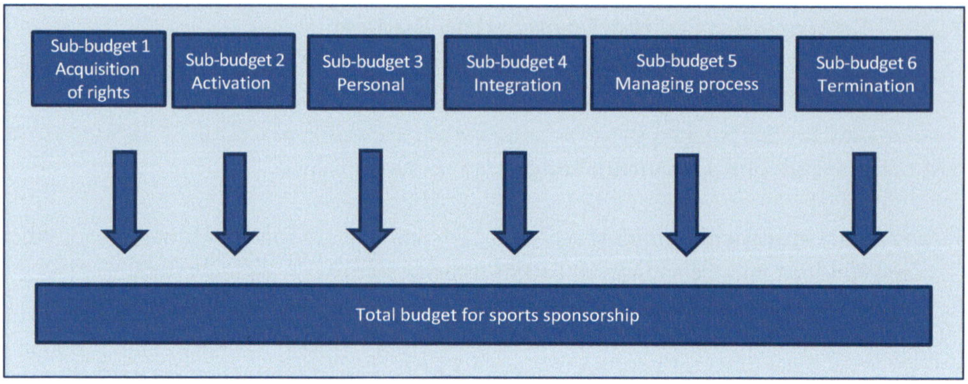

Fig. 7.1 Sub-budgets in sports sponsoring

Cost types	Output items	Sample figures in EUR
Preparation	Planning and conception	50,000
Actual sponsorship rights	Premium partner of a first division soccer team	2,500,000
Action budget	Design of the sports sponsorship: VIP room, perimeter boards, sales stands, etc.	1,250,000
Personnel costs	Seconded employees or organization team, photographers, hostesses, etc.	500,000
Follow-up costs for networked communication	Advertisements, TV commercials, press/public relations, production of advertising material, promotion	750,000
Control and follow-up work	Execution of impact studies and regular press releases, documentation	100,000
Commissions, fees	Marketing agencies involved, intermediary or consultant	250,000
Termination	Possible expense at the end of sponsorship	50,000
Projected total costs for sports sponsorship		5,450,000

Fig. 7.2 Example of a calculation in sports sponsoring

sponsored party has been steadily growing since 1998, while the proportion invested in communication and implementation of the measures has decreased from 27.2 to 20.7%. In 2012, according to company surveys, up to 80% of the expenses went directly to the sponsored party, while the rest was invested in the implementation (Bagusat, 2013,

p. 63). In addition to the communicative marketing of a sponsoring, additional costs arise mainly through personnel costs. The often incurred commission rates for sponsoring consultants and intermediaries are—depending on the service—about 15 to 20% of the sponsoring budget. Furthermore, about two percent of the budget should be provided for regular success controls (Reischauer, 1997, p. 61).

7.3 Determining Budget Size and Budget Allocation

The budgeting of sponsoring refers to the calculation of the total sponsoring budget and the allocation to individual sponsoring measures. This involves determining the total costs incurred by the company's sponsoring activities. Ideally, the budget is set simultaneously with the planning of individual measures, as the cost is largely dependent on the chosen sponsorings. Similar to advertising budgeting, it is necessary in sponsoring to budget all expenses associated with the measures for a planning period (month, year). In budgeting, these two **decision problems** arise:

- Determination of the amount of the sponsoring budget **(budget size)**,
- Distribution of the sponsoring budget in terms of content and time **(budget allocation)**.

Budget Size In general, p the **methods for determining the budget size** can be distinguished into analytical and heuristic procedures (Bruhn, 2018, p. 65).

Analytical procedures are based on the determination of advertising response functions and optimization approaches. They are therefore fundamentally suitable for providing precise information for the calculation of the communication budget. However, since they involve extensive information and planning efforts and thus also significant costs, they are rarely used in practice. Specifically for the budgeting of sponsoring, it is further complicated by the fact that the sales volume, which is central in these procedures, shows only a low responsiveness to the use of sponsoring, so that no meaningful success functions can be modeled (see the explanations on event marketing by Nufer, 2006, p. 73).

For this reason, the determination of the sponsoring budget size mainly uses **heuristic procedures**, which are mostly based on the subjective experiences and intuition of the sponsoring managers. However, a large part of the heuristics commonly used in practice, e.g. percentage of sales, orientation towards sales volumes, competitive parity method (Tietz & Zentes, 1980, pp. 288 ff.; Rogge, 2004, p. 142; Kotler & Bliemel, 2007, pp. 913 ff.; Bruhn, 2019, pp. 246 ff.) are of little use from a business perspective for determining the budget, as a cause-effect relationship between the sponsoring activities and the pursued goals is not taken into account.

Another method for determining the budget size is the **goal-measure method**, as it most closely meets the theoretical requirements for a logically justified decision-making procedure. This method calculates the costs incurred based on the set sponsoring goals, which sponsoring activities are to be carried out to achieve the goals. In addition to the difficulties in determining costs, this method is associated with the problem of gathering sufficient information about the effect of the sponsorings that can be used to achieve the goals (Bruhn, 2018).

Budget Allocation After determining the total budget size, **criteria for budget allocation** are set, i.e. the distribution of the budget according to packages of measures, time units, regions, etc. As part of the budget allocation, it must be decided according to content and time criteria which part of the budget is spent when for the individual sponsorings. The temporal budget allocation is closely linked to the established sponsoring strategy, as the decision on the sponsoring timing already determines the temporal distribution of the budget. The content-related budget allocation is primarily carried out from an economic perspective based on a cost-benefit analysis. As a consequence, sponsorings that make a disproportionate contribution to achieving the goals should be budgeted disproportionately (Schweiger & Schrattenecker, 2013, pp. 223 ff.).

For illustration, Fig. 7.3 shows an example of the **distribution of a company budget** across three sports sponsoring projects. In the context of the sponsoring commitments, which all fulfill the company fit to varying degrees, the company sets a clear priority for Project A.

The planning and implementation of sponsorings sometimes lead to numerous budgeting problems in companies when other internal budgets are affected by the sponsoring commitment. However, company surveys indicate that the use of sponsoring leads to an increase in communication budgets in a large part of companies and more and more companies have their own **sponsoring budgets** (Pilot Checkpoint, 2008; Nielsen Sports—formerly Repucom, 2015). This contradicts the thesis that sponsoring is at the expense of "classic" communication tools.

Sports sponsorship	Project A	Project B	Project C	Total
Acquisition of rights	3.5	1.2	1.0	5.7
Activation	3.0	0.8	0.5	4.3
Budget in EUR million	6.5	2.0	1.5	10.0
Company fit	90 %	80 %	75 %	

Fig. 7.3 Example of a budget allocation in sports sponsoring (figures in million EUR)

7.4 Budgeting Methods in Practice

In the media, speculations and estimates about the budgets of individual engagements in sports sponsoring are regularly mentioned. These are sometimes closer and sometimes further away from the true sum. However, what is much more important for the success of a sponsoring is not the absolute sum for a specific usage right in sports, but how the total cost volume for is composed. This can be differentiated as rights budget and activation budget. The rights budget refers to the sum that the sponsor pays the sponsored party for the respective rights package. For the sponsored party, these are revenues, for the sponsoring party, they are expenses. The **activation or implementation budget** includes all costs that are additionally available to the sponsor to use and activate his purchased rights or to "fill them with life" (Hohenauer, 2016). These can include, among other things, production costs for advertising materials, personnel or agency costs, as well as media costs.

The first question, therefore, is about the **costs for certain sponsoring rights**. In sponsoring pricing, two economic organizations essentially face each other (B2B level) and here, different forms of price determination or pricing usually apply than on the end consumer side (B2C level). For the respective provider and demander of sponsoring rights, it is about finding the "right" price for an agreement. This is often a difficult and complex undertaking. Often, it is relatively arbitrarily and not very comprehensibly determined how much the sponsoring will cost and what services are associated with it. The lack of transparency about the **value of the rights** often lies in the fact that there is often no clear offer and demand behavior in sponsoring, which is why an exact price determination in advance is only possible to a limited extent. While the official or verifiable costs of an event could be calculated and passed on to the sponsors, the allocation of voluntary services, for example, is just as difficult as the exact evaluation of qualitative components. Even the exact calculation of media minutes does not help much or at all here, as they only represent a very superficial indicator and do not reflect the quality of the sports event.

For a marketing concept and the willingness to sponsor by companies, the **prices of sponsoring packages** play a central role. There are no general guidelines and rules for price determination. Rather, a number of influencing factors must be taken into account, which ultimately result in the price. There are different possibilities for the **methods of price determination**. The following procedures are of particular importance in practice:

- Calculation of the cost-benefit ratio,
- Alignment with market prices,
- Calculation of opportunity costs.

Calculation of the Cost-Benefit Ratio A "right" or "fair" price always results when the cost-benefit ratio is balanced, i.e. when the benefit is considered justified compared to the costs or prices. The costs, for example, include the effort for conception, implementation, control, and documentation. It will be particularly difficult to put the effort in relation to the financial or material benefit of the partner. The benefit of the partner is not only to be measured in quantitative criteria (e.g. reach, cost per thousand, etc.), but also contains qualitative criteria (e.g. transfer of image values). An adequate cost-benefit ratio or the value of the sponsoring package is achieved when the cost-benefit ratio is at least balanced.

Alignment with Market Prices Sponsoring packages are bundles of services, where both the competing service offers and the specific demand behavior must be taken into account. So the question is who offers similar offers in sports sponsoring at what prices and who demands these at what prices. The focus here is on the price willingness of the demanding sponsoring interested parties. This results primarily from the (subjectively evaluated) benefit of a sports right for a purchaser. Here it can be helpful to think in analogies and to orient oneself to similar market prices or "industry-standard" prices for the targeted benefit.

Calculation of Opportunity Costs With opportunity costs, it is necessary to check which costs would be incurred by companies willing to sponsor with other or similar advertising opportunities. Prices for other sponsorings can provide orientation. There are attempts to evaluate sponsoring using market research studies in sports. Advertising equivalence calculations and cost per thousand contact prices are used (see also the example of Rakuten in Sect. 6.1 of this book). Even elaborate sponsoring evaluations by specific models of sports agencies are carried out, but these can ultimately only calculate the value of the sponsoring package to a limited extent.

Expert studies or agency evaluations often cannot provide sufficient decision-making bases for the sports sponsor. Therefore, other ways must be found to achieve an appropriate evaluation of the sponsoring offers based on the simultaneous consideration of the cost-benefit ratio, alignment with market prices, and the inclusion of opportunity costs. One possibility, for example, is to orient oneself to the offer prices of other sponsored parties or comparable market prices. Meanwhile, science has also increasingly turned to the problem of price determination in sports business and developed approaches to this (Chatrath & Wengler, 2009).

7.5 Budgeting as a Basis for Negotiations

A central element in sponsoring budgeting is the price determination of the offer. This can be seen as the subject of negotiations to determine the value of the offer. This so-called **value-analytical approach** (Chatrath & Wengler, 2009) aims at determining the value drivers of an offered sponsoring package from the perspective of a potential customer.

To **determine the value drivers** of a sponsoring offer, the price determination is similar to that in similarly structured project business and is based on a classic cost-benefit analysis. The first step is to start with a calculation of the price based on the self-costs incurred by the seller. The goal is to determine the economic price lower limit (Pu) using appropriate calculation methods. As shown in Fig. 7.4, to determine the price policy leeway of a seller, it is necessary in a second step to determine or estimate the buyer's price upper limit (Po). It is necessary to determine the price the buyer would be willing to pay at most. This is often how it works in sponsoring. Even if you have set a price for your sponsoring offer, this does not mean that this price will be paid by the partner in the end. Whenever there are concrete negotiations regarding the contents of a cooperation, the sponsored parties will find that in addition to changes in the offered services, there are also modifications in the (financial) counter-services of the sponsor. This is due, among other things, to the fact that each partner starts the negotiation from different conditions and interests and thus competition does not allow for price dictation.

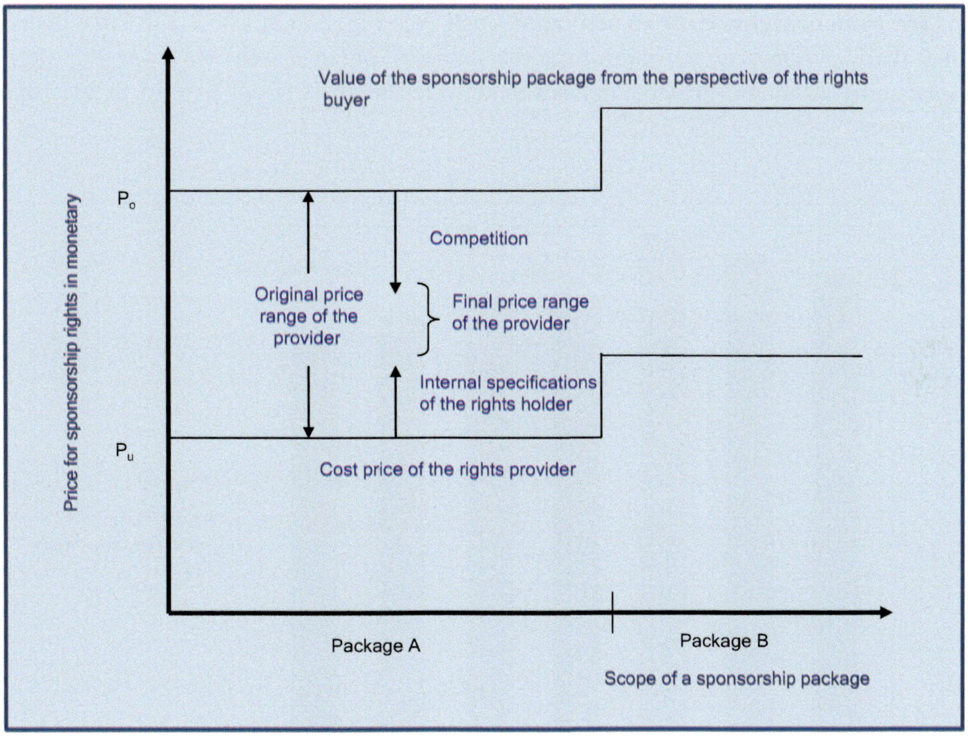

Fig. 7.4 Price determination in sponsoring as a negotiation model. (*Source:* Chatrath & Wengler, 2009)

7.6 Budgeting of Activation Costs

In addition to the price determination for the sponsoring packages, the costs for the implementation of the sponsorings to achieve the planned sponsoring goals play an important role. These so-called **activation costs of sponsoring** are still the determining basis and adjustment screw for success in the eyes of decision-makers. Therefore, sponsors are generally willing to invest at least the same amount—if not even more than the rights amount—for the activation of their sponsoring in traditional or digital media as well as other advertising measures.

Of course, the **target of the sponsoring** plays an important role in terms of the share of the activation budget. For example, a pure perimeter advertising presence in football can achieve reach and awareness, even without using an excessive activation budget. A networked sponsoring, which sometimes pursues many different targets (besides image and awareness also goals like customer loyalty, sales targets, CSR etc.), needs a much stronger activation. An old rule says that the total sponsoring budget should at least double the amount of funding determined for the partner.

The **ratio of rights costs to activation costs** (see Fig. 7.5) of 1 to 1.2 in 2018 underlines the importance of activation from the sponsors' point of view. However, this value is declining again after a stable upward trend in recent years (from 1 to 0.5 in 2010 and

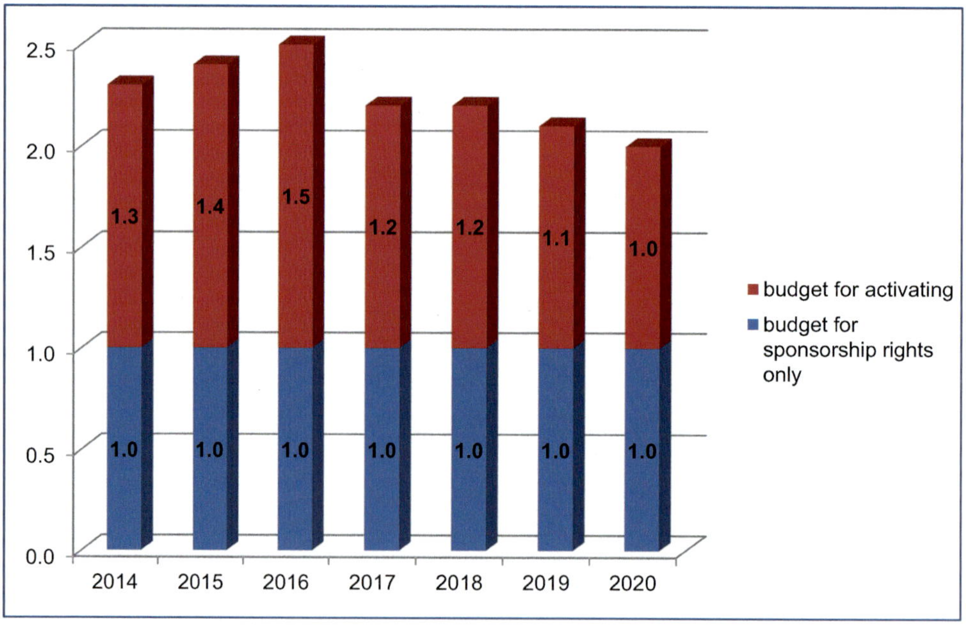

Fig. 7.5 Ratio of rights and activation costs in sponsoring. (*Source:* Nielsen Sponsor Reports, 2014–2018; own estimates 2019–2020)

from 1 to 1.5 in 2016 to about 1 to 1 in 2020). The current tendency to save in companies and especially in certain sectors (automobiles, finance) is also taking its toll in the financing and activation of sponsoring commitments. The Corona pandemic in 2020 and 2021 is unlikely to have reduced this downward trend. If you take the average of the past years, the activation budget was about 25% higher than the rights budget.

Also, because the above-mentioned cost ratios apply to all forms of sponsoring, it can be assumed that efforts will likely be even higher in the most competitive sports markets. In addition to the rights costs, sports sponsors have recently spent up to half more on implementation than on the acquisition of rights, so that the total costs for a sports sponsoring have more than doubled. The strong eagerness to implement and the will to succeed are evaluated positively on the one hand, but on the other hand, the ratio does not yet say anything about whether the rights budget or the associated activation budget is appropriate.

How important a networked **activation for successful sponsoring** is, was determined in a survey on sports sponsoring (Nielsen, 2018b). Social media is attributed the greatest importance by far with 90% (previous year: 61%). But all other areas also increase to some extent, which is likely to result in growing investments in the networking and activation of sponsoring, especially through networked activation with other departments in the company (see Fig. 7.6).

The necessity for the activation of sports sponsoring is ultimately also reflected in the **assessment of decision-makers on budget development** (VSA, 2021). Without activation, the instrument of sponsoring cannot unfold its power. Therefore, financial resources must be provided for this—otherwise, the acquisition of certain usage rights in sports would be inconsistent and not purposeful. However, the willingness for well-activated sponsoring is seen as quite large by the surveyed experts: 62% consider the projection "Sponsors will provide more budget for activation than for the acquisition of rights" likely. Also, in terms of the dimensions "desirability" (with 5.5 on a 7-point scale) and "extent" (4.8), the statement was rated above average positive (see Fig. 7.7).

The company survey was conducted during the Corona pandemic, which has also posed many problems and challenges for the sports sponsoring market. At the same time, the crisis has shown how sports, despite all adversities, could trigger positive emotions in people. Therefore, it can be assumed that a certain trend towards activation in 2019 and 2020 was only temporary. As a rough rule of thumb for budgeting, the previously presented relations can therefore be used as reliable determinants for successful sports sponsoring by companies.

The many opportunities of well-activated sponsoring, however, are also faced with one or other internal hurdles. This concerns the question of internal **participation of departments in the sponsoring budget**. This also raises important questions such as the coordination between the involved company areas in terms of target and task division, the ongoing and efficient control of the project, the involvement of agencies and service providers, etc. It seems obvious that complex tasks like a larger sponsoring need flexible structures and processes to be successfully implemented.

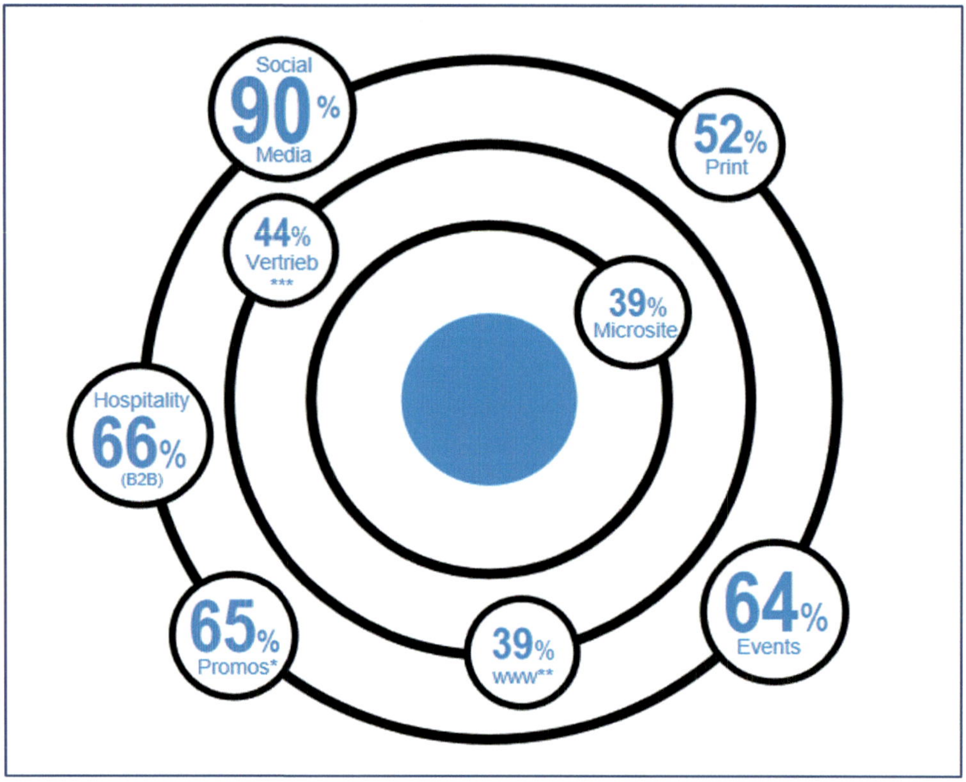

Fig. 7.6 Successful sports sponsoring through networked activation (* Promotion actions in the event environment/** on general pages on the Internet/*** new distribution channels via sponsoring partners). (*Source:* Nielsen, 2018a, p. 14)

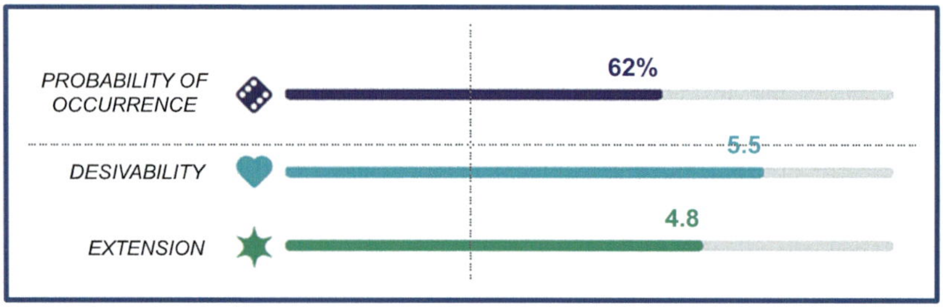

Fig. 7.7 Importance of activation for successful sports sponsoring (agreement on a 7-point scale). (*Source:* VSA, 2021, p. 16)

The sometimes very high prices demanded in the sports sponsoring market for dominant team sports and major events usually reflect the demand—nevertheless or perhaps for this very reason, it is worth for sponsors of all kinds to look into the numerous **niche sports**. This applies to corporations and medium-sized companies alike. In sports areas that are less in the spotlight, there are considerable advertising opportunities that are still largely neglected by many potential sponsors. Even if the quantitative reach cannot compete with that of the "big sports": If the right products are placed in the right target group with an ideal "fit", one can expect a higher return-on-sponsoring-investment (ROSI) for a small budget. In other words: With a high reach, as is consistently the case with an engagement in the Football Bundesliga, the scatter loss for some sponsors often bears no relation to the extensive sponsoring budget.

In the age of increasing digitalization, sports sponsoring is one of the few marketing tools that offers brands the opportunity to reach consumers on a broad scale. This explains why big and well-known brands are willing to pay millions of dollars to build a relationship with the fan communities of sports clubs, sports events, and sports organizations. According to a YouGov study, which conducted a consumer survey on the **suitability of industries as sports sponsors** in 17 markets worldwide at the end of 2021 (YouGov, 2022a), brands from certain industries may be better positioned or accepted than others to benefit from the platform of sports sponsoring. Worldwide, automobile manufacturers are most likely to be seen as suitable for sports sponsoring. Over a third of consumers (36%) consider car manufacturers to be suitable sponsors of professional sports clubs, leagues, or athletes. Technology (34%) and telecommunications brands (34%) follow closely behind. Three out of five consumers also consider banks and insurance brands (31%) as well as companies in the tourism industry (31%) to be suitable sponsors in sports (see Fig. 7.8).

In this study, despite the close and long-standing connections of the gambling industry to the sports business, interestingly only 12% of consumers stated that they can be seen as "appropriate sponsors of professional sports clubs, sports leagues, or athletes". Cryptocurrencies have recently signed a number of notable contracts for sports sponsoring, but only one in ten consumers thinks they are suitable partners (10%).

Opinions on how appropriate it is for certain industries to engage in sports sponsoring can vary greatly in different markets. Britons and Germans are least likely to believe that cryptocurrencies are suitable as sports sponsors (6%), while Americans (11%) accept this much more. One fifth of consumers in France (20%) and Mexico (20%) consider it appropriate for gambling brands to participate in sports sponsoring. Consumers in the UK (7%) and Italy (7%) are at the other end of the spectrum.

Taking into account therefore also **attitudes of fans**, it would be appropriate for some sponsors to reconsider their sponsoring commitments and the associated budgets. The target group obviously denies many of them the suitability as a sports sponsor from the outset. Of course, a brand from an industry with low acceptance for sports sponsoring can still enter effective partnerships in the sports industry. But consumer attitudes are a factor that marketers have to consider when they develop plans to engage in sports and with sports sponsoring.

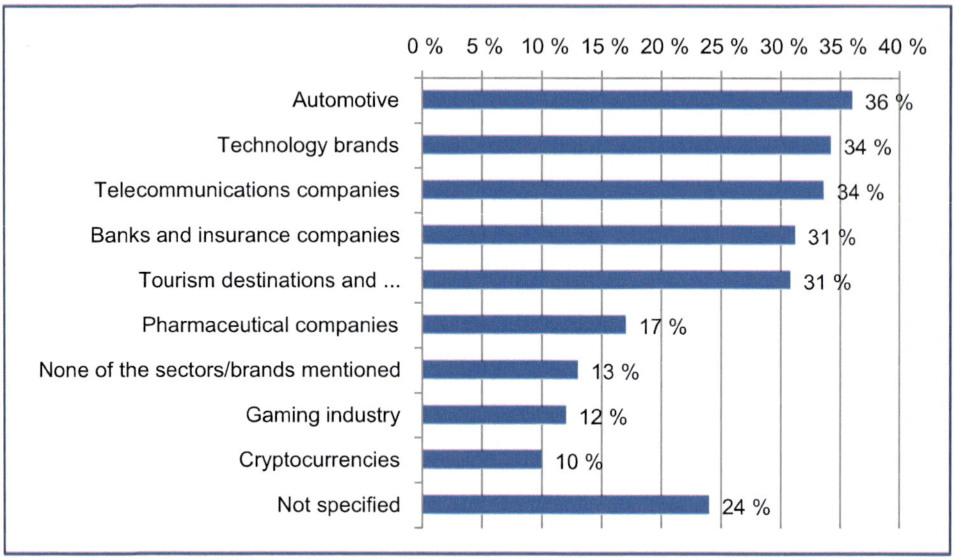

Fig. 7.8 Industry and brand suitability for sports sponsoring. (*Source:* YouGov, 2022a)

7.7 Sponsoring Volumes in Practice

It is often difficult to have an approximate order of magnitude in mind when it comes to operating a promising in sports. Therefore, an **examination of the sports sponsoring market** according to the most committed companies and industries is interesting.

In the past seven years, the top 10 **companies with the largest sports sponsoring volumes** in Germany have increased their expenditures to around 770 million EUR, or by a third (see Fig. 7.9). This leads to the conclusion that sports sponsoring is still considered a very suitable means of achieving marketing goals, but it also becomes clear that in the premium class of sports sponsoring, the expenditures of individual commitments are constantly increasing.

In both rankings (2014/2015 and 2021/2022), it is noticeable that car manufacturers and sports equipment manufacturers dominate in this respect. This already indicates that certain industries apparently use this tool particularly intensively in their marketing work. If you also look at the top 10 industries in terms of **sponsoring expenditures in German professional football**, the same picture is confirmed in a similar way (see Fig. 7.10). Of the approximately 530 million EUR, half is accounted for by the sports equipment and automobile industries.

Even when looking at the **sponsoring volumes from the perspective of the sponsored**, there are quite different results regarding the scope and structure of the supported. The differences can be clearly illustrated using examples from three Bundesliga football clubs (see Fig. 7.11). It is easy to see that the expectations of the sponsoring companies

Rank	2014/15	Volume of sports sponsorship
1	Volkswagen/Audi	140.0
2	Savings banks	91.0
3	Mercedes-Benz	85.0
4	Adidas	85.0
5	German Telekom	50.0
6	Bayer AG	39.0
7	BMW	30.0
8	Alliance	21.0
9	Coca-Cola	19.0
10	Nike	19.0
	Top 10	**579.0**

Rank	2021/22	Volume of sports sponsorship
1	Volkswagen/Audi	160.0
2	Adidas	136.0
3	Savings banks	100.0
4	Alliance	98.0
5	Mercedes-Benz	75.0
6	German Telekom	67.0
7	Puma	43.0
8	Bayer AG	40.0
9	Coca-Cola	25.0
10	Nike	25.0
	Top 10	**769.0**

Fig. 7.9 Companies with the largest sports sponsoring volumes in Germany (figures in million EUR). (*Source:* Repucom, Nielsen Sports; PR MARKETING)

Fig. 7.10 The strongest sponsoring industries in German professional football (figures in million EUR). (*Source:* Media information and PR MARKETING)

1st + 2nd German Soccer League	2021/22
Sporting goods	138.0
Automotive	129.0
Telecommunications	71.0
Beverages	63.0
Insurances	48.0
Banks	23.5
Industry/Mechanical Engineering	22.5
Energy	14.5
Food (incl. retail)	10.5
Real estate	9.0
Top 10	**529,0**

are different solely based on the value of the sponsorings per sponsoring category. The proportion of foreign sponsors in the clubs also shows that the appeal and value of sponsoring relationships place very different demands on the budgets of interested companies.

7.8 Key Points

Successful sports sponsoring requires professional and precise budgeting. It is advisable to keep a close eye on certain topics.

	FC Bayern München	
Sponsoring category	Number of sponsors	Sponsorship amount (in EUR million)
1st category	4	141.0
2nd category	8	49.0
3rd category	3	6.0
4th category	18	11.0
Total	33	207.0
	Domestic sponsors	Foreign sponsors
1st-4th category	19	14
Pro rata	58 %	42 %

	Borussia Dortmund	
Sponsoring category	Number Sponsors	Sponsorship amount (in EUR million)
1st category	4	70.0
2nd category	10	27.0
3rd category	11	8.0
4th category	23	9.0
Total	48	114.0
	Domestic sponsors	Foreign sponsors
1st-4th category	41	7
Pro rata	85 %	15 %

	1st FC Cologne	
Sponsoring category	Number Sponsors	Sponsorship amount (in EUR million)
1st category	4	14.0
2nd category	4	4.0
3rd category	4	1.5
4th category	11	4.0
Total	23	23.5
	Domestic sponsors	Foreign sponsors
1st-4th category	21	2
Pro rata	91 %	9 %

Fig. 7.11 Scope and structure in sports sponsoring from the perspective of the sponsored in the 2020/2021 season. (*Source:* Club information and PR MARKETING)

Key Points

1. A crucial basis for the budgeting of sports sponsoring is a **strategic guideline** that provides orientation for the necessary financial resources for planning, implementation, and control of the sponsoring budget.
2. The budgeting of the sponsoring initially refers to the **calculation of the total sponsoring budget**. In addition to the expenses for the sponsored party, the own costs for activating the sponsorings must be taken into account.
3. The **budget size** is dependent on the pursued sponsoring goals and special strategic considerations (including which sports, which performance level, which markets). In addition, company-specific factors (including industry, size, competition) play a significant role.
4. Once the total budget for sports sponsoring is set, a **budget allocation** must be made. The sponsoring budget is to be distributed according to factual and temporal criteria as well as taking into account priorities.
5. Various methods can be used for **pricing sponsoring packages**, such as the calculation of cost-benefit ratios, market prices, and opportunity costs. In addition to using these methods, pricing is usually the result of price negotiations.
6. A sponsoring budget for a specific commitment consists of several **cost components**, including sponsoring rights, activation costs, personnel, follow-up and post-processing effort. These costs need to be calculated carefully and generously.
7. The **activation of a sponsoring** is a determining basis and the most important lever for the success of sponsorings in sports. As a rule of thumb, at least the same amount—if not even a higher amount than the rights costs—should be used for the activation of the sponsoring in traditional and digital media as well as other advertising measures.

8. Integrated activation is essential for successful sponsoring, especially the inclusion of digital media. In this context, a sufficient **sponsoring budget can be mentioned as a crucial prerequisite**.
9. The sometimes very high prices demanded on the sports sponsoring market for dominant team sports and major events usually reflect the demand, but it is worthwhile to also deal with the **niche sports**. They often provide an adequate counter value for the sponsoring budget.
10. There are always certain industry waves and **trends in sports sponsoring**. Especially then, potential sponsors should not engage with partners who make unrealistic promises for a given budget. In this case, it is advantageous if relevant experience values are available.

References

B

Bagusat, A. (2013). *Sponsoring trends 2012*. https://www.ostfalia.de/export/sites/default/de/ispm/Blickpunkt_Sportmanagement/Sponsoring_Trends_2012.pdf. Accessed: 17. Febr. 2016.

Bruhn, M. (2018). *Sponsoring. Systematische Planung und integrativer Einsatz* (6. Aufl.). https://doi.org/10.1007/978-3-658-13313-9.

Bruhn, M. (2019). *Kommunikationspolitik. Systematischer Einsatz der Kommunikation für Unternehmen* (9. Aufl.). https://doi.org/10.15358/9783800648924.

C

Chatrath, S., & Wengler, S. (2009). Preisfindung für und Bewertung von Sportssponsorings, Ausgabe 5 von Berliner Reihe zum Marketing. Freie Universität Berlin, Marketing-Department.

D

Dreisbach, J. (2018). *Erfolgsfaktoren der Sponsoringumsetzung und -aktivierung – Eine empirische Analyse aus Management- und Konsumentenwirkungsperspektive im Kontext der Fußball-Bundesliga*. Springer Gabler. https://doi.org/10.1007/978-3-658-24519-1.

H

Hohenauer, R. (2016). *Sponsoring-Wirkung auf das Kaufverhalten*. https://doi.org/10.1007/978-3-658-15573-5.

K

Kotler, P., & Bliemel, F. (2007). *Marketing Management. Analyse, Planung und Verwirklichung* (11. Aufl.). Schäffer-Poeschel.

N

Nielsen Sports. (2015). Sponsor-Trend 2015: Status und Trends im Sponsoringmarkt in Deutschland, Österreich und Schweiz. http://www.marketing.ch/Portals/0/Wissen/Allgemein/Repucom%20Insights_Sponsor-Trend%202015_DACH_SFS.pdf. Accessed: 17. Febr. 2016.

Nielsen Sports. (2018a). Sponsor-Trend 2018: Status und Trends im Sponsoringmarkt in Deutschland, Österreich und Schweiz.

Nielsen Sports. (2018b). *World football report 2018*.

Nufer, G. (2006). *Event-Marketing: theoretische Fundierung und empirische Analyse unter besonderer Berücksichtigung von Imagewirkungen* (2. Aufl.). Deutscher Universitäts Verlag.

P

Pilot Checkpoint. (2008). *Sponsor visions 2008*.

R

Reischauer, C. (1997). Mit Sportsponsoring die gewünschte Wirkung zu erreichen, wird immer schwieriger. *Wirtschaftswoche, 51*(6), 60–65.

Rogge, H. -J. (2004). *Werbung* (6. Aufl.). NWB.

S

Salzer, F. (2022). *Beendigungsmanagement von Sponsoringbeziehungen – Konzeption und empirische Analyse eines Wirkungsmodells*. https://doi.org/10.1007/978-3-658-37778-6.

Schweiger, G., & Schrattenecker, G. (2013). *Werbung* (8. Aufl.). UVK.

T

Tietz, B., & Zentes, J. (1980). *Die Werbung der Unternehmung*. Rowohlt.

V

VSA. (2021). Delphi-Studie: Zukunft 2030 – Sportsponsoring im Wandel, WHU – Otto Beisheim School of Management, Center for Sports and Management, Düsseldorf.

Y

YouGov. (2022a). *Global: Which industries are best suited for sports sponsoring?* https://sport.yougov.com/global-which-industries-are-best-suited-for-sports-sponsoring/. Accessed: 2. Nov. 2021.

Selection of Engagements in Sports Sponsoring

8

Contents

Abstract

The selection of Sponsorings in sports sponsoring is both a strategic and a tactical decision. Initially, a strategic process of rough selection of sports is described, in which connection lines to the product, to the target group, and to the desired image are sought according to the affinity concept. The fine selection involves the choice of specific sponsorings in sports. For this decision, the company provides selection criteria, which are often also documented in guidelines and principles. The chapter includes a case study of Mercedes-Benz on the termination of the sponsoring with the DFB, as well as numerous practical examples from the companies Homeday, Deutsche Telekom, AOK, Skinfit, Gazprom, Rewe, and the IOC.

M. Bruhn and P. Rohlmann, *Sports Sponsoring*,
https://doi.org/10.1007/978-3-658-44171-5_8

8.1 Levels of Selection Decisions

The selection of sports sponsorings follows a staged process. A special importance is attached to the determination of the sponsored party. This is done with the rough selection of sports and the fine selection of specific sponsorings. So it is about **sponsoring decisions on two levels**:

- The **rough selection** encompasses the choice of sports. This is about the decision regarding the sports suitable for the company, such as tennis, archery or rowing.
- As part of the **fine selection** the choice of sponsoring forms is made. The focus is on the decision about the form of support in the respective sports. Possible are, for example, the sponsoring of individuals, groups, institutions, projects or events.

8.2 Rough Selection of Sports

In the **phase of rough selection** of sports, criteria must be defined on the basis of which the suitability of the sports for the communicative task of the company can be checked. A central role is played by possible connection lines ("links") between the sponsoring company and sports. According to the **affinity concept**, the following three **connection lines** are conceivable (see Bruhn, 2018, pp. 153 ff.):

- **Product affinity:** The sports has a certain relationship to the product or service of the sponsor. The sports affinity of individual products and brands is primarily determined by the dominant product-benefit dimensions. While technically functional products, such as sports equipment, are most likely to be classified as sports-affine, pleasure goods, such as cigarettes and alcoholic beverages, have a low sports affinity. The example of the numerous sports sponsoring activities of various beer brands shows that even products and brands in this category can achieve a higher sports affinity and corresponding image change through sports-oriented communication.
- **Target group affinity:** The sports finds special interest in a certain target group, which is also important for the sponsor. Fig. 8.1 illustrates, for example, that men aged 50 and over with an above-average income and higher education have a pronounced interest in golf (AWA, 2016).
- **Image affinity:** The image of the sports is similar to the image of the company (Corporate Image), the umbrella or individual brand (Product Image, Brand Image) or a similarity can be associated.

Other conceivable connection lines are, for example, the common **location reference** of sponsor and sponsored party or similarly perceived "externals" of both sponsoring partners (Bassenge, 2000, pp. 108 f.). For example, the Badische Staatsbrauerei Rothaus is

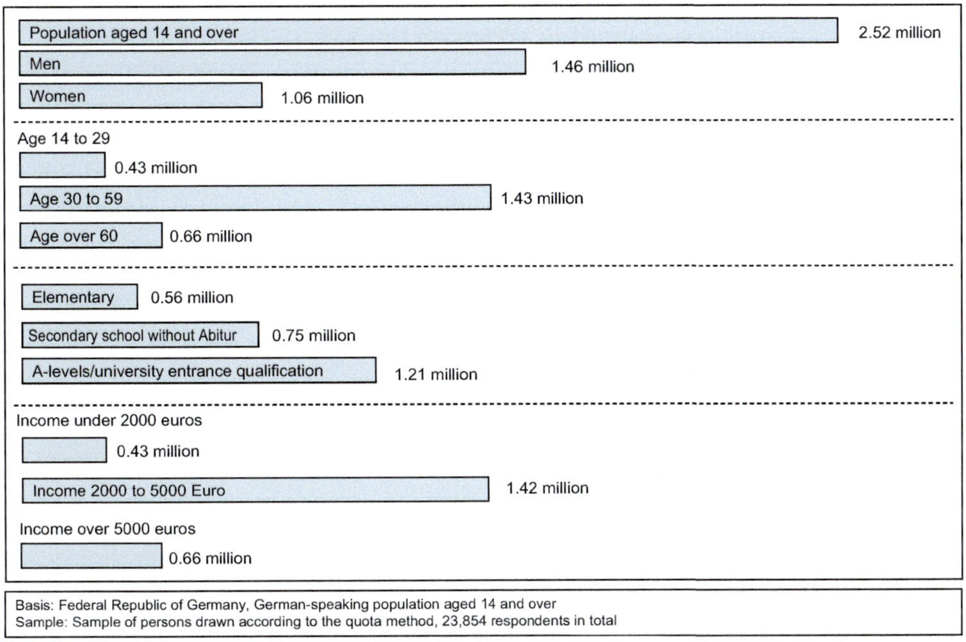

Fig. 8.1 Sociodemographic distribution of golf players. (*Source:* AWA, 2016)

primarily involved in its home market Baden-Württemberg, especially the Black Forest region, and acts there as a sponsor of numerous clubs such as the Bundesliga football club SC Freiburg (since 2005) and the ice hockey club EHC Freiburg (since 1996).

Possible affinities between companies and sports need to be examined in more detail. To support this methodically, it is advisable to use the **point rating method**.

This is illustrated by the example of the **analysis of image affinities**. The examination is carried out in three steps:

- Determination of the image characteristics relevant to the company and to be aimed for (product/company) with a weight of importance,
- Evaluation of the various sports with regard to the individual image characteristics,
- Rough selection of some sports (e.g., based on the height of the point values) that are to be further analyzed.

In Fig. 8.2, the **scheme for a point evaluation method** for the rough selection of sports is exemplarily represented. The method is equally used for the rough selection of types of sponsoring. The procedure is based on the fact that evaluations are made for the individual sports at each stage.

Since image dimensions are fundamentally determined by the category of a sponsoring engagement, an engagement in sports already results in a first rough positioning for

Sponsoring areas	Image dimensions						Weighted points			Total points
	Dimension 1		Dimension 2		Dimension 3		1	2	3	
		Weight		Weight		Weight	Point x Weight	Point x Weight	Point x Weight	
	Point value	0.5	Point value	0.2	Point value	0.3				
e.g. squash	4	0.5	6	0.2	10	0.3	2	1.2	3	6.2
Total										
Weight: total 100 %; point values 1 = very low to 10 = very high										

Fig. 8.2 Use of point evaluation methods for the rough selection of sports

a company. Thus, characteristics such as healthy, young, fast, and lively are associated with "sports in general", while other forms of sponsoring (e.g., socio-, environmental, and media sponsoring) fundamentally stand for other dimensions. The specification of a desired positioning is carried out through the analysis of the relevant image dimensions of individual sports (Meenaghan & Shipley, 1999, p. 341). In individual cases, three different **image dimensions** can be distinguished:

- **Image of the sports institution:** for example, image characteristics of clubs or associations,
- **Image of the sponsored person:** for example, the image of a sports personality and their suitability as a role model or testimonial,
- **Image of the sports:** for example, image characteristics such as endurance, fitness, aesthetics of the individual sports, etc.

After specifying the desired image dimensions, the circle of potential sports for the company is reduced by the descriptive characteristics. The specific **image characteristics of the selected sports** or sports events then also affect the image of the sports sponsors. A study on the image profile of the sports Formula 1 came to the results shown in Fig. 8.3. The sports Formula 1 is associated with positive associations such as "high quality", "dynamic" and "combative".

In a similar way, market research institutes conduct image profiles of top athletes and sports institutions. Fig. 8.4 shows **image profiles of selected sports associations**. For example, the German Tennis Federation (DTB) is seen as particularly high-performing and successful. The German Football Association (DFB) was rated as credible and trustworthy. Whether this is still the case after the last Football World Cups remains to be seen.

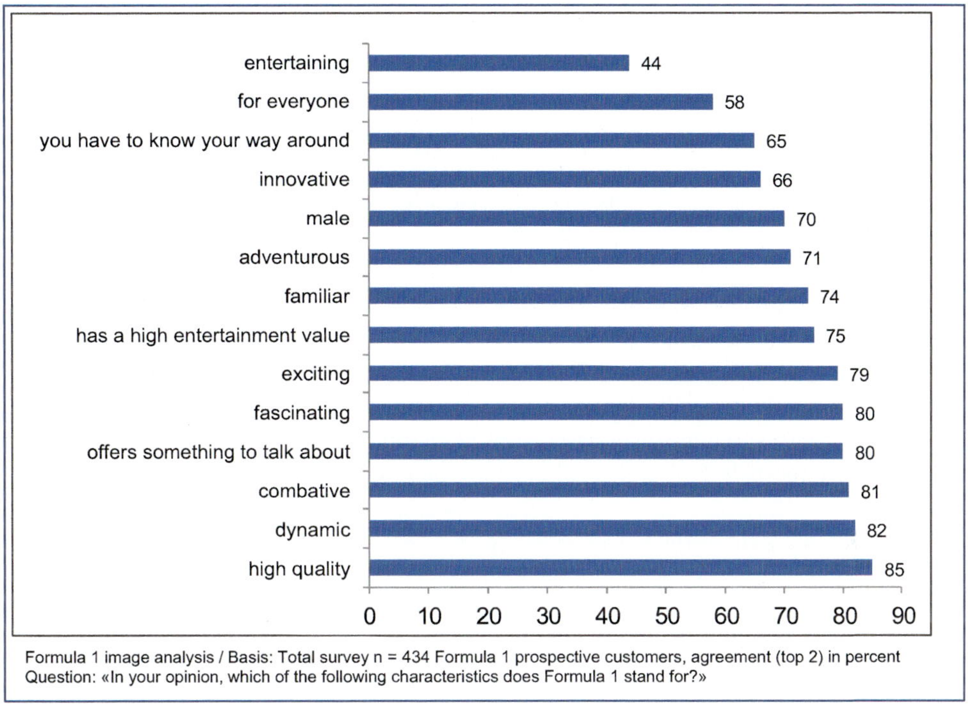

Fig. 8.3 Image profile of Formula 1. (*Source:* Mediengruppe RTL Deutschland, 2015, p. 10)

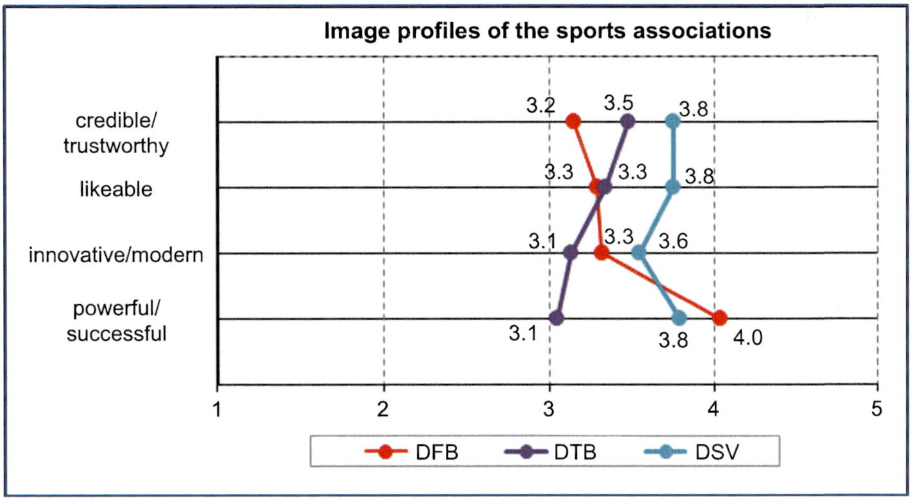

Fig. 8.4 Image profiles of selected sports associations. (*Source:* Daumann et al., 2011)

The **selection of a sponsoring** based solely on the image characteristics of a sport, however, is not sufficient for every sport. There are sports with a strong call to action, where the sport itself becomes the point of reference for an image dimension. In other sports, however, athletes or teams are in the foreground and form the link between sports and spectators. For example, the image of cycling is significantly more influenced by doping incidents (e.g., Lance Armstrong, Jan Ullrich, and Alberto Contador) than by terms such as speed and performance.

Such complex relationships are often studied by media research, including TV broadcasters and/or sports associations, by capturing the image that a sport has with the viewer as a construct of past experiences and diverse connotations (DSF, 1999; Hackforth, 2010). In this context, the **perception of brands** is interesting. For example, in football, it is evident that its image is significantly shaped by emotions and aesthetics, but certain brands are rarely spontaneously associated with football by the viewer; and this, even though major football sponsors regularly rank among the most well-known sponsors in Germany. Only the events and clubs seem to form the connection points to brands, while brands play only a subordinate role in the sport itself.

In addition to existing affinities between the sponsoring company and the different sports, the rough selection of sports is also interested in the extent to which a sponsoring commitment in the various sports meets **acceptance by consumers**. Figure 8.5 provides an overview of which sports welcome sponsoring engagement or meet with increased rejection. Another criterion can be the **size of the fan base** of a sport. Figure 8.6 shows the most popular sports worldwide.

Depending on the communicative task, the **trend potential of a sport** is also decisive for engagement. However, it is important to closely observe how trends develop within the respective target group, as these are sometimes short-lived and often based on non-sport-originating trend elements. Trend indicators include specific sports equipment and facilities as well as special clothing, and media that are closely tailored to the sport. In addition, companies planning to engage in the trend sports sector need to carefully examine the image characteristics of the respective sports. Within different trend sports, the specific image characteristics can vary. For example, basketball is predominantly perceived as technical and exciting by young people and stands for a sense of community, while the image of inline skating is primarily "in" and "young".

Another criterion for engagement in trend sports is the **"fitting" between the sponsor's industry and the trend sport**. A good example of a sponsor fit is the brand Red Bull with extreme and fun sports or individual athletes (Future Institute, 2014; Steinkirchner, 2016). Both sides embody the attributes of activity, energy, dynamism or vigor and fit, among other things, to a central leitmotif: "... revitalizes body and mind". However, there is also a risk for sponsors regarding certain sports trends. "E-Skateboarding", "Plogging" or "Hyrox" are familiar to many young people, but these supposed trend sports are still not or only minimally practiced. Instead, there is a strong

	Rejection	Acceptance
Disabled sports	13 %	78 %
Athletics	19 %	71 %
Swimming	21 %	68 %
Soccer	23 %	68 %
Handball	22 %	66 %
Ski jumping	25 %	65 %
Biathlon	25 %	64 %
Cross-country skiing	24 %	63 %
Basketball	25 %	63 %
Nordic combined	26 %	62 %
Marathon	26 %	61 %
Gymnastics	28 %	61 %
Figure skating	29 %	59 %
Rowing	30 %	58 %
Formula 1	34 %	57 %
Triathlon	29 %	57 %
Ice hockey	30 %	56 %
Volleyball	30 %	56 %
Table tennis	30 %	56 %
Equestrian sports	33 %	56 %
Cycling	35 %	53 %
Tennis	35 %	52 %
Boxing	38 %	52 %
Golf	48 %	39 %

Fig. 8.5 Acceptance of sponsoring in various sports. (*Source:* Ipsos GmbH, 2014)

trend towards more retro. Numerous market observers hold the opinion that normal and traditional sports apparently have a resurgence, also and especially among younger age groups.

The **result of the rough selection** is one or more sports that are particularly attractive for the company. These identified sports are then analyzed in more detail in the fine selection process.

Fig. 8.6 Most popular sports worldwide. (*Source:* World Atlas, 2022)

	Sport type	Million fans worldwide
1	Soccer	4000
2	Cricket	2500
3	Field hockey	2000
4	Tennis	1000
5	Volleyball	900
6	Table tennis	875
7	Basketball	825
8	Baseball	500
9	Rugby	475
10	Golf	425

8.3 Fine Selection of Sponsorings

The **phase of fine selection** includes the analysis and selection of various sponsoring alternatives within the defined sports. This also includes the decision about the different **forms of sponsorings,** such as:

- Individuals,
- Teams,
- Organizations,
- Events.

Decisions about these forms are primarily operational, but sometimes also strategic decisions. This is especially true when aligning sponsorings over a period of several years, such as multi-year contracts with top athletes or organizers of sporting events.

For the specific selection of individuals, sports organizations or sports events, decision criteria must be formulated that allow a comparison of alternative offers. The focus is on the following **decision criteria**:

Individuals and Teams

- Previous performances and successes of the athlete or team,
- Fame, credibility and sympathy in the target group,
- Evaluation and acceptance by the target group,
- Media presence at Sports events,
- Opportunities for integration into further communication measures,
- Inclusion of digital expansion possibilities (e.g. virtual),
- Costs among others.

Example: Decision for top athletes at Skinfit

For the company **Skinfit**, collaboration with top athletes from various sports is of particular interest. Decisive criteria for the selection of individual athletes are results and a performance record at national or international level, at least two results in the top 10 overall at a competition with at least 200 participants in the last 12 months, a target time that is only a maximum of 10% slower than the winning time (overall), a good network in the local sports world and regular (at least ten times a year) appearances in the press (the internet is excluded; Skinfit, 2016). ◀

Sports organizations

- Management qualification in the organization and in the association,
- Public Relations work by the sports organization,
- Interest in cooperation,
- Additional digital usage possibilities,
- Costs among others.

Sports events

- Expected media presence of the sports event,
- Participation of certain personalities and top sports people at the sports event,
- Experience with the responsible representatives of the event organization,
- Possibility of awarding predicates, licenses and titles,
- Position of the sponsor compared to other companies,
- Use of advertising opportunities before, during and after the Sports events,
- "Expansion possibilities" according to periods and channels (especially digital additional opportunities),
- Costs for sports sponsoring including the costs for preparation and follow-up among others.

Example: IOC and the Adjustment of the Sponsoring Strategy

The **International Olympic Committee (IOC)** is among the world leaders in sponsoring marketing. Behind the massive numbers lies a new approach to sponsoring that can promise increased revenue for many smaller sports rights providers. Despite numerous changes in the economic and social environment, the traditional appearance of sports sponsoring, which often still relies on media presence, TV reach, and cost per thousand contacts, can be found to this day. Especially against the backdrop of advancing digitalization, performance marketing, and the goal of companies to turn fans into customers, the question arises whether this is sufficient and whether new and modern sponsoring services need to be developed. In recent years, the International

Olympic Committee (IOC) has given this some thought and has already achieved considerable success. A growth to three billion USD is already pre-programmed for the upcoming marketing cycle (2021–2024).

The IOC's figures are particularly impressive because both the TV broadcasts of the Olympic Games are almost completely free of advertising and the viewing figures are usually lower than for games of a major football tournament. The basis for the IOC's billion-dollar sponsoring revenues is the so-called TOP program, which was launched after the 1984 Summer Olympics in Los Angeles. This is the global marketing program for the IOC's strategically long-term partners and the Olympic movement. The companies are not only partners of the IOC, but also partners of the Olympic Games taking place during the contract period and their organizing committees, as well as all 206 National Olympic Committees. At its core, three fundamental **changes in the IOC's marketing concept** were initiated:

- Instead of event sponsoring with many, towards multi-year Olympic sponsoring in a limited circle of partners (quality before quantity of participating companies).
- Expansion of sponsoring rights (for example, each TOP partner of the IOC from the rights period 2021 to 2024 also receives rights to the International Paralympic Committee (IPC) and the Paralympic Games).
- Moving away from traditional advertising services towards digital 360° marketing (strong individualization of the packages according to the philosophy that a sponsoring package should become an individual business case for the partner).

In the future, the IOC wants to go one step further with the concept expansion "Deep Integration" and position itself as a data-based communication platform for its advertising partners. The advantage is then not only to earn from the sponsoring rights, but also from the activation of the packages in the IOC's own media ecosystem, consisting among other things of a website, app, and Olympic Channel. ◄

Another important decision criterion in the selection of the form of sponsorings are the **activities of competitors**. Target of most companies is to choose a sports and organizational form that allows them to differentiate themselves from competitors and build independent image dimensions. Since image effects only set in over a longer period of time, sponsorings are to be planned for the long term and the image to be conveyed through the sponsoring commitment must also be reflected in other marketing instruments. Only through such a uniform presentation of the image dimensions can it be prevented that competing companies achieve comparable effects with similar sponsoring strategies and the communication instrument sponsoring can be developed into a business success factor. However, if one looks at Fig. 8.7 at the sports sponsoring measures of various breweries, it becomes clear that many breweries are involved in ball sports, making it increasingly difficult to profile the brands independently.

The company	Sports
Bitburger	Soccer, basketball, badminton, handball, marathon
Licher	Basketball, soccer, handball, endurance sports, ice hockey
Warsteiner	Motor sport, soccer, balloon sport, handball, equestrian sport
Hasseröder	Ice hockey, soccer
Holsten	Ice hockey, soccer, handball
Jever	Marathon, surfing, skiing

Fig. 8.7 Sports of brewery sponsoring

8.4 Termination of Sponsorings (Incl. Case Study Mercedes-Benz and DFB)

Sponsoring represents a special form of business relationships and, like any other contractual B2B relationship, is described by a beginning and an end. Therefore, one can also speak of a kind of **sponsoring lifecycle**. In this respect, relationships in sports sponsoring can usually be divided into a formation, realization, and termination phase distinguish (Salzer, 2022, p. 7). Figure 8.8 illustrates an ideal-typical course of a sponsoring relationship, taking into account the relationship level between the sponsor and the sponsored as well as the sponsor and the target group. In the ideal-typical course, it

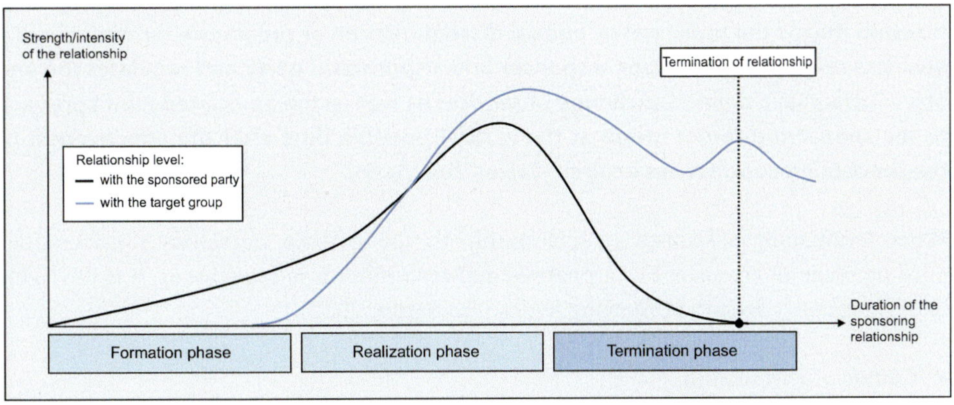

Fig. 8.8 Ideal-typical lifecycle of sponsoring relationships. (*Source:* Based on Bruhn, 2016, p. 66)

is assumed that a sponsoring contract is concluded and the contractual relationship is not prematurely terminated.

Accordingly, relationships in sports sponsoring initially go through a **formation phase**, which is characterized by preliminary discussions and contract negotiations between the party to be sponsored (rights holder) and the sponsor (rights acquirer). The relationship level with the sponsoring target group only begins with an official (public) announcement of a contractual agreement between both parties. The **realization phase** of the sponsoring relationship, characterized by the implementation of the contractual services and thus by the target group approach, starts with the beginning of the contract (Bruhn, 2016, p. 66).

Due to a usually pre-scheduled contract end, every sponsoring relationship regularly goes through a **termination phase** (Dreisbach, 2018, p. 90). This can directly lead into a renewed realization phase through a contract extension and/or even be transformed into another form of relation (e.g., as an investor). If there is no intention to continue the relationship between the sponsor and the sponsored party, the sponsoring relationship ends with the expiration of the contract term. In the ideal-typical course, the relationship with the (previous) target group does not break off in the termination phase due to targeted measures of termination management of sponsoring relationships, but an attempt is made to maintain it.

In this context, a long-term sponsor benefits from the fact that in sports sponsoring there is a certain **residual effect** among large parts of the target group, i.e., its supposed assignment to its favorite team in a phase when the relationship no longer exists. Thus, in market surveys of the first years after the turn of the millennium, many FC Bayern fans still considered Opel to be a main sponsor of the Munich team, although the car manufacturer had withdrawn at the end of the 2001/2002 season after 13 years and has been replaced by Telekom to this day. This phenomenon of the longer-term brand recall of previous sponsors is also a scientifically researched topic (Edeling et al., 2017).

▶ **Termination of Sponsoring Relationship** **The termination of a sponsoring relationship means the unilateral or mutual discontinuation or premature termination of a business relationship between a sponsor and a sponsored party and regulates the end of a contractually defined exchange of services as well as the associated joint approach to the sponsoring target group at the earliest possible time after the effectiveness of the sponsoring contract has expired (Salzer, 2022, p. 9).**

When terminating a sponsoring relationship by the sponsor, numerous considerations must be made in advance. For a **professional termination management**, it is advisable to deal primarily with the following topics (see Salzer, 2022):

- Causes of termination,
- Termination situations,
- Termination communication.

The reasons for terminating sponsoring relationships are diverse. In a survey of sponsors and sponsored parties, the following **causes of termination** were identified (Walzel & Schubert, 2018, p. 267; Salzer, 2022, pp. 89 ff.):

- Strategic realignment of the company,
- Insufficient value generation in the collaboration,
- Misconduct of the sponsored party,
- Financial difficulties due to budget cuts in the company,
- Counteroffer from a competitor,
- Achievement of the target,
- Economic crisis,
- Natural contractual end,
- Personnel changes among the participants,
- Inappropriate demands by the sponsored party,
- Lack of sporting success,
- Signaling to society,
- Lack of personnel in the company, etc.

In addition to dealing with the cause of termination, it is important for the sponsor to deal with the specific **termination situation** in which the company finds itself. This situation will be characterized by the question of whether the cause of termination is not, only partially, or fully comprehensible to the participants. On the other hand, the risk and opportunity associated with the separation from the sponsored party should also be assessed for the situation. It could be harmonious, carefree, prejudiced, tense, understanding-free, or escalating termination situations (Salzer, 2022, p. 192). Each of these situations requires a specific termination strategy.

Professional behavior is the norm when terminating a contract between sponsoring partners. This includes, among other things, a coordinated substantive, temporal, and formal approach to the public communication of a termination decision. From the sponsor's perspective, various different **communication strategies** are conceivable, which differ in terms of the types of address, openness, and target group orientation, such as (Salzer, 2022, p. 201):

- Gratitude strategy,
- Content positioning,
- Factual information,
- Announcement of the successor sponsor,
- Concealment of the cause,
- Withheld information,
- "Letting it expire".

However, there are also other constellations—especially when one of the contract partners feels disadvantaged by the termination of the relationship and there is "bad" talk about the departing sponsor. In such constellations, the comprehensibility of the cause of termination is crucial, as the target group perceives the termination decision (Salzer, 2022, p. 181).

The different communication strategies must be seen in the context of the specific termination situation in which the sponsor finds itself. Therefore, a **determination of the communication strategy depending on the termination situation** must be considered. Figure 8.9 shows and indicates which communication strategy can be considered suitable in which termination situation.

The termination of sponsoring relationships must therefore be seen in the overall context for the sponsor. This is made clear by an **impact model of termination management** developed based on theoretical and empirical findings (see Fig. 8.10). The causes of termination and the manner in which the sponsoring is terminated are judged by the target groups in terms of fairness. This results in psychological effects (e.g., brand attitude, brand image, brand trust), which ultimately also influence behavior (e.g., brand loyalty, buying behavior, negative or positive word-of-mouth communication). These effects are partly uncontrollable (e.g., relationship attitude, consequences for the sponsored, etc.), but also can be influenced by the sponsor (e.g., through a suitable communication strategy, compensation activities, etc.). The impact model illustrates which

			Communication strategy						
Termination type		Setting	Gratitude strategy	Positioning in terms of content	Factual information	Announcement of the successor sponsor	Concealing the cause	Information withheld	"Allow to expire"
Opportunity-maximizing approach	Harmonious termination situation	positive	✓	+ ✓					
		negative				✓		✓	✓
	Carefree termination situation	positive	✓	+ ✓					
		negative				✓		✓	✓
	Prejudiced termination situation	positive	✓	+ ✓					
		negative				✓		✓	✓
Risk-minimizing approach	Tense termination situation	positive	✓				+ ✓		
		negative				✓		✓	✓
	Comprehension-free termination situation	positive	✓				+ ✓		
		negative				✓		✓	✓
	Escalating termination situation	positive	✓				+ ✓		
		negative				✓		✓	✓

Fig. 8.9 Determination of communication strategies depending on termination situations. (*Source:* Salzer, 2022, p. 201)

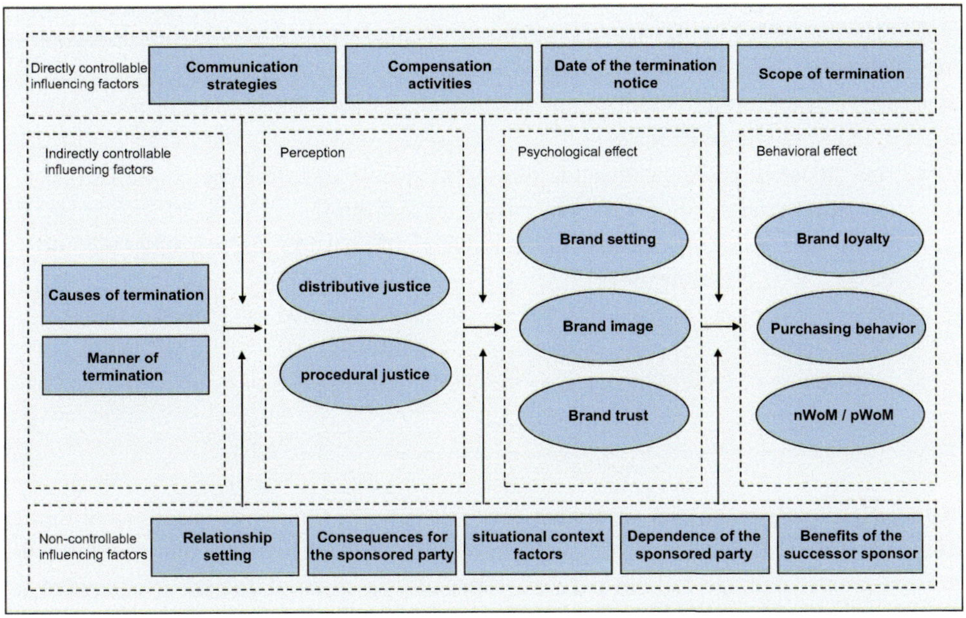

Fig. 8.10 Impact model for the termination management of sponsoring relationships. (*Source:* Salzer, 2022, p. 218)

influencing factors and consequences can be associated with the termination of sponsoring relationships.

In order to manage the termination of a relationship in sports sponsoring as "harmlessly" as possible for all parties involved, it can be helpful to structure the individual situation and include the subsequent effects for both partners. A checklist can help, among other things, to consider the most important points in a **termination management in sports sponsoring**:

Checklist for an optimal termination of a sports sponsoring project:

- Is there a strategic realignment for the sponsored party or the sponsor? For example, is there no longer a sponsor fit, is the focus shifting more towards international rather than national markets?
- Is the desired or hoped-for value generation missing? Is it due to wrong expectations, poor goal achievement, or deficiencies in the implementation?
- Is there misconduct among the partners? For example, is there a violation by the sponsored party against certain values (including doping, lifestyle) or a code of conduct (e.g., sports betting)? Is the sponsor involved in dubious, perhaps even criminal, activities (e.g., climate damage, money laundering)?
- Are there financial difficulties of a partner (e.g., insolvency)?

- Has the target of the partnership been reached? Is the cost-benefit ratio still correct?
- Do constraints such as an economic crisis (e.g., recession, energy crisis) require a new strategic direction?
- Are changes in laws and guidelines coming up that affect the continuation of the current partnership (e.g., advertising restrictions)?
- Are personnel changes decisive (e.g., change of decision-makers, CEO with different sports preferences)?
- Are the sporting results from the sponsor's perspective no longer given (e.g., relegation)?
- Is it necessary to send a signal to the public and target groups through changes (e.g., new trends, mainstream, niches)?

A thorough **analysis of exit scenarios** depending on the causes of termination, the termination situation, and termination communication can be used to find measures that prevent greater damage to both parties—especially in cases of forced or unwanted terminations. Even though each termination scenario is individual, the following practical examples can provide clues for successful and less successful measures.

Example: Homeday and the separation from Hertha BSC

The main sponsoring between Hertha BSC and **Homeday**, limited to only five months, is exceptional, as market research shows. The central challenge for the online broker Homeday from Berlin was to quickly increase its brand awareness. As a young company that had not long outgrown its start-up status, Homeday set itself an ambitious goal: The awareness values should increase significantly in as short a time as possible in order to catch up with the industry leader, Engel & Völkers. Against this background, the extraordinary sponsoring situation at the capital club Hertha BSC turned out to be a stroke of luck for all involved: Because the main sponsoring on the jersey was still available due to the pandemic, the opportunity arose for sponsor Homeday to conclude one of the most valuable partnerships in the highest league of German football with the club during the already ongoing Bundesliga season. The effects of the sponsoring were impressive. The conclusion (ESB, 2021):

- Within just five months (January to May 2021), the Homeday brand was able to increase its awareness by 14 percentage points to 32%.
- Among football enthusiasts, the largest community among the respondents, awareness also grew by 78%. The value increased by 18 percentage points from 23 to 41%.

In the aforementioned case, several influencing factors (including achieved goals, contacts with the targeted target group, manageable use of resources) were decisive for Homeday to end the sponsoring with Hertha after a short time. ◄

Example: Deutsche Telekom and the separation from cycling

The **Deutsche Telekom** tolerated the doping problems in the difficult phase of cycling for many months, certainly also because of its 16-year commitment. However, due to increasing brand endangerment, it finally terminated its cycling sponsoring with immediate effect. The company announced this decision of the board in November 2007. They wanted to distance themselves from doping in cycling and not risk any (further) damage to the corporate brand (Stern, 2007).

The Telekom case vividly illustrates how a brand in sports sponsoring is affected by negative influences. If the actual values of the brands are not to be contradicted, a quick or rigorous separation often remains the only solution. In this context, reference is also made to Chap. 15 in this book. ◄

Example: AOK and the Separation from the German Handball Federation (DHB)

Changing legal regulations can also lead to the involuntary end of long-standing and good commitments in sports sponsoring. The sports sponsoring of health insurance companies was never completely uncontroversial. However, since a law change in April 2021, no image or brand advertising was allowed to increase awareness. Instead, it is mandatory that factual information is at the forefront. How this is to be interpreted was not clearly defined. This led to the green **AOK** logo being replaced on the national jerseys with the slogan "Vaccination saves lives". For seven years, players of the German handball national teams wore AOK jerseys. Now the so-called health partnership with the health insurance company ended (Der Spiegel, 2021). The responsible AOK Federal Association in Berlin wanted to extend the agreement in a different form, said a spokesperson, but could not agree on the financial conditions with the German Handball Federation (DHB) (previously, the AOK had spent around 1.2 million EUR per year for the sponsoring). Even the upcoming men's European Championship did not help, and the partnership between AOK and DHB came to an end. ◄

Example: UEFA and the Separation from Gazprom

The European Football Union UEFA apparently could no longer avoid a separation from its Russian major sponsor **Gazprom** (N-TV, 2022). According to information from the English daily newspaper "The Times", work on dissolving the contract, which runs until 2024, began shortly after the Russian attack on Ukraine. The separation of UEFA from the Russian gas company was a very drastic reaction to the invasion of Russian troops. The ten-year cooperation with Gazprom had only been extended by another three years in 2021, including the 2024 European Championship final round in Germany. Estimates suggest that UEFA has so far received up to 48 million EUR per year from Gazprom. As part of the rapid separation, the Russian energy company was no longer present at the games in the European Cup competitions from March. At the same time, UEFA moved the Champions League final scheduled for May 28, 2022, from St. Petersburg to the Stade de France in Paris. Spartak Moscow, RB Leipzig's opponent in the Europa League round of 16, also had to play its "home game" on neutral ground. Apparently, in this case too, the sponsored parties found themselves in a value conflict with the sponsor, whose resolution they saw as possible only with a quick termination of the cooperation. ◄

Example: Rewe and the Separation from the German Football Association (DFB)

A double-edged example of termination management can be found with DFB sponsor **Rewe** (Zeit online, 2022a, b). The Cologne-based food retailer ended its cooperation with the DFB, the termination of which the retail group had already informed the association leadership in October for the end of 2022. The company announced the early termination on November 22, 2022, in a detailed press release. The background was that the captain of the German national team, Manuel Neuer, did not wear the "One Love" armband as initially announced in the opening match against Japan. The retail group wanted to clearly distance itself from the attitude of the world federation FIFA and the statements of its president Gianni Infantino. As a result, Rewe received extraordinarily strong attention and enormous approval from many football fans. However, the (transparent) action turned out to be a "own goal" due to the already mentioned termination at the end of the year. Therefore, Rewe's behavior was not so credible and was seen in numerous comments as a pure PR action. ◄

When a termination of a previous sponsoring relationship is imminent, it is essential to maintain clear and credible communication in order to keep negative consequences for all, especially for the departing sponsor, relatively small. To achieve this, the sponsor has several **withdrawal strategies** available (Salzer, 2022, p. 60, 95). For both main participants in sports sponsoring, the respective separation or termination strategy depends on individual circumstances, which is why such decisions can only be ideally represented. Companies have the opportunity to actively influence the effects in the target group through the following **factors and measures**:

- **Extent of termination** (gradual withdrawal such as changing the sponsoring level or completely and without further connection),
- **Timing of termination notification** (as early as possible or short-term, with longer preparation and alternatives or spontaneously),
- **Compensation activities within the club** (e.g., switching from men's to women's football or E-sports) or with third parties (switching to a competitor or out of sports itself),

- **Authentic and transparent information campaign** (for better acceptance of the relationship's end by the target groups).

Often a sponsoring partnership ends harmoniously, but occasionally there are many (sometimes unnecessary) "side noises", i.e., negative side effects due to the separation. If a company has been involved in the youth work of a sports club or in a fringe sport for years, the withdrawal of a company from this sponsoring sector quickly leads to negative press. This is partly due to the general termination problem, and it weighs even more heavily the more target groups and the public see a disadvantage for the sponsored party (e.g., because it is difficult for the sponsored parties to find a successor or to maintain the sports operation at all). Unilateral separation messages and/or blame can quickly lead to the destruction of a multi-year sponsoring commitment and a trust relationship built up over years.

Because on the one hand the type of termination is important, but on the other hand its communicative representation for the target groups is even more important, some **communication strategies** can be derived taking into account various separation scenarios (see Fig. 8.9). If there is a positive attitude of the target group towards a sponsoring cooperation, a so-called gratitude strategy seems sensible regardless of the type of termination. In this respect, a direct target group approach is considered the best approach. If the sponsor also sees a chance maximization in the separation, it may make sense to combine the gratitude strategy with the strategy of its own content positioning (Salzer, 2022, p. 201).

If one interprets communication strategies for public termination notification as an exchange service between the sponsor and the target group (Bruhn, 2016; Salzer, 2022), it is possible to better estimate the **effects on the relevant target groups**. This allows one to deduce that a target group only evaluates a communication strategy if a benefit of a functional or emotional nature is perceived in the sponsoring relationship and in the communicative measure. On the other hand, one gains the insight that the degree of directness of a communication (e.g., at a live event or via social media) is responsible for its (positive) effects (Salzer, 2022, pp. 181 ff.).

In addition, in the **public communication** in connection with the separation of sponsoring relationships, it should be taken into account to what extent negative consequences for the sponsored party arise from the termination, whether and which successor sponsor is already fixed, and whether situational context factors, such as the sporting relegation of a club, exist (Salzer, 2022, pp. 216 ff.).

Of course, there will always be changes and shifts in the diverse sponsoring relationships in sports. However, considerations regarding the termination of sponsoring relationships make it clear that there are numerous risks for the sponsor. Therefore, from the perspective of the Sponsor, it is necessary to pay attention to **critical points during the separation** from the sponsored party. These include, for example, the following activities where serious mistakes could be made:

- Announcement of termination,
- Timing of termination,
- Traceability of the cause of separation,
- Handling of partners during the separation,
- Scope of termination,
- Compensation activities,
- Consequences for the sponsored party,
- Benefits for the successor sponsor,
- Situational context factors,
- Communication strategies, among others.

The selection of sponsorings is not just an important operational decision that requires diverse decision criteria—both in the choice and in the termination of sponsorings. The decision about it and the associated contractual design are also prerequisites for the effect in terms of effectiveness and success in terms of efficiency to occur in the sponsoring commitment. The integration of sports sponsoring into marketing and corporate communication is also of particular importance for effectiveness.

Case Study Mercedes-Benz—Termination of the sponsoring with the DFB

The following case study was compiled by **Dr. Felix Salzer**, marketing consultant at Mercedes Benz Consulting GmbH, and **Dr. Peter Rohlmann** and is made with the kind support and permission of Mercedes-Benz AG (formerly Daimler AG).

Mercedes-Benz AG is a German manufacturer of passenger cars and commercial vehicles, which also offers mobility and financial services. The company's best-known brand is **Mercedes-Benz**. On October 1, 2021, a majority of shareholders decided to spin off Daimler Truck AG from Daimler AG as of December 1, 2021, and to list it as an independent company on the stock exchange and to operate under a new (old) name.

Initial Situation for the Sponsoring and Its End

In the marketing communication of the **Mercedes-Benz brand**, activities in sports sponsoring have been used for decades primarily to reach their target group in an emotional environment like sports and to influence the brand image in terms of perceived sportiness. During this time, different sponsoring strategies were pursued, with the long-term cooperation with the German Football Association (DFB) occupying a central position within the sponsoring portfolio.

The **contract with the DFB**, which ran until 2018, was extended in 2011. The partnership began in 1972. At that time, German football was under a particularly good star: Germany won the European Football Championship for the first time, the DFB and Mercedes-Benz began a loose cooperation on a partnership basis. The cooperation was expanded on the occasion of the 1990 World Cup, since then Mercedes-Benz has been the general sponsor of the DFB.

As part of the **cooperation with the DFB**, Mercedes-Benz particularly supported the men's and women's national teams of the DFB. Buses were available for the teams and their supervisors for trips to international matches or training sessions (Fig. 8.11). In addition to classic activation measures during international matches (playing of advertising spaces in the stadium), a driver service was provided at home games. Jerseys and leisure clothing of national players, female players and coaching staff were adorned with the logo and lettering of Mercedes-Benz.

In 2018, the DFB had for the first time made a **tender** for the automobile partnership (for the period between 2019 and 2024), Mercedes-Benz participated in the procedure. Different views on the scope of sponsoring and the financial framework led to Mercedes-Benz and the DFB ending the sponsoring relationship in 2019.

In the course of the separation, the then CEO of Daimler AG, Dieter Zetsche, commented very promptly: "Over the course of our decades-long partnership, German football has achieved a lot. It was fantastic to have been there with Mercedes-Benz. This end now also offers us the opportunity for a realignment. What does not change: We remain passionate fans of the national team".

Origins of the Sponsoring Termination between Mercedes-Benz and the DFB

The collaboration with the DFB has provided Mercedes-Benz with a suitable framework for presenting the brand in international top-level sports for many years. The **termination situation** presented itself to Mercedes-Benz and the DFB as follows:

Fig. 8.11 Mercedes-Benz as a partner of the DFB over decades. (*Source:* Mercedes-Benz)

- It was the first time that the DFB had officially tendered the automotive partnership sponsoring package in 2017. Previously, the sponsoring contract with Mercedes-Benz had been extended several times without considering competitors.
- The tendered sponsoring package from the DFB stipulated that the future partner, in addition to the national teams (scope of the sponsoring package with Mercedes-Benz), should also become a partner of the DFB-Pokal. In this context, the DFB's counter-services in connection with the national team deteriorated in the tendered package.
- As part of the tendering process, Volkswagen AG (VW) reportedly offered a sum of 25 to 30 million EUR for the sponsoring package, including the rights to the DFB-Pokal. Mercedes-Benz had increased the sponsoring sum of the previous contract (approx. 8 million) for the new package by about 2 to 3 million EUR and had exclusively focused on the sponsoring package of the national teams (Deutschlandfunk, 2017).
- The DFB had offered Mercedes-Benz the opportunity to outbid VW's offer in order to win the contract. Mercedes-Benz did not further increase the financial offer in this context.
- The DFB ultimately decided in favor of VW's offer. In addition to financial reasons, the possibility of gaining a partner for both the national teams and the DFB-Pokal was another reason for the decision. Moreover, the then DFB president Reinhard Grindel justified the decision for VW by stating that he saw VW as a strong or stronger partner in terms of internationalization with regard to market penetration in China (Finanzen100, 2017).

A **comparison between Mercedes-Benz and Volkswagen** as the main sponsor is shown in Fig. 8.12 based on the criteria: length of cooperation, sponsoring value, company turnover, market share in the Asian market, and intensity of cooperation.

Termination Management by Mercedes-Benz

Internally at Mercedes-Benz, the termination not to outbid VW was received positively, even though employees were not pleased about the end of the sponsoring both emotionally and in terms of content. Nevertheless, Mercedes-Benz saw a communicative opportunity in the end of the sponsoring and developed a **communication strategy** that pursued the following **goals**:

- Transparency regarding the cause of termination and the associated process,
- Generation of a harmonious farewell in public,
- Positive look back and gratitude for the shared journey including the achieved successes,
- Communicative "fireworks" through extensive termination measures.

Criteria	Mercedes-Benz	Volkswagen
Familiarity/collaboration	1972–2018 (46 years)	2019–2024
Sponsorship value	EUR 8–9 million	EUR 25–30 million (of which allegedly EUR 6–7 million for the DFB Cup)
Turnover in EUR billion	167.4 (2018)	235.8 (2018)
Expansion of the Asian market	market share China 25 % (2018)	market share China 39 % (2018)
Intensity of cooperation	National teams	National teams DFB Cup Amateur soccer DFB Academy

Fig. 8.12 Previous and new main sponsor of the DFB in comparison

Based on this target, Mercedes-Benz published a press release on the end of the sponsoring shortly after the decision, in which Dieter Zetsche, former CEO of the then Daimler AG, commented. "This hurts every football fan in our company—including me" (Businessinsider, 2017). At the same time, however, he also spoke about "reason and proportionality". He chose open words to explain the **termination of the relationship** with the DFB: "As a company, we are not responsible for fee payers, but we also have to examine every sponsoring very carefully with regard to employees and shareholders." Why Mercedes-Benz finally did not want or could not be a partner of the DFB at any cost, Zetsche justified as follows: "The package in question included fewer services than the previous one. To get it, however, we would have had to pay significantly more." Because of the formula of less performance for more money, we could not agree to the DFB package. Especially since the company would not have been guaranteed exclusivity. "Even with a contract award, we would not have remained the main sponsor, but only one of several partners," said Zetsche. At the same time, the head of Mercedes-Benz still thanked for the shared time: "We are proud of the decades-long successful partnership with the DFB and of course wish the national team much success with the new automotive partner."

Furthermore, the sports marketing team at Mercedes-Benz created a **special jersey for the farewell** from the DFB, which combined various iconic designs from the past (Fig. 8.13). For each "stellar moment" of the DFB, a star was placed on the national team's jersey, including for the shared World Cup titles. The production of the jersey was documented in the form of a film and played out in different formats on social media. These were the introductory measures, in addition to the preliminary press information, for the communication activities around the end of the sponsoring.

The international match of the German national football team against the Netherlands in November 2018 marked the public end of the relationship and was therefore used as a central communicative launch. For this purpose, all the advertising spaces in the stadium in Gelsenkirchen were used to thank the DFB for the shared time. In addition, a TV spot was released on the day of the international match. In the **film "The Journey"**, the DFB team bus provided by Mercedes-Benz drives through Germany, reviewing the shared experiences with the national team. The film then went online on various Mercedes-Benz channels (see Fig. 8.14). Mercedes-Benz also made its farewell performance on social networks under the hashtag #dfbye.

In a **total evaluation**, the communicative measures of Mercedes-Benz were very positively received in the target group, as an internal market survey and an evaluation of social media comments in the context of the termination had shown.

Fig. 8.13 Farewell with an "All-Star Jersey". (Photo: Joko Schmidt, 2017)

This is mainly due to the comprehensibility of the cause of termination and the communicative positioning through the "gratitude strategy". Because an disproportionate counteroffer from a competitor led to the termination, the actors of the target group did not blame Mercedes-Benz for the termination. Rather, there were numerous critical voices towards the DFB regarding the commercialization of football (Handelsblatt, 2017). This situational context factor also positively influenced the perception of consumers for Mercedes-Benz, as the company consciously decided against an "disproportionate" financial offer. In addition, when it was announced that VW would be the new automotive partner of the DFB, the VW emissions scandal was at its peak. This circumstance also positively influenced the perception of the target group for Mercedes-Benz. The tarnished image and the associated symbolic value for the target group was significantly lower at this time than the symbolic value represented by the image of Mercedes-Benz. On social media channels, Mercedes-Benz was genuinely mourned.

For the sponsoring strategy of Mercedes-Benz, the termination with the DFB had significant **impacts on sports sponsoring**. Activities in football have since been pursued exclusively for location policy reasons at VfB Stuttgart and at the Mercedes-Benz JuniorCup. The global focus is on motorsport involvement in Formula 1 as well as activities in golf and eSport. Individual sponsorings in tennis, such as the Laver Cup and the commitment with Roger Federer, are continued for historical reasons. In addition, there are market-specific activities in other sports, such as the sponsoring of the German market at the CHIO Aachen equestrian tournament.

Fig. 8.14 Stylish farewell through a film about the shared journey. (*Source:* Mercedes-Benz)

8.5 Key Points

The selection of sponsorings in sports sponsoring involves both strategic and operational decisions. Some fundamental points must be considered in all phases of planning and implementation of the sponsorings.

Key Points

1. The **selection of a sponsoring** usually follows a **step-by-step process**, which begins with a rough selection as a strategic decision and continues with a fine selection as an operational decision.
2. In the context of the **rough selection of sports**, criteria must be established on the basis of which the suitability of the sports for the communicative task of the company can be checked (e.g., affinity concept, proximity to location, etc.).
3. Also, consumers play an important role in the selection of sponsorings, which includes the **acceptance of sponsoring by the target groups**, but also the size of the fan community associated with the sports.
4. In the question of engagements in traditional sports or trendy sports, the **question of permanence and sustainability** must also be examined.
5. In the **fine selection**, the various sponsoring alternatives within the defined sports(s) are to be examined. This includes decisions on whether individuals, teams, organizations and/or events could be suitable partners.
6. Often, **competition-related criteria** are also important for the selection of a sport and an organizational unit to be sponsored. This allows the sponsor to differentiate itself from competitors and build independent image dimensions.
7. Every sponsoring commitment has a contractual term. If this is a decision to be made, the **termination of the sponsoring relationship** should be prepared in good time.
8. Professional behavior is generally normal among sponsoring partners when a contract is terminated. This includes a coordinated content, timing, and formal approach to the public **communication of a termination decision**.
9. It is helpful to have discussions with the sponsored party in the final phase of a partnership to send **signals for termination** in good time.
10. Special **withdrawal and communication strategies** can help a departing sponsor avoid many negative side effects.

References

A

Allensbacher Markt- und Werbeträgeranalyse (AWA 2016). Sportarten, Fußballvereine. http://sportfive.comsulting.de. Accessed: 19. Dec. 2016.

B

Bassenge, C. (2000). *Dienstleister als Sponsoren. Imageprofilierung durch kommunikatives Engagement im Sport*. https://doi.org/10.1007/978-3-322-89616-2.

Bruhn, M. (2016). *Relationship Marketing. Das Management von Kundenbeziehungen* (5. Aufl.). https://doi.org/10.15358/9783800651849.

Bruhn, M. (2018). *Sponsoring. Systematische Planung und integrativer Einsatz* (6. Aufl.). https://doi.org/10.1007/978-3-658-13313-9.

Businessinsider. (2017). Zetsche packt aus: Darum hört Mercedes wirklich als DFB-Sponsor auf; Beitrag vom 18.07.2017. https://www.businessinsider.de/wirtschaft/zetsche-packt-aus-darum-hoert-mercedes-wirklich-als-dfb-sponsor-auf-2017-7/.

D

Daumann, F., Esipovich, L., & Römmelt, B. (2011). Imageprofile im Sport – Sportverbände, Sportler, Fußballclubs und im Sport werbende Marken, Jenaer Sportmanagement Surveys, Friedrich-Schiller-Universität Jena. https://www.mba-sportmanagement.com/service/jenaer-kommentare/65-master-sportmanagement-image-survey.

Deutsches Sport Fernsehen (DSF 1999). Imagetrends. Ismaning.

Deutschlandfunk. (2017). VW löst Daimler als DFB-Sponsor ab – „Man kann kaum prominenter werben in Deutschland", Beitrag vom 14.07.2017. https://www.deutschlandfunk.de/vw-loest-daimler-als-dfb-sponsor-ab-man-kann-kaum-100.html.

Dreisbach, J. (2018). *Erfolgsfaktoren der Sponsoringumsetzung und -aktivierung – Eine empirische Analyse aus Management- und Konsumentenwirkungsperspektive im Kontext der Fußball-Bundesliga*. Springer Gabler. https://doi.org/10.1007/978-3-658-24519-1.

E

Edeling, A., Hattula, S., & Bornemann, T. (2017). Over, out, but present: Recalling former sponsorings. *European Journal of Marketing, 51*(7/8), 1286–1307. https://doi.org/10.1108/ejm-05-2015-0263.

ESB. (2021). Best case: HOMEDAY x Hertha BSC, Beitrag vom 04.11.2021. https://www.esb-online.com/business-guides/artikel/best-case-homeday-x-hertha-bsc/.

F

Finanzen100. (2017). 30 Millionen Euro pro J. https://www.deutschlandfunk.de/vw-loest-daimler-als-dfb-sponsor-ab-man-kann-kaum-100.htmlahr: Warum der DFB-Deal für Volkswagen so wichtig ist, Beitrag vom 14.07.2017. https://www.finanzen100.de/finanznachrichten/wirtschaft/sponsoring-30-millionen-euro-pro-jahr-warum-der-dfb-deal-fuer-volkswagen-so-wichtig-ist_H417380626_442964/.

H

Hackforth, J. (2010). *Imageträger Fußball – Werte, Wert und Wertschätzung, in: Auf den Spuren der Nationalmannschaft*, DFB (Hrsg.), Frankfurt.

Handelsblatt. (2017). VW sticht Mercedes bei Nationalmannschaft aus, Beitrag vom 14.07.2017. http://www.handelsblatt.com/sport/fussball/dfb-sponsor-vw-sticht-mercedes

I

Ipsos GmbH. (2014). Grundlagenstudie Sponsoring 2014, Hamburg.

M

Mediengruppe RTL Deutschland. (2015). Formel 1 – Imageanalyse. Accessed: 31. May 2016.

Meenaghan, T., & Shipley, D. (1999). Media effect in commercial sponsoring. *European Journal of Marketing, 33*(3/4), 328–347. https://doi.org/10.1108/03090569910253170.

N

n-tv. (2022). UEFA will Geldgeber Gazprom loswerden, Beitrag vom 25.02.2022. https://www.n-tv.de/sport/fussball/UEFA-will-Geldgeber-Gazprom-loswerden-article23156507.html.

S

Salzer, F. (2022). *Beendigungsmanagement von Sponsoringbeziehungen – Konzeption und empirische Analyse eines Wirkungsmodells*. https://doi.org/10.1007/978-3-658-37778-6

Schmidt, J. (2017). Foto Allstar Jersey. http://www.jokoschmidt.com/portfolio/allstar-jersey.

Skinfit. (2016). *Sponsoring*. http://www.skinfit.eu/ch/de/teams-sponsoring.html. Accessed: 8. June 2016.

Spiegel. (2021). AOK beendet umstrittenes Trikot-Sponsoring, Beitrag vom 21.12.2021. https://www.spiegel.de/sport/handball/handball-nationalmannschaft-aok-beendet-umstrittenes-trikot-sponsoring-a-bd0f5df6-f150-4156-a596-4068d5ece8bd.

Steinkirchner, P. (2016). Wie das Red-Bull-Imperium die Sportwelt erobert, in: Wirtschaftswoche vom 13.05.2016.

Stern. (2007). Telekom zieht die Reißleine, Beitrag vom 27.11.2007. https://www.stern.de/sport/sportwelt/sponsoring-ausstieg-telekom-zieht-die-reissleine-3218652.html

W

Walzel, S., & Schubert, M. (2018). *Sportsponsoring – Grundlagen, Konzeption und Wirkungen*. Springer Gabler. https://doi.org/10.1007/978-3-662-55246-9.

World Atlas. (2022). *The most popular sports in the world*. https://www.worldatlas.com/articles/what-are-the-most-popular-sports-in-the-world.html.

Z

Zeit. (2022a). Investor Kühne erwirbt Namensrechte am Volksparkstadion, Beitrag vom 31.03.2022. https://www.zeit.de/news/2022-03/31/investor-kuehne-erwirbt-namensrechte-am-volksparkstadion.

Zeit. (2022b). Rewe und der DFB: „Das hätte man als PR-Aktion auch nicht besser planen können", Beitrag vom 23.11.2022. https://www.zeit.de/wirtschaft/unternehmen/2022-11/rewe-dfb-kooperation-pr-aktion-one-love-binde.

Zukunftsinsitut. (2014). Die Red-Bullisierung des Sports. Trend Update 6/2014. https://www.zukunftsinstitut.de/artikel/sport/die-red-bullisierung-des-sports/.

Integration of Sports Sponsoring into Marketing and Corporate Communication

9

Contents

Abstract

In addition to planning individual measures, a major concern of the sponsoring planner is to achieve an integration of the sports sponsoring strategy into the communication and marketing strategy. Synergistic effects can only be achieved through a strategic and operational interlocking of the various communication instruments. In particular, the use of sports sponsoring offers a multitude of possibilities for a systematic networking with other instruments of marketing and corporate communication. This necessitates examining the possibilities of integration in detail and making various adjustments in marketing and corporate communication. This is evident not only from the detailed case study of Deutsche Telekom, but also from other company examples such as ABB, BMW, Coca-Cola, Commerzbank, Mercedes-Benz, Milka and others.

M. Bruhn and P. Rohlmann, *Sports Sponsoring*,
https://doi.org/10.1007/978-3-658-44171-5_9

9.1 Integration into the Communication Mix

The subject of **inter-instrumental integration** is the connection of sports sponsoring with the other instruments of marketing and corporate communication. Regardless of the internal difficulties in networking the instruments, the activities within the framework of sports sponsoring should be taken up within the other communication instruments in order to meaningfully enhance the impact of overall communication.

The integration of sports sponsoring into marketing and corporate communication makes sense from various perspectives, as cost reduction potentials can be realized and synergy effects can be used through the integrated use of the instruments. The following are examples of the possibilities for **integrating sports sponsoring with communication instruments** of marketing and corporate communication:

Sports sponsoring and Public Relations
The integration of the instruments sports sponsoring and Public Relations takes place, for example, in the form that a company active in the field of sports sponsoring specifically points out its sporting commitment through press information, press conferences, and references in company brochures. The widest possible media resonance regarding the sponsoring commitment is achieved in particular when the sponsoring company also actively contributes to the media receiving background information, for example about a tournament series or an athlete, which they consider it sensible to report on.

For instance, the car manufacturer Porsche has been the main sponsor of the young tennis player Angelique Kerber since 2012 and actively provides press information about the athlete's respective successes, such as at the Australian Open 2016 in Melbourne (see Fig. 9.1). Porsche appears both in public relations and in sponsoring with Kerber as a brand ambassador (Porsche AG, 2016).

An extension or prolongation of sponsorings is now offered by digital media, in which individual players, but occasionally also clubs themselves, send partner connections and emotional moments directly from the locker room via various channels (Absatzwirtschaft, 2017). Finally, documentaries have become modern, in which professional filmmakers provide so-called "stories behind ...". Sponsors also appear in this world of sports from new perspectives time and again. Fans can follow their sports idols up close in impressive documentaries, investigative reports, and authentic portraits (Taz, 2021). Director Paul Verhoeven accompanied Bayern for over 100 shooting days from the summer of 2020 to the end of the 2020/2021 season for the documentary "FC Bayern—Behind the Legend".

Sports sponsoring and Media advertising
A networking of sports sponsoring and media advertising is possible in different forms. For example, the sponsoring company points out its sports sponsoring through classic print, television, and radio advertising and picks up images or themes from sponsored

Fig. 9.1 Porsche and its brand ambassador Angelique Kerber. (*Source:* Porsche, 2016)

events in media advertising. Furthermore, it can be increasingly observed that companies use teams and individual athletes as so-called "testimonials" in media advertising, who communicate that they themselves use certain brands or are customers of a specific service. Figure 9.2 shows Jürgen Klopp as a testimonial for the brand Nivea Men. As another example, Coca-Cola launched a TV commercial shortly before the 2016 European Football Championship, which focused on the shared experience and celebration of the tournament. The spot shows that young and old, football fans and many others meet on the street and make their way to the stadium together to support the German team. In addition to the TV spot, Coca-Cola advertises with outdoor posters showing German national players and their limited Coca-Cola cans (see Fig. 9.3). The posters are complemented by humorous word games tailored to the respective players, such as "Die und keine André!" or "Geh Reus und hol sie dir!" (About Drinks, 2016).

Sporting goods manufacturers approach the presentation of new club jerseys with extreme creativity and often humor. To this end, equipment sponsors often choose video clips with more or less appealing content to show their club loyalty to fans on YouTube and encourage them to purchase the new outfit (see the launch of the new BVB jersey on YouTube in Fig. 9.4).

Sports sponsoring and sales promotion

Sports sponsorings are used in the context of sales promotion, for example, by conducting targeted promotional actions (e.g., autograph sessions, competitions, lectures, and

Fig. 9.2 Jürgen Klopp as a testimonial for Nivea Men. (*Source:* Horizont, 2021)

tours) with athletes in retail or at other central locations. In addition, some sponsors (e.g., beverage manufacturers) also have opportunities to specifically promote the sale of their products in the context of sporting events. For example, Emmi links its commitment in sports sponsoring with sales promotion measures. During the hosting of

Fig. 9.3 Coca-Cola and its advertising campaign for UEFA EURO 2016 with the DFB-Elf. (*Source:* Coca-Cola, 2016)

Fig. 9.4 Puma and the launch of the new BVB jersey on YouTube. (*Source:* Puma-BVB, 2022)

various skiing events, Emmi uses the event to conduct product presentations, in the form of free giveaways of the coffee drink "Emmi Caffè Latte", at the event location (Ringle, 2003, pp. 201 ff.; Emmi Group, 2019). In a similar way, Melitta used its sponsoring with Manchester United. Here alone, over 200 fully automatic Melitta coffee machines were installed within the Executive Club Boxes and catering areas. In addition, the Red Café, where Melitta products are offered, was completely redesigned by Melitta. As a result, almost half a million people who visit Old Trafford annually get to enjoy Melitta's special coffee specialties. On match days, Melitta serves up to 7500 VIP guests and tens of thousands of stadium visitors outside of match days. For the company, Manchester United is like a showcase customer: alone in the first season 2017/2018, 40% more coffee was sold at Old Trafford than in the past (Melitta, 2020).

Another form of integrating sports sponsoring into sales promotion is the use of athletes as testimonials for the sponsor's products. In Fig. 9.5, the example of Coca-Cola and some Bayern players shows how the club sponsor conducts specific sales promotion for its brand mezzo mix using a competition.

Sports sponsoring and Direct Marketing

A connection of sports sponsoring with Direct Marketing is conceivable, for example, in the form that selected members of the public as well as trade and business partners are informed about the sporting events sponsored by the sponsor via mailings and possibly

Fig. 9.5 Integration of sports sponsoring into sales promotion. (*Source:* Coca-Cola, 2020)

invited. Often, tickets for a sponsored parties event are also raffled off as part of a competition. In addition, for example, after a sponsored parties sports event, documentaries about the tournament and the sponsor's commitment are sent to selected target groups. The European airline Turkish Airlines, for example, is active as a sponsor of various sporting events. The company's customers are regularly informed about the events, such as the European Football Championship or the Porsche Tennis Grand Prix, via personal letters. There is often the opportunity to obtain tickets at reduced prices or to participate in competitions to win tickets (Turkish Airlines, 2016).

A vivid example of the link between sports sponsoring and Felix Neureuther is provided by the company Firestixx through a broad-based direct marketing campaign with personal letters and apps (see Fig. 9.6).

Sports Sponsoring and Customer Care

Events of sports sponsoring often offer the opportunity to rent premises in the vicinity of the event. Key customers and opinion leaders are invited by the sponsor and cared for as part of hospitality measures before, during, and after the event. Most top events have these so-called VIP rooms and are made available to sponsors in a sponsoring package. Deutsche Telekom, as the main sponsor of the football club FC Bayern Munich, for

Fig. 9.6 Linking sports sponsoring with Direct Marketing using the example of Firestixx. (*Source:* Sein und Haben Advertising Agency GmbH)

example, uses its Hospitality rights for customer invitations to the Bundesliga matches of FC Bayern and special Sports Events, such as the Champions League or the UEFA Cup (Althoff, 2007, pp. 90 ff.; Deutsche Telekom AG, 2016). Especially in Formula 1, the topic of hospitality and customer care by the sponsors is at the top of the agenda (see Fig. 9.7). For example, the Mercedes hospitality for the races on a Grand Prix weekend is fully booked. This means for the example of the US Grand Prix in Austin: The team welcomes more than 1000 guests over the course of the three-day race weekend. From Friday to Sunday, 210 VIPs enjoy the luxury of the Silver Arrow Lounge or the team's Paddock Club Suite overlooking the Silver Arrow Box. In addition, 40 more guests are catered for in the team's Paddock Hospitality each of the three days. International media representatives are also welcome here. This increases the number of people the team welcomes here to 150 people per day—and all this without the advantages of the spacious motorhomes. Over the course of a fully booked week at the US Grand Prix, the team serves around 1700 meals. That's 500 meals per day from Friday to Sunday for media representatives, Paddock Club guests, and other team VIPs. The program can therefore quite keep up with that of the engineers. To accomplish this, 14 marketing staff

Fig. 9.7 Mercedes-Benz Lounge at the Nürburgring as an important part of customer care. (*Source:* Mercedes-Benz, 2022)

are on duty at the track for the team—starting with executives from partner services to the hospitality manager. They are supported by 13 hospitality staff who together speak six languages (Motorsport Total, 2017).

Precisely because hospitality is an integral part of many marketing and sponsoring concepts, some uncertainties have arisen in the context of new compliance regulations by companies. In order to continue to use this important element of sports promotion and to support the legal certainty of the invitation practice, the S20 sponsors' association and the VSA—Association of sports sponsoring providers—in cooperation with the Federal Ministry of the Interior (BMI) in 2017, adapted and further developed a new, expanded edition of the guide "Hospitality and Criminal Law" after legal changes (VSA et al., 2017).

The fact that image transfer is often given more importance than awareness in these measures is illustrated by the increase in sponsoring commitments in elite sports such as golf, sailing, horse riding, or polo. In these sports, companies encounter an upscale target audience, which is assumed to have above-average preferences for high-quality goods and services. In Swiss polo sport, for example, only exclusive companies such as Land Rover, Cartier, and Dom Perignon are involved, who reach their target groups specifically through this niche segment. Engagement in golf, for example, is shown by the car manufacturer BMW, which offers test drives in the latest models to guests—primarily national and international business partners—during the BMW International Open golf tournament (BMW AG, 2016).

Sports Sponsoring and Internal Communication

Sponsoring also offers the opportunity to increase the motivation of employees and their identification with the company. It plays a central role to inform them in a timely and detailed manner about the reasons and plans regarding sponsoring commitments through measures of employee communication. If the employees are not sufficiently informed, there is a risk of counterproductive effects within the company. Systematic clarification and active involvement in sports commitments prevent these resistances within the company. In this way, positive effects on the sports activities of the employees themselves are conceivable through sports sponsoring, for example, if the company sports of the employees are actively promoted in parallel to external sponsorings. The use of a sports commitment within internal communication takes place in various ways. For example, employees are regularly informed about the company's sponsoring activities through in-house announcements or company magazines. It also seems sensible to involve employees in decisions regarding new sponsorings in order to promote internal acceptance of sports sponsoring. Last but not least, the company's own employees are also invited to the relevant sports events (either as spectators or active participants) or sponsored athletes or sports teams participate in festivities within the company. Since 2003, for example, employees of Deutsche Telekom have had the opportunity to participate in the "Fit like the Bayern" fitness program, which was developed by physiotherapists from FC Bayern and is provided via the intranet. In addition, the "T-Block" was introduced at

Fig. 9.8 Audience on site as a human "T"—creative sponsoring measure of Deutsche Telekom and hit on YouTube. (*Source:* Nufer & Rützel, 2016, p. 13)

FC Bayern home games. Deutsche Telekom bought contiguous season tickets in the stadium of FC Bayern Munich and formed an oversized human "T" on the stands through the appropriate seating arrangement of the trainees (Althoff, 2007, pp. 90 ff.; tz Munich, 2013). Figure 9.8 shows the human "T" in the stadium during a game scene. The energy company ABB, as a sponsor of Special Olympics Germany e.V., the sports movement for people with intellectual and multiple disabilities, also involves its employees in its sponsoring activities. At the "National Games", which take place annually as summer or winter games, employees of the company support the participating athletes. This involvement has positive effects on the social behavior of the employees. Some of them made contact with facilities for mentally disabled people with the goal of supporting local actions (e.g., parties or training) (ABB, 2016; see Fig. 9.9).

A study by the University of Linz examined the effects of sports sponsoring on employees at a company in Austria (Hofer, 2013). It was found that sports sponsoring has a positive effect on employee motivation. The positive effects were shown in the following areas: increase in employee satisfaction, job motivation and pride in the company, increase in employee loyalty and emotional attachment to the company (Hofer, 2013).

Sports Sponsoring and Social Media Communication

The integration of sports sponsoring and social media communication is considered particularly advantageous as it can extend the duration of a sponsoring commitment. Another advantage is the opportunity for emotional interaction with target groups associated with the integration of social media. Compared to the display of logos or lettering on banners or jerseys, more content can be communicated (Panten, 2013, p. 10). Furthermore, the integration of social media activities into sports sponsoring offers the possibility of cost savings, as expensive advertising campaigns can be avoided (Cotting, 2011, p. 18). In the field of Social Media Communication, there are numerous multimedia networking opportunities with a company's sponsoring activities. Many companies use social media platforms such as Facebook, YouTube, and Twitter to inform about their sponsoring activities, communicate event dates, or provide information about sponsored individuals. Social media users can then individually select and retrieve such information that corresponds to their specific interest. In addition to announcing sports events and providing sponsoring-related information, social media platforms also offer the opportunity to broadcast special sponsoring occasions live on the internet for specific user groups (e.g., sports events), offer internet users virtual visits to a sponsored event (e.g., a sports competition), or provide coverage after a sponsoring event (Cotting, 2011, p. 17). Commerzbank is a sponsor of the German Football Association (DFB). References to the sponsoring commitment can be found, for example, in a blog of the financial service provider on the topic "Meeting People" or on the corporate homepage. Here, the company explicitly refers to joint activities within the framework of the sponsoring. For example, a blog post reported on the new TV spot by DFB and Commerzbank for the 2016 European Championship or—as is currently the case—informed about the special

Fig. 9.9 ABB employees at the Special Olympics. (*Source:* ABB, 2020)

Fig. 9.10 Cheeky Commerzbank video clip in the run-up to the Women's Football World Cup 2019. (*Source:* YouTube Commerzbank, 2019)

cooperation with the women's national team. Information and videos about current sports sponsoring commitments can also be found on their Facebook and YouTube pages. See Fig. 9.10, in which the DFB women are provoked by sponsor Commerzbank with a cheeky commercial.

In addition, some companies use online presentation platforms to network sponsoring and social media. For example, during its DFB sponsoring, the Bitburger Brewery Group created such a platform for the Bitburger Fan Force One to get fans excited about the 2016 European Football Championship. After purchasing a promotional case, the receipt could be uploaded to the online platform, and with a bit of luck, a seat on the Fan Force One plane (Fig. 9.11) could be won for the international match (Bitburger Brewery Group GmbH, 2016).

Example: Integration of Sports Sponsoring with the Confectionery Brand Milka

Successful networking is also achieved by the company Mondelez International with the confectionery brand **Milka**. Both the German Ski Association (DSV) and the skiers Viktoria Rebensburg (GER), Michaela Kirchgasser (AUT), Tina Maze (SLO), and Tessa Worley (FRA) are sponsored by Milka (2022). The sponsored parties team of ski athletes is called "Milka Ski Stars".

On the internet site, the consumer receives all current information about the individual athletes as well as the current results in the World Cup. The homepage is directly linked to various social media platforms (such as YouTube, Facebook, and

Fig. 9.11 Fan Force One plane from DFB sponsor Bitburger. (*Source:* Bitburger Brewery Group GmbH, 2016)

Twitter), so that fans can get in touch with the company. In addition, Milka commercials are shown and Milka competitions are offered in the context of events. In addition to the sponsoring, the topic of ski jumping is taken up in its own events. In cooperation with the DSV, Milka organized, among other things, the junior competition titled "DSV Milka German Pupil Cup".

Milka is now also active in football as a sponsor (FC Milka) and has been an official partner of the two football leagues and the Supercup since January 2021. Special Milka experiences are available for children entering the Bundesliga games, at barbecue events with Bundesliga legends, and at professional training weekends. Milka aims to build an additional (year-round) platform that sets strong impulses in retail and at the point of sale. The company wants to activate the partnership in such a way that exciting concepts and experiences are created for the customer in the end. ◀

Sports Sponsoring and Event Marketing

Sports sponsoring is linked with the communication tool Event Marketing in such a way that important events within the framework of sports sponsoring are used as an occasion to hold own events. For example, athletes sponsored by the company are hired to participate in independently initiated events. The asset manager J.P. Morgan Asset Management long supported sailing and annually organized its own events, such as the "J.P. Morgan

Asset Management Round the Island Race" (J.P. Morgan Asset Management, 2016). The DIY store chain Bauhaus was one of the sponsors of the football club Fortuna Düsseldorf. The sports area was also reflected in its own events. Thus, the company annually conducted the Bauhaus Cup, a sports tournament for young people, in various sports (e.g., football, sailing, athletics).

Example: Coca-Cola and the Christmas Truck

The beverage manufacturer **Coca-Cola** is active as a sponsor with many partners from the sports sector, and the Christmas Coca-Cola truck is also well-known from years of advertising during the Advent season. This is the reason to combine both activities of the brand. At such an event, the festively decorated vehicles drive to the respective location to surprise people on site (About Drinks, 2021). With the B2B event marketing action, Coca-Cola creates a very memorable experience for loyal buyers, potential customers, and of course also for the fans of the sponsored. The timing of the event in the contemplative pre-Christmas period is ideal. It evokes positive feelings and memories in people, which they later associate with the Coca-Cola brand (and also their favorite club). On site, Coca-Cola takes visitors on a journey through a sensory landscape (including a visit from Santa Claus in the cozy fireplace room, a virtual sleigh ride, or the opportunity to have their picture taken in a snow globe). For 25 years, Coca-Cola has been hosting the Christmas truck event, which continues to strongly shape the company's image (Fig. 9.12). The event promotion is supported by further measures such as television advertising, email, and social media campaigns. In connection with the sponsored, the core activity (Christmas truck) can thus be further enhanced. ◀

Fig. 9.12 Coca-Cola and the Christmas truck on tour. (Coca-Cola, 2022)

Fig. 9.13 Title sponsoring by Audi at the Ingolstadt Triathlon 2022. (*Source:* Audi AG)

Since 2010, the Audi Triathlon Ingolstadt has been held regularly, with the car manufacturer as the founder of the event providing an example of successful sponsoring in the immediate neighborhood. The competition, with now 3000 athletes, is among the top 3 of its kind in Germany. From 2022, Audi will also be the title sponsor and wants to further develop and reposition the Ingolstadt triathlon together with the other partners and the organizer (Fig. 9.13). This sports event, well-known far beyond the region, is an important component of the corporate citizenship commitment of the Four Rings at the Ingolstadt location.

Sports Sponsoring and Trade Fairs & Exhibitions

A sports sponsoring commitment is used within the framework of trade fairs and Exhibitions to inform about sponsoring commitments. Supported by appropriate information materials, initiatives, their backgrounds, and their goals are pointed out on site. Often, the sponsored teams or individual athletes are available at the company's trade fair stands for discussions with visitors. Such a concentrated, direct encounter with the target group allows for direct exchange of ideas and feedback, thus forming an important source of information about the effects of sponsoring commitments. Depending on the sponsored sports, there is also the possibility that sports activities, such as a beach volleyball show, are integrated into the program schedule at the trade fair stand. For example, the Daimler AG brand smart succeeded in linking its sponsoring activities with its trade fair appearance with the "smart Beach" campaign at the IAA. The company has been active in beach volleyball for over ten years and is committed to the smart beach

Fig. 9.14 Smart beach volleyball teams visiting the IAA. (*Source:* Mercedes-Benz, 2013)

tour in Germany, among other things. For the IAA, the company set up a beach volleyball field right in the middle of the Frankfurt exhibition grounds (see Fig. 9.14), with a comprehensive supporting program (Mercedes-Benz, 2013).

Sports Sponsoring and Personal Communication

The use of sports sponsoring provides a good basis for personal contact with target groups relevant to the company. Invitations to receptions or the allocation of VIP tickets to attend sponsored sports events open up the opportunity for intensive conversations in a relaxed atmosphere. This was already made clear when considering the integration of sports sponsoring and customer care, where the possibilities of hospitality measures were also explained. In the context of personal communication, key customers, opinion leaders, media representatives, etc. are in the foreground. However, there are also other forms of personal communication to mention, where the company's sports sponsoring can be reported. These include consultation talks, conversations between customers and contact employees in services, sales talks in sales, etc. Here, on the one hand, an exchange about the positive aspects of the company's sponsorings can take place and, on the other hand, the negative and controversial aspects in the perception of the conversation partners can be taken up. The company representatives have the opportunity to make the sponsor's point of view clear and to solicit understanding for certain behaviors of the sponsor. The fact that a systematic integration of sports sponsoring activities into the communication

Fig. 9.15 Sports sponsoring and direct customer approach using the example of Coca-Cola fan club card of the DFB. (*Source:* DFB)

mix is carried out by both large and medium-sized companies and is at the center of the networking of brands as well as teams or new products is illustrated by two further case studies.

Example: Integration of sports sponsoring at Coca-Cola

Another example of networking sponsoring is the brand **Coca-Cola**, which is involved in various sports events. The company relies on long-term partnerships: Coca-Cola has been actively supporting the Olympic Games since 1928 and football in various ways for 60 years, including partnerships with the DFB and various Bundesliga clubs, sponsoring at the World and European Championships, and fan activities.

At such events, the brand works with various communication tools. Advertising boards at the edge of the pitch and free PR samples on Coca-Cola buses, as well as the sale of Coca-Cola in the stadiums, ensure appropriate attention. At home, the brand message is brought to the target groups, for example, during a football World Cup in the form of TV spots on television. But also in the cities, various posters can be observed to convey the brand message. Extensive reporting is done via the website and social media platforms such as Facebook. Competitions with ticket raffles for individual events are also offered. In addition, Coca-Cola is very close to the customer with the help of its own fan club and thus benefits from a positive image gain (The Coca-Cola Company, 2013, 2015). The image in Fig. 9.15 shows the corresponding fan club card of the German national football team. ◀

Empirical Study

An empirical study on the integration of sponsoring with other communication tools shows that sponsoring is primarily coordinated with Public Relations (81.4%), Internal Communication (69.9%), and Event Marketing (65.5%). Compared to previous years, the networking of sponsoring with online (55.3%) and Social Media Communication (39.4%) has been intensified (Bagusat, 2013, p. 26). Similarly, companies have increasingly to consider certain success factors of a social media presence, which become increasingly important as the abundance of information and company appearances in social media increases. In addition to basic requirements for the timeliness, clarity, optics, etc. of a social media presence, it is particularly aspects such as "cross-mediality", "(sporting) success", "activation" and the offer of sponsoring-related interaction possibilities that decide the success of a social media presence (Haupt, 2014). In addition, the creation of sponsoring-related added value and additional benefits is in the focus. Another study (VSA, 2019) confirms a certain leadership role of sponsoring within the communication mix, here Red Bull could be mentioned as an example.

The importance of a consistent integration of sponsoring measures becomes particularly clear in very competitive competitive environments, such as in Formula 1. Day-after-recall tests, in which viewers are asked about the awareness of sponsors the day after the event, suggest that isolated sponsoring measures often barely exceed the perception threshold of the recipients and thus the building of awareness or the transport of a communicative message is not achieved (Klewenhagen, 2001, p. 16). Therefore, the **networking of sponsoring** is of great importance. A consistent integration of sponsoring measures is particularly important when many companies in an industry are active in the same sports and there is a risk that sponsoring leads to pure industry advertising instead of promoting the brand profiling of individual sponsors.

In the following, a distinction must be made between two **forms of integration** of sports sponsoring:

- The **networking with other communication instruments (inter-instrumental integration)** deals with the question of integrating sponsoring into the communication mix of the company, i.e., the networking of sports sponsoring with traditional communication instruments such as media advertising, public relations, sales promotion, internal communication, etc.
- The **networking of various sponsorings in sports sponsoring (intra-instrumental integration)** investigates the question of how a standardization of the various commitments in a company's sports sponsoring—i.e., different sports, athletes, sports events, etc.—can be achieved.

9.2 Integration of Sports Sponsoring into the Sponsoring Mix

Crucial for achieving strong effects with the targeted target groups of sports sponsoring is equally the intra-instrumental Integration of sponsoring activities, i.e., the **networking of various sponsorings within sports sponsoring** by the company. According to this requirement, decisions regarding the concept and design of the company's sponsoring commitments must be networked and coordinated with each other.

This does not mean that every sponsoring activity must be carried out in the same way; rather, the specifics of each measure or the different expectations of the respective sponsoring target groups must be taken into account. The **content, formal, and temporal dimensions** can be distinguished as dimensions of integration decisions, analogous to inter-instrumental integration (Bruhn, 2018, pp. 181 f.).

The **content dimension** of intra-instrumental integration primarily refers to the specification of an overarching umbrella theme for all sponsorings. It is of paramount importance that the communicative guiding idea, or the overarching theme, is a central component of all promoted areas, so that synergies can be built and used accordingly. By defining a focus underlying all activities, such as supporting dynamic ball sports, the credibility of the commitment is enhanced and a corresponding image transfer is brought about. When selecting the overarching theme, it is important to consider the needs and desires of the targeted target groups to ensure the necessary theme-related acceptance. The selection of the theme spectrum thus also represents a significant strategic decision that sets the framework for all further planning and implementation decisions.

The **formal dimension** of intra-instrumental integration includes all decisions aimed at the uniform and consistent design implementation of the defined theme in individual sports sponsorings. To make the most of synergy potentials, all sponsored events or sponsors should maintain a consistent formal appearance of the company; it is advisable, for example, to repeatedly use certain colors and shapes and to use uniform typefaces. In addition, the repeated use of logos and slogans is a central aspect of formal integration.

In a study, the formal question of the fit of the brand colors was investigated (Cheong et al., 2019). It turned out that a visual congruence, i.e., a color match of the sponsor's message (e.g., logo) and the respective team colors, had a positive effect on the respondents' attitude towards the sponsor. In particular, when the sponsor adapted its own color to the team color, there were more positive responses from the respondents than when the sponsor color was randomly the same as the team color. In both cases, the respondents' view that the sponsor's activities supported their own team was a significant mediator between visual congruence and positive attitude.

The **temporal dimension** of intra-instrumental integration concerns both the coordination of individual sponsoring measures within a planning period and between different planning periods. The goal here is to achieve repetition and learning effects in the target groups through continuity in sponsoring commitments and to ensure through integrative measures that the individual activities support each other in their effect.

From a temporal perspective, questions also need to be clarified as to whether and how year-round or only sporadic sports events are to be accompanied (e.g., league operation in team sports and one-off short-term sports tournament) and how to deal with weather-endangered sports sponsorings (e.g., cancellation of winter sports activities due to lack of snow). Due to the narrow time window of limited sports activities (especially major sports events), it is necessary to check in good time how and with what intensity a temporal extension of the sponsoring measures is carried out in order to increase effectiveness without burdening the actual event period through wear and tear.

9.3 Decision Levels for Sports Sponsoring in the Corporate Hierarchy (Incl. Case Study Deutsche Telekom)

When using sponsoring as an integrative instrument of marketing and corporate communication, both sponsored parties and sponsoring agencies face the question of which **instance within the corporate hierarchy** is responsible for sponsorings. In practice, it is shown that the responsibilities and competencies regarding the initiation of a sponsoring commitment are very widely spread within individual companies. This is strongly related to the question of communication organization and budget responsibility. The results of a company survey on the position of the main responsible persons for sponsoring are shown in Fig. 9.16.

It is useful to differentiate between the different sponsoring areas (e.g. sports, culture, etc.) and the respective **functions** (stimulation, planning, decision, implementation, etc.). As a rule, various people from different departments are involved in sponsorings. The responsibilities and tasks of the various hierarchy levels and departments are therefore to be considered in terms of the phases of stimulation, planning, decision and implementation.

As far as **sports sponsoring** is concerned, the marketing and advertising departments in particular have essential functions for the stimulation, planning, decision and implementation of sponsorings, with guidelines for the basic strategy often also coming from the company management. In addition, more and more companies have special sponsoring departments, which are used much more frequently in sports sponsoring than in other types of sponsoring.

The decision on sports sponsoring is a **strategic element in corporate or brand communication**, so that in addition to the basic decision for or against it, the corresponding guidelines and budget availabilities are also to be made at the top corporate level (Horizont, 2009). These are the results of a study in which the professional association sponsoring (FASPO) has examined sponsoring structures in companies. In just over three fifths of the companies surveyed, there are special sponsoring departments. The same number operates on the basis of a long-term sponsoring concept. In 80% of

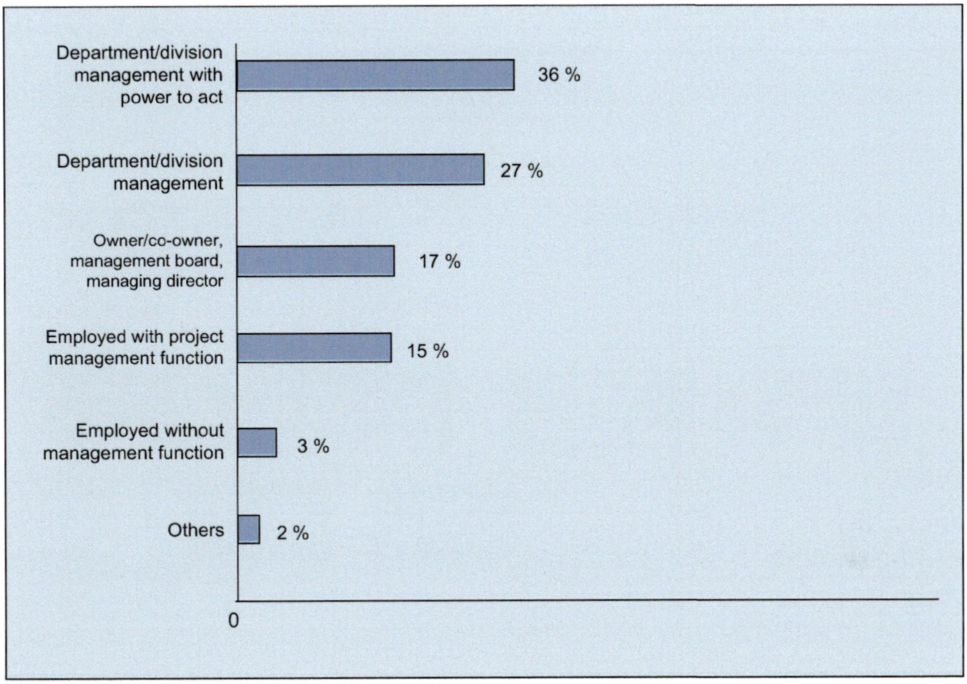

Fig. 9.16 Position of the main responsible person for sponsoring. (*Source:* ZHAW, 2015, p. 11)

cases, sponsoring is a matter for the boss: here, the management or the board decides on commitments. In 60% of companies, sponsoring is firmly established as a communication tool and is fundamentally not questioned. For 54%, it is important that their own employees support a sponsoring commitment, and 29% use sponsoring as part of their location marketing.

However, the further the planning process, which is supported by checklists and network plans, and the creative process of using new and unusual communicative possibilities progress, the more the **responsibilities shift from the generalists to the specialists**. Against this background, a top-down management style is usually found in sports sponsoring, i.e., business processes are determined by the upper management levels, starting with the board or Chief Executive Officer (CEO). The decision-making process is initially in the hands of a few decision-makers and is usually then delegated within the company or passed on to independent planning and decision-making units (see Fig. 9.17).

Depending on the company and the scope of the sponsoring commitment, such responsibilities can also change over time, i.e., under the leadership of a project manager, for example, a certain number of employees or several teams are then responsible for one or more sponsoring partnerships. In the case of a **change of responsibilities**, this affects, for example, teams that then differ in structure, size and their tasks. Each sponsor has to

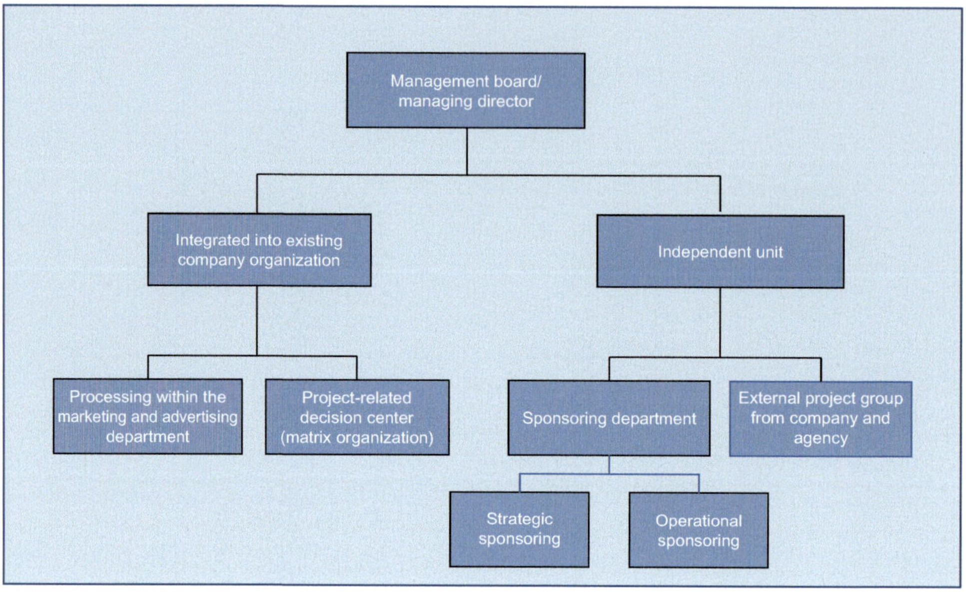

Fig. 9.17 Responsibility for sports sponsoring in the company

decide which organizational anchoring is best suited for their own company. In general, a sponsor must ensure that all necessary measures, both external and internal to the company, are carefully planned. The latter applies both to the use of their own communication tools and to the planning of personnel and organizational resources.

Already in the planning of sports sponsoring engagements, their **coordination within the company** must be taken into account. Successful sponsoring is only possible if a sponsor has qualified personnel for the right selection and optimal support of sponsoring measures. Internally, especially in small and medium-sized companies, there is rarely a separate sponsoring department that carries out the detailed coordination of individual measures. The responsibility for sponsoring in German companies, according to a company survey, lies 70% with the marketing and advertising departments (pilot checkpoint, 2002, p. 72). Especially in medium-sized companies, it is often the owners or managing directors who decide on the sponsoring and only in about 15% of these companies it is the press or public relations departments. With increasing budgets for sponsoring, companies are increasingly creating special organizational units, such as departments for operational and strategic sponsoring. Regardless of the existing organizational structure in the company, it must be ensured that the coordination of individual measures is guaranteed through the development of certain process and decision-making processes, the use of cross-departmental sponsoring teams, etc. Fig. 9.18 shows the tasks and areas of responsibility in coordinating sponsoring measures between various internal departments, including a sponsoring agency.

Sponsorship Coordinator

Jobs / Dimension bundle of measures	Advertising department	PR or public affairs department (public relations)	Sale, Sales promotion	Sponsorship Consultant or Agencies	Market research
Purchase of Media (e.g. sideline signs, advertisements)	In coordination with the consultant through advertising agency	***	***	Responsible to coordinator for conception, coordination, organization of measures	Possible study before using the media
Providing of promotional and advertising material	Responsible to coordinator for conception, organization and provision	Possibly postcards, brochures, program design in consultation with advertising department and consultant	In coordination with the advertising department (e.g. displays for sales promotion measures)	In coordination with PR and advertising department, possibly also sales promotion department	***
Inviting and looking after guests	Possibly suggestions to PR department	Responsible to the coordinator for considering/inviting and looking after guests from all target groups	Guest list to the PR department; possibly provision of a supervisor	Support of the PR department through own guest list, suggestions	Target group analysis, if applicable
Press contacts (press kit, press conferences)	***	Close cooperation with the consultant	***	Responsible to the coordinator in close coordination with the PR department and the sponsors	***
Organization and support for publicity shots, autograph sessions, etc.	Responsible to the coordinator in coordination with all other departments	***	***	Possible support of the advertising department in arranging appointments, etc.	"Protest" before a measure is implemented, if applicable
Design and provision of e.g. – Stickers – Sportswear	In consultation with sales promotion if necessary Suggestions, specification to consultant	***	Possibly suggestions to advertising department	Responsible to the coordinator in close coordination with the advertising department	***
Organization, support and control on site	Possibly support of the PR department	Responsible to the coordinator in coordination with the consultant, sales promotion, sales and advertising department	If necessary, provision of a local representative to support key accounts, trading partners	In accordance with the PR or sales department	***
Follow-up measures	Responsible to the coordinator in close coordination with sales promotion, sales and PR	In accordance with the advertising department	Building on publicity for the sponsorship, e.g. visits by representatives, trade fairs	***	Organization and implementation of controls, e.g. media reactions

Fig. 9.18 Coordination of sponsoring measures in the company. (*Source:* Bruhn, 2018, p. 74)

The various **responsibilities within the company** make it clear that sponsoring is not the domain of a specific communication department. Rather, the responsibility varies depending on the sponsoring area, the communicative situation of the company, the power of individual departments, and the personal interests of managers. The marketing and advertising department is usually responsible for sports sponsoring. This clearly shows the advertising character of sports sponsoring.

Case Study Deutsche Telekom—sponsoring and brand communication

The following case study was compiled by **Stephan Althoff**, Head of Corporate Sponsoring, and Hiro Kishi, Sports Marketing Division, with the kind support and permission of Deutsche Telekom.

The **Deutsche Telekom** is Europe's largest and leading telecommunications company with a turnover of approximately 114 billion EUR (2022) and a market value of 97 billion EUR (12/2022). The company is among the 20 most valuable brands worldwide and its main markets are Europe and the USA.

Initial Situation

Deutsche Telekom operates in three **strategic fields**. Fig. 9.19 shows that the areas of sports in various fields, CSR/culture, and music are particularly central.

Fig. 9.19 Deutsche Telekom and sponsoring in Germany—Three strategic fields. (*Source:* Deutsche Telekom)

For Deutsche Telekom, sports sponsoring has been an important component of the communication strategy for decades. What began in 1991 as the largest sponsor in German cycling has now developed into a central component of the company's overall communication. While in the early years cycling and the participation of its own team, among others at the Tour de France (Team Telekom), dominated the sports sponsoring, other sports such as basketball were gradually targeted. The company decided to establish a second pillar alongside cycling (Team Telekom) and to support its international brand building (T-Mobile) through football, which was to be achieved by a strong position in sports. When Opel's main sponsoring with FC Bayern Munich ended in 2002, Deutsche Telekom saw the opportunity to achieve the desired international competitive positioning through the collaboration of two European market leaders and the interaction of two power brands.

Fig. 9.20 shows the long-standing cooperation between **FC Bayern Munich** and Deutsche Telekom. The sponsorings have been in place since 2002 and have been continuously expanded.

With the start of the 2002/2003 season, Deutsche Telekom promoted the different business divisions and products of the group on the jersey of the German record champion. Since the restructuring of the brand architecture, only the Telekom logo has adorned the club jersey since the 2010/2011 season. In addition to the **main sponsoring with FC Bayern Munich**, the group has been **"Official Partner of the DFB and its A national team"** since 2005 and premium partner of the traditional club Borussia Mönchengladbach since 2013. In addition to the exclusive partnership with Hamburger Sportverein (Autumn 2020), 1. FC Köln has also been part of the German Telekom's football portfolio since 2021. The football commitment is complemented by extensive content partnerships, which are bundled in the TV offer of "MagentaSport": All matches of the 3rd league as well as the women's Bundesliga, all matches of the highest German ice hockey league including the playoffs—a total of up to 419 matches, top matches of the German ice hockey national team and all matches of the Deutschland Cup, all matches of the Basketball Bundesliga, the MagentaSport BBL Cup and the Euroleague. Also included are all matches of the German basketball national team and events such as FIBA EuroBasket 2022. But also in basketball (commitments with the Telekom Baskets Bonn) and in disabled sports (German Disabled Sports Association) as well as with Deutsche Sporthilfe, there are sponsoring commitments.

Goals and Target Groups

In the new environment of football, Deutsche Telekom saw great opportunities to develop better than the competition shortly after the turn of the millennium. Its goal was to position the brand in an emotional and performance-related football environment in such a way that both psychographic and economic goals would be realized better and faster. The following **sponsoring goals** were particularly central:

Fig. 9.20 FC Bayern Munich and Deutsche Telekom. (*Source:* Deutsche Telekom)

- Strengthening Telekom's reputation,
- Expanding market leadership in Germany and Europe,
- Direct sales into fan target groups and gaining market shares across all segments,
- Generating important content for distribution via own channels,
- International brand awareness (T-Mobile),
- Employee motivation,
- Creation of new markets (e.g. Club-TV, StadiumVision etc.).

From the previously formulated goals for sponsoring commitments, it is clear that a wide range of target groups had to be addressed in both the B2C and B2B markets, after all, the sponsoring was supposed to have an effect not only externally, but also internally. Specifically, Telekom's sponsoring was intended to address these various **target groups**:

- Existing private customers, business customers, system customers (national/international) with the goal of customer retention,
- Potential customers with the goal of acquiring new customers,
- Media and similar multipliers (e.g. influencers),
- Politics, associations, institutions (e.g. NGOs),
- Executives and employees.

Strategic Orientation and Selection

Following the **company's sponsoring guidelines**, commitments in sports sponsoring of Deutsche Telekom must be aligned with the brand values, communication strategy, and the desired image of Telekom. Over the years, Deutsche Telekom has become one of the most well-known and largest national sports sponsors in Germany, supporting athletes, associations, clubs, and events with the goal of conveying the image dimensions of team spirit, willingness to perform and success, as well as the brand values of competence, innovation, simplicity, and service.

Sports sponsoring is a firm **component of the marketing strategy**, and football in particular plays a prominent role in the sponsoring portfolio as a strategic communicative instrument. The reasons for this are obvious: Far more than 30 million people in Germany consider themselves football fans, over seven million people form the largest football association in the world with the DFB, football is played in over 25,000 German clubs, no other sport is as popular.

The following criteria or facts speak for **football as the number 1 sponsoring platform** from Telekom's point of view:

- Expansion of Telekom's position in the most important and widest-reaching sport in Europe (= football),
- Availability of Bayern Munich—one of the most valuable assets in football—after Opel's withdrawal,
- Brand strength and fit with FC Bayern Munich,
- Long-term and extensive sponsoring contract (initially six years: 2002 to 2008, the term has since been extended to 2027),
- All important advertising and content rights are usable, including jersey, training clothing, comprehensive ticket package, usage rights to players, TV-relevant branding areas, etc.

Implementation and Results

In addition to the broad use of the core rights listed above, Telekom has also launched its own **activation measures for sports sponsoring** with FC Bayern Munich, in particular:

- Initiation of the Telekom Cup with FC Bayern as the main attraction,
- Advertising campaigns with players (TV, social media, etc.),
- Joint TV channel "FC Bayern.tv live",
- Fan rates (FC Bayern Mobile),
- Creation of a unique multimedia experience space (StadiumVision),
- Sales actions offline/online.

The **Telekom Cup** plays a special role in the sponsoring of FC Bayern. Fig. 9.21 gives an impression of the competition that has been in existence for years.

At FC Bayern Munich, the group advertises on jerseys and banners, as well as with many exciting fan actions and new formats (e.g., StadiumVision). Telekom also introduced the first 24-hour TV channel of a German football club, with daily live reports, unique communication content, and exclusive behind-the-scenes insights available seven days a week on **"FC Bayern.tv live"**. Exclusive club content is integrated into the information and entertainment platforms of the Telekom Group. Since 2009, Telekom has been organizing its own football tournament. Four Bundesliga teams, including FC Bayern Munich, compete in an attractively cast competition during the summer or winter break to determine the winner of the Telekom Cup. The media presence alone and the associated effects are worth many times what Telekom invests in the partnership.

Fig. 9.21 Telekom Cup as part of the FC Bayern sponsoring. (*Source:* Deutsche Telekom)

The **networking of sports sponsoring** with other communication tools is particularly evident in the sponsoring of FC Bayern Munich. In addition to branding measures on the game and training clothing and in the stadium, the players and management of FC Bayern are deliberately integrated into TV spots and as testimonials in print advertisements. The Magenta TV campaign by Deutsche Telekom with FC Bayern professionals can be cited as an example. The campaign focused on football artist Andrew Cassidy and the Bundesliga players of FC Bayern Munich. In addition, Telekom is present on the club website and actively integrates the internet and social media into its sponsoring activities. For example, background information on the sponsoring of FC Bayern Munich can be found on the website and social media channels of Deutsche Telekom. Telekom also set standards with the comprehensive coverage of the Allianz Arena with 5G mobile technology—see Fig. 9.22 for this (Deutsche Telekom AG, 2021).

A **networking with other marketing disciplines** has continuously taken place, among other things through the following measures:

- Use of players/officials in advertising campaigns (all types of advertising),
- Appearances of players at trade fairs (IFA, Mobile World Congress, etc.),
- Appearances of officials at internal major events and others.

Fig. 9.22 5G campaign as part of the FC Bayern sponsoring. (*Source:* Deutsche Telekom)

Given the strong commitment to football, the "decision-making threads" converge in the **Sports Marketing Department**, which has brought on board the Mataracan agency from Munich for conception and implementation.

In an overall assessment, Deutsche Telekom comes to a thoroughly positive **result of its commitment** to the German football record champion. Qualitative controls have shown that those recipients who know Telekom as a sponsor of FC Bayern rate the Telekom brand significantly better than the rest of the population. The group of these sponsoring connoisseurs is significantly larger than 50% of the population. In the course of quantitative media research, it was found that the media output of the partnership, even when using the strictly weighted Nielsen QI index, is many times the financial input.

The **overall assessment** of the 20-year sponsoring commitment to FC Bayern Munich is therefore clearly positive. Sales effects through sales measures in the private and business customer sector have not even been taken into account. The involvement of employees in the partnership is also highly valued. The internal support for the main sponsoring is therefore very good and finds broad support.

9.4 Key Points

To best integrate sports sponsoring into corporate and brand communication, several important aspects must be considered when integrating sports sponsoring into the communication and sponsoring mix.

Key Points

1. The integration of sports sponsoring into a company's communication strategy involves achieving sufficient synergy effects through a **strategic and operational interlocking of various communication instruments**, and creating the conditions for the desired sponsoring success.
2. Two fundamental forms of integration of sports sponsoring should be pursued: The **networking with other instruments in the communication mix** (inter-instrumental integration) and the **networking within the sponsoring mix** (intra-instrumental integration).
3. The subject of inter-instrumental Integration is the **connection of sports sponsoring with marketing and communication instruments**. Here, Possibilities should be sought to increase the impact across the entire communication mix.
4. The most important **instruments from the communication mix** are public relations, media advertising, sales promotion, direct marketing, customer care, internal communication, social media activities, event marketing, trade fairs and exhibitions, and personal communication. Sports sponsoring offers numerous interesting starting points for networking.

5. The **intra-instrumental integration** deals with whether and to what extent a standardization of the various commitments in sports sponsoring can be achieved. This should be pursued in order to increase the overall effect.
6. In the case of intra-instrumental integration, **content-related, formal, and temporal measures** can be taken to present a unified appearance for sports sponsoring to the outside world.
7. A frequently overlooked question concerns the **decision-making levels** and clarity about which instance within the corporate hierarchy is responsible for sponsorings. This should be taken into account when planning sponsorings.
8. In general, **responsibilities and competencies** regarding the undertaking of a sponsoring commitment are very differently regulated at the company level. Certain influencing factors are also important, such as the type and scope of the sponsoring, phase of the decision-making process, etc. A potential sponsor must adjust to this.
9. The decision on sports sponsoring is a strategic element in corporate or brand communication. The basic decision is usually made at a higher decision-making level. **Guidelines and budget availability** must be taken into account.
10. Even when planning sports sponsoring commitments, their **coordination within the company** must be taken into account. Successful sponsoring is only possible if a sponsor has qualified personnel for the correct selection and optimal support of sponsoring measures.

References

A

ABB. (2016). ABB und Special Olympics. http://new.abb.com/de/ueber-uns/nachhaltigkeit/special-olympics. Accessed: 9. June 2016.

ABB. (2020). 100 ABB-Mitarbeiter bei Special Olympics, Beitrag vom 10.03.2020. https://new.abb.com/news/de/detail/58318/100-abb-mitarbeiter-bei-special-olympics.

About Drinks. (2016). Gemeinsam durch den Fußballsommer: Coca-Cola startet die Kampagne zur UEFA EURO 2016. http://www.about-drinks.com/coca-cola-startet-die-kampagne-zur-uefa-euro-2016/. Accessed: 8. June 2016.

About Drinks. (2021). Die Coca-Cola Weihnachtstrucks starten ihre Tour durch Deutschland. https://www.about-drinks.com/die-coca-cola-weihnachtstrucks-starten-ihre-tour-durch-deutschland/.

Absatzwirtschaft. (2017). Authentisches aus der Kabine: Warum der FC Bayern München in den sozialen Medien erfolgreicher ist als andere, Beitrag vom 06.06.2017. https://www.absatzwirtschaft.de/authentisches-aus-der-kabine-warum-der-fc-bayern-muenchen-in-den-sozialen-medien-erfolgreicher-ist-als-andere-216251/.

Althoff, S. (2007). Das Sportsponsoring der Telekom – und was dahinter steckt. In D. Ahlert, D. Woisetschläger, & Vogel, V. (Hrsg.), *Exzellentes Sponsoring. Innovative Ansätze und Best Practices für das Markenmanagement* (2. Aufl., S. 77–100). https://doi.org/10.1007/978-3-8350-9639-4_4.

B

Bagusat, A. (2013). *Sponsoring trends 2012.* https://www.ostfalia.de/export/sites/default/de/ispm/Blickpunkt_Sportmanagement/Sponsoring_Trends_2012.pdf. Accessed: 17. Febr. 2016.

Bitburger Braugruppe GmbH. (2016). *Fan force one.* https://www.fanforceone.de/.

BMW AG. (2016). *BMW International Open.* http://www.bmw-golfsport.com/en/tournaments/bmw-international-open/home/tournament.html. Accessed: 8. March 2016.

Bruhn, M. (2018). *Sponsoring. Systematische Planung und integrativer Einsatz* (6. Aufl.). https://doi.org/10.1007/978-3-658-13313-9.

C

Cheong, C., Do, Y. P., & Ho, K. L. (2019). Sponsoring and advertising in sport: A study of consumers' attitude. *European Sport Management Quarterly, 19*(3), 287–311. https://doi.org/10.1080/16184742.2018.1517271.

Coca-Cola. (2016). Coca-Cola Dosen Werbung UEFA EURO 2016 TV-Spot Europameisterschaft Manuel Neuer. https://www.youtube.com/watch?v=VfISpAROnT4.

Coca-Cola. (2020). mezzo mix erfüllt gemeinsam mit dem FC Bayern München Fan-Träume, Beitrag vom 16.12.2020. https://www.presseportal.de/pm/7974/4792707.

Coca-Cola. (2022). Volle Ladung Vorfreude! Coca-Cola Trucktour 2022. https://www.coca-cola-deutschland.de/unterhaltung/weihnachten/truck-tour-2021. Accessed: 8. Dec. 2022.

Cotting, P. (2011). Interview Medien. http://www.sponsoringextra.ch/file/archiv/Interview_Medien/Social%20Media%20im%20Sponsoring-06-2011.pdf. Accessed: 2.Febr. 2016.

D

Deutsche Telekom AG. (2016). Deutsche Telekom startet Entertain-Kampagne mit FC Bayern Profis und Ballkünstler Andrew Cassidy. https://www.telekom.com/innovation/ifa-2014/246628. Accessed: 10. June 2016.

Deutsche Telekom AG. (2021). Engagement im Fußball zahlt sich aus. https://www.telekom.com/de/konzern/details/engagement-im-fussball-zahlt-sich-aus-336788.

E

Emmi Group. (2019). Emmi Caffè Latte ist neuer Hauptsponsor von Wendy Holdener, Beitrag vom 12.07.2019. https://group.emmi.com/che/de/medien-investoren/medienmitteilungen/emmi-caffe-latte-ist-neuer-hauptsponsor-von-wendy-holdener.

H

Haupt, T. (2014). Social Media Marketing und Kapitalisierungsmöglichkeiten im Spitzensport – Eine empirische Erfolgsfaktorenanalyse im Rahmen der 1. Fußball-Bundesliga. In C. Werner & F. Kainz (Hrsg.), *Schriftenreihe des internationalen Hochschulverbunds IUNworld* (Bd. 6, S. 109–136). https://doi.org/10.1007/978-3-642-54884-0_29.

Hofer, K. (2013). Auswirkungen des Sport-Sponsorings auf die Mitarbeiter des Unternehmens, Studie des Instituts für Handel, Absatz und Marketing an der Johannes-Kepler-Universität Linz 2013. https://news.observer.at/4-sport-business-circle-2013-messbarkeit-und-effizienz-von-sponsoring/.

Horizont. (2009). Unternehmen bemängeln Qualität von Sponsoringpaketen. Studie vom Fachverband Sponsoring (FASPO), in: Horizont vom 27.11.2009. https://www.horizont.net/marketing/nachrichten/-Studie-Unternehmen-bemaengeln-Qualitaet-von-Sponsoringpaketen-88771.

Horizont. (2021). Jürgen Klopp wird Botschafter von Nivea Men – Jogi Löw soll an Bord bleiben, Beitrag vom 07.09.2021. https://www.horizont.net/marketing/nachrichten/beiersdorf-juergen-klopp-wird-botschafter-von-nivea-men%2D%2D-jogi-loew-soll-an-bord-bleiben-194220.

J

J.P. Morgan Asset Management. (2016). *J.P. Morgan asset management round the island race*. https://am.jpmorgan.co.uk/sponsoring/RoundTheIslandRace.aspx.

K

Klewenhagen, M. (2001). Vernetzte Kommunikation. Eine verstrickte Sache. *Sponsors, 6*, 14–22. https://doi.org/10.1007/978-3-8349-8078-6_8.

M

Melitta. (2020). Melitta und Manchester United verlängern Partnerschaft. https://www.melitta-group.com/de/Melitta-und-Manchester-United-verlaengern-Partnerschaft-4207.html.

Mercedes-Benz. (2013). Smart Beachvolleyball-Teams zu Besuch auf der IAA in Frankfurt, Beitrag vom 11.09.2013. https://group-media.mercedes-benz.com/marsMediaSite/de/instance/ko/smart-Beachvolleyball-Teams-zu-Besuch-auf-der-IAA-in-Frankfurt.xhtml?oid=9918934.

Mercedes-Benz. (2022). In der Lounge von Mercedes-AMG den Nürburgring erleben, Beitrag vom 09.05.2022. https://mbpassion.de/2022/05/in-der-lounge-von-mercedes-amg-den-nuerburgring-erleben/.

Milka. (2022). Milka Ski Sponsoring. https://www.milka.de/uber-milka/milka-ski-sponsoring. Accessed: 8. Nov. 2022.

Motorsport Total. (2017). Hinter den Kulissen: So geht es in der Mercedes-Hospitality zu, Beitrag vom 16.10.2017. https://www.motorsport-total.com/formel-1/news/hinter-den-kulissen-so-geht-es-in-der-mercedes-hospitality-zu-17101611.

N

Nufer, G., & Rützel, F. (2016). Best Practices im Sportsponsoring, Nachspielzeit – die Schriftenreihe des Deutschen Instituts für Sportmarketing, herausgegeben von Gerd Nufer & André Bühler, Nr. 2016–7.

P

Panten, D. (2013). Sponsoring goes Social Media – Aktivierung von Zielgruppen im digitalen Zeitalter. *Media 41 – Journal für Media & Marketing, 41*(5), 6–10.

Pilot Checkpoint. (2002). *Sponsor visions 2002.*

Porsche AG. (2016). Rendezvous der Supersportler, Beirag vom 13.09.2016. https://newsroom.porsche.com/de/unternehmen/porsche-tennis-angelique-kerber-markenbotschafterin-us-open-titel-panamera-turbo-12886.html.

Puma-BVB. (2022). BVB-Heimtrikot 22/23|Different From Day One. https://www.youtube.com/watch?v=KND_kjdtPJw.

R

Ringle, T. (2003). Vernetzung von Sportevents. In A. Hermanns & F. Riedmüller (Hrsg.), *Sponsoring und Events im Sport* (S. 193–207). Vahlen Franz GmbH.

T

Taz. (2021). Trend Sport-Dokumentationen: Bis unter die Dusche, Beitrag vom 22.02.2021. https://taz.de/Trend-Sport-Dokumentationen/!5750323/.

The Coca-Cola Company. (2013). Der 12. Mann auf dem Platz: Fan Club Nationalmannschaft. http://www.coca-cola-deutschland.de/stories/seit-10-jahren-der-12-mann-auf-dem-platz-fan-club-nationalmannschaft.

The Coca-Cola Company. (2015). *CocaCola journey.* http://www.coca-cola-deutschland.de/#sport.

Turkish Airlines. (2016). *Sponsorings.* http://www.turkishairlines.com/en-int/corporate/sport-club.

Tz München. (2013). Wer sind eigentlich diese Fans im „T"? http://www.tz.de/sport/fc-bayern/telekom-t-allianz-arena-fc-bayern-muenchen-wer-sind-fans-bewerben-meta-2853149.html.

V

VSA. (2019). Sportsponsoring: Volltreffer mit gezielter Wirkung, Berlin. Accessed: 1. May 2022.
VSA, S 20, BMI. (2017). *Hospitality und Strafrecht – ein Leitfaden* (2. Aufl.). https://cdn.dosb.de/alter_Datenbestand/fm-dosb/downloads/recht/Hospitality-und-Strafrecht-ein-Leitfaden_2017.pdf.

Y

YouTube Commerbank. (2019). Frecher Commerzbank Video-Clip. https://www.youtube.com/watch?v=fZL1D-ybye8.

Z

ZHAW. (2015). (Zentrum für Kulturmanagement, School of Management and Law, Zürcher Hochschule für Angewandte Wissenschaften. „Sponsor-Visions 2014/15"- Eine empirische Studie zum Sponsoringmarkt Schweiz. http://www.swa-asa.ch/de-wAssets/docs/artikel-print-medien/2015/Studie_Sponsor_Visions_Schweiz_2014-15.pdf. Accessed: 17. Febr. 2016.

Operational Design of Sports Sponsoring 10

Contents

Abstract

Sponsoring requires, above all, a convincing, i.e., widely accepted realization for successful realization. Certain design dimensions play an important role, which can be described with the terms sponsoring quantity and sponsoring quality. Both the relevant factors for the required sponsoring quantity and for the sponsoring quality are explained. Numerous individual measures need to be considered for the activation of sports sponsoring. These are detailed for the sponsor as well as the potential counter-services of the sponsored party. Finally, content, formal, and temporal design issues of sports sponsoring are addressed. The essential points of the operational design of sports sponsoring are summarized in the form of key points. The chapter contains a case study of Mercedes-Benz and the Laver Cup.

M. Bruhn and P. Rohlmann, *Sports Sponsoring*,
https://doi.org/10.1007/978-3-658-44171-5_10

10.1 Design Dimensions of Sports Sponsoring

The selection of sponsorings in sports sponsoring and their integration into the overall marketing and corporate communication are central strategic decisions in sports sponsoring, which significantly influence the success of sponsoring. However, success also depends on the **design of the sponsorings**. Not only are there numerous degrees of freedom, but it also lies in the creative potential of the participants (sponsor, sponsored parties, agencies) to generate ideas and measures for successful use of the sponsorings.

In the context of describing a sports sponsoring engagement, the terms "sponsoring quantity" and "sponsoring quality" are often used, implicitly assuming certain design dimensions, with whose different characteristics the interaction in a specific extent and certain properties is meant (cf. Bruhn & Batt, 2012). The perceived **sponsoring quantity** consistently refers to the pressure or presence with which sponsoring measures are implemented. It results on the one hand from the demand-side perceived frequency or duration of sponsoring activities, which can also be measured in financial terms. On the other hand, it results from the integration of the sponsoring into the communication mix. The perceived **sponsoring quality**, which is expressed in creative and credible design, includes the positive assessment of the sponsoring engagement by the demander(s) and can be determined by certain degrees of effectiveness.

The so-called **Mere-Exposure-Effect** plays a particular role here. The effect states that an object is rated more positively the more often an individual is exposed to this object (Zajonc, 1968). The mere repetition thus improves the attitude towards this object. In relation to sponsoring, this insight leads to the conclusion that continuous sponsoring engagement and the favorable conditions of a sporting event lead to positive effects on the viewer. It can be observed that the Mere-Exposure-Effect is stronger due to the positively stimulating atmosphere at a sporting event than under other circumstances (Bennett, 1999). Against this background, the influence of the duration of a sponsoring activity and the conditions of contact on the effectiveness of the sponsoring was examined (e.g. Shilbury & Berriman, 1996; Turco, 1996; Grohs et al., 2004). It was found that the duration of a sponsoring measure and participation in the sponsored event have a positive influence on effectiveness.

It was also observed that sponsoring is perceived more consciously when it is used in **connection with other communication instruments**(e.g. Lardinoit, 1998, 1999; Quester & Thompson, 2001). By establishing a content-related reference of the advertising and the use of official logos or similar, a close connection between the event or sponsoring object and the sponsor can be established and thus the effectiveness of the sponsoring can be increased. Although the state of research in this area is still in flux, it seems significant for the perception of the sponsoring activity, so that the sponsoring integration is taken into account in the conceptualization of the sponsoring quantity. This can also be measured by the importance of a particular commitment within the totality of all sponsorings (see also Chap. 9).

A positive **evaluation of the sponsoring object**(e.g. in terms of image) by customers is of great importance, because the sponsoring object itself becomes a part of the communication between the company and the target group. The influence of a positive attitude of the customer towards the sponsoring object in achieving a positive communication effect has already been empirically proven. Thus, Huber and Matthes (2007) show in their study that a positive attitude of the consumer towards a sponsored individual as a sponsoring object has a positive effect on the attitude towards the sponsor. D'Astous and Bitz (1995) found that an event rated as attractive or interesting by the customer positively influences the image of the sponsor.

The **fit between the sponsor and the sponsoring object**perceived by the consumer represents the most frequently studied theoretical construct within the sponsoring literature (e.g. Ferrand & Pages, 1995; Gwinner, 1997; Musante et al., 1999; Speed & Thompson, 2000; Becker-Olsen & Simmons, 2002). The fit between a sponsor and the sponsoring object depends on the perceived congruence within this relationship (Simmons & Becker-Olsen, 2006; Rodgers, 2007). Congruence exists when two objects perceived in a positive mutual relationship are classified as equal. The level of sponsoring fit can be determined based on the target group, product and image affinity.

The sponsoring company can design numerous parameters itself so that the quantity and quality of its sports sponsoring commitments can unfold their promising effect. However, there are also individual **adjustment screws for the design**, the adjustment of which is not solely up to the sponsor, as Fig. 10.1 illustrates.

If a company wants to use sports sponsoring to increase the brand visibility, image transfer, and demand intensification of itself and its products through the sponsored party, the basic strategic consideration is that sports provide a suitable platform for this. The actual **design of the sponsoring** is then determined by decisions about the intensity

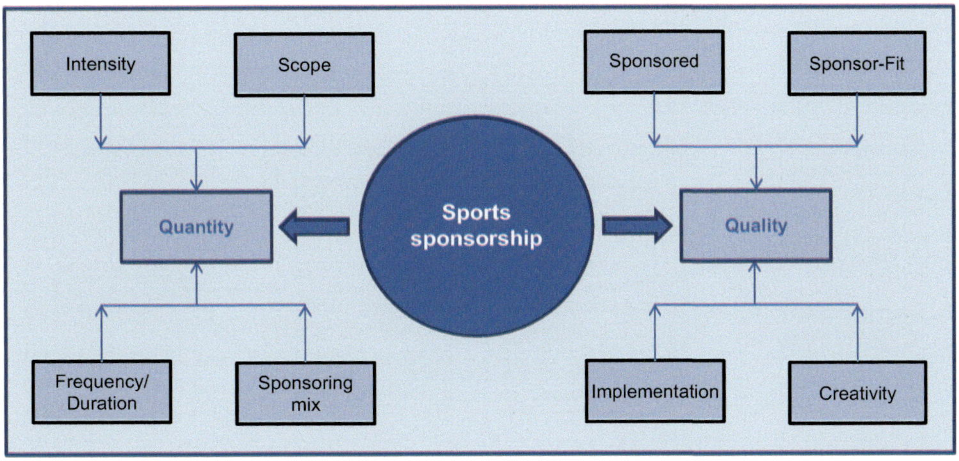

Fig. 10.1 Design dimensions in sports sponsoring from the perspective of the sponsoring companies

and duration of the commitments, their frequency or repetitions, which ultimately depends on the amount and regularity of the sponsoring expenses and their share of the total marketing budget. The latter also applies to the quality of the sponsoring, because the activation of the sponsoring (implementation and creativity) has a decisive influence on the effect, as does the (as exact as possible) fit of the sponsoring company with the sponsored party. Finally, the success in sports sponsoring is also measured by the extent to which negative (e.g., scandals, failures) or positive parameters (e.g., star transfer, sports successes) of the sponsored party can have an influence.

From empirical studies, some important **recommendations for action** can be derived for sports sponsoring (Bruhn & Batt, 2012, pp. 40 f.):

- The quality of sponsoring has proven to be a superior influence factor of the emotional brand image than the quantity of sponsoring.
- To ensure a high quality of sponsoring, the fit or compatibility of the image between the sponsor and the sponsoring object is of central importance.
- Due to the desired image transfer from the sponsoring object to the sponsor, it is important to ensure that the image of the sponsoring object corresponds to or is complementary to the image of the sponsor's brand.
- The credibility and sympathy of the sponsoring object are also relevant for ensuring a high quality of sponsoring.

The interplay between sponsoring and a sponsor brand is shown in Fig. 10.2.

However, the design dimensions of sponsoring quantity and quality also apply with regard to the **(counter-) performances of the sponsored party**. Thus, a sponsored party can also positively influence mutual success in sports sponsoring using the parameters of quantity and quality. Particularly noticeable are factors whose general consideration can also be described as a basic rule when granting sponsorings. The sponsoring quantity from the perspective of the sponsored party is primarily determined by the scope of

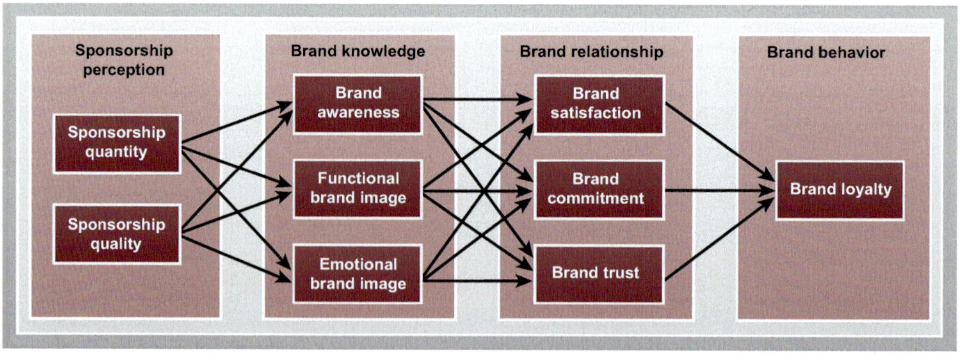

Fig. 10.2 Interplay between sponsoring and sponsor brand. (*Source:* Bruhn & Batt, 2012, p. 38)

services, which is embedded in the number and structure of the entire sponsoring, and thus refers to the position of the individual sponsor within the other partners. The scope of services can be upgraded by planned (e.g., B2B events) and unplanned additional services (e.g., random success in sports). In addition, the sponsored parties have means to influence the quality of sponsoring. This results from the nature of the sponsor relationship (including individual sponsor contact and individual appreciation) and of course from the quality of the service implementation, which includes professionalism and creativity in realizing the counter-performance (fulfillment of the performance promise) as well as creative add-ons (e.g., content on social media accounts). The design dimensions in sports sponsoring from the perspective of the sponsored party are shown in Fig. 10.3.

10.2 Development of Individual Measures for Sports Sponsoring

Once the decision for a specific sponsoring has been made after appropriate selection (see also Chap. 8), a detailed action plan must be drawn up, which includes all the individual measures necessary for the implementation of the sponsoring commitment. This includes, in addition to the definition of services and counter-services, the legal design of the sponsoring, the calculation of costs, and possibly the selection of an agency to support the sponsoring planning and implementation. In Fig. 10.4, the development and implementation of individual measures in sports sponsoring are differentiated in the individual phases.

With regard to the determination of services and counter-services between both parties, it must be clarified on the part of the sponsors what **services the company** provides

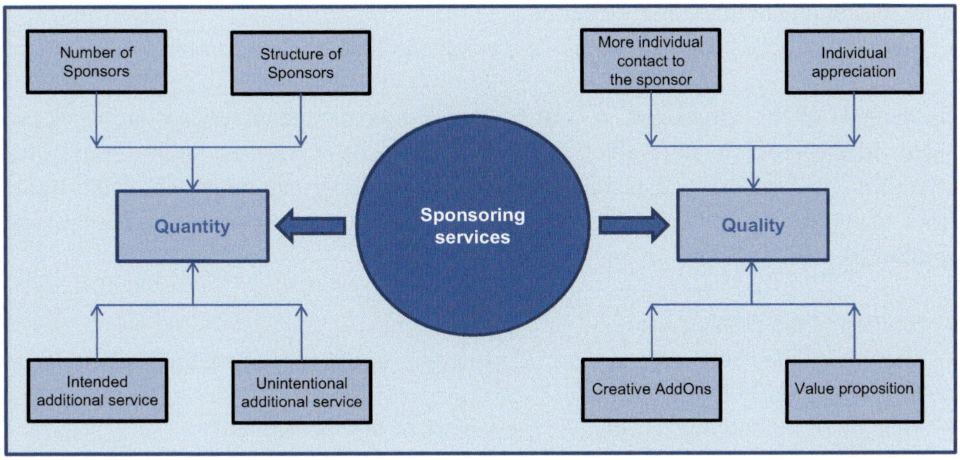

Fig. 10.3 Design dimensions in sports sponsoring from the perspective of the sponsored party

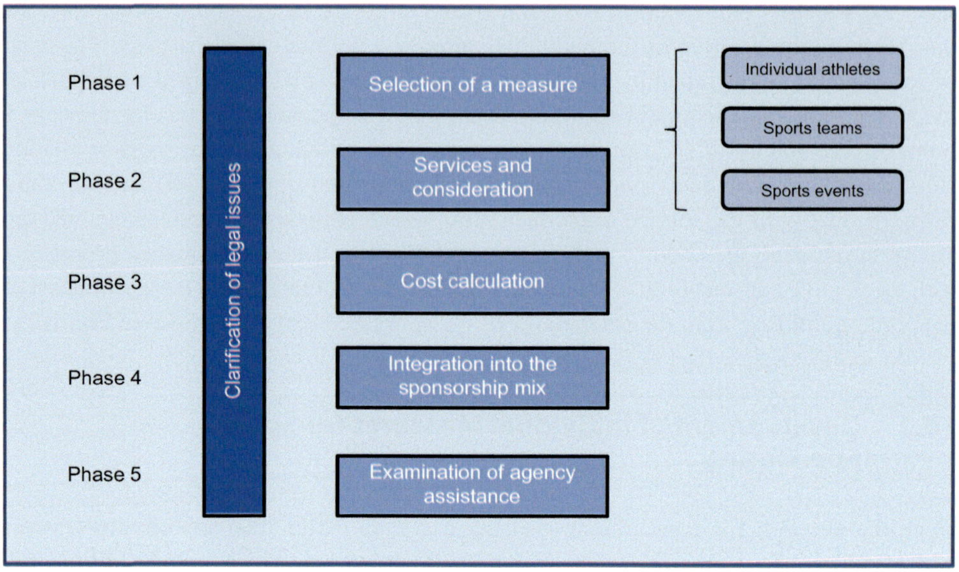

Fig. 10.4 Development and implementation of individual measures in sports sponsoring

to the sponsored party or parties (see Bruhn, 2018, pp. 163 ff.). The following are examples of **individual services provided by sponsors** (see also Fig. 10.5):

- Subsidies for the financing of events, projects, actions, organizations, associations, or individuals,
- Release of employees to support partner organizations (secondments),
- Assumption of material (e.g., printing of brochures or annual reports) or services (e.g., administration, event execution),
- Purchase of objects or properties that are made available to the partner, among others.

On the **side of the sponsored**, it must be clarified what counter-services are to be provided. In the professional marketing of events in sports, potential sponsors are often offered a "package", i.e., a bundle of various advertising measures within the framework of the event. The following are examples of **counter-services provided by the sponsored**:

- Naming of the sponsor at events,
- Mention of the sponsor on brochures, programs, books, social media platforms (e.g., Facebook), the website, etc.,
- Mention of the sponsor through the press work of the sponsored,
- Advertisements of the sponsor in program booklets, annual reports, catalogs, etc.,
- Awarding of predicates, emblems, titles, signs,

Sponsored	Exemplary advertising opportunities and cooperation with sponsors
Clubs and associations	• License rights (predicates, titles for competitions and leagues) • Naming (stadium/hall/competition venue; training center/boarding school) • Provision of equipment • Assumption of sponsorships • VIP activities (lounges, hospitality, contacts) • Advertising with spectators (flags, caps) • Advertising at the sporting event (see below)
Teams	• Shirt advertising • Media advertising (testimonials) • Customer and employee events (hospitality) • Equipment with play and training clothing and sports equipment • Equipped with going out clothes • Advertising on the team bus
Sports events	• License rights (predicates, titles) • Perimeter advertising • Display and video boards • Flags, banners • Print products (program booklets, posters, tickets) • VIP opportunities • Press conferences • Loudspeaker announcements • Marking of stadium components/tracks as well as utility and equipment items, including transport vehicles • Organization of competition breaks
Individual athletes	• Advertising space for men and women • Media advertising (testimonials, personal rights) • Sales promotion (autograph sessions, competitions) • Equipment contract
Media	• TV program sponsoring • Competitions • TV graphics • Category sponsoring in print media • Online/Internet sponsoring • Banner advertising • Virtual advertising (new media)

Fig. 10.5 Selection of individual measures by the participants in sports sponsoring

- Implementation of actions in the company with employees,
- Granting the possibility of hospitality measures,
- Product presentations during an event,
- Tolerance of advertising measures of the sponsor within the framework and environment of an event, e.g., mention of the sponsoring in press releases and in advertising, among others.

For the planning and selection of the individual measures of the sponsoring commitment, the following **checklist** should beconsulted:

- Placement of various media and advertising materials as part of sponsorings, e.g., poster advertising, company logo on tickets, flyers, online ads, and billboards,

- Joint press work by the sponsored party and the sponsor before, during, and after the event, for example through the use of press releases, press conferences, and press kits,
- Placement of advertisements and other advertising materials by the sponsor to draw attention to the event and the sponsoring,
- Use of social media communication to announce the sponsoring (e.g., via Twitter messages),
- Provision of products and promotional materials such as images, stickers, promotional items, product samples, promotional gifts, brochures,
- In connection with "hospitality", the invitation and care of company-relevant individuals at events, e.g., invitation, reception, care, catering, and transport of honored guests,
- Planning of own actions during and after the event (e.g., autograph sessions, draws, competitions, and own product presentations),
- Implementation of consumer-oriented sales promotion measures such as sweepstakes and special offer actions, at the sponsored event and/or accompanying in retail,
- Implementation of trade-oriented sales promotion measures to involve wholesalers and retailers,
- Involvement of employees in the sponsorings through invitations or other forms of participation,
- Measures for the follow-up of the sponsorings, especially press work, implementation of impact measurements, calculation of the cost-benefit ratio, field service visits, among others.

The **planning and selection of individual measures** should be carried out depending on the size of the sponsorings, their relative importance, the legally agreed possibilities, and the available budgets. The more intensively the sponsors use their sponsorings through various individual measures, the higher the effectiveness and efficiency of achieving their goals will be. In sponsoring, many sponsors still limit themselves to the exclusive use of advertising opportunities with the sponsored party. The potential that lies in the networking of sponsorings with other instruments of product, sales, and communication policy is often underestimated.

The **development of sponsoring measures** is both a systematic, planning process, supported by checklists and network plans, and a creative process of using new and unusual communicative possibilities. In general, a sponsor must ensure that all necessary measures, both external and internal to the company, are carefully planned. This applies both to the use of their own communication instruments and to the planning of personnel and organizational resources.

When planning individual measures, their **coordination within the company** must be ensured. Internally, especially in small and medium-sized companies, there is rarely a separate sponsoring department that carries out the detailed coordination of individual measures. The responsibility for sponsoring in larger German companies is predominantly in the hands of the marketing department (see also Fig. 9.17 and 9.18 in Chap. 9).

Regardless of existing organizational structures in the company, it must be ensured that the coordination of individual measures is guaranteed—be it through certain procedures, or with the help of cross-departmental working groups such as sponsoring project teams or similar.

Even though sponsoring has now become an everyday accompaniment at sports events and in sports reporting, and the design of sponsoring measures is part of the daily routine of companies, overstrains and **limits of sports sponsoring** must also be taken into account. Many market participants try to maximize their benefit in the implementation of sponsorings, leading to phenomena that can be described as "sponsoring overload" and "sponsoring overkill".

Especially when offering limited availability sponsoring rights, it is occasionally tempting to dilute the potential impact of this marketing measure by having a very (too) high density of sponsors. In this context, one can also speak of a "**sponsoring-overload**". While the sponsor recipient primarily aims to generate as much revenue as possible from the allocation of his sponsoring rights, the sponsor provider wants to place as efficient advertising as possible, which is often no longer possible due to an overly dense concentration of sponsor logos on too small an area. This dilemma can only be solved by a clever selection of the potential sponsoring elements on the one hand (from the sponsor provider's point of view) and by a trusting, fair partnership on the other hand (from the sponsor recipient's point of view). Often, such contrasting approaches can also be exaggeratedly described as a problem between "advertising graveyard" and "efficiency marketing".

Regardless of the fact that due to the ever-increasing competition, every company interested in sports sponsoring wants and needs to use its funds effectively, it seems to be always tempting to also acquire **sponsoring rights without special status**, where a partner does not belong to a small circle of a few chosen ones or even has exclusivity status. Commitments such as being the 145th business partner of Club XY may possibly allow access to tickets, hospitality, etc., which is otherwise not so easy, but they do not stand up to efficient and penetrating brand presentation as a partner of Club XY.

The same applies to the sometimes attractive "somehow-presence" on the **playing kit of sports teams** of Club XY, the number of jersey sponsors is only limited by a ultimately limited clothing area. While there are clear rules for advertising on the playing kit in German sports, especially in football, this is not always the case in other countries (e.g. Austria, Mexico) and in other sports (e.g. handball, volleyball, biathlon). The specifications for jersey flocking or jersey printing are given in German football by the DFB or the respective football state association or the DFL (DFB, 2018; DFL, 2022). This also determines the size of the advertising for the jersey flocking.

For the **size of the advertising** or the company logo, the area in cm^2 is decisive. However, the size of an advertisement or a sponsor logo on the playing kit is not the only specification. There are also other requirements to be met for sponsor advertising on football jerseys. The main concern is not to violate the ethical or moral principles of the association. Political statements with an advertising logo on the jersey are also not allowed. Also, the number of advertising companies or their logos is limited. However, a club can apply for a change at the DFB or the DFL once per season.

The extent to which ingenuity and excess are sometimes used in the context of sponsor advertising on sports clothing is evident from the following compilation alone. Without claiming to be exhaustive, the following advertising on **team sports clothing** are included, with the logo of the equipment supplier and the club logo also to be taken into account (see Fig. 10.6):

Jersey front:

- Center chest (1)
- Upper chest, right and left (2)
- Sleeves, right and left (3)
- Lower abdomen (4)
- Side panel right and left (5)

Fig. 10.6 Placement of sponsor logos in jersey advertising

- Collar attachment right and left (12)
- Shoulder right and left (13)

Jersey back:

- Upper back (7)
- Lower back (8)

Shorts front:

- Leg, side, right and left (6)

Shorts back:

- Buttocks (9)
- Leg, side, right and left (10)

Socks:

- front, side and/or back (11)

The boundaries to a "sponsoring overload" are often fluid. This is easy to see when following equestrian tournaments through the numerous banners or at Formula 1 races through the numerous banners at the event location. These **extreme examples from sports practice** can quickly show the limits. It is likely to give many sponsoring experts food for thought, let alone be particularly appealing to fans when buying merchandising items. For example, the Austrian football Bundesliga team Wolfsberger AC presented a curious jersey for the 2018/19 season, even in the eyes of well-meaning fans, which was "record-breaking" in a non-sporting sense with regard to the well over ten sponsor logos (see Fig. 10.7).

Apart from the sports competition legal requirements and the maximum conceivable **advertising placements on a game outfit**, the sponsor's expectation is of course first and foremost, i.e., which goals a company wants to achieve with the sponsoring commitment as a jersey sponsor and which cost-benefit ratio is (still) acceptable from its point of view. Especially the latter premise for a commitment with sole or multiple jersey advertising usually sets tight limits to the density of sponsors on the game or athlete's clothing.

Another danger to successful sports sponsoring threatens when there is too much **intervention by sponsors in the sports sector**. Here too, the limits of corporate sponsoring commitments must be taken into account. Especially at sports events, there is a risk of a "**sponsoring overkill**". This can have the following reasons, for example:

- Overly strong advertising presence of sponsors, so that the sports event fades into the background,

Fig. 10.7 "Sponsoring overload" using the example of jersey advertising by Wolfsberger AC. (*Source:* Sky sports, 2018)

- Influence of sponsors on the execution of the sports event, especially on the location, the timing, and the composition of the audience,
- Excessive commercialization of sports, which can further intensify the competition and lead to negative side effects (e.g., doping and bribery allegations),
- Over-commercialization of television broadcasts of sports events by broadcasters, who have to "recoup" the prices for the broadcasting rights through commercials and other measures, thereby causing frustration among the target group.

A "sponsoring overkill" initially results in negative attitudes towards the affected sports forming among the target groups and a **negative image transfer** to the sponsors. This results in sponsors withdrawing from the "endangered" sports.

Furthermore, it is pointed out that sports sponsoring also involves **dangers for sports**, which have intensified particularly in recent years. The following aspects are particularly worth mentioning:

- Excessive commercialization among top athletes, sports associations and clubs, and sports events,
- Growing competition for sponsoring money between sports,
- Exaggerated sense of entitlement among athletes,
- Declining voluntary commitment in clubs,
- Risks of sports clubs and associations losing their non-profit status,
- Increase in public criticism of certain manifestations of sports events (e.g., football matches or tennis tournaments with excessive admission fees),
- Decreasing willingness of government agencies to promote sports,
- Neglect of grassroots sports and youth development by sports clubs and associations,
- Criticism of officials due to opaque marketing of sponsoring and broadcasting rights to sports events,
- Declining self-determination of sports associations and clubs, which have passed on their rights to the marketing of sports events to sports agencies and individuals.

10.3 Content, Formal and Temporal Design (Incl. Case Study Mercedes-Benz and Laver Cup)

Of particular importance is the **coordination of the various individual measures** in the individual sponsoring projects. The projects must be functionally, temporally, and hierarchically coordinated with each other in order to achieve the highest possible communication effect. It should also be noted that different focuses are set in the advertising use in the following forms of sports sponsoring:

- Sponsoring of individual athletes,
- Sponsoring of sports teams,
- Sponsoring of sports events.

Sponsoring of Individual Athletes

Top athletes usually enjoy high popularity and a specific image that has developed over the course of their career. With a series of individual measures, companies try to achieve a positive image transfer to the company itself or certain products within the framework of sponsoring individual athletes. Athletes are also involved in sales promotion. For example, there is the possibility that athletes give autograph sessions at the point of sale during a new product launch or that raffles are initiated, in which activities with the athletes are drawn as prizes (e.g., Meet & Greet). Another possible use of athletes is in the context of personal communication. Meetings with important customers, opinion leaders, and other people relevant to the company often involve prominent sports personalities.

Sponsoring of Sports Teams

In the sponsoring of sports teams, the same advertising forms can be observed that are also applied in the sponsoring of individual athletes. The sponsoring of sports events offers a wide range of advertising uses. In professional marketing of sports events, potential sponsors are often offered a so-called total package, i.e., a bundle of various advertising and other measures within the framework of the event. Under the umbrella of certain sponsor predicates, the value of different commitments such as being a global top partner, official partner for a certain sports category, or regional partner is summarized.

Sponsoring of Sports Events

There are certain risks associated with the sponsoring of individual athletes and sports teams, which are linked to the sporting success of these athletes and teams. This is less risky when sponsoring a sports event fewer. Here, the sponsor supports the entire event—regardless of who the winners or losers are in the end. Sponsors of sports events can use different forms of advertising during the event, such as the presentation of new products, the implementation of sales promotion measures, the invitation of important people to hospitality services, etc. Here too, a total package is agreed with the organizer in order to be able to use the event in a targeted manner.

Even though sports sponsoring projects usually offer attractive opportunities for achieving corporate and communication goals, such a commitment is not a "self-runner"

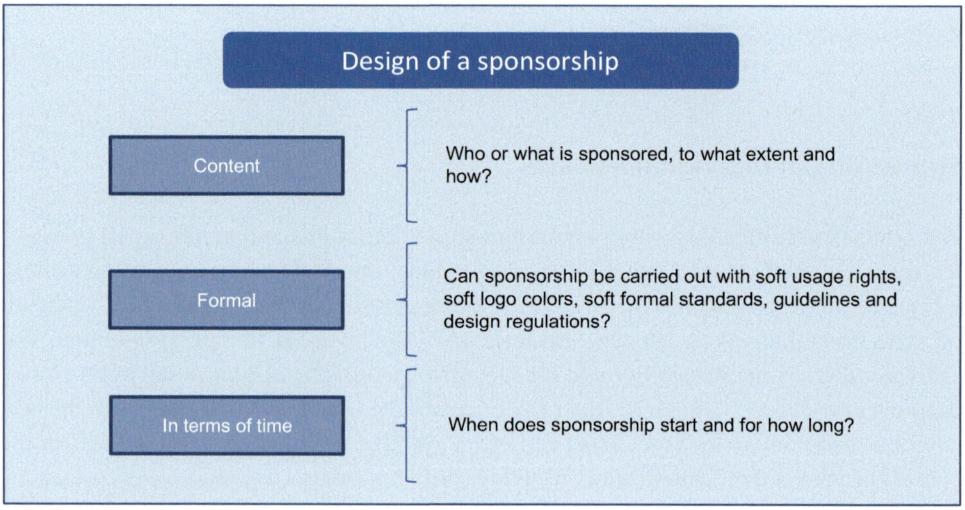

Fig. 10.8 Sponsoring design according to content, formal and temporal criteria

for a sponsor. Rather, it requires a detailed sponsoring design (see Bruhn, 2018, pp. 181 f.) according to content, formal and temporal criteria (see Fig. 10.8).

In the **content design**, the individual sponsoring measures are thematically linked and their context is established with marketing and corporate communication. The thematic coordination in sports sponsoring takes into account the sponsored person or persons as well as the scope and type of individual measures. The key is the presentation and communication of a uniform appearance of the sponsor, based on the central communication goals. Uniform core messages, core arguments and key images can be used as corresponding connecting lines for application. Specifically, it may become necessary to address the different directions (functional, instrumental, horizontal and vertical) in the content design of sponsoring.

The **formal criteria** set the legally relevant framework for the sponsoring commitment. They organize the sponsoring of the sponsored person as well as the use of sponsoring by the sponsor and standardize all individual measures within the sponsoring relationship. Examples include the use of uniform trademarks and logos by all participants as well as the scope of the sponsoring. Formal standards and guidelines are consistently binding. This is how the size, color and font type for certain advertising measures of the sponsor are specified. Such formal criteria make the sponsoring communication more easily perceptible for the target group(s) and better sponsoring successes can be achieved. In practice, formal design specifications are particularly used when using classic sponsoring measures, such as perimeter and media advertising. However, when coordinating new instruments, such as virtual sponsoring, there are still fewer clear lines and guidelines.

Finally, a **temporal coordination** is necessary, i.e. both at the beginning and between different sponsoring periods. Through the clearly fixed starting and (anticipated) end points, all participants know which sponsoring measures need to be regulated by certain dates. In the temporal coordination between different individual measures in sponsoring, the goal of the sponsoring company is that the different activities of the sponsoring use support each other through coordinated use.

Case Study Mercedes Benz and Laver Cup for the Activation of Sponsoring

The following case study was compiled by **Dr. Felix Salzer**, Consultant Performance Marketing of Mercedes Benz Consulting, and is made with the kind support and permission of the Mercedes-Benz Group (formerly Daimler AG).

The Mercedes-Benz Group AG is a German manufacturer of passenger cars and commercial vehicles, which also offers mobility and financial services. As a parent company based in Stuttgart, the Mercedes-Benz Group AG assumes governance, strategy and control functions as well as group-wide services for the two legally independent subsidiaries Mercedes-Benz AG and Mercedes-Benz Mobility AG, which are responsible for the operational business. The most famous brand of the group is Mercedes-Benz. On October 1, 2021, a majority of shareholders decided to spin off Daimler Truck AG from Daimler AG as of December 1, 2021 and to list it as an independent company on the stock exchange.

Initial Situation and Selection of Sponsoring

In the marketing communication of Mercedes-Benz, activities in sports sponsoring have been predominantly used for over 50 years to reach the target group in an emotional, sporting environment and to influence the brand image in terms of perceived sportiness. During this time, different sponsoring strategies were pursued, which have led to the fact that today different sports sponsorings are operated, such as motorsport, football, golf, eSports or tennis (see Fig. 10.9).

The peak phase of activities in the field of tennis was between 1996 and 2008 for Mercedes-Benz through the official partnership with the ATP (Association of Tennis Professionals). This led to further commitments in tennis sponsoring, such as the automotive partnership at the US Open or with brand ambassador Roger Federer. In 2016, the existing partnership with Roger Federer opened up the opportunity to become a global automotive partner at the newly founded **Laver Cup**. Roger Federer's management agency "TEAM8" is the organizer of the Laver Cup. The special thing about this format is that it is a team competition and has a unique international orientation in tennis. A team of six players from Europe

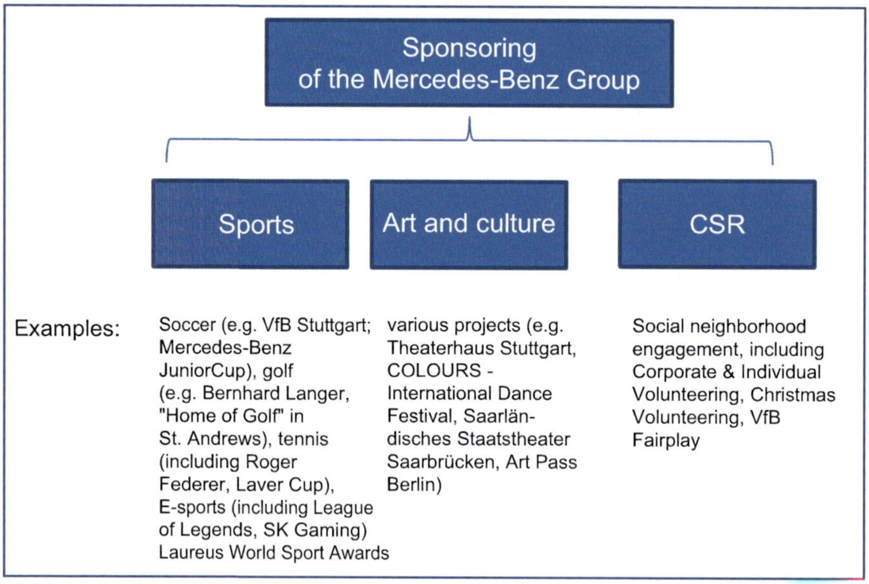

Fig. 10.9 Sponsoring selection of the Mercedes-Benz Group. (*Source:* Mercedes-Benz Group)

"Team Europe" competes on three tournament days against six players from the rest of the continents "Team World". The venue alternates annually between North America (2018: Chicago. 2021: Boston. 2023: Vancouver) and Europe (2017: Prague. 2019: Geneva. 2022: London. 2024: Berlin). The reasons for Mercedes-Benz to engage in the sponsoring of the Laver Cup were essentially:

- High global relevance in the media,
- Activation platform for brand ambassador Roger Federer,
- Placement of the brand in the environment of luxury brands (e.g. Rolex, Moët & Chandon),
- Integration of different markets annually,
- Authentic integration of products.

Activation of the Laver Cup 2019 in Geneva
The third edition of the Laver Cup took place from September 20-22, 2019 at the exhibition center in Geneva, Switzerland. As a result, the implementation of the measures on site was realized with the Swiss market (Mercedes-Benz Switzerland AG). The Laver Cup provided the Swiss market with the benefit of creating physical brand experiences and making contact with customers. On the one hand, exhibition stands set up in front of the arena served for physical interaction with the target group. There, visitors could charge electric vehicles in a virtual tennis game and learn about the new products. On the other hand, exclusive customer

Fig. 10.10 Activation example at the Laver Cup. (*Source:* Mercedes-Benz Group)

invitations in the non-purchasable hospitality area of the Laver Cup and "meet-and-greets" with the tournament players offered special customer experiences.

In addition, the sponsoring in 2019 included analog and digital advertising spaces, extensive usage rights for global social media reporting and activation. It should be emphasized at this point that the brand ambassador contract with Roger Federer was used in this context to make brand-related content more relevant within the framework of the Laver Cup, thus achieving a higher and better target group approach (Fig. 10.10). In return, the "Laver Cup" platform offers the opportunity to activate the brand ambassador in an authentic environment on a broad scale.

Based on the existing activation possibilities, Mercedes-Benz pursued the target with the Laver Cup 2019 to position the electric brand "EQ" as well as the vehicle model "EQC". For this purpose, a communication strategy was developed to publicize the electric brand or the vehicle model. This included different stages of communication. It was planned to play out all digital content via the then social media channel "MercedesSports" (Instagram, Facebook and YouTube) and highlight postings via the official Mercedes-Benz social media channels (global and country-specific channels).

In addition, the official social media channels of the Laver Cup and Roger Federer helped to extend the highlight postings. For this purpose, a production with Roger Federer and several vehicles took place two weeks before the event. The focus of the production was on shooting a commercial and press content for the vehicle model "EQC" in connection with Roger Federer and the Laver Cup. Furthermore, physical activation measures on site were planned in consideration of the communication strategy, such as the aforementioned exhibition stands, branding elements and vehicle placements throughout the event, as well as the provision of vehicles (40 EQC) as tournament shuttles.

In summary, the following **activation measures**were implemented in three stages of communication.

Stage 1: Preliminary Communication

Teaser from advertising clip on social media,
Publication of press content with Roger Federer for the Laver Cup,
Announcement postings for the Laver Cup on social media.

Stage 2: Measures at the Beginning and during the Event

- Active reporting from the tournament and brand-related content on social media,
- Physical brand experiences on the event grounds,

- Customer invitations and "meet-and-greets",
- Vehicles wrapped in team colors to represent the current score,
- (Media-effective) branding elements on event areas,
- Driving experience with EQC for participants and guests of the Laver Cup through a driving service.

Stage 3: Measures at the End of the Event

- Winner postings on social media,
- Broadcast of the commercial after the last game of the Laver Cup as a highlight posting on social media.

To control the implemented measures, key figures were established in the planning phase of the sponsoring realization, which were analyzed and prepared after the event. Of central importance was the media value generated by the global broadcast of the games, press coverage, and social media activities. For this purpose, a media equivalence value was determined by a market research company, which—based on the type of media—multiplied different values with the visibility of the logo or brand-related content. In addition, traditional evaluations of social media postings were carried out based on "impressions" or "interactions". Furthermore, the physical contact points with potential customers in the form of rides in the vehicles and in the form of interactions at the physical brand appearances were recorded. In total, the control of the measures showed that the costs incurred for the sponsoring (sponsoring fee and activation costs) were significantly lower than the generated counter values through the sponsoring.

10.4 Key Points

The operational decisions of a sports sponsoring relate to the specific design of the commitment and therefore require many detailed decisions and the use of a broad range of measures. Various points are of particular importance in this context.

Key Points

1. In sports sponsoring, both **quantitative and qualitative aspects** are important for the operational design of the sponsoring: Within the framework of sports sponsoring, attention must be paid to both sufficient visibility (presence or pressure of the commitment) and a convincing perception of the relationship (creativity and credibility of the appearance).
2. In the case of **sponsoring quantity**, decisions about the intensity and duration of the commitments, their frequency or repetitions are to be made—based on

the scope of services. This ultimately also influences the amount and regularity of sponsoring expenditures.

3. Sports sponsoring is perceived more consciously when it is used in **connection with other communication tools**. Individual measures must be coordinated within the other sponsoring commitments, but also with the entire communication.
4. The **sponsoring quality** andof the sponsoring fit are closely related, as a high sponsoring quality is particularly the result of fit or compatibility of the image between the sponsor and the sponsoring object.
5. The **combination of different levers**brings success. The strength of a sponsoring commitment is also expressed by the fact that the sponsored parties offer the sponsor various support and opportunities within the framework of the design.
6. The **planning and selection of individual measures** are to be made depending on the size of the sponsorings, their relative importance, the legally agreed possibilities and the available budgets.
7. For the **coordination of individual measures**, the various activities must be individually coordinated for each individualsponsoring project and coordinated functionally, temporally and hierarchically among each other.
8. The size of the sponsoring, its relative importance, the legal environment and the budget set the **framework for sports sponsoring**, within which the operational implementation of the sponsoring can take place.
9. The systematic planning and implementation of individual measures is important, as successful engagement for a sponsor is not a "self-runner". All the more, a **detailed sponsoring design** according to content, formal and temporal criteria is to be carried out.
10. In particular, through **formal criteria** (including the use of uniform trademarks, logos, certain fonts and sizes, certain color schemes, etc.), the sponsoring communication becomes easier and better perceptible for the target groups.

References

B

Becker-Olsen, K. L., & Simmons, C. J. (2002). When do social sponsorings enhance or dilute equity? Fit, message source, and the persistence of effects. *NA – Advances in Consumer Research, 29*, 287–289.

Bennett, R. (1999). Sport sponsorings. *European Journal of Marketing, 33*(3/4), 291–313. https://doi.org/10.1108/03090569910253071.

Bruhn, M. (2018). *Sponsoring. Systematische Planung und integrativer Einsatz* (6. Aufl.). https://doi.org/10.1007/978-3-658-13313-9.

Bruhn, M., & Batt, V. (2012). Der Einfluss von Sponsoring auf den Erfolg von Luxusmarken. *Marketing Review St. Gallen, 29*(1), 36–41.

D

D'Astous, A., & Bitz, P. (1995). Consumer evaluations of sponsoring programs. *European Journal of Marketing, 29*(12), 6–22.

Deutscher Fußball-Bund (DFB). (2018). Durchführungsbestimmungen zur Spielordnung. https://www.dfb.de/fileadmin/_dfbdam/16443-07_Durchfuehrungsbestimmungen_14.pdf.

Deutsche Fußball Liga (DFL). (2022). Anhang IV zur LO: Richtlinie für Spielkleidung und Ausrüstung. https://media.dfl.de/sites/2/2018/11/anhang-IVzur-LO-2018-07-01.pdf. Accessed: 2. Nov. 2021.

F

Ferrand, A., & Pages, M. (1995). Image sponsoring. A methodology to match event and sponsor. *Journal of Sport Management, 10*(3), 278–291. https://doi.org/10.1123/jsm.10.3.278.

G

Grohs, R., Wagner, U., & Vsetecka, S. (2004). Assessing the effectiveness of sport sponsorings. An empirical examination. *Schmalenbach Business Review, 56*(2), 119–138. https://doi.org/10.1007/bf03396689.

Gwinner, K. (1997). A model of image creation and image transfer in event sponsoring. *International Marketing Review, 14*(3), 145–158. https://doi.org/10.1108/02651339710170221.

H

Huber, F., & Matthes, I. (2007). Sponsoringwirkung auf Einstellung und Kaufabsicht. Theoretische Grundlagen und Ergebnisse einer empirischen Studie. *Marketing ZFP, 29*(2), 90–104. https://doi.org/10.15358/0344-1369-2007-2-90.

L

Lardinoit, T. (1998, May). Effet modérateur de limplication durable sur l'efficacité mémorielle de la conjonction des parrainages terrain et T.V. In *Proceedings of the 14th Congress of the French Marketing Association (AFM)* (S. 261–276). Association Française de Marketing.

Lardinoit, T. (1999, May 19–21). Interaction des parrainages terrain et TV: impact sur deux niveaux de mémorisation. In *Proceedings of the 15th Congress of the French Marketing Association (AFM)*, (S. 585–602). Association Française de Marketing.

M

Musante, M. D., Milne, G. R., & McDonald, M. (1999). Sport sponsoring: Evaluating the sport and brand image match. *International Journal of Sports Marketing & Sponsoring, 1*(1), 24–39. https://doi.org/10.1108/ijsms-01-01-1999-b004.

P

Quester, P. G., & Thompson, B. (2001). Advertising and promotion leverage on arts sponsoring effectiveness. *Journal of Advertising Research, 41*(1), 33–47. https://doi.org/10.2501/jar-41-1-33-47.

R

Rodgers, S. (2007). Effects of sponsoring congruity on e-sponsors and e-newspapers. *Journalism & Mass Communication Quarterly, 84*(1), 24–39. https://doi.org/10.1177/107769900708400103.

S

Shilbury, D., & Berriman, M. (1996). Sponsoring awareness: A study of St. Kilda football club supporters. *Sport Marketing Quarterly, 5*(1), 27–33.

Simmons, C. J., & Becker-Olsen, K. L. (2006). Achieving marketing objectives through social sponsorings. *Journal of Marketing, 70*(4), 154–169.

Sky Sport. (2018). Wolfsberger AC präsentiert kurioses Trikot, Beitrag vom 14.07.2018. https://sport.sky.de/fussball/artikel/dezent-ist-anders-wac-trikot-blueht-voller-sponsoren/11437033/34271.

Speed, R., & Thompson, P. (2000). Determinants of sports sponsoring response. *Journal of the Academy of Marketing Science, 28*(2), 225–238. https://doi.org/10.1177/0092070300282004.

T

Turco, D. M. (1996). The effects of courtside advertisingon product recognition and attitude change. *Sport Marketing Quarterly, 5*(4), 11–15.

Z

Zajonc, R. B. (1968). Attitudinal effects of mere exposure. *Journal of Personality and Social Psychology, Monograph Supplement, 9*, 1–27. https://doi.org/10.1037/h0025848.

Success Control in Sports Sponsoring 11

Contents

Abstract

Success monitoring plays a crucial role in the planning process of sponsoring. The outlined processes of strategic alignment, budgeting, the selection of specific sponsorings, the integration into the communication mix, and the operational design of sports sponsoring are essential prerequisites for an evaluation of the deployment to take place at the end of the planning process. Numerous methods of success monitoring are available for this purpose in science and practice. It will be of decisive importance which data basis a success monitoring can refer to in order to carry out a sponsoring evaluation. The following will show the possibilities and limitations of various methods. This chapter will present examples of the sponsors Rockets, Indeed, and Deutsche Telekom AG.

M. Bruhn and P. Rohlmann, *Sports Sponsoring*,
https://doi.org/10.1007/978-3-658-44171-5_11

11.1 Methodological Approach to Success Control

Initially, in the success measurement of sports sponsorsing, various **decisions regarding the methodological approach to success control** can be identified in terms of a systematic analysis—regardless of the different forms of success control (cf. Bruhn, 2018, pp. 75 ff.):

- Methods of data collection,
- Timing of the measurement,
- Type of measurement,
- Type of test situation.

Methods of data collection

Regarding the methods of data collection for gathering data on the success of sponsoring, one-time studies, for example in the form of surveys and observations, as well as regular success analyses based on panel data and methods of Social Media Monitoring can be distinguished (Hermanns et al., 2016; Werner, 2013).

- **Surveys:**Determination of recall and recognition values as well as image profiles of sponsoring areas through written, oral or telephone surveys. The use of memory protocols and memory images is also recommended for measuring cognitive reactions and association chains in the context of image transfers.
- **Observations:**Determination of contacts through video recordings during television broadcasts or use of the eye tracking method to measure the information intake of brand symbols in sports. The frequency, duration, order and pattern of fixations are particularly examined.
- **Panel data:**Regular impact analyses are carried out. Ongoing surveys include, among others, media analyses of print media (e.g., AG Media Analyses), television (e.g., GfK Television Research) and databases, for example from ONE8Y.
- **Social Media Monitoring:** Continuous recording of published social media content and screening of direct expressions of opinion by stakeholder groups on the topic of sponsoring provide information about perception and knowledge increases as well as the attitude of different target groups. The evaluation of user-generated content does not take place through surveys, but through content analyses and web tracking. From simple forms of analysis, such as the quantitative evaluation of user activities, the number of recommendations and the summarization and categorization of topic-specific expressions of opinion according to content parameters (e.g., tonalities, actors), complex forms of analysis are also applied. These include, for example, key figures

such as the acceptance quotient and the identification of opinion leaders, distribution paths and trends, relevant hashtags, mentions of competitors, etc.

Timing of the measurement

For success measurement, companies conduct studies during and after the implementation of the sponsorings. Examples include:

- **Pre-Tests**: They include the use of target group data (especially attitudes) before the start of a sponsoring measure. However, this is less about advertising impact control and more about basic target group parameters that are later measured and used for success control.
- **Inbetween-Tests:** The measurements are taken during the ongoing sponsoring (e.g., at sports competitions). The focus is on measuring memory values and opinions of visitors (e.g., opinion leaders).
- **Post-Tests**: The measurements are carried out after the completion of a sponsoring. For example, subsequent memory values and contact frequencies with a medium as well as media performances including costs (e.g., cost per thousand contacts) are examined.

Type of Measurement

In reference to the control of advertising success, the success control of sports sponsoring can be carried out both quantitatively and qualitatively:

- **Quantitative Analyses:** Using statistical methods, computational results are developed, for example, regarding the achieved viewing figuresduring broadcasts or the change in image profiles and levels of awareness.
- **Qualitative Analyses:** Verbal statements regarding the sponsoring are collected through expert interviews and other exploratory studies. For example, the satisfaction with the various measures of contact maintenance (special invitations, care, driving service, information, etc.) is asked of specially invited, company-relevant individuals (e.g., key customers, opinion leaders, opinion multipliers).

Type of Test Situation

Success controls can be carried out in different test situations, for example, through the use of laboratory and field experiments:

- **Laboratory Experiment**: Presentation of video recordings, presentation of images, etc. related to the company's commitment in the sports sector. In addition to capturing spontaneous reactions of the target persons, there is also the possibility of a detailed survey (e.g., image and motive analyses).
- **Field Experiment:** Surveys before, during or after a sports event, for example, regarding the memory or assessment of sponsoring measures.

Depending on the experimental arrangement (with or without control groups), various types of experiments can be used to measure the communicative success in sports sponsoring.

The overview of the methodological possibilities and alternatives for success control in sponsoring makes it clear that basic **decisions about the procedure** must also be made in order to obtain meaningful evaluations of the success of sports sponsorings. General studies on success indicators for sponsoring engagements in sports are provided by various sports market research institutes (including Nielsen Sports).

Another fundamental decision to be made is which **forms of success control** are important for the sponsor at which stage of sports sponsoring in order to substantiate his decisions about the use of sports sponsoring. The process, effectiveness and efficiency controls are of particular importance here.

11.2 Forms of Success Control

Following the respective sports sponsorings, a success control must be carried out with regard to the achievement of the targeted goals. A comprehensive **evaluation of the success effectiveness** of the individual sports sponsorings is carried out through process control as well as through the control of effectiveness and efficiency (see Bruhn, 2018, pp. 75 ff., 182 ff.):

- **Process Controls:** As part of the process control, the implementation of sports sponsorings is controlled. The monitoring includes all necessary activities for the preparation and course of a company's appearance at a sponsored sports event.
- **Effectiveness Controls:** The effectiveness controlrefers to the control of the sponsorsing effects on the recipients according to psychological and economic criteria. This involves measuring the degree of target achievement (response) realized due to certain communication measures (stimuli), i.e., the degree of achieving the communicative goals.
- **Efficiency Controls:** Efficiency controls are carried out in the sense of a cost-benefit comparison to assess the sponsoring activities, i.e., the costs incurred for all sponsoring activities are compared to the realized benefits. The efficiency controlof sports sponsoring is about an economic evaluation of the individual sponsoring measures and means. The benefits of the sponsoring include all services that were achieved with

the sports sponsoring, such as visitor numbers at sponsored party sports events, television ratings and reach of print media.

Based on these three forms of success control, the methods that can be used in the context of sports sponsoring are presented below. The individual procedures are illustrated with examples.

11.3 Methods of Process Control

The **process control in sports sponsoring** deals with the implementation of various processes, including organizational, temporal, and financial ones, which are related to the planned sponsorings. The various forms of process control are closely related to a **project organization** or a **project management** (see Bruhn, 2018, pp. 183 ff.).

The subject and content of the process controls are primarily the analysis of the temporal sequence of the sponsorings **(control of the schedule planning)** as well as the progress of the task **(control of the activities planning)**. In addition, the resources used in the form of employees, services, and cost budgets allocated or claimed for the sponsoring **(control of resource planning)** must be taken into account. These control contents need to be carefully planned, especially for larger sponsorings in sports.

As analysis tools within the framework of process controls, numerous methods have emerged in sports sponsoring in recent years. The following **process control methods** are mentioned as examples (Bruhn, 2014):

- Checklists (Checklist),
- Bar charts and network planning technique,
- Point evaluation methods (Scoring models),
- Mini-Audit,
- Process-Audit,
- Balanced sponsoring Scorecard,
- Sponsoring Dashboard.

The use of these process control methods largely depends on the **maturity level of sports sponsoring** in the company. It is up to each company to decide which methods can provide valuable assistance for the sponsoring.

Checklists (Checklist)

The simplest form of process control consists in creating a **checklist**, in which the essential requirements for monitoring the sponsoring project are recorded. This so-called **catalog of questions for review** contains the essential points in the form of target expectations that need to be met in the project. Here, particular attention must be paid to the completeness of the checklist. An example of this is shown in Fig. 11.1.

Bar Charts and Network Planning Technique

In a **bar chart**, the sub-activities of the sponsoring project are listed on the time axis. Even more precise monitoring is possible if the factual and temporal relationships and dependencies of the sub-activities are represented in the form of a **network planning technique**. Based on this, the project progress can be controlled on the time axis and corresponding deficits can be identified. How the decision-making process in sports sponsoring can be monitored and controlled using the network planning technique is exemplified in Fig. 11.2. It shows, among other things, that a systematically made sponsoring decision requires a not to be underestimated time requirement and, as shown in the example of the figure, requires at least three quarters of a year lead time until the start.

Point Evaluation Method (Scoring Models)

The **point evaluation method** is a classic tool for planning and control, used to evaluate activities. In sports sponsoring, for example, the degree of integration of the sponsoring into the company's, marketing, and brand communication could be examined. For this, it would be necessary to determine criteria as indicators within the framework of

Checklist for the use of sports sponsoring in the company:

1. Which specialist departments in the company have used sports sponsoring to date?
2. Were all formal guidelines, organizational and design principles adhered to in the design of the sports sponsoring?
3. Did the specialist departments comply with the guidelines on the combined use of communication tools in sports sponsoring?
4. Can a change in content and form achieve more intensive use in sponsoring?
5. Can or perhaps even must other specialist departments be involved?
6. Are all employees informed about the possibilities of using sports sponsoring in the company?
7. Is there any information on the impact of sports sponsoring that could be used as an argument for increased integrative use of communication?
8. Does the specific sponsoring commitment also include references to and links with the company's other means of communication?
9. Are the opportunities for internal networking of sponsoring used by employees?
10. Are sufficient resources provided to measure the impact of the sponsorships?

Fig. 11.1 Checklist for reviewing the use and design of sports sponsoring in the company

No.	Process	Predecessor	Duration (in weeks)
A	Decision for sports sponsorship from company X	–	4
B	Preselection sport	A	4
C	Strategic analysis, selection of processes	A, B	10
D	Sponsor search and contacts	B	8
E	Concrete decision	C, D	1
F	Adopt targets and budget	E	4
G	Provide resources	F	3
H	Internal communication within the company and with partners	F	4
I	Removing obstacles/networking	G	3
J	Develop and prepare activation	H	5
K	Roll out, possibly external service providers	I, J	3
L	Monitoring success, planning improvements	K	6

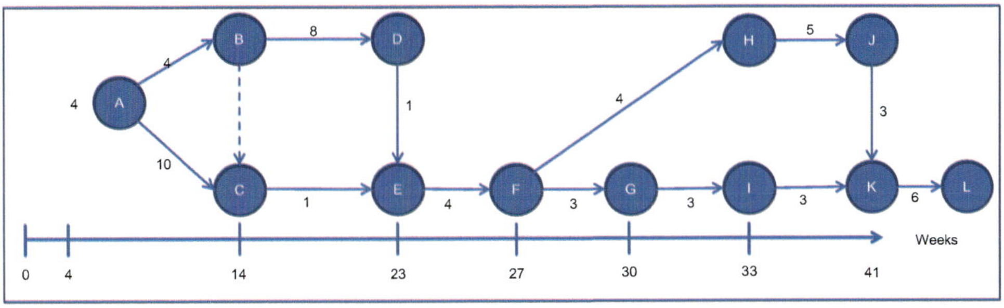

Fig. 11.2 Network planning technique as a monitoring and control instrument in sports sponsoring

the **creation of a scoring model**, to provide them with weighting factors, and to evaluate them on a point scale. The project progress for the integration of sports sponsoring could, for example, be carried out annually.

This requires certain **criteria** or **indicators**, which are recorded in their characteristics and weighting and allow the comparison of the point totals (scoring values) to identify the respective status of sports sponsoring in a company. For example, various content-conceptual, organizational-structural, and personnel-cultural indicators could be used to check the development status of sports sponsoring in the company. In Fig. 11.3, various indicators in the three areas are listed as examples. These could be included in the point evaluation method.

Mini-Audit

An evaluation of the work on sponsoring projects can regularly be carried out through so-called **mini-audits**. In this process, for example, the sponsoring manager creates various questions based on the current status of the project and addressing the further process flow. These questions are discussed in workshops with the participants (e.g., employees from various departments, agency representatives) and worked on in teams.

Content-related conceptual indicators	Organizational-structural indicators	Personnel and cultural indicators
Existence of a systematic planning process for integrated communication and inclusion of (sports) sponsoring	Existence of organizational assignments for integrated sponsoring in the organizational and operational structure	Extent of the value and need for integration of sponsorship among employees
Degree of involvement of various specialist departments for an integrated sponsoring concept	Responsible position for integrated sponsoring in the company	Knowledge and experience of integrated sponsoring, especially in sport
Existence of a concept paper on integrated communication and sponsorship guidelines	Regulatory scope of instruction and decision-making powers in sponsoring	Involvement of employees in an integrated sponsoring concept (active and communicative)
Existence of a strategic positioning for the company's brand and for (sports) sponsoring	Degree of formalization of coordination processes between the parties involved in integrated communication work	Information status on activities within the scope of integrated communication activities in the company
Degree to which the integration potential of sponsoring is taken into account in budgeting	Existence of project teams or interdisciplinary teams with integration tasks	Willingness to cooperate and coordinate between departments and employees
Knowledge of relationships and functions of sponsoring in relation to other communication instruments	Number and degree of involvement of external service providers in sponsoring (especially agencies)	Communication style in the company and between the hierarchy levels
Existence of a system for integrating the sponsored party's own content into the company's integrated sponsorship	Existence of a partner-centered organizational structure in the case of diverse sponsoring, formation of project teams	Employees' level of experience with digital forms of communication and integration into ongoing sponsorship activities

Fig. 11.3 Indicators for assessing and measuring the degree of integration of sponsoring into a company's communication mix

As a **result of the mini-audits**, deficits, weaknesses, and barriers in the project process are identified, which are important for future work. Although these mini-audits, which can be carried out several times as needed in the project timeline, make very subjective assessments, the main advantage is that quick results are generated and the processes of sports sponsoring can be optimized. In Fig. 11.4, an example of a mini-audit of sports sponsoring in a company's communication is shown. The topics listed there form the basis for identifying potential improvements in the sponsoring planning process.

Process Audit

In addition to a mini-audit, which can be carried out quickly and without much effort, a **process audit** is designed to monitor the basic structures of the processes in sports sponsoring. This includes, for example, the selection of the implementers and participants of the projects as well as the starting point and the instruments of the audit. These are the essential **structural features of an audit system**, with which the activities of sports sponsoring are monitored comprehensively and regularly. Conclusions for future

Sports sponsorship mini-audit	Characteristics Never				Always
1. Organizational requirements/infrastructure					
• Decision-making and execution processes for positioning the the risks and opportunities for companies through sports sponsorship are regulated in a cross-divisional responsibility that includes other areas in addition to marketing.	1	2	3	4	5
• All employees in the sponsoring/communications department have a good understanding of the strengths and weaknesses of the key communication tools and their integrated use.	1	2	3	4	5
• Not only internally (within the company itself), but also externally (e.g. agencies) there is a regular and good exchange on the specific sports sponsorship project.	1	2	3	4	5
2. Dissemination of our mission statement					
• The mission statement of our company and our brand are given strong consideration in our sponsoring planning.	1	2	3	4	5
• Our mission statement and our commitment to sport provide an additional reason for all our stakeholders to trust our messages and continue to support our company.	1	2	3	4	5
3. Strategic consistency					
• We regularly review all of our planned sports sponsorship measures to determine the extent to which they are in line with our strategic positioning.	1	2	3	4	5
• Our current sponsorship concept is broad enough to integrate coordinated sub-campaigns and new commitments.	1	2	3	4	5
4. Planning and evaluation					
• We use a SWOT analysis to determine the strengths and opportunities we have and to identify the weaknesses and risks we need to address as part of our sports sponsorship planning.	1	2	3	4	5
• We carry out annual tracking studies to evaluate the quality of our sponsoring relationship in sport and make any necessary adjustments.	1	2	3	4	5
• Our sponsorship highlights the particular strengths of the various communication tools.	1	2	3	4	5

Fig. 11.4 Exemplary mini-audit of sports sponsoring in a company's communication

engagements in sports sponsoring can be drawn from the findings. An appropriate example of the characteristics of a process audit of sports sponsoring is shown in Fig. 11.5.

Balanced Sponsoring Scorecard

When creating a **sponsoring Scorecard**, the basic idea of the Balanced Scorecard (BSC) is adopted. For sports sponsoring, it will be necessary to identify the fundamental **dimensions for controlling the processes of sports sponsoring**. As a rule, this can be derived from the strategy of sports sponsoring. These could be, for example, the following dimensions:

Features	Recommendations
Audit performer	External experts
Audit participants	All employees in the areas of marketing and communication (internal and external)
Audit starting point	All documents such as sponsoring guidelines, sponsoring concepts, sponsoring plans
Audit instruments	• Internal standardized surveys (e.g. knowledge about brand fit with sponsored party, sponsorship goals, etc.) • Sponsoring network analysis • Content analysis (including sponsoring measures) • Contact point analysis (including reach in which areas) etc.

Fig. 11.5 Characteristics of a process audit for sports sponsoring

- Success factors for the strategy,
- Drivers of effects,
- Internal integration,
- Operational value drivers.

According to the functionality of the BSC, for this **sports sponsoring Scorecard**, the corresponding **goals, metrics, specifications, and measures** are developed from the basic four dimensions or perspectives. In this sense, the strategy of sports sponsoring is "broken down" to the operational level of measures. This allows the processes of sports sponsoring to be operationally controlled according to these four dimensions. In Fig. 11.6, the approach of a **Balanced sponsoring Scorecard** for the sports sector is schematically illustrated.

Sponsoring Dashboard

A dashboard is a graphical representation where the central data can be relatively easily and quickly captured through visualization. For the use of a **sponsoring Dashboard**, it will be necessary to display the relevant data for the success of sports sponsoring (e.g., media data, costs, etc.) in an overview and update it regularly.

In a **Dashboard for sports sponsoring**, the essential Key Performance Indicators (KPIs) are included. These are taken from the relevant metrics from the effectiveness and efficiency control. These are presented in the following sections. In Fig. 11.7, a (fictitious) example of the media effectiveness of sports sponsoring is shown.

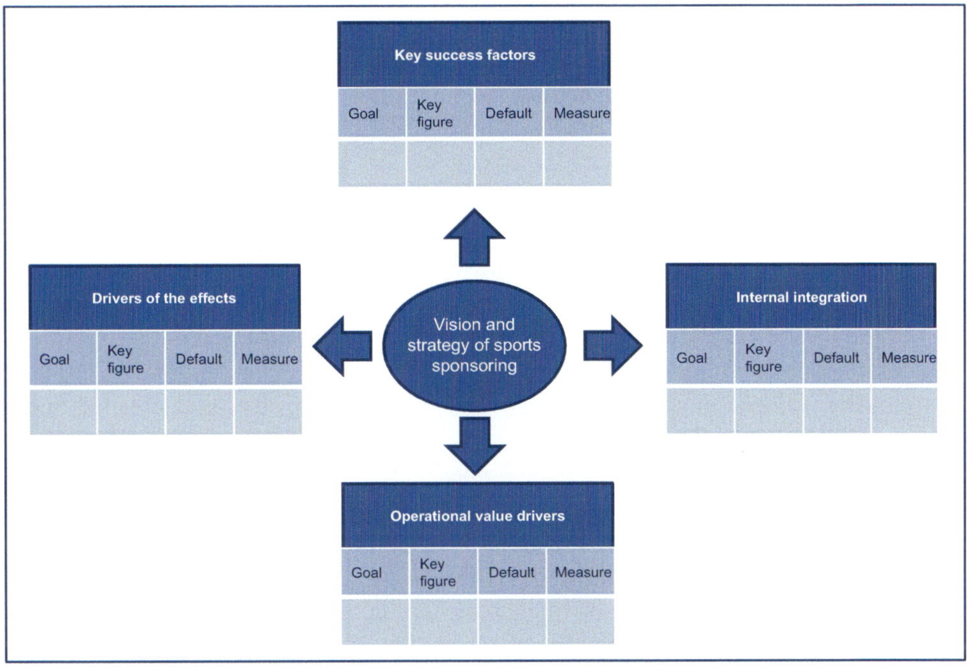

Fig. 11.6 Balanced sponsoring Scorecard in sports sponsorings

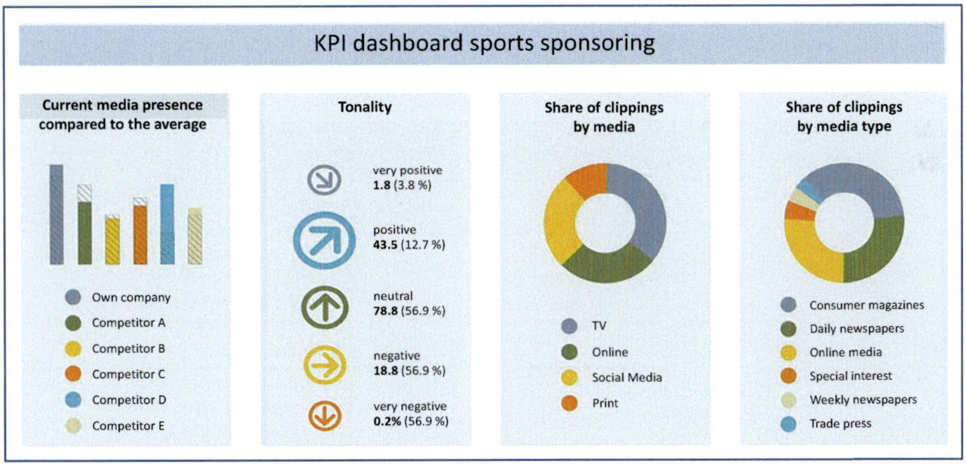

Fig. 11.7 Sports sponsoring-Dashboard as a (fictitious) example of the media effectiveness of a company's sports sponsoring

Overall, the process control methods are suitable not only for controlling schedules and critical activities in the planning process of sponsoring, but also for tracking the overall process of sponsorings in sports.

11.4 Methods of Effectiveness Control

For the proof of communicative effects, classical market research methods have proven to be effective, with which various reactions in the target groups can be checked. The following **types of reactions** are particularly noteworthy (see Bruhn, 2018, pp. 183 ff.):

- **Cognitive effects** aim at knowledge and remembering the measures of sports sponsoring,
- **Affective effects** include the feelings when perceiving sports sponsoring, i.e., the emotions and evaluations of the sponsorings,
- **Conative effects** consider the actions or behavioral intentions of the target groups, such as purchasing or information behavior.

These effect categories can be determined by methods of observation and questioning. In Fig. 11.8, different **measurement methods of effectiveness control in sports sponsoring** are listed according to the cognitive, affective, and conative communication effects. Individual and frequently used methods are explained in more detail below.

Categories of communication impact / Type of measuring method	Observation	Survey
Cognitive effects	• Eye tracking • Observation of the absorption behavior	• Recall tests (day-after-recall test, top-of-mind test) • Recognition tests (day-after recognition test, impact test) • Rating scales
Affective effects	• Eye tracking • Other instrumental procedures	• Verbal and non-verbal experience measurements • Attitude and image scales • Imagery research • Semantic differential
Conative effects	• Behavioral registration • On-screen time • Click behavior	• Remembered behavior • Survey by product preference and behavioral intention

Fig. 11.8 Measurement methods of effectiveness control in sports sponsoring

For the **measurement of cognitive success factors**, recall tests (recording of unaided memory) and recognition tests (recording of recognition values by presenting the advertising materials of the sponsorings) are primarily used in sports sponsoring, which are often used as day-after-(recall/tecognition)-test. In these tests, the target persons are asked as by word of mouth or by telephone about the advertised brands or companies a few hours or a day after an event or television broadcast of a sports event.

At the heart of **measuring affective success factors** is the control of image effects, as image profiling represents a central sponsoring goal. A tool often used for this purpose in sponsoring is the Semantic Differential. Here, the test subjects evaluate a sponsoring object with regard to various attitude-relevant characteristics (dynamics, team spirit, etc.) on a multi-level, bipolar rating scale. The image profile of the object resulting from the mean values of the characteristics provides information on whether the desired image effects were achieved through engagement in sports, or whether a deviating profile is the result, so that a change in current activities should be considered.

The greatest difficulties in sponsoring are the **measurement of conative variables**, as changes in behavior of the target groups (e.g., an increase in purchases of a sponsor's products or the recommendation of the sponsor) can rarely be directly attributed to sponsoring activities. However, some studies have shown positive effects of sponsoring on purchase intent (Serviceplan/Sky Media Network, 2013; SevenOne Media, 2015; Hohenauer, 2016; Papadimitriou et al., 2016; Charitomeni et al., 2018). Behavioral effects are primarily to be expected with sports-related products (e.g., sports equipment, beverages).

The comparatively most common **forms of impact measurement** for effectiveness control in sports sponsoring can be seen in the following methods:

- Measurement of the perception of sponsoring measures,
- Measurement of the memory effect,
- Conducting image surveys,
- Determination of contact numbers.

Measurement of the Perception of Sponsoring Measures

In addition to capturing memory values following an event, another focus of impact analysis in sports sponsoring is the measurement of sponsoring message perception. A method used for this purpose in sports sponsoring is **eye tracking**. For this purpose, test subjects are shown, for example, video recordings of sports eventsand their eye movements are recorded while watching the video. By evaluating the dwell time on certain points, a sponsor receives hints on the optimal placement and design of a message (Hermanns & Marwitz, 2008, pp. 151 f.; Breuer et al., 2013; VSA, 2019).

In sports sponsoring, the possibilities to convey a complete message are rather limited, as often no more than the logo of a brand or at most a short claim can be placed.

Digital boards may allow for one or two additional images, but beyond that, messages are rarely possible in a sports sponsor presentation at the competition venue (Falkenau, 2013, p. 14).

Measurement of the Memory Effect

For the measurement of **knowledge and memory effects**, recall tests (recording of unaided memory) and recognition tests (recording of recognition values by providing the advertising media) are particularly suitable in sports sponsoring.

The **recall test** is used to measure communicative memory effects. A few hours or a day after the end of the sponsoring event, for example when leaving a sports event or after a tennis TV broadcast, target persons are asked orally or by phone about the advertised brands or companies. This approach is also referred to as a **"Top-of-Mind" test**, in which the test persons name the sponsors that they remember best (Witt, 2000, p. 181; McAlister et al., 2012). In addition, there is the possibility to conduct the tests based on written surveys (as omnibus surveys or exploratory).

As an **example** of such a "Top-of-Mind"-Test, a study by the market research institute Ipsos can be cited, which surveyed about 15,000 people from 26 countries during the sponsor advertising campaigns on the occasion of the 2014 Football World Cup. The participants were asked in an online survey to name all the official FIFA partners and sponsors of the 2014 World Cup that they noticed in the run-up to the sports event and that they remember. The winner of this study was the long-standing FIFA partner Coca-Cola, which was named first by every second respondent worldwide (Horizont, 2014). In a study on the 2018 Football World Cup in Russia, the result was not much different: Coca-Cola, Adidas and McDonalds. These brands make up the top 3 when it comes to which the German citizens perceive as sponsors of the Football World Cup (Splendid Research, 2018).

A **TV recall test**, for example, is conducted in such a way that selected test persons are confronted with a sponsoring event via television transmission in a studio. Subsequently, the task of the test persons is to indicate the remembered trademarks or sponsors. This method is particularly popular in perimeter advertising (Nufer, 2008), but is also used for sponsoring reports in the media.

Another recall test, which is often used in sports sponsoring in a modified form, is the so-called **Impact Test**. The memory effect of sponsoring measures is measured by presenting visitors to sports events with different lists of sponsor logos. One list contains the original form of the logos, another shows sponsor names in uniform black-and-white print, another list contains partially difficult to decipher sponsoring messages that the test persons have to complete. In addition, names of companies that were not represented as sponsors at the respective event are added to the lists. When the test persons' memory of the sponsors is queried, conclusions can be drawn about which groups of people remember which advertisements how intensively, which elements of an advertisement are particularly memorable, and what impressions the advertisement leaves on the individual persons.

In addition to the characteristics of the sponsoring message, other **factors influencing the memory effects** of the spectators on the sponsors of sporting events are effective. These include the interest in sports, the duration of attendance or broadcast time of an event, the duration of the brand logo's display, and the size of the audience. Depending on the characteristics of the individual variables, different memory values result for the different sports with regard to the sponsoring companies. Studies have found that the highest memory values are found in those sports that attract the largest direct or indirect audience numbers. However, these influencing factors are not considered independently of each other. Fig. 11.9 shows the memory of sponsors depending on the size of the audience for different sports. It is noticeable that in figure skating and gymnastics, an above-average number of spectators have difficulty remembering a sponsor (Walliser, 1995, pp. 161 ff.).

In a **critical appraisal of the memory effect**, it is necessary to point out some problems in practice. In this context, it should first be pointed out that memory values are a

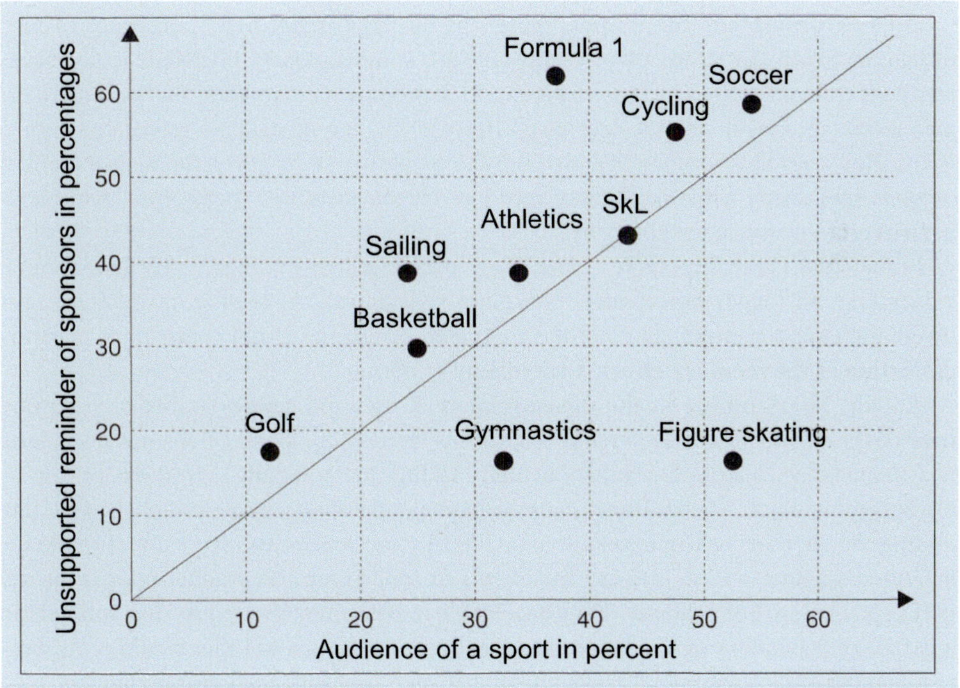

Fig. 11.9 Audience of different sports and memory effect of sponsoring. (*Source*: Walliser, 1995, p. 172)

relatively rough indicator of communication effect. They should only be used as a measure if the main goal of the sponsor is to stabilize or increase its level of awareness.

Furthermore, surveys have found that the sponsors of events often do not gain the expected awareness for their commitment, or even the competitors of the actual sponsors are remembered as sponsors. Obviously, recall and recognition values are influenced by factors that make the interpretation of the results of such tests difficult.

Studies have shown that it is particularly dependent on the **"prominence" of a company** or a brand—in the sense of a high level of awareness and importance in the market—whether a particular company is remembered as a sponsor of an event; regardless of whether it is actually a sponsor (Hermanns & Marwitz, 2008, pp. 48 f.). Prominent companies or brands are more likely to be associated with an event, as their sponsoring activities are more efficiently "learned" by the target groups and thus better remembered.

However, prominence alone is not sufficient for correct recall of a sponsor. The **memory power of a consumer** also proved to be equally important. Only in the case that a consumer is not convinced of his memory power, does prominence exert an unconscious influence; but not when consumers trust their memory. How great the memory power of a consumer is, is largely determined by how difficult or easy it is to "learn" a sponsor. At events that are sponsored by a multitude of companies, the memory of individual sponsors is comparatively poor, so that again prominent companies are more likely to be remembered, even if they did not appear as sponsors.

For **less prominent companies**, these relationships imply that sponsoring of large events, in which numerous other companies are simultaneously involved, is not necessarily an efficient way to increase awareness. Well-known companies, on the other hand, gain advantages even without their own efforts if they are mistakenly associated with an event. However, these companies also run the greatest risk of overestimating the effects of their sponsoring activities if they rely less on the measures themselves than on the general prominence of the company.

For success control in sports sponsoring, the presented findings imply that memory values may no longer reflect mere consumer speculation. At least in recognition tests, where the fame (or prominence) of the compared companies is not comparable, a certain **distortion of the memory effect** is very likely to occur.

Another **shortcoming in the measurement of memory values** is that brand awareness or the memory of the sports sponsoring of certain companies does not necessarily and immediately lead to consumers actually testing the company's products or non-users becoming users. Such a direct causal relationship could only be established by integrating the sponsoring commitments into sales promotion measures or direct marketing activities. Another way to measure the effects of sponsorings on product sales is through event sponsoring. For example, it is conceivable to determine the sponsoring amounts for a company depending on the achieved sales of the company, but this would represent a realignment of the contractual cooperations between sponsors and event organizers.

Conducting Image Studies

Against the background of the special importance of the image goal in sponsoring, image studies also have a high priority. A tool that is regularly used for this purpose in sports sponsoring is the **"Semantic Differential"**. On a multi-level, bipolar rating scale, for example, visitors to a sports event assess a sponsoring object with regard to various attitude-relevant characteristics (dynamics, aesthetics, etc.). The mean values of the various characteristics can be combined into an image profile of the sponsoring object and transferred to the sponsor (Hermanns & Marwitz, 2008, pp. 156 ff.; Grohs & Reisinger, 2014). See also the image profiles of various sports in Chap. 8, Fig. 8.4.

Determination of Contact Numbers

The measurement of the memory effect as well as the perception of sponsoring measures and image studies is based on the subjective statements of the test persons. In contrast, the determination of contact numbers is based on objective units of measurement.

Referring to classical advertising impact research, the sizes Contact Frequencyand Contact Qualityare used as **units of measurement** for measuring the communicative effect in sports sponsoring:

- **Contact Quantityor Frequency/Reach:** The Contact Quantity shows the frequency of the target persons' contact with the sponsoring measures. These metrics are used in various forms (e.g., reach) in media planning (advertising contact).
- **Contact Quality***:* This involves an evaluation of the sponsoring measures and results in qualitative terms.

A **measurement of contact frequencies**is carried out in sponsoring measures by various indicators of the use of advertising media. These include:

- **Attendance numbers** at sports events.
- **Television ratings** for the broadcast of sports events in terms of gross and net reach. The gross reach refers to the total duration of the broadcast(s) on various television programs. The net reach includes the inclusion of audience analyses (especially reach overlaps) in the broadcast. Both reaches are essentially contact probabilities.
- **Reachof print media** in sports reporting. Here, the usual values in readership research (e.g., circulation number x reader-per-issue value) are used.
- **Reachof internet activities** in sports reporting. These result from the number of users who have seen a post on the internet and are measured based on the click rate on the internet or on social media pages.
- **On-screen time** as the duration of the sponsor's visibility during the broadcast of sports events.

- **Interactions** regarding a sports event on various social media channels. The greater the number of interactions on a post, the more interesting it is for the recipients. An increased number of likes, shared content, comments, or hashtags indicates increased contact frequency with the sponsor.

As examples of different values of contact frequencies , studies on the gross reach of sports events on television are primarily used. Thus, the contact numbers of sports competitions, the media potential of sports teams, and interview durations with athletes or coaches are recorded. Fig. 11.10 summarizes the results of these media analyses, with football being separately listed due to its dominance in TV presence.

Furthermore, **company-specific detailed studies** are also conducted regarding the contacts achieved at individual sports events and in the context of cooperation with a sports team. For a sponsor with jersey and perimeter advertising, the **contact frequenciesof various advertising media** are to be added up (contact sum calculation). For example, if the contact sum of a perimeter and jersey advertiser at a football club is to be determined, an addition of the contacts that arise via stadium visitors, television viewers, and newspaper readers is made. In this case, assumptions are made for the calculations regarding the contacts that visitors and television viewers have with the perimeter and jersey advertising. If the contact prices are not determined for specific target groups, the results are unweighted cost per thousand contacts. In a comparison with the contact prices of other advertising media, the financial advantages and disadvantages of

	Soccer competitions	TV Contacts	Other competitions	TV Contacts	Bundesliga clubs	IFM-Index*	Interview partner soccer	Interview duration h:mm:ss	Interviewee other	Interview duration h:mm:ss
1	1st Bundesliga	7,214.03	Formula 1	5,429.72	Bayern Munich	100	Ottmar Hitzfeld	25:44:51	Michael Schumacher	17:05:29
2	UEFA Champions-League	1,951.41	Ski Jumping World Cup	1,627.97	Dortmund	72	Rudi Völler	17:14:09	Ralf Schumacher	10:46:01
3	World Cup qualification	1,814.59	Tour de France	1,220.08	Leverkusen	56	Uli Hoeneß	16:00:11	Niki Lauda	10:00:33
4	Bundesliga 2	1,233.24	Biathlon World Cup	888.24	Berlin	48	Eduard Geyer	12:57:39	Norbert Haug	8:07:34
5	General	1,068.43	Professional boxing in general	665.56	Schalke	42	Franz Beckenbauer	11:17:03	Jan Ullrich	6:57:58
6	UEFA Cup	770.26	Alpine World Ski Championships	546.06	Fribourg	36	Klaus Augenthaler	11:08:10	Jutta Kleinschmidt	6:57:18
7	DFB Cup	624.16	Alpine Skiing World Cup	509.08	Kaiserslautern	21	Oliver Kahn	10:53:59	Martin Schmitt	6:37:57
8	World Cup reviews	514.84	Athletics WM	474.45	Hamburg	17	Werner Lorant	10:50:02	Erik Zabel	6:27:50
9	International matches	512.18	Boxing World Championship Professionals	473.64	Mönchengladbach	15	Felix Magath	9:06:29	Franziska Van Almsick	5:50:29
10	Regional league	488.93	DEL-The 1. Bundesliga	457.07	Nuremberg	14	Jürgen Röber	8:55:38	Sven Ottke	5:46:53

*The IFM Index shows the media potential (broadcasting times and TV contacts) of a club. Example: The club Bayern Munich achieved the highest media potential in the 2001/2002 preliminary round = index 100. The following clubs have a correspondingly lower potential.
Basis: All competitions/home and away matches/all TV programs in Germany
Survey period: Preliminary round: 1.7.2001-31.12.2001)

Fig. 11.10 Top 10 media presence in football and other sports. (*Source*: Institute for Media Analyses GmbH, 2002)

the sponsoring commitment compared to alternative advertising media can be clearly demonstrated.

Example: Rakuten and its NFL Sponsoring

The question for those willing to sponsor is often, how much would it cost to transfer the visibility of the brand to advertising on TV or the internet instead of the sponsoring? This essentially involves a comparison between the logo presence in the media and payable spot bookings. The kit sponsoring at the NBA series champion Golden State Warriors by **Rakuten**—one of the largest online retailers from Japan—allegedly costs 20 million USD and is allegedly worth 40 million USD per year. The benefit or equivalence amount is composed as follows: 19 million USD annually are the images and videos with the Golden State Warriors on social networks, which mainly result from postings on other pages, e.g., in the form of sports news. 21 million USD is the presence of the team on television (Global Sports, 2019). According to this evaluation, this would be a doubling of the sponsoring sum that Rakuten pays to the Golden State Warriors to be allowed to attach a rather small logo to their game jerseys. ◀

11.5 Methods of Efficiency Control

The main goal of success control is, in addition to capturing psychological target effects through effectiveness control, to carry out a cost-benefit analysis in the form of a**efficiency control of sports sponsoring** (see Bruhn, 2018, pp. 183 ff.). For the economic evaluation of sponsoring measures, costs and benefits must be compared:

- **Costs of Sponsoring:** The costs are recorded as expenses for the respective sponsoring. These arise both internally and externally and will need to be calculated individually. The costs are also a benchmark for the budgeting of sports sponsoring.
- **Benefits of Sponsoring:** The benefits of sponsorings are often determined in such a way that the cognitive, affective, and conative effects are recorded as realized benefits. In addition, other benefit categories can be considered.

The primary goal of efficiency controls is to obtain indications of the **economic efficiency of sports sponsoring**. For this purpose, cost-benefit comparisons are made in various ways to assess sponsoring activities within the framework of efficiency controls.

Efficiency control is therefore about attempting an economic evaluation of individual sponsoring measures and means in sports. However, not only the control of the entire sponsoring commitment is in focus, but also the **evaluation of individual sponsoring measures and means**. The results are therefore of particular importance for engagements in sponsoring, as conclusions can be drawn from the value for a redistribution of budgets to increase the efficiency of sports sponsoring.

Various methods are available for efficiency control in sports sponsoring. Fig. 11.11 lists selected **measurement methods for efficiency control in sports sponsoring**. These refer to the initially isolated measurements of costs and benefits and their comparison in the form of a cost-benefit comparison. Some of the methods for cost-benefit comparison are explained in more detail below.

The **measurement of costs in sports sponsoring** can be done in different ways. Various cost components need to be considered, such as:

- **External Costs:** These are the direct costs that have to be paid, such as the sponsoring contributions for the sponsored party, costs for media placements, implementation costs, agency fees, etc.
- **Internal Costs:** These indirect costs include the calculation of internal costs for the planning, implementation, and control of sports sponsoring, especially personnel, travel, and material costs, etc.

Depending on the calculation, the total sponsoring budget or the budget for individual sponsoring projects is determined (see also Chap. 7 for budgeting sports sponsoring).

Efficiency controls in sports sponsorship			
Measurement of costs	Measuring the benefit		
• Total sponsorship budget • Sponsorship budget of individual sponsoring measures • Personnel expenses for sponsoring • Time budget • and more.	**Cognitive effects:** • Brand awareness • Information status • Attention • and more.	**Affective effects:** • Brand appeal • Brand attitude • Customer satisfaction • Image • and more.	**Conative effects:** • Increase in sales • Purchase intention • On-screen time • and more.
Cost-benefit comparison			
• Determination of cost-benefit ratios, • Determination of cost-performance diagrams, • Use of activity-based costing, • Calculation of thousand-sponsoring contact price (TSCP) • Calculation of advertising value, • Calculation PR value, • Calculation of target group affinity, • Calculation of index points, • Calculation of return on sponsorship investment (ROSI), • Sponsorship value analysis (SVA), • Data Envelopment Analysis (DEA).			

Fig. 11.11 Measurement methods for efficiency control in sports sponsoring

The **measurement of benefits in sports sponsoring** involves recording benefit components as part of effectiveness control. These are the **cognitive effects** (e.g., brand awareness, attention), the **affective effects** (e.g., brand sympathy, brand attitudes), and the **conative effects** (e.g., purchase intention, sales increases) of engagements in sports sponsoring. In the specific case of individual sponsorings, all effects or services achieved with the sponsoring, such as visitor numbers at sponsored party events, television ratings, and reach of print media, count as benefits of sports sponsoring. In sports sponsoring, the on-screen time of a sponsor is often used for efficiency measurement. It determines the duration of visibility of the sponsor (or its name or logo) during the broadcast of sports events.

As **analysis tools for a cost-benefit comparison** to calculate the profitability of sports sponsorings, there are numerous methods that have been developed over the past decades. The following **efficiency control methods** can be mentioned:

- Determination of cost-benefit ratios,
- Determination of cost-performance diagrams,
- Use of process cost accounting,
- Calculation of thousand sponsoring contact price (TSCP)
- Calculation of advertising value,
- Calculation of PR value,
- Calculation of target group affinity,
- Calculation of index points,
- Calculation of Return on sponsoring Investment (ROSI),
- Sponsoring value analysis (SVA),
- Digital advertising values: Adjusted Ad Value (AAV),
- Data Envelopment Analysis (DEA),
- Benchmarking.

Determination of Cost-Benefit Ratios

A classic form of examining the profitability of sponsoring engagements is the **determination of cost-benefit ratios**. In this process, cost and/or benefit figures are put into relation. These can be created in different forms:

- **Cost ratios:** For example, budget sports sponsoring in relation to the total sponsoring budget, budget sports sponsoring in relation to the total communication budget, etc.
- **Benefit ratios:** For example, increase in awareness through sports sponsoring between two periods, change in spatial and quantitative reach in annual comparison, etc.

- **Cost-benefit ratios:** Increase in brand awareness through sports sponsoring in relation to the costs of sports sponsoring, etc.

For the various ratios, **comparison standards** can then be used. If the corresponding data are available, examples of **ratio comparisons** include:

- Comparison of sports sponsorings,
- Comparison of sports,
- Time comparisons between planning periods,
- Comparison with other types of sponsoring,
- Comparison between communication tools,
- Competitor and industry comparisons,
- Regional comparisons, etc.

The question of which **ratios are best suited for efficiency evaluation** in sponsoring has not yet been clearly answered by either science or practice. However, it can be stated that for sponsoring measures that are characterized by a high media presence, such as sports sponsoring in attractive sports, ratios such as PR value calculation, event index, and sponsor index are generally also suitable. These provide auxiliary sizes for sports sponsoring to obtain an indicator of the efficiency of sports sponsoring.

Example: Indeed—Sponsoring with Eintracht Frankfurt Leads to Market Leadership

In 2008, the job exchange **Indeed** started in Germany. In July 2017, they became the main and shirt sponsor of the Bundesliga club Eintracht Frankfurt. Since then, the two partners have made impressive progress (sponsors, 2022e).

Indeed initially started the partnership with the goal of increasing brand awareness in Germany. Through the main sponsoring with Eintracht and in combination with other marketing measures, this was quickly achieved, after which the goals were continuously adjusted and now KPIs much further at the end of the brand funnel are in focus. The most important value currently is the "Unaided Consideration", i.e., how many people consider the job site Indeed when they are looking for a new job. For people who are aware of the Eintracht sponsoring, this KPI is 50% higher. With this value, which clearly shows an effect on the actual business, Indeed is very satisfied. In addition, Indeed also clearly focuses on economic targets, e.g., how much revenue can/will be generated from discussions and negotiations on match days in the box.

All in all, every euro of the sponsoring is very efficient for Indeed, which is also shown by the recent extension of the partnership until 2026. The new sponsoring agreement includes all women's football teams, the U21, and the e-sports area of Eintracht, in addition to the previous scope of services. This is also because Indeed, together with Eintracht, is committed to more diversity in society, in sports, and in working life. It also speaks to the fact that a great hype has arisen around women's football, through which Indeed can engage with new target groups. And with the e-sports area, they can especially reach young, gaming-affine people. ◀

Determination of Cost-Performance Diagrams

In addition to the relatively isolated cost-performance indicators, a set of performance indicators (KPI) of sports sponsoring can also be determined in the form of a **cost-performance diagram**. This diagram can be used to evaluate and compare different sports sponsorings. The process is carried out in various **steps**:

- Compilation of the relevant KPIs for the individual sponsorings in sports,
- Creation of a scoring model with the KPIs as criteria and indication of the importance of the criteria,
- Evaluation of the individual sponsorings in sports in the scoring model by assigning points and adding the individual points to a total point value for a sports sponsoring (as a performance indicator),
- Calculation of the costs of the individual sponsorings,
- Representation of the different sponsorings in a cost-performance diagram.

In Fig. 11.12, an example of a **cost-performance diagram** is shown. The performance indicators of the different sponsorings are shown on the abscissa (maximum 100%), and the external and internal costs of the individual sponsorings in the considered planning period are shown on the ordinate. The **sponsoring experience curve** shown within the diagram provides information on the efficiency of the individual sponsorings. The sponsorings below the experience curve are considered efficient, those above the curve as less efficient or as "too expensive". Based on the results, appropriate redistributions in the sports sponsoring budget can be made for the future.

Of central importance for the determination of cost-benefit indicators and cost-performance diagrams is a reliable measurement of the costs of sports sponsorings. Process cost accounting can provide valuable assistance in this regard.

Use of Process Cost Accounting

Process cost accounting emphasizes the **process-oriented view of costs** of engagement in sports sponsoring. The methodology captures all specific costs of each individual activity. A distinction is made between the main process and the sub-processes.

The **main process** is considered to be the engagement in sports sponsoring. The **sub-processes** consist of the individual activities of the sponsoring planning process (analysis, planning, implementation, control). These are broken down into individual activities and assigned to the corresponding cost centers (Fig. 11.13). The cost

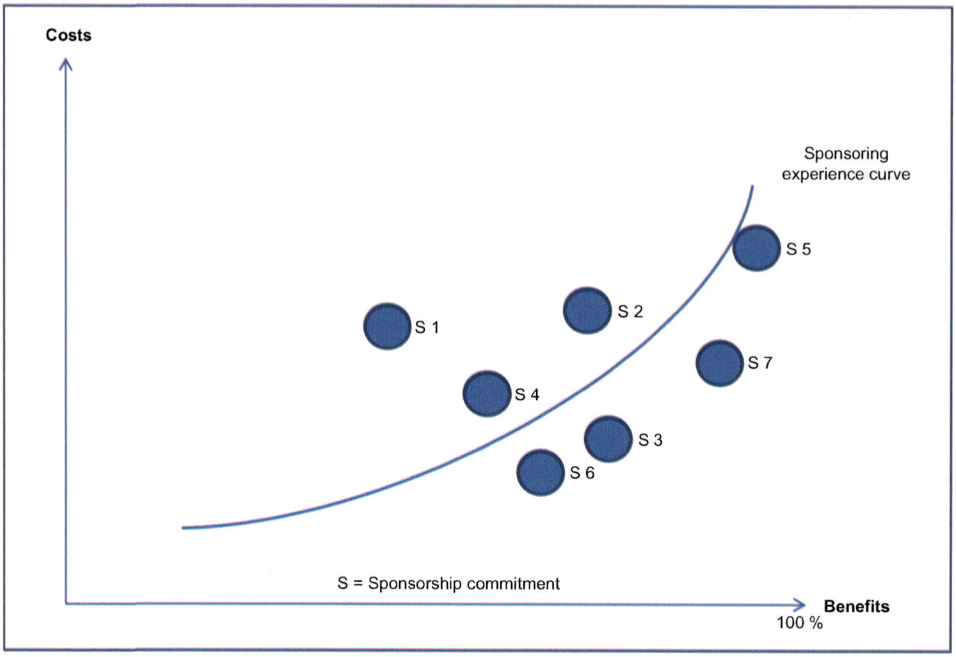

Fig. 11.12 Cost-performance diagram for efficiency evaluation in sports sponsoring

Cost element/cost center	Sponsorship costs
Concept and selection	120,000
Sponsorship rights	1,000,000
Personnel costs activation (networking, hospitality, etc.)	200,000
Material costs activation (networking, media costs, hospitality, etc.)	850,000
Internal control and reporting/documentation	45,000
External control	75,000
Total process costs	**2,290,000**

Fig. 11.13 Exemplary representation of process cost accounting in sports sponsoring

influencing factors or reference variables are also analyzed. These are identified as cost drivers (e.g., media use in sports sponsoring).

The **result of process cost accounting** is a detailed analysis of the cost situation of sports sponsorings. This provides cost transparency over the main process, the sub-processes, the individual activities, and the relevant cost centers. This is the basis for efficiency evaluations of sports sponsorings and allows conclusions to be drawn about efficiency improvements.

Calculation of Thousand Sponsoring Contact Price (TSCP)

The **Thousand Sponsoring Contact Price** essentially corresponds to the thousand contact price of classic advertising success control and is a proven key figure for assessing the efficiency of communicative measures. For example, an evaluation of the **sponsoring broadcasts on television** can be carried out. The key figures for advertising media contact and advertising media contact opportunity, which are taken from media advertising, can also be determined in a similar way in sports sponsoring.

The weighting of the thousand contact price is carried out via the exposure time of the sponsors' perimeter advertising. For example, the **thousand contact price in sponsoring** provides information about the cost of 30 seconds of advertising duration (on-screen time) to reach 1000 viewer contacts. Since this method usually involves standard values from analyses of exemplary broadcasts, the key figures primarily serve to evaluate performance in advance of the sponsoring measures (comparable to media planning in media advertising). However, the problem is that the comparability of contacts is not always given (e.g., perimeter in close-up and long shot). In addition, the focus on perimeter advertising means that other important carriers of sponsor advertising (e.g., jerseys, flags) are not sufficiently taken into account.

When calculating cost-benefit ratios, it should be critically noted that promising thousand prices(or also advertising and PR values) are no guarantee for successful sponsoring, as these do not include competition in the analysis. If the appearances of sponsors are perceived as interchangeable from the consumer's point of view, then even less attractive thousand prices contribute to driving brand profiling (Brannasch, 2001).

Advertising Value Calculation

The calculation of an advertising value in sponsoring corresponds to the basic idea of the **opportunity cost approach**. Here, the advertising benefit is calculated as an opportunity cost point by first compiling the performance data of a sponsoring. In a second step, based on experience and available data, it is determined what costs would have had to be paid for the service if it were to be purchased "normally". To take into account the different quality of impact, a percentage discount could be considered from these calculated opportunity costs.

The **advertising value** thus informs a sponsor how much he would have to pay for a normal media advertising placement to achieve the same on-screen time as with sports sponsoring. Essential calculation factors are the advertising duration, the time of broadcast of the contribution, and the broadcasting television station (see also the example of Rakuten in section 11.4).

As an **example of the calculation of advertising value** of sports engagements, an analysis of sports sponsoring in Austria is used. In Fig. 11.14, the advertising value of the sports sponsoring market, calculated according to the advertising value in TV, print, and online, is presented. This value has remained relatively stable despite the Corona pandemic and significantly fewer sports events. The advertising value fell by 9% to 1.04 billion EUR in 2020 according to the market research institute Focus compared to the previous year. Adjusted for the major events in 2019 (alpine and Nordic Ski World Championships), there was an increase of 4% despite all Corona measures in the previous year. Of the total sports sponsoring advertising value, the largest shares are in Alpine skiing (35%) and football (almost 22%). In terms of media, 749 million EUR went to TV, 231 million EUR to print, and 62 million EUR to online images. Advertising top performer and tennis player Dominic Thiem achieved an advertising value of 8.9 million EUR for his sponsors, followed by skiers Matthias Mayer (3.7 million EUR) and Vincent Kriechmayr (3.2 million EUR). In 2019, skier Marcel Hirscher, who had retired in the summer, was still in first place with 7.9 million EUR (market research institute Focus according to Wiener Zeitung, 2021).

The **measurement of advertising duration** is often used by companies as a criterion for the effectiveness of a sponsoring, as it is relatively easy to measure and

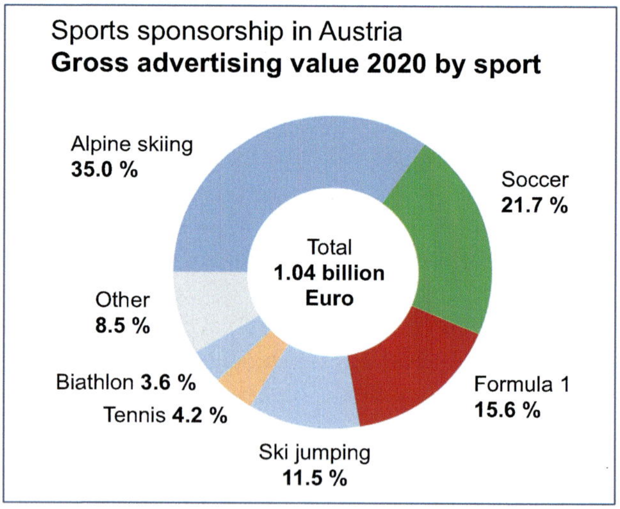

Fig. 11.14 Advertising value of sports in Austria. (*Source*: Wiener Zeitung, 2021; information according to market research Focus)

interpret. However, behind this criterion is ultimately nothing more than the extent of publicity achieved through a sponsoring measure. However, the consequences in terms of brand-relevant effects that actually result from contact with the target group are not recorded.

At this point, the so-called **False-Consensus Hypothesis** ("fallacy hypothesis") comes into play, according to which—applied to sports sponsoring—individual people tend to adopt attitudes towards a sponsor that they believe the majority of the rest of the audience of a sponsored event or a fan community represents (Ross et al., 1977; Engelmann & Strobel, 2012). This results in four essential **consequences***for a sponsor:*

- People who overestimate the percentage of consumers of a certain sponsor brand are also more likely to buy this brand themselves.
- Image characteristics that a sports fan projects onto a sponsor and that are based solely on a sponsored event, sports, or team, are internalized in such a way that they are still associated with a sponsor even when interest in the sponsored parties object has already decreased.
- Individuals tend to perceive their affection for the products of a sponsor as normal, rational, and objective, but perceive alternative opinions as incorrect, thus increasing their self-confidence for their own evaluation.
- Finally, it was found that such a "fallacy" of an individual increases their memory and they better recognize messages from the sponsor.

The hypothesis was confirmed by surveys of English football fans, proving at least for this target group that sponsoring measures not only have positive effects at the cognitive level by increasing awareness and recognition of the sponsor, but also positively influence the consumption of the products of the sponsoring company at the conative level.

Calculation of PR Value

The so-called **PR value calculation** relates the total time of sponsor visibility on television and the time-equivalent advertising placement mathematically to each other based on a 30-second spot. This could also occur in the case of print media coverage, if an advertisement is considered equivalent.

The result shows the amount that "would" have had to be spent on traditional advertising to achieve the on-screen time of the sponsoring. This is also referred to as **"opportunity costs"**. However, the direct comparability of sponsoring with traditional advertising and public relations measures is problematic, as the communication tools differ significantly in their abilities to convey messages, reach target groups, and in their communication goals. In sports sponsoring, the advertising measures receive "secondary attention", as the "primary attention" is mainly focused on the sporting event.

Calculation of Target Group Affinity

In the context of success control, **target group affinity** is understood as the quotient of the proportion of a certain target group in the user base of the medium and the proportion in the total population. When affinities are calculated in sports sponsoring, the primary task is to assess to what extent certain target group segments disproportionately often follow certain sports, events or broadcasts on television (target group affinity). This could also be an indicator of the efficiency of the target group selection. In this regard, the annual surveys of the Allensbach Market and Advertising Carrier Analysis (AWA, 2021) provide current and reliable data. Good conclusions can be drawn from the ratio of the proportion of certain population groups to the proportion of interested parties in a sport.

Calculation of Index Points

The on-screen time also forms the basis for the calculation of a so-called **event index**, where in this case the transmission duration of a specific sports event is measured. Taking into account corresponding viewing figures, this is summed up to an event index. This primarily allows the TV presence of individual sports to be compared.

The **sponsor index** determines the on-screen time of a sponsor's advertising space(s) during the transmission time and multiplies it by the viewing figures. This allows a comparison with other sponsorings. Both the sponsor and event index are plagued with the problem that no distinction is made between more or less relevant TV times.

Calculation of Return on Sponsoring Investment (ROSI)

The performance indicators presented often only allow a purely quantitative evaluation of sponsoring efficiency. Only the calculation of a **Return on Sponsoring Investment** (ROSI) opens up the possibility of integrating qualitative criteria into the efficiency control of the sponsoring. This was long determined by Serviceplan/Sky Media Network, currently Nielsen Sports has taken on the task (Nielsen Sports, 2017). In a first step, a so-called sponsoring index is calculated, which consists of the components awareness, authenticity, emotionality, brand lift, and preference. By summing the weighted averages of the individual components to 100, the sponsoring index is then transformed in a second step. The actual efficiency evaluation, i.e. the calculation of the Return on Sponsoring Investment, takes place in a final step by comparing the sponsoring index with the rights expenditures for sponsoring measures (costs of sponsoring in Germany; Serviceplan/Sky Media Network, 2013).

Sponsoring Value Analysis (SVA)

The method of **Sponsoring Value Analysis** is based on the Communication Value Analysis (Bruhn, 2014, pp. 487 ff.) as well as the basic idea of cost-benefit analysis and overhead cost value analysis. The core consists of examining the "value" of the costs and benefits of sponsorings in sports. Through the analysis, one hopes to find indications of potential rationalizations and other efficiency increases.

The sponsoring value analysis is carried out in the form of a **project work**, which is characterized by four **phases**:

- **Preparation phase:** At the start of the project work, the participants of the project group are to be determined. They should come from all areas that are involved in the sports sponsoring. Also, the individual steps of the project work are to be assigned with personnel responsibilities.
- **Inventory phase:** The actual project work consists of compiling all cost components and benefits of the sponsorings. This is done in the sense of a status quo analysis from the perspective of the participants. Both the cost and the benefit components must be proven with evidence.
- **Negotiation and decision phase:** At the heart of the project work is the discussion about the measures and consequences of changing the sponsoring budget. On the one hand, cost-saving measures are discussed if the budget were to be cut by a certain percentage (e.g., 10%). On the other hand, measures are discussed if the budget could be increased by a corresponding percentage and what performance increases could be expected. On this basis, negotiations about the measures are conducted. Of particular importance are the available information and data to prove potential savings or performance increases.
- **Realization phase:** At the end of the project work, the substantive implementation of the agreed measures by the responsible persons and the project control takes place.

With the help of the sponsoring value analysis, the **thinking in cost and benefit categories** is strengthened. Through the project work and the evidence, transparency about the costs and performance values is increased. This can generate indications of potential improvements (cost-saving measures and performance increases) for sponsorings in sports.

In Fig. 11.15, the **procedure of a sponsoring value analysis** with the individual phases is exemplarily shown.

Digital Advertising Values: Adjusted Ad Value (AAV)

As a further outlook for determining the total sponsoring effect, a new method is to be mentioned, which is based on the posts and dialogues on social networks. This value is

Phases	Activities
1. preparation	• Definition of the sponsoring project team • Definition of sponsorship objectives • Target planning • Information
2. inventory	• Actual recording of sponsorship costs • Analysis of sponsorship benefits from a departmental perspective (performance data) • Analysis of the sponsorship benefit from a market perspective
3. negotiation and decision	• Specification of fictitious measures for budget changes • Negotiations on budget changes • Decision on new sponsorship budget
4. realization	• Implementation of the sponsoring measures • Control by project team and possibly external agency

Fig. 11.15 Procedure of a sponsoring value analysis in sports. (*Source*: based on Bruhn, 2014, p. 487)

also referred to as **digital advertising value** or **adjusted ad value** (Adjusted Ad Value, AAV), because it captures digital activations of followers to the manifestations and visibilities of well-known brands in sports. The data collected for this purpose comes from social media platforms, including Facebook, Instagram, TikTok, Twitter, Twitch, VK, Weibo, and YouTube. Such well-known studies focus on up to 8000 brands that sponsor large professional sports leagues, teams, and athletes. Through computer vision and advanced machine learning, each post of these sports objects and individuals is analyzed to consciously advertise a brand through direct mention, hashtag, or keyword in the text of the post, as well as brand logos in the images and videos (KORE & SportsPro, 2022).

In connection with the new media and the additional sponsoring effect beyond the classic manifestations, this so-called **Social Sports sponsoring Value** is of increasing importance. Especially the expansion of the sponsoring space into the digital world, initiated by fans and participants themselves, creates additional confrontations of the target groups with the sponsoring partnership, so it is particularly important to also capture and measure such impressions and reactions in relation to the sponsor brand. First steps towards this have already been realized, further reliable control methods for the digital extension in sports sponsoring remain to be seen. Overall, the experts determined a social sponsoring value for the top 50 brands in sports 2022 of around 8.6 billion USD, thus again reaching the pre-Corona level of 8.5 billion USD in 2019 (see Fig. 11.16)

It is also interesting in which sectors of sports such additional sponsoring effects mainly occur. As Fig. 11.16. shows, football also proves its dominant position in sports sponsoring under this analysis focus. Its share has now risen to 49%, seven percentage points more than three years ago, while motorsport has lost three percentage points in this respect.

Sports	2019	Pro rata	...	2022	Pro rata
Soccer	3,570	42 %		4,200	49 %
Motorsport	1,270	15 %		1,000	12 %
Basketball	1,100	13 %		655	7.6 %
Cricket				469	5.4 %
American Football	500	6 %		288	3.3 %
Top 5 sports				6,612	77 %
All sports	8,500			8,600	100 %

Fig. 11.16 Adjusted Ad Value (AAV)—adjusted advertising values of brands in sports sponsoring on digital platforms. (*Source*: KORE & SportsPro, 2022; figures in million USD)

RANK	YoY RANK CHANGE	BRAND	CATEGORY	PROMOTERS	BRANDED POSTS	VALUE RECEIVED (AAV)
1	<	Nike	Sporting Goods & Apparel	16,903	566,435	$527,834,422
2	<	Adidas	Sporting Goods & Apparel	9,865	274,932	$331,098,859
3	<	Emirates	Travel	2,420	87,856	$290,276,097
4	+1	Red Bull	Beverage	4,566	108,179	$198,809,073
5	+1	Puma	Sporting Goods & Apparel	5,290	172,979	$154,716,439
6	-2	Santander	Financial	1,108	86,681	$152,644,975
7	+3	Heineken	Beverage	1,304	20,780	$143,300,205
8	+3	PlayStation	Consumer Electronics	1,678	13,963	$124,144,617
9	-1	Monster Energy	Beverage	2,586	71,089	$110,024,898
10	+4	Mastercard	Financial	1,101	13,557	$93,256,537

Fig. 11.17 Top 10 of the most activated sponsor brands in sports on digital platforms. (*Source*: KORE & SportsPro, 2022, p. 10)

The top 10 of the most benefiting brands in sports sponsoring alone attract a quarter of this additional effect and achieve an advertising equivalent value or a social sponsoring value—generated by social media posts—of over 2.1 billion USD (see Fig. 11.17).

In an overall **critical appraisal of the digital additional effect in sports sponsoring**, it should be noted that despite astonishing starting points, a comprehensive and uniform framework for effect control for sports sponsoring in the digital space is not yet available. This may in part also be due to the fact that it is not yet conclusively clear to what extent digital activities of the target group actually allow conclusions to be drawn about the preference and willingness to buy brands. In addition, it should be noted that known social media channels are also subject to certain time trends and thus different target group relevance.

It is definitely positive to note that the digital effects can also be recorded for comprehensive sponsoring controlling. Especially developments over time of such control values allow the attractiveness of a brand to be made additionally visible through sports sponsoring (see Fig. 11.18).

Data Envelopment Analysis (DEA)

As a prospect, it should be added at this point that one way to determine the efficiency of sponsoring in the future lies in the application of the **Data Envelopment Analysis (DEA)**. This methodology has only spread in research practice (especially in the field of advertising efficiency and sales efficiency) in recent years (cf. on the subject of DEA in detail Cooper et al., 2006; Bauer et al., 2006; Cooper et al., 2011; cf. on communication efficiency Schwarz, 2012; cf. on advertising efficiency e.g. Büschken et al., 2007, pp. 51 ff.; Bauer et al., 2010, cf. on sales efficiency e.g. Büschken, 2004; Michaelis & Woisetschläger, 2011).

In connection with the **efficiency measurement in sponsoring**, the DEA has not yet been used. However, the strengths of the DEA can also come into play for the efficiency control in sponsoring. The DEA model is characterized by its comprehensiveness, processing multiple inputs (e.g., advertising expenditures, sponsoring expenditures) and outputs (e.g., brand awareness, brand sympathy) simultaneously. The DEA thus allows the verification of which instruments are how efficient. Furthermore, the DEA has the advantage of circumventing the often-occurring problem in marketing of combining monetary and non-monetary sizes by using both sizes in the model. For the efficiency control of sponsoring, this means that sizes such as sales increase or customer satisfaction can be

Brands in sport	2019	pro rata	...	2022	pro rata	Growth in 3 yrs.
Period of data collection	1.8.2018 - 1.8.2019			1.9.2021 - 1.9.2022		
Nike	462.0	6.60%		527.8	6.14%	65.8
adidas	228.0	3.26%		331.1	3.85%	103.1
Emirates	252.0	3.60%		290.3	3.38%	38.2
Red Bull	114.0	1.63%		198.8	2.31%	84.4
Puma	75.0	1.07%		154.7	1.80%	79.7

Fig. 11.18 Digital advertising values (AAV) of selected brands in sports sponsoring in comparison over time. (*Source*: KORE & SportsPro, 2022; figures in million USD)

taken into account simultaneously. A test of endurance for the DEA in sports sponsoring is still pending.

Benchmarking

A new variant for success control is the benchmarking of a consulting firm, in which the economic situation of the 18 German first division teams of the 2021/2022 season has been analyzed for the first time in a Bundesliga benchmarking. Over months, key figures on the most important value levers in professional football were evaluated. All results were condensed into a total point value in a table, but individual evaluations such as for sponsoring are quite meaningful (Sinn et al., 2022).

Example: Sponsoring Benchmark and Bundesliga Football

In sponsoring, according to the Bundesliga benchmarking of the consulting firm Bain & Company, FC Bayern Munich plays in a league of its own. Success with sponsors is measured in this Bundesliga benchmarking with two key figures: revenue per sponsor and share of international sponsors. In both respects, Bayern outperforms the competition. In fact, on average, more than six million EUR per sponsor flows into the coffers of the record champion. And with the contract extension, which Bayern agreed with their main sponsor this year and which is now expected to bring them 50 million EUR annually, new standards have been set. For comparison: At the second-placed RB Leipzig, it is 3.5 million EUR per sponsor, at Borussia Dortmund 1.7 million EUR and at the also successful Freiburgers for years 230,000 EUR. At the same time, almost a third of the funds come from international sponsors at the serial champion from Munich and Champions League regular, at SC Freiburg it is 1.4% (Fig. 11.19). ◄

In an overall **critical appraisal of efficiency control in sports sponsoring**, it can be noted that a uniform systematic approach to efficiency control for sports sponsoring does not yet exist. This is mainly due to the fact that there is uncertainty in all approaches as to the extent to which a realistic sum of contact opportunities can be represented through these. Furthermore, qualitative evaluation criteria for a cost-benefit assessment are becoming increasingly important. Against this background, special attention should be paid to a measurement and evaluation system of the professional association for sponsoring and special advertising forms(FASPO, 2005), which, in addition to quantifiable contacts, also includes non-quantifiable services of a sponsoring, such as media resonance and evaluation of the reached target group, in the calculation of a total value for the contract sum of a sponsoring. In addition, it seems essential for the future to also examine other qualitative dimensions of contact evaluation, such as differences in

TURNOVER PER SPONSOR

Place	Team	in million euros
1	Bayern Munich	6.1
2	RB Leipzig	3.5
3	VfL Wolfsburg	2.0
4	Borussia Dortmund	1.7
5	Bayer Leverkusen	1.5
6	1. FC Cologne	1.5
7	Eintracht Frankfurt	1.0
8	VfB Stuttgart	1.0
9	Borussia Mönchengladbach	1.0
10	FSV Mainz 05	0.8
11	TSG Hoffenheim	0.7
12	Hertha BSC Berlin	0.6
13	Union Berlin	0.4
14	Arminia Bielefeld	0.3
15	FC Augsburg	0.3
16	SC Freiburg	0.2
17	VfL Bochum	0.1
18	Greuther Fürth	0.1

PERCENTAGE SHARE OF INTERNATIONAL SPONSORS

Place	Team	in percent
1	Bayern Munich	32.4
2	Borussia Dortmund	30.2
3	RB Leipzig	29.6
4	Bayer Leverkusen	22.6
5	Borussia Mönchengladbach	22.6
6	Hertha BSC Berlin	21.1
7	1. FC Cologne	20.0
8	VfL Wolfsburg	20.0
9	TSG Hoffenheim	19.4
10	Arminia Bielefeld	10.7
11	Union Berlin	10.5
12	FSV Mainz 05	10.3
13	Eintracht Frankfurt	9.7
14	VfB Stuttgart	9.1
15	VfL Bochum	7.0
16	FC Augsburg	6.5
17	Greuther Fürth	4.4
18	SC Freiburg	1.4

Fig. 11.19 Bundesliga Benchmarking 2021/2022. (*Source*: Sinn et al., 2022)

camera guidance, the stimulus strength of advertising media and competitive stimuli on the screen.

In the future, there is a **need for new approaches to success control** for sponsoring controlling. These need to be worked out and empirically tested. Despite the increasing growth rates in the last decade, which can largely be explained by the innovativeness of the communication instrument and its specific advantages over media advertising, the economic efficiency of different sponsoring measures will be the focus in the future. This development requires professional controlling instruments to subject the company's sponsoring portfolio to a systematic effectiveness and efficiency analysis. Consequently, the importance of efficiency control of sports sponsoring will continue to increase.

11.6 Success Control in Practice

With reference to the application of **success control in practice**, divergent results are available. Thus, the results of two studies conducted in Germany show that in 2012, almost 32% of companies did not carry out any success control. This represents a significant decrease in the implementation of sponsoring controls. In 2004, only 12.1% refrained from doing so (BBDO Live, 2010, p. 47; Bagusat, 2013, p. 31). Those companies that control the success of their sponsoring commitments most frequently carry out media and reach analyses. Some companies also measure efficiency and memory effect with the help of recall and recognition tests. But event checks and social media monitoring are also used. Impact tracking, day-after recalls and tracking are also carried out, albeit less frequently (Bagusat, 2013, p. 34; ZHAW, 2015).

A different result emerges from surveys with companies in Switzerland and Austria. The study conducted in Switzerland reveals that 75% of companies control the achievement of their sponsoring goals. The verification of awareness and image goals is of central importance here (ZHAW, 2015, p. 21). For Austrian companies, a share of only 4% of companies is reported that do not carry out any success control. A good third of the companies (37%) always check their sponsoring activities (sports + Markt AG, 2013, p. 44).

Example: Deutsche Telekom AG and FC Bayern Munich

Deutsche Telekom AG is the parent company of Europe's largest telecommunications company, headquartered in Bonn, and one of the largest sports and music sponsors in Germany. Through its diverse sponsoring commitment (see also Chap. 9), the group inspires people with enthusiasm and assumes social responsibility.

In 2002, Telekom replaced the car manufacturer Opel after 13 years as the main sponsor and has thus been the main sponsor of FC Bayern Munich (FCB) for over 20 years. The start of this sponsoring coincided with the third phase of Deutsche Telekom AG's corporate development, internationalization (Althoff, 2007, p. 82). The partnership with the increasingly international FC Bayern Munich was therefore a strategically important measure to further increase the brand awareness and brand value of Deutsche Telekom. The target was that Deutsche Telekom and FC Bayern Munich intended to enter into a strategic partnership from the second half of 2002. The current focus for Deutsche Telekom was to increase the awareness and value of the T-Mobile brand internationally through joint sponsoring activities (Deutsche Telekom, 2002). Today, Telekom is one of the most important financial backers of the German football record champion. However, the Telekom company does not hold shares in FC Bayern Munich AG.

Telekom has prematurely extended its kit sponsoring with record champion FC Bayern Munich, which has been in place for 20 years now, and has once again extended the contract, which was previously limited until 2023, as the main and shirt sponsor for another five years until the end of the 2027/2028 season. The official confirmation took place at the first home game of FC Bayern in mid-2022. In this context, the trustful and long-standing partnership with the Magenta Group was highlighted.

The media (including SportBild) have already speculated a sponsoring amount of 50 million EUR per year compared to 45 million EUR previously, which would ultimately mean 250 million EUR for the new contract term. Telekom or its sponsoring head did not comment on such figures. However, some experts have certain doubts about the amount, they assume a maximum of 40 million EUR per year. Regardless of this, Telekom's sponsoring management is convinced that the once again more expensive FC Bayern investment pays off. Reference is made to Telekom's brand value of 60 billion EUR, and that sports sponsoring has certainly contributed to this value. For example, the presence of the "T" in connection with the FC Bayern sponsoring is regularly measured. In 2021, the "T" was visible for over 5000 minutes on TV alone due to the successes of FC Bayern—and that was not even its most successful year. If this fact is put into relation to the prices for classic 20-second commercials (e.g. the cheapest spot price of the afternoon and early evening ARD advertising), this results in an advertising equivalent value of over 90 million EUR from the visibility of the "T" on television alone (see Fig. 11.20).

In terms of brand value, Telekom is also very satisfied with the partnership with FCB, although the development of the brand value is not exclusively due to sports sponsoring. Although the Telekom "T" was already one of the most well-known brands in Germany in 2002 with a value estimated by experts at 20 billion EUR at the time, it has tripled this value to date (see Fig. 11.20 and 11.21). ◄

Visibility minutes of the "T" 2021/22 on television	Ø 20-second price (e.g. for ARD TV advertising in the afternoon and early evening program Ø between 6000 and 42,000 EUR per 20 sec)	Advertising value of jersey sponsorship only on TV
> 5000	min. 18,000 EUR/min	> EUR 90.0 million

	2002	...	2006	...	2012	...	**2022**
Brand value of the "T" (EUR billion)	20.0		23.4		26.0		60.0

Fig. 11.20 Deutsche Telekom and control figures of the sponsoring with FC Bayern Munich. (*Sources*: Deutsche Telekom, 2002; Sponsor News, 2022a, b; Brand Finance Global 500)

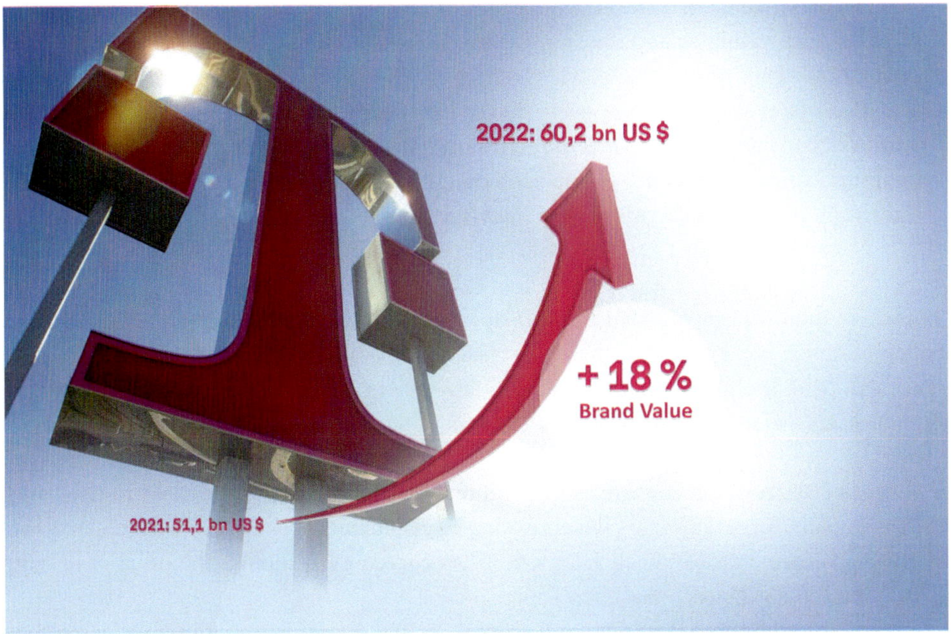

Fig. 11.21 Increase in brand value of Deutsche Telekom in a time comparison 2022 to 2021. (*Sources*: Deutsche Telekom, 2022; Sponsor News, 2022a, b)

11.7 Problems of Success Control in Sports Sponsoring

The **success controlin sports sponsoring** has about the same importance in practice as advertising effectiveness research with regard to media advertising: It is partly underestimated in its importance by those affected and not carried out with the necessary consistency. A large number of companies primarily see the costs that come with sponsoring control (the price for a day-after-recall with 300 respondents amounts to about 10,000 EUR upwards), but are not aware of the benefits and the absolute necessity of ex-post and ex-ante market research.

A growing number of sponsors are now demonstrating a **professionalization of success control**. In a 1993 survey, about a third of companies reported regularly conducting impact assessments to measure success, and a quarter said they did not conduct any checks (Bruhn & Pristaff, 1993, p. 33). By 2012, approximately 60% of the companies surveyed were checking the success of their sponsoring commitments. The primary control instrument used is outcome control, but performance and efficiency controls are also frequently used (Bagusat, 2013, p. 31).

Like the entire field of advertising impact research, the impact control of sports sponsoring is fraught with methodological and substantive problems. In this context, two **peculiarities in sports sponsoring** should be noted:

- **Secondary attention effect:** The attention of the target individuals is primarily directed at the athletes and the sporting event, not at the brand symbols of products or companies. This form of selective, "automatic" attention attributes only a secondary attention effect to sports sponsoring due to the specific environment.
- **Limited communication statement:** Sports sponsoring allows only a very limited communication statement, as the advertising possibilities are often reduced to the indication of the brand symbol. A very differentiated transmission of product information is usually excluded.

Overall, it should be noted that there is still little information available about some of the communicative processes that take place in sports sponsoring. Further research is needed. This includes, for example, the analysis of the following open **problems of impact analysis** (see Bruhn, 2018, pp. 194 ff.):

- **Effect of sponsoring measures over time:** It is important for sponsors to determine learning and forgetting rates in sponsoring engagements as well as possible carry-over effects. In some cases, recall rates are still recorded even though the product or company no longer appears as a sports sponsor.
- **Cumulative effects of sponsoring use:** It is also necessary to capture those effects that occur with multiple contacts with the advertising message. In sports sponsoring, too, the effect must be examined depending on the generated advertising/sponsoring pressure.
- **Synergy effects of sponsoring use:** Sports sponsorings are not used in isolation. Their impact must be analyzed in conjunction with other advertising media, further sponsoring commitments of the company, and the successful integration of the sponsoring into the company's marketing and corporate communication.
- **Inclusion of media behavior:** For an impact analysis in sports sponsoring, it is not sufficient to calculate a calculative (advertising) benefit without taking into account more detailed information about media behavior. Advertising impact research in the television, social media, and print sectors needs to conduct in-depth studies to better assess media impact.
- **Purchase relevance of sports sponsoring:** In the medium to long term, information about the influence of sports sponsoring on changes in purchasing willingness and behavior is of interest.
- **Attention measurement of brand symbols:** Specifically for measuring the attention effect of brand symbols in the sports environment, newer theoretical approaches to advertising impact research will initially be worked out and empirically tested in the future to arrive at more precise statements. This includes in particular information processing psychology and specifically the concept of image information processing, which deals with the processing of images in certain situations (Kroeber-Riel & Gröppel-Klein, 2019). This involves both brain research (hemispheric specialization

of pictorial elements by the right hemisphere) and analyses regarding the formation and effect of inner images on human behavior (imagery research).
- **Image effect and image transfer:** It is necessary to capture the effects of sports sponsoring in terms of changes in the image perceived by target individuals. Above all, it is of interest whether the intended image transfers from the sponsored party to the sponsor have actually taken place.

The **success control of image transfer** is of paramount importance for sponsoring. In principle—according to current research—the possibility of an image transfer from the sponsored party to the sponsor exists. However, to realize and make use of this for the sponsor, special psychological prerequisites must be observed, which enable an image transfer in sports sponsoring in the first place, as well as target group and sponsoring-specific determining factors that condition the course and success of an image transfer.

The fundamental **mechanism of image transfer in sports sponsoring** can be identified as the associative learning of conscious content. From this specific form of learning, requirements for the perception process of image transfer in sports sponsoring emerge, which are concretized in the conscious perception of the sponsoring message, the attention given, and a high action-specific involvement. The image transfer itself is in turn influenced by a multitude of conditions that affect the recipient of a sponsoring message (e.g., awareness of the sponsor and strength of the sponsoring involvement) and relate to the characteristics of the sponsoring or sponsor (e.g., duration of the sponsoring and design of the sponsoring message).

Fig. 11.22 summarizes the psychological **prerequisites for image transfer** and the determining factors that can be derived from them (Glogger, 1999, p. 200).

The presented **findings on image transfer** are also useful for the management practice of sports sponsoring by assigning the determining factors to individual phases in the sponsoring planning process, in which they each provide guidance for the planning and design of sponsoring activities. For example, Fig. 11.23 shows that the awareness of a company as a sponsor provides indications as to whether a sponsoring commitment can be considered promising at all, while the number of sponsors and the image fit between sponsor and sponsored provide clues for the fine selection of a sponsoring (Glogger, 1999, p. 223; Wiedmann & Gross, 2013; Nufer, 2015).

Sports sponsoring is a communication tool for companies to achieve certain goals. For analysis, various methods for checking the degree of target achievement are to be used in the **control phase of sports sponsoring**. In addition to process controls, effectiveness controls (checking the communicative effects) and efficiency controls (checking the economic efficiency of sports sponsoring) play a central role. It should be noted that in a comprehensive success control, the interrelationships with other instruments of corporate and marketing communication must be taken into account.

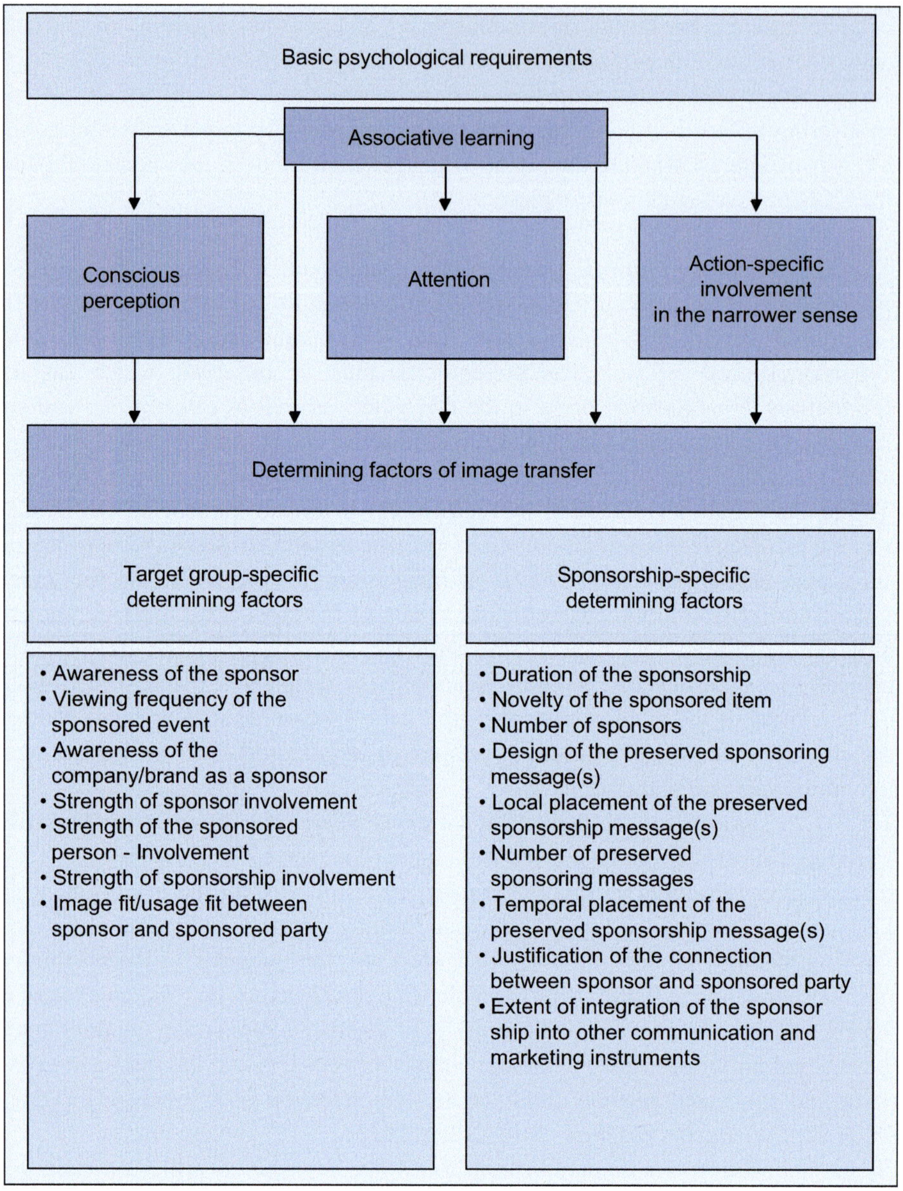

Fig. 11.22 Psychological prerequisites for image transfer. (*Source*: Glogger, 1999, p. 200)

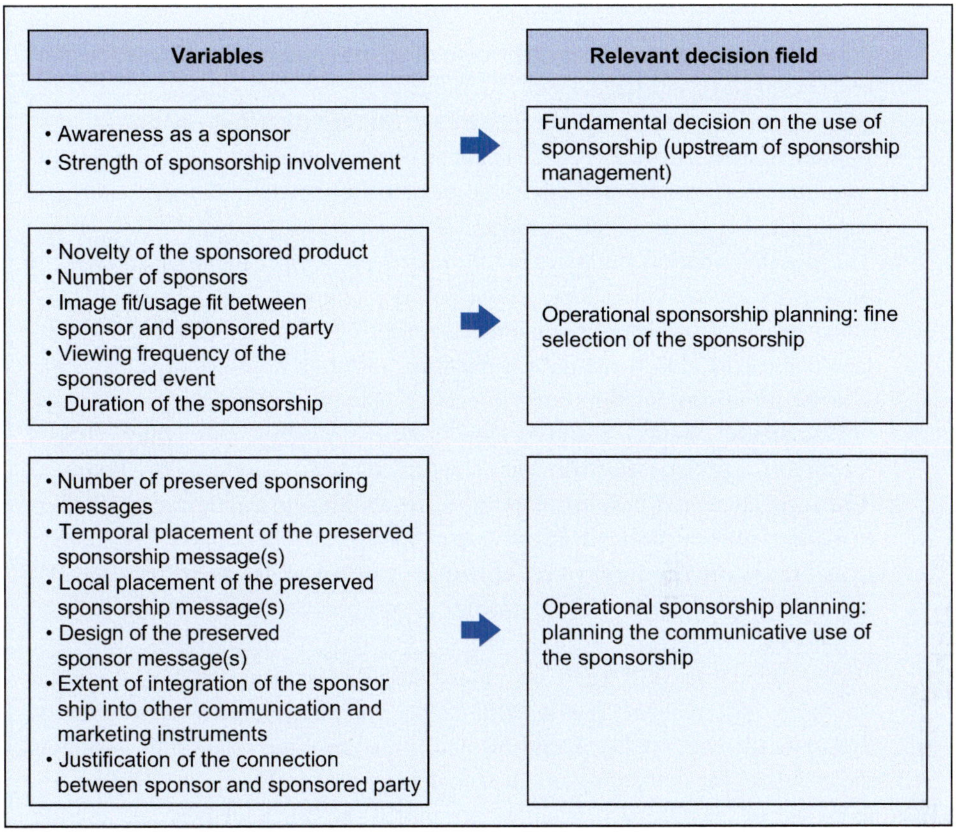

Fig. 11.23 Determining factors of image transfer and decision-making fields of sponsoring management. (*Source*: Glogger, 1999, p. 230)

11.8 Key Points

The success control in sports sponsoring pursues the goal of enabling an evaluation of the commitment at the end of the planning process. There are some points to pay particular attention to.

Key Points

1. The **control of sponsoring success** ideally forms the conclusion of the planning process in sports sponsoring. It should not be neglected throughout the planning process, but requires intensive analysis.
2. At the center of success control, both the examination of the communicative effect through the sponsoring on the target groups **(effectiveness control)** and

the examination of the cost-benefit ratio of sports sponsorings (**efficiency control**) should be considered.

3. In the success control of sports sponsoring, **quantitative and qualitative performance criteria** should be considered. Statistical methods are suitable for quantitative analyses. Qualitative analyses are carried out in the form of expert surveys and other exploratory studies.
4. The **process control** in sports sponsoring deals with the implementation of various processes, including organizational, temporal, and financial ones, which are associated with the planned sponsorings. The various forms of process control are closely related to project organization or project management.
5. For the proof of communicative effects by means of **effectiveness controls**, classic market research methods have proven successful, with which various reactions (cognitive, affective, conative) can be checked in the target groups.
6. The main goal of a success control is, in addition to capturing psychological target effects through effectiveness control, to carry out a cost-benefit consideration in the form of an **efficiency control** of sports sponsoring. For the economic evaluation of sponsoring measures, costs and benefits must be compared.
7. When calculating a **Return on sponsoring Investment** (ROSI), it should be taken into account that in addition to components such as awareness, authenticity, emotionality, brand lift and preference, the relation to the rights expenditures for sponsoring measures can be considered.
8. It should be checked whether not only media and reach analyses are used in the **methods of success control** of sponsoring commitments, but also methods of efficiency evaluation and the measurement of memory effect with the help of recall and recognition tests. Event checks and social media monitoring can also be applied, as well as advertising equivalent calculations.
9. Similar to the entire advertising impact research, the impact control of sports sponsoring is also fraught with **methodological and content-related problems**. In this context, two peculiarities must be taken into account in success control: the secondary attention effect and the limited communication statement.
10. The **success control of image transfer** is of outstanding importance for the sponsoring, the image transfer is to be considered as given. However, when providing evidence for an image transfer, the special context of the advertising effect and the framework conditions of sports sponsoring must be taken into account.

References

A

Allensbacher Markt- und Werbeträgeranalyse (AWA 2011–2021). Allensbacher Marktanalyse Werbeträgeranalyse Codebuch.

Althoff, S. (2007). Das Sportsponsoring der Telekom – und was dahinter steckt. In D. Ahlert, D. Woisetschläger, & Vogel, V. (Hrsg.), *Exzellentes Sponsoring. Innovative Ansätze und Best Practices für das Markenmanagement* (2. Aufl., S. 77–100). https://doi.org/10.1007/978-3-8350-9639-4_4

B

Bagusat, A. (2013). *Sponsoring trends 2012.* https://www.ostfalia.de/export/sites/default/de/ispm/Blickpunkt_Sportmanagement/Sponsoring_Trends_2012.pdf. Accessed: 17. Febr. 2016.

Bauer, H. H., Staat, M., & Hammerschmidt, M. (Hrsg.). (2006). *Marketingeffizienz. Messung und Steuerung mit der DEA – Konzept und Einsatz in der Praxis.* https://doi.org/10.15358/9783800643387.

Bauer, H. H., Hammerschidt, M., Hartung, R., & Shenawai, N. (2010). Messung und Analyse der Online-Werbeeffizienz. *Controlling – Zeitschrift für erfolgsorientierte Unternehmenssteuerung, 22*(2), 83–88. https://doi.org/10.15358/0935-0381-2010-2-83.

BBDO Live GmbH. (2010). Sponsoring Trends 2010, Studie in Zusammenarbeit mit dem Institut für Marketing, Universität der Bundeswehr München, Bonn.

Brannasch, A. (2001). Milliarden verpulvert – wenn Marken Pech haben im Sportsponsoring. Vortrag im Rahmen der Medientage München (Werben & Verkaufen), 18.10.2001.

Breuer, C., Rumpf, C., & Kurz, S. (2013). Ein Bewertungsmodell zur Analyse von Sponsoring-Alternativen. *Marketing Review St. Gallen, 30*(1), 72–81. https://doi.org/10.1365/s11621-013-0190-5.

Bruhn, M. (2014). *Integrierte Unternehmens- und Markenkommunikation* (6. Aufl.). Schäffer-Poeschel.

Bruhn, M. (2018). *Sponsoring. Systematische Planung und integrativer Einsatz* (6. Aufl.). https://doi.org/10.1007/978-3-658-13313-9.

Bruhn, M., & Pristaff, J. (1993). *Sponsoring in Deutschland. Ergebnisse einer Unternehmensbefragung*. Arbeitspapier Nr. 14. Institut für Marketing, European Business School, Schloß Reichartshausen/Rheingau.

Büschken, J. (2004). *Higher profits through customer lock-in*. Thomson.

Büschken, J., Voeth, M., & Weiber, R. (Hrsg.). (2007). *Innovationen für das Industriegütermarketing. Festschrift für Professor Klaus Backhaus*. Schäffer-Poeschel.

C

Charitomeni, T., Papadimitriou, D., & Parganas, P. (2018). The influence of sport sponsoring on brand equity and purchase behavior. *Journal of Strategic Marketing, 26*(1), 85–105. https://doi.org/10.1080/0965254x.2017.1374299.

Cooper, W., Seiford, L., & Tone, K. (2006). *Introduction to data envelopment analysis and its uses: With DEA solver software and references* (2. Aufl.). https://doi.org/10.1007/978-0-387-45283-8.
Cooper, W., Seiford, L., & Zhu, J. (2011). *Handbook on data envelopment analysis* (2. Aufl.). https://doi.org/10.1007/978-1-4419-6151-8.

D

Deutsche Telekom. (2002). Sport-Engagement stärkt zusätzlich die Kraft der Marke: Sponsoring – strategische Partnerschaft mit FC Bayern München. *Forum T-Aktie „direkt", 6*(2), 5.
Deutsche Telekom. (2022). Telekom-Markenwert auf Rekordniveau. https://www.telekom.com/de/medien/medieninformationen/detail/telekom-markenwert-auf-rekordniveau-645052.

E

Engelmann, D., & Strobel, M. (2012). Deconstruction and reconstruction of an anomaly. *Games and Economic Behavior, 76*(2), 678–689. https://doi.org/10.1016/j.geb.2012.07.009.

F

Falkenau, J. (2013). *Sportsponsoring. Wirkung und Erfolgsfaktoren aus neuropsychologischer Sicht*. Haufe.
FASPO (Fachverband für Sponsoring-Agenturen und Dienstleister e. V.). (2005). FASPO-Konvention zur Ermittlung und Verrechnung von Leistungswerten im Sponsoring: Eventkontakte, Medienkontakte, Dokumentation, Zertifikation, Begriffsdefinitionen, Berechnungsbeispiele.

G

Global Sports. (2019). Rakuten – ein Beispiel für effektives Sponsoring im Sport, Beitrag vom 02.12.2019. https://intelligence.globalsportsjobs.de/rakuten-ein-beispiel-f%C3%BCr-effekives-sponsoring-im-sport
Glogger, A. (1999). *Imagetransfer im Sponsoring: Entwicklung eines Erklärungsmodells*. Lang.
Grohs, R., & Reisinger, H. (2014). Sponsoring effects on brand image: The role of exposure and activity involvement. *Journal of Business Research, 67*(5), 1018–1025. https://doi.org/10.1016/j.jbusres.2013.08.008.

H

Hermanns, A., & Marwitz, C. (2008). *Sponsoring. Grundlagen, Wirkungen, Management, Markenführung* (3. Aufl.). Vahlen.

Hermanns, A., Marwitz, C., & Schubert, M. (2016). Messung der Wirkung von Sponsoringmaßnahmen. In F.-R. Esch, M. Bruhn, & T. Langner (Hrsg.), *Handbuch Controlling der Kommunikation* (2. Aufl., S. 507–538). Springer Gabler. https://doi.org/10.1007/978-3-8349-3857-2_23.

Hohenauer, R. (2016). *Sponsoring-Wirkung auf das Kaufverhalten*. https://doi.org/10.1007/978-3-658-15573-5.

Horizont. (2014). Coca-Cola schlägt sie alle, Beitrag vom 12.06.2014. http://www.horizont.net/marketing/nachrichten/Bekanntheit-der-WM-Sponsoren-Coca-Cola-schlaegt-sie-alle-120907.

K

KORE & SportsPro. (2022). Battle of the brands. Why are the best promoted sports sponsors on social? *Whitepaper*. https://50mm.sportspromedia.com/wp-content/uploads/2020/10/HOOKIT-SportsPro-50MM-Brands-2020-whitepaper-Oct-2020.pdf.

Kroeber-Riel, W., & Gröppel-Klein, A. (2019). *Konsumentenverhalten* (11. Aufl.). Vahlen.

M

McAlister, A. R., Kelly, S. J., Humphreys, M. S., & Cornwell, T. B. (2012). Change in a sponsoring alliance and the communication implications of spontaneous recovery. *Journal of Advertising, 41*(1), 5–16. https://doi.org/10.2753/joa0091-3367410101.

Michaelis, M., & Woisetschläger, D. M. (2011). Innovatives Vertriebscontrolling in interorganisationalen Vertriebssystemen mit Hilfe der Data Envelopment Analysis. *Controlling, 23*(4/5), 242–247. https://doi.org/10.15358/0935-0381-2011-4-5-242.

N

Nielsen Sports. (2017). Wie Nielsen Sports die Wirkung von Sponsoring messbar machen will, Beitrag vom 10.03.2017. https://www.horizont.net/marketing/nachrichten/Return-on-Sponsoring-Investment-Wie-Nielsen-Sports-die-Wirkung-von-Sponsoring-messbar-machenwill-156477. https://nielsensports.com/return-on-sponsoring-investment-so-gelingt-die-ganzheitliche-messung/. Accessed: 2. Nov. 2021.

Nufer, G. (2008). Marken-Recall-Werte bei Fußball-Weltmeisterschaften, Beitrag vom 20.03.2008. https://www.marktforschung.de/marktforschung/a/marken-recall-werte-bei-fussball-weltmeisterschaften/.

Nufer, G. (2015). Creating an image transfer through event marketing: Principles, requirements and consequences. *European Journal of Business and Social Sciences, 3*(12), 1–18.

P

Papadimitriou, D., Kaplanidou, K. K., & Papacharalampous, N. (2016). Sport event-sponsor fit and its effects on sponsor purchase intentions: A non-consumer perspective among athletes, volunteers and spectators. *Journal of Business & Industrial Marketing, 31*(2), 247–259. https://doi.org/10.1108/jbim-09-2014-0187.

R

Ross, L., Greene, D., & House, P. (1977). The „false consensus effect“: An egocentric bias in social perception and attribute processes. *Journal of Experimental Social Psychology, 13*(3), 279–301. https://doi.org/10.1016/0022-1031(77)90049-x.

S

Schwarz, J. (2012). *Messung und Steuerung der Kommunikations-Effizienz: Eine theoretische und empirische Analyse durch den Einsatz der Data Envelopment Analysis.* https://doi.org/10.1007/978-3-658-00279-4.

Serviceplan/Sky Media Network. (2013). From the Heart to the Brain. Der Deutsche Sponsoring-Index 2013, München/Unterföhring. Accessed: 16. Dec. 2013.

SevenOne Media. (2015). Opel Adam: Begleitforschung „Germany's next Topmodel“ (Staffel 10). https://www.sevenonemedia.ch/documents/20182/400450/Opel_Adam_GNT_2015.pdf/33c15753-624b-47dc-89a8-5edb382d42af. Accessed: 20. May 2016.

Sinn, W., Dowling, P., Richau, L., & Ellenrieder, D. (2022). *Bain-Bundesliga-Benchmarking: Union Berlin, Dortmund und Köln jagen die Bayern.* Bain & Company.

Splendid Research. (2018). Coca-Cola und Adidas bekannteste Sponsoren der Fußball-WM, Beitrag von Juni 2018. https://www.splendid-research.com/de/statistiken/studie-sponsoren-wahrnehmung-fu%C3%9Fball-wm.

Sponsors. (2022a). Fußball-Bundesliga: Das Social-Media-Ranking der Saison 2021/22, Beitrag vom 30.05.2022. https://www.sponsors.de/news/fussball/fussball-bundesliga-das-social-media-ranking-der-saison-202122.

Sponsors. (2022b). Virtuelle Werbung: Zusatzerlöse von 100 Millionen Euro für die Bundesliga? Beirag vom 15.09.2022. https://www.sponsors.de/news/themen/virtuelle-werbung-zusatzerloese-von-100-millionen-euro-fuer-die-bundesliga.

Sponsors. (2022e). Indeed: Übers Eintracht-Hauptsponsoring zum Marktführer in Deutschland, Beitrag vom 12.12.2022. https://www.sponsors.de/news/themen/indeed-uebers-eintracht-hauptsponsoring-zum-marktfuehrer.

Sport + Markt AG. (2013). Sponsoring Barometer Österreich 2012/2013, Köln.

V

VSA. (2019). Sportsponsoring: Volltreffer mit gezielter Wirkung, Berlin. Accessed: 1. May 2022.

W

Walliser, B. (1995). Sponsoring. Bedeutung, Wirkung und Kontrollmöglichkeiten, Wiesbaden. https://doi.org/10.1007/978-3-663-12376-7.

Werner, A. (2013). *Social Media – Analytics & Monitoring. Verfahren und Werkzeuge zur Optimierung des ROI.* dpunkt.

Wiedmann, K.-P., & Gross, P. (2013). Image transfer in a sponsoring alliance. *Marketing Review St. Gallen, 30*(1), 22–35. https://doi.org/10.1365/s11621-013-0186-1.

Wiener Zeitung. (2021). Sport-Sponsoring-Markt trotzt Corona-Krise, Beitrag vom 16.02.2021. https://www.wienerzeitung.at/nachrichten/sport/mehr-sport/2093100-Sport-Sponsoring-Markt-trotzt-Corona-Krise.html.

Witt, M. (2000). *Kunstsponsoring. Gestaltungsdimensionen, Wirkungsweise und Wirkungsmessungen.* Schmidt.

Z

ZHAW. (2015). (Zentrum für Kulturmanagement, School of Management and Law, Zürcher Hochschule für Angewandte Wissenschaften. „Sponsor-Visions 2014/15"- Eine empirische Studie zum Sponsoringmarkt Schweiz. http://www.swa-asa.ch/de-wAssets/docs/artikel-print-medien/2015/Studie_Sponsor_Visions_Schweiz_2014-15.pdf. Accessed: 17. Febr. 2016.

Legal Aspects in Sports Sponsoring 12

Contents

Abstract

The collaboration between sponsor and sponsored is regulated in a sponsoring contract. This is indispensable for a rights holder in every sponsor acquisition. With the contract, the sponsor and the sponsored party seal their partnership and their specific fulfillment in terms of services and counter-services. The basis for the design of sponsoring contracts is the general law of obligations regulated in the BGB (§§ 241–432 BGB). The general law of obligations stipulates that the two contracting parties (e.g., sponsor and sports club) can individually determine the content of the agreement made. Therefore, a sponsoring contract in sports does not require a specific contract form. This chapter outlines the contracting parties, types of contracts, forms, and content of a sponsoring contract in sports, as well as the regulations in case of disputes. In addition, tax aspects in sports sponsoring are discussed.

M. Bruhn and P. Rohlmann, *Sports Sponsoring*,
https://doi.org/10.1007/978-3-658-44171-5_12

12.1 Contractual Parties in Sports Sponsoring

The legal basis for a sports sponsoring relationship is formed by sponsoring contracts, which are intended to reconcile the different interests of the sponsors and the sponsored parties and to avoid disputes. Especially in the phase leading up to the final start of the sponsoring project, third parties involved can be involved—this includes, for example, sports sponsoring agencies or lawyers—it is necessary to clearly and legally describe who acts as the **sponsor** and who as the **sponsored party**. Against the background that the legal form constructions in sports as in business are sometimes quite complex, it must be ensured that the sponsored parties actually have the rights to the sponsoring measures to be provided and that the sponsoring party also has the legal jurisdiction and responsibility to fulfill in the form of the agreed consideration.

Practice shows that the contractual partners rarely regulate all essential points concerning a sponsoring in detail. The legal uncertainty arising from the **lack of relevant legal regulations** can largely be excluded by a detailed contractual regulation between those involved in a sponsoring. Primarily, it can prove disadvantageous for the usually economically weaker sponsored party to emphasize mutual trust too much and not to consider potential conflict potentials before the conclusion of the contract.

12.2 Types of Contracts in Sports Business

As a minimum content, the sponsoring contract regulates the performance of the sponsor as well as the consideration to be provided by the sponsored party according to type, place, time and other modalities of performance. Furthermore, the contract must record the entry into force and the duration, as well as provisions on extension options and extraordinary reasons for termination (see Bruhn, 2018, pp. 167 ff.). Based on this basic structure, a sponsoring contract must always be adapted to the individual case due to the variety and diversity of sports sponsoring conditions, depending on the form of the sponsored party (individual, team, association, event) and the type of consideration (Bruhn & Mehlinger, 1995, 1999). Basically, four types of contracts can be distinguished (see Fig. 12.1).

- **Advertising contract**
  The advertising contract (also: sponsoring contract) is to be concluded either between the sponsor and the athlete or between the sponsor and the organizer of a sports event. In an individual contract with a top athlete, the advertising contract regulates the services (e.g. autograph sessions, use in commercials) and counter-services (payment of a sum of money) in free contract design. To agree on a sponsor's participation in a sports event, a kind of advertising contract is also concluded. In addition to

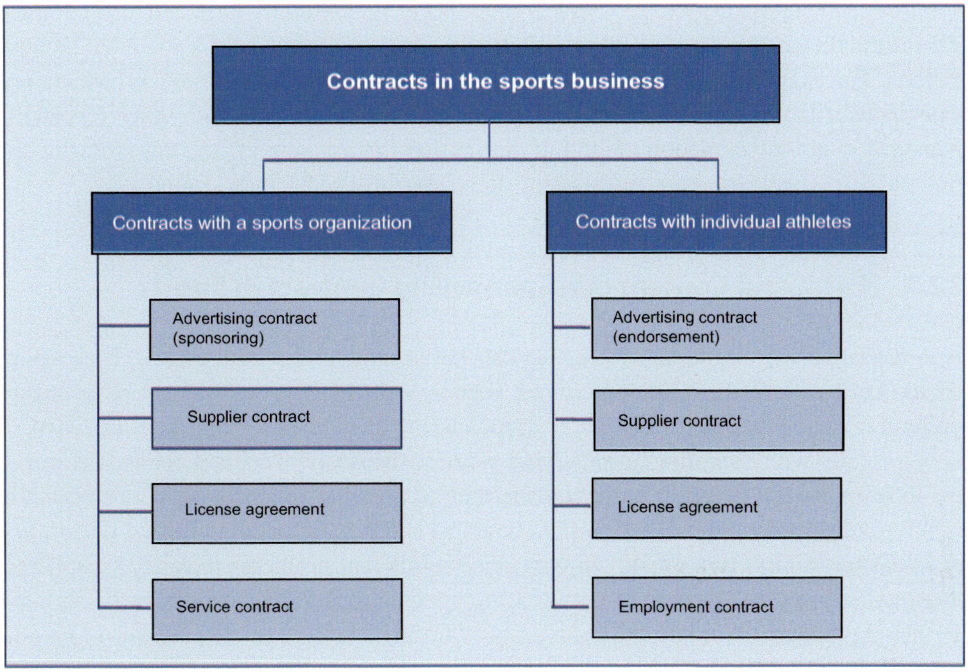

Fig. 12.1 Contract types in sports

the payment of the sponsoring amount, the provision of advertising measures by the organizer for the sponsor is listed in detail.

- **Equipment contract**
  The equipment contract ("endorsement") is concluded between the provider of sports clothing, shoes and equipment and certain individual athletes. It regulates the sponsoring amounts (in-kind and cash benefits) in connection with support at competitions as well as victory premiums and the like.
- **License contract**
  If a top athlete provides his name for a special product line of a sports goods provider, such as football shoes, tennis rackets or sports clothing, a license contract is concluded. The manufacturer usually offers the athlete a fixed fee and a sales-dependent commission for the naming.
- **Employment contract**
  In the case of professional athletes in certain sports, employment contracts are concluded between sports clubs and athletes. This is done, for example, in the top leagues of team sports such as football, ice hockey, etc. The contracts regulate the obligations (jersey advertising, advertising campaigns with the club, equipment with sports clothing and equipment) and rights of the athletes (degrees of freedom for their own advertising contracts).

The above-mentioned types of contracts often occur in combined form and also contrary. Therefore, they occasionally lead to disputes or more or less successful so-called ambush actions. For example, in football, during player transfers, some newcomers, whose private sponsor is not identical to the equipment partner of the new club, have repeatedly managed to put the competing brand in the spotlight in a media-effective way during the first public presentation, thus pushing the club sponsor into the background.

12.3 Form and Content of a Sponsoring Contract in Sports

It is fundamentally important to distinguish between a and a **oral and written sponsoring contract**. There is no doubt that a written contract in sports sponsoring is always preferable to an oral one. In Fig. 12.2, various forms of sponsoring contracts are listed.

Especially with **"smaller" sponsoring relationships**, sponsors and sponsored parties try to keep the cooperation as unbureaucratic as possible. Sponsoring cooperations in oral form and/or by implied action (i.e., conclusive behavior or tacit bilateral declaration of intent) are simple and quick, but can cause significant problems in case of dispute. If there are serious disagreements between the sponsor and the sponsored party during a sponsoring relationship, this can potentially result in a costly legal dispute. As a rule, this exceeds the costs of creating a written sponsoring contract many times over.

Sponsors and also sponsored parties show their lack of commitment and a lack of professionalism with the **waiver of a written sponsoring contract**. If sponsoring

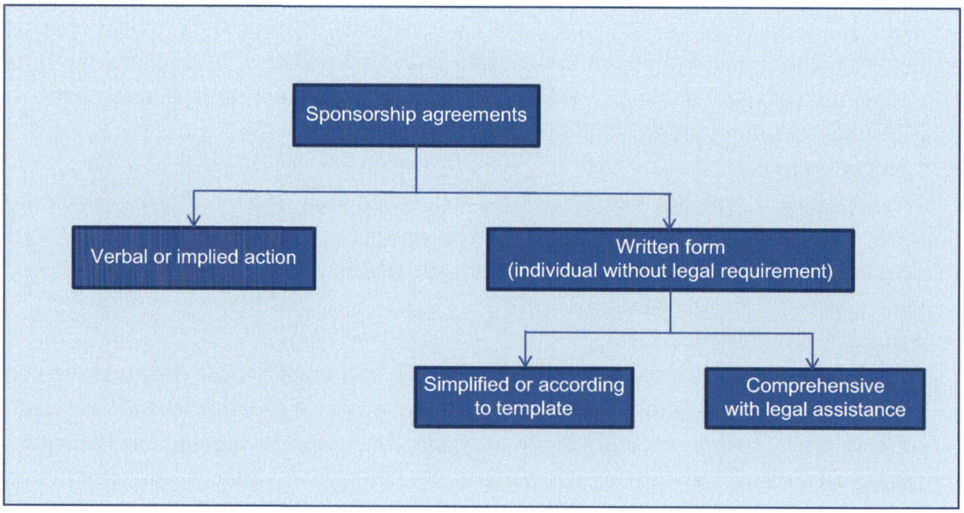

Fig. 12.2 Forms of sponsoring contracts

partners do not want to conclude a written contract, the reasons for this waiver should be investigated.

For the aforementioned reasons, a **written sponsoring contract** is actually the rule for a professional sponsoring relationship (see Bruhn, 2018, pp. 167 ff.). Although the legal design of such contracts involves effort and costs, it also brings indispensable **advantages through the formulation of the sponsoring contract**:

- **Protection against rashness**: The written elaboration of a sponsoring contract protects the contracting parties from immature or hasty decisions. During the contract formulation, practice- and contract-relevant questions always arise that can be clarified in advance.
- **Contract subject matter**: The sponsoring contract describes exactly what the sponsoring cooperation includes and what it does not. This allows third parties (lawyers, courts, etc.) to quickly familiarize themselves with the sponsoring relationship in case of conflict and to understand and clarify it in detail.
- **Rights and obligations**: The sponsoring contract definitively regulates all rights and obligations of the sponsoring partners and securely records the agreed contract contents. This can also become relevant for other matters (e.g., tax law questions).

The **contract design** is usually undertaken by the sponsored parties. They usually find it easier to design the content of the contract than the sponsor, as they are more familiar with the specific sponsoring rights and their usage possibilities. If the contract design is in the hands of the sponsor, the sponsored parties will have the contract checked by a lawyer they trust before signing. The risk of not recognizing potentially disadvantageous contract clauses and misjudging the consequences is too great.

The **formulation of a legally valid sponsoring contract** is not an easy task for both laypersons and lawyers. Sponsoring recipients are usually not lawyers and lack legal knowledge. It is difficult for them to assess the legal facets of such a contract. A legal advisor often has problems correctly grasping the relevant facts if he is not familiar with the topic of sports sponsoring. Therefore, both a good knowledge of the sponsoring project and legal knowledge are required. In practice, rights holders therefore resort to a competent specialist lawyer in sports sponsoring. For initial discussion points regarding a written agreement, sponsors and sponsored parties can sometimes also use corresponding **sample contracts**. These sample contracts contain essential cornerstones for the legal regulations.

Even though the peculiarities of each sponsoring relationship, which in sports includes many opportunities but also restrictions, require individual regulations, there are numerous contract elements that need to be regulated in any case. For this purpose, the state sports associations also provide corresponding **template forms**. These contract points can be named as follows (Poser & Backes, 2010):

(1) Preamble
(2) Sponsoring contract
  a) Sponsor's performance
  b) Counter-performance of the sponsored party
  c) Exclusivity
  d) Good conduct, notification, confidentiality, purpose limitation, doping
  e) Personal performance, assignability
  f) Disclaimer, interest in performance
  g) Security, contractual penalty, offsetting
  h) Entry into force, term, option rights
  i) Early termination of contract, restitution of performances
  j) Written form, receipt of declarations, severability clause
  k) Applicable law, place of performance, jurisdiction
  l) Attachments

Writing a **preamble** is not mandatory when creating a sponsoring contract, but it is useful. The preamble serves the purpose of a declaration function. It clarifies who the contract parties are, what the purpose of the sponsoring contract is, and which activities are being sponsored.

Under the contract point **Sponsor's performance**, the monetary, material, or service contributions that the sponsor provides for the performance of the sponsored party are defined. This is then detailed in the sponsoring contract by specifying the amounts of money or other services, the handling of payment modalities, etc.

The **performance of the sponsored party** also needs to be fixed. Since the principle of sponsoring is based on performance and counter-performance, the counter-performances to be provided by the sponsored party are also defined in the sponsoring contract. As a counter-performance for the sponsor's services, the services that the sponsored parties have to provide are listed in detail in the sponsoring contract.

Although some sponsoring commitments in sports can have an idealistic background (especially in grassroots and recreational sports), the main intention of a sponsor is to **improve their own communication and sales goals**. Competitors or too many sponsors diminish the achievement of these goals. Also, activities of the sponsored party for other partners, who appear similar or not at all as sponsors, reduce the value of the advertising performance for sponsors. Therefore, in the interest of the sponsor, the sponsoring contract should regulate under the point **exclusivity** whether there are other sponsors besides the sponsor. It also determines whether the sponsor has exclusive rights and to what extent the sponsored parties may work for other advertising partners. A violation of this is considered by the sponsor as a serious breach of contract, and can lead to the sponsor withdrawing early and possibly making claims for damages.

In the context of a sponsoring cooperation, the sponsor understandably insists on **good conduct** in the sense that the sponsored party behaves publicly in the interest of the sponsor. At the very least, it is expected that they will not act detrimentally to the sponsor. The sponsored party has an interest in the sponsor not restricting them in the execution of their activities or the achievement of their goals.

In the context of a cooperation in sports sponsoring, situations can arise (see e.g. Corona pandemic, energy crisis) that can influence the sponsoring commitment in some way. Therefore, the contract parties often agree on a mutual **notification and coordination of influencing factors** that can affect the sponsoring contract, and also provide for an agreement, i.e. to inform each other in a timely and active manner about changes in the situation in the cooperation.

Despite the common goal of communicating the cooperation between sponsor and sponsored party to the public, there are non-public, confidential agreements between the contract parties. These include, for example, price agreements or the goals pursued by the sponsor. In the **confidentiality agreement**, it is therefore also regulated who (financial authorities, courts, etc.) may inspect the sponsoring contract under what conditions.

In the field of sports sponsoring, sponsors are confronted with potential **problem situations** (e.g., doping, betting fraud, bribery). Such offenses by individual athletes, teams, or officials generally have a detrimental effect on the sponsoring commitment. Therefore, such topics are often part of the sponsoring contract in sports engagements. Regarding corresponding contract formulations, reference can be made, among other things, to the respective national Anti-Doping Code of the World Anti-Doping Agency (WADA) or the corresponding German institution (NADA).

The sponsoring contract has a peculiarity with regard to the **individual performance**. In normal economic life, a contractually guaranteed service can sometimes be passed on to a subcontractor. However, a sponsor has a sole interest in the agreed service being provided by the sponsored parties and not by a third party. He would not agree if not the sponsored parties, but a third party appeared with his company logo. The service for the sponsor would be provided with the advertising space provided, but not by the one who is supposed to provide the service. This would be to the disadvantage of the sponsor. Therefore, the sponsoring contract regulates the service to be provided by the sponsored party itself.

The **assignment of contractual claims** to third parties also poses a problem in the sponsoring contract. After all, both contract parties in the sponsoring have an interest in dealing exclusively with the respective contract partner and not with other third parties. Nevertheless, it can make sense to include an assignment agreement in the sponsoring contract, which includes an option of assigning the claim rights after written agreement. This makes sense, for example, in the case of owner changes when selling companies or similar.

The sponsoring contract regulates in the case of **exclusions of liability**, whether and for what the sponsor is liable to the sponsored party due to slight negligence, gross negligence, or intent. Actually, it is not possible for third parties (for example, in the execution of a sports event) to hold the sponsor liable for his participation. After all, there are no contractual regulations between these parties. Here, the general terms and conditions of the organizer apply.

However, there are cases where a **sponsor can be held liable**. This can be the case if the sponsor provides products, services, or employees as part of the implementation of a sponsoring project. A sponsor pursues communicative goals with his commitment in sports and demands corresponding services from the sponsored party. However, these also depend on unforeseeable factors that the sponsored party cannot always influence, such as media presence, number of viewers/followers, etc. Therefore, it is important for the sponsored party to be excluded from liability regarding the achievement of the sponsor's communicative goals, unless they are the main part of the agreed service. Excluded from this is the culpable violation of contractual obligations.

The **interest in performance** refers to the interest of the sponsored party in the proper fulfillment of the contract towards the sponsor. The formulation of an interest in performance in the sponsoring contract helps the sponsored party to limit claims for damages for culpable behavior on their part to a certain amount. If the amount of damage can be quantified and measured due to culpable behavior of the sponsored party, the sponsor will claim the damage from the sponsored party. To minimize this risk, the contract limits the amount of the interest in performance towards the sponsor.

The consideration of **contractual penalties** in the sponsoring contract serves to sanction non-performed services. They must not be disproportionately high. The formulation of contractual penalties is mainly found in the field of sports sponsoring application, as there is the possibility of damaging the sponsor in certain offenses. For example, a contractual penalty for doping or fraud offenses could consist of reclaiming the sponsoring services of the past two years.

For reasons of legal certainty, the **time limits** must also be regulated in the sponsoring contract. This concerns the question of when the agreement comes into effect. This can be the time of signature, but also another time. The sponsoring contract regulates not only its entry into force but also the termination of the sponsoring relationship. Accordingly, termination is not necessary. Unlimited sponsoring contracts contain corresponding termination clauses. The following **termination rules** are common in sponsoring contracts:

- Termination of the contract without ordinary termination (ordinary termination before the end of the contract term is not possible),
- Termination of the contract with ordinary termination (ordinary termination before the end of the contract term is possible),
- Automatic extension of the sponsoring contract (contract automatically extends under the same conditions if one of the contracting parties does not terminate in due time),
- Indefinite contracts (should include a right to ordinary termination, otherwise the statutory notice periods apply),
- Extraordinary termination of the contract.

Renegotiating and regulating sponsoring contracts after termination or expiration involves considerable time and financial effort. Therefore, clauses are often included in the contract that automatically extend the cooperation after the contract term has expired. This allows both parties to keep an **extension of the contract** under the same conditions open. With option rights, the sponsor is granted the right to unilaterally extend the contract within a specified period. This is advantageous for the sponsor, but can be disadvantageous for the sponsored party if circumstances have changed significantly.

A contract within the framework of sports sponsoring is a legally unregulated, so-called **atypical contract**. In the event of a **performance disturbance** (non-fulfillment of agreed performance), general contract law applies to this type of contract. The conditions and legal consequences for an **early termination of the contract** by ordinary or extraordinary termination without legal regulation are usually agreed separately.

Not only breaches of the contract agreements allow for an **immediate termination**. Violations of game and competition rules, club or association regulations, or violation of laws can also lead to an immediate termination of the contract. An immediate termination can also occur for an important reason. The **reasons for an immediate termination** include, for example:

- Implementation of the sponsoring contract not possible (e.g., cancellation of the sponsored sports event, illness or injury of the sponsored athlete, etc.),
- Changes in the basic conditions at the sponsor (e.g., change of ownership, company transformations, change of shareholder, etc.),
- Unreasonable change in the conditions at the sponsor, thereby negatively affecting the interests of the sponsored party (e.g., image problems of the sponsor, reorientation of the company, etc.),
- Intentional discontinuation of the sponsored activities by the sponsored party,
- Prohibition of contractually agreed sponsoring measures by legal regulations,
- Changed communication strategy of the sponsor,
- Insolvencies, etc.

In addition to the termination regulations, the sponsoring contract must specify the **consequences of a termination**. This raises the question of whether and to what extent already granted services are to be refunded. If there is no agreement, a refund is not applicable and thus poses a risk for both contract parties.

12.4 Dispute Resolution

It is by no means uncommon for different views on the implementation of the collaboration to arise during a sponsoring relationship. It is not even the supposed important reasons for a disagreement, but often it is simply small annoyances in everyday life that can lead to larger dis. Therefore, a regulation is agreed upon for such cases, which as soon as possible ensures a constructive fulfillment of the partnership again in a time- and cost-saving manner, before both parties suffer damage. An overview of the **dispute resolution** of sponsoring contracts is shown in Fig. 12.3.

Unless disagreements are resolved through **direct talks**, an **arbitration procedure** could otherwise be agreed upon, ranging from the mediator to the appointed arbitrator. In a **mediation**, the mediator helps the parties find a solution themselves, in an arbitration procedure the arbitrator decides on a dispute between two parties.

Since January 1, 2008, the **German Sports Arbitration Court** has been located at the DIS (German Institution for Arbitration). It is based on a joint initiative of the National Anti-Doping Agency (NADA) Foundation and the DIS. The DIS Sports Arbitration Rules (DIS-SportSchO) were specifically developed for the resolution of disputes related to sports, e.g., doping offenses, disputes in connection with sports events, transfer disputes, license contracts, sponsoring contracts, club disputes, etc. (see also https://www.dis-sportschiedsgericht.de).

12.5 Tax Aspects in Sports Sponsoring

In addition to contractual design, **tax aspects** also need to be considered in sports sponsoring. For the sponsor, the central question is whether they can claim the expenses incurred with the sponsoring commitment as tax advantages. From the perspective of the sponsored party, the primary interest is whether the payments or monetary benefits flowing from the sponsor are taxable. The sponsor's expenses are generally considered as **business expenses** according to § 4 paragraphs 4 and 5 of the Income Tax Act (EStG). The basis for the tax treatment of sponsoring was created on 18.02.1998 in the so-called

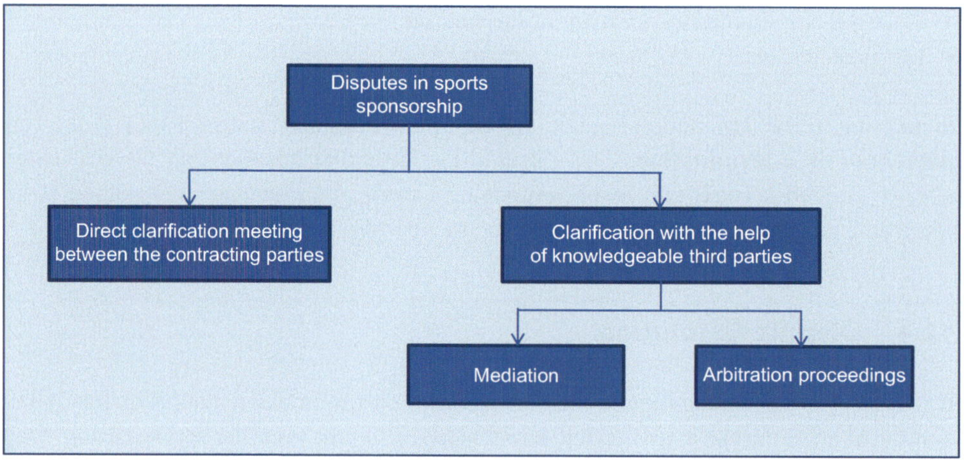

Fig. 12.3 Dispute resolution in sponsoring contracts

"sponsoring decree" of the Federal Ministry of Finance. This decree has significantly eased the burden for companies involved in sponsoring (see Bruhn, 2018, pp. 167 ff.).

Sponsoring expenses are considered fully **deductible business expenses,** "if the sponsor seeks economic benefits, which lie particularly in securing or increasing his corporate reputation, for his company or wants to advertise for products of his company" (BMF letter of 18.02.1998 IV B 2–S 2144–40/98; Federal Ministry of Finance, 1998, p. 212). Applied to practice, this means that any consideration that has an advertising effect for the sponsor is suitable as a justification for a business expense. However, various borderline questions remain open in the classification of sponsoring expenses as deductible business expenses, and no reliable criteria for differentiation have been developed to date. The problem of differentiating between a pure attention effect for the sponsor—which is not considered a business purpose—on the one hand, and image advertising as a business expense on the other, is mentioned as an example (Mitschke, 2007, pp. 133 f.; Klatt-Wenderodt, 2016).

Tax aspects also come into play for the sponsored parties, with the taxation of the received funds depending on whether the sponsored parties are non-profit or not. On the side of **non-profit sponsored party**, it is necessary to distinguish, among other things, whether the sponsored parties provide active or passive advertising services for the sponsor, enter into cooperation with the sponsor or act independently. The inflows to **non-charitable sponsored party** will be income from trade, self-employed or non-self-employed work, or considered as rental income, depending on the design of the sponsoring contract, resulting in different taxation models.

As a rule, a clear **separation between charitable and economic activities** (e.g., by founding an advertising GmbH that belongs to the non-profit association) is necessary. Only with a precise separation of the financial flows are tax problems avoided.

So-called VIP measures also require **special tax treatment** in sponsoring, for example when free tickets are given to business friends or customers. A basic deduction as a business expense is only considered in these cases if the invited guests are considered potential customers or contact persons for maintaining business relationships (Bruhn & Mehlinger, 1995, 1999; Klatt-Wenderodt, 2016). To meet this requirement, the measures must take place within an appropriate framework for business discussions. The tax treatment is different again if tickets are given away for private use, and the business expenses are gifts (i.e., according to § 4 paragraph 5, sentence 1 No. 1 EStG), which are deductible according to the amount limit mentioned there (Klatt-Wenderodt, 2016).

12.6 Key Points

The collaboration between the sponsored party and the sponsoring company should ideally be cast into a legally binding and clear agreement. Accordingly, there are certain legal aspects to consider in sports sponsoring.

Key Points

1. The sponsor and the sponsored party seal their partnership on the **basis of the general law of obligations regulated in the BGB (German Civil Code)**, the regulations there must be observed.
2. Both contract parties (e.g., sponsor and sports club) can **individually determine the contents of their agreement**, therefore, interests should be considered in advance.
3. The more individual points of the collaboration are regulated in advance, the fewer problems can be expected afterwards. The **possible legal uncertainty** due to lack of statutory regulations can be largely excluded by a detailed contractual regulation.
4. A **written contract in sports sponsoring** is always preferable to a verbal one, i.e., the written agreement is the standard in sports sponsoring.
5. The **contract design** is usually undertaken by the sponsored parties. The content formulation is generally easier for them than for the sponsor, as they are more familiar with the specific sponsoring rights and their usage possibilities. The sponsor has to deal intensively with the rights and contract rules.
6. When designing the contract, it is advisable to involve **legal experts** such as experienced lawyers in addition to the directly involved parties.
7. Under the contract point **performance of the sponsor**, the sponsor will have to check whether, in addition to monetary amounts, goods or services can also be provided for the performance of the sponsored party.
8. Also, the **performance of the sponsored party** needs to be fixed, i.e., to avoid misunderstandings and misinterpretations of the sponsoring rights, these need to be detailed and comprehensively recorded.
9. Further **central contract points** need to be considered, such as the position of the sponsor in the sponsoring structure, contractual penalties, and geographical and temporal scope.
10. The legal and other bases for the **tax treatment** of the sponsoring need to be considered and designed accordingly. These have brought significant relief for companies engaged in sponsoring in recent years.

References

B

Bruhn, M. (2018). *Sponsoring. Systematische Planung und integrativer Einsatz* (6. Aufl.). https://doi.org/10.1007/978-3-658-13313-9.

Bruhn, M., & Mehlinger, R. (1995). *Rechtliche Gestaltung des Sponsoring. Vertragsrecht, Steuerrecht, Medienrecht, Wettbewerbsrecht* (Bd. I, Allgemeiner Teil, 2. Aufl.). Beck.

Bruhn, M., & Mehlinger, R. (1999). *Rechtliche Gestaltung des Sponsoring. Sport-, Kultur-, Sozial-, Umwelt- und Programmsponsoring* (Bd. II, Spezieller Teil, 2. Aufl.). Beck.

Bundesministerium der Finanzen (BMF 1998). Ertragssteuerliche Behandlung des Sponsoring vom 18.02.1998 IV B 2–S 2144–40/98 (BStBl I S. 212). https://esth.bundesfinanzministerium.de/esth/2016/C-Anhaenge/Anhang-16/IV/inhalt.html.

K

Klatt-Wenderodt, S. (2016). Steuerliche Aspekte von Sponsoring insbesondere auch bei Hospitality-Leistungen und VIP-Logen. https://www.hk24.de/produktmarken/beratung-service/recht_und_steuern/steuerrecht/ertrag_lohnsteuer/einkommen_koerper_steuer/steuern-sponsoring/1167790#titleInText1. Accessed: 8. June 2016.

M

Mitschke, M. (2007). Rechtliche Grenzen des Sponsoring. Ahlert, D., Woisetschläger, D., & Vogel, V. (Hrsg.), *Exzellentes Sponsoring. Innovative Ansätze und Best Practices für das Markenmanagement* (2. Aufl., S. 119–135). https://doi.org/10.1007/978-3-8350-9639-4_6.

P

Poser, U., & Backes, B. (2010). *Sponsoringvertrag: Bd. 26. Beck'sche Musterverträge.* Beck.

Services of Sports Agencies 13

Contents

Abstract

As a rule, sports agencies have a proven marketing expertise and a larger customer or client base. Their focus can concentrate on certain sports areas (e.g., winter sports). However, in many cases, they cover all sports and all topics related to sports sponsoring. Sports agencies can provide important support for sponsored parties as well as sponsors in partner acquisition and sponsoring implementation. The involvement of a sports agency is a make-or-buy decision. The chapter presents various types of sports agencies and their services. However, special aspects must also be considered when working with agencies. The agency Sportfive in cooperation with Hertha BSC is described as an example.

M. Bruhn and P. Rohlmann, *Sports Sponsoring*,
https://doi.org/10.1007/978-3-658-44171-5_13

13.1 Sports Sponsoring as a Make-or-Buy Decision

For the rights holders, the fundamental question arises whether a cooperation with a sports marketing agency is even a consideration for him or whether he can or wants to handle the task in sponsoring independently. In principle, this is a **Make-or-buy decision**. In a make decision, an in-house solution is sought, i.e., own organizational units carry out the engagements in sports sponsoring for the company using on-board resources. In contrast, a buy decision means that various agencies take over the task of carrying out the sponsorings. In Fig. 13.1, the differences as well as the associated advantages and disadvantages are listed. Cooperation with a sponsoring or sports marketing agency is especially important for the sponsored party, the less experienced he is and the less his expertise, which is indispensable today for the professional handling of a sponsoring project.

If one looks at for example the **cooperation in German professional football** in recent years, two central tendencies can be observed. On the one hand, there is a tendency towards self-marketing. On the other hand, if external marketing is sought, the

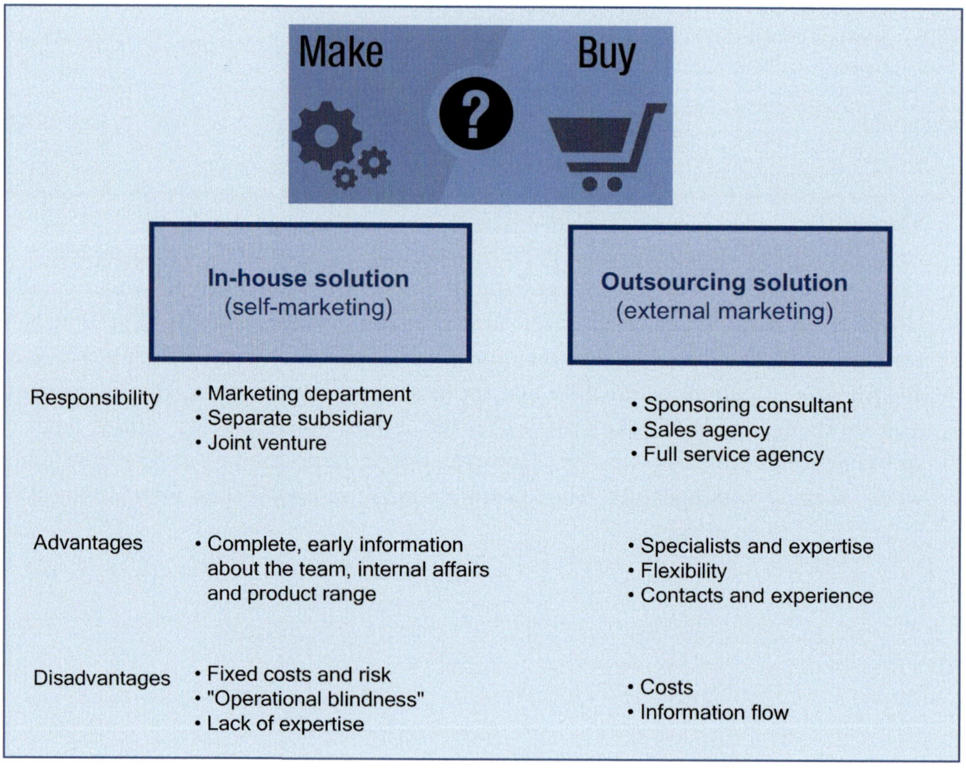

Fig. 13.1 Basic decision on the involvement of a sports agency in sponsoring

market is dominated by a few marketing agencies. This marketer situation is shown in Fig. 13.2 in the first and second Bundesliga.

Once the decision for external marketing has been made, the great challenge lies in selecting the right choice from a multitude of marketing agencies active in the sports sector. With such a large number, it is not easy for an (inexperienced) sports provider to make a selection among the agencies. Here, a structured approach is advisable. The sponsoring provider first has to make a decision about which services the agency has to provide for him. In a further step, it must be determined which qualifications the agency must bring for his specific concern. The sports actor will define these qualifications in the form of **selection criteria for the agency** or within a checklist. In the context of rights marketing, the following questions are relevant, for example:

- Does the agency have experience in the acute marketing topic, i.e. sponsoring?
- Does it have contacts with potential interested parties?
- What business contacts does the agency have?
- How extensive is the agency's range of services, possibly as a full-service offer in terms of planning, implementation and control?
- How can the seriousness/credibility of the agency be assessed?
- What are the strengths and weaknesses of the agency?
- What references can the agency provide?
- On which sponsoring projects has the agency worked so far?
- What reputation does the agency have in the sports industry?
- Do the agency's fees correspond to market conditions?
- Does the agency offer individual and creative advice?
- among others.

Bundesliga	**2011/12**	**2016/17**	**2017/18**	**2018/19**	**2019/20**	**2020/21**	**2021/22**
Self-marketing	6	5	6	9	7	8	9
Sportfive incl. predecessor	8	6	7	7	4	6	6
Infront	3	5	5	2	6	4	3
Other	1	2			1		
All clubs	18	18	18	18	18	18	18
Bundesliga 2	**2011/12**	**2016/17**	**2017/18**	**2018/19**	**2019/20**	**2020/21**	**2021/22**
Self-marketing	5	5	5	8	10	11	9
Sportfive incl. predecessor	7	7	6	4	5	4	6
Infront	2	3	2	3	2	3	3
Other	4	3	5	3	1		
All clubs	18	18	18	18	18	18	18

Fig. 13.2 Marketer situation in German professional football. (*Sources*: Stadionwelt and PR-Marketing)

In the sales area, sports actors need numerous cooperation partners, where sports marketing agencies can provide valuable assistance. This will be better the more accurately a detailed requirement profile is used by the rights holders in the selection. However, in most sponsoring relationships, more than one agency is involved because both parties in sports sponsoring each bring their "specialist agency" with their specific tasks. Nevertheless, it is advisable that the immediate partners of the sponsoring engagement reserve the "final say". In Fig. 13.3, the **relationship structure of agencies in sports sponsoring** is shown.

13.2 Selection of Sports Agencies

Sports agencies are marketing companies that act as intermediaries between sports, media, and business. These agencies are either "full-service providers", i.e., from consulting to mediation to implementation, or "specialists", i.e., they focus on areas such as

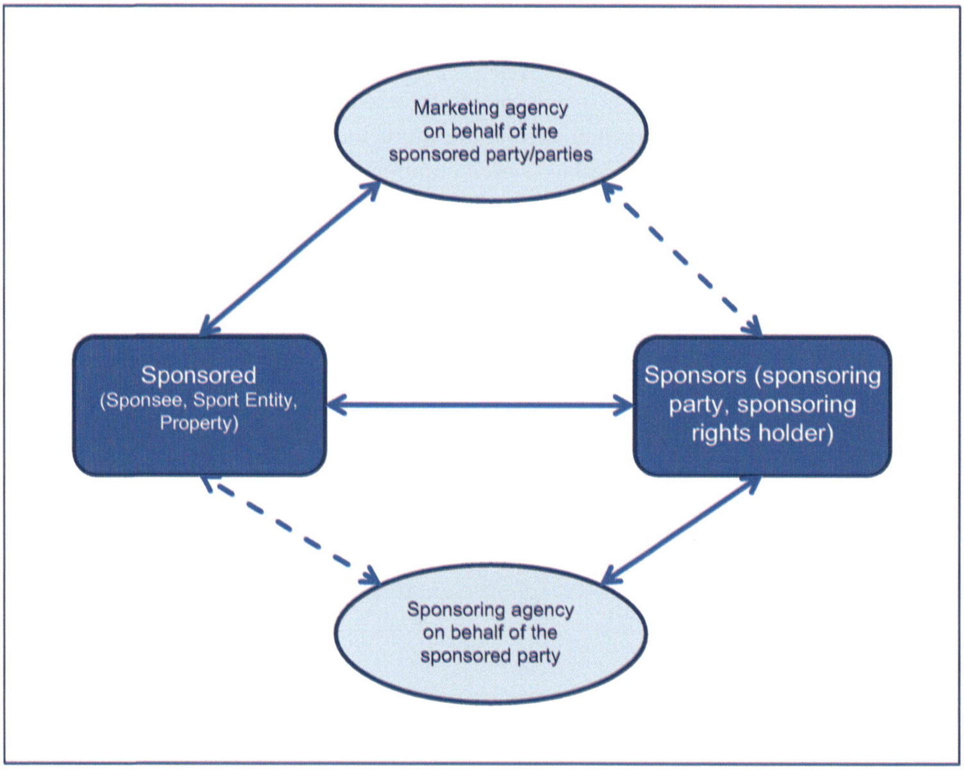

Fig. 13.3 Agency relationships in sports sponsoring. (*Source*: based on Walzel & Schubert, 2018, p. 24)

the development of sponsoring concepts, rights and/or advertising space sales, license exploitation, athlete marketing, etc.

The **competency and service catalog** of sports agencies will vary depending on their orientation, for example, the following services can be listed:

- Responsible management of a client's sports marketing including concept and control of the sponsoring volume,
- Creation of sports communication concepts in analog and digital space,
- Planning and execution of events,
- Exploitation of sports marketing rights and licenses,
- Placement and sale of analog and digital advertising spaces,
- Marketing of television and other media rights,
- Acquisition and support of sponsored parties and sponsors,
- Consultation of sponsored parties and sponsors,
- Management of athletes, etc.

The motivation of specialized agencies for a sponsoring commitment arises from the economic success opportunities that they derive from their specialization in advising on sponsorings. Accordingly, sponsoring agencies see themselves as service companies that are rewarded for their services by the constitutive elements of sponsoring, i.e., sponsors and/or sponsored parties (Drees, 1989, p. 89).

The **advantages** that speak for the use of external consultants in sports sponsoring include additional know-how and experience, as well as the presence of a network of contacts. Also worth highlighting are the possibilities of mediation between the sponsor and the sponsored party and the receipt of an objective and realistic recommendation about entering into a sports sponsoring. This is contrasted with various **disadvantages**, such as additional costs, no B provision of funds for initial services of an agency on the part of the sponsored parties, the dependence on agencies in the assurance of exclusive rights, and the risk of falling into "unscrupulous" intermediaries.

As a general guideline for the selection of a sports marketing agency, the following **requirement profile** serves as an example (Bruhn, 2018, p. 75): Profound experiences in the field of marketing and communication, expertise or "insider knowledge" in sports topics and sports so as well as personal contacts to institutions, associations, and important persons in sports (network) are expected. Also, contacts to the media, full-service offers regarding the implementation and execution of sponsoring measures as well as objective advice, free from marketing interests, and seriousness or credibility regarding persons and concepts are important (Mussler, 1989).

13.3 Types and Services of Sports Agencies

In the market of sports agencies, there are not only tendencies towards concentration, but also the tendency towards specialization of service offers. In principle, the following **types of sports agencies** can be distinguished (see the following Bruhn, 2018, pp. 73 f., 504 ff.):

- Consulting agencies,
- Mediation agencies,
- Implementation agencies,
- Athlete agencies.

These agencies offer a broad and deep range of services for sponsors and sponsored parties in their respective fields.

Consulting Agencies
Consulting agencies focus on the conceptual support of a sponsoring company or a sponsored sports actor. Their main **tasks** include:

- Getting to know and understanding the company willing to sponsor or the one to be sponsored regarding the use of sports sponsoring (data collection, conversations, etc.),
- Developing solutions for specific objectives of a company or the one to be sponsored (conceptual proposals),
- Evaluations of sports sponsoring or individual rights and price ideas for the one to be sponsored,
- Presentation, discussion, and adoption of a sponsoring concept,
- Determination and control of a company's sports sponsoring budget (acquisition costs and activation),
- Support/guidance during the implementation,
- Sponsor coordination, final control, and possible learnings for the sponsored party.

For the conceptual and accompanying work in sports sponsoring, such consulting agencies usually receive a fixed fee according to the usual daily rates. Less often, success-dependent participation commissions on the realized sponsoring engagements are agreed upon in addition to a fixed basic amount. However, success-dependent payments are more common when advising individual athletes.

Brokerage Agencies
Brokerage agencies—also called **rights brokers**—are agencies that are commissioned by sports clubs, sports associations, athletes, and/or sports teams, media, etc., to sell certain usage rights (e.g., advertising, broadcasting, and licensing rights) to sponsors, media, advertising material producers, etc. Occasionally, such agencies also buy the

rights themselves (exclusively acquired usage rights for unrestricted implementation) to then resell them to specific rights users (e.g., companies willing to sponsor). Many sports clubs want to rely on the help of sports agencies for sponsor acquisition. The cooperation is particularly useful when the rights holders and clients themselves do not have the necessary sponsoring experience, the resources (experts), and the time for acquisition, and have few contacts with potential sponsors. For the acquired sponsoring revenues, brokerage agencies receive an agency commission of at least 10 to 25%. In-kind services and barter deals (bartering) are usually included in the total amount of a sports sponsoring engagement.

An **example** of this is provided by Borussia Dortmund. In 2017, the club and Sportfive (then known as Lagardère Sports) prematurely extended their successful cooperation until 30.06.2026. Since 1999, the sports rights agency has been the overall marketing partner of the traditional club and has been responsible for all the club's marketing activities. With the new sales or brokerage partnership, which began in July 2020, Borussia Dortmund and the leading European sports marketing agency want to jointly pursue the Bundesliga club's ambitious growth targets in the commercial sector.

Implementation Agencies

Implementation agencies—often also **event agencies**—help with the implementation, which includes legal design, event and athlete management, press work, etc., as needed. For example, certain specialized agencies can take over the entire contract work (from individual sponsoring contracts to complete events), the entire implementation of stadium advertising (from the boards to the loudspeakers to the video board) or the digital spaces (account management, content management, etc.). Many sports venue and event service providers work according to international quality standards and set trends, especially in TV-oriented brand and sponsor representation. Here, the leading international marketers, organizers, sponsors, or arena operators usually rely on certain companies that have been successful in the industry for years.

Athlete Agencies

A special feature in this category are athlete agencies, which have to work much more elaborately than the other types of agencies. The activities can be described in more detail using the example of athlete management. Here, the agency representatives as advisors or intermediaries are important advisors and competent contacts in almost all areas relevant to the athletes. These include the following **services**:

- Acquisition of sponsors and advertising partners,
- Acquisition of equipment contracts,
- Contract negotiations,
- Arranging autograph sessions, appearances at sports press festivals, trade fairs, sales-promoting measures, gala evenings, television shows, etc.,

- Financial management,
- Career planning (times during and after the active sports career),
- Tax and other legal advice,
- Public relations/media contacts, etc.

Especially in athlete management, agencies wish for a long-term contract, and to conclude it early, in order to benefit from potential performance developments of their athlete. The payment of athlete agencies is similar to the payment of an artist agent. Such are usually paid on the basis of an agency fee, but there are also mixed forms (fixed salary, success components, cost reimbursement, etc.).

Actors in the sports agency sector are often subject to ownership changes and acquisitions, resulting in a high turnover in this market.

13.4 Sports Agencies in Practice

The **market for sports agencies** has developed very strongly over the past decades, depending on the attractiveness of various sports. This is accompanied by **concentration trends** among sports agencies. The 40 most valuable sports agencies in the world conducted business worth more than 56 billion USD in 2020 and were able to collect commissions worth 2.9 billion USD, representing an increase of 10% compared to 2019 and a growth of 55% since 2015. The annual contract values consist of both sponsoring contracts and player transfers. Of the contracts concluded in 2020, 60% were accounted for by the ten largest sports agencies alone. These sports agencies are listed in Fig. 13.4.

The renowned Creative Artists Agency (CAA) leads the Forbes ranking with more than 8.8 billion USD in managed contract value and 419 million USD in commission (Forbes, 2020). Wasserman follows in second place. The agency increased its business by 37% to 5.7 billion USD in contracts and 331 million USD in commissions, largely thanks to the introduction of a number of smaller firms, which are also mentioned in the ranking in Fig. 13.4, including the football agencies Key Sports, Top Value and Mondial Promotion as well as the hockey boutiques Acme World Sports and Orr Hockey Group.

Agents in sports, who act as **advisors and intermediaries for athletes**, are very important in the professional sports market and a significant influence group in the business. Especially football agents play a crucial role in the development of a professional footballer. They broker most of the million-dollar contracts in the football world. In doing so, they deliver the largest possible deals that fulfill the players' desire to play for the desired team. While they handle the business with the clubs, most player agents are generously rewarded financially. Selected agents sometimes earn more than coaches and players combined.

In Fig. 13.5, the top 10 highest-earning **football agents in the world** are listed according to their managed player values, which is always a snapshot, as the market

Agency	Contract Value	Commission	Ø Rate	Sport
Creative Artists Agency (CAA)	8850	419.3	4.7 %	Basketball, Football, Hockey, Baseball, Soccer
Wasserman Media Group LLC	5700	331.4	5.8 %	Basketball, Football, Hockey, Baseball, Golf, Soccer
Excel Sports Management	4000	191.9	4.8 %	Basketball, Baseball, Golf
Boras Corporation	3200	161.1	5.0 %	Baseball
ICM Stellar Sports	1400	142.6	10.2 %	Football, Soccer
Octagon	2400	112.4	4.7 %	Football, Hockey, Basketball, Baseball, Golf, Tennis
Gestifute	1000	104.0	10.4 %	Soccer
Athletes First	4400	85.2	1.9 %	Football
Mino Raiola	848	84.7	10.0 %	Soccer
Newport Sports	1900	77.6	4.1 %	Hockey
Top 10	33,698	1,710.2	5.1 %	

Fig. 13.4 Contract values and commission revenues of the ten largest sports agencies. (*Sources*: forbes.com and transfermarkt.com; figures for 2020 in million USD)

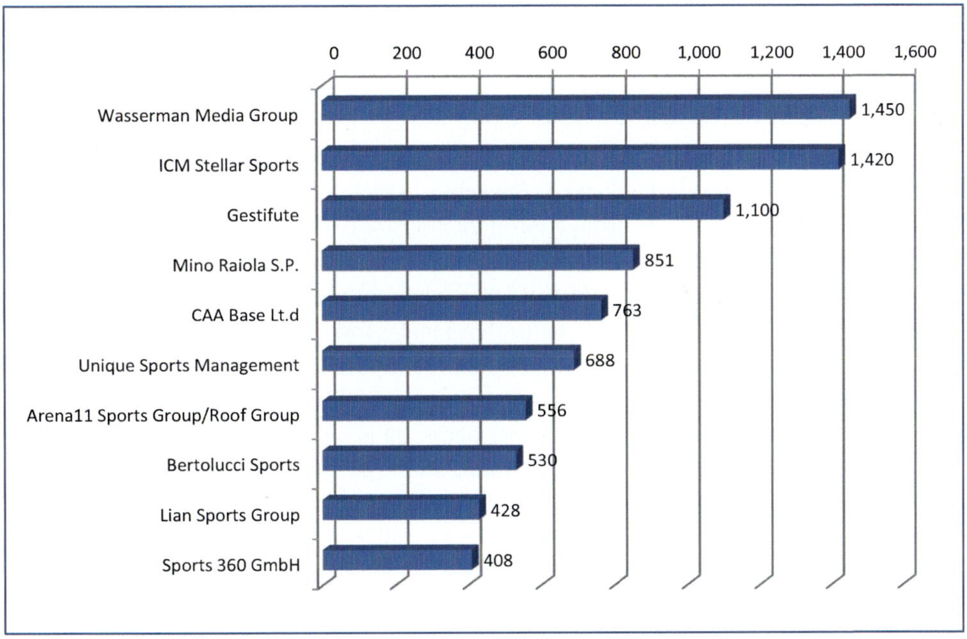

Fig. 13.5 Contract values of the ten largest football agencies worldwide. (*Sources*: Statista 2022d; forbes.com and transfermarkt.com; figures in million EUR)

values of individual footballers can change very quickly. The top 10 in the industry alone account for a contract value of approximately 8.2 billion EUR. The leading player agency worldwide is the American agency Wasserman Media Group, which has systematically acquired ambitious smaller agencies in recent years, and especially has many players from the UK under contract.

Barnett's ICM Stellar Sports and Wasserman Media Group—both operating their global football activities from London—are among the most successful agencies in this sport. There is overall strong **competition among sports agencies**, especially between the industry giants (ESPN, 2017). There are also major differences in the type of marketing, for example in the design of relationships with athletes and their environment.

13.5 Agency Collaboration in Discussion

There are not too many highly specialized agencies in the sports market. They usually have been working in this field for decades, and there are arguments for their inclusion when sponsors and sponsored parties do not want to be negligent. This is also due to the fact that **differences between sports** exist. Football is quite different from rugby, sailing, motorsport, and athletics. It's not about rules and sports applications, but rather about goals and usage possibilities, about different communication goals and values associated with the sport. It is no coincidence that, for example, Deutsche Telekom is particularly strongly involved in football, Prada is active in sailing (Luna Rossa in the America's Cup), and Mapei has been associated with the world of cycling for years.

In the current **market for sports sponsoring**, which has also developed into a data-based, cross-platform, and multi-layered marketing tool, success is more likely to occur the more professionally the processes of sports sponsoring are planned and implemented. However, some sports actors do not have the necessary prerequisites and can only build them up gradually (e.g., rapid rise to professional sports; personnel changes, etc.). In such cases, sports sponsoring agencies are (almost) indispensable, as decisions are based more on rational than on "gut-driven" foundations.

However, collaboration with sponsoring agencies is also associated with **controversies** and is accordingly discussed (see Bruhn, 2018, p. 504 ff.). The following **advantages** are mainly mentioned for a connection with external consultants:

- Experts bring time, know-how, and experience that are beneficial for systematic and professional work.
- Consultants have a network of contacts that they bring into their work.
- With the help of consultants, the participants manage to understand the specific mindset of their counterpart and to take it into account in their own decisions.
- Independent consultants give sponsors and those sponsored objective and realistic recommendations regarding the entering of sponsorings, based on knowledge of the sponsoring market.

On the other hand, **disadvantages** are also mentioned that are associated with such cooperation. Here are some examples:

- The use of consultants incurs additional costs.
- The sponsored parties lack—less in sports, but more in areas such as culture, social and environment—the funds to finance the necessary initial services of the agency (e.g., creation of a sponsoring concept) from their own resources.
- For the sponsored parties, there is a dependency on consultants or intermediaries if they have been granted certain exclusive rights.

In the sponsoring market, there are also occasionally "unscrupulous" intermediaries and consultants who pick up sponsoring as a topic for "quick money" and are not able to provide solid and well-founded work.

The type of **consultation** companies currently use in the field of sponsoring is shown in Fig. 13.6. It becomes clear that rarely the classic creative and media agencies are used, but rather specialized sponsoring agencies. While sponsoring planning is mainly carried out by internal departments—but also by specialist agencies in many cases—specialist agencies for sponsoring or events are particularly hired for implementation. For contract design, companies also seek support from lawyers and law firms, while market research institutes and specialist institutes for recording and evaluating media presence are mainly used for success control.

Despite the multitude of agencies that have now included sponsoring in their range of services, there is often still a **deficit of consulting or communication agencies** that are capable of developing sponsoring concepts and simultaneously networking them with other communication tools in terms of content, form, and timing. However, as sponsoring companies will increasingly demand complexly networked sponsoring strategies in the future, agencies will also come under increasing pressure to meet these requirements.

The fact that traditional media agencies are increasingly recognizing the increased **importance of sponsoring** makes it clear that sponsoring is now accepted as a serious marketing tool. At the same time, this also creates new competition for established sponsoring agencies to effectively sell their specialization in the future. In addition to the deficit of full-service providers, given the high importance of sponsoring in international communication and the communication of an international market presence, it also becomes clear that there are currently too few internationally experienced sponsoring agencies or sponsoring managers. Here too, the pressure on the international agency scene to design and implement appropriate concepts for customers will increase.

	Contract design	Planning	Implementation	Performance review
PR agency(ies)	11 %	30 %	36 %	23 %
Specialist agency/ agencies for sponsoring and events	23 %	40 %	53 %	21 %
Full service agency(ies)	3 %	12 %	15 %	8 %
Creative agency(ies)	1 %	18 %	23 %	1 %
Media agency(ies)	5 %	23 %	20 %	11 %
Lawyer(s), law firm(s)	30 %	5 %	2 %	2 %
Market research institute(s)	1 %	9 %	5 %	44 %
Specialized institute(s) for recording and evaluating media presence	0 %	2 %	1 %	43 %
Mainly carried out by internal departments	35 %	29 %	29 %	19 %

Fig. 13.6 Subject and frequency of cooperation with sponsoring agencies. (*Source*: Pilot Checkpoint, 2002, pp. 69 f.)

Example: Sportfive and Hertha BSC Berlin

Hertha BSC—also known as Hertha or "old lady"—is a well-known professional football club from Berlin. After a sporting decline in the 1980s down to the 3rd league, the Herthaners have been playing in the 2nd Bundesliga since 1990, but without really making sporting and economic progress. As early as 1992, the Bertelsmann subsidiary Ufa-Sports (predecessor of Sportfive) acquired the advertising rights in the Olympic Stadium—at that time Hertha was in the middle of the second league. In 1994, the club was on the verge of ruin. During this time, in 1994, the first comprehensive marketing commitment of the Hamburg sports rights marketer Ufa Sports emerged. Despite the precarious situation, the marketers had recognized that a strong Hertha would have great potential. So a contract was concluded, which was initially valid until 2003. All revenues from the marketing were initially divided in a ratio of 60 (Hertha) to 40 (Ufa), from 2000 in a ratio of 80 to 20. Advance payments and excellent sales connections of the agency then initiated the turnaround. At the end of the 1996/1997 season, the club was promoted to the top league.

Between 2009 and 2014, Hertha proved to be a "yo-yo team" with constant changes between the 1st and 2nd Bundesliga, which put extreme strain on the

Hertha BSC	1995/96	…	2000/01	….	2015/16	2016/17	2017/18	2018/19	2019/20	2020/21
Marketing income (sponsorship, hospitality, merchandising) in EUR million	2.0		21.1		30.3	30.0	32.1	33.6	33.4	22.2
League	2. BL		BL		BL	BL	BL	BL	BL	BL

Fig. 13.7 Marketing revenues of Hertha BSC Berlin with agency support. (*Source*: Club and media information)

financial situation in the club and repeatedly led to new conditions with the agency (i.e., infusion of fresh money or advance payments) and changed rights assignments. Despite interim changes in the ownership structure of the agency and in the scope of cooperation (including 2005, 2014), Germany's leading sports rights agency Sportfive has currently extended its comprehensive marketing contract with Hertha BSC until 2025. This makes Sportfive a strong partner alongside the capital club, which was relegated to the 2nd league in 2023, even after the entries of the international financial investor KKR (already exited) and the Tennor Holding by Lars Windhorst (also exited by sale to Triple 7). As part of the cooperation, Sportfive is responsible for the marketing of marketing and TV rights as well as hospitality and new media services. According to industry circles, the agency currently receives the usual 15–20% of the marketing revenues achieved and benefits from UEFA television money in the event of participation in a European competition. The marketing revenues of Hertha BSC are listed in Fig. 13.7. ◀

13.6 Key Points

The following are the most important aspects to consider when potential sponsoring partners collaborate with service agencies.

Key Points

1. The **collaboration of a participant in sports sponsoring with knowledgeable third parties** should fundamentally be examined and considered. Especially the less experience a partner can bring into the relationship, the more advantageous the collaboration with professional agencies is.
2. Engaged sports sponsoring agencies require a **clear mandate**: The sponsoring partner(s) must specify which tasks an agency should specifically perform.
3. When **selecting an agency**, a **requirement profile** is indispensable. The more comprehensive and clear the qualification criteria for the agency are defined and applied, the more promising the result of the agency's work will be.
4. Sports agencies are marketing companies that act as intermediaries between sports, media, and business. The **diversity of agencies** is large—from

full-service providers to specialized agencies. It is necessary to check what the sponsored parties or sponsor really needs.

5. The **focus of agency collaboration** for those to be sponsored lies in sales. The normal everyday life in a sports club will rarely allow extensive and time-consuming sales activities, so the involvement of specialists can be advantageous here.
6. In the **activation and specific implementation** of sponsorings in sports, agencies can provide quick and reliable support for the sponsor. Here too, the involvement of experts can be beneficial.
7. **Specialists and service providers** do cause costs, but they also bring enormous advantages. The use of various specialist agencies serves the purpose of making the sports sponsoring relationship a success, both for sponsors and for sponsored parties. This is often a consideration that pays off in view of the duration of a partnership.
8. Collaboration with agencies does not relieve the sponsoring participants from their own **participation** in terms of planning, designing, and controlling a sponsoring relationship: It's not just about workload relief, but also about a certain "learning by doing" and a better understanding of the interrelationships for a successful sponsoring in the sense of a "win-win" situation.
9. The **costs of sports sponsoring agencies** vary with the scope of their tasks and can be agreed upon partly as a fixed fee and partly depending on success. Here, the advantage of the remuneration needs to be checked.
10. In the future, increasingly complex networked sponsoring strategies will be demanded. Due to **new challenges**, some agencies may come under increased pressure to meet these requirements. Therefore, a continuous review of the collaboration with agencies is necessary.

References

B

Bruhn, M. (2018). *Sponsoring. Systematische Planung und integrativer Einsatz* (6. Aufl.). https://doi.org/10.1007/978-3-658-13313-9.

D

Drees, N. (1989). *Sportsponsoring*. https://doi.org/10.1007/978-3-663-06737-5

E

ESPN. (2017). Meet the men behind football's biggest deals, Beitrag vom 15.06.2017. https://www.espn.com/soccer/english-premier-league/23/blog/post/3143956/premier-league-and-la-liga-stars-like-gareth-bale-turn-to-these-agents-for-their-deals.

F

Forbes. (2020). The World's Most Valuable Sports Agencies 2020: CAA On Top, Wasserman Closes The Gap, Beitrag vom 22.12.2020. https://www.forbes.com/sites/jasonbelzer/2020/12/22/the-worlds-most-valuable-sports-agencies-2020-caa-on-top-as-wasserman-closes-the-gap/?sh=310827af136f.

M

Mussler, D. (1989). Organisation und Durchführung des Sponsoring. In A. Hermanns (Hrsg.), *Sport- und Kultursponsoring* (S. 29–38). Vahlen.

P

Pilot Checkpoint. (2002). *Sponsor visions 2002.*

S

Statista. (2022d). *Soccer agencies with the highest total market value of players worldwide as of March 2022.* https://www.statista.com/statistics/1125816/soccer-agencies-total-market-value/.

W

Walzel, S., & Schubert, M. (2018). *Sportsponsoring – Grundlagen, Konzeption und Wirkungen.* Springer Gabler. https://doi.org/10.1007/978-3-662-55246-9.

Trends in the Use of Sports Sponsoring 14

Contents

Abstract

The framework conditions of recent years have repeatedly made it clear how quickly changes in the environment and new topics arise that have a high impact on sports sponsoring activities. These and other topics, which have also been confirmed in a Delphi study, become relevant at different levels and must be taken into account in their entirety in future sponsoring decisions. Corresponding developments and trends are viewed from the perspective of the sponsoring participants, i.e., trends from the perspective of sports, companies, media, and agencies. In addition, trends among so-called "Sponvestors" are highlighted when companies engage as both investors and sponsors in sports. Concrete examples from sports clubs (FC St. Pauli, 1. FC Köln) and companies (Deutsche Telekom) as well as case studies from Viessmann and Red Bull illustrate the explanations.

M. Bruhn and P. Rohlmann, *Sports Sponsoring*,
https://doi.org/10.1007/978-3-658-44171-5_14

Sports Sponsoring has developed very dynamically over the last four decades. It has significantly increased in diversity and creativity. This is true both in terms of breadth **(Broadening)** and depth **(Deepening)** of sports Sponsoring. It can be assumed with certainty that this process will continue in the future. Therefore, an attempt is made here to highlight various trends from different perspectives.

Given the expected continued dynamic development, it can be assumed that this is merely a snapshot, as the economic, legal, technological, and other framework conditions are constantly changing. Nevertheless, some important **future topics in sports Sponsoring** are addressed below (see Fig. 14.1). These include topics such as the accuracy of target group targeting, the opening up of new markets, the internationalization of concepts, the consideration of sustainability aspects, the generation of new opportunities through digitization, the increasing importance of e-sports, and topics such as deepening and conversion, among others.

The following will highlight selected trends**trends of the actors involved in sports sponsoring**. These are trends from the perspective of sports, companies, media, and agencies. In addition, attention is drawn to a phenomenon that represents an intertwining of sports investors and sports sponsors and in which companies take on a new role as so-called "Sponvestors".

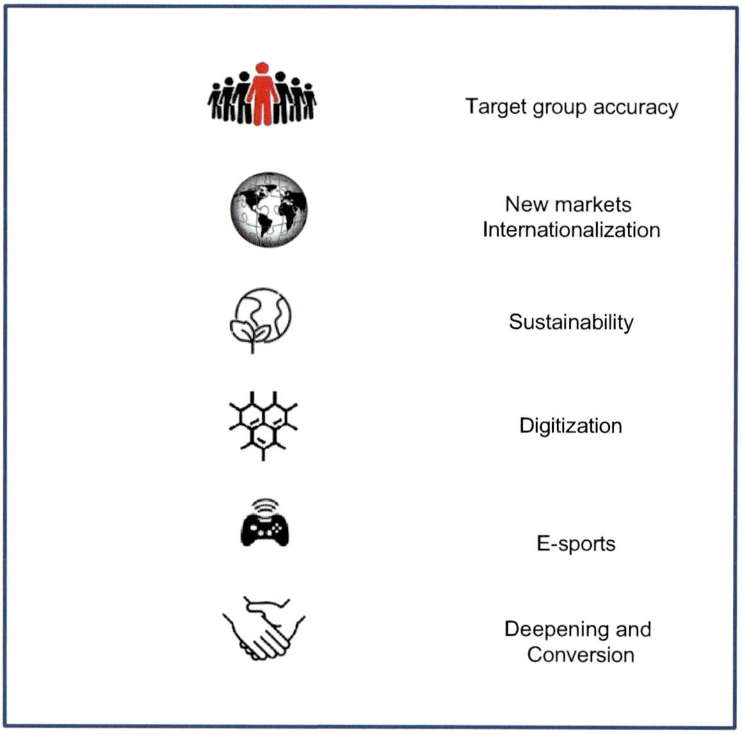

Fig. 14.1 Important future topics in sports Sponsoring. (*Source*: VSA, 2021)

14.1 Trends from a Sports Perspective

Changes in the environment constantly result in **adaptation requirements** for both the sponsoring actors and new challenges for decision-makers and service providers. Given the multitude of differentand not only isolated parameters, their consideration is made according to the categories of rights partners and competition as well as environment and technology (see Fig. 14.2).

In some areas of sports (e.g., football), the public image and the image of the professional sector are already damaged, and revenues are also declining in some cases. Many sports actors are working on a turnaround, especially away from the top. This is not only because certain megatrends exert clearer constraints, but also because other **stakeholders in sports sponsoring** such as fans, sponsors, and investors exert pressure (Gürtler & Möthe, 2022). In sports, however, the scope, duration, and credibility of the sponsors are also at the center of attention. The competition among sports actors forces constant investments (squad, coach, functional team, infrastructure, etc.), which should preferably be made through own funds and not through debts.

Fig. 14.3 shows which topics are associated with the accompanying**role change of rights holders in sports**. At the core are the necessary investments in the areas of

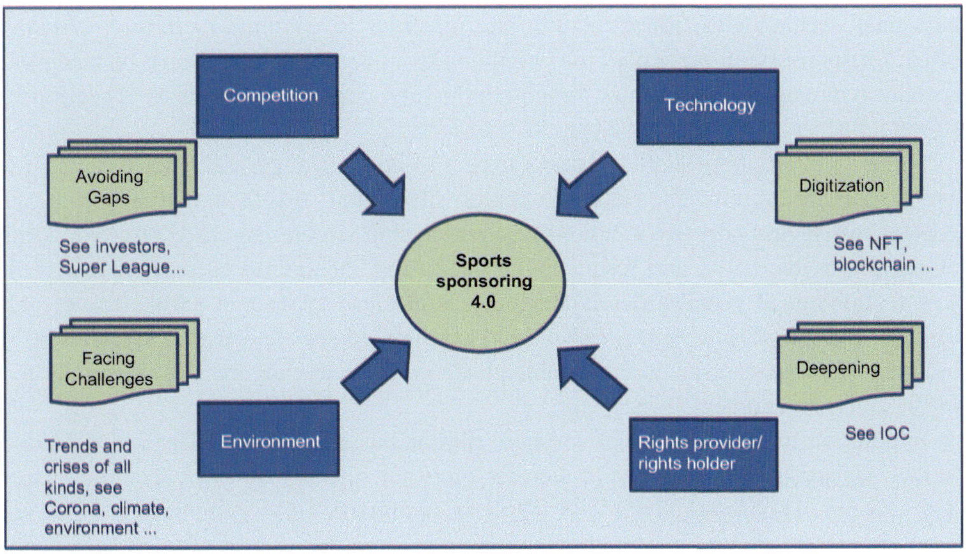

Fig. 14.2 Important influencing parameters in the sports sponsoring of the future

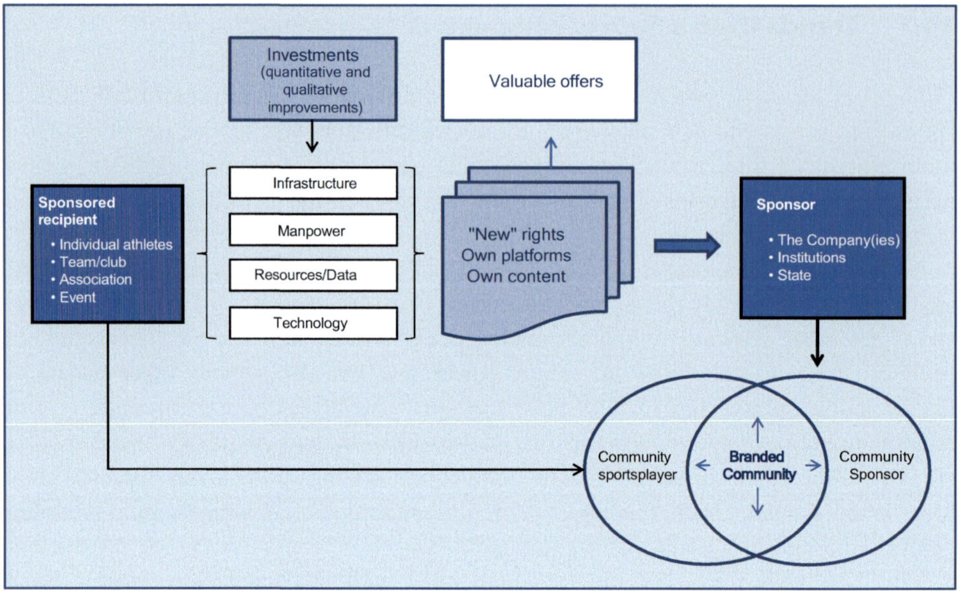

Fig. 14.3 Role change of rights holders in sports

personnel, technologies, infrastructure, etc., in order to continue to develop valuable offers for sponsors. In particular, the communities of the participants must be taken into account (community sports actor, brand community, community sponsor). They have a strong influence on the markets of sports sponsoring.

Sponsors and the associated partners expect technological prerequisites to be able to use the full spectrum of engagement—analog and digital—for their (partially changed) goals. Creative and effective solutions of a partnership require increased efforts in terms of manpower, expertise, and resources on the part of the sponsored parties. Especially new **technological possibilities** could increasingly lead sponsored parties to not only identify and award new rights, but also to produce content and media themselves, in order to offer a sponsoring party valuable platforms for achieving their goals, similar to a media house or a content agency.

In addition to new sources of revenue, **digital business models**offer rights holders further advantages that can lead to increased revenue downstream. One example is new data and new knowledge about fans. With an optimized CRM system, new types and forms of presentation of information (receptive or interactive offers) can be specifically transmitted to fans. In this way, new **community activities** of the clubs can also be increased in the future with the help of additional fan data. Synergies are also possible outside of the primary new business model.

The **social media activities of sports clubs** also offer even better exploitable potential. Clubs are finding it increasingly difficult to reach their fans today because analog advertising services are wearing out and organic reach on platforms such as Facebook is decreasing. As a result, clubs often cannot convey the full strength of their own fan community to their sponsors. Decreasing values on social media can even cause guaranteed services, such as reach and interactions, to no longer be fulfilled as planned or promised. This could mean that sports clubs have to put their own money into advertising spendings to make the specific services fulfillable.

Due to the shared interests and associations with a brand from sports, it is often easier to form and maintain communities for companies and/or consumer brands. If a sponsor (but also the sponsored parties) communicates and interacts specifically with a community (e.g., German national team or DFB), then one can speak of a **brand community**. Brand communities are based on shared interests, such as interest in a sports club or a sports event, with the sponsor itself taking a back seat.

Example: FC St. Pauli with New Topics in Sports Sponsoring

Despite the pandemic, **FC St. Pauli** has increased its marketing revenues. The revenues from sponsoring and hospitality at FC St. Pauli amounted to 15–16 million EUR before the pandemic and are heading towards revenues of 18 million EUR. A key to this is that the club focuses on sustainability and creates new offers for partners and sponsors that fit into the club's value cosmos. Thus, FC St. Pauli should not only be perceived as a football club, but ideally also as a sustainability platform. The societal task that the club has identified for itself, combined with the needs of the sponsors, is a key factor for success. Thus, FC St. Pauli is one of the best-marketed clubs, not only in the 2nd Bundesliga, but also in both DFL leagues overall (Sponsors, 2022f). In addition, FC St. Pauli has agreed on a multi-year cooperation with the University of Bayreuth. The team of the Chair for Marketing & Sports Management will support FC St. Pauli in the future with scientific analyses of brand management. ◀

A special development and increasing interest has been found in the **E-sports market**. Hardly any sub-area within the sports industry has developed as quickly and as value-increasing as E-sports. The E-Sportbund Deutschland e. V. (ESBD) understands this to mean the direct competition between human players using suitable video and computer games on various devices and digital platforms under defined rules. In 2021, the global E-sports market was estimated at just over one billion USD, a further increase compared to the previous year (see Fig. 14.4). The majority was made up of sponsoring and advertising deals and the sale of media rights. The global audience has risen to almost 500 million. In addition, it was predicted that the global market revenues of the E-sports industry will grow to up to 1.6 billion USD by 2024. Asia and North America currently represent the largest E-sports markets in terms of revenue, with China alone accounting for almost a fifth of the market.

According to an **E-sports study** by PwC, a turnover of 113.2 million EUR was achieved in Germany in 2021. By 2024, market growth is forecast to exceed 150 million

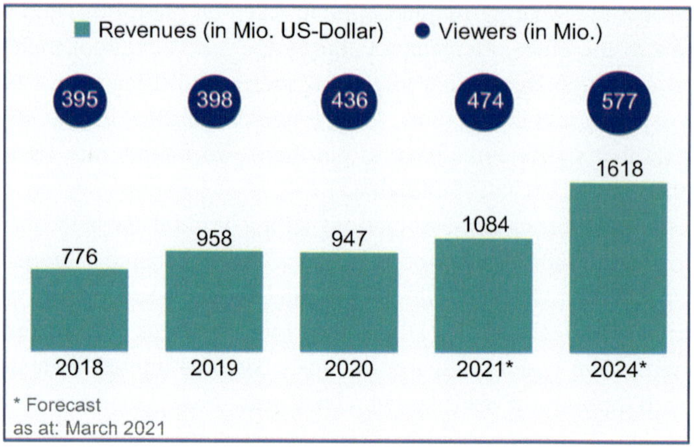

Fig. 14.4 E-sports as a dynamically growing market in the sports industry worldwide. (*Source*: Statista, 2021c)

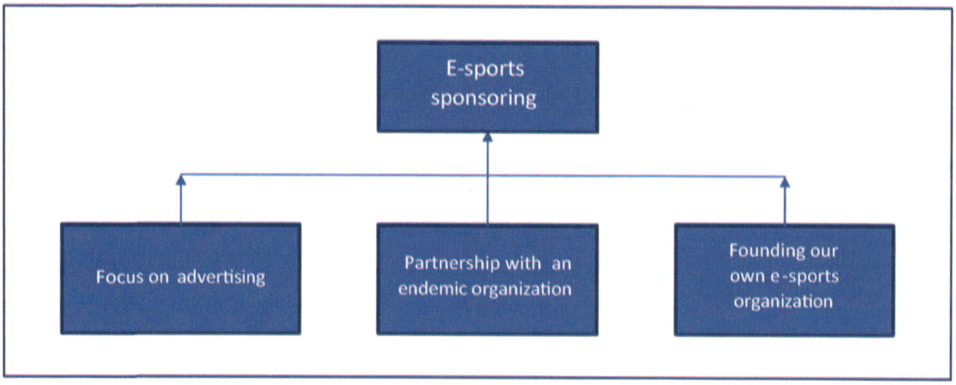

Fig. 14.5 Strategy approaches in E-sports sponsoring. (*Source*: PwC, 2018)

EUR (esports.com, 2021). The annual increase is more than 20%. In Western Europe, Germany accounts for about 50% of total sales. Germany is also the largest E-sports market in Europe and holds its own against followers such as France or Spain. In the global ranking, Germany is in fourth place.

A large portion of the revenue comes from sponsoring (significantly over 50%) and a good third is generated through TV and streaming (PwC, 2018). However, market dynamics and the increasing interest of the younger, spendthrift generation promise much more in the future. After more and more analog or real sports units (including almost all professional football clubs) have founded their own E-sports departments, there was early consideration of what corresponding **strategy approaches in E-sports sponsoring** could look like. Various approaches are possible and make sense (see Fig. 14.5).

In **E-sports sponsoring**, two groups can be distinguished in particular (PwC, 2018). The so-called "endemic partners" include companies with products or services that are essential for the E-sports industry, such as game and hardware manufacturers like Intel, HyperX, or Ubisoft. They invest directly in the success of E-Sports. Since 2020, for example, more than 27 different crypto and blockchain companies have entered the global E-sports market as sponsors. Non-endemic companies do not directly deal with their products and services with the E-sports industry. They initially played a secondary role and come from different sectors, but often see there the opportunity for important target group access. Nielsen Sports reported that 42% of E-sports brand sponsors worldwide were non-endemic in the second quarter of 2017. The participation of Wüstenrot as the main sponsor of the ESL Spring Championship 2016 was surprising (but successful), and since then, more and more non-endemic companies have followed. In the future, there will probably be no surprising, non-endemic sponsors anymore (PwC, 2018).

The **success story of E-sports sponsoring** has parallels to that of football, as success there also developed in small steps. The naming of teams is also found in E-sports. Just as in football the company name can be part of the club name, E-sports teams with names like Samsung Galaxy or SK Telecom T1 can also be found. The sponsoring revenues of the E-sports teams are not yet comparable to those of football clubs, but the development is clearly and quickly moving in this direction. In this extremely growing sports sector, the sponsoring volume has more than doubled in the last four years. Fig. 14.6 shows the revenues in E-sports through sponsoring.

The sponsors particularly target the so-called **Generations Y and Z**, as the media usage behavior has changed significantly, especially in the young group. This means for companies that have these target groups in focus, not to be left out of this development. It is also about the question of the relevant platforms through which the target groups can be reached authentically. Sponsoring can help strengthen the trust of target groups in brands. Therefore, E-sports sponsoring is a suitable means of building trust, despite or precisely because of the differences compared to traditional sports.

Interest in **E-sports as a marketing platform** remains consistently high. Since the beginning of the Corona pandemic, the proportion of new E-sports partnerships in the total number of all new signings in sports sponsoring has increased. This underlines the high relevance of E-Sports for advertising companies to communicate with their target groups. In the first pandemic year 2020 alone, the number of new contracts in E-sports

	2017	2018	2019	2020	2021
E-Sport sponsoring (billion USD)	266	354	471	584	641
Share of revenues	38 %	39 %	43 %	61 %	59 %

Fig. 14.6 Sponsoring as a source of income in E-sports. (*Source*: Statista, 2021d)

could be more than doubled with an increase of 103% compared to the previous year. In the annual comparison 2021 to 2020, there was an increase of still 45%. Compared to traditional sports, E-sports was able to maintain many contractual relationships in sports sponsoring and the number of new signings remained largely constant, especially during the first pandemic measures (ESB, 2022).

More and more well-known brands from numerous sectors and product categories are recognizing the **marketing potential** of teams or events in E-sports due to the available data and market insights. These include companies from the financial and automotive sectors, supermarket chains and food manufacturers, telecommunications companies, but also younger industries such as betting providers in Germany.

14.2 Trends from a Corporate Perspective (incl. Viessmann Case Study)

Sports sponsoring has changed because the companies and their brands have also changed have. In the past, for sports actors, it was primarily about selling brand visibility and reach, among other things, with the help of advertising on the edge of the field and on the chest of the player jerseys. Now, however, rights holders or sponsors are increasingly asking for **closer and deeper target group relationships** and want to see this proven by conversion rates, i.e., who exactly the fans are, how they can best be reached (analogously or digitally), and where the best monetization opportunities lie. Conversion is understood as the transformation of a target person's status into a new status, e.g., from a fan to a prospect, from a prospect to a customer, and from a customer to a brand ambassador.

Fig. 14.7 shows the **role and goal changes in sports sponsoring** due to environmental changes. Based on the three central marketing constructs (brand awareness, brand image, brand use), it is expected that sponsoring will evolve from a "broadening" towards "targeting" and "deepening" (Sponsors, 2020; Sportfive, 2022).

In the course of the transformation processes in sports sponsoring, various **marketing trends** can be used, which will play an important role in the **sports sponsoring of the future** (cf. Hackl, 2021):

- Purpose Driven Marketing,
- Content Marketing,
- Omnichannel Marketing,
- Experience Marketing,
- Engagement Marketing.

These **marketing trends** have already significantly changed the marketing appearance in the areas of product management, communication, dialogue, sales, etc., and it is expected that these marketing trends will also affect sports sponsoring. Some aspects of this will be highlighted below.

Purpose Driven Marketing

In the future, sponsors will use sponsoring commitments to communicate their corporate purpose believably, generate high-quality and relevant content, and emotionalize and make their brand promise tangible in the form of "storyliving". **Purpose orientation**—essentially the actual "justification" for corporate activity—as an important corporate focus has received additional interest in public discussion due to the Corona pandemic. The crisis has ensured that companies and society were forced to rethink and partially reevaluate prevailing values. In situations of high stress and low security, increasing revenues are suddenly no longer the sole focus.

In turbulent times, people look to brands for stability. Brands become significant orientation aids in everyday life. A study by the consulting firm Deloitte showed that consumers turn to brands that fulfill a purpose in uncertain times (Deloitte, 2020a, b, pp. 7 ff.). It is essentially about focusing on a higher purpose and the common good of society (Blache, 2020; Brendel, 2020; Stumpf, 2020, pp. 26 ff.). For purpose-oriented

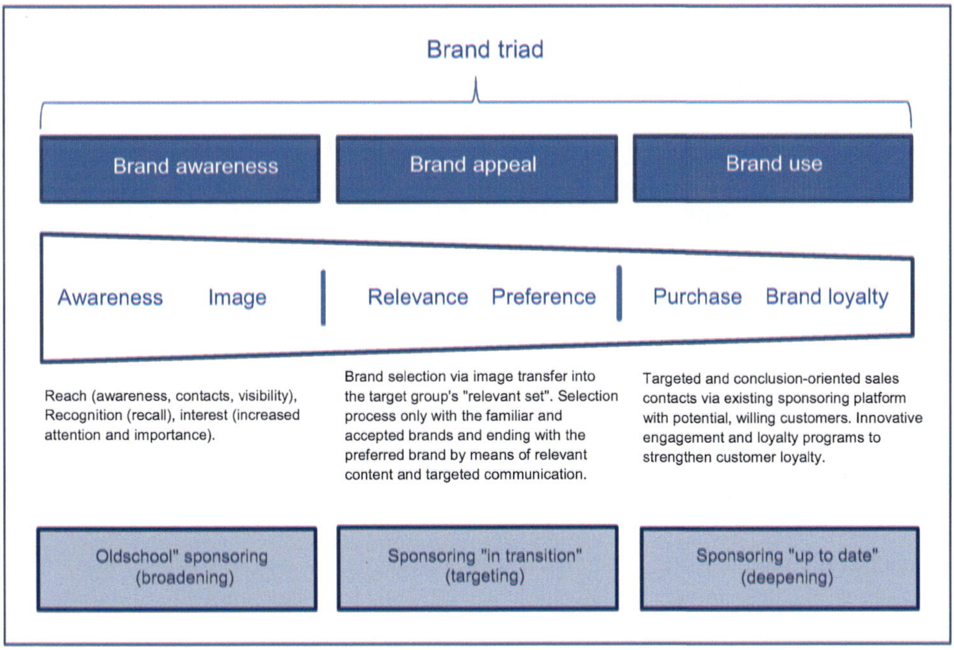

Fig. 14.7 Role and goal change of sports Sponsoring in a changing environment. (*Source*: Own representation based on Sportfive, 2022)

companies, making a positive contribution to societal challenges is on an equal footing with the intention to make a profit (Brendel, 2020).

The purpose idea must be authentically anchored in the corporate culture, only then is the external communication credible. Purpose-driven companies not only talk and claim, they also act accordingly consistently. However, it becomes critical when the purpose orientation is only superficially used as a marketing action. This causes considerable damage (for example through "greenwashing"), because in times of digital transparency, consumers can easily see through the appearance and content of a brand (Blache, 2020).

Content Marketing

The relevance of content marketing in sponsoring can be explained by the fact that it is becoming increasingly difficult to reach target groups with conventional advertising. On the one hand, consumers' acceptance and credibility of traditional advertising is steadily declining. Consumers tend to turn to their closer social environment such as family and circles of friends to get an honest recommendation for a product or a brand (Stumpf, 2020, p. 132). On the other hand, the increasing sensory overload ("information overload") means that many messages no longer really reach consumers.

Content marketing differs significantly from conventional communication strategies and advertising techniques. Unlike usual advertising messages—with the goal to sell—content marketing does not put the company or the products in the foreground, but offers content that provides added value and helps customers achieve their own personal and professional goals (Kotler et al., 2017, p. 150). Thus, content marketing aims to win and retain customers without, however, appearing intrusive and "ad-like" (Lammenett, 2019, p. 80).

The conveyance of emotions and information in the context of a brand often takes place through **"storytelling"**. Storytelling is a frequently used tool of content marketing: by using "small stories", content is conveyed simply and vividly (Gutting, 2020, p. 41). In addition to emotional messages, content marketing content can also be informative, advisory or entertaining. All have the goal of arousing the interest of the recipients, initiating interactions and building relationships in order to ultimately convince consumers of products and services.

Omnichannel Marketing

Omnichannel stands for the parallel use of several (sales and communication) channels—both physical and digital (Kotler et al., 2017, p. 168). In contrast to the multichannel or cross-channel approach, the sales and communication channels are linked. The **interlocking of the channels** ensures that there is no loss of customer information on the company side despite a channel change by the consumer. Omnichannel marketing aims to offer the customer a consistent experience across all channels (Stumpf, 2020, p. 165).

The omnichannel approach is characterized by a strong customer orientation, where the needs and wishes of consumers are at the center, to guarantee them a seamless shopping experience. From a company's perspective, the omnichannel concept helps to gain valuable insights from the collected customer data about the holistic behavior of consumers in order to continuously improve the company's offer. Accordingly, the implementation of a cross-channel CRM system in the company is an essential prerequisite for omnichannel marketing.

Customer Experience

There is a broad consensus in marketing that it is not enough to satisfy customers. The focus is less and less on customer satisfaction, but on the goal of **customer delight**. Products and offers are often interchangeable, the providers only differ marginally with theirs, and the attention of customers is declining (Gutting, 2020, p. 62). Only brands that manage to achieve a so-called "wow effect" will find the necessary attention and stand out from the crowd (Kotler et al., 2017, p. 41).

Therefore, it is becoming increasingly important for companies to focus on customer experience in their activities. Customer experience—a kind of special customer perception—is to be understood as a subjective customer reaction that occurs with every direct or indirect contact with a company. The direct contact usually takes place during purchase, use and service and is usually initiated by the customers. Indirect contact includes unplanned encounters with products or services of a company, and occurs for example in the form of word-of-mouth recommendations, advertising or PR contributions. Customer experience is therefore about much more than just the subjective perception of customers in relation to products and services. Instead, it includes everything that consumers perceive along the respective customer journey and at all touchpoints with a specific brand (Stumpf, 2020, p. 256).

Customer Engagement

In order to be able to compete as a brand in an increasingly competitive environment, business and marketing strategies are aimed at building a deeper **connection between brand and customers**. Such a strategy is described with the term Customer Engagement (Kotler et al., 2017). Customer Engagement refers to the degree of personal commitment that a consumer brings to a product, a company, or a brand. As part of Customer Engagement, companies consciously motivate their customers to act as ambassadors or advocates of the brand. Customers are actively involved in the marketing process and actively participate in the design and development of a brand. The consulting firm

Deloitte, which examined the most important current and upcoming marketing trends in its 2022 marketing report, has described Customer Engagement as one of the most significant global marketing trends of the future (Deloitte, 2022).

Consumers fulfill important functions when they act as loyal brand ambassadors. There are a number of different customer engagement approaches that can be used. The goal of all approaches is to promote interactions with the customer. The approaches differ in their intensity and the degree of participation levels. In the first stage, it is primarily about triggering conversations, user-generated messages, and increasing the interaction between customers and companies through methods such as gamification or apps (Kotler et al., 2017, p. 183).

To intensify the customer base at this stage, the use of mobile apps or gamification is suitable, among other things. The approach of **Co-Creation** reaches the next level of intensification of Customer Engagement. This is also used by sports clubs in merchandising (Rohlmann, 2023). Co-Creation refers to the direct involvement of customers in the service creation process, for example in the form of idea generation for product development. Companies use crowdfunding approaches, prototyping, and collaborative platforms to incorporate customer inputs into various product designs and product development phases. The trend towards an increased intensification of the Customer Experience is closely related to Customer Engagement and the two approaches complement each other.

In summary, **sports sponsoring as a marketing platform** can be understood as an entry point and as a bracket for numerous marketing activities of companies. It can be used in different areas of a company and fulfills a wide range of goals: sponsoring is a platform with which goals in the areas of marketing, sales, and personnel can be achieved. Classic sponsoring engagements aim at brand awareness, image, and branding. Sponsorings can also contribute to customer loyalty, employee recruitment, and employee motivation.

The strength of sponsoring can be seen, among other things, in the fact that content can be conveyed and more complex topics and relationships can be explained, which are often not adequately conveyed in classic advertising campaigns. Sports sponsoring has to face changes such as digitization and various trends in order to continue to be attractive. It becomes particularly difficult when the target system of the sponsored differs from the target system of the companies, because then a (negative) sponsoring result is preprogrammed. This can not only lead to negative consequences for the sponsoring brand, but also for the sports actors, if some decision-makers no longer consider sponsoring to be a multifunctional and effective communication tool.

Case Study Viessmann—Sports Sponsoring as a Pioneer and Brand Enhancer

The following case study was compiled by **Georg van der Vorst**, Head of sports sponsoring, and is carried out with the kind support and permission of the Viessmann Group.

Viessmann is a fourth-generation family business with a focus on developing and manufacturing heating, cooling, and ventilation systems: Viessmann ensures optimal climate and develops intelligent and sustainable energy systems and cooling solutions—for residential buildings, industry, and commerce. With 22 production companies in 12 countries and worldwide sales companies, representations, and trading partners in 74 countries, Viessmann has a strong international orientation and employs over 13,000 people.

Initial Situation

At the beginning of the 1990s, a development of the heating market from a seller to a buyer market was observed. Before that, market processing was almost exclusively directed at the implementation partners in the end consumer market (heating companies). At the same time, the company began the phase of internationalization, so that numerous foreign markets also had to be taken into account in marketing work.

Viessmann recognized the potential of sports sponsoring and the importance of athletes as brand ambassadors about 30 years ago. Commitment, taking responsibility, and thinking in terms of a team are essential components of the corporate culture. Viessmann supports athletes, officials, and associations. The promotion of young talent is of particular importance. In this respect, sponsoring for Viessmann is a long-term tool for the continuous further development of the brand. Such activities primarily pay into the upper area of the marketing funnel (Awareness—Interest—Consideration), i.e., a well-structured and played marketing funnel simplifies the sales process.

Viessmann has been active in winter sports sponsoring for almost 30 years. As one of the first sponsors in winter sports, Viessmann strategically occupied a previously dormant field in brand communication and is considered a pioneer of winter sports sponsoring. Viessmann supports three sports, two international associations, and more than 20 athletes as a reliable partner (Fig. 14.8).

Football passed its "acid test" in 2016, first in the English Premier League with Huddersfield Town FC and then through the sponsoring of FC Bayern Munich. The German record champion has become an important part of Viessmann's sports commitment. The international partnership of the two global players, both market leaders in their industry, began in China, where Viessmann became the Official Regional Partner of FC Bayern in 2018. In response to the successful partnership, Viessmann expanded its commitment with FC Bayern to Southeast Asia in 2021, and in the same year became the official climate partner of FC Bayern Munich in selected European markets (France, Spain, Poland, BeNeLux, and Russia). At the start of the 2022/2023 season, the cooperation with FC Bayern Munich was expanded as a global partnership.

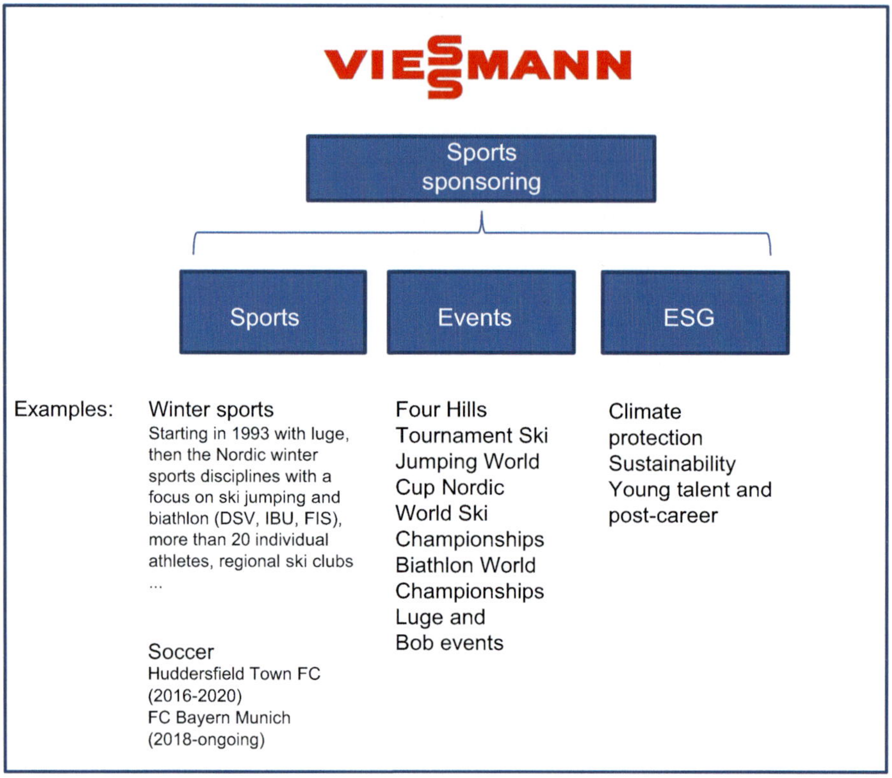

Fig. 14.8 Viessmann's commitments in sports sponsoring. (*Source*: Viessmann)

Goals and Target Groups

In the context of sports sponsoring, Viessmann focuses on brand and communication-related **goals**. These include in particular:

- Increasing and building brand awareness,
- Building and expanding company-related image values,
- Platform for customer and employee identification to emotionalize the brand.

With regard to the target groups, the company addresses its two traditionally important **target group levels** through sports sponsoring:

- Homeowners and potential homeowners (age 30-69 years, B2C),
- Partners from the installation trade (B2B).

Strategic Orientation and Selection

The strategic priorities of Viessmann include, in accordance with the strategic corporate orientation, primarily three **core topics**:

- Commitment to international sports with high TV presence,
- Possibility of dominant branding to increase the probability of recall,
- Partnership with athletes to adapt image values and use for storytelling.

In line with Viessmann's consistent brand and marketing orientation, the sponsoring department is integrated into the marketing area, which also facilitates short decision-making paths and constant coordination or networking.

Implementation and Results

Above all, winter sports with various sports and events fits perfectly with the company's DNA, which deals with the basic need for warmth. Consequently, Viessmann's **sports sponsorings at various levels** have been and continue to be the focus (see Figs. 14.9 and 14.10):

- Associations,
- Athletes,
- Events.

Such **sponsoring agreements** have been and are usually concluded with terms of two to four years in order to achieve the sponsoring rights for the fulfillment of the

Fig. 14.9 Viessmann—it all started with luge and Georg Hackl. (*Source*: Viessmann)

Fig. 14.10 Viessmann—in winter sports with climate protection on first-name terms. (*Source*: Viessmann)

strategic orientation. This also includes event invitations and exclusive "behind-the-scenes" moments, which are highly appreciated by customers. Viessmann sees a special plus for itself especially in athlete sponsoring. This starts with the promotion of young athletes and then goes beyond the active career. Because all sponsoring contracts include a clause that allows athletes to undergo training or dual studies at Viessmann after the end of their active career. The same applies to juniors who do not make it to the World Cup.

As already indicated, Viessmann sees a successful sponsoring as being given by the fact that there is fundamentally a **networking of sponsoring commitments** with other marketing disciplines, e.g. integration at trade fairs & events, advertising measures of different kinds with the use of sponsored party athletes, with occasional competitions for the fans being included. This also involves a certain change in the implementation of sponsoring. In the past, sponsoring for Viessmann was very strongly associated with the topic of branding. Today, the company is more about telling stories. This development can be partly explained by the fact that as a sponsor today you can use completely different opportunities. In particular, digital channels and social media give a company new and optimally usable opportunities. This can be clearly shown using the following specific implementation examples.

Example: Viessmann—Live Show "Viessmann Daheim"

In this live show, various athletes are used who present special events as Viessmann ambassadors. In the 3rd live show from the Viessmann studio in March 2021, cross-country skier Tobias Angerer was a guest. Together, presenter Tom Meiler and Tobias Angerer watched the current highlight of winter sports—the Nordic World Ski Championships in Oberstdorf. With Johannes Rydzek, Eric Frenzel and Markus Eisenbichler, the absolute top athletes of the Viessmann combined team were live from Oberstdorf, as well as Katharina Althaus and Richard Freitag from the ski jumping team. Studio Vi was not only supposed to take a look at the sporting events in Oberstdorf, but also behind the scenes. Johannes Rydzek reported on his beginnings in Nordic Combined, and what and who inspired him to take the path as a competitive athlete. From Eric Frenzel, the viewers learned how the team spirit is lived in Nordic Combined, and Richard Freitag told how he wanted to fight his way back from his current performance low.

Expert Tobias Angerer is not only a long-time Viessmann brand ambassador and former world-class cross-country skier, but also DSV vice-president, and strongly committed to the youth. Together with Viessmann marketing director Ivo Hoevel and Tom Meiler, he spoke about the promotion of young talent in the German Ski Association, the modernized sports facilities in Oberstdorf and what Viessmann has contributed to it. For the two new facilities in Oberstdorf, the ski jumping and cross-country skiing stadium, the choice fell on climate solutions from Viessmann. ◀

Example: Homestory #Start Daheim

As part of the digital Homestory series #Start Daheim, prominent brand ambassadors of the manufacturer of climate and energy solutions provide interesting and exciting insights into both their private lives (including Viessmann solutions in their own home) and their commitment to climate protection.

During her biathlon career, snowy landscapes, snow-covered forests and white hills provided an impressive backdrop for Laura Dahlmeier's successes. Two Olympic victories, seven world championship titles and 33 World Cup victories made the Garmisch-Partenkirchnerin one of the most successful biathletes of all time. But for Dahlmeier, nature has always been more than just the appropriate scenery for her sports. Home, connection to nature, the mountains! These are the topics that the 28-year-old, who already made a name for herself during her active time in the summer months with spectacular mountain tours, stands for like hardly anyone else. It goes without saying that this passion is also an important part of her everyday life after her retirement from biathlon. That's why Dahlmeier is giving a lot of thought to sustainability and environmental compatibility when building a house. Viessmann accompanied Laura and her mother Susi Dahlmeier in the planning and preparation of the house construction in January 2022 and is at their side with climate and energy solutions tailored specifically to their needs. In three exciting videos, the Dahlmeiers were accompanied in their considerations and planning. The three-part video series "Daheim am Start" with Laura Dahlmeier was watched by over a million people in total.

As far as the internal cooperation of different departments is concerned, Viessmann uses the neighboring departments Media, Social Media, Trade Fairs & Events, B2B Marketing for networking. Due to the traditionally strong and grown dominance of winter sports sponsoring, which has almost made Viessmann sponsoring a generic term for winter sports promotion, there is so far no networking with other sponsorings (cf. in this context Fig. 14.11). ◄

Success Measurement, Selected Insights and Outlook

Of course, nobody at Viessmann wants to rely solely on gut feeling and just positive headlines. Therefore, various **methods of impact and success control** are used:

- Regular measurement of defined KPIs for sponsorings, including Brand Awareness, Relevant Set, First choice, NPS, sponsoring Awareness, Uplift Relevant Set (acquaintances of Viessmann sponsoring vs. non-acquaintances), Uplift Image (acquaintances of Viessmann sponsoring vs. non-acquaintances),
- Regular media analyses,

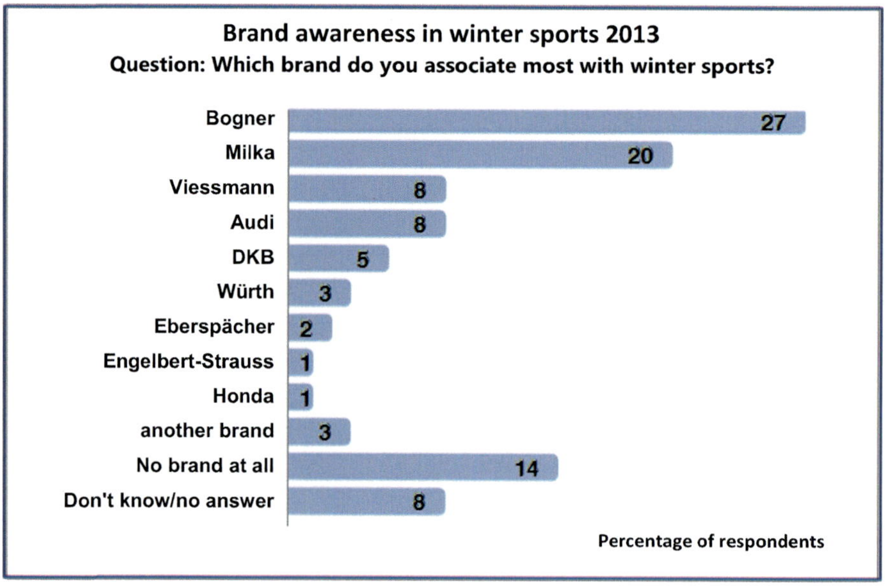

Fig. 14.11 Brand awareness in winter sports 2013. (*Source*: Statista, 2013)

Fig. 14.12 Brand status of Viessmann. (*Source*: YouGov & Handelsblatt, 2021)

Brand of the year 2021

Energie & Wärme

Rank	Brand	Score
1.	Viessmann	34,4
2.	Vaillant	31,3
3.	Buderus	30,7
4.	Bosch (Junkers)	27,0
5.	Stiebel Eltron	25,9

Other brands (sorted alphabetically):
E wie einfach, e.on, EnBW, Eprimo, EWE, Gazprom, Innogy, Lichtblick, RheinEnergie, RWE, Stromio, Vattenfall, Yello Strom

- Reach measurements regarding the overall brand and logo presence as well as differentiated by advertising media,
- Social media audit with reach and engagement in own and other channels as well as evaluation of media equivalence values.

In Fig. 14.12, the so-called **brand status of Viessmann** is shown. The point value of a brand contained therein stands for its average performance among its brand connoisseurs on six different evaluation dimensions: General impression, Quality, Price-performance ratio, Customer satisfaction, Recommendation readiness, and Employer image.

The interim **expansion of sports sponsoring to football** goes back to the company's expansion per se. The additional commitment in sports sponsoring is particularly important for Viessmann in order to transport its communication messages internationally. Winter sports alone are not enough for this. Especially in growth markets like Southeast Asia, other platforms are needed to be successful on the sponsor's side. The importance of sponsoring for Viessmann is also evident from the fact that seven employees now take care of the sponsoring in winter sports and at FC Bayern. In addition, external partners are added as needed, who support the Viessmann team in the areas of sponsoring, social media activities, and content production.

14.3 Trends from a Media Perspective

The trends discussed so far are also important for sports sponsoring from a media perspective. This raises many questions, for example, about the **use of analog and digital media** within the framework of a sponsoring commitment. It will have to be examined how and with which media or message carriers a rights provider can guarantee its sponsor even better performance. The various technical aids are also important for the value of sponsorings.

However, it's not just about typical media platforms—whether externally controlled or initiated by the club—but also about advertising in and around the stadium, which, after jersey advertising, is one of the most well-known and significant forms of sports sponsoring. Fig. 14.13 simplifies which **developments of advertising elements in sports sponsoring**, starting from the first advertising formats in sports venues in the early 1970s to today, have taken place and what can be expected in the future due to technical developments with digitization.

Regardless of **technological advances**, those involved in sports sponsoring always ask themselves the question of a balanced cost-benefit ratio and the quality of digital expansions. The application of cameras on the athlete's body is also considered a further step in using technology partnerships within the framework of sports sponsoring.

Example: Technology Partnership Deutsche Telekom and 1. FC Köln

During the summer break 2022, the Cologne Bundesliga team welcomed the multiple Italian champion AC Milan to its stadium for a friendly match. This so-called **Telekom Cup** was/is part of the technology partnership of 1. FC Cologne with Deutsche Telekom and presented numerous new technologies and features as an "Innovation Game" (ZDF heute, 2022a). Both the TV viewers on Magenta TV and the fans and partners in the stadium were offered a completely new experience. FC

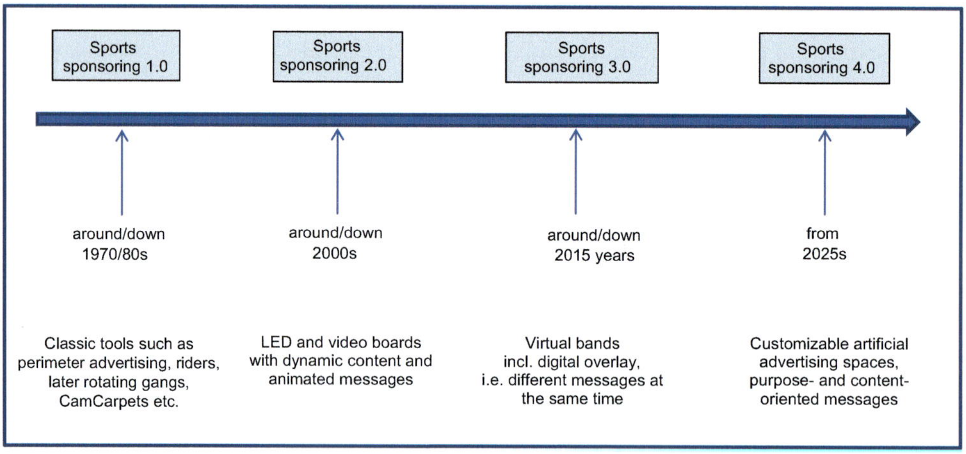

Fig. 14.13 Development of advertising formats within the framework of sports sponsoring in Germany

fans could be virtually up close and follow the encounter from completely new perspectives. For example, the game was shown from the perspective of an FC player using special bodycams. In addition, some FC professionals were wired on the field, automated highlights were created, and exciting data feeds were offered. The stadium experience was also improved for FC fans by meeting the fans' wish from 2021 for better connectivity and a controlled distribution of spectators. A strategic crowd management system informed stadium visitors about which entrance, which kiosk, or which toilet currently has the shortest queue. Thanks to the technology partnership with Telekom, fans could also look forward to a 5G network in the stadium. To what extent such data and image collections will actually become "normal reality" in sports or serve more than occasionally as a demonstration object for technology-savvy sponsors remains to be seen. ◄

14.4 Trends from the Agency Perspective

Similar to the rights holders selbst—the sports actors—the rights brokers and rights service providers—the sports agencies—will also have to make considerable efforts and investments to meet the new challenges in terms of structural and personnel prerequisites as well as data basing and technology affinity. Because it is primarily the fans and their behavior that set new standards (Nielsen Sports, 2022). This applies to all agencies in sports in the same way.

Some **challenges may affect different types of agencies** differently. Some developments are mentioned below:

- **Consulting agencies:** In the conception and selection phase, not only the consideration of basic paradigm shifts (see the mentioned general societal and development trends) is part of it, but also the pre-planning of feasibility within the framework of activation with the help of experts and specialized service providers including budgeting. In the future, cooperation with a consulting agency could become even more important for some sports actors to be sponsored, because especially those without a large own planning and organization background can hardly manage all facets of a sponsoring award. Therefore, there might be a trend from "do it yourself" to professional sponsoring marketing with the help of a sports marketing agency.
- **Brokerage agencies:** A mere partner matchmaking will hardly be sufficient to initiate successful and lasting partnerships. Rather, it also requires creative agency contributions and detailed elaborations for activation as well as the specification of success parameters and suggestions for their measurability and control.
- **Implementation agencies:** The same applies to service agencies, which contribute to the success of sponsoring by taking over certain activation measures. Especially here, more and more suggestions for technological innovations (including digital formats, content) and creative implementations will be required, which go beyond the mere execution of an implementation order.

- **Athlete agencies:** A holistic view and marketing of a successful and prominent athlete even after his active career will be particularly in focus in the future, especially when such an athlete can continue to work as a senior expert both as a brand ambassador of a sponsor and/or bring his experiences into optimizable engagements of the company in sports sponsoring of any kind.

In addition, in sports sponsoring, the **demands and complexity** are increasing, which many sports actors on the one hand do not see as their core area, and on the other hand will also make their limits felt, so that sports agencies in this context will be given increasing assistance and support from sponsors, but also from sponsors. In addition, many sports actors depend on successful and swift demand generation by competent salespeople. To what extent full-service agencies or more specialized niche agencies will be used more intensively will be seen. However, with the requirement of increasing specialized knowledge and the corresponding equipment with technology and infrastructure, some "all-rounders" might reach their limits, and compared to specialized niche agencies, they might be at a disadvantage, which in turn would increase the control span of the sports actors.

Some also see a certain **danger for sports agencies** that focus solely on (national) sports (German Bundestag, 2018). Especially the European sports rights market is currently exposed to hostile takeovers from China, the Arab region, and the USA. For example, in the agency market, it can be observed that Chinese companies have been buying up European sports rights agencies for some time. The purchase of the sports agency Infront by the Chinese conglomerate Dalian also the transfer of know-howWanda can be mentioned as an example.

14.5 Trends in "Sponvestors" (incl. Red Bull Case Study)

For a long time, there was a clear separation between Investors, the investing in sports (e.g., Sports goods companies) and sponsors who use sports to achieve marketing and communication goals for their brand (e.g., car manufacturers, banks, beverage manufacturers, private equity firms, etc.). In the meantime, there is an increasing trend to observe that so-called **"sponvestors"** are getting involved in the sports market. This refers to the trend that companies from the non-sports sector invest in sports to realize both economic and sports as well as communicative goals. This future of sponsoring is already observable in many countries.

For example, according to the economic database Pitchbook, private equity firms invested 51 billion USD worldwide in sports in 2021. Of this, 22 billion flowed to Europe, only three billion to the USA. There, the US professional leagues like NBA or MLS only allow minority stakes (Deutschlandfunk, 2022). Similarly, the **legal situation**

for sports investments in Germany's largest sports, football, as well as in Austria, but no longer in most UEFA member nations. According to this, a team participating in official football matches (registered association or corporation) may not have a majority of people or organizations not affiliated with the club. Only very few exceptions in Germany (Bayer AG/Bayer 04 Leverkusen, Volkswagen AG/VfL Wolfsburg, Dietmar Hopp/TSG 1899 Hoffenheim) were allowed.

Experts assess the situation of sports investments in such a way that investments in sports values in the USA have become increasingly difficult. This is also due to the high entry prices and the associated high capital requirement for an engagement (Deutschlandfunk, 2022). Therefore, many companies from the USA are involved in European sports. The **European sports market** is more attractive for sports investments than sports markets in non-European areas.

The **future of sports Sponsoring between traditional sports investors and sponvestors** will depend on numerous factors. These interconnections are currently being tested in many areas and the experiences and learning effects remain to be seen. When assessing future prospects, the following factors should be taken into account:

- Search for lucrative investments by investors,
- Critical voices and moods towards investors,
- Investor participation from the perspective of the sports actor,
- Sports participation from an investor's perspective.

In the following, the arguments of the actors involved in the sports market will be presented in detail. It can be assumed that especially internationally active large companies and private equity firms will increasingly have an interest in getting involved as Sponvestors.

Search for lucrative Investments by Investors

Many investment firms have numerous financial resources and are increasingly showing **financial interest** in the world's most popular sport, football. They are thus also following the interest of private billionaires, Middle Eastern countries and Chinese investors who have discovered football as an investment object. They have been continuously buying into the football market over the last two decades. The latest wave of investors are private equity firms and hedge funds.

Not only the **search for high-yield capital investments** makes sports and sports actors attractive to investors, but also external negative developments such as economic crises and pandemics can drive professional sports towards such partnerships. In football, for example, the pandemic-related losses were highest because that's where the most money is turned over. In a situation report published in May 2021, UEFA alone estimated the corona-related economic damage at club level in the ticketing sector at four billion EUR (UEFA, 2021, p. 102). Since a cumulative shortfall of 2.7 billion EUR was also expected in sponsoring and a deficit of 1.4 billion in media rights, the total loss amounted to more than eight billion EUR.

Many clubs could often only prevent insolvency with state guarantees or state aid. Additional funds were required. Financing with conventional borrowed capital from banking institutions is rarely possible due to unfavorable conditions. Therefore, it was and is the interest of the sports industry to also examine **alternative sources of financing**. One of the alternatives to borrowed capital is private equity, which has increasingly come into the focus of companies in recent years. In recent years, there has been an almost constant increase in the number of sports industry-related private equity transactions (Hufnagel, 2011).

▶ **Private Equity** As **Private Equity**we refer to equity capital. Private equity companies are entrepreneurial investors who provide their own or raised capital to companies of various types, most recently also increasingly in top-class sports, for a certain period of time. They profit from the profit when the investment is sold later, while the sports actor opens up new opportunities for further development. Private equity differs from pure financiers such as banks because they provide more than just capital.

So **Private Equity for the sports industry** means not only the influx of fresh capital, but also the transfer of know-how to other industries and other technologies. Especially in the area of international marketing as well as in digitization and especially in streaming, there is great potential for further development of sports organizations with the help of experienced investors (Sponsors, 2021).

In many areas of sports, sponsors and investors have become common terms. It is particularly noticeable in countries with strong traditions and socially relevant sports that both actors are often met with great skepticism from the base.

Critical Voices and Mood Towards Investors

On the one hand, many fans see an **increasing commercialization** of their sport, even if they are aware that without sufficient marketing revenues, there are hardly any chances at the top of the sport. Club supporters regret, among other things, the loss of a certain closeness to their idols, the increase in event visitors in the stadiums in the form of box rentals and VIP seat marketing, less influence on the officials than the business club partners, the decision on event times more according to commercial aspects than fan friendliness, etc.

On the other hand, numerous financial arrangements of the decision-makers and concessions of the sponsored take place without sufficient transparency and often in "back rooms". Due to **lack of transparency and participation** as well as the appearance of influence by financiers on sports, not a few fans get the impression that they are locked out of events and developments of their club.

These fundamental **reservations against financial commitments** are particularly carried into the public eye nationally and internationally by the so-called Ultras of sports clubs, by launching general protest actions or targeted attacks against such committed individuals, groups, and organizations. Therefore, it is of great importance for every professional sports actor to dispel certain "half-truths" through dialogue and open discussions and to carry decisions more transparently into the fan community.

In addition, it is not only about involving the fans, but also other stakeholders such as long-standing and highly committed sponsors, when financial requirements could suggest cooperation with investors in professional sports. It can also be useful to consider not only "non-sports investments" (pure financial investors) (derogatorily referred to as "locusts"), but also to think about "sponvestors". The **different participation commitments** in sports are characterized by different goals or motives, with a company often starting as a sponsor and later ending as an investor (see Fig. 14.14).

With these different participation commitments, the **role and position of companies in sports**—and thus the opportunities and risks—change significantly. Therefore, it is important to distinguish more clearly between sponsors, investors, and sponvestors.

Sponsor: A **sponsor** is a private individual, an organization, or a company that promotes a sponsored party through money, goods, or services. It is a mutual agreement, i.e., obligations for counter-services for services, between a sponsor and a sponsored

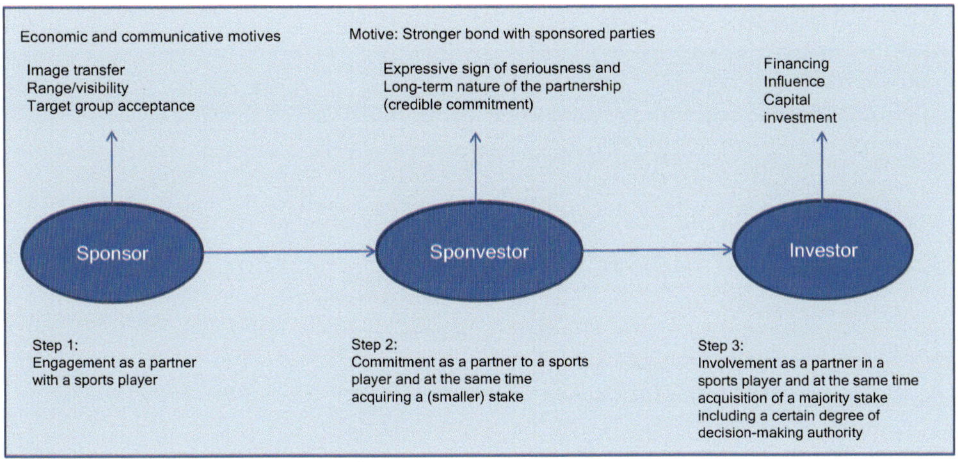

Fig. 14.14 Sponsors, sponvestors, and investors in sports

party in the sports sector. The motivation is marketing and sales-driven. Its targets are primarily based on economic and communicative improvements of its own position (example: Rakuten/FC Barcelona). A sponsor is therefore not a patron or donor.

Investor: An **investor** wants to invest his capital profitably in sports and at the same time promote the sporting performance of the respective sports actor. He is a shareholder in the equity of a sports object. The main aim is to create a win-win situation over several years, based on grown values. His motivation is entrepreneurial activity, to do something better than before. When the investor's goals are achieved or the performance promise is fulfilled, a withdrawal and a resale of the capital investment can/will occur. The target of an investor is purely financial, in order to realize an appropriate ROI at the end (example: KKR or Tennor Holding/Hertha BSC; Glazer Family/Manchester United FC).

Sponvestor: A **sponvestor** is a private individual, an organization, or a company that, in addition to its commitment as a sports sponsor, also acquires a more or less large stake in the equity. The motives are based on underpinning the connection to the sports actor and serious efforts to improve his sporting performance through this commitment. The focus continues to be on pursuing economic and communicative goals (example: Allianz/FC Bayern Munich; Evonik Industries/BVB).

Looking at the various possibilities for sports actors or sports units to generate additional financial resources, it is also possible to identify **subtypes** among the various basic types that can play a role in the decision of sports objects. Fig. 14.15 shows the main

Sponsors in sport	Subspecies	Central motives	Participation and scope in the equity of a sports property
Sponsor	a) Main sponsor b) Co-sponsor c) Advertising partner	Improvement of own market position and image transfer	No
Investor	a) Strategic investor b) Financial investor c) Private investor (patron)	a) Increasing company value and helping to shape the competitive strength of sports properties b) Pure financial goals through multiplication of the property value c) Social recognition	Yes, partially up to 100%
Sponvestor	a) More sponsor, less investor b) More investor, less sponsor c) Of equal rank	Improvement of own market position, influence on further development of the sports property, CSR	Yes, mostly minority interest

Fig. 14.15 Differences between sponsors, investors, and sponvestors in sports

differences between sponsors, investors, and sponvestors in terms of their central motives and the extent of their involvement in the sports object.

The possibility in sports to shape through a strong financial commitment from investors is, however, limited in some areas (including the USA, Austria, Germany). For example, the **50+1 rule** (sometimes also called: 50+1 regulation) is a binding provision in the statutes of the German Football League (DFL). According to this rule, capital investors are not able to take over the majority of votes in corporations into which football clubs have outsourced their professional department. This only applies in very few UEFA member countries (e.g., Germany and Austria), which leads to a competitive disadvantage in generating additional financial resources. Although minority shares in German football corporations can be sold to interested private individuals and companies, this remains far below the possibilities of free foreign investments. An overview of the related change in the sports landscape in Europe can be found, among other things, in a recently completed dissertation (Brenner, 2022).

An interesting insight into the history of investors in German football is provided by Fig. 14.16. It becomes clear that the **entry of investors into German football** has been taking place for decades, albeit with different focuses and intensities.

Furthermore, in the course of transforming a sports club into a corporation, it is important which **form of company** is chosen and whether a possibly chosen stock corporation is listed on the stock exchange or not. Regarding the German football scene, Fig. 14.17 shows that among the legal forms, the GmbH & Co. KGaA obviously has the greatest attractiveness. Within the Football Bundesliga 2022/2023, there are only four out of 18 clubs or 22% in the form of a registered association, which clearly indicates the **end of the traditional club structure in professional football**. If you add the corporations completely owned by the association to the e. V. clubs, currently only eight out of 18 Bundesliga clubs or 44% are completely without external influence. With six out of

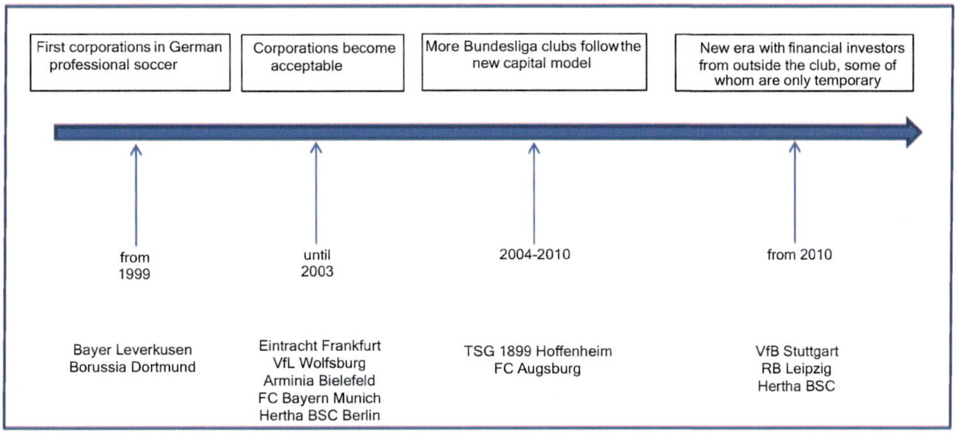

Fig. 14.16 Entry of investors into German football

German professional soccer clubs	Type of company	Status since	Shareholders and shareholdings
Bayer 04 Leverkusen	Bayer 04 Leverkusen Fußball GmbH	1999	Bayer AG (100 %)
Borussia Dortmund	Borussia Dortmund GmbH & Co. KGaA	1999	Evonik Industries (9,83 %), Bernd Geske (9,35 %), Ballspielverein Borussia 09 e. V. Dortmund (5,53 %), Signal Iduna (5,43 %), Puma (5 %) and Ralph Dommermuth Beteiligungen GmbH (1&1) (5,004 %), free float(59,86 %)
Eintracht Frankfurt	Eintracht Frankfurt Fußball AG	2000	Eintracht Frankfurt e. V. (67,89 %), Freunde des Adlers GmbH (16,81 %), Friends of Eintracht Frankfurt AG (7,30 %), Herzschlag Eintracht GmbH (5,00 %), Steubing AG (3,00 %)
VfL Wolfsburg	VfL Wolfsburg-Fußball GmbH	2001	Volkswagen AG (100 %)
Arminia Bielefeld	DSC Arminia Bielefeld GmbH & Co. KGaA	2001	DSC Arminia Bielefeld e.V. (71,4 %), Bündnis Ostwestfalen (28,6 %)
FC Bayern München	FC Bayern München AG	2001	FC Bayern München e.V. (75 %), adidas (8,33 %), AUDI (8,33 %), Allianz (8,33 %)
Hertha BSC Berlin	Hertha BSC Berlin GmbH & Co. KGaA	2002	Peil Investment B.V. (66,6 %), Hertha BSC e. V. (33,3 %); later KKR und Tenor Holding
1. FC Cologne	1. FC Köln GmbH & Co. KGaA	2002	1. FC Köln e. V. (100 %)
SpVgg. Greuther Fürth	SpVgg. Greuther Fürth GmbH & Co. KGaA	2003	SpVgg Greuther Fürth e. V. (100 %)
Borussia Mönchengladbach	Borussia VfL 1900 Mönchengladbach GmbH	2003	Borussia Verein für Leibesübungen 1900 e. V. (100 %)
Werder Bremen	SV Werder Bremen GmbH & Co. KGaA	2003	SV Werder e. V. (100 %)
1899 Hoffenheim	TSG 1899 Hoffenheim Fußball-Spielbetriebs GmbH	2005	Dietmar Hopp (96 %; 1989 start of promotion by Dietmar Hopp in the e.V.), TSG Hoffenheim 1899 e.V. (4 %)
FC Augsburg	FC Augsburg 1907 GmbH & Co. KGaA	2006	Hofmann Investoren GmbH (99,4 %; davon 45 %: Bolt Football Holdings von David Blitzer; 30,56 %: Klaus Hofmann; 20,37 %: Project Green GmbH von Michael Reuss; 4,07 %: Thilo Sautter), FC Augsburg e.V. (0,6 %)
1860 München	TSV 1860 München GmbH & Co. KGaA	2011	HAM International Limited (60 %), TSV 1860 München e. V. (40 %)
VfB Stuttgart	VfB Stuttgart 1893 AG	2014	VfB Stuttgart e. V. (87,09 %), Daimler AG (11,75 %) und Jako AG (1,16 %)
RB Leipzig	RasenBallsport Leipzig GmbH	2014	Red Bull GmbH (99 %), RB Leipzig e. V. (1 %)
VfL Bochum	VfL Bochum GmbH & Co. KGaA	2018	VfL Bochum e. V. (100 %)

Fig. 14.17 Corporations and their shareholders in German football clubs. (Season 2021/2022)

English Premier League	Company name	Status since	Club-Investoren (majority shareholder)
FC Arsenal London	Arsenal Holdings Limited with 100% subsidiary Tochter The Arsenal Football Club plc	April 2011	Kroenke Sports & Entertainment LLC (100%)
FC Chelsea London	Chelsea FC Holdings Limited	May 2022	Clearlake Capital Group (60%), Todd Boehly, Mark Walter and Hansjörg Wyss
Liverpool FC	The Liverpool Football Club and Athletic Grounds Ltd.	October 2010	UKSV Holdings Company Ltd (Fenway Sports Group LLC, 90%)
Manchester City F.C.	Manchester City Limited	September 2008	City Football Group (Umbrella company of Abu Dhabi United Group Investment and Development Limited)
Manchester United FC	Manchester United Football Club Ltd., a wholly owned subsidiary of Manchester United plc	May 2005	Glazer family with over 70% of the shares and additional increased voting power
Tottenham Hotspur	Tottenham Hotspur Ltd.	February 2001	ENIC International Ltd. (85% Kapitalanteil via Lewis Family Trusts)
Newcastle United	Newcastle United Ltd.	October 2021	Public Investment Fund (80%), PCP Capital Partners and RB Sports & Media

Fig. 14.18 Ownership situation of the top clubs in the English top football league

18 clubs, the GmbH & Co. KGaA is most represented, followed by five as GmbH and three as stock corporations.

In other, in this respect "more liberal" football countries like England, the situation of investor supremacy is even more pronounced. This is shown by Fig. 14.18, which depicts the **ownership situation of the top clubs in the English top football league**. Here, a multitude and diversity of club investors can be observed.

However, the question of the **integrity and seriousness of majority shareholders** is highly relevant in order to avoid disappointments and unpleasant side effects (e.g., shady business, money laundering). Some transactions in England in the recent past have shown this. The traditional Austrian club FC Wacker Innsbruck, for example, had to experience this painfully (Mein Bezirk, 2021). Therefore, there is much to be said for subjecting the particularly majority influence of large financial partners in a sports club to an objective and serious examination in advance, if this cannot be completely prevented according to the statutes (Heun, 2016).

Example: Eagle Football Holdings

A special example is Eagle Football Holdings, a multi-club group controlled by US businessman John Textor. According to media reports, this group plans to go **public via a Special Purpose Acquisition Company (SPAC),** which would be a premiere for the football industry (Financial Times, 2023). Eagle Football and Textor completed the acquisition of French Ligue 1 club Olympique Lyon at the end of 2022 and already own Brazilian professional club Botafogo FR and Belgian second division club RWD Molenbeek. The group also owns a 40% stake in Premier League team Crystal Palace. Allegedly, Eagle Football is aiming for a valuation of 1.2 billion USD and wants to go public in 2023. SPACs, also known as blank check companies, are publicly traded and raise money with the explicit goal of merging with another company within a certain period of time. ◄

Investor Participation from the Perspective of the Sports Actor

When deciding for or against the inclusion of an investor by a sports actor, different, sometimes contrary arguments need to be examined. Various aspects speak in favor of a strong participation of investors in sports, the following **advantages** are particularly worth mentioning:

- Creation of more competitive equality for all participants in a sport.
- Generation of financial resources that are often not achievable otherwise (e.g., through own funds).
- Medium to long-term improvement of all areas—from the sporting and organizational infrastructure to sporting performance.
- Safety backup for difficult club times.

However, there are also some criteria to consider that can completely or partially negate the previously mentioned advantages. The following **disadvantages** should be highlighted:

- Impairment of event, club or athlete image, because investors have a rather bad reputation in the eyes of the most important stakeholders, the fans.
- Difficult to dispel prejudice that there are (too) many "black sheep" who only want to "plunder" athletes, a club and its assets or want to afford a "toy" as a person (Buschmann & Wulzinger, 2017).
- Withdrawal of sponsors who feel disadvantaged by the sports partner compared to investors.
- Fear of loss of self-determination or co-determination of the sports actor, which could be damaged or even lost.

Sports Participation from an Investor's Perspective

Similarly, investors will have to ask themselves whether and under what conditions participation in a sports actor is attractive for them and which points must be met in order to identify a tradable investor business. The aspects that are mainly cited as **reasons for an investment** in the sports sector include the following points:

- Assistance in creating equal opportunities in a sporting competition contributes to a positive image and strengthens one's own market position, as private equity competitors also work with it.
- With sports investments experience shows that money can be made and the provision of financial resources offers corresponding co-decision opportunities in the use of money.
- Entrepreneurial experience/expertise from outside as well as constructive influences typically bring improvements in all areas of the sports actor over 3–5 years—from the infrastructure to sporting success, which in turn also benefits one's own image and return.

However, opposing aspects can often curb the previously described euphoria. The following can be mentioned as **reasons against an investment**:

- Short-term capital injections help neither the sports actor nor the investor.
- There is no guarantee of success and return in fundamentally unpredictable sports competitions.
- Fear of loss of self-determination or co-determination of the sports actor, i.e., he is no longer master of his decisions or the pressure from outside (including fans and the public) becomes too great.

Sports Participation from the Perspective of Competition Organizers

National and international competition organizers, such as the respective sports associations, view the increasing activity of externally motivated investors with mixed feelings, as they fear for the integrity of sports, especially in cases of multiple participations in the same sports. For instance, UEFA has warned against the increasing rise of investments in multiple clubs in football and stated that this could jeopardize the integrity of their European club competitions (Sportspromedia, 2023).

The European football association has issued such a warning in its annual Club Licensing Benchmarking Report. Multi-club ownership, where individuals own shares in more than one football team, has become a popular business model among investors, with UEFA identifying more than 180 clubs worldwide by the end of 2022 that will be part of a multi-club structure. This is almost double the number from four years ago. "The rise of multi-club investments has the potential to pose a significant threat to the integrity of European club competitions, with a growing risk of two clubs with the same owner or investor facing each other on the field," UEFA explained.

Member-determined sports clubs and the negative evaluation of investors are particularly significant issues in German football clubs, often fueled by the conservative ultra-movement. In other countries, however, the issue of investors is much more objectified and less heated. However, German football officials will have to ask themselves to what extent the so-called 50+1 rule (the Federal Cartel Office has called on German football associations to establish a uniform regulation) and the issue of investor admission need to be regulated for the future. Some thoughts on possible **solutions for new financing and ownership models in professional football** are summarized in Fig. 14.19.

An investor accepted by the club stakeholders will therefore respect the **culture and heritage of a sports actor**, value decisions in dialogue with stakeholders (including fans), focus on a balance of goals of all participants, and increase the sporting

General conditions and requirements:
- Investor participation not as an end in itself, but with the aim of developing a sports club in a comprehensible manner.
- Different objectives (e.g. sporting success and fans' wishes, decision-making and power) of different shareholders (members vs. financial backers, management vs. fans, etc.) must be reconciled.

Solution approaches:
- No decisions only in the case of a sporting and economic emergency.
- Forward-looking and broad discussion of topics in a sports club.
- Development of a sustainable concept for the future, also for the purpose of reducing emotionality.
- Communicative clarification of potential investors (type, origin, shares, use of funds).
- External support in the decision-making process (moderator and consultant role).

Fig. 14.19 Solutions for new financing and ownership models in professional football competitiveness of the partner in a competition where the financial gap (Gap) between the few tops and many followers is anyway getting bigger. All this could lead to ambitious sports clubs analyzing their sponsor portfolio more closely in the future and not only seeing the extreme poles on the sponsor-investor scale (see again Fig. 14.14), but increasingly thinking about **Sponvestors**. But investors like private equity firms can also be important (especially for sports associations) to take the next growth steps. The majority of sports clubs are only partially able to finance further growth due to collapsing or fluctuating revenues. Their focus is on their core business. For some clubs, it is easier to think about the future with the help of external financiers. Because private equity partners are also always temporary shareholders and a planned exit is clear before the entry, sports actors also need suitable structures to fill such forms of cooperation with life in a targeted manner.

Case Study Red Bull—a Classic "Sponvestor"

A typical example of the integration of sponsor and investor functions is Red Bull. **Red Bull**, the well-known energy drink company, is one of the most active sponsors in sports, and also owns its own sports organizations and sports venues and organizes its own sports events. In this sense, it acts like a classic **"sponvestors"**. The company owns, among others, Red Bull Salzburg in Austria and RB Leipzig in Germany in the top German-speaking football leagues. In addition, the company has a sponsoring contract with the New York Red Bulls—a franchise club of the professional Major League Soccer in the USA. The extensive and diverse commitment of Red Bull as a sponsor and investor is illustrated in Fig. 14.20.

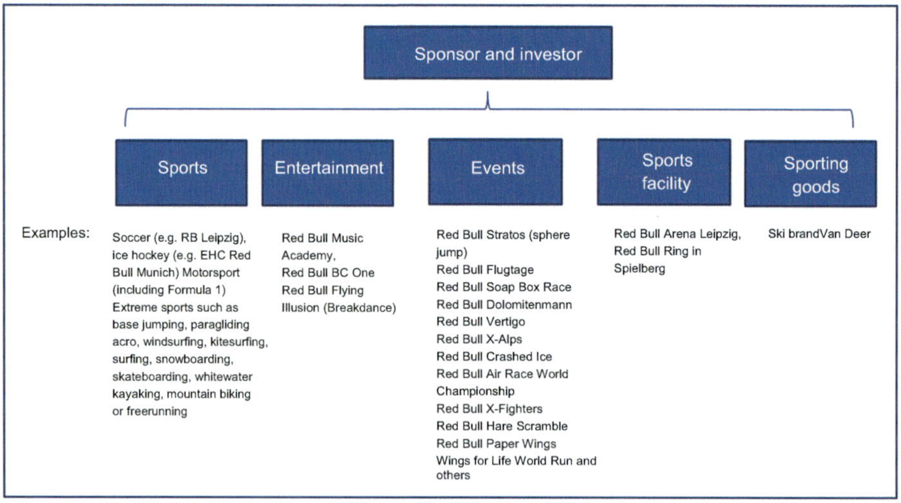

Fig. 14.20 Engagement of Red Bull as a sponsor and investor. (*Source*: Red Bull)

Red Bull pays quite high sums per year to present sports teams and athletes. The share of marketing expenses is 30 to 35% of sales, half of which is estimated to flow into sponsoring. But it obviously pays off, as Red Bull has now become a fixed size in sports and has also made a name for itself in ice hockey and "quirky" sports like soapbox racing and the Red Bull Flugtag.

In addition to kit sponsoring, Red Bull also spends millions on naming rights for stadiums and other marketing initiatives. What distinguishes Red Bull in many areas from sports-supporting companies like "normal" sponsors is the "project-like" nature of their commitment. Simply sticking the logo on a piece of sports clothing or a vehicle was always too little for the now deceased CEO of Red Bull, Dietrich Mateschitz. According to him, Red Bull's commitments were always about meaningfulness, even if it perhaps only confirmed itself in retrospect (ORF, 2022; Fürweger, 2023). Initially, Red Bull targeted mainly younger target groups through extreme athletes, but now, thanks to attractive sports like football and others, there are no restrictions on sports or age limits when addressing target groups. The rapid development of Red Bull's sports commitment with sponsoring and investments can be easily traced over time using Fig. 14.21.

For better visibility, Red Bull aimed to standardize the logos of the (formerly traditional) sports clubs in their engagements as a Sponvestor. Fig. 14.22 shows some examples of the old club logos and the standardizations by Red Bull. This approach can also be observed in other engagements and underlines the formal networking of Red Bull's sports commitments.

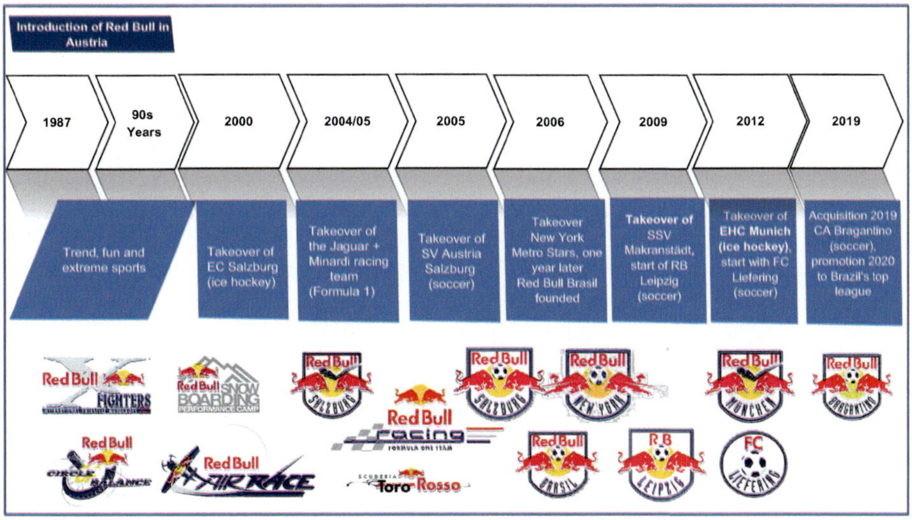

Fig. 14.21 Red Bull as a sponvestor over time. (*Source*: Red Bull)

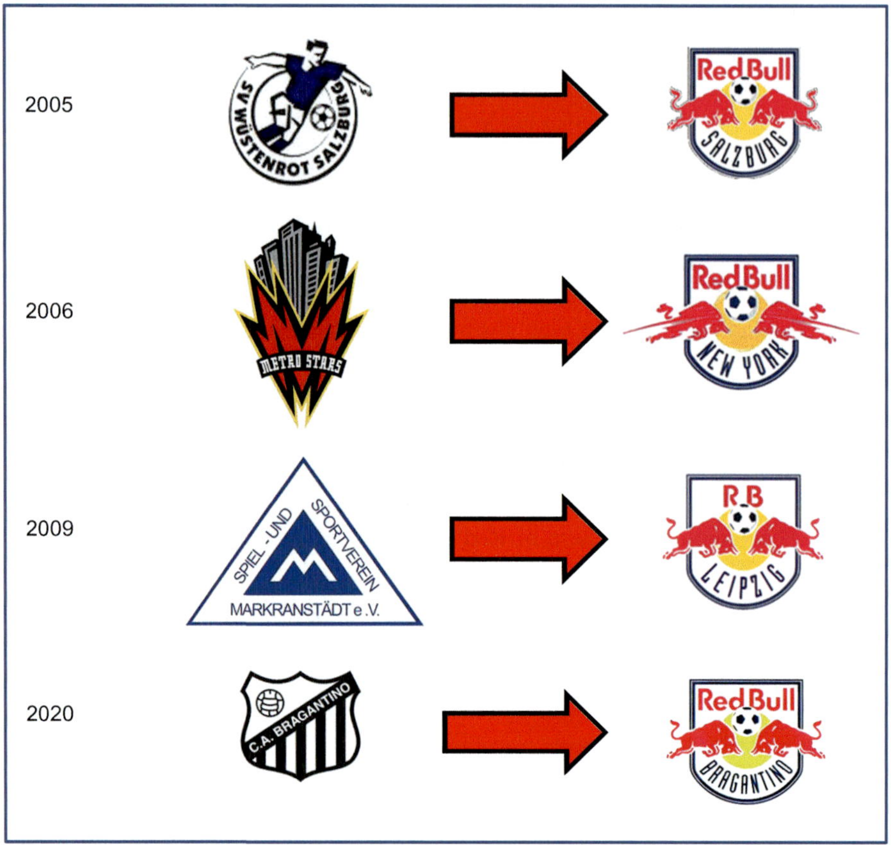

Fig. 14.22 Examples of the standardization of logos of well-known football clubs by Red Bull. (*Source*: Red Bull)

However, Red Bull is also a media conglomerate, as evidenced by television stations, glossy magazines, documentaries, etc. The company finances and stages the most adventurous projects, not everything has to be extreme and dangerous, as long as it can be underpinned with impressive images and stories. This type of brand staging in the world of extreme and consumer sports could only be achieved through extraordinary sponsoring and investment activities. Brand recognition values close to 100%, a brand value of 17 billion EUR (see Fig. 14.23) and a digital advertising value (AAV) of almost 200 million USD are impressive success figures for the engagements.

While since the mid-2010s the new flagship club RB Leipzig has been "on course" mainly through loans from the energy drink manufacturer, i.e. has been able to establish itself at the top of football, Red Bull as the main sponsor and

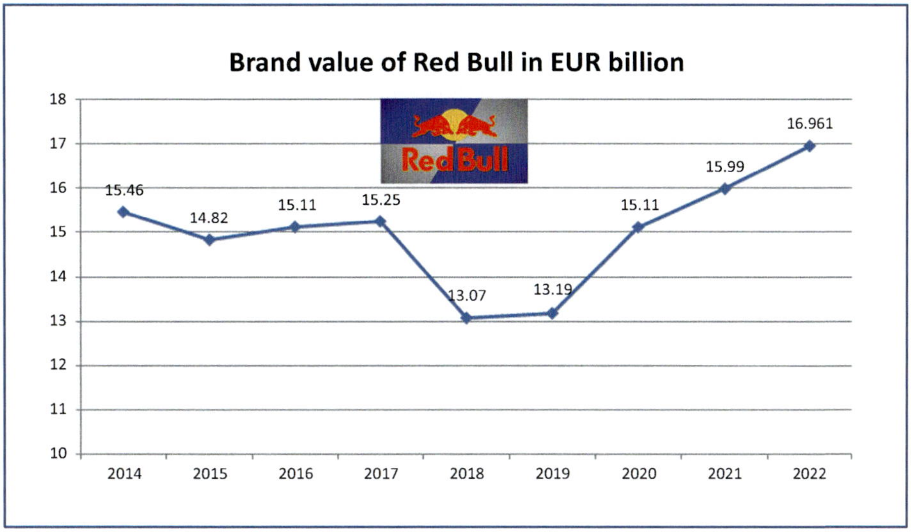

Fig. 14.23 Development of Red Bull's brand value. (*Source*: European Brand Institute)

RasenBallsport Leipzig GmbH	2014/15	...	2017/18	2018/19	2019/20	2020/21
League affiliation	2. BL		1. BL	1. BL	1. BL	1. BL
Total revenue in EUR million	76.5		245.2	270.8	322.3	371.6
Sponsorship income in EUR million	41.0		90.0	95.0	107.0	100.0
- of which Red Bull in EUR million	20.0		45.0	78.0	58.0	50.0
Equity in EUR million	3.1		6.6	108.2	111.0	112.1
Liabilities in EUR million	58.9		149.1	124.4	164.3	227.7
- of which Red Bull loan in EUR million	52.4		121.3	86.3	68.4	59.5
Red Bull's share of the club's sponsorship	**49 %**		**50 %**	**82 %**	**54 %**	**50 %**
Red Bull share of liabilities	**89 %**		**81 %**	**69 %**	**42 %**	**26 %**

Fig. 14.24 Sponsoring and capital investment by Red Bull in RasenBallsport Leipzig GmbH. (*Source*: Annual reports of RasenBallsport Leipzig GmbH; Research PR MARKETING)

99-percent shareholder of the so-called RasenBallsport Leipzig GmbH has written off a total of 100 million EUR in debt for the football club according to the 2018/2019 annual report and converted it into equity. This reclassification increased the equity ratio from four to 44% and had positive effects due to the elimination of interest and repayment payments. This significantly improved the financial leeway for the club. Fig. 14.24 shows the sponsoring amounts and the capital investment by Red Bull in RasenBallsport Leipzig GmbH for the seasons 2014/2015 to 2020/2021.

14.6 Key Points

Changes in the environment of the participants and new topics in society and the economy clearly show that they can have significant effects on the happenings in sports sponsoring. Consequently, their ongoing observation is an important task in sports sponsoring, in order to create an attractive basis for the future. In this context, some points need to be particularly considered.

Key Points

1. In general, for the future of sports sponsoring, it is important to ensure that the **central marketing and communication trends** are recognized in time. Anticipating these and integrating them into the work of sports sponsoring represents a central challenge.
2. The previously significant target variables in sports sponsoring (e.g., brand awareness, brand image) will continue to exist in the future. However, **long-term targets** regarding customers and employees should also be considered, such as customer and employee retention.
3. For sponsors and sponsored parties, it is important to deal with the **future topics of sports sponsoring**. These include topics such as target group accuracy, development of new markets, internationalization, sustainability, digitalization, development of e-sports, deepening, conversion, etc.
4. For the purpose of seamless **contacting of target groups**, more attention will need to be paid to a mix of analog and digital formats—whether they are operated by the sports actor themselves or by external media.
5. For the future, it is important to continue developing **valuable offers** to remain attractive to sponsors. This means creating new values beyond the usual happenings, in the sense of maximum value generation for all involved stakeholders, as this will be the basis for legitimizing engagements in sports.
6. In sports sponsoring, there are increasingly opportunities for **data-based activities and omni-channel interactions**. They not only increase chances of revenue and further goal achievement probabilities, but also enhance the quality of bonding with the target groups.
7. Creative **experience marketing**, i.e., the emotionalization and experience of brands, is increasingly being discovered and can be used for stronger fan engagement.
8. Regardless of technological advances, participants in sports sponsoring should always question a balanced **cost-benefit ratio** and the **quality of digital expansions**.
9. The **digital worlds**—from online-based experience islands to the complex metaverse—will gain more space and importance in sports sponsoring. They

should be included in sponsoring considerations by the participants at an early stage.

10. Increasingly, **sports sponsoring can be used as a marketing platform**. It should be checked whether sponsors can be offered opportunities to use the platform for numerous activities in the areas of marketing, sales, personnel, etc. This also applies to the so-called **"sponvestors"**, who participate in sports both as investors and sponsors.

References

B

Blache, C. (2020). Ist ein höherer Sinn für Marken sinnvoll? https://www.horizont.net/news/p/180111.

Brendel, D. (2020). Was steckt wirklich hinter dem Marketing-Buzzword Purpose? https://www.horizont.net/news/p/180197.

Brenner, P. (2022). *Zwischen e. V. und (Sport-)Kapitalgesellschaft. Organisationsrechtliche Überlegungen zur Ausübung professionellen Sports am Beispiel des Lizenzfußballs*. Baden-Baden.

Buschmann, R., & Wulzinger, M. (2017). *Football Leaks: Die schmutzigen Geschäfte im Profifußball*. Deutsche Verlags-Anstalt.

D

Deloitte. (2020a). *Sponsoring sports in today's digital age*. Deloitte.

Deloitte. (2020b). 2021 global marketing trends: Find your focus. https://www2.deloitte.com/content/dam/insights/us/articles/6963_global-marke-ting-trends/DI_2021-Global-Marketing-Trends_US.pdf.

Deloitte. (2022). 2022 global marketing trends. Thriving through customer centricity. https://www2.deloitte.com/us/en/insights/topics/marketing-and-sales-operations/global-marketing-trends.html.

Deutscher Bundestag. (2018). Europas Sportrechte unter Druck, Beitrag vom 07.11.2018. https://www.bundestag.de/webarchiv/presse/hib/2018_11/577542-577542.

Deutschlandfunk. (2022). Investoren im Sport. Lieber Europa als USA, Beitrag vom 07.08.2022. https://www.deutschlandfunk.de/tv-rechte-bundesliga-investoren-100.html.

E

ESB. (2022). Sponsoring im eSport-Markt, Beitrag vom 13.04.2022. https://www.esb-online.com/business-guides/artikel/sponsoring-im-esport-markt/.

Esports.com. (2021). So professionell ist der Esport im Jahr 2021 in Deutschland wirklich, Beitrag vom 27.11.2021. https://www.esports.com/de/so-professionell-ist-der-esport-im-jahr-2021-in-deutschland-wirklich-295103.

F

Financial Times. (2023). New Olympique Lyonnais owners plan Spac listing, Beitrag vom 18.01.2023. https://www.ft.com/content/c74b5e96-c1ab-463e-9c4f-3e469e543d6d.

Fürweger, W. (2023). *Die Red-Bull-Story – Der unglaubliche Erfolg des Dietrich Mateschitz* (12. Aufl.). Haymon.

G

Gürtler, T., & Möthe, A. (2022, August 20). Gegenentwurf zu Geld und kurzfristigem Glamour: Der Fußball entdeckt sein Gewissen wieder. *Handelsblatt*. https://www.handelsblatt.com/unternehmen/handel-konsumgueter/sport-sponsoring-gegenentwurf-zu-geld-und-kurzfristigem-glamour-der-fussball-entdeckt-sein-gewissen-wieder/28583060.html.

Gutting, D. (2020). *Interkulturelles Marketing im digitalen Zeitalter: Strategien für den globalen Markterfolg*. Springer Gabler. https://doi.org/10.1007/978-3-658-29429-8.

H

Hackl, K. (2021). Sponsoring im Zeitalter Marketing 4.0: Wie können Trends und Erkenntnisse aus dem Marketing 4.0 im Sponsoring der Zukunft angewandt werden? Masterthesis der Universität Basel.

Heun, V. (2016). *Assetklasse Fußball: Chancen und Risiken für Investoren im Fußball*. BoD – Books on Demand.

Hufnagel, J. (2011). Private Equity-Aktivitäten in der Sportbranche: Bestandsaufnahme und Analyse, Deutsche Sporthochschule Köln, Dissertation, Köln.

K

Kotler, P., Kartajaya, H., & Setiawan, I. (2017). *Marketing 4.0: Der Leitfaden für das Marketing der Zukunft*. Campus.

L

Lammenett, E. (2019). *Praxiswissen Online-Marketing: Affiliate-, Influencer-, Content- und E-Mail-Marketing, Google Ads, SEO, Social Media, Online- inklusive Face book-Werbung* (7. Aufl.). Springer Gabler. https://doi.org/10.1007/978-3-658-25135-2.

M

Mein Bezirk. (2021). FC Wacker: Entschuldigung für die falsche Investorentscheidung; Beitrag vom 01.06.2021. https://www.meinbezirk.at/innsbruck/c-sport/entschuldigung-fuer-die-falsche-investorentscheidung_a4679879.

N

Nielsen Sports. (2022). Sportmarketing-Trends 2022: So verändern Fans das Sportbusiness, Köln.

O

ORF. (2022). Mateschitz-Erfolg eng mit Sport verbunden, Beitrag vom 23.10.2023. https://sport.orf.at/stories/3101092.

P

PricewaterhouseCoopers. (2018). Digital Trend Outlook 2018: Esport-Studie 2018. https://www.pwc.de/de/technologie-medien-und-telekommunikation/digital-trend-outlook-2018-esport/sponsoring-im-esport-markt.html.

R

Rohlmann, P. (2023). *Sportmerchandising – Konzeptionelle Grundlagen, Marktdaten und Trends.* ESV-Verlag.

S

Sponsors. (2020). Business Case statt Bande: Was die Bundesliga vom IOC lernen kann, Beitrag vom 14.07.2020. https://www.sponsors.de/news/themen/ioc-vermarktung.

Sponsors. (2021). Warum Private Equity zunehmend in den Sport investiert, Beitrag vom 20.07.2021. https://www.sponsors.de/news/themen/warum-private-equity-zunehmend-in-den-sport-investiert.

Sponsors. (2022f). SPOBIS Podcast „Sports, Business & Players“ mit Bernd von Geldern, Beitrag vom 24.08.2022. https://www.sponsors.de/news/fussball/spobis-podcast-sports-business-players-mit-bernd-von-geldern.

Sportfive. (2022). Mehr Sales durch Sportsponsoring, Beitrag vom 09.05.2022. https://beyond-the-match.com/sponsoring/mehr-sales-durch-sportsponsoring/.

Sportspromedia. (2023). Uefa warns multi-club ownership threatens 'integrity' of soccer, Beitrag vom 13.02.2023. https://www.sportspromedia.com/news/uefa-soccer-multi-club-ownership-investment-model-ceferin/.

Statista. (2013). Welche Marke verbinden Sie am meisten mit Wintersport? Beitrag vom 18.12.2013. https://de.statista.com/statistik/daten/studie/283776/umfrage/bekannteste-marken-im-wintersport-2013-2014/.

Statista. (2021c). Das Milliardengeschäft mit dem digitalen Sport. https://de.statista.com/infografik/8643/esport-umsatz-und-zuschauer-weltweit/.

Statista. (2021d). E-Sport-Sponsoring widersteht Coronakrise, Beitrag vom 25.01.2021. https://de.statista.com/infografik/26671/prognostizierter-jahresumsatz-mit-e-sports-nach-quelle/.

Stumpf, M. (2020). *Die 10 wichtigsten Zukunftsthemen im Marketing* (2. Aufl.). Haufe Group.

U

UEFA. (2021). Die europäische Klubfußballlandschaft – Benchmarking-Bericht zur Klublizenzierung. Mit der Pandemie leben, Nyon.

V

VSA. (2021). Delphi-Studie: Zukunft 2030 – Sportsponsoring im Wandel, WHU – Otto Beisheim School of Management, Center for Sports and Management, Düsseldorf.

Y

YouGov, & Handelsblatt. (2021). Marke des Jahres.Ranking 2021. https://commercial.yougov.com/rs/464-VHH-988/images/YouGov-Germany-Marke-des-Jahres-Ranking-October-2021.pdf?mkt_tok=NDY0LVZISC05ODgAAAGAY-Cpv-RsvLbZQDJh2IfHsg1iPYmm7637P48oTvc_KZPYBa-HxsGrcF98khHEI304ZmkYuK0OwgjCrFWQ_P3lifsnNjYAvaKxaHFBzDoYLZc4.

Z

ZDF heute. (2022a). Skepsis nach Testlauf in Köln, Beitrag vom 20.07.2022. https://www.zdf.de/nachrichten/sport/fussball-bundesliga-technologisierung-datenerfassung-body-camera-1-fc-koeln-ac-mailand-100.html.

2022 FIFA World Cup in Qatar—Lessons for Future Sports Sponsoring? 15

Contents

Abstract

The awarding of the 21st and 22nd Men's Football World Cup in 2018 and 2022 took place jointly following the decision of the FIFA World Football Association. FIFA announced the decision on the awarding of the two final rounds on December 2, 2010, in Zurich. Upon conclusion, it was confirmed that the 2018 World Cup would be held in Russia and the 2022 World Cup in Qatar, which had already hosted the Asian Football Championships in 1988 and 2011. No World Cup in Europe has been discussed as much and as controversially in advance as the one in Qatar. Although there was also criticism in earlier years (for example, when Russia and Brazil were the host countries), these debates largely faded into the background with the start of the tournaments. The events that had an impact on the sponsors, how they dealt with them, and the consequences that resulted from them, are made apparent through further explanations and extensive numerical data. This chapter refers to sponsors such as Budweiser, Adidas, Rewe, Hummel, and the non-sponsor Brewdog. This acknowledges the current relevance of the topic in order to discuss implications for upcoming major sporting events.

M. Bruhn and P. Rohlmann, *Sports Sponsoring*,
https://doi.org/10.1007/978-3-658-44171-5_15

15.1 Qatar 2022 in Public Discussion

The hosting of the 2022 Football World Cup was the pinnacle and crowning achievement of a long-term planned "sports offensive" for Qatar. The World Cup (WC) 2022 project started 14 years ago and has been pursued at a considerable pace ever since. As early as 2008, the **development plan "Qatar National Vision"** was launched. Qatar, governed like a monarchy, wanted to use sports as a power tool for contacts and acceptance around the world. For the implementation of this strategy, the gas- and oil-rich country made large expenditures (Image, 2022).

In 2014, the Swimming World Championships took place in Qatar, followed by the Handball World Championships in 2015. Even in these years, there were "purchased" cheering fans from Spain. This was followed by the Cycling World Championships in 2016, the Gymnastics World Championships in 2018, and the Athletics World Championships in 2019. Qatar was awarded these World Championships because the emirate provided the world federation with sponsoring money amounting to almost 40 million EUR (Image, 2022).

Dubious and opaque circumstances surrounding the awarding of the World Cup, workers injured during the multi-year stadium construction, restricted human rights of the population, and regarding numerous visitors: The Football World Cup in Qatar caused many, decidedly **controversial discussions**. For example, statements about the sexual orientations of people by a Qatari World Cup ambassador caused outrage. Federal Minister of Justice Marco Buschmann, among others, responded to these remarks, reminding Qatar of the security guarantees for fans during the tournament, the non-exclusion of homosexual people, and the observance of ethical values in connection with human rights. Many statements with similar content from high-ranking federal politicians of various parties have shown how early the public and emotional discussion began.

These and similar **statements by politicians** and other public figures fueled the discussion in Germany. In the strongly emotionally driven debate, various expressions of opinion led to a lively dispute. Examples show various headlines about the Football World Cup in Qatar (see Fig. 15.1). Also, the fact that the Qataris deployed around 1600 "purchased" fans from all over the world (program name: "Fan Leader Network") to spread good vibes and post positive and impressive news on social media fits into the overall picture of a World Cup marked by points of contention and peculiarities.

As if issues such as the rescheduling of the World Cup tournament to winter or in the middle of the usual league football season, the human rights situation, worker exploitation, corruption, and sports washing were not enough contentious points (Spiegel, 2022), the World Cup host showed a **struggle for dominance at the World Cup** in contrast to agreements with FIFA. Two days before the start of the tournament, the Qataris won the power struggle over the alcohol ban around the World Cup stadiums against FIFA, thereby sabotaging one of the global World Cup sponsors, the beer brewer

Fig. 15.1 Headlines about the 2022 football world cup in Qatar. (*Source*: various media)

Anheuser-Busch with its brand Budweiser. As FIFA itself announced, no alcoholic beer was allowed to be served near the eight arenas, contrary to previous agreements. This confirmed the media reports that the Qatari royal family Al Thani had demanded from the world federation not to serve any alcoholic beer in the stadiums and around the arenas at all. Apparently, moving the beer sales points to less conspicuous locations than in and around the stadiums was not enough, as there were also advertising restrictions, including the awarding of the Budweiser Cup "Man of the Match".

Some media (e.g., The Times) wrote of a "shock" for FIFA caused by the late **intervention of the World Cup organizers**. After all, it was more than unusual for significant changes to a contract with a sponsor (no sale of alcoholic beverages around the stadiums) to be made so shortly before the start of a major event. Moreover, FIFA thereby violated a multi-million dollar contract (a sum of 75 million USD for the four-year cycle is reported). The beer brand Budweiser, which has been an official FIFA sponsor at Football World Cups since Mexico 1986, is one of the largest donors and was neither visible at the games this year, nor was Anheuser-Busch allowed to sell its brand there. It was allowed for the beer to be served in the fan zones in Doha and in the VIP areas of the stadiums, which caused additional resentment and protests among the "normal" fans.

The short-term nature of the ban not only made waves because of the **emotionally charged debate** about beer. It became apparent that FIFA complied with the will of the desert emirate in several respects, contrary to the agreements with the sponsors. Corresponding comments by FIFA President Gianni Infantino and a press conference one day before the opening of the World Cup suggested that FIFA had given in to the demands of the host country, apparently to not jeopardize the hosting of the World Cup. The impression was created that FIFA could no longer assert its leadership role, but the host country was able to enforce its own claims.

Another example regarding the **shifted power relations** was the opening match, which was moved forward by one day to November 20, 2022, just a few months earlier, so that Qatar could play the first match of the tournament. The next example was the short-term FIFA ban on the "One Love" captain's armband (similar to the rainbow colors of the LGBTQ+ movement). Ten European participating countries (England, Holland, Belgium, Switzerland, Wales, France, Denmark, Norway, Sweden, and Germany) had jointly designed this and wanted their team captains to wear it as a sign against any form of discrimination during the games (Spox, 2022). Although this had been communicated to FIFA since September and officially requested, the world football association only reacted one day before the first match day, announcing that due to a violation of the FIFA dress code, rigorous sanctions could be expected (yellow card for the player, fine up to exclusion from the tournament for the team). As a result, all involved

Points of contention	Reproaches	Justifications	Consequences for related sports sponsorships
Awarding of the 2022 World Cup	Irregular and non -transparent	Decision-making process within the framework of FIFA regulations.	General negative effect simply due to proximity to Qatar.
Execution in winter	Disruption of league soccer, because in the middle of its usual season, risk of overloading the players.	Professional footballers have to do their job like all professionals.	Problematic overlap with Christmas
Human rights	Violation of all basic principles (equality of all people, women's rights), disregard for freedom of expression, discrimination against the local population and foreign fans.	At the time of the award, the host was already exactly the same as it is now – namely a state that cannot be compared with the standards of the West.	Mixing politics and sport.
Stadium construction	Catastrophic working conditions (allegedly thousands of deaths) and gross violations in terms of sustainability (white elephants).	The Qataris have promised to dismantle numerous stadiums, FIFA and Qatar have announced a climate -neutral World Cup, it remai ns to be seen.	Negative effect due to participation in reckless waste of money (costs of EUR 220 billion for the most expensive World Cup of all time).
Corruption	Strong suspicion of corruption and proven bribery from start to finish– from the award ceremony to the presentation ceremony.	Things are different in Arab countries than in many other countries around the world, and a certain tolerance on the part of Western circles is also part of it.	Major sponsorships come directly from Qatar and the Arab world, with opaque cash flows casting a shadow.
Sportswashing	Attempt to improve the image of one's own country by organizing major sporting events and their positive reputation without actually making any changes.	Why are so many people only really crying out now, when it was no different with major sporting events in Russia and China.	A clear opposing position and distancing oneself from others can be expected to win sympathy.
Supremacy of the hosts	Compliant and submissive behavior on the part of FIFA officials, including the restriction of sponsorship rights (Budweiser).	The World Cup organizer has ceded the World Cup rights to the host, so the host also has the say.	Loss of rights and communication sovereignty.

Fig. 15.2 Summary of the controversial points about the 2022 world cup in Qatar

associations, including the DFB, cooperated, and the team captains wore the "standard" captain's armbandsprovided by FIFA.

If one summarizes the different discussion points with their accusations and justifications, a complete picture emerges that can explain why the anticipation and interest of the fans experienced a significant decrease. In Fig. 15.2, a **summary of the controversial points** about the 2022 World Cup 2022 in Qatar can be found. Based on various topics (tournament allocation, winter hosting, human rights, stadium construction, corruption, sportswashing, preference of the host), the accusations, the justifications, and possible consequences for related sports sponsorings are listed. For the sponsors, it was particularly serious that the overall interest in the World Cup among the population decreased significantly.

The controversial debates, especially in Germany, caused a stir and also led to corresponding **changes in opinion and behavior in the population**. The anticipation was always very high at previous World Cups. However, opinion polls show that anticipation and expectations have decreased this year. In Fig. 15.3, the results of a study representative for Germany are presented, showing the interest in sports, football, and the World Cup at the last four World Cups.

15.2 Reactions of the Participants and Effects on Sports Sponsoring

The World Cup is a global event in which not only the general population and the fans in particular are involved. Rather, a **network of sponsors** is involved in a World Cup, who have very different interests. As shown in Fig. 15.4, several levels with different involvements (organizers, hosts, participants, visitors) can generally be distinguished at a World Cup. Accordingly, various categories of sponsors are involved, such as global

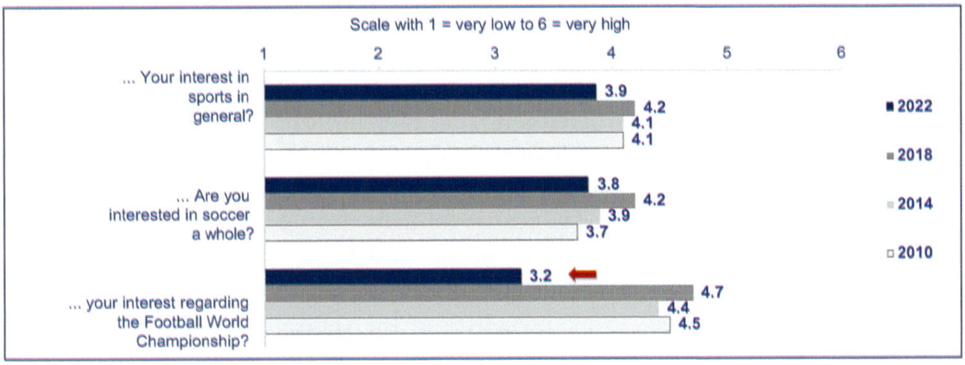

Fig. 15.3 Interests and expectations for the last four world cups. (*Source*: Voeth & Urbitsch, 2022, Volume 1, p. 7)

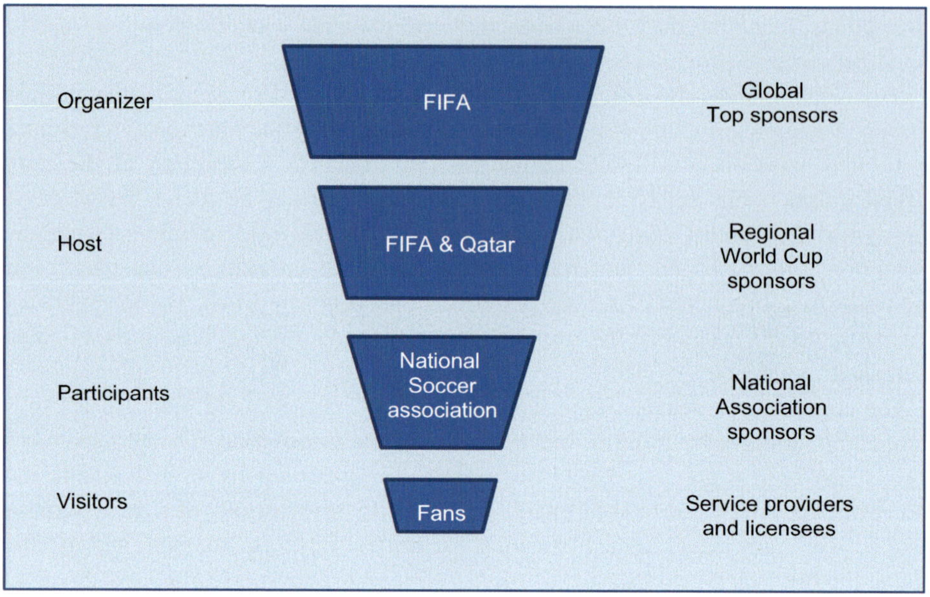

Fig. 15.4 Sponsors and other participants in the 2022 world cup in Qatar

top sponsors, regional World Cup sponsors, national association sponsors, and service providers and licensees. Many of these sponsors—some more, some less—are faced with the question of how to deal with and cope with such new situations. Among the various sponsors, there is a varying degree of concern.

The World Cup in Qatar almost turned into a "nightmare" for sponsors even before it started, noting that this is particularly true for those from Western countries, especially the European football nations. The numerous **criticisms and negative headlines** such as allegations of corruption, human rights violations, dead migrant workers—all this damaged the image of the sponsors and their proximity to this unique major sports event in many ways.

Furthermore, these topics dominated the media landscape and also mobilized the public. Many marketing and sponsoring professionals could not detect any enthusiasm among their target groups and the public. Therefore, some sponsors also tried to establish as little direct reference to the tournament in Qatar as possible. It was not in the sponsors' interest that the **sporting aspect was not the focus** of the tournament, but rather societal and political discussions. The reason for participating in a sponsoring—the fascination and enthusiasm for the rare tournament—receded into the background, and this could not and cannot be in the interest of the sponsors.

It was noticeable that due to the **structure of the sponsors**—especially the global and regional World Cup 2022 sponsors—and also due to the country-specific different

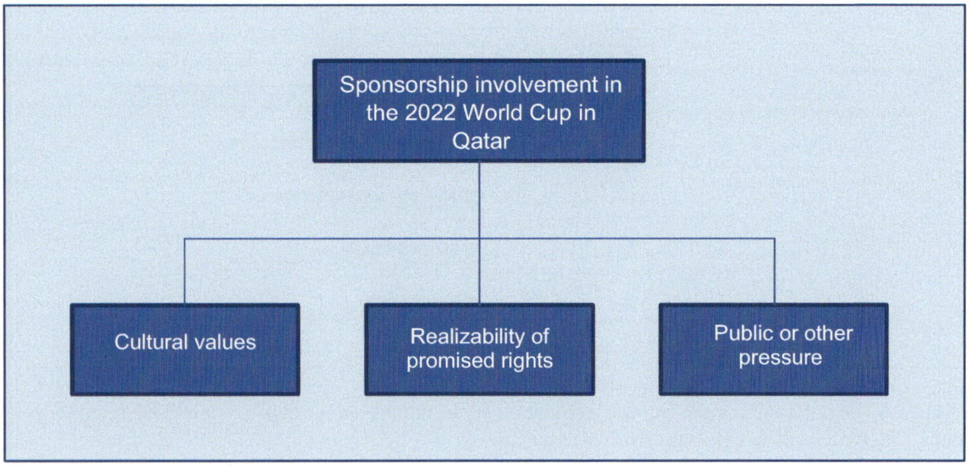

Fig. 15.5 Influencing factors of sponsor impact at the 2022 world cup in Qatar

handling of the World Cup in Qatar, only a few companies were seriously affected, but these were then quite significantly, as described in the Budweiser case. Fig. 15.5 shows the central influencing factors of the **impact on sponsors** at the World Cup in Qatar. These were primarily the affected cultural circle and the associated canon of values, the actual feasibility of the promised rights, and public and media pressure. It is also interesting that most of the regional World Cup sponsors came from the Asian-Arabic region, while only one European company remained among the global partners (Bruhn & Rohlmann, 2021).

The short-term imposed **restriction of the sponsoring rights** of the American brewing corporation Anheuser-Busch InBev with its brand Budweiser and the subsequent, particularly sharp criticism articulated in Germany, including calls for boycotts, were particularly noticeable. The latter could count on broad support among the fans, as empirical studies showed before the tournament. The majority of fans did not want to follow the World Cup live—a clear indication of what opinion the fans had of the World Cup in Qatar and FIFA (Voeth & Urbitsch, 2022; FanQ, 2022a). Throughout the year, fans were repeatedly asked how much they were **looking forward to the tournament** in Qatar. While in February 2022 only 6.5% of fans stated that they were "very much" looking forward to it, this number continued to decrease throughout the World Cup year. In the survey from November 2022, only 4.3% of respondents stated that they were "very much" looking forward to it (FanQ, 2022b).

In the summer of 2022, the **calls for a boycott of the World Cup** became louder (YouGov, 2022b). In total, 48% of respondents were in favor of the DFB team withdrawing, 28% were of the opinion that the DFB team should not miss the start of the World

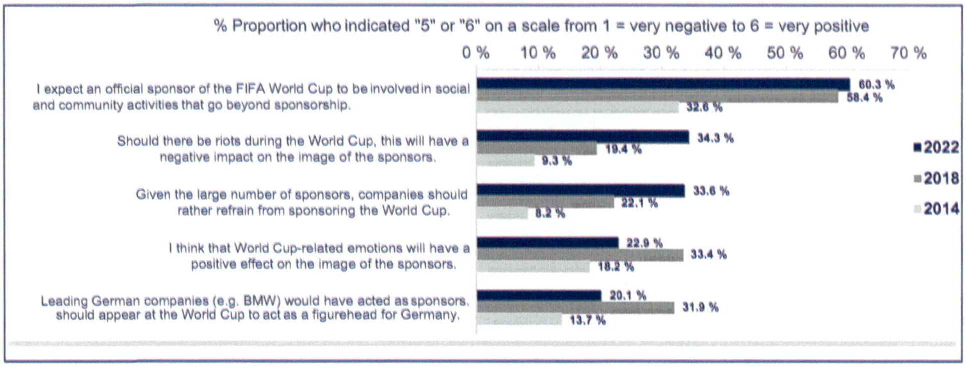

Fig. 15.6 Expectations of the German population regarding the sponsors of the last three football world cups. (*Source*: Voeth & Urbitsch, 2022, Volume 2, p. 8)

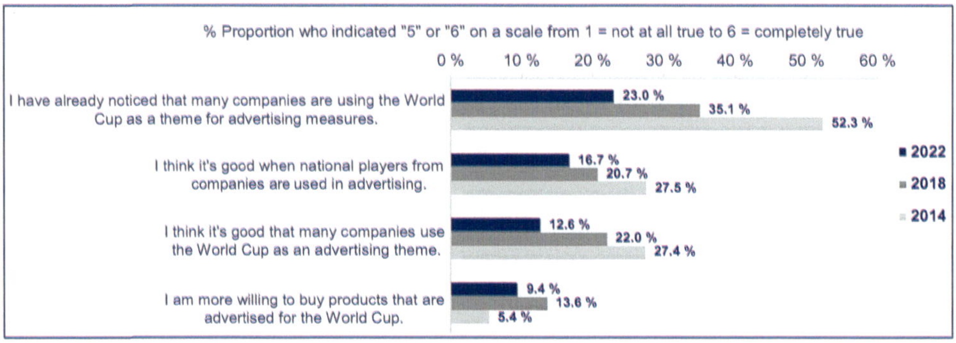

Fig. 15.7 Attitude of the German population towards world cup-related advertising activities of the last three football world cups. (*Source*: Voeth & Urbitsch, 2022, Volume 3, p. 9)

Cup in the fall. The proportion of people who did not provide any information was 24%. Also with regard to **World Cup-related advertising activities** by companies, the skepticism of the German population was as high as never before. Figs. 15.6 and 15.7 show the results of a representative survey in the population regarding the World Cup sponsors of the last three football World Cups. It becomes clear that the expectations of the population towards sponsors could not be reconciled with the events in Qatar.

In a similar way, the opinion of the Germans developed regarding advertising measures in connection with the World Cup in Qatar. As Fig. 15.7 shows with the results of a representative survey, compared to the last three football World Cups, the **World Cup-related advertising activities** were no longer rated so positively. Here too, the German population took a critical stance towards the World Cup sponsors.

The **DFB** and German **politicians** issued opposing statements in the run-up to the tournament (including DFB President Bernd Neuendorf regarding a "clear stance" and "showing edge"), only to later defensively bow to the short-term FIFA decisions. Visits by politicians and other public figures to Qatar to build contacts and networks were critically eyed by "normal" fans. Federal Interior Minister Nancy Faeser, on the other hand, had the courage to demonstratively place herself next to FIFA President Gianni Infantino at the first group match of the Germans with the "One-Love-Band" on her arm, which was forbidden by FIFA for the teams.

Examples: Creative Handling of Dress Codes in Connection with the 2022 World Cup

Actually, the DFB and six other European associations wanted to set a sign with the armband action. After the world federation FIFA had announced sanctions such as yellow cards for the players, the associations withdrew their project one day before their World Cup start, which caused widespread astonishment. All the more striking was an action by the Danish sports goods company Hummel, which set a special sign for the World Cup with the help of the jersey design for its own national team.

Thus, the Danish national team wore jerseys at the 2022 World Cup in Qatar that criticized the human rights situation in the host country. Equipment supplier Hummel provided a total of three jersey variants for the Danish Football Association (Dansk Boldspil-Union, DBU) (home, away, and alternate version). All three were intended to draw attention to the human rights and worker situation in the host country Qatar. But especially the completely black alternate version was supposed to honor the migrant workers who died in Qatar. Neither the company logo nor the association emblem of the DBU were supposed to stand out in color. The sponsor explained that they did not want to be visible on the jersey in view of the deaths during the construction measures at the tournament, and that while they supported the Danish national team, they did not support Qatar as the host country. Last but not least, sponsor Hummel donated a percentage of its total online revenues (including sales of the Denmark jerseys) to Amnesty International. The Danish fans were totally thrilled and the sales figures of the World Cup jerseys exceeded everything seen before.

Host Qatar was outraged by the action, which was celebrated on social media. The fact that Hummel had no problem with the Handball World Cup 2015 in Qatar, as well as with the sponsoring of Qatari teams until at least 2020, was obviously forgotten (Die Welt, 2022). ◀

The **athletes** (players and coaches) were the participants with the least action possibilities in connection with the demanded protests and boycott calls. Ironically, things were demanded of the people for whom a World Cup is a highlight in their sporting life and experience, things they had not caused and which belonged in the responsibility of others. However, neither FIFA officials nor politicians have found a solution to this over many years to this day.

However, **consequences from World Cup sponsors** could already be observed earlier. This is particularly because the sponsors, from their basic understanding, did not agree with the agreed developments within the framework of the FIFA World Cups. **Continental** was already a sponsor of the tournament in 2006, 2010 and 2014, but did not continue the relationship. The British oil company **Castrol** sponsored two tournaments (2010 and 2014), but did not return in 2018, and **Johnson & Johnson** from the USA was also a main sponsor in 2014, but not in 2018. These "western" sponsors were partly replaced by local partners, with the Russian energy company **Gazprom** being an additional sponsor for the 2018 World Cup. Gazprom was an enthusiastic supporter of football tournaments and teams and until the war in Ukraine at the end of February 2022 also a sponsor of the UEFA Champions League. It made the company a participant in the international football world. Since Russian money was no longer available, and some western sponsors continued to stay away from Qatar, the 2022 World Cup has focused heavily on Chinese sponsoring contracts.

The Japanese electronics corporation **Sony** and the airline **Emirates** from Dubai had already not renewed their contract with FIFA at the end of 2014—among other things because of the allegations of corruption in the awarding of the 2022 World Cup to Qatar. The remaining sponsors **Hyundai** and **Coca-Cola** had already expressed "quiet" criticism of FIFA's behavior in between.

The sponsors pay relatively high sponsoring amounts over many years in order to achieve their goals with the international fame and reputation of this major event. Therefore, it is understandable that a **waiver of their own presence** and a return on their

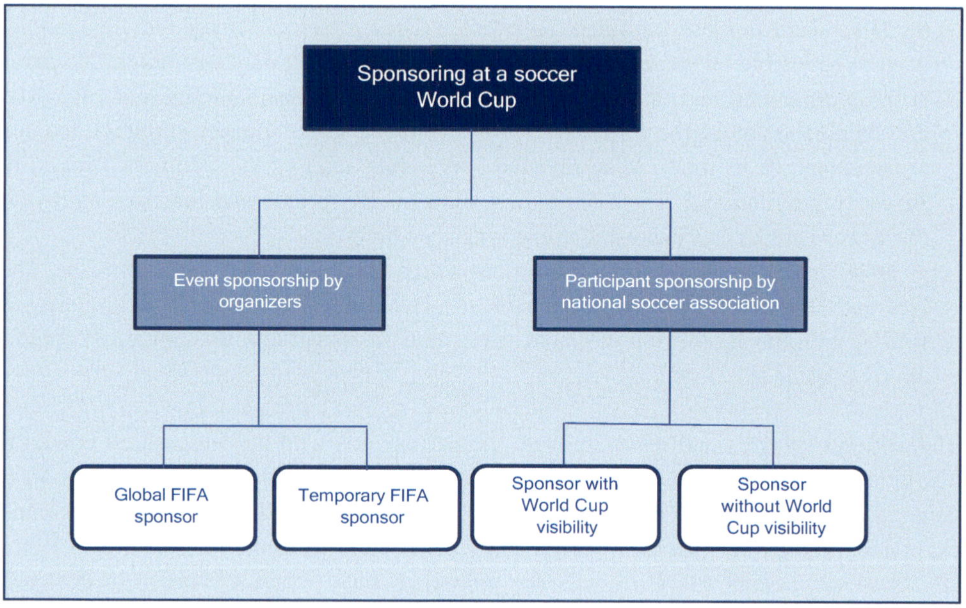

Fig. 15.8 Types of sponsors at a football world cup

sponsoring commitment due to different value systems of larger groups does not seem feasible for them. It is also necessary to check whether a current waiver may lead to long-term disadvantages for the waiving sponsor (e.g., no contract extension at the less criticized follow-up event, or a competitor takes over the role of the retiring sponsor). However, certain sympathy gains could also arise among the arguing target group, without the sponsor having the guarantee that this will last in the medium to long term.

The most important group alongside the rights holders for the broadcasting rights are the **sponsor companies**, which commit to this World Cup according to agreements with FIFA. In total, there are currently 22 companies, 14 of which are top sponsors. Fig. 15.8 shows different **types of sponsors at a World Cup**. In addition to global and regional FIFA sponsors, various forms of participant sponsoring can also be observed and taken into account among the national football associations.

Among the 14 top sponsors, there is only one company from Europe (Adidas), while a South Korean (Hyundai/Kia) and four more American companies can be attributed to Western culture and society. Fig. 15.9 lists the **changes in the sponsor structure at the Football World Cups** in recent years. It becomes clear that the "Asian" share as well as the share of "authoritarian governed" states has increased significantly. This in turn means that FIFA had no really significant problems with the official sponsor partners for the World Cup despite possibly smaller "demands" regarding the design of the tournament, especially since most of these partners concluded or extended their contract early and knowing the venue and tournament time. However, at least the sponsors from the Western-oriented countries must have been aware that the **sponsoring of the World Cup in Qatar is associated with reputation risks**, which, however, was completely irrelevant for the Chinese and Qatari companies.

	WM 2002	WM 2006	WM 2010	WM 2014	WM 2018	WM 2022
Europe	3	10	4	3	7	2
America	7	7	5	13	4	7
Africa/Middle East	0	1	6	1	2	6
Asia	9	3	4	3	8	7
Total	19	21	19	20	21	22

	WM 2002	WM 2006	WM 2010	WM 2014	WM 2018	WM 2022
Europe share	16 %	48 %	21 %	15 %	33 %	9 %
America share	37 %	33 %	26 %	65 %	19 %	32 %
Asia/MEA share	47 %	19 %	53 %	20 %	48 %	59 %

Authoritarian countries	0	1	2	2	15	10
Pro rata	0 %	5 %	11 %	10 %	71 %	45 %

Fig. 15.9 Changes in the sponsor structure at the football world cups over the past 20 years. (*Source*: FIFA reports; Bruhn & Rohlmann, 2021)

According to a study (Global Data, 2022), **Chinese companies** provided more sponsoring money at the 2022 World Cup than companies from any other country ($1.4 billion from Chinese companies compared to $1.1 billion from US companies during the four-year tournament cycle). Even when considering the annual value of these sponsoring sums, China is the largest sponsor for FIFA 2022—and that without its own team at the World Cup.

For the American beer brand and **World Cup sponsor Budweiser**, the beer ban in Qatar meant less revenue and limited advertising presence. As a result, the company did not receive the services promised by FIFA, but it was a global topic of conversation and achieved a lot of reach in old and new media worldwide. At the same time, the company made a virtue out of necessity and had a clever solution for the unsold beer: Budweiser announced that it wanted to host the ultimate championship celebration for the winning country (Der Westen, 2022). After the initial disappointment, Budweiser reconsidered and turned the initially negative situation into a positive one with a new tweet, "the beer will go to the future world champion and his fans".

Each country qualified for the 2022 World Cup canalso grant sponsoring rights. The **national football associations with their own sponsors** are in the slipstream of their national team and benefit from their successes or a successful tournament participation of their team. These approximately 500 companies do not have sponsoring rights to the FIFA World Cup and are therefore dependent on designing their advertising communication exclusively in connection and direct reference to the sponsored association team.

This also applies to the **equipment suppliers**. At the World Cup tournament in Qatar, nine sports equipment companies were represented, which equipped the 32 World Cup participants. In addition to the so-called **Big 3 (Adidas, Nike and Puma)**, which not only sponsored over 80% of the participating nations, but also carried 97% of the total equipment sponsoring, Hummel, Kappa, Le Coq Sportif, Majid, Marathon and New Balance were also present. Fig. 15.10 shows the suppliers of the last six football World Cups and thus the dominance of the Big 3. Fig. 15.11 shows the expenditures of the equipment sponsors of these World Cups and shows the growth rates and the level of commitments.

	Korea/Japan	Germany	South Africa	Brazil	Russia	Qatar	20 years	
Supplier	WC 2002	WC 2006	WC 2010	WC 2014	WC 2018	WC 2022	2002-2022	Ø /WC
adidas	10	6	12	9	12	7	56	9.3
Nike	8	8	10	10	10	13	59	9.8
Puma	4	12	7	8	4	6	41	6.8
Other brands	10	6	3	5	6	6	36	6.0
Teams	32	32	32	32	32	32		32

Fig. 15.10 Suppliers of football world cups 2002–2022. (*Source*: FIFA and PR MARKETING)

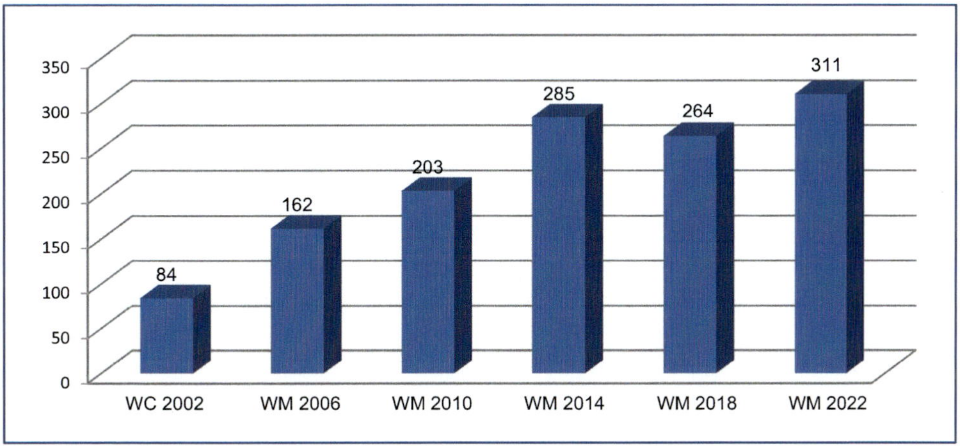

Fig. 15.11 Expenditures of equipment sponsors at a football world cup. (Source: PR MARKETING; in million EUR)

Since the **association and equipment sponsors of the participating teams** were not allowed to advertise directly with the event (exception Adidas, because the supplier is also a World Cup sponsor), they took a step back and, through clever communication in their target groups, focused more on the team qualified for the World Cup and less on the tournament itself. This allowed them to somewhat deflect the accusation of supporting Qatar in any way.

Examples: Developments of DFB Sponsorings in Connection with the 2022 World Cup

A rather flimsy example of a protest stance against FIFA and Qatar can be found with the Cologne food retailer **Rewe** (Zeit online, 2022b). It ended its cooperation with the DFB "spontaneously" in its opinion, although the termination at the end of 2022 had already been communicated to the association leadership by the retail group in October. The company announced the early termination shortly before the start of the tournament with a high-profile press release. The background was that the German national team did not use the "One Love" captain's armband for in the opening match against Japan as initially announced.

DFB sponsor **Flyeralarm** (contract until 2024) also issued a statement, saying that it had exchanged views in an open conversation with the DFB leadership around President Bernd Neuendorf and Managing Director Dr. Holger Blask. In this context, the partners had the opportunity to express their disappointment and expectations directly to the DFB.

Coca-Cola wants to "continue its commitment with the DFB". Because experience shows that changes take time and can be achieved through sustainable cooperation and active engagement.

Also **VW** and the other DFB sponsors view the current debate about the banned captain's armband critically and regret the current development. They do not accept FIFA's behavior from their point of view. ◀

According to a survey, the majority of German football fans did not want to watch the World Cup at all and even planned to refrain from buying sponsor products and brands (Sponsors, 2022d). The latter could also become problematic for the DFB's sponsor partners if they fail to meet the challenge between (desired) World Cup participation and (perceived) host support.

From the fans' point of view, not only was there a risk of damage to their brand image for the World Cup sponsors, but they also ran the risk of **sales losses due to a sponsoring in Qatar**. Fig. 15.12 shows the results of a survey in which a large majority of 58.2% of respondents stated that a sponsoring at the World Cup in Qatar would negatively affect their personal willingness to buy products from World Cup sponsors.

It seemed as if there was no royal road for World Cup sponsors in this complex situation that had already arisen from the awarding in 2010. If the fans had had their say, the

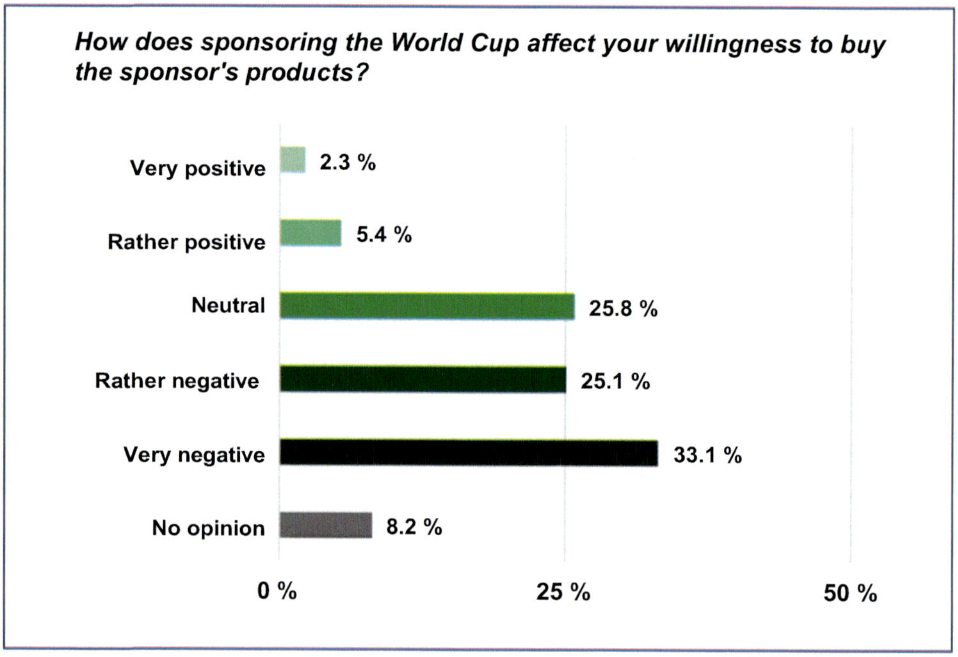

Fig. 15.12 Products of the world cup sponsors in Qatar lose attractiveness. (*Source*: FanQ, 2022a, p. 18)

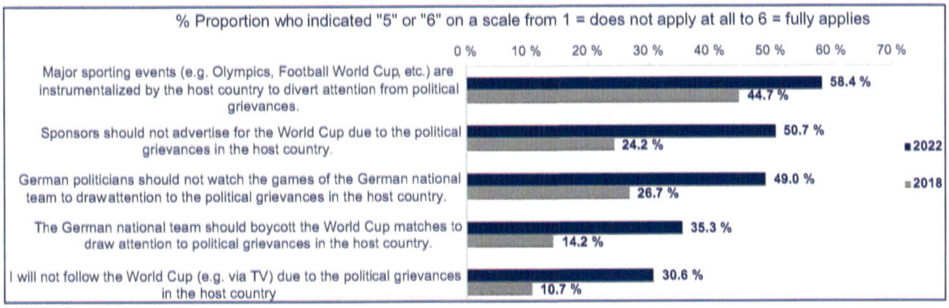

Fig. 15.13 Sponsoring as well as politics and society in connection with the football world cup from the fans' perspective. (*Source*: Voeth & Urbitsch, 2022, Volume 4, p. 6)

only solution for them would have been a **renunciation of sponsoring in Qatar** as a way out of the dilemma. However, this highly idealistic problem solution was not an option on the sponsor side. Instead, some sponsors chose to leave their advertising spaces unused or empty; others renounced provided ticket contingents and hospitality packages. Current statements from fans on the topic of World Cup sponsoring as well as politics and society suggest that from the fans' perspective, the proximity of companies and politics to major sporting events will not be problem-free in the future. Fig. 15.13 shows the results of a representative survey in Germany, reflecting the critical opinions of the fans.

15.3 Review and Outlook Regarding the 2022 World Cup

Looking back at the World Cup tournament in Qatar, different insights emerge depending on the perspective. If one considers the results for sponsored parties including the host on the one hand, and sponsors and participating nations on the other, the following **summary** can be drawn as an interim status (Spring 2023):

- **Hosts and organizers**: Qatar and FIFA promised the best World Cup ever, mutually praised each other for the best execution after the conclusion, but also received praise from third parties. Western countries strongly criticized the tournament at the beginning—Germany in particular (Focus, 2022). During the course of the games, there were many politically influenced debates and contradictions, but also occasionally differentiating statements. FIFA achieved its best result in sponsoring to date, and Qatar was perceived worldwide as one of the most ambitious and best-organized countries in the Arab world. Whether there will actually be a stronger anchoring of ESG criteria in the awarding and execution of mega sporting events in the face of noticeable protests is uncertain. This is likely to be the case, not least because it is to be expected that host countries will continue to use established sporting events for their own purposes.

- **Participating nations**: The sporting results at the 2022 Football World Cup brought many surprises. For example, the division of the football world into "big and small" no longer holds true, if it ever did. Most sponsors fully utilized the tightness of the event space, the perfect organization in the country, and the global attention for their campaigns. Only in Western Europe—and especially in Germany—there were some discordant notes from sponsors (e.g., Rewe in Germany, Hummel in Denmark).
- **Sponsors**: FIFA announced unilateral and extremely short-term changes to agreements with sponsors several times. Protests and criticism from sponsors of national (especially European) associations were ineffective or quickly disappeared from the headlines due to sporting miseries. FIFA's commercial growth of around 30% shows that sponsors overall were not deterred by protests and criticism regarding Qatar, or did not find the conditions on site as worthy of criticism as some other participants. Nevertheless, the incidents in Qatar teach that sponsoring companies of major sporting events should also consider an alternative strategy in the future if the framework conditions cannot be clearly considered as secured.

Although the tournament in Qatar was not as successful as desired for some FIFA partners and some team sponsors in relation to the target groups in Germany, the general **conclusion of the World Cup sponsors** remains predominantly positive, which may be partly due to their origin from Eastern cultures. Looking at the very World Cup-critical Germany, it can be noted that anticipation and interest in the 2022 Football World Cup were significantly lower than in other countries. If, for example, TV viewers and their market shares are used as a criterion for fan interest, more or less surprising results are shown. According to AGF video research, the **viewing figures in Germany** for the public broadcasters have dropped drastically, thus reducing the reach of the sponsors, even though the actual viewing figures were probably higher due to digital viewers. Magenta TV also broadcast the 2022 World Cup games, but the reach of this broadcaster is not published. In addition, streaming views via media libraries, apps, and websites were not counted in 2022. Fig. 15.14 shows the TV viewing figures by viewers and market shares of the last three Football World Cups.

The German disinterest in football goes hand in hand with the performance of the DFB team for some time. Looking at the international matches of 2022 as a whole, the viewing figures here are also far from those of previous years. In addition to the criticism of Qatar, a certain fan **alienation from the national team** can also be observed. Fig. 15.15 shows the viewing figures for various games of the German national team.

Recent surveys during the World Cup in Qatar have yielded relatively poor **polling results for the participants** in Germany. When asked how the image of Qatar, FIFA, and DFB has changed due to the course of the World Cup so far, the results for the actors after the first tournament week were not pleasing. Fig. 15.16 shows the results of the ARD-Deutschlandtrend survey on the perception of the host country and football associations by the German population at the 2022 World Cup. Given these relatively poor values, it was all the more understandable that numerous sponsors have tried to behave

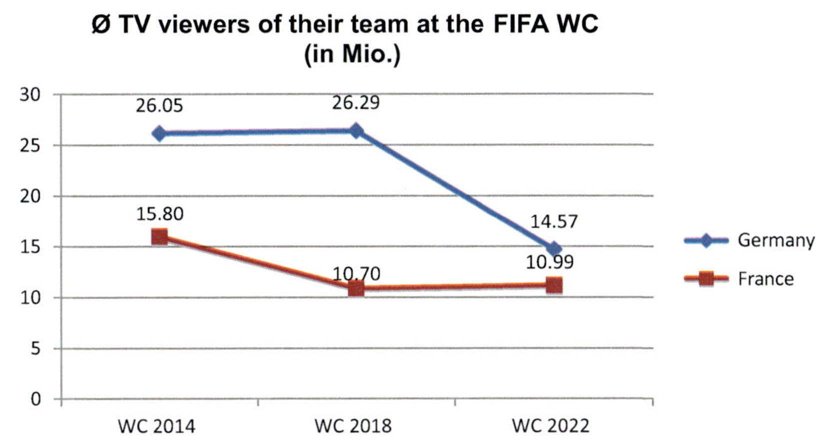

Ø TV viewers			
Group stage	WC 2014	WC 2018	WC 2022
Germany (Mio. viewers)	26.05	26.29	14.57
France (Mio. viewers)	15.80	10.70	10.99
Ø Market shares			
Group stage	WC 2014	WC 2018	WC 2022
Germany	80.8 %	81.7 %	54.2 %

Fig. 15.14 TV viewing figures by viewers and market shares at football world cups. (*Source*: AGF, 2014–2022)

	Number of games	Mio. TV-viewers	Market share
Test matches 2022	3	6.48	25.1 %
Nations League 2022	6	7.63	31.7 %
WC 2022 Qatar 2022	3	14.57	54.3 %

Fig. 15.15 TV viewing figures for all games of the German national team in 2022. (*Source*: AGF, 2022)

as quietly as possible to avoid attracting negative attention and being too much drawn into the negative image trend of the tournament in Germany.

Similarly, there was a certain **division of the fan base** regarding the question of political statements in football. Fig. 15.17 shows the results of the ARD-Deutschlandtrend survey on the protest attitude of footballers as perceived by the German population at the 2022 World Cup. While a slight majority advocated for a clear (protesting) appearance

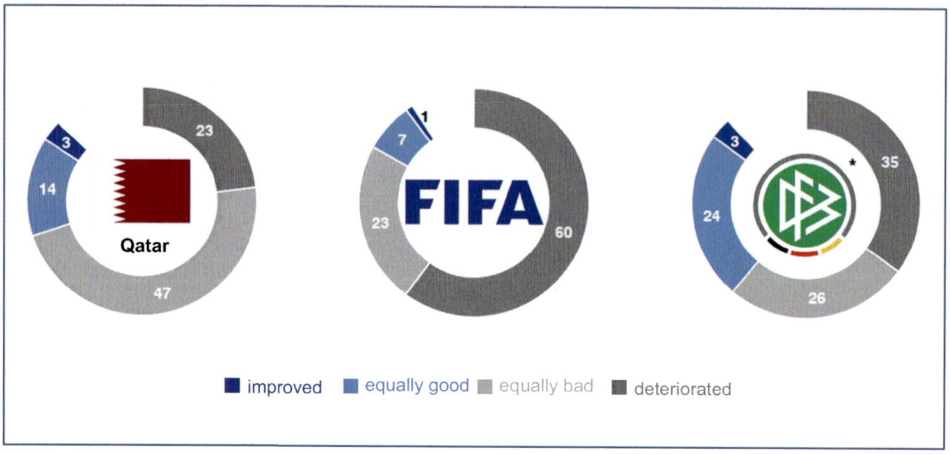

Fig. 15.16 Perception of the host country and football associations by the German population at the 2022 world cup. (Source: ARD, 2022)

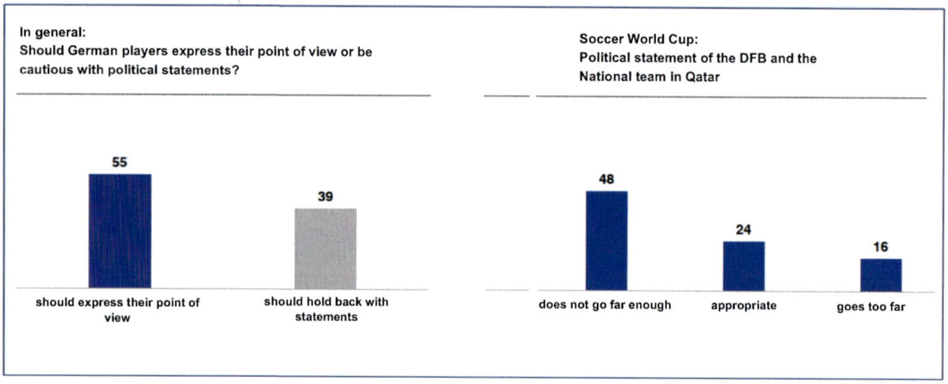

Fig. 15.17 Opinion of the German population on the protest attitude of footballers at the 2022 world cup. (*Source*: ARD, 2022)

(the German national team posed at the first group match with the gesture of a covered mouth), almost half of the respondents did not consider this gesture protest enough.

The low interest in the 2022 World Cup in Germany was also felt by most retailers who, in addition to FIFA World Cup 2022 items, also had **fan merchandise of the German national team** on offer. Added to this is the fact that the tournament fell right in the middle of the Christmas season and energy prices and inflation heavily burdened consumers. These conditions reduced a lucrative merchandising business for FIFA and its licensees.

Experts estimate that the 2022 World Cup generated **revenues for FIFA** of over 7.5 billion USD this year (Handelsblatt, 2022). About a quarter of the revenue comes from marketing rights (approx. 1.8 billion USD for partner, sponsor, and regional support categories). FIFA licensee Legends, who ran the e-commerce shop, also had winter World Cup items on offer. However, the buying mood was not as high and the range was not as extensive as usual. Thus, among others, the Handelsblatt headlined on 01.11.2022 "No trace of football fever", the Merkur announced on 07.11.2022 "Kaufland is already selling off fan utensils before the World Cup in Qatar" and Wallstreet-Online knew as early as 12.11.2022 "Economy expects a gloomy World Cup business".

World Cup and DFB sponsor Adidas is likely to have been unimpressed by the poor sales figures. At the end of August 2022, the DFB and its equipment supplier Adidas presented the new **Germany jersey**. Fans could buy the shirt in the official DFB fan shop at a price that remained constant compared to the previous tournament, while prices for shorts (+ 12.6%), socks (+ 27.9%), and finishing (+ 20%) had risen sharply. But not even eight weeks later, jersey discounts of a third were standard. As early as mid-November, even the DFB fan shop offered the adult shirt with a 20% discount. In some cities, the item now dubbed a "shelf warmer" was even available at the retail purchase price of 36 EUR. After the DFB's preliminary round exit, even equipment supplier Adidas reduced the item by 40% on its own webshop.

Another evidence of rather weak or half-hearted protests by sponsors was an **action by human rights organizations** Human Rights Watch, Amnesty International, and FairSquare (web.de, 2022). In the summer of 2022 (the award to Qatar was already 12 years ago), they contacted 14 companies and World Cup sponsors of the FIFA football association and asked them to address human rights issues with FIFA and Qatar. They wanted to ensure that compensation payments were made to workers (or their families) who had died, been injured, or exploited during the construction of the World Cup stadiums. The result: Only four companies responded, specifically Anheuser-Busch InBev/Budweiser, Adidas, Coca-Cola, and McDonald's. This also means: Ten companies remained silent, specifically Visa, Hyundai-Kia, the Wanda Group, Qatar Energy, Qatar Airways, Vivo, Hisense, Mengniu, Crypto, and Byju's.

The very restrained **response of sponsors to human rights violations** showed an obviously clear stance that has not yet existed in this extreme form. This is probably also because sponsors usually did not express criticism, e.g., most recently at the 2021 Olympic Games in Beijing. It seems to be a widespread maxim in the **connection of sports and politics** to take a restrained position as a sponsor and not to participate in the discussion in order to avoid risks. All this is combined with the hope that the specific tensions will subside and the next (less or non-controversial) sports event will take place soon. By then, any negative headlines or vibrations would have long been forgotten. It remains to be seen whether this attitude will also be confirmed after the World Cup in Qatar.

Another interesting aspect will be how sponsors deal with major events in the future, i.e., whether they will show a sensitization to difficult and controversial issues or whether the **adaptation processes of the sponsors** will remain. They are caught in a tension between striving for communicative impact through the World Cup and public discussion and pressure generated by certain parts of politics, the media, and the public. If this pressure does not persist after the tournament and subsides in favor of other issues, this shows only a temporary interest of the public, and then actions against sponsors of the World Cup in Qatar will no longer be worthwhile (web.de, 2022).

Case Study: Brewdog—World Cup sponsoring in changing times

While for decades sponsoring participation in a Football World Cup was seen as a successful marketing campaign and value-enhancing competitive positioning, the 2022 World Cup in Qatar also brought up contrary examples. The Scottish beer brand **Brewdog** made a statement against the World Cup in Qatar with its campaign. On posters and in social media, the company called itself "proud Anti-Sponsor of the World F*Cup" (Tageskarte, 2022). A poster of Brewdog's anti-World Cup campaign is reproduced in Fig. 15.18. Critics, however, accuse Brewdog of hypocrisy because the company apparently wanted to profit from the World Cup.

Fig. 15.18 Anti-World Cup Campaign 2022 by Brewdog. (Source: Tageskarte, 2022)

With its striking poster campaign, the "Craft Brewer" caused a worldwide sensation in Europe. The company positioned itself against the World Cup in Qatar and openly denounced, among other things, the violation of fundamental human rights. In addition, Brewdog promised that it would donate the proceeds from the sold beer brand "Lost Lager" to charitable organizations. Critics, on the other hand, accused the beer brand of double standards—also because it was reported last year that there was a "culture of fear" at Brewdog. Critics also claim that Brewdog would only want to benefit from the World Cup in Qatar, instead of boycotting it. Not only were the World Cup games still shown in Brewdog pubs, but it also became known that the brewer had concluded an agreement with the host country Qatar about the World Cup through a third party just a few months ago (Meedia, 2022). ◄

15.4 Implications for Upcoming Major Sporting Events

In addition to the Football World Cup, the Olympic Games and the European Football Championships are among the most watched worldwide—and in terms of sponsoring—the largest sporting events in the world. The next events have already been awarded or

Jahr	Sportevent	Gastgeber	Zeitraum
2024	European Football Championship	Germany, 10 cities (GER)	14.06.-14.07.24
2024	Olympic Summer Games	Paris (FRA)	26.07.-11.08.24
2026	Winter Olympics	Milan-Cortina d'Ampezzo (ITA)	06.02.-22.02.26
2026	Soccer World Cup	Canada, Mexico, USA	08.06.-03.07.26
2028	European Football Championship	Great Britain and Ireland	June/July
2028	Summer Olympics	Los Angeles (USA)	14.07.-30.07.28
2030	Soccer World Cup	Portugal, Spain and Morocco as well as Argentina, Paraguay, Uruguay	08.06.-21.07.30
2032	Summer Olympics	Brisbane (AUS)	23.07.-08.08.32
2032	European Football Championship	Italy and Turkey	June/July

Fig. 15.19 Major sporting events of the near future

are in planning, the **major sporting events** for the years 2024 to 2032 are shown in Fig. 15.19.

For the sponsoring financiers, the **interplay between sports and politics** remains a dilemma in the future, both morally and conceptually and financially. On the one hand, there is concern that a negative image of a sporting event may also be associated with a negative image transfer, and the brand may be heavily burdened as a result. If one criticizes too harshly, there is a risk that the original idea behind the commitment will not (any longer) come to the fore. However, the sporting mega-events also offer many companies a platform that allows them to achieve global goals relatively quickly, as seems hardly possible elsewhere. Therefore, the attractiveness of such commitments in sports sponsoring is unlikely to decrease in the future, and the sponsoring revenues of the rights holders will continue to grow.

However, major sporting events like those in Qatar, Russia, and China have shown that the **influence of non-sporting interests** particularly comes into play in the sponsoring situation and thus the sponsoring effect when the host countries have significantly different political and/or cultural orientations than the Western (often sports- and economically stronger) nations. The upcoming major events do not seem to have to fear this "systemic" danger, which is why the European Football Championship in Germany will also be a successful event for all sponsors and fans.

If the major international sports associations want to attract less criticism in the future or expect further increasing approval from business and society, some **lessons for the awarding of World Championships**—also due to the experiences from past awards for hosting—seem necessary. In this context, the following should be mentioned:

- The criteria catalogs, which are generally or globally accepted, include fair and transparent examinations and decisions about the award for a major sporting event.
- Enforcement of agreed sponsor services and adherence to the respective contracts by the rights holder for the rights holder and this also in the extreme case against the resistance of the hosts.
- Respect and fair play for all participants, because sports and not politics should be in the foreground, and this without restrictions.

The review and outlook of the Football World Cup 2022 in Qatar has shown how extremely different the positions of the participants were at this event. The significant cultural differences between the host country and other (essential) countries have further exacerbated the positions. This was particularly clearly articulated in Germany and also publicly discussed by politics, the media, the associations, and many others. Whether this will have **effects on sports sponsoring** remains to be seen, and these will initially refer to the major events in sports.

It will be interesting to observe whether lessons will actually be learned from the World Cup 2022 in Qatar, i.e., whether the participants will deal with a **"learning curve"** and avoid the negative aspects in advance, or whether a **"forgetting curve"** will set in among the participants, by quickly fading out the negative aspects and continuing to conduct major events of this kind according to their own rules and principles.

For the affected sports sponsors, this means increasingly dealing with a **risk management** and thinking in alternatives, so that the opportunities and risks for the sponsor remain calculable.

References

A

AGF. (2014–2022). Tägliche Top 10-Sendungen mit der höchsten Sehbeteiligung sowie Marktanteile, AGF Videoforschung in Zusammenarbeit mit GfK. https://www.agf.de/daten/tv-daten.

ARD. (2022). ARD-DeutschlandTREND Dezember 2022. Eine repräsentative Studie im Auftrag der tagesthemen. https://www.tagesschau.de/inland/deutschlandtrend/deutschlandtrend-pdf-105.pdf.

B

Bild. (2022). Korrupte Fifa-Mitglieder stopften sich doppelt die Taschen voll, Beitrag vom 18.11.2022. https://www.bild.de/sport/fussball/fifa-wm-2022/wm-2022-in-katar-skandal-korrupte-fifa-mitglieder-stopften-sich-doppelt-die-tasc-81989888.bild.html.

Bruhn, M., & Rohlmann, P. (2021). Instrumentalisierung im Fußball und Auswirkungen auf die Stakeholder. *Absatzwirtschaft online, 64*(11). Accessed: 15. Nov. 2021.

D

Der Westen. (2022). Katar: Bier-Verbot bei WM 2022 – jetzt reagiert Budweiser drastisch, Beitrag vom 27.11.2022. https://www.derwesten.de/sport/fussball/katar-wm-budweiser-bier-id300199270.html.

Die Welt. (2022). Der etwas scheinheilige Katar-Protest mit dem dänischen Trikot, Beitrag vom 30.09.2022. https://www.welt.de/sport/article241346503/WM-in-Katar-Der-etwas-scheinheilige-Protest-mit-dem-daenischen-Trikot.html.

F

FanQ. (2022a). Erwartungen an die WM 2022 in Katar. Eine Studie aus Perspektive der Fans. https://fanq-app.com/wp-content/uploads/2022/05/fanq-studie-erwartungen-wm-katar-endversion-1.pdf.

FanQ. (2022b). Studienreihe zur WM 2022 in Katar. https://fanq.com/studienreihe-zur-wm-2022-in-katar-vorfreude-ist-bei-jungen-fussball-fans-groesser/.

Focus. (2022). ARD-Reporterin nach Rückkehr: Katar-Kritik „hatten wir Deutsche exklusiv", Beitrag vom 14.12.2022. https://www.focus.de/kultur/kino_tv/ard-reporterin-nach-rueckkehr-aus-katar-kritischen-blick-hatten-wir-exklusiv_id_180454664.html.

G

Global Data. (2022). Business of the FIFA World Cup 2022 – Property Profile, Sponsoring and Media Landscape, Beitrag vom 11.11.2022. https://www.globaldata.com/store/report/fifa-world-cup-business-analysis/.

H

Handelsblatt. (2022). FIFA plant mit Umsatzsteigerung auf elf Milliarden US-Dollar, Beitrag vom 16.12.2022. https://www.handelsblatt.com/dpa/fifa-plant-mit-umsatzsteigerung-auf-elf-milliarden-us-dollar/28873240.html.

M

Meedia. (2022). Wenn Haltung nur bis zum Claim reicht, Beitrag vom 10.11.2022. https://meedia.de/2022/11/10/wenn-haltung-nur-bis-zum-claim-reicht/.

S

Spiegel. (2022). Darum ist die WM in Katar so in Verruf, Beitrag vom 18.11.2022. https://www.spiegel.de/sport/fussball/fussball-wm-2022-in-katar-warum-die-weltmeisterschaft-so-umstritten-ist-a-2e06d0b8-6f2d-4c1f-bad1-4ad4d3b57ff4.

Sponsors. (2022d). FIFA WM 2022: Wie Sponsoren mit öffentlicher Kritik umgehen könnten, Beitrag vom 29.09.2022. https://www.sponsors.de/news/themen/fifa-wm-2022-wie-sponsoren-mit-oeffentlicher-kritik-umgehen-koennten.

Spox. (2022). Kommentar zur Farce um die One-Love-Binde: Das Einknicken von DFB und Co. ist frustrierender als die schauerliche Machtdemonstration der FIFA, Beitrag vom 21.11.2022. https://www.spox.com/de/sport/fussball/wm/wm2022/2211/Artikel/kommentar-farce-one-love-binde-einknicken-neuendorf-dfb-fa-niederlande-frustrierender-fifa-ftr.html.

T

Tageskarte. (2022). „Anti-Sponsor“ Brewdog für „World F*Cup“-Kampagne gefeiert und kritisiert, Beitrag vom 16.11.2022. https://www.tageskarte.io/detail/anti-sponsor-brewdog-fuer-world-fcup-kampagne-gefeiert-und-kritisiert.html.

V

Voeth, M., & Urbitsch, Y. (2022). *Studie zur FIFA WM 2022 in Katar. Was denkt die deutsche Bevölkerung?* (Bd. 1–4). Universität Hohenheim.

W

Web.de. (2022). Sponsoren der Fußball-WM am Pranger: Wie heftig sind die Image-Folgen für Adidas, Coca-Cola und Co.? Beitrag vom 05.11.2022. https://web.de/magazine/sport/fussball/wm/sponsoren-fussball-wm-pranger-heftig-folgen-adidas-coca-cola-co-37387076.

Y

YouGov. (2022b). Umfrage des Meinungsforschungsinstituts YouGov im Auftrag der Deutschen Presse-Agentur, Beitrag vom 03.07.2022. https://www.sportbuzzer.de/artikel/umfrage-wm-katar-grossteil-der-deutschen-fur-ruckzug-der-nationalmannschaft/.

Z

Zeit. (2022a). Investor Kühne erwirbt Namensrechte am Volksparkstadion, Beitrag vom 31.03.2022. https://www.zeit.de/news/2022-03/31/investor-kuehne-erwirbt-namensrechte-am-volksparkstadion.

Zeit. (2022b). Rewe und der DFB: „Das hätte man als PR-Aktion auch nicht besser planen können“, Beitrag vom 23.11.2022. https://www.zeit.de/wirtschaft/unternehmen/2022-11/rewe-dfb-kooperation-pr-aktion-one-love-binde.

References

A

ABB. (2016). ABB und Special Olympics. http://new.abb.com/de/ueber-uns/nachhaltigkeit/special-olympics. Accessed: 9. June 2016.

ABB. (2020). 100 ABB-Mitarbeiter bei Special Olympics, Beitrag vom 10.03.2020. https://new.abb.com/news/de/detail/58318/100-abb-mitarbeiter-bei-special-olympics. Accessed: 2. Nov. 2021.

About Drinks. (2016). Gemeinsam durch den Fußballsommer: Coca-Cola startet die Kampagne zur UEFA EURO 2016. http://www.about-drinks.com/coca-cola-startet-die-kampagne-zur-uefa-euro-2016/. Accessed: 8. June 2016.

About Drinks. (2021). Die Coca-Cola Weihnachtstrucks starten ihre Tour durch Deutschland. https://www.about-drinks.com/die-coca-cola-weihnachtstrucks-starten-ihre-tour-durch-deutschland/. Accessed: 2. Nov. 2021.

Abratt, R., Clayton, B. C., & Pitt, L. F. (1987). Corporate objectives in sports sponsoring. *International Journal of Advertising, 6*(4), 299–312. https://doi.org/10.1080/02650487.1987.11107030.

Abril Barrie, C., Sánchez Herrera, J., & Recio Naranjo, T. (2018). Does Wall Street love sports sponsoring? Stock market reactions to the announcement of global official sponsorings. *Journal of Advertising Research, 58*(3), 297–310. https://doi.org/10.2501/jar-2017-016.

Abril, C., Sanchez, J., & Recio, T. (2018). How does Wall Street react to global sports sponsoring announcements?: An analysis of the effect on sponsoring companies' stock market prices. *Journal of Advertising Research, 58*(3), 297–310. https://doi.org/10.2501/jar-2017-016.

Absatzwirtschaft. (2017). Authentisches aus der Kabine: Warum der FC Bayern München in den sozialen Medien erfolgreicher ist als andere, Beitrag vom 06.06.2017. https://www.absatzwirtschaft.de/authentisches-aus-der-kabine-warum-der-fc-bayern-muenchen-in-den-sozialen-medien-erfolgreicher-ist-als-andere-216251/. Accessed: 2. Nov. 2021.

Adidas. (2016). Adidas und FC Chelsea beenden Partnerschaft vorzeitig, Pressemitteilung vom 11.05.2016. https://www.adidas-group.com/de/medien/newsarchiv/pressemitteilungen/2016/adidas-und-fc-chelsea-beenden-partnerschaft-vorzeitig/. Accessed: 02.11.2021.

AGF. (2014–2022). Tägliche Top 10-Sendungen mit der höchsten Sehbeteiligung sowie Marktanteile, AGF Videoforschung in Zusammenarbeit mit GfK. https://www.agf.de/daten/tv-daten. Accessed: 2. Nov. 2021.

M. Bruhn and P. Rohlmann, *Sports Sponsoring*,
https://doi.org/10.1007/978-3-658-44171-5

Ahlert, D., Vogel, V., & Woisetschläger, D. (2007). Ist Sponsoring der Zaubertrank einer starken Marke? In D. Ahlert, D. Woisetschläger, & Vogel, V. (Hrsg.), *Exzellentes Sponsoring. Innovative Ansätze und Best Practices für das Markenmanagement* (2. Aufl., S. 3–32). https://doi.org/10.1007/978-3-8350-9639-4_1.

Allensbacher Markt- und Werbeträgeranalyse. (AWA 2016). Sportarten, Fußballvereine. http://sportfive.comsulting.de. Accessed: 19. Dec. 2016.

Allensbacher Markt- und Werbeträgeranalyse. (AWA 2011–2021). Allensbacher Markt- und Werbeträgeranalyse Codebuch.

Allianz Arena. (2014). Allianz stellt Kooperation mit FC Bayern München auf langfristige Basis, Beitrag vom 13.02.2014. https://allianz-arena.com/de/news/2014/02/allianz-steigt-beim-fc-bayern-munchen-ein. Accessed: 2. Nov. 2021.

Althoff, S. (2007). Das Sportsponsoring der Telekom – und was dahinter steckt. In D. Ahlert, D. Woisetschläger, & Vogel, V. (Hrsg.), *Exzellentes Sponsoring. Innovative Ansätze und Best Practices für das Markenmanagement* (2. Aufl., S. 77–100). https://doi.org/10.1007/978-3-8350-9639-4_4

Angermair, T. (2021). Best Case Sponsoring: Der außergewöhnliche Fall HOMEDAY x Hertha BSC. https://beyond-the-match.com/sponsoring/best-case-sponsoring-homeday-x-hertha-bsc/. Accessed: 2. Nov. 2021.

AOK.de. (2016). AOK und Deutscher Handballbund: Ein starkes Team. https://www.aok.de/inhalt/starkes-doppel-aok-kooperiert-mit-dem-dhb-1/. Accessed: 20. Dec. 2016.

ARD. (2022). ARD-DeutschlandTREND Dezember 2022. Eine repräsentative Studie im Auftrag der tagesthemen. https://www.tagesschau.de/inland/deutschlandtrend/deutschlandtrend-pdf-105.pdf. Accessed: 2. Nov. 2021.

AUDI. (2022). Audi stärkt Region als „guter Nachbar" und wird Titelsponsor beim Ingolstädter Triathlon, Beitrag vom 21.02.2022. https://www.audi-mediacenter.com/de/pressemitteilungen/audi-staerkt-region-als-guter-nachbar-und-wird-titelsponsor-beim-ingolstaedter-triathlon-14507. Accessed: 2. Nov. 2021.

B

Bagusat, A. (2013). *Sponsoring trends 2012*. https://www.ostfalia.de/export/sites/default/de/ispm/Blickpunkt_Sportmanagement/Sponsoring_Trends_2012.pdf. Accessed: 17. Febr. 2016.

Bagusat, A., & Marwitz, C. (2008). Sponsoring. Faszinierendes Instrument der Marketingkommunikation. In A. Bagusat, C. Marwitz, & M. Vogl (Hrsg.), *Handbuch Sponsoring. Erfolgreiche Marketing- und Markenkommunikation* (S. 3–15). Erich Schmidt.

Bassenge, C. (2000). *Dienstleister als Sponsoren. Imageprofilierung durch kommunikatives Engagement im Sport*. https://doi.org/10.1007/978-3-322-89616-2.

Bauer, H. H., Staat, M., & Hammerschmidt, M. (Hrsg.). (2006). *Marketingeffizienz. Messung und Steuerung mit der DEA – Konzept und Einsatz in der Praxis*. https://doi.org/10.15358/9783800643387.

Bauer, H. H., Hammerschidt, M., Hartung, R., & Shenawai, N. (2010). Messung und Analyse der Online-Werbeeffizienz. *Controlling – Zeitschrift für erfolgsorientierte Unternehmenssteuerung, 22*(2), 83–88. https://doi.org/10.15358/0935-0381-2010-2-83.

BBDO Live GmbH. (2010). Sponsoring Trends 2010, Studie in Zusammenarbeit mit dem Institut für Marketing, Universität der Bundeswehr München, Bonn.

Becker-Olsen, K. L., & Hill, R. P. (2006). The impact of sponsor fit on brand equity. The case of nonprofit service providers. *Journal of Service Research, 9*(1), 73–83. https://doi.org/10.1177/1094670506289532.

Becker-Olsen, K. L., & Simmons, C. J. (2002). When do social sponsorings enhance or dilute equity? Fit, message source, and the persistence of effects. *NA – Advances in Consumer Research, 29,* 287–289.

Bennett, R. (1999). Sport sponsorings. *European Journal of Marketing, 33*(3/4), 291–313. https://doi.org/10.1108/03090569910253071.

Bennett, R., & Gabriel, H. (1999). Schools sponsoring: Corporate philanthropy or integrated marketing communications weapon? *Journal of Communication Management, 4*(2), 135–158. https://doi.org/10.1108/eb023514.

Berliner Zeitung. (BZ 2015). Hertha verliert Bahn als Trikotsponsor vom 14.01.2015. https://www.bz-berlin.de/archiv-artikel/trikotwerbung-deutsche-bahn-geht-von-der-hertha-brust. Accessed: 2. Nov. 2021.

Berrett, T., & Slack, T. (2001). A framework for the analysis of strategic approaches employed by non-profit sport organisations in seeking corporate sponsoring. *Sport Management Review, 4*(1), 21–45. https://doi.org/10.1016/s1441-3523(01)70068-x.

Bhuiyan, M. A. H., Darda, M. A., & Hossain, M. B. (2022). Corporate social responsibility (CSR) practices in Islamic banks of Bangladesh. *Social Responsibility Journal, 18*(5), 968–983. https://doi.org/10.1108/srj-07-2020-0280.

Bild. (2022). Korrupte Fifa-Mitglieder stopften sich doppelt die Taschen voll, Beitrag vom 18.11.2022. https://www.bild.de/sport/fussball/fifa-wm-2022/wm-2022-in-katar-skandal-korrupte-fifa-mitglieder-stopften-sich-doppelt-die-tasc-81989888.bild.html. Accessed: 2. Nov. 2021.

Bitburger Braugruppe GmbH. (2016). *Fan force one.* https://www.fanforceone.de/. Accessed: 2. Nov. 2021.

Blache, C. (2020). Ist ein höherer Sinn für Marken sinnvoll? https://www.horizont.net/news/p/180111. Accessed: 2. Nov. 2021.

Blackshaw, I. S., & Hogg, G. (1993). *Sports marketing Europe: The legal and tax aspects.* Kluwer Law International.

Blake, J., Fourie, S., & Goldman, M. (2018). The relationship between sports sponsorings and corporate financial returns in South Africa. *International Journal of Sports Marketing and Sponsoring, 20*(1), 2–25. https://doi.org/10.1108/IJSMS-12-2016-0088.

BMW AG. (2016). *BMW International Open.* http://www.bmw-golfsport.com/en/tournaments/bmw-international-open/home/tournament.html. Accessed: 8. March 2016.

Bob Bomliz Group. (2008). Sponsoring Trends 2008, Studie in Zusammenarbeit mit dem Institut für Marketing, Universität der Bundeswehr München, Bonn.

Brand Finance. (2022). Deutsche Telekom: 2nd place among telecoms brands globally, Beitrag vom 08.06.2022. https://brandfinance.com/insights/brand-spotlight-deutsche-telekom-2022. Accessed: 2. Nov. 2021.

Brannasch, A. (2001). Milliarden verpulvert – wenn Marken Pech haben im Sportsponsoring. Vortrag im Rahmen der Medientage München (Werben & Verkaufen), 18.10.2001.

Breitbarth, T. (2016). Unternehmerischer Nutzen von Sponsoring und sozialem Engagement im Sport-Im olympischen Rio wie in der heimischen Region. *Industrieanzeiger, 17*(6), 24–26.

Brendel, D. (2020). Was steckt wirklich hinter dem Marketing-Buzzword Purpose? https://www.horizont.net/news/p/180197. Accessed: 2. Nov. 2021.

Brenner, P. (2022). *Zwischen e. V. und (Sport-)Kapitalgesellschaft. Organisationsrechtliche Überlegungen zur Ausübung professionellen Sports am Beispiel des Lizenzfußballs.* Baden-Baden.

Breuer, C., Rumpf, C., & Kurz, S. (2013). Ein Bewertungsmodell zur Analyse von Sponsoring-Alternativen. *Marketing Review St. Gallen, 30*(1), 72–81. https://doi.org/10.1365/s11621-013-0190-5.

Bruhn, M. (1987). Sponsoring. Mäzenatentum oder Schleichwerbung? *Harvard Manager, 9*(3), 46–52.

Bruhn, M. (1990a). *Sozio- und Umweltsponsoring. Engagements von Unternehmen für soziale und ökologische Aufgaben*. F. Vahlen.

Bruhn, M. (1990b). Sponsoring als Instrument der Unternehmenskommunikation. Erscheinungsformen, Planungskonzepte und Integrationsaspekte. In H. Meffert & H. Wagner (Hrsg.), *Arbeitspapier Nr. 55 der Wissenschaftlichen Gesellschaft für Marketing und Unternehmensführung e. V.* (S. 3–14). Insitut für Marketing Münster.

Bruhn, M. (1996). Sponsoring. In L. G. Poth (Hrsg.), *Marketing* (S. 1–57). Gabler.

Bruhn, M. (2003). Denk- und Planungsansatz der Integrierten Marketing-Kommunikation. In A. Hermanns & F. Riedmüller (Hrsg.), *Sponsoring und Events im Sport. Von der Instrumentalbetrachtung zur Kommunikationsplattform* (S. 23–44). Vahlen.

Bruhn, M. (2012). *Marketing für Nonprofit-Organisationen. Grundlagen, Konzepte, Instrumente* (2. Aufl.). W. Kohlhammer GmbH.

Bruhn, M. (2014). *Integrierte Unternehmens- und Markenkommunikation* (6. Aufl.). Schäffer-Poeschel.

Bruhn, M. (2016). *Relationship Marketing. Das Management von Kundenbeziehungen* (5. Aufl.). https://doi.org/10.15358/9783800651849.

Bruhn, M. (2018). *Sponsoring. Systematische Planung und integrativer Einsatz* (6. Aufl.). https://doi.org/10.1007/978-3-658-13313-9.

Bruhn, M. (2019). *Kommunikationspolitik. Systematischer Einsatz der Kommunikation für Unternehmen* (9. Aufl.). https://doi.org/10.15358/9783800648924.

Bruhn, M. (2022). *Relationship Marketing. Das Management von Kundenbeziehungen* (6. Aufl.). Vahlen.

Bruhn, M., & Ahlers, G. M. (2003). Ambush Marketing. „Angriff aus dem Hinterhalt" oder intelligentes Marketing? *Jahrbuch der Absatz- und Verbrauchsforschung, 49*(3), 271–294.

Bruhn, M., & Ahlers, G. M. (2004). Ambush marketing. "Attack from behind". *Yearbook of Marketing and Consumer Research, 2*(1), 40–61.

Bruhn, M., & Batt, V. (2012). Der Einfluss von Sponsoring auf den Erfolg von Luxusmarken. *Marketing Review St. Gallen, 29*(1), 36–41.

Bruhn, M., & Dahlhoff, H. D. (Hrsg.). (1990). *Sponsoring für Umwelt und Gesellschaft. Neue Instrumente der Unternehmenskommunikation*. BDW Service- und Verlagsgesellschaft Kommunikation GmbH.

Bruhn, M., & Mehlinger, R. (1995). *Rechtliche Gestaltung des Sponsoring. Vertragsrecht, Steuerrecht, Medienrecht, Wettbewerbsrecht* (Bd. I, Allgemeiner Teil, 2. Aufl.). Beck.

Bruhn, M., & Mehlinger, R. (1999). *Rechtliche Gestaltung des Sponsoring. Sport-, Kultur-, Sozial-, Umwelt- und Programmsponsoring* (Bd. II, Spezieller Teil, 2. Aufl.). Beck.

Bruhn, M., & Pristaff, J. (1993). *Sponsoring in Deutschland. Ergebnisse einer Unternehmensbefragung*. Arbeitspapier Nr. 14. Institut für Marketing, European Business School, Schloß Reichartshausen/Rheingau.

Bruhn, M., & Rohlmann, P. (2021). Instrumentalisierung im Fußball und Auswirkungen auf die Stakeholder. *Absatzwirtschaft online, 64*(11). Accessed: 15. Nov. 2021.

Bruhn, M., & Rohlmann, P. (2022). *Sportmarketing. Grundlagen – Strategien – Instrumente*. Springer Gabler. https://doi.org/10.1007/978-3-658-37176-0.

Bruhn, M., Batt, V., & Holzer, M. (2013). Der Einfluss des Sponsoring auf das Markenverhalten von Mitarbeitenden. *Die Unternehmung, 67*(3), 289–308.

Bruhn, M., Martin, S., & Schnebelen, S. (2014). *Integrierte Kommunikation in der Praxis – Entwicklungsstand in deutschsprachigen Unternehmen*. Springer Gabler.

Bundesministerium der Finanzen. (BMF 1998). Ertragssteuerliche Behandlung des Sponsoring vom 18.02.1998 IV B 2–S 2144–40/98 (BStBl I S. 212). https://esth.bundesfinanzministerium.de/esth/2016/C-Anhaenge/Anhang-16/IV/inhalt.html. Accessed: 2. Nov. 2021.

Burton, N., & Chadwick, S. (2009). Ambush marketing in sport: An analysis of sponsoring protection means and counter-ambush measures. *Journal of Sponsoring, 2*(4), 303–315.

Busch, R., Dögl, R., & Unger, F. (2008). *Integriertes Marketing. Strategie, Organisation, Instrumente* (4. Aufl.). Gabler.

Büschken, J. (2004). *Higher profits through customer lock-in*. Thomson.

Büschken, J., Voeth, M., & Weiber, R. (Hrsg.). (2007). *Innovationen für das Industriegütermarketing. Festschrift für Professor Klaus Backhaus*. Schäffer-Poeschel.

Buschmann, R., & Wulzinger, M. (2017). *Football Leaks: Die schmutzigen Geschäfte im Profifußball*. Deutsche Verlags-Anstalt.

Business Insider. (2013). *Why brands like Nike stuck with Tiger Woods through his scandal*. https://www.businessinsider.com/tiger-woods-a-tale-of-two-images-2013-4?IR=T. Accessed: 2. Nov. 2021.

Businessinsider. (2017). Zetsche packt aus: Darum hört Mercedes wirklich als DFB-Sponsor auf; Beitrag vom 18.07.2017. https://www.businessinsider.de/wirtschaft/zetsche-packt-aus-darum-hoert-mercedes-wirklich-als-dfb-sponsor-auf-2017-7/. Accessed: 2. Nov. 2021.

C

Carat. (2019). Carat Fantypologie 2019 vom 16.08.2019. https://www.dentsu.com/de/de/carat-fantypologie-2019. Accessed: 2. Nov. 2021.

Charitomeni, T., Papadimitriou, D., & Parganas, P. (2018). The influence of sport sponsoring on brand equity and purchase behavior. *Journal of Strategic Marketing, 26*(1), 85–105. https://doi.org/10.1080/0965254x.2017.1374299.

Chatrath, S., & Wengler, S. (2009). Preisfindung für und Bewertung von Sportsponsorings, Ausgabe 5 von Berliner Reihe zum Marketing. Freie Universität Berlin, Marketing-Department.

Cheong, C., Do, Y. P., & Ho, K. L. (2019). Sponsoring and advertising in sport: A study of consumers' attitude. *European Sport Management Quarterly, 19*(3), 287–311. https://doi.org/10.1080/16184742.2018.1517271.

Christensen, S. R. (2006). Measuring consumer reactions to sponsoring partnerships based upon emotional and attitudinal responses. *International Journal of Market Research, 48*(1), 61–80. https://doi.org/10.1177/147078530604800105.

Clark, J., Lachowetz, T., Irwin, R. L., & Schimmel, K. (2003). Business-to-business relationships and sport: Using sponsoring as a critical sales event. *International Journal of Sports Marketing and Sponsoring, 5*(2), 38–53. https://doi.org/10.1108/ijsms-05-02-2003-b004.

Cliffe, S. J., & Motion, J. (2005). Building contemporary brands: A sponsoring-based strategy. *Journal of Business Research, 58*(8), 1068–1077. https://doi.org/10.1016/j.jbusres.2004.03.004.

Coca-Cola. (2016). Coca-Cola Dosen Werbung UEFA EURO 2016 TV-Spot Europameisterschaft Manuel Neuer. https://www.youtube.com/watch?v=VfISpAROnT4. Accessed: 2. Nov. 2021.

Coca-Cola. (2020). mezzo mix erfüllt gemeinsam mit dem FC Bayern München Fan-Träume, Beitrag vom 16.12.2020. https://www.presseportal.de/pm/7974/4792707. Accessed: 2. Nov. 2021.

Coca-Cola. (2022). Volle Ladung Vorfreude! Coca-Cola Trucktour 2022. https://www.coca-cola-deutschland.de/unterhaltung/weihnachten/truck-tour-2021. Accessed: 8. Dec. 2022.

Commerzbank. (2022). *Sponsoring*. https://www.commerzbank.de/de/hauptnavigation/konzern/sponsoring/01_dfb_premium_partner/dfb_partner.html. Accessed: 2. Nov. 2021.

Cooper, W., Seiford, L., & Tone, K. (2006). *Introduction to data envelopment analysis and its uses: With DEA solver software and references* (2. Aufl.). https://doi.org/10.1007/978-0-387-45283-8.

Cooper, W., Seiford, L., & Zhu, J. (2011). *Handbook on data envelopment analysis* (2. Aufl.). https://doi.org/10.1007/978-1-4419-6151-8.

Corkindale, D., & Hastings, G. B. (1985). The role of sponsoring for marketing. *International Journal of Advertising, 4*(4), 371–372. https://doi.org/10.1080/02650487.1985.11106945.

Cornwell, B. T., & Maignan, I. (1998). An international review of sponsoring research. *Journal of Advertising, 27*(1), 1–21.

Cornwell, B. T., Clinton, S. W., & Donald, P. R. (2005). Sponsoring-linked marketing: Opening the black box. *Journal of Advertising, 34*(2), 21–42. https://doi.org/10.1080/00913367.2005.10639194.

Cornwell, T. B., & Relyea, G. E. (2000). Understanding long-term effects of sports sponsoring: Role of experience, involvement, enthusiasm and clutter. *International Journal of Sports Marketing and Sponsoring, 2*(2), 39–55. https://doi.org/10.1108/ijsms-02-02-2000-b005.

Cornwell, T. B., Roy, D. P., & Steinard, E. A., II. (2001). Exploring managers' perceptions of the impact of sponsoring on brand equity. *Journal of Advertising, 30*(2), 41–51. https://doi.org/10.1080/00913367.2001.10673636.

Cotting, P. (2003). Entwicklung einer Sponsoring Scorecard als strategisches Entscheidungs- und Controllinginstrument. In A. Hermanns & F. Riedmüller (Hrsg.), *Sponsoring und Events im Sport* (S. 93–115). Vahlen.

Cotting, P. (2011). Interview Medien. http://www.sponsoringextra.ch/file/archiv/Interview_Medien/Social%20Media%20im%20Sponsoring-06-2011.pdf. Accessed: 2. Febr. 2016.

Crawford, C. T. (1992). IRS attacks exempt organization income from corporate sponsoring fees. *The Journal of Taxation, 76*(4), 230–234.

Crompton, J. L. (1993). Sponsoring of sport by tobacco and alcohol companies: A review of the issues. *Journal of Sport & Social Issues, 17*(2), 148–167. https://doi.org/10.1177/019372359301700210.

Crompton, J. L. (1994). Measuring the return on sponsoring investments at major recreation events. *Journal of Park and Recreation Administration, 12,* 73–73.

Cuneen, J., & Hannan, M. J. (1993). Intermediate measures and recognition testing of sponsoring advertisIng at an LPGA tournament. *Sport Marketing Quarterly, 2*(1), 47–56.

D

D'Astous, A., & Bitz, P. (1995). Consumer evaluations of sponsoring programs. *European Journal of Marketing, 29*(12), 6–22.

Daumann, F., Esipovich, L., & Römmelt, B. (2011). Imageprofile im Sport – Sportverbände, Sportler, Fußballclubs und im Sport werbende Marken, Jenaer Sportmanagement Surveys, Friedrich-Schiller-Universität Jena. https://www.mba-sportmanagement.com/service/jenaer-kommentare/65-master-sportmanagement-image-survey. Accessed: 2. Nov. 2021.

Davey, T. (2021). Wie Sie attraktive Sponsoring-Pakete für Ihre Online-Veranstaltungen erstellen, Beitrag vom 17.12.2021. https://www.eventtia.com/de/blog/wie-sie-attraktive-sponsoring-pakete-fur-ihre-online-veranstaltungen-erstellen. Accessed: 2. Nov. 2021.

Dees, W. (2011). New media and technology use in corporate sport sponsoring: Performing activational leverage from an exchange perspective. *International Journal of Sport Management and Marketing, 10*(3–4), 272–285. https://doi.org/10.1504/ijsmm.2011.044795.

Deloitte. (2020a). Sponsoring sports in today's digital age. Deloitte. https://www2.deloitte.com/content/dam/Deloitte/lu/Documents/sports-consulting/lu-sponsoring-sports-today-digital-age.pdf.

Deloitte. (2020b). 2021 global marketing trends: Find your focus. https://www2.deloitte.com/content/dam/insights/us/articles/6963_global-marke-ting-trends/DI_2021-Global-Marketing-Trends_US.pdf. Accessed: 2. Nov. 2021.

Deloitte. (2021). Let's Play! 2021. The European esports market. Deloitte. https://www2.deloitte.com/content/dam/insights/articles/de154437-lets-play-2021/DI_Lets-Play-2021.pdf.
Deloitte. (2022). 2022 global marketing trends. Thriving through customer centricity. https://www2.deloitte.com/us/en/insights/topics/marketing-and-sales-operations/global-marketing-trends.html. Accessed: 2. Nov. 2021.
Demirel, A. (2020). CSR in sport sponsoring consumers' perceptions of a sponsoring brand's CSR. *International Journal of Sports Marketing and Sponsoring, 21*(2), 371–388.
Der Westen. (2022). Katar: Bier-Verbot bei WM 2022 – jetzt reagiert Budweiser drastisch, Beitrag vom 27.11.2022. https://www.derwesten.de/sport/fussball/katar-wm-budweiser-bier-id300199270.html. Accessed: 2. Nov. 2021.
Deutsche Fußball Liga (DFL). (2022). Anhang IV zur LO: Richtlinie für Spielkleidung und Ausrüstung. https://media.dfl.de/sites/2/2018/11/anhang-IV-zur-LO-2018-07-01.pdf. Accessed: 2. Nov. 2021.
Deutsche Telekom. (2002). Sport-Engagement stärkt zusätzlich die Kraft der Marke: Sponsoring – strategische Partnerschaft mit FC Bayern München. *Forum T-Aktie „direkt", 6*(2), 5.
Deutsche Telekom. (2022). Telekom-Markenwert auf Rekordniveau. https://www.telekom.com/de/medien/medieninformationen/detail/telekom-markenwert-auf-rekordniveau-645052. Accessed: 2. Nov. 2021.
Deutsche Telekom AG. (2016). Deutsche Telekom startet Entertain-Kampagne mit FC Bayern Profis und Ballkünstler Andrew Cassidy. https://www.telekom.com/innovation/ifa-2014/246628. Accessed: 10. June 2016.
Deutsche Telekom AG. (2021). Engagement im Fußball zahlt sich aus. https://www.telekom.com/de/konzern/details/engagement-im-fussball-zahlt-sich-aus-336788. Accessed: 2. Nov. 2021.
Deutscher Bundestag. (2018). Europas Sportrechte unter Druck, Beitrag vom 07.11.2018. https://www.bundestag.de/webarchiv/presse/hib/2018_11/577542-577542. Accessed: 2. Nov. 2021.
Deutscher Fußball-Bund (DFB). (2018). Durchführungsbestimmungen zur Spielordnung. https://www.dfb.de/fileadmin/_dfbdam/16443-07_Durchfuehrungsbestimmungen_14.pdf. Accessed: 2. Nov. 2021.
Deutscher Olympischer Sportbund. (2016). Attraktives Erhrenamt im Sport. https://ehrenamt.dosb.de/attraktives-ehrenamt#akkordeon-11739. Accessed: 2. Nov. 2021.
Deutscher Olympischer Sportbund. (2018). Die Geschichte der „Trimm-Dich" – Bewegung. https://www.dosb.de/sonderseiten/news/news-detail/news/trimm-dich-hob-die-sport-aktiven-quote. Accessed: 2. Nov. 2021.
Deutscher Olympischer Sportbund. (2021). Bestandserhebung 2021, Fassung vom 01.10.2021, Frankfurt am Main.
Deutsches Sport Fernsehen (DSF 1999). Imagetrends. Ismaning.
Deutschlandfunk. (2017). VW löst Daimler als DFB-Sponsor ab – „Man kann kaum prominenter werben in Deutschland", Beitrag vom 14.07.2017. https://www.deutschlandfunk.de/vw-loest-daimler-als-dfb-sponsor-ab-man-kann-kaum-100.html. Accessed: 2. Nov. 2021.
Deutschlandfunk. (2022). Investoren im Sport. Lieber Europa als USA, Beitrag vom 07.08.2022. https://www.deutschlandfunk.de/tv-rechte-bundesliga-investoren-100.html. Accessed: 2. Nov. 2021.
Dick, C. (2018). Gradual vs entire sponsoring termination. *International Journal of Sports Marketing and Sponsoring, 19*(4), 433–449.
Die Welt. (2014). *Die Nationalmannschaft sprengt alle TV-Rekorde*. http://www.welt.de/sport/article135215406/Die-Nationalmannschaft-sprengt-alle-TV-Rekorde.html. Accessed: 5. Apr. 2016.
Die Welt. (2022). Der etwas scheinheilige Katar-Protest mit dem dänischen Trikot, Beitrag vom 30.09.2022. https://www.welt.de/sport/article241346503/WM-in-Katar-Der-etwas-scheinheilige-Protest-mit-dem-daenischen-Trikot.html. Accessed: 2. Nov. 2021.

Dircks, M. (2022). Regionales Sportmarketing: Ihr Unternehmen im Fokus der Region. https://beyond-the-match.com/sponsoring/regionales-sportmarketing-ihr-unternehmen-im-fokus-der-region/. Accessed: 2. Nov. 2021.

Djaballah, M., Hautbois, C., & Desbordes, M. (2017). Sponsors' CSR strategies in sport: A sensemaking approach of corporations established in France. *Sport Management Review, 20*(2), 211–225. https://doi.org/10.1016/j.smr.2016.07.002.

Dolphin, R. R. (2003). Sponsoring: Perspectives on its strategic role. *Corporate Communications: An International Journal, 8*(3), 173–186. https://doi.org/10.1108/13563280310487630.

Drees, N. (1989). *Sportsponsoring*. https://doi.org/10.1007/978-3-663-06737-5.

Drees, N. (2003). Bedeutung und Erscheinungsformen des Sportsponsoring. In A. Hermanns & F. Riedmüller (Hrsg.), *Sponsoring und Events im Sport* (S. 47–66). Vahlen.

Drees, N., & Trautwein, S. (2008). Erscheinungsformen des Sponsoring. In A. Bagusat, C. Marwitz, & M. Vogl (Hrsg.), *Handbuch Sponsoring. Erfolgreiche Marketing- und Markenkommunikation* (S. 89–112). Schmidt.

Dreisbach, J. (2018). *Erfolgsfaktoren der Sponsoringumsetzung und -aktivierung – Eine empirische Analyse aus Management- und Konsumentenwirkungsperspektive im Kontext der Fußball-Bundesliga*. Springer Gabler. https://doi.org/10.1007/978-3-658-24519-1.

E

Easton, S., & Mackie, P. (1998). When football came home: A case history of the sponsoring activity at Euro'96. *International Journal of Advertising, 17*(1), 99–114. https://doi.org/10.1080/02650487.1998.11104708.

Edeling, A., Hattula, S., & Bornemann, T. (2017). Over, out, but present: Recalling former sponsorings. *European Journal of Marketing, 51*(7/8), 1286–1307. https://doi.org/10.1108/ejm-05-2015-0263.

Eisdorfer, A., & Kohl, E. (2017). Corporate sport sponsoring and stock returns: Evidence from the NFL. *Critical Finance Review, 6*, 179–209. https://doi.org/10.1561/104.00000041.

Emmi Group. (2019). Emmi Caffè Latte ist neuer Hauptsponsor von Wendy Holdener, Beitrag vom 12.07.2019. https://group.emmi.com/che/de/medien-investoren/medienmitteilungen/emmi-caffe-latte-ist-neuer-hauptsponsor-von-wendy-holdener. Accessed: 2. Nov. 2021.

Engelmann, D., & Strobel, M. (2012). Deconstruction and reconstruction of an anomaly. *Games and Economic Behavior, 76*(2), 678–689. https://doi.org/10.1016/j.geb.2012.07.009.

ESA. (2022). *The 2022 ESA sponsoring market overview*. ESA.

ESB. (2021). Best case: HOMEDAY x Hertha BSC, Beitrag vom 04.11.2021. https://www.esb-online.com/business-guides/artikel/best-case-homeday-x-hertha-bsc/. Accessed: 2. Nov. 2021.

ESB. (2022). Sponsoring im eSport-Markt, Beitrag vom 13.04.2022. https://www.esb-online.com/business-guides/artikel/sponsoring-im-esport-markt/. Accessed: 2. Nov. 2021.

Eschenbach, F. (2011). Erfolgsfaktoren des Ambush-Marketing. Eine theoretische und empirische Analyse am Beispiel der Fußball-Europameisterschaft 2008. Wiesbaden. https://doi.org/10.1007/978-3-8349-6624-7.

ESPN. (2017). Meet the men behind football's biggest deals, Beitrag vom 15.06.2017. https://www.espn.com/soccer/english-premier-league/23/blog/post/3143956/premier-league-and-la-liga-stars-like-gareth-bale-turn-to-these-agents-for-their-deals. Accessed: 2. Nov. 2021.

Europäische Sponsoring Börse (ESB 2021). Best Case: HOMEDAY x Hertha BSC, Beitrag vom 04.11.2021. https://www.esb-online.com/business-guides/artikel/best-case-homeday-x-hertha-bsc/. Accessed: 2. Nov. 2021.

Europäische Sponsoring Börse (ESB)/Gfs-Forschungsinstitut. (2000). Sponsoringstudie 2000, Zürich.

Esports.com. (2021). So professionell ist der Esport im Jahr 2021 in Deutschland wirklich, Beitrag vom 27.11.2021. https://www.esports.com/de/so-professionell-ist-der-esport-im-jahr-2021-in-deutschland-wirklich-295103. Accessed: 2. Nov. 2021.

F

Fahy, J., Farrelly, F., & Quester, P. (2004). Competitive advantage through sponsoring: A conceptual model and research propositions. *European Journal of Marketing, 38*(8), 1013–1030. https://doi.org/10.1108/03090560410539140.

Falkenau, J. (2013). *Sportsponsoring. Wirkung und Erfolgsfaktoren aus neuropsychologischer Sicht.* Haufe.

FanQ. (2022a). Erwartungen an die WM 2022 in Katar. Eine Studie aus Perspektive der Fans. https://fanq-app.com/wp-content/uploads/2022/05/fanq-studie-erwartungen-wm-katar-endversion-1.pdf. Accessed: 2. Nov. 2021.

FanQ. (2022b). Studienreihe zur WM 2022 in Katar. https://fanq.com/studienreihe-zur-wm-2022-in-katar-vorfreude-ist-bei-jungen-fussball-fans-groesser/. Accessed: 2. Nov. 2021.

FanQ/Intelligent Research in Sponsoring. (2020). *Regionalität liegt auch bei Fußballfans voll im Trend!* (FanQ/IRIS 2020). https://fanq-app.com/wp-content/uploads/2020/01/pressemitteilung_sponsorenstudie2019_final.pdf. Accessed: 2. Nov. 2021.

Farrelly, F., & Quester, P. (2003). The effects of market orientation on trust and commitment: The case of the sponsoring business-to-business relationship. *European Journal of Marketing, 37*(3/4), 530–553. https://doi.org/10.1108/03090560310459078.

Farrelly, F., Quester, P., & Greyser, S. A. (2005). Defending the co-branding benefits of sponsoring B2B partnerships: The case of ambush marketing. *Journal of Advertising Research, 45*(3), 339–348. https://doi.org/10.1017/s0021849905050348.

Farrelly, F. J., Quester, P. G., & Burton, R. (1997). Integrating sports sponsoring into the corporate marketing function: An international comparative study. *International Marketing Review, 14*(3), 170–182. https://doi.org/10.1108/02651339710170249.

FASPO (Fachverband für Sponsoring-Agenturen und Dienstleister e. V.). (2005). FASPO-Konvention zur Ermittlung und Verrechnung von Leistungswerten im Sponsoring: Eventkontakte, Medienkontakte, Dokumentation, Zertifikation, Begriffsdefinitionen, Berechnungsbeispiele.

FASPO (Fachverband für Sponsoring-Agenturen und Dienstleister e. V.). (2016). http://www.faspo.de/media/files/isa_2016/Ausschreibungsunterlagen_Sponsporing-Award_2016_18.03.pdf. Accessed: 28.06.2016.

FAZ. (2006). Von nun an herrscht freie Schuhwahl. Beitrag vom 31.08.2006. https://www.faz.net/aktuell/sport/fussball/nationalmannschaft-von-nun-an-herrscht-freie-schuhwahl-1358153.html. Accessed: 2. Nov. 2021.

FC Bayern München AG. (2014). Allianz beteiligt sich an FC Bayern München AG, Pressemitteilung vom 11.02.2014. https://fcbayern.com/de/news/2014/02/allianz-beteiligt-sich-an-fc-bayern-munchen-ag. Accessed: 2. Nov. 2021.

Ferrand, A., & Pages, M. (1995). Image sponsoring. A methodology to match event and sponsor. *Journal of Sport Management, 10*(3), 278–291. https://doi.org/10.1123/jsm.10.3.278.

FIFA. (2011). FIFA-Finanzbericht 2010, Zürich.

FIFA. (2015). FIFA-Finanzbericht 2014, Zürich.

FIFA. (2016). Programm zum Schutz der Fifa-Markenrechte. http://de.fifa.com/about-fifa/marketing/brand-protection/index.html. Accessed: 2. Nov. 2021.

Financial Times. (2023). New Olympique Lyonnais owners plan Spac listing, Beitrag vom 18.01.2023. https://www.ft.com/content/c74b5e96-c1ab-463e-9c4f-3e469e543d6d. Accessed: 2. Nov. 2021.

Finanzen100. (2017). 30 Millionen Euro pro J. https://www.deutschlandfunk.de/vw-loest-daimler-als-dfb-sponsor-ab-man-kann-kaum-100.htmlahr: Warum der DFB-Deal für Volkswagen so wichtig ist, Beitrag vom 14.07.2017. https://www.finanzen100.de/finanznachrichten/wirtschaft/sponsoring-30-millionen-euro-pro-jahr-warum-der-dfb-deal-fuer-volkswagen-so-wichtig-ist_H417380626_442964/. Accessed: 2. Nov. 2021.

FNP. (2022). 48 Stunden vor Beginn der WM 2022: Spektakuläre Wende – Kein Bier in Katar. Beitrag vom 18.11.2022. https://www.fnp.de/sport/fussball/wm-2022-spektakulaere-kehrtwende-kein-bier-katar-fans-fifa-druck-fra-91924584.html. Accessed: 02. Nov. 2021.

Focus. (2022). ARD-Reporterin nach Rückkehr: Katar-Kritik „hatten wir Deutsche exklusiv", Beitrag vom 14.12.2022. https://www.focus.de/kultur/kino_tv/ard-reporterin-nach-rueckkehr-aus-katar-kritischen-blick-hatten-wir-exklusiv_id_180454664.html. Accessed: 2. Nov. 2021.

Footgoal. (2022). *Top 10 Bundesliga football clubs with most fans in the world in 2022.* https://footgoal.pro/top-10-bundesliga-football-clubs-with-most-fans-in-the-world-in-2022/. Accessed: 2. Nov. 2021.

Forbes. (2020). The World's Most Valuable Sports Agencies 2020: CAA On Top, Wasserman Closes The Gap, Beitrag vom 22.12.2020. https://www.forbes.com/sites/jasonbelzer/2020/12/22/the-worlds-most-valuable-sports-agencies-2020-caa-on-top-as-wasserman-closes-the-gap/?sh=310827af136f. Accessed: 2. Nov. 2021.

Freyer, W. (2018). *Sportmarketing – Modernes Marketingmanagement für die Sportwirtschaft* (5. Aufl.). Schmidt.

Fuchs, W., & Unger, F. (2014). *Management der Marketing-Kommunikation* (5. Aufl.). Springer Gabler.

Funk. (2022). Sportinvestoren verdienen mehr Geld als Fußballer, Beitrag vom 27.11.2022. https://www.funk.net/channel/highperformerhenning-12276/sportinvestoren-verdienen-mehr-geld-als-fussballer-highperformerhenning-1854765. Accessed: 2. Nov. 2021.

Furlong, R. (1994). Tobacco advertising legislation and the sponsoring of sport. *Australian Business Law Review, 22*(3), 159–189.

Fürweger, W. (2023). *Die Red-Bull-Story – Der unglaubliche Erfolg des Dietrich Mateschitz* (12. Aufl.). Haymon.

G

Gardner, M. P., & Shuman, P. J. (1987). Sponsoring: An important component of the promotions mix. *Journal of Advertising, 16*(1), 11–17. https://doi.org/10.1080/00913367.1987.10673055.

Gilbert, D. (1988). Sponsoring strategy is a drift. *The Quarterly Review of Marketing, 14*(1), 6–9.

Global Data. (2022). Business of the FIFA World Cup 2022 – Property Profile, Sponsoring and Media Landscape, Beitrag vom 11.11.2022. https://www.globaldata.com/store/report/fifa-world-cup-business-analysis/. Accessed: 2. Nov. 2021.

Global Sports. (2019). Rakuten – ein Beispiel für effektives Sponsoring im Sport, Beitrag vom 02.12.2019. https://intelligence.globalsportsjobs.de/rakuten-ein-beispiel-f%C3%BCr-effekives-sponsoring-im-sport. Accessed: 2. Nov. 2021.

Glogger, A. (1999). *Imagetransfer im Sponsoring: Entwicklung eines Erklärungsmodells.* Lang.

Grass, A., & Backhaus, C. (2007). Theorie und Praxis des Sportstättensponsorings am Beispiel der Allianz Arena. In D. Ahlert, D. Woisetschläger, & V. Vogel (Hrsg.), *Exzellentes Sponsoring. Innovative Ansätze und Best Practices für das Markenmanagement* (2. Aufl., S. 141–157). Deutscher Universitätsverlag. https://doi.org/10.1007/978-3-8350-9639-4_7.

Grimes, E., & Meenaghan, T. (1998). Focusing commercial sponsoring on the internal corporate audience. *International Journal of Advertising, 17*(1), 51–74. https://doi.org/10.1080/02650487.1998.11104705.

Grohs, R., & Reisinger, H. (2014). Sponsoring effects on brand image: The role of exposure and activity involvement. *Journal of Business Research, 67*(5), 1018–1025. https://doi.org/10.1016/j.jbusres.2013.08.008.

Grohs, R., Wagner, U., & Vsetecka, S. (2004). Assessing the effectiveness of sport sponsorings. An empirical examination. *Schmalenbach Business Review, 56*(2), 119–138. https://doi.org/10.1007/bf03396689.

Gundacker, L. (2021). Sportsponsoring im Zeitalter der Digitalisierung Erfolgsfaktoren für Vereine im deutschen Profifußball, Bachelorarbeit der Hochschule Mittweida.

Gürtler, T., & Möthe, A. (2022, August 20). Gegenentwurf zu Geld und kurzfristigem Glamour: Der Fußball entdeckt sein Gewissen wieder. *Handelsblatt.* https://www.handelsblatt.com/unternehmen/handel-konsumgueter/sport-sponsoring-gegenentwurf-zu-geld-und-kurzfristigem-glamour-der-fussball-entdeckt-sein-gewissen-wieder/28583060.html.

Gutting, D. (2020). *Interkulturelles Marketing im digitalen Zeitalter: Strategien für den globalen Markterfolg.* Springer Gabler. https://doi.org/10.1007/978-3-658-29429-8.

Gwinner, K. (1997). A model of image creation and image transfer in event sponsoring. *International Marketing Review, 14*(3), 145–158. https://doi.org/10.1108/02651339710170221.

H

Habitzreuter, A. M., & Koenigstorfer, J. (2021). The impact of environmental CSR-linked sport sponsoring on attitude toward the sponsor depending on regulatory fit. *Journal of Business Research, 124*, 720–730. https://doi.org/10.1016/j.jbusres.2018.11.040.

Hackforth, J. (2010). *Imageträger Fußball – Werte, Wert und Wertschätzung, in: Auf den Spuren der Nationalmannschaft*, DFB (Hrsg.), Frankfurt.

Hackl, K. (2021). Sponsoring im Zeitalter Marketing 4.0: Wie können Trends und Erkenntnisse aus dem Marketing 4.0 im Sponsoring der Zukunft angewandt werden? Masterthesis der Universität Basel.

Haibach, M. (2012). *Handbuch Fundraising. Spenden, Sponsoring, Stiftungen in der Praxis* (4. Aufl.). Campus.

Hamburger Sport Verein (HSV). (2022). Fakten zum Stadion. https://www.hsv.de/unser-hsv/ueber-den-hsv/geschichte/stadion. Accessed: 2. Nov. 2021.

Handelsblatt. (2014). Die Weltmeister der inoffiziellen Werbung. http://www.handelsblatt.com/unternehmen/handel-konsumgueter/fussball-wm-in-brasilien-nur-fussball-und-brasilien-reicht-nicht-fuer-gute-werbung/9816614-3.html. Accessed: 2. Nov. 2021.

Handelsblatt. (2015). Aus der Imtech-Arena wird wieder das Volksparkstadion. http://www.handelsblatt.com/sport/fussball/fussball-tempel-aus-der-imtech-arena-wird-wieder-das-volkspark-stadion/10272992.html. Accessed: 2. Nov. 2021.

Handelsblatt. (2017). VW sticht Mercedes bei Nationalmannschaft aus, Beitrag vom 14.07.2017. http://www.handelsblatt.com/sport/fussball/dfb-sponsor-vw-sticht-mercedes. Accessed: 2. Nov. 2021.

Handelsblatt. (2022). FIFA plant mit Umsatzsteigerung auf elf Milliarden US-Dollar, Beitrag vom 16.12.2022. https://www.handelsblatt.com/dpa/fifa-plant-mit-umsatzsteigerung-auf-elf-milliarden-us-dollar/28873240.html. Accessed: 2. Nov. 2021.

Harrison, V. S., Vafeiadis, M., & Bober, J. (2022). Greening professional sport: How communicating the fit, proximity, and impact of sustainability efforts affects fan perceptions and supportive intentions. *Sustainability (Switzerland), 14*(6). https://doi.org/10.3390/su14063139.

Hastings, G. B. (1984). Sponsoring works differently from advertising. *International Journal of Advertising, 3*(2), 171–176. https://doi.org/10.1080/02650487.1984.11105012.

Haupt, T. (2014). Social Media Marketing und Kapitalisierungsmöglichkeiten im Spitzensport – Eine empirische Erfolgsfaktorenanalyse im Rahmen der 1. Fußball-Bundesliga. In C. Werner & F. Kainz (Hrsg.), *Schriftenreihe des internationalen Hochschulverbunds IUNworld* (Bd. 6, S. 109–136). https://doi.org/10.1007/978-3-642-54884-0_29.

Henkel. (2022). *Sponsoring*. https://www.henkel.de/unternehmen/sponsoring. Accessed: 8. Dec. 2022.

Henseler, J., Wilson, B., Götz, O., & Hautvast, C. (2007). Investigating the moderating role of fit on sports sponsoring and brand equity. *International Journal of Sports Marketing and Sponsoring, 8*(4), 34–42. https://doi.org/10.1108/ijsms-08-04-2007-b005.

Henseler, J., Wilson, B., & Westberg, K. (2011). Managers' perceptions of the impact of sport sponsoring on brand equity: Which aspects of the sponsoring matter most? *Sport Marketing Quarterly, 20*(1), 7–21.

Hermanns, A., & Marwitz, C. (2008). *Sponsoring. Grundlagen, Wirkungen, Management, Markenführung* (3. Aufl.). Vahlen.

Hermanns, A., & Riedmüller, F. (2008). *Management Handbuch Sportmarketing* (2. Aufl.). Vahlen.

Hermanns, A., Marwitz, C., & Schubert, M. (2016). Messung der Wirkung von Sponsoringmaßnahmen. In F.-R. Esch, M. Bruhn, & T. Langner (Hrsg.), *Handbuch Controlling der Kommunikation* (2. Aufl., S. 507–538). Springer Gabler. https://doi.org/10.1007/978-3-8349-3857-2_23.

Heun, V. (2016). *Assetklasse Fußball: Chancen und Risiken für Investoren im Fußball*. BoD – Books on Demand.

Hofer, K. (2013). Auswirkungen des Sport-Sponsorings auf die Mitarbeiter des Unternehmens, Studie des Instituts für Handel, Absatz und Marketing an der Johannes-Kepler-Universität Linz 2013. https://news.observer.at/4-sport-business-circle-2013-messbarkeit-und-effizienz-von-sponsoring/. Accessed: 2. Nov. 2021.

Hohenauer, R. (2016). *Sponsoring-Wirkung auf das Kaufverhalten*. https://doi.org/10.1007/978-3-658-15573-5.

Horizont. (2009). Unternehmen bemängeln Qualität von Sponsoringpaketen. Studie vom Fachverband Sponsoring (FASPO), in: Horizont vom 27.11.2009. https://www.horizont.net/marketing/nachrichten/-Studie-Unternehmen-bemaengeln-Qualitaet-von-Sponsoringpaketen-88771. Accessed: 2. Nov. 2021.

Horizont. (2012). Nike liefert zum Olympiastart Geniestreich im Ambush-Marketing. http://www.horizont.net/marketing/nachrichten/-Nike-liefert-zum-Olympiastart-Geniestreich-im-Ambush-Marketing%2D%2D109033. Accessed: 2. Nov. 2021.

Horizont. (2014). Coca-Cola schlägt sie alle, Beitrag vom 12.06.2014. http://www.horizont.net/marketing/nachrichten/Bekanntheit-der-WM-Sponsoren-Coca-Cola-schlaegt-sie-alle-120907. Accessed: 2. Nov. 2021.

Horizont. (2020). Beachvolleyball: Liga-Blaupause in Düsseldorf, Beitrag vom 25.06.2020. https://www.horizont.net/media/media/32/2026_Sportbusiness_II.pdf-319324.pdf. Accessed: 2. Nov. 2021.

Horizont. (2021). Jürgen Klopp wird Botschafter von Nivea Men – Jogi Löw soll an Bord bleiben, Beitrag vom 07.09.2021. https://www.horizont.net/marketing/nachrichten/beiersdorf-juergen-klopp-wird-botschafter-von-nivea-men%2D%2D-jogi-loew-soll-an-bord-bleiben-194220. Accessed: 2. Nov. 2021.

Huber, F., & Matthes, I. (2007). Sponsoringwirkung auf Einstellung und Kaufabsicht. Theoretische Grundlagen und Ergebnisse einer empirischen Studie. *Marketing ZFP, 29*(2), 90–104. https://doi.org/10.15358/0344-1369-2007-2-90.

Hufnagel, J. (2011). Private Equity-Aktivitäten in der Sportbranche: Bestandsaufnahme und Analyse, Deutsche Sporthochschule Köln, Dissertation Köln.

Huth, R., & Pflaum, D. (2005). *Einführung in die Werbelehre* (7. Aufl.). Kohlhammer.

I

INRA Deutschland GmbH. (2000). Grundlagenuntersuchung Sponsoring XIII, Mölln.

International Event Group (IEG). (2007). http://www.sponsoring.com/About-IEG/Press-Room/Sponsoring-Spending-To-Total-$14.93-Billion-In-20.aspx. Accessed: 17. Febr. 2016.

International Event Group (IEG). (2015a). http://www.sponsoring.com/About-IEG/Press-Room/IEG-Projects-North-American-Sponsoring-Spending-t.aspx. Accessed: 17. Febr. 2016.

International Event Group (IEG). (2015b). *Sponsoring spending report 2015*. http://www.sponsoring.com/IEG/files/4e/4e525456-b2b1-4049-bd51-03d9c35ac507.pdf. Accessed: 17. Febr. 2016.

International Event Group (IEG). (2010–2020). *IEG sponsoring report*. https://sponsoring.com. Accessed: 2. Nov. 2021.

International Olympic Comitee (IOC). (2022). *Olympic marketing*. https://olympics.com/ioc/partners/coca-cola-mengniu. Accessed: 2. Nov. 2021.

International Olympic Committee (IOC). (2012). *London 2012 – Report and accounts*.

International Olympic Committee (IOC). (2016). *Olympic marketing*. http://www.olympic.org/sponsors/coca-cola. Accessed: 23. Febr. 2016.

Ipsos Deutschland/ESB. (2002). Regionales Sport-Sponsoring. www.esb-online.com/literatur/SportSponsoringRegional2002.pdf. Accessed: 2. Nov. 2021.

Ipsos GmbH. (2014). Grundlagenstudie Sponsoring 2014, Hamburg.

J

J. P. Morgan Asset Management. (2016). *J.P. Morgan asset management round the island race*. https://am.jpmorgan.co.uk/sponsoring/RoundTheIslandRace.aspx. Accessed: 2. Nov. 2021.

Javalgi, R. G., Traylor, M. B., Gross, A. C., & Lampman, E. (1994). Awareness of sponsoring and corporate image: An empirical investigation. *Journal of Advertising, 23*(4), 47–58. https://doi.org/10.1080/00913367.1943.10673458.

Jensen, J. A., Cobbs, J. B., & Turner, B. A. (2016). Evaluating sponsoring through the lens of the resource-based view: The potential for sustained competitive advantage. *Business Horizons, 59*(2), 163–173. https://doi.org/10.1016/j.bushor.2015.11.001.

K

Kalamadi, S. (2012). Intellectual property and the business of sports management. *Journal of Intellectual Property Rights, 17*(5), 437–442.

Klatt-Wenderodt, S. (2016). Steuerliche Aspekte von Sponsoring insbesondere auch bei Hospitality-Leistungen und VIP-Logen. https://www.hk24.de/produktmarken/beratung-service/recht_und_steuern/steuerrecht/ertrag_lohnsteuer/einkommen_koerper_steuer/steuern-sponsoring/1167790#titleInText1. Accessed: 8. June 2016.

Klewenhagen, M. (2001). Vernetzte Kommunikation. Eine verstrickte Sache. *Sponsors, 6*, 14–22. https://doi.org/10.1007/978-3-8349-8078-6_8.

Klincewicz, K. (1998). Ethical aspects of sponsoring. *Journal of Business Ethics, 17*(9/10), 1103–1110. https://doi.org/10.1023/a:1006027601493.

Koch, M., & Müller, P. (2021). Startpfiff für digitale Vermarktung, Beitrag vom 09.08.2021. https://www.sponsors.de/news/gastbeitraege/startpfiff-fuer-digitale-vermarktung. Accessed: 2. Nov. 2021.

KORE & SportsPro. (2022). Battle of the brands. Why are the best promoted sports sponsors on social? *Whitepaper*. https://50mm.sportspromedia.com/wp-content/uploads/2020/10/HOOKIT-SportsPro-50MM-Brands-2020-whitepaper-Oct-2020.pdf. Accessed: 2. Nov. 2021.

Koronios, K., Psiloutsikou, M., Kriemadis, A., Zervoulakos, P., & Leivaditi, E. (2016). Sport sponsoring: The impact of sponsor image on purchase intention of fans. *Journal of Promotion Management, 22*(2), 238–250. https://doi.org/10.1080/10496491.2016.1121739.

Koth, M. (2000). *Soziosponsoring von Krankenhäusern – Potenzielle Gewinnbringung eines Marketinginstruments*. Deutscher Universitätsverlag.

Kotler, P., & Bliemel, F. (2007). *Marketing Management. Analyse, Planung und Verwirklichung* (11. Aufl.). Schäffer-Poeschel.

Kotler, P., & Keller, K. L. (2016). *Marketing management*. https://doi.org/10.1556/9789630597784.

Kotler, P., Kartajaya, H., & Setiawan, I. (2017). *Marketing 4.0: Der Leitfaden für das Marketing der Zukunft*. Campus.

Kottke, M. (2022). Mehr als nur ein Name: Naming Rights Sponsoring, Beyond the match – Insights von Sportfive 09.03.2022. https://beyond-the-match.com/insights/mehr-als-nur-ein-name-naming-rights-sponsoring/. Accessed: 1. May 2022.

Kroeber-Riel, W., & Gröppel-Klein, A. (2019). *Konsumentenverhalten* (11. Aufl.). Vahlen.

Kuske, T. (2014). Deutsche Bahn mit Ambush-Kampagne zur WM vom 13.05.2014. http://www.tobiaskuske.de/2014/05/13/deutsche-bahn-ueberzeugt-mit-wm-kampagne/. Accessed: 2. Nov. 2021.

L

Lammenett, E. (2019). *Praxiswissen Online-Marketing: Affiliate-, Influencer-, Content- und E-Mail-Marketing, Google Ads, SEO, Social Media, Online- inklusive Face book-Werbung* (7. Aufl.). Springer Gabler. https://doi.org/10.1007/978-3-658-25135-2.

Lang, R., & Haunert, F. (1995). *Handbuch Sozial-Sponsoring. Grundlagen, Praxisbeispiele, Handungsempfehlungen*. Beltz.

Lardinoit, T. (1998, May). Effet modérateur de limplication durable sur l'efficacité mémorielle de la conjonction des parrainages terrain et T.V. In *Proceedings of the 14th Congress of the French Marketing Association (AFM)* (S. 261–276). Association Française de Marketing.

Lardinoit, T. (1999, May 19–21). Interaction des parrainages terrain et TV: impact sur deux niveaux de mémorisation. In *Proceedings of the 15th Congress of the French Marketing Association (AFM)*, (S. 585–602). Association Française de Marketing.

Liebetrau, M. (2007). Ambush Marketing – eine qualitative Analyse am Beispiel der FIFA Fußballweltmeisterschaft 2006. *Erfurter Hefte zum angewandten Marketing, 15,* 13–23.

Limbach, M. (2020). Erfassung der Effektivität von Sportsponsoring als Marketingkommunikationsinstrument auf der impliziten und expliziten Verarbeitungsebene von Konsumenten als Handlungsgrundlage für operative und strategische Managemententscheidungen. Gottfried Wilhelm Leibniz Universität Hannover, Dissertation. https://doi.org/10.15488/9802.

Lobo, A., Meyer, D., & Chester, Y. (2014). Evaluating consumer response associated with sponsoring of major sporting events in Australia. *Sport, Business and Management: An International Journal, 4*(1), 52–70. https://doi.org/10.1108/sbm-05-2011-0043.

Lyberger, M. R., & McCarthy, L. (2001). An assessment of consumer knowledge of, interest in, and perceptions of ambush marketing strategies. *Sport Marketing Quarterly, 10*(2), 130–137.

M

Markenartikel. (2021). E-Sport-Publikum ist für Unternehmen eine attraktive Zielgruppe, Beitrag vom 20.10.2021. https://www.markenartikel-magazin.de/_rubric/detail.php?rubric=marke-marketing&nr=43281. Accessed: 2. Nov. 2021.

Marshall, D. W., & Cook, G. (1992). The corporate (Sports) sponsor. *International Journal of Advertising, 11*(4), 307–324. https://doi.org/10.1080/02650487.1992.11104507.

Mattmüller, R., & Oettgen, N. (2008). Der Einsatz des Sponsoring im Handelsmarketing. In A. Bagusat, C. Marwitz, & M. Vogl (Hrsg.), *Handbuch Sponsoring. Eine erfolgreiche Marketing- und Markenkommunikation* (S. 287–297). Schmidt.

Mazodier, M., & Merunka, D. (2012). Achieving brand loyalty through sponsoring: The role of fit and self-congruity. *Journal of the Academy of Marketing Science, 40*(6), 807–820. https://doi.org/10.1007/s11747-011-0285-y.

McAlister, A. R., Kelly, S. J., Humphreys, M. S., & Cornwell, T. B. (2012). Change in a sponsoring alliance and the communication implications of spontaneous recovery. *Journal of Advertising, 41*(1), 5–16. https://doi.org/10.2753/joa0091-3367410101.

McDonald, C. (1991). Sponsoring and the image of the sponsor. *European Journal of Marketing, 25*(11), 31–38. https://doi.org/10.1108/eum0000000000630.

McDonald, J., & Davidson, J. (2002). Avoiding surprise results at the olympic games. *Managing Intellectual Property, 115,* 22–27.

McKelvey, S., & Grady, J. (2008). Sponsoring program protection strategies for special sport events: Are event organizers outmaneuvering ambush marketers. *Journal of Sport Management, 22*(5), 550–586. https://doi.org/10.1123/jsm.22.5.550.

Mecking, C. (2010). Corporate Giving. Unternehmensspende, Sponsoring und insbesondere Unternehmensstiftung. In H. Backhaus-Maul, C. Biedermann, S. Näahrlich, & J. Polterauer (Hrsg.), *Corporate Citizenship in Deutschland: Gesellschaftliches Engagement von Unternehmen* (S. 371–387). *Bilanz und Perspektiven*. VS Verlag.

Mediengruppe RTL Deutschland. (2015). Formel 1 – Imageanalyse. http://www.ip.de/loadfile.cfm-l?file=%3D9P.HPHW%23IX%22K%40%22%40%2C%3B094I*AUI*Z%40S%3FW%28QD*%2FFYD%20%0A&type=application%2Fpdf&sendcontent=true. Accessed: 31. May 2016.

Meedia. (2022). Wenn Haltung nur bis zum Claim reicht, Beitrag vom 10.11.2022. https://meedia.de/2022/11/10/wenn-haltung-nur-bis-zum-claim-reicht/.

Meenaghan, T. (1983). Commercial sponsoring. *European Journal of Marketing, 17*(2), 5–73. https://doi.org/10.1108/eum0000000004825.

Meenaghan, T., & Flood, P. R. (1983). *Commercial sponsoring. The misunderstood corporate art* (Special report). Dublin College of Marketing & Design.

Meenaghan, T., & Shipley, D. (1999). Media effect in commercial sponsoring. *European Journal of Marketing, 33*(3/4), 328–347. https://doi.org/10.1108/03090569910253170.

Meenaghan, T., McLoughlin, D., & McCormack, A. (2013). New challenges in sponsoring evaluation actors, new media, and the context of praxis. *Psychology & Marketing, 30*(5), 444–460. https://doi.org/10.1002/mar.20618.

Mein Bezirk. (2021). FC Wacker: Entschuldigung für die falsche Investorentscheidung; Beitrag vom 01.06.2021. https://www.meinbezirk.at/innsbruck/c-sport/entschuldigung-fuer-die-falsche-investorentscheidung_a4679879. Accessed: 2. Nov. 2021.

Melitta. (2019). 111 Jahre Melitta Sportsponsoring. Beitrag vom 16.07.2019.

Melitta. (2020). Melitta und Manchester United verlängern Partnerschaft. https://www.melitta-group.com/de/Melitta-und-Manchester-United-verlaengern-Partnerschaft-4207.html. Accessed: 2. Nov. 2021.

Mercedes-Benz. (2013). Smart Beachvolleyball-Teams zu Besuch auf der IAA in Frankfurt, Beitrag vom 11.09.2013. https://group-media.mercedes-benz.com/marsMediaSite/de/instance/ko/smart-Beachvolleyball-Teams-zu-Besuch-auf-der-IAA-in-Frankfurt.xhtml?oid=9918934. Accessed: 2. Nov. 2021.

Mercedes-Benz. (2020). *Mercedes-Benz junior cup*. https://group-media.mercedes-benz.com/marsMediaSite/de/instance/ko/Mercedes-Benz-Junior-Cup.xhtml?oid=9265680. Accessed: 2. Nov. 2021.

Mercedes-Benz. (2022). In der Lounge von Mercedes-AMG den Nürburgring erleben, Beitrag vom 09.05.2022. https://mbpassion.de/2022/05/in-der-lounge-von-mercedes-amg-den-nuerburgring-erleben/. Accessed: 2. Nov. 2021.

Michaelis, M., & Woisetschläger, D. M. (2011). Innovatives Vertriebscontrolling in interorganisationalen Vertriebssystemen mit Hilfe der Data Envelopment Analysis. *Controlling, 23*(4/5), 242–247. https://doi.org/10.15358/0935-0381-2011-4-5-242.

Milka. (2022). Milka Ski Sponsoring. https://www.milka.de/uber-milka/milka-ski-sponsoring. Accessed: 8. Nov. 2022.

Miragaia, D. A. M., Ferreira, J., & Ratten, V. (2017). Corporate social responsibility and social entrepreneurship: Drivers of sports sponsoring policy. *International Journal of Sport Policy, 9*(4), 613–623. https://doi.org/10.1080/19406940.2017.1374297.

Mitschke, M. (2007). Rechtliche Grenzen des Sponsoring. In D. Ahlert, D. Woisetschläger, & Vogel V. (Hrsg.), *Exzellentes Sponsoring. Innovative Ansätze und Best Practices für das Markenmanagement* (2. Aufl., S. 119–135). https://doi.org/10.1007/978-3-8350-9639-4_6.

Motorsport Total. (2017). Hinter den Kulissen: So geht es in der Mercedes-Hospitality zu, Beitrag vom 16.10.2017. https://www.motorsport-total.com/formel-1/news/hinter-den-kulissen-so-geht-es-in-der-mercedes-hospitality-zu-17101611. Accessed: 2. Nov.2021.

Musante, M. D., Milne, G. R., & McDonald, M. (1999). Sport sponsoring: Evaluating the sport and brand image match. *International Journal of Sports Marketing & Sponsoring, 1*(1), 24–39. https://doi.org/10.1108/ijsms-01-01-1999-b004.

Mussler, D. (1989). Organisation und Durchführung des Sponsoring. In A. Hermanns (Hrsg.), *Sport- und Kultursponsoring* (S. 29–38). Vahlen.

N

Nagel, S. (2012). Sponsoring und Vermarktungsrechte der Sportler und der Verbände. *Causa Sport, 1,* 55–63.

Nebenzhal, I. D., & Jaffe, E. D. (1998). Ethical dimensions of advertising executions. *Journal of Business Ethics, 17*(7), 805–815. https://doi.org/10.1023/a:1005850812845.

Nicholls, J. A. F., Roslow, S., & Dublish, S. (1999). Spectator recall and brand preference at sponsored Golf and Tennis tournaments. *European Journal of Marketing, 33*(3/4), 365–386. https://doi.org/10.1108/03090569910253198.

Nielsen Sports. (2015). Sponsor-Trend 2015: Status und Trends im Sponsoringmarkt in Deutschland, Österreich und Schweiz. http://www.marketing.ch/Portals/0/Wissen/Allgemein/Repucom%20Insights_Sponsor-Trend%202015_DACH_SFS.pdf. Accessed: 17. Febr. 2016.

Nielsen Sports. (2016). Sponsor-Trend 2016: Status und Trends im Sponsoringmarkt in Deutschland, Österreich und Schweiz.

Nielsen Sports. (2017). Wie Nielsen Sports die Wirkung von Sponsoring messbar machen will, Beitrag vom 10.03.2017. https://www.horizont.net/marketing/nachrichten/Return-on-Sponsoring-Investment-Wie-Nielsen-Sports-die-Wirkung-von-Sponsoring-messbar-machen-will-156477. https://nielsensports.com/return-on-sponsoring-investment-so-gelingt-die-ganzheitliche-messung/. Accessed: 2. Nov. 2021.

Nielsen Sports. (2018a). Sponsor-Trend 2018: Status und Trends im Sponsoringmarkt in Deutschland, Österreich und Schweiz.

Nielsen Sports. (2018b). *World football report 2018*.

Nielsen Sports. (2021). Sportsponsoren in Deutschland 2020/21. https://nielsensports.com/sportsponsoren-in-deutschland-2020-2021. Accessed: 1. May 2022.

Nielsen Sports. (2022). Sportmarketing-Trends 2022: So verändern Fans das Sportbusiness, Köln.

Nielsen Sports/Repucom. (2015). Sportsponsoren in Deutschland 2014/15, Köln.

Nieschlag, R., Dichtl, E., & Hörschgen, H. (2002). *Marketing* (19. Aufl.). Duncker & Humblot.

Nike. (2016). *Tiger Woods*. http://news.nike.com/tiger-woods. Accessed: 23. Febr. 2016.

n-tv. (2014). Trittbrett-Werbung bei der WM. Wenn Neymars Schlüpfer die Fifa empört. http://www.ntv.de/sport/fussball_wm_2014/Wenn-Neymars-Schluepfer-die-Fifa-empoert-article13173361.html. Accessed: 27. May 2016.

n-tv. (2022). UEFA will Geldgeber Gazprom loswerden, Beitrag vom 25.02.2022. https://www.n-tv.de/sport/fussball/UEFA-will-Geldgeber-Gazprom-loswerden-article23156507.html. Accessed: 2. Nov. 2021.

Nufer, G. (2005). Ambush Marketing. Angriff aus dem Hinterhalt oder eine Alternative zum Sportsponsoring? In H. D. Horch, G. Hovemann, S. Kaiser, & K. Viebahn (Hrsg.), *Perspektiven des Sportmarketing. Besonderheiten, Herausforderungen, Tendenzen* (S. 209–227). Institut für Sportökonomie und Sportmanagement Köln.

Nufer, G. (2006). *Event-Marketing: theoretische Fundierung und empirische Analyse unter besonderer Berücksichtigung von Imagewirkungen* (2. Aufl.). Deutscher Universitäts Verlag.

Nufer, G. (2008). Marken-Recall-Werte bei Fußball-Weltmeisterschaften, Beitrag vom 20.03.2008. https://www.marktforschung.de/marktforschung/a/marken-recall-werte-bei-fussball-weltmeisterschaften/. Accessed: 2. Nov. 2021.

Nufer, G. (2010). *Ambush Marketing im Sport: Grundlagen – Strategien – Wirkungen*. Schmidt.

Nufer, G. (2015). Creating an image transfer through event marketing: Principles, requirements and consequences. *European Journal of Business and Social Sciences, 3*(12), 1–18.

Nufer, G., & Bühler, A. (2014). Ambush Marketing im Sport – Wie Nicht-Sponsoren Sportveranstaltungen zur Markenkommunikation nutzen. In H. Preuss, F. Huber, H. Schunk, & T. Könecke (Hrsg.), *Marken und Sport* (S. 145–164). Gabler.

Nufer, G., & Bühler, A. (2015). Wie Erfolg in der Formel 1 die Marke Mercedes pusht. Nachspielzeit – die Schriftenreihe des Deutschen Instituts für Sportmarketing, herausgegeben von Gerd Nufer & André Bühler, Nr. 2015–2.

Nufer, G., & Rützel, F. (2016). Best Practices im Sportsponsoring, Nachspielzeit – die Schriftenreihe des Deutschen Instituts für Sportmarketing, herausgegeben von Gerd Nufer & André Bühler, Nr. 2016–7.

O

O'Sullivan, P., & Murphy, P. (1998). Ambush marketing: The ethical issues. *Psychology & Marketing, 15*(4), 349–366. https://doi.org/10.1002/(sici)1520-6793(199807)15:4<349::aid-mar5>3.0.co.2-8.

Oediger, F. (2022). Virtuelle Werbung: Zusatzerlöse von 100 Millionen Euro für die Bundesliga? Beitrag vom 15.09.2022. https://www.sponsors.de/news/themen/virtuelle-werbung-zusatzerloese-von-100-millionen-euro-fuer-die-bundesliga. Accessed: 2. Nov. 2021.

Off-the-pitch. (2022). Interview: New AS Roma Executive on commercial revolution in the Eternal city, Beitrag vom 18.05.2022. https://offthepitch.com/a/interview-new-roma-executive-commercial-revolution-eternal-city. Accessed: 2. Nov. 2021.

Olkkonen, R. (2001). Case study: The network approach to international sport sponsoring arrangement. *Journal of Business & Industrial Marketing, 16*(4), 309–329. https://doi.org/10.1108/eum0000000005503.

Olkkonen, R., Tikkanen, H., & Alajoutsijärvi, K. (2000). Sponsoring as relationships and networks: Implications for research. *Corporate Communications: An International Journal, 5*(1), 12–19. https://doi.org/10.1108/13563280010317532.

ORF. (2022). Mateschitz-Erfolg eng mit Sport verbunden, Beitrag vom 23.10.2023. https://sport.orf.at/stories/3101092.

Oschmann, A. (1997). Viel Image für gutes Geld. *Der Handel, 26*(4), 12–14.

P

Panten, D. (2013). Sponsoring goes Social Media – Aktivierung von Zielgruppen im digitalen Zeitalter. *Media 41 – Journal für Media & Marketing, 41*(5), 6–10.

Papadimitriou, D., Kaplanidou, K. K., & Papacharalampous, N. (2016). Sport event-sponsor fit and its effects on sponsor purchase intentions: A non-consumer perspective among athletes, volunteers and spectators. *Journal of Business & Industrial Marketing, 31*(2), 247–259. https://doi.org/10.1108/jbim-09-2014-0187.

Pechtl, H. (2007). Trittbrettfahren bei Sportevents: Das Ambush-Marketing. Wirtschaftswissenschaftliche Diskussionspapiere, (1), Rechts- und Staatswissenschaftliche Fakultät, Universität Greifswald.

Perform Media Deutschland GmbH. (2010). Woods: Verlust von 50 Millionen Dollar. http://www.spox.com/de/sport/golf/1004/News/tiger-woods-verliert-durch-eskapaden-50-millionen-dollar-skandal-affaere-verlust-sponsoren.html. Accessed: 23. Febr. 2016.

Pham, M. T. (1991). The evaluation of sponsoring effectiveness: A model and some methodological considerations. *Gestion 2000, 7*(4), 47–65.

Pilot Checkpoint. (2000). *Sponsor visions 2000*.

Pilot Checkpoint. (2002). *Sponsor visions 2002*.

Pilot Checkpoint. (2008). *Sponsor visions 2008.*

Pommer, J., & Kaiser, D. (2014). Beko Basketball Bundesliga – die Schaffung und Positionierung einer neuen Marke. In H. Preuß, F. Huber, H. Schunk, & T. Könecke (Hrsg.), *Marken und Sport – Aktuelle Aspekte der Markenführung im Sport und mit Sport* (S. 465–483). Gabler.

Pope, N. K. L., & Voges, K. E. (1994). Sponsoring evaluation: Does it match the motive and the mechanism? *Sport Marketing Quarterly, 3*(4), 37–45.

Porsche AG. (2016). Rendezvous der Supersportler, Beirag vom 13.09.2016. https://newsroom.porsche.com/de/unternehmen/porsche-tennis-angelique-kerber-markenbotschafterin-us-open-titel-panamera-turbo-12886.html. Accessed: 2. Nov. 2021.

Porter, M. E., & Kramer, M. R. (2003). Wohltätigkeit als Wettbewerbsvorteil. *Harvard Business Manager, 3*(März), 40–56.

Poser, U., & Backes, B. (2010). *Sponsoringvertrag: Bd. 26. Beck'sche Musterverträge.* Beck.

PricewaterhouseCoopers. (2018). Digital Trend Outlook 2018: Esport-Studie 2018. https://www.pwc.de/de/technologie-medien-und-telekommunikation/digital-trend-outlook-2018-esport/sponsoring-im-esport-markt.html. Accessed: 2. Nov. 2021.

PricewaterhouseCoopers. (2020). Studie PwC's Sports Survey 2020 – Deutsche Ausgabe.

Puma-BVB. (2022). BVB-Heimtrikot 22/23|Different From Day One. https://www.youtube.com/watch?v=KND_kjdtPJw. Accessed: 2. Nov. 2021.

Quester, P. G., & Thompson, B. (2001). Advertising and promotion leverage on arts sponsoring effectiveness. *Journal of Advertising Research, 41*(1), 33–47. https://doi.org/10.2501/jar-41-1-33-47.

R

Reischauer, C. (1997). Mit Sportsponsoring die gewünschte Wirkung zu erreichen, wird immer schwieriger. *Wirtschaftswoche, 51*(6), 60–65.

Ringle, T. (2003). Vernetzung von Sportevents. In A. Hermanns & F. Riedmüller (Hrsg.), *Sponsoring und Events im Sport* (S. 193–207). Vahlen.

Roche. (2022). Spenden und Sponsoring bei Roche in Deutschland. https://www.roche.de/ueber-roche/verantwortung-dialog/gesellschaft-umwelt/sponsoring-roche-deutschland. Accessed: 2. Nov. 2021.

Rodgers, S. (2007). Effects of sponsoring congruity on e-sponsors and e-newspapers. *Journalism & Mass Communication Quarterly, 84*(1), 24–39. https://doi.org/10.1177/107769900708400103.

Rogge, H. -J. (2004). *Werbung* (6. Aufl.). NWB Verlag.

Rohlmann, P. (2016). Sportsponsoring – Wachstum ohne Grenzen? Sponsoring als unverzichtbarer Bestandteil der Sportvermarktung. *Stadionwelt INSIDE*, Sonderheft Sponsoring, S. 79.

Rohlmann, P. (2018). Ausrüsterverträge im Fußball gestern – heute – morgen. Marktdaten, Akteure, Strategien, Nutznießer und Trikotabsatz aus den TOP 5-Ligen Europas sowie einem Ausblick in die Zukunft des Fußballartikelmarktes, Rheine/St. Gallen.

Rohlmann, P. (2021). Red Bull und Fußball – Eine Analyse der Fußballaktivitäten des Red Bull Konzerns (Red Bull Global Soccer), Rheine/St. Gallen.

Rohlmann, P. (2022a). Sportklubs und Sportartikelhersteller – eine Schicksalsgemeinschaft besonderer Art, Rheine/St. Gallen.

Rohlmann, P. (2023). *Sportmerchandising – Konzeptionelle Grundlagen, Marktdaten und Trends.* ESV-Verlag.

Ross, L., Greene, D., & House, P. (1977). The „false consensus effect": An egocentric bias in social perception and attribute processes. *Journal of Experimental Social Psychology, 13*(3), 279–301. https://doi.org/10.1016/0022-1031(77)90049-x.

Rothe, C. (2001). Kultursponsoring und Image-Konstruktion. Interdisziplinäre Analyse der rezeptionsspezifischen Faktoren des Kultursponsoring und Entwicklung eines kommunikationswissenschaftlichen Imageapproaches, Bochum.

Rowley, J., & Williams, C. (2008). The impact of brand sponsoring of music festivals. *Marketing Intelligence & Planning, 26*(7), 781–792. https://doi.org/10.1108/02634500810916717.

RP-Online. (2017). Bitburger beendet Partnerschaft mit DFB, Beitrag vom 20.01.2017. https://rp-online.de/sport/fussball/nationalelf/bitburger-beendet-partnerschaft-mit-dfb_aid-19135133. Accessed: 2. Nov. 2021.

Ryan, A., & Fahy, J. (2003). A relationship marketing perspective on the sponsoring of the arts in Ireland: A Galway arts festival-nortel networks case study. *Irish Marketing Review, 16*(1), 31–42.

S

S20. (2021). Responsible Sport-Sponsoring. Modernes Sportsponsoring – verantwortungsvoll, nachhaltig und relevant. Whitepaper der S20 e. V. Bonn.

Salzer, F. (2022). *Beendigungsmanagement von Sponsoringbeziehungen – Konzeption und empirische Analyse eines Wirkungsmodells.* https://doi.org/10.1007/978-3-658-37778-6.

Santomier, J. (2008). New media, branding and global sports sponsoring. *International Journal of Sports Marketing and Sponsoring, 10*(1), 9–22. https://doi.org/10.1108/ijsms-10-01-2008-b005.

Scharf, A., Schubert, B., & Hehn, P. (2015). *Marketing. Einführung in Theorie und Praxis* (7. Aufl.). Stuttgart. https://doi.org/10.34156/9783799269506.

Schaub, R. (2008). *Sponsoring und Doping. Beendigung von Sponsoringverträgen wegen Verfehlungen des Gesponserten, insbesondere in Dopingfällen, Göttingen.* Universitätsverlag Göttingen. https://doi.org/10.17875/gup2008-175

Schmidt, J. (2017). Foto Allstar Jersey. http://www.jokoschmidt.com/portfolio/allstar-jersey. Accessed: 2. Nov. 2021.

Schmitgen, A., & Schilhaneck, M. (2016). Fallstudie – Sponsoring im Mittelstand: Sweetheart-Deal vs. strategisches Investment? Sciamus – Sport und Management, Nr. 1, S. 20–28.

Schröder, S. (2019). Sportsponsoring und Social Media – die neue Herausforderung für die Erfolgskontrolle, Beitrag vom 29.01.2019. https://www.marktforschung.de/marktforschung/a/sportsponsoring-und-social-media-die-neue-herausforderung-fuer-die-erfolgskontrolle/. Accessed: 2. Nov. 2021.

Schwarz, J. (2012). *Messung und Steuerung der Kommunikations-Effizienz: Eine theoretische und empirische Analyse durch den Einsatz der Data Envelopment Analysis.* https://doi.org/10.1007/978-3-658-00279-4.

Schweiger, G., & Schrattenecker, G. (2013). *Werbung* (8. Aufl.). UVK Verlagsgesellschaft.

Seibert, J., & Wiese, M. (2013). Sponsoring kann die Neukundengewinnung unterstützen. *Marketing Review St. Gallen, 30*(1), 6–10. https://doi.org/10.1365/s11621-013-0184-3.

Serviceplan/Sky Media Network. (2013). From the Heart to the Brain. Der Deutsche Sponsoring-Index 2013, München/Unterföhring. Accessed: 16. Dec. 2013.

SevenOne Media. (2015). Opel Adam: Begleitforschung „Germany's next Topmodel" (Staffel 10). https://www.sevenonemedia.ch/documents/20182/400450/Opel_Adam_GNT_2015.pdf/33c15753-624b-47dc-89a8-5edb382d42af. Accessed: 20. May 2016.

Shilbury, D., & Berriman, M. (1996). Sponsoring awareness: A study of St. Kilda football club supporters. *Sport Marketing Quarterly, 5*(1), 27–33.

Simkins, J. (1980). Sponsoring 1980/81, Rockville.

Simmons, C. J., & Becker-Olsen, K. L. (2006). Achieving marketing objectives through social sponsorings. *Journal of Marketing, 70*(4), 154–169.

Sinn, W., Dowling, Ph., Richau, L., & Ellenrieder, D. (2022). *Bain-Bundesliga-Benchmarking: Union Berlin, Dortmund und Köln jagen die Bayern.* Bain & Company.

Sirgy, M. J., Lee, D. J., Johar, J. S., & Tidwell, J. (2008). Effect of self-congruity with sponsoring on brand loyalty. *Journal of Business Research, 61*(10), 1091–1097.

Skinfit. (2016). *Sponsoring.* http://www.skinfit.eu/ch/de/teams-sponsoring.html. Accessed: 8. June 2016.

Sky Sport. (2018). Wolfsberger AC präsentiert kurioses Trikot, Beitrag vom 14.07.2018. https://sport.sky.de/fussball/artikel/dezent-ist-anders-wac-trikot-blueht-voller-sponsoren/11437033/34271. Accessed: 2. Nov. 2021.

SLC. (2021). Beliebtheitsstudie zur Fußball Bundesliga 2021, 7. Erhebung, Nürnberg.

Speed, R., & Thompson, P. (2000). Determinants of sports sponsoring response. *Journal of the Academy of Marketing Science, 28*(2), 225–238. https://doi.org/10.1177/0092070300282004.

Spiegel. (2016). Korruptionsskandal: Adidas zieht sich offenbar als Sponsor aus der Leichtathletik zurück, Beitrag vom 25.01.2016. http://www.spiegel.de/sport/sonst/adidas-zieht-sich-laut-bbc-als-sponsor-aus-leichtathletik-zurueck-a-1073684.html. Accessed: 2. Nov. 2021.

Spiegel. (2021). AOK beendet umstrittenes Trikot-Sponsoring, Beitrag vom 21.12.2021. https://www.spiegel.de/sport/handball/handball-nationalmannschaft-aok-beendet-umstrittenes-trikot-sponsoring-a-bd0f5df6-f150-4156-a596-4068d5ece8bd. Accessed: 2. Nov. 2021.

Spiegel. (2022). Darum ist die WM in Katar so in Verruf, Beitrag vom 18.11.2022. https://www.spiegel.de/sport/fussball/fussball-wm-2022-in-katar-warum-die-weltmeisterschaft-so-umstritten-ist-a-2e06d0b8-6f2d-4c1f-bad1-4ad4d3b57ff4. Accessed: 2. Nov. 2021.

Splendid Research. (2018). Coca-Cola und Adidas bekannteste Sponsoren der Fußball-WM, Beitrag von Juni 2018. https://www.splendid-research.com/de/statistiken/studie-sponsoren-wahrnehmung-fu%C3%9Fball-wm. Accessed: 2. Nov. 2021.

Sponsor Partners (Hrsg.). (2000). Sponsoring Trends 2000. Studie in Zusammenarbeit mit dem Institut für Marketing der Universität der Bundeswehr München, Bonn.

Sponsor.news. (2022a). Banken. Mit einer Reihe von Neuabschlüssen fallen Regionalbanken in einem ansonsten schwierigen Marktumfeld auf, Ausgabe 2, S. 4–5.

Sponsor.news. (2022b). „Telekom und FC Bayern: „Unser ‚T' kommt über 5.000 Minuten ins Bild", Ausgabe Aug./Sept., S. 4.

Sponsors. (2020). Business Case statt Bande: Was die Bundesliga vom IOC lernen kann, Beitrag vom 14.07.2020. https://www.sponsors.de/news/themen/ioc-vermarktung. Accessed: 2. Nov. 2021.

Sponsors. (2020a). Warum Clubs ihren Fokus mehr auf digitales Sponsoring legen sollten, Beitrag vom 30.06.2020. https://www.sponsors.de/news/themen/clubs-digitales-sponsoring?active=1. Accessed: 2. Nov. 2011.

Sponsors. (2021). Warum Private Equity zunehmend in den Sport investiert, Beitrag vom 20.07.2021. https://www.sponsors.de/news/themen/warum-private-equity-zunehmend-in-den-sport-investiert. Accessed: 2. Nov. 2021.

Sponsors. (2022a). Fußball-Bundesliga: Das Social-Media-Ranking der Saison 2021/22, Beitrag vom 30.05.2022. https://www.sponsors.de/news/fussball/fussball-bundesliga-das-social-media-ranking-der-saison-202122. Accessed: 2. Nov. 2021.

Sponsors. (2022b). Virtuelle Werbung: Zusatzerlöse von 100 Millionen Euro für die Bundesliga? Beirag vom 15.09.2022. https://www.sponsors.de/news/themen/virtuelle-werbung-zusatzerloese-von-100-millionen-euro-fuer-die-bundesliga. Accessed: 2. Nov. 2021.

Sponsors. (2022c). *Sponsors data*. https://sites.sponsors.de/data/. Accessed: 2. Nov. 2021.

Sponsors. (2022d). FIFA WM 2022: Wie Sponsoren mit öffentlicher Kritik umgehen könnten, Beitrag vom 29.09.2022. https://www.sponsors.de/news/themen/fifa-wm-2022-wie-sponsoren-mit-oeffentlicher-kritik-umgehen-koennten. Accessed: 2. Nov. 2021.

Sponsors. (2022e). Indeed: Übers Eintracht-Hauptsponsoring zum Marktführer in Deutschland, Beitrag vom 12.12.2022. https://www.sponsors.de/news/themen/indeed-uebers-eintracht-hauptsponsoring-zum-marktfuehrer. Accessed: 2. Nov. 2021.

Sponsors. (2022f). SPOBIS Podcast „Sports, Business & Players“ mit Bernd von Geldern, Beitrag vom 24.08.2022. https://www.sponsors.de/news/fussball/spobis-podcast-sports-business-players-mit-bernd-von-geldern. Accessed: 2. Nov. 2021.

Sponsor-Service. (2022). Sponsor-Service, der internationalen Sponsorbörse. http://www.sponsor-service.com/german.htm. Accessed: 2. Nov. 2021.

Sport + Markt AG. (2013). Sponsoring Barometer Österreich 2012/2013, Köln.

Sportbusiness Consulting. (2021). *Stadium naming rights report*. https://www.sportbusiness.com/stadium-naming-rights-report/. Accessed: 2. Nov. 2021.

Sportbuzzer. (2020). 100 Millionen Euro Schuldenerlass für RB Leipzig: „Nicht ungewöhnlich und nicht zu bemängeln“, Beitrag vom 09.06.2020. https://www.sportbuzzer.de/artikel/100-millionen-euro-schuldenerlass-rb-leipzig-zuelch-erklaerung-schenkung-uefa/. Accessed: 2. Nov. 2021.

Sportcal. (2020). *The 2020–21 European club Soccer kit supply report*.

Sportfive. (2022). Mehr Sales durch Sportsponsoring, Beitrag vom 09.05.2022. https://beyond-the-match.com/sponsoring/mehr-sales-durch-sportsponsoring/. Accessed: 2. Nov. 2021.

Sportspromedia. (2023). Uefa warns multi-club ownership threatens ‘integrity’ of soccer, Beitrag vom 13.02.2023. https://www.sportspromedia.com/news/uefa-soccer-multi-club-ownership-investment-model-ceferin/. Accessed: 2. Nov. 2021.

Spox. (2022). Kommentar zur Farce um die One-Love-Binde: Das Einknicken von DFB und Co. ist frustrierender als die schauerliche Machtdemonstration der FIFA, Beitrag vom 21.11.2022. https://www.spox.com/de/sport/fussball/wm/wm2022/2211/Artikel/kommentar-farce-one-love-binde-einknicken-neuendorf-dfb-fa-niederlande-frustrierender-fifa-ftr.html. Accessed: 2. Nov. 2021.

Stadionwelt. (2019). Besitzverhältnisse der Bundesligastadien, Beitrag vom 20.11.2019. https://www.stadionwelt.de/news/19697/besitzverhaeltnisse-der-bundesligastadien. Accessed: 2. Nov. 2021.

Stadionwelt. (2020). Besitz- und Betriebsverhältnisse: Profifußball Deutschland. https://imageserver.stadionwelt.de/Image/6/6/49a4586f70d05ac618ecfce11f8563ed1230bf78beb17ea2d774-e64f50f203/Besitz-_und_Betriebsverh%C3%A4ltnisse_Profifu%C3%9Fball_Deutschland.pdf. Accessed: 2. Nov. 2021.

Stadionwelt INSIDE. (2015). Naming Right für Stadien und Arenen: intensive Beziehung mit hohem Potenzial, Ausgabe Mai, S. 44–51.

Stadtwerke Tübingen. (2022). Sponsoring-Leitlinien der SWT. https://www.swtue.de/fileadmin/user_upload/4Unternehmen/Verantwortung/GesEngagement/220413_swt-Sponsoring_Leitlinien.pdf. Accessed: 2. Nov. 2021.

Statista. (2013). Welche Marke verbinden Sie am meisten mit Wintersport? Beitrag vom 18.12.2013. https://de.statista.com/statistik/daten/studie/283776/umfrage/bekannteste-marken-im-wintersport-2013-2014/. Accessed: 2. Nov. 2021.

Statista. (2016a). Investitionsvolumen auf dem deutschen Sponsoringmarkt im Jahr 2014 und Prognosen für 2015 und 2016 (in Milliarden Euro). http://de.statista.com/statistik/daten/studie/4789/umfrage/investitionsvolumen-fuer-sponsoring-prognose/. Accessed: 17. Febr. 2016.

Statista. (2016b). Welche Sportarten schauen Sie gerne im Fernsehen? https://de.statista.com/statistik/daten/studie/235067/umfrage/die-beliebtesten-sportarten-im-tv/. Accessed: 2. Nov. 2021.

Statista. (2017). Anteil des Sponsoring am Kommunikationsbudget von deutschen Unternehmen im Jahresvergleich 2013 und 2016. https://de.statista.com/statistik/daten/studie/302340/umfrage/anteil-des-kommunikationsbudget-von-unternehmen/. Accessed: 1. May 2022.

Statista. (2019). In diese Sportarten fließt das Geld (Werte in Milliarden US-Dollar pro Jahr). https://www.horizont.net/marketing/nachrichten/statista-studie-30-milliarden-dollar-fuer-sportsponsoring%2D%2D-und-so-wenig-fliesst-in-den-frauensport-178891. Accessed: 2. Nov. 2021.

Statista. (2021a). Anteil der Sportarten an den Sportsponsoring-Investitionen der Top-100-Sponsoren in Deutschland in der Saison 2020/2021. Accessed: 9. Sept. 2022.

Statista. (2021b). Bevölkerung in Deutschland nach Häufigkeit des Sporttreibens in der Freizeit von 2017 bis 2021. https://de.statista.com/statistik/daten/studie/171911/umfrage/haeufigkeit-sport-treiben-in-der-freizeit/. Accessed: 2. Nov. 2021.

Statista. (2021c). Das Milliardengeschäft mit dem digitalen Sport. https://de.statista.com/infografik/8643/esport-umsatz-und-zuschauer-weltweit/. Accessed: 2. Nov. 2021.

Statista. (2021d). E-Sport-Sponsoring widersteht Coronakrise, Beitrag vom 25.01.2021. https://de.statista.com/infografik/26671/prognostizierter-jahresumsatz-mit-e-sports-nach-quelle/. Accessed: 2. Nov. 2021.

Statista. (2022a). Investitionen in Sportsponsoring in Deutschland von 2000 bis 2020 (in Milliarden Euro). https://de.statista.com/statistik/daten/studie/167709/umfrage/ausgaben-fuer-sponsoring-in-sport-und-kultur/. Accessed: 2. Nov. 2021.

Statista. (2022b). Marktwert der teuersten Fußball-Bundesligaprofis in der Saison 2022/2023 (Quelle: transfermarkt.de). https://de.statista.com/statistik/daten/studie/1454/umfrage/marktwert-der-teuersten-bundesligaprofis/. Accessed: 2. Nov. 2021.

Statista. (2022c). Bevölkerung in Deutschland nach Häufigkeit des Sporttreibens in der Freizeit von 2017 bis 2021.

Statista. (2022d). *Soccer agencies with the highest total market value of players worldwide as of March 2022*. https://www.statista.com/statistics/1125816/soccer-agencies-total-market-value/. Accessed: 2. Nov. 2021.

Statista. (2022e). Sportsponsoring-Ausgaben in Deutschland nach Sportarten 2020/2021. https://de.statista.com/statistik/daten/studie/431355/umfrage/formen-des-sport-sponsorings-in-deutschland-oesterreich-und-der-schweiz/. Accessed: 02.11.2021.

Steinkirchner, P. (2016). Wie das Red-Bull-Imperium die Sportwelt erobert, in: Wirtschaftswoche vom 13.05.2016.

Stern. (2007). Telekom zieht die Reißleine, Beitrag vom 27.11.2007. https://www.stern.de/sport/sportwelt/sponsoring-ausstieg-telekom-zieht-die-reissleine-3218652.html. Accessed: 2. Nov. 2021.

Stipp, H., & Schiavone, N. P. (1996). Modeling the impact of Olympic sponsoring on corporate image. *Journal of Advertising Research, 36*(4), 22–28.

Streppelhoff, R., & Pohlmann, A. (2020). *Sportgroßveranstaltungen in Deutschland. Band 1: Bewegende Momente*. Sonderpublikation des Bundesinstituts für Sportwissenschaft.

Stumpf, M. (2020). *Die 10 wichtigsten Zukunftsthemen im Marketing* (2. Aufl.). Haufe Group.

Sudolska, A., & Łapińska, J. (2020). Implementation of the CSR concept through sport sponsoring: The case of the polish chemical capital group. *Journal of Physical Education and Sport, 20,* 1100–1105.

Sung, M., & Lee, W. Y. (2016). What makes an effective CSR program? An analysis of the constructs of a cause-related participant sport sponsoring event. *International Journal of Sports Marketing and Sponsoring, 17*(1), 56–77. https://doi.org/10.1108/ijsms-02-2016-004.

T

Tageskarte. (2022). „Anti-Sponsor" Brewdog für „World F*Cup"-Kampagne gefeiert und kritisiert, Beitrag vom 16.11.2022. https://www.tageskarte.io/detail/anti-sponsor-brewdog-fuer-world-fcup-kampagne-gefeiert-und-kritisiert.html. Accessed: 2. Nov. 2021.

Taz. (2021). Trend Sport-Dokumentationen: Bis unter die Dusche, Beitrag vom 22.02.2021. https://taz.de/Trend-Sport-Dokumentationen/!5750323/. Accessed: 2. Nov. 2021.

The Coca-Cola Company. (2013). Der 12. Mann auf dem Platz: Fan Club Nationalmannschaft. http://www.coca-cola-deutschland.de/stories/seit-10-jahren-der-12-mann-auf-dem-platz-fan-club-nationalmannschaft. Accessed: 2. Nov. 2021.

The Coca-Cola Company. (2015). *Coca-Cola journey*. http://www.coca-cola-deutschland.de/#sport. Accessed: 2. Nov. 2021.

Tietz, B., & Zentes, J. (1980). *Die Werbung der Unternehmung*. Rowohlt.

Townley, S., & Grayson, E. (1984). *Sponsoring of sport, arts and leisure: Law, tax and business relationships*. Sweet & Maxwell.

Townley, S. E. (1993). Some legal issues associated with international sports marketing. *Sport Marketing Quarterly, 2*(2), 31–42.

Turco, D. M. (1996). The effects of courtside advertisingon product recognition and attitude change. *Sport Marketing Quarterly, 5*(4), 11–15.

Turkish Airlines. (2016). *Sponsorings*. http://www.turkishairlines.com/en-int/corporate/sport-club. Accessed: 2. Nov. 2021.

Two Circles. (2020). Sponsoring's Digital Revolution, Beitrag vom 18.05.2020. https://twocircles.com/eu-en/sponsorings-digital-revolution/. Accessed: 2. Nov. 2021.

Tz München. (2013). Wer sind eigentlich diese Fans im „T"? http://www.tz.de/sport/fc-bayern/telekom-t-allianz-arena-fc-bayern-muenchen-wer-sind-fans-bewerben-meta-2853149.html. Accessed: 2. Nov. 2021.

U

UEFA. (2021). Die europäische Klubfußballlandschaft – Benchmarking-Bericht zur Klublizenzierung. Mit der Pandemie leben, Nyon.

V

van Berkel, M. (2017). „The more you know, the more you enjoy"? – Empirische Überprüfung von medialen Sportangeboten. *Journal für Sportkommunikation, 2*(1), 31–45. https://doi.org/10.25968/JSkMs.2017.1.31-45

von Berkel, M. (2017). „The more you know, the more you enjoy"? – Empirische Überprüfung von Netzwerkeffekten in medialen Sportangeboten. *Journal für Sportkommunikation und Mediensport, 2*(1), 31–45. https://doi.org/10.25968/JSkMs.2017.1.31-45.

Vignali, C. (1997). The MIXMAP-model for international sport sponsoring. *European Business Review, 97*(4), 187–193. https://doi.org/10.1108/09555349710175315.

Voeth, M., & Urbitsch, Y. (2022). *Studie zur FIFA WM 2022 in Katar. Was denkt die deutsche Bevölkerung?* (Bd. 1–4). Universität Hohenheim.

Vogelsang, F. (2019). Das Virtuelle digitaler Medien ist nie nur virtuell. Es ist Teil der menschlichen Realität. https://frank-vogelsang.de/2019/03/28/ist-die-kommunikation-in-digitalen-medien-nur-virtuell-was-ist-dann-real/. Accessed: 2. Nov. 2021.

VSA. (2019). Sportsponsoring: Volltreffer mit gezielter Wirkung, Berlin. Accessed: 1. May 2022.

VSA. (2021). Delphi-Studie: Zukunft 2030 – Sportsponsoring im Wandel, WHU – Otto Beisheim School of Management, Center for Sports and Management, Düsseldorf.

VSA, S 20, BMI. (2017). *Hospitality und Strafrecht – ein Leitfaden* (2. Aufl.). https://cdn.dosb.de/alter_Datenbestand/fm-dosb/downloads/recht/Hospitality-und-Strafrecht-ein-Leitfaden_2017.pdf. Accessed: 2. Nov. 2021.

W

Web.de. (2022). Sponsoren der Fußball-WM am Pranger: Wie heftig sind die Image-Folgen für Adidas, Coca-Cola und Co.? Beitrag vom 05.11.2022. https://web.de/magazine/sport/fussball/wm/sponsoren-fussball-wm-pranger-heftig-folgen-adidas-coca-cola-co-37387076. Accessed: 2. Nov. 2021.

W&V (Verlag Werben und Verkaufen GmbH). (2012). Sponsor Visions 2012: Sport-Sponsoring boomt. http://www.wuv.de/medien/sponsor_visions_2012_sport_sponsoring_boomt. Accessed: 17. Febr. 2016.

W&V (Verlag Werben und Verkaufen GmbH). (2017). 8 Wege, im Sport-Sponsoring Geld zu verbrennen, Beitrag vom 11.08.2017. https://www.wuv.de/Archiv/8-Wege,-im-Sport-Sponsoring-Geld-zu-verbrennen. Accessed: 2. Nov. 2021.

Waite, N. (1979). Sponsoring in Context. Unveröffentlichte PhD-Thesis. Cranefield Institute of Management, Cranfield.

Wall Street Journal. (2012). Ambush Marketing: Die Raubritter bei Olympia. http://www.wsj.de/nachrichten/SB10001424052702304181204579368573188797410. Accessed: 2. Nov. 2021.

Walliser, B. (1995). Sponsoring. Bedeutung, Wirkung und Kontrollmöglichkeiten, Wiesbaden. https://doi.org/10.1007/978-3-663-12376-7.

Walliser, B. (2003). An international review of sponsoring research. Extension and update. *International Journal of Advertising, 22*(1), 5–40. https://doi.org/10.1080/02650487.2003.11072838.

Walraven, M., Bijmolt, T. H., & Koning, R. H. (2014). Dynamic effects of sponsoring: How sponsoring awareness develops over time. *Journal of Advertising, 43*(2), 142–154. https://doi.org/10.1080/00913367.2013.835754.

Walzel, S., & Schubert, M. (2018). *Sportsponsoring – Grundlagen, Konzeption und Wirkungen.* Springer Gabler. https://doi.org/10.1007/978-3-662-55246-9.

Watson. (2022). WM 2022: Budweiser reagiert auf Bier-Verbot, Beitrag vom 22.11.2022. https://www.watson.de/sport/wm%202022/297800342-wm-2022-budweiser-reagiert-auf-bier-verbot-in-katar. Accessed: 2. Nov. 2021.

Weeks, C. S., Cornwell, T. B., & Drennan, J. C. (2008). Leveraging sponsorings on the internet: Activation, congruence, and articulation. *Psychology & Marketing, 25*(7), 637–654. https://doi.org/10.1002/mar.20229.

Wegner, R. (2020). Zur Genese und Entwicklung von Trendsportarten angesichts wirtschaftlicher Paradigmenwechsel und digitaler Informationsmöglichkeiten, Dissertation der Technischen Universität Kaiserslautern.

Werner, A. (2013). *Social Media – Analytics & Monitoring. Verfahren und Werkzeuge zur Optimierung des ROI*. dpunkt.

Wichert, J., & Leda, L. (2001). Namensrechte an Stadien und Arenen. *Sponsors, 6*(Ausgabe März), 45–46.

Wiedmann, K.-P., & Gross, P. (2013). Image transfer in a sponsoring alliance. *Marketing Review St. Gallen, 30*(1), 22–35. https://doi.org/10.1365/s11621-013-0186-1.

Wiener Zeitung. (2021). Sport-Sponsoring-Markt trotzt Corona-Krise, Beitrag vom 16.02.2021. https://www.wienerzeitung.at/nachrichten/sport/mehr-sport/2093100-Sport-Sponsoring-Markt-trotzt-Corona-Krise.html. Accessed: 2. Nov. 2021.

Witcher, B. J., Craigen, G., Culligan, D., & Harvey, A. (1991). The links between objectives and function in organizational sponsoring. *International Journal of Aduertising, 10*(1), 13–21. https://doi.org/10.1080/02650487.1991.11104431.

Witt, M. (2000). *Kunstsponsoring. Gestaltungsdimensionen, Wirkungsweise und Wirkungsmessungen*. Schmidt.

Woisetschläger, D. M., & Michaelis, M. (2012). Sponsoring congruence and brand image: A pre-post event analysis. *European Journal of Marketing, 46*(3/4), 509–523. https://doi.org/10.1108/03090561211202585.

World Atlas. (2022). The most popular sports in the world. https://www.worldatlas.com/articles/what-are-the-most-popular-sports-in-the-world.html. Accessed: 2. Nov. 2021.

Y

YouGov. (2021). Finanzdienstleister-Studie: Sport-Sponsoring zahlt schon nach kurzer Zeit auf das Markenimage ein, Beitrag vom 04.05.2021. https://yougov.de/news/2021/05/04/finanzdienstleister-studie-sport-sponsoring-zahlt-/. Accessed: 2. Nov. 2021.

YouGov. (2022a). Global: Which industries are best suited for sports sponsoring? https://sport.yougov.com/global-which-industries-are-best-suited-for-sports-sponsoring/. Accessed: 2. Nov. 2021.

YouGov. (2022b). Umfrage des Meinungsforschungsinstituts YouGov im Auftrag der Deutschen Presse-Agentur, Beitrag vom 03.07.2022. https://www.sportbuzzer.de/artikel/umfrage-wm-katar-grossteil-der-deutschen-fur-ruckzug-der-nationalmannschaft/. Accessed: 2. Nov. 2021.

YouGov, & Handelsblatt. (2021). Marke des Jahres.Ranking 2021. https://commercial.yougov.com/rs/464-VHH-988/images/YouGov-Germany-Marke-des-Jahres-Ranking-October-2021.pdf?mkt_tok=NDY0LVZISC05ODgAAAGAYCpv-RsvLbZQDJh2IfHs-g1iPYmm7637P48oTvc_KZPYBa-HxsGrcF98khHEI304ZmkYuK0OwgjCrFWQ_P3lifsnNjYAvaKxaHFBzDoYLZc4. Accessed: 2. Nov. 2021.

YouTube Commerbank. (2019). Frecher Commerzbank Video-Clip. https://www.youtube.com/watch?v=fZL1D-ybye8. Accessed: 2. Nov. 2021.

Z

Zafer Erdogan, B., & Kitchen, P. J. (1998). Managerial mindsets and the symbiotic relationship between sponsoring and advertising. *Marketing Intelligence & Planning, 16*(6), 369–374. https://doi.org/10.1108/02634509810237578.

Zajonc, R. B. (1968). Attitudinal effects of mere exposure. *Journal of Personality and Social Psychology, Monograph Supplement, 9*, 1–27. https://doi.org/10.1037/h0025848.

ZAW (Zentralverband der Deutschen Werbewirtschaft). (2006–2021). Werbung in Deutschland, Bonn.

ZDF heute. (2022a). Skepsis nach Testlauf in Köln, Beitrag vom 20.07.2022. https://www.zdf.de/nachrichten/sport/fussball-bundesliga-technologisierung-datenerfassung-body-camera-1-fc-koeln-ac-mailand-100.html. Accessed: 2. Nov. 2021.

ZDF heute. (2022b). Buschmann: Homosexualität ist keine Krankheit, Beitrag vom 08.11.2022. https://www.zdf.de/nachrichten/politik/katar-fussball-wm-homosexualitaet-buschmann-kritik-100.html. Accessed: 2. Nov. 2021.

Zeit. (2022a). Investor Kühne erwirbt Namensrechte am Volksparkstadion, Beitrag vom 31.03.2022. https://www.zeit.de/news/2022-03/31/investor-kuehne-erwirbt-namensrechte-am-volksparkstadion. Accessed: 2. Nov. 2021.

Zeit. (2022b). Rewe und der DFB: „Das hätte man als PR-Aktion auch nicht besser planen können", Beitrag vom 23.11.2022. https://www.zeit.de/wirtschaft/unternehmen/2022-11/rewe-dfb-kooperation-pr-aktion-one-love-binde. Accessed: 2. Nov. 2021.

ZHAW. (2015). (Zentrum für Kulturmanagement, School of Management and Law, Zürcher Hochschule für Angewandte Wissenschaften. „Sponsor-Visions 2014/15"- Eine empirische Studie zum Sponsoringmarkt Schweiz. http://www.swa-asa.ch/de-wAssets/docs/artikel-print-medien/2015/Studie_Sponsor_Visions_Schweiz_2014-15.pdf. Accessed: 17. Febr. 2016.

Zimmer, J. (2020). Beachvolleyball: Liga-Blaupause in Düsseldorf. Horizont Nr. 26 vom 25.06.2020. S. 14. https://www.horizont.net/media/media/32/2026_Sportbusiness_II.pdf-319324.pdf. Accessed: 2. Nov. 2021.

Zollinger, H. (1995). In T. Tomczak, F. Müller, & R. Müller (Hrsg.), *Die Nicht-Klassiker der Unternehmenskommunikation* (S. 118–124). THEXIS.

Zukunftsinsitut. (2014). Die Red-Bullisierung des Sports. Trend Update 6/2014. https://www.zukunftsinstitut.de/artikel/sport/die-red-bullisierung-des-sports/. Accessed: 2. Nov. 2021.

Further reading

The sources listed in the bibliography have been incorporated and cited accordingly in the book. Additionally, there are other literary sources that address specialized aspects of sports sponsorship and may be of interest to readers. Therefore, the following sources are provided, which may be helpful in specific cases.

Aguiló-Lemoine, A. E., Rejón-Guardia, F., & García-Sastre, M. A. (2020). Congruence effects on the effectiveness of sponsoring of sport event websites: An experimental approach. *Sustainability (Switzerland), 12*(19). https://doi.org/10.3390/su12198173.

de Alcântara, J. N., de Benedicto, G. C., & da Silva, S. S. (2019). Possible key factors for Brazilian publicly traded companies to adopt a sponsoring strategy. *Journal of Strategy and Management, 12*(4), 429–446. https://doi.org/10.1108/JSMA-04-2018-0029.

Alonso Dos Santos, M., Calabuig Moreno, F., Rejón Guardia, F., & Pérez Campos, C. (2016). Influence of the virtual brand community in sports sponsoring. *Psychology and Marketing, 33*(12), 1091–1097. https://doi.org/10.1002/mar.20943.

Alonso Dos Santos, M., Rejón Guardia, F., & Calabuig Moreno, F. (2018). Sponsoring image transfer theory in virtual brand communities. *Industrial Management and Data Systems, 118*(6), 1287–1302. https://doi.org/10.1108/IMDS-08-2017-0349.

Alonso Dos Santos, M., Calabuig Moreno, F., & Crespo-Hervás, J. (2019). Influence of perceived and effective congruence on recall and purchase intention in sponsored printed sports advertising: An eye-tracking application. *International Journal of Sports Marketing and Sponsoring, 20*(4), 617–633. https://doi.org/10.1108/IJSMS-10-2018-0099.

Alonso Dos Santos, M., Pérez Campos, C., & Crespo Hervás, J. (2020). The effectiveness of advertising alcohol products in sports sponsoring. *Psychology and Marketing, 37*(4), 556–563. https://doi.org/10.1002/mar.21325.

Alonso Dos Santos, M., Sánchez-Franco, M. J., & Prado Gascó, V. (2020). The effect of articulated sports sponsoring on recall and visual attention to the brand. *International Journal of Sports Marketing and Sponsoring, 22*(3), 493–506. https://doi.org/10.1108/IJSMS-11-2019-0129.

Alonso Dos Santos, M., Huertas-Serrano, M., Sánchez-Franco, M. J., & Torres-Moraga, E. I. (2021). Alcohol versus sponsoring: Effectiveness in sports posters. *British Food Journal, 123*(7), 2398–2413. https://doi.org/10.1108/BFJ-06-2020-0541.

Alonso-Dos-Santos, M., Vveinhardt, J., Calabuig-Moreno, F., & Montoro-Rios, F. J. (2016). Involvement and image transfer in sports sponsoring. *Engineering Economics, 27*(1), 78–89. https://doi.org/10.5755/j01.ee.27.1.8536.

Alonso-Dos-Santos, M., Rejón Guardia, F., Pérez Campos, C., Calabuig-Moreno, F., & Ko, Y. J. (2018). Engagement in sports virtual brand communities. *Journal of Business Research, 89*, 273–279. https://doi.org/10.1016/j.jbusres.2017.12.053.

Anestos, K., Gargalianos, D., & Thamnopoulos, Y. (2016). Exploring the issue of naming rights of public sports facilities in Greece. *Journal of Facilities Management, 14*(2), 125–138. https://doi.org/10.1108/JFM-06-2015-0019.

Angell, R., Bottomley, P., Brečić, R., Filipović, J., Gorton, M., Logkizidou, M., & White, J. (2021). Configuring perceived fit to mitigate consumer animosity in the context of cross-border sport sponsorings. *European Sport Management Quarterly, 21*(4), 605–624. https://doi.org/10.1080/16184742.2020.1765828.

Ballouli, K., Koesters, T. C., & Hall, T. (2018). Leverage and activation of sport sponsoring through music festivals. *Event Management, 22*(2), 123–133. https://doi.org/10.3727/152599518X15173355843299.

Batty, R. J., & Gee, S. (2019). Fast food, fizz, and funding: Balancing the scales of regional sport organisation sponsoring. *Sport Management Review, 22*(1), 167–179. https://doi.org/10.1016/j.smr.2018.06.014.

Batty, R. J., Palmer, F., Nauright, J., & Davies, J. (2018). The business of rugby in the twenty-first century: An introduction to this special issue. *Journal of Global Sport Management, 3*(3), 209–214. https://doi.org/10.1080/24704067.2018.1455152.

Bee, C., King, J., & Stornelli, J. (2021). Are you with us or against us? The role of threat and anger in sport sponsoring. *Journal of Business Research, 124*, 698–707. https://doi.org/10.1016/j.jbusres.2019.02.048.

Binnewies, B., & Hertwig, D. (2019). Sport Sponsoring. *Die Aktiengesellschaft, 64*(21), 782–783. https://doi.org/10.9785/ag-2019-642114.

Biscaia, R., Trail, G., Ross, S., & Yoshida, M. (2017). A model bridging team brand experience and sponsoring brand experience. *International Journal of Sports Marketing and Sponsoring, 18*(4), 380–399. https://doi.org/10.1108/IJSMS-07-2016-0038.

Bjerke, R., & Kirkesaether, E. (2020). How should sponsoring activation work? A sports event and athlete-based brand building framework (sea-bb) capturing an internal and external route. *Event Management, 24*(6), 711–733. https://doi.org/10.3727/152599519X15506259856002.

Blake, J., Fourie, S., & Goldman, M. (2019). The relationship between sports sponsorings and corporate financial returns in South Africa. *International Journal of Sports Marketing and Sponsoring, 20*(1), 2–25. https://doi.org/10.1108/IJSMS-12-2016-0088.

von Borcke, Y., & Konnowski, N. (2021). Sponsoring und Sportsponsoring. In *eSport-Sponsoring: Erfolgsfaktoren – Herausforderungen – Potenziale* (S. 5–15). Springer Fachmedien. https://doi.org/10.1007/978-3-658-33747-6_2.

Boyle, B. A. (2017). Multiple sports sponsorings: Is more always better? An abstract. In P. Rossi & N. Krey (Hrsg.), *Marketing transformation: Marketing practice in an ever changing world* (S. 83–83). Springer International Publishing. https://doi.org/10.1007/978-3-319-68750-6_23.

Bragg, M. A., Miller, A. N., Roberto, C. A., Sam, R., Sarda, V., Harris, J. L., & Brownell, K. D. (2018). Sports sponsorings of food and nonalcoholic beverages. *Pediatrics, 141*(4). https://doi.org/10.1542/peds.2017-2822.

Branikas, I. (2019). *Advertising exposure and portfolio choice: Estimates based on sports sponsorings* (2019 academic research colloquium for financial planning and related disciplines). EARIE.

Breuer, C., Boronczyk, F., & Rumpf, C. (2021). Message personalization and real-time adaptation as next innovations in sport sponsoring management? How run-of-play and team affiliation affect viewer response. *Journal of Business Research, 133*, 309–316. https://doi.org/10.1016/j.jbusres.2021.05.003.

Brochado, A., Dionísio, P., & Leal, M. C. (2018). Sponsoring the football national team. *Journal of Business and Industrial Marketing, 33*(5), 625–637. https://doi.org/10.1108/JBIM-03-2017-0076.

Brown, K. (2016). Association between alcohol sports sponsoring and consumption: A systematic review. *Alcohol and Alcoholism, 51*(6), 747–755. https://doi.org/10.1093/alcalc/agw006.

Brüggemann, K. (2022). Sponsoring: Aufgaben und Macht der Vermarkter. In *Die Fußballblase: Hinter den Kulissen eines Milliardengeschäfts* (S. 65–79). Springer. https://doi.org/10.1007/978-3-662-64327-3_5.

Bruhn, M., & Rohlmann, P. (2022). Kommunikationsthemen im Sportmarketing. In *Sportmarketing: Grundlagen – Strategien – Instrumente* (S. 63–70). Springer Fachmedien. https://doi.org/10.1007/978-3-658-37176-0_6.

de Bruijn, A., Tanghe, J., de Leeuw, R., Engels, R., Anderson, P., Beccaria, F., Bujalski, M., Celata, C., Gosselt, J., Schreckenberg, D., Słodownik, L., Wothge, J., & van Dalen, W. (2016). European longitudinal study on the relationship between adolescents' alcohol marketing exposure and alcohol use. *Addiction, 111*(10), 1774–1783. https://doi.org/10.1111/add.13455.

Bukvič, V. (2018). Cost-benefit analysis as the most appropriate method for estimation of corporate financial support to sports clubs. *Advances in Business Related Scientific Research Journal, 9*(1), 44–67. https://www.scopus.com/inward/record.uri?eid=2-s2.0-85061281862&partnerID=40&md5=e1aefb7f050b272b8c0566e727981a9a.

Buser, M., Woratschek, H., & Schönberner, J. (2022). 'Going the extra mile' in resource integration: Evolving a concept of sport sponsoring as an engagement platform. *European Sport Management Quarterly, 22*(4), 548–568. https://doi.org/10.1080/16184742.2020.1820061.

Buszko, M. (2020). Sports sponsoring in cooperative banks –terms, scope and goals based on the example of cooperative bank in Torun. *Journal of Physical Education and Sport, 20*, 2892–2898. https://doi.org/10.7752/jpes.2020.s5392.

Buszko, M. (2020). Sports sponsoring in cooperative banks–terms, scope and goals based on the example of cooperative bank in Torun. *Journal of Physical Education and Sport, 20*(Suppl. 5), 2892–2898. https://doi.org/10.7752/jpes.2020.s5392.

Castyana, B., Amali, Z., Hartono, M., Pujianto, A., Rahayu, T., Ali, M. A., & Anggita, G. M. (2022). The role of committee attitude on company's decision for sponsoring sports events. *Journal Sport Area, 7*(1), 89–95. https://doi.org/10.25299/sportarea.2022.vol7(1).7969.

Chadwick, S., Widdop, P., & Burton, N. (2022). Soft power sports sponsoring–A social network analysis of a new sponsoring form. *Journal of Political Marketing, 21*(2), 196–217. https://doi.org/10.1080/15377857.2020.1723781.

Chambers, T. (2020). Alcohol sponsoring and esports: Reinforcing the need for legislative restrictions on alcohol sponsoring. *Alcohol and Alcoholism, 55*(2), 144–146. https://doi.org/10.1093/ALCALC/AGZ104.

Chambers, T., Signal, L., Carter, M. A., McConville, S., Wong, R., & Zhu, W. (2017). Alcohol sponsoring of a summer of sport: A frequency analysis of alcohol marketing during major sports events on New Zealand television. *New Zealand Medical Journal, 130*(1448), 27–33. https://www.scopus.com/inward/record.uri?eid=2-s2.0-85010901193&partnerID=40&md5=fbbcf32d50e6f2b8827d14afa9240abe.

Chambers, T., Stanley, J., Signal, L., Pearson, A. L., Smith, M., Barr, M., & Mhurchu, C. N. (2018). Quantifying the nature and extent of children's real-time exposure to alcohol marketing in their everyday lives using wearable cameras: Children's exposure via a range of media in a range of key places. *Alcohol and Alcoholism, 53*(5), 626–633. https://doi.org/10.1093/alcalc/agy053.

Chang, Y. (2018). Exploring the patterns of dual attitude changes in the context of athlete endorsement: The interplay of fit, evaluative conditioning, and introspection focus. *Journal of Sport Management, 32*(5), 413–425. https://doi.org/10.1123/jsm.2017-0149.

Chelladurai, P. (2016). Introduction to the second inaugural issue of the journal of global sport management. *Journal of Global Sport Management, 1*(3–4), 67–69. https://doi.org/10.1080/24704067.2016.1245514.

Cheong, C., Pyun, D. Y., & Leng, H. K. (2019). Sponsoring and advertising in sport: A study of consumers' attitude. *European Sport Management Quarterly, 19*(3), 287–311. https://doi.org/10.1080/16184742.2018.1517271.

Chiu, C., & Pyun, D. Y. (2020). Investigating brand image transfer in sport sponsoring of a participation sport event in Singapore. *Event Management, 24*(2–3), 263–275. https://doi.org/10.3727/152599518X15403853721240.

Cobbs, J., & Groza, M. D. (2020). Reverse effects of sponsoring: Establishing sport brand equity. *Managing Sport and Leisure.* https://doi.org/10.1080/23750472.2020.1848445.

Cody, K., & Jackson, S. (2016). The contested terrain of alcohol sponsoring of sport in New Zealand. *International Review for the Sociology of Sport, 51*(4), 375–393. https://doi.org/10.1177/1012690214526399.

Coelho, M. G. R., de Amorim, J. G. B., & de Almeida, V. M. C. (2019). Sports mega-event sponsoring: The impact of FIFA reputation and world cup image on sponsor brand equity. *BAR – Brazilian Administration Review, 16*(1). https://doi.org/10.1590/1807-7692bar2019180071.

Couttenier, M., & Hatte, S. (2016). Mass media effects on non-governmental organizations. *Journal of Development Economics, 123,* 57–72. https://doi.org/10.1016/j.jdeveco.2016.07.001.

Cui, G. Q., Lee, J. Y., & Jin, C. H. (2019). The role of sports sponsoring in negative new stories about a brand: Approach the halo effect. *Cogent Business and Management, 6*(1). https://doi.org/10.1080/23311975.2019.1699284.

Datson, P., Ozuem, W., Howell, K., & Lancaster, G. (2021). Beyond the game: Perceptions and practices of sports sponsoring in German SMEs. *Qualitative Market Research, 24*(5), 632–652. https://doi.org/10.1108/QMR-12-2020-0148.

Demirel, A. (2020). CSR in sport sponsoring consumers' perceptions of a sponsoring brand's CSR. *International Journal of Sports Marketing and Sponsoring, 21*(2), 371–388. https://doi.org/10.1108/IJSMS-09-2019-0108.

Demirel, A., & Erdogmus, I. (2016). The impacts of fans' sincerity perceptions and social media usage on attitude toward sponsor. *Sport, Business and Management: An International Journal, 6*(1), 36–54. https://doi.org/10.1108/SBM-07-2014-0036.

Desmarais, F., Boobyer, K., & Bruce, T. (2021). Lingering effects of sponsor transgression against a national fan base: The importance of respect in relationship management. *Sport Management Review*, 1–31. https://doi.org/10.1080/14413523.2021.1880743.

Dietl, H. M., Özdemir, A., & Schweizer, N. (2017). Outsourcing sports sponsoring activities: A multi-theoretical approach. *Sport, Business and Management: An International Journal, 7*(1), 77–96. https://doi.org/10.1108/SBM-09-2014-0041.

Dixon, H., Scully, M., Wakefield, M., Kelly, B., & Pettigrew, S. (2018). Community junior sport sponsoring: An online experiment assessing children's responses to unhealthy food v. pro-health sponsoring options. *Public Health Nutrition, 21*(6), 1176–1185. https://doi.org/10.1017/S1368980017003561.

Dixon, H., Scully, M., Wakefield, M., Kelly, B., Pettigrew, S., Chapman, K., & Niederdeppe, J. (2018). The impact of unhealthy food sponsoring vs. pro-health sponsoring models on young adults' food preferences: A randomised controlled trial. *BMC Public Health, 18*(1). https://doi.org/10.1186/s12889-018-6298-4.

Dixon, H., Scully, M., Wakefield, M., Kelly, B., Pettigrew, S., Chapman, K., & Niederdeppe, J. (2020). Can counter-advertising protect spectators of elite sport against the influence of unhealthy food and beverage sponsoring? A naturalistic trial. *Social Science and Medicine*. https://doi.org/10.1016/j.socscimed.2020.113415.

Djohari, N., Weston, G., Cassidy, R., Wemyss, M., & Thomas, S. (2019). Recall and awareness of gambling advertising and sponsoring in sport in the UK: A study of young people and adults. *Harm Reduction Journal, 16*(1). https://doi.org/10.1186/s12954-019-0291-9.

Doellman, T. W., Walkup, B. R., Bouchet, A., & Chabowski, B. R. (2022). A dichotomy of sport sponsorings: Does the nature of competition among sponsors matter? *Journal of Sport Management, 36*(2), 188–198. https://doi.org/10.1123/jsm.2020-0203.

Donaldson, A., & Nicholson, M. (2020). Attitudes of sports organisation members to junk food sponsoring. *Public Health, 185,* 212–217. https://doi.org/10.1016/j.puhe.2020.04.043.

Donaldson, A., Reimers, J. L., Brophy, K. T., & Nicholson, M. (2019). Barriers to rejecting junk food sponsoring in sport – A formative evaluation using concept mapping. *Public Health, 166*, 1–9. https://doi.org/10.1016/j.puhe.2018.09.021.

Dreisbach, J. (2019). *Erfolgsfaktoren der Sponsoringumsetzung und-aktivierung: Eine empirische Analyse aus Management- und Konsumentenwirkungsperspektive im Kontext der Fußball-Bundesliga.* Springer Gabler. https://doi.org/10.1007/978-3-658-24519-1.

Dreisbach, J., Woisetschläger, D. M., Backhaus, C., & Cornwell, T. B. (2021). The role of fan benefits in shaping responses to sponsoring activation. *Journal of Business Research, 124*, 780–789. https://doi.org/10.1016/j.jbusres.2018.11.041.

Dróżdż, M. (2021). Legal aspects of sponsoring sports by state-owned companies. *Journal of Physical Education and Sport, 21*(Suppl. 2), 1071–1075. https://doi.org/10.7752/jpes.2021.s2134.

Dróżdż, M. (2021). Legal aspects of sponsoring sports by state-owned companies. *Journal of Physical Education and Sport, 21,* 1071–1075. https://doi.org/10.7752/jpes.2021.s2134.

Edeling, A., Hattula, S., & Bornemann, T. (2017). Over, out, but present: Recalling former sponsorings. *European journal of marketing, 51*(7–8), 1286–1307. https://doi.org/10.1108/EJM-05-2015-0263.

Edwards, M. R. (2016). The Olympic effect: Employee reactions to their employer's sponsoring of a high-profile global sporting event. *Human Resource Management, 55*(4), 721–740. https://doi.org/10.1002/hrm.21702.

Eisdorfer, A., & Kohl, E. (2017). Corporate sport sponsoring and stock returns: Evidence from the NFL. *Critical Finance Review, 6,* 179–209. https://doi.org/10.1561/104.0000041.

Ennis, S., Marck, M., Paul, C., & Radon, A. (2019). *Social sponsorings in sport: Context and potential.* Conference Proceedings, ANZMAC 2019: Winds of Change, Wellington, New Zealand.

Erguder, T., Bilir, N., Özcebe, H., Irmak, H., Tasti, E., İlter, H., Palipudi, K. M., Andes, L. J., Asma, S., Khoury, R. N., & Talley, B. (2016). Exposure to anti- and pro-tobacco advertising, promotions or sponsorings: Turkey, 2008. *Global Health Promotion, 23*(2), 58–67. https://doi.org/10.1177/1757975913502369.

Erichsen, M., Stiklestad, T., Holum, M., & Jakobsen, T. G. (2022). Added value for sponsors: A study of network in football 2011–2018. *Sport, Business and Management: An International Journal, 12*(4), 421–439. https://doi.org/10.1108/SBM-11-2020-0119.

Ertz, E., Frey Cordes, R. V., & Buettgen, M. (2020). Does ambushing pay off? Comparing the effectiveness of event sponsoring, team sponsoring, and ambush marketing. *International Journal of Sports Marketing and Sponsoring, 21*(1), 191–204. https://doi.org/10.1108/IJSMS-03-2018-0021.

Eshghi, K. (2022). Are sports sponsoring announcements good news for shareholders? A meta-analysis. *International Journal of Research in Marketing, 39*(1), 268–287. https://doi.org/10.1016/j.ijresmar.2021.04.003.

Eshghi, K., Shahriari, H., & Ray, S. (2022). Sports sponsoring announcements and marketing capability. *Journal of Sport Management, 36*(2), 171–187. https://doi.org/10.1123/jsm.2020-0294.

Evans, R. D., Jr., Deitz, G. D., Sherrell, D. L., & Rocco, R. A. (2018). Do investors prefer new or existing sponsoring relationships: Evidence from sponsoring interorganizational relationship formation and maintenance on firm stock returns. *Journal of Marketing Theory and Practice, 26*(4), 329–338. https://doi.org/10.1080/10696679.2018.1487768.

Fiedler, D. (2017). *Sportsponsoring und Arbeitsrecht: Arbeitsrechtliche Selbstvermarktungsgrenzen.* Springer Gabler. https://doi.org/10.1007/978-3-658-19379-9.

Fischer, D., & Schmidli, F. (2022). *Sponsor Visions Schweiz 2022: Trends und Entwicklungen im Schweizer Sponsoring-Markt der letzten zehn Jahre.* ZHAW Zürcher Hochschule für Angewandte Wissenschaften. https://doi.org/10.21256/zhaw-24757.

Ford, J. B. (2018). What do we know about sports sponsorings? *Journal of advertising research, 58*(3), 257–258. https://doi.org/10.2501/JAR-2018-033.

Förg, C. (2018). Krisenfestigkeit in der Sponsoringpartnerschaft: Eine Analyse von Kommunikationsstrategien in der Sportbranche. In C. M. Schmidt (Hrsg.), *Werbekommunikation in der Wirtschaft: Mediengerecht, praxisorientiert und interdisziplinär* (S. 307–339). Springer Fachmedien. https://doi.org/10.1007/978-3-658-20815-8_11.

Ge, Q., & Humphreys, B. R. (2021a). Athlete misconduct and team sponsor stock prices: The role of incident type and media coverage. *Journal of Sport Management, 35*(3), 216–227. https://doi.org/10.1123/JSM.2020-0106.

Ge, Q., & Humphreys, B. R. (2021b). Athlete off-field misconduct, sponsor reputation risk, and stock returns. *European Sport Management Quarterly, 21*(2), 153–172. https://doi.org/10.1080/16184742.2020.1728778.

Gee, S., Thompson, A. J., & Batty, R. J. (2018). Rules of engagement: Sport sponsoring, anti-ambush marketing legislation, and alcohol images during the 2011 Rugby World Cup. *Journal of Global Sport Management, 3*(3), 266–283. https://doi.org/10.1080/24704067.2018.1432991.

Gillooly, L., Anagnostopoulos, C., & Chadwick, S. (2017). Social media-based sponsoring activation – A typology of content. *Sport, Business and Management: An International Journal, 7*(3), 293–314. https://doi.org/10.1108/SBM-04-2016-0016.

Górecka, D. (2021). Applying the mars method to the sponsor contract negotiations. *Journal of Physical Education and Sport, 21,* 3109–3116. https://doi.org/10.7752/jpes.2021.s5413.

Harrison, V. S., Vafeiadis, M., & Bober, J. (2022). Greening professional sport: How communicating the fit, proximity, and impact of sustainability efforts affects fan perceptions and supportive intentions. *Sustainability (Switzerland), 14*(6), 3139. https://doi.org/10.3390/su14063139.

Hermanns, A., Marwitz, C., & Schubert, M. (2016). Messung der Wirkung von Sponsoringmaßnahmen. In F.-R. Esch, T. Langner, & M. Bruhn (Hrsg.), *Handbuch Controlling der Kommunikation: Grundlagen – Innovative Ansätze – Praktische Umsetzungen* (S. 507–537). Springer Fachmedien. https://doi.org/10.1007/978-3-8349-3857-2_23.

Herold, E., Boronczyk, F., & Breuer, C. (2021). Professional clubs as platforms in multi-sided markets in times of COVID-19: The role of spectators and atmosphere in live football. *Sustainability (Switzerland), 13*(4), 1–16. https://doi.org/10.3390/su13042312.

Herrmann, J. L., Kacha, M., & Derbaix, C. (2016). „I support your team, support me in turn!" The driving role of consumers' affiliation with the sponsored entity in explaining behavioral effects of sport sponsoring leveraging activities. *Journal of Business Research, 69*(2), 604–612. https://doi.org/10.1016/j.jbusres.2015.05.016.

Hino, Y., & Takeda, F. (2020). Market reactions to sport sponsoring announcements: Comparison between sponsors and their rivals. *Sport Management Review, 23*(3), 401–413. https://doi.org/10.1016/j.smr.2019.02.002.

Hohenberger, C., & Grohs, R. (2020). Old and exciting? Sport sponsoring effects on brand age and brand personality. *Sport Management Review, 23*(3), 469–481. https://doi.org/10.1016/j.smr.2019.05.002.

Hsiao, C. H., Tang, K. Y., & Su, Y. S. (2021). An empirical exploration of sports sponsoring: Activation of experiential marketing, sponsoring satisfaction, brand equity, and purchase intention. *Frontiers in Psychology.* https://doi.org/10.3389/fpsyg.2021.677137.

Huang, T., & Zhou, T. (2017). Construction and analysis of the operation model of mass sports marketing planning. *Boletin Tecnico/Technical Bulletin, 55*(15), 36–41. https://www.scopus.com/inward/record.uri?eid=2-s2.0-85037813286&partnerID=40&md5=0f725a800b23b9823118b78700d5352b.

Huettermann, M., Trail, G. T., Pizzo, A. D., & Stallone, V. (2020). Esports sponsoring: An empirical examination of esports consumers' perceptions of non-endemic sponsors. *Journal of Global Sport Management.* https://doi.org/10.1080/24704067.2020.1846906.

Hundt, S., & Horsch, A. (2019). Sponsoring of the FIFA world cup, shareholder wealth, and the impact of corruption. *Applied Economics, 51*(23), 2468–2491. https://doi.org/10.1080/00036846.2018.1545082

Hüttermann, M., Bearth, A., & Hannich, F. (2018). Sportsponsoring als employer-branding-tool. *Marketing Review St. Gallen, 35*(6), 76–83. https://doi.org/10.21256/zhaw-2096.

Ifsits, C. (2019). *Strafrechtliche Risiken des Sponsoring: Zur Strafbarkeit von Sponsor und Gesponsertem wegen Untreue und Korruption.* Springer. https://doi.org/10.1007/978-3-658-25665-4.

Inoue, Y., Havard, C. T., & Irwin, R. L. (2016). Roles of sport and cause involvement in determining employees' beliefs about cause-related sport sponsoring. *International Journal of Sports Marketing and Sponsoring, 17*(1), 3–18. https://doi.org/10.1108/IJSMS-02-2016-001.

Ireland, R., Muc, M., Bunn, C., & Boyland, E. (2021). Marketing of unhealthy brands during the 2018 Fédération Internationale de Football Association (FIFA) World Cup UK broadcasts – a frequency analysis. *Journal of Strategic Marketing.* https://doi.org/10.1080/0965254X.2021.1967427.

Jensen, J. A. (2017). Assessing corporate demand for sponsoring: Marketing costs in the financial services industry. *Marketing Letters, 28*(2), 281–291. https://doi.org/10.1007/s11002-016-9410-5.

Jensen, J. A., & Cornwell, T. B. (2017). Why do marketing relationships end? Findings from an integrated model of sport sponsoring decision-making. *Journal of Sport Management, 31*(4), 401–418. https://doi.org/10.1123/jsm.2016-0232.

Jensen, J. A., & Head, D. (2020). An advancement in the study of marketing partnership longevity: Analysing sport sponsoring survival. *International Journal of Sport Management and Marketing, 20*(1–2), 64–91. https://doi.org/10.1504/IJSMM.2020.109761.

Jensen, J. A., & Turner, B. A. (2018). Event history analysis of longitudinal data: A methodological application to sport sponsoring. *Sport in Society, 21*(2), 376–393. https://doi.org/10.1080/17430437.2016.1179728.

Jensen, J. A., Walsh, P., & Cobbs, J. (2018). The moderating effect of identification on return on investment from sponsor brand integration. *International Journal of Sports Marketing and Sponsoring, 19*(1), 41–57. https://doi.org/10.1108/IJSMS-10-2016-0077.

Jin, C. H. (2017). Retrospection and state of sports marketing and sponsoring research in IJSMS from 1999 to 2015. *International Journal of Sports Marketing and Sponsoring, 18*(4), 363–379. https://doi.org/10.1108/IJSMS-04-2016-0002.

Kagerbauer, L., Naskrent, J., & Rüttgers, C. (2016). Spitzensportmonitor Würzburg: Empirische Analyse über Image, Sponsoringangebote und strategische Handlungsfelder der regionalen Spitzensportvereine. K. K. f. M. M. FOM Hochschule für Oekonomie & Management.

Kamath, G. B., Ganguli, S., & George, S. (2020). Attachment points, team identification and sponsoring outcomes: Evidence from the Indian Premier League. *International Journal of Sports Marketing and Sponsoring, 22*(3), 429–452. https://doi.org/10.1108/IJSMS-01-2020-0008.

Kamath, G. B., George, S., & Ganguli, S. (2020). Consequences of event-sponsor fit in sport sponsoring: Evidence from the Indian Premier League. *International Journal of Economics and Business Research, 20*(3), 348–363. https://doi.org/10.1504/IJEBR.2020.110439.

Kang, S. H., Kim, J. G., & Yang, M. H. (2019). The effects of sports sponsoring recognition on corporate image, purchasing intention and brand identification. *Journal of Distribution Science, 17*(10), 49–59. https://doi.org/10.15722/jds.17.10.201910.49.

Kang, T., & Matsuoka, H. (2022). Sponsoring many or few sports properties? Moderated mediation effect of perceived sponsor ubiquity depending on sponsor – property fit. *Journal of Business & Industrial Marketing*, ahead-of-print(ahead-of-print). https://doi.org/10.1108/JBIM-10-2021-0500.

Karjaluoto, H., & Paakkonen, L. (2019). An empirical assessment of employer branding as a form of sport event sponsoring. *International Journal of Sports Marketing and Sponsoring, 20*(4), 666–682. https://doi.org/10.1108/IJSMS-10-2018-0103.

Kelly, S., & Ireland, M. (2021). The alcohol–sport nexus and how consumers are affected through sponsoring. *International Journal of Sport Communication, 12*(1), 79–103. https://doi.org/10.1123/ijsc.2018-0153.

Kelly, S., Ireland, M., & Mangan, J. (2017). Alcohol sponsoring and its impact on sports participants' consumption. *Sport in Society, 20*(7), 848–860. https://doi.org/10.1080/17430437.2016.1221930.

Kelly, S. J., Ireland, M., Mangan, J., & Williamson, H. (2018). Can alcohol sponsoring be diluted by health messaging? *Sport in Society, 21*(3), 434–451. https://doi.org/10.1080/17430437.2017.1346617.

Kelly, S. J., Cornwell, B., & Singh, K. (2019). The gladiatorial sponsoring arena: How ambushing impacts memory. *Marketing Intelligence and Planning, 37*(4), 417–432. https://doi.org/10.1108/MIP-07-2018-0271.

Kim, D., Walker, M., Heo, J., & Koo, G. Y. (2017). Sport league website: An effective marketing communication tool for corporate sponsors. *International Journal of Sports Marketing and Sponsoring, 18*(3), 314–327. https://doi.org/10.1108/IJSMS-08-2017-097.

Kim, D., Ko, Y., Lee, J. L., & Kim, Y. C. (2020). The impact of CSR-linked sport sponsoring on consumers' reactions to service failures. *International Journal of Sports Marketing and Sponsoring, 21*(1), 70–90. https://doi.org/10.1108/IJSMS-01-2019-0011.

Kim, M., Oja, B. D., Kim, H. S., & Chin, J. H. (2020). Developing student-athlete school satisfaction and psychological well-being: The effects of academic psychological capital and engagement. *Journal of Sport Management, 34*(4), 378–390. https://doi.org/10.1123/JSM.2020-0091.

Kim, Y., Kim, S., Lee, S., & Cho, S. (2019). A structural validation of brand personality scale: Assessing the congruence effects of sport sponsoring. *Measurement in Physical Education and Exercise Science, 23*(4), 351–363. https://doi.org/10.1080/1091367X.2018.1523794.

King, J., & Madrigal, R. (2018). Improved articulation of incongruent sponsor-property partnerships using analogy. *Journal of Sport Management, 32*(5), 464–472. https://doi.org/10.1123/jsm.2017-0290.

Koch, N. (2020). The geopolitics of Gulf sport sponsoring. *Sport, Ethics and Philosophy, 14*(3), 355–376. https://doi.org/10.1080/17511321.2019.1669693.

Kolhoff, L. (2017). Sponsoring und Fundraising als Mittel der Eigenfinanzierung. In *Finanzierung der Sozialwirtschaft: Eine Einführung* (2. Aufl., S. 99–117). Springer. https://doi.org/10.1007/978-3-658-15410-3_5.

Kończak, J. (2020a). Rights in sports sponsoring. *Journal of Physical Education and Sport, 20,* 2918–2923. https://doi.org/10.7752/jpes.2020.s5396.

Kończak, J. (2020b). Sponsoring communication and the sport sponsoring market in poland. *Journal of Physical Education and Sport, 20,* 1225–1229. https://doi.org/10.7752/jpes.2020.s2170.

Kończak, J. (2021). Sports themes in advertising. *Journal of Physical Education and Sport, 21,* 1179–1184. https://doi.org/10.7752/jpes.2021.s2149.

Konstantoulaki, K., Rizomyliotis, I., Giovanis, A., Conti, V., & Kallandranis, C. (2017). Sponsoring sports teams with low media exposure: An exploratory investigation on small and medium sized B2B firms. *International Journal of Marketing Studies, 9*(5), 77–94. https://doi.org/10.5539/ijms.v9n5p77.

Koo, J., & Lee, Y. (2019). Sponsor-event congruence effects: The moderating role of sport involvement and mediating role of sponsor attitudes. *Sport Management Review, 22*(2), 222–234. https://doi.org/10.1016/j.smr.2018.03.001.

Koronios, K., & Dimitropoulos, P. (2020). Examining sponsoring's effectiveness over the internet: A conceptual framework for researchers and practitioners. *International Journal of Innovation and Technology Management, 17*(4). https://doi.org/10.1142/S0219877020500273.

Koronios, K., Dimitropoulos, P., Travlos, A., Douvis, I., & Ratten, V. (2020). Online technologies and sports: A new era for sponsoring. *Journal of High Technology Management Research, 31*(1). https://doi.org/10.1016/j.hitech.2020.100373.

Koronios, K., Vrontis, D., & Thrassou, A. (2021). Strategic sport sponsoring management – A scale development and validation. *Journal of Business Research, 130*, 295–307. https://doi.org/10.1016/j.jbusres.2021.03.031.

Koronios, K., Ntasis, L., & Dimitropoulos, P. E. (2022). Sponsoring-linked marketing: Sport consumers' attitudes and behaviors. *International Journal of Innovation and Technology Management, 19*(5). https://doi.org/10.1142/S0219877022410085.

Koronios, K., Ntasis, L., Dimitropoulos, P., & Ratten, V. (2022). Not just intentions: Predicting actual purchase behavior in sport sponsoring context. *Sport, Business and Management: An International Journal, 12*(1), 4–28. https://doi.org/10.1108/SBM-03-2021-0034.

Koronios, K., Thrassou, A., Ntasis, L., & Sakka, G. (2022). Participant or spectator? Comprehending the sport sponsoring process from different perspectives. *EuroMed Journal of Business*. https://doi.org/10.1108/EMJB-03-2022-0062.

Kramer, K., Wagner, D., & Scheck, B. (2021). Reaping the digital dividend? Sport marketing's move into esports: Insights from Germany. *European Journal of International Management, 15*(2–3), 339–366. https://doi.org/10.1504/EJIM.2021.113265.

Krebs, M. (2017). Die Einstellung kulturinteressierter Personen gegen-über Sponsoren kultureller Events–Eine qualitative Studie. *Junior Management Science, 2*(2), 84–96. https://doi.org/10.5282/jums/v2i2pp84-96.

Kucharski, M., Kot, S., & Kot, S. (2017). Cost of recognisability of a sponsor's brand achieved through TV broadcasts. *Oeconomia Copernicana, 8*(3), 447–461. https://doi.org/10.24136/oc.v8i3.28.

Kwon, H., & Shin, J. E. (2020). Effects of brand exposure time duration and frequency on image transfer in sport sponsoring. *International Journal of Sports Marketing and Sponsoring, 21*(1), 170–190. https://doi.org/10.1108/IJSMS-04-2019-0042.

Larson, D. J., Wetherbee, J. C., & Branscum, P. (2019). Crossfit athletic identity's relationship to sponsor recall, recognition, and purchase intent. *International Journal of Kinesiology and Sports Science, 7*(3), 6–15. https://doi.org/10.7575/aiac.ijkss.v.7n.3p.6.

Lee, J. Y., & Jin, C. H. (2019). The effect of sponsor's brand on consumer-brand relationship in sport sponsoring. *Global Business and Finance Review, 24*(1), 27–43. https://doi.org/10.17549/gbfr.2019.24.1.27.

Lee, S., & Suh, Y. I. (2021). The severity of a sports-related accident and sponsoring effects: Focusing on the fear appeal theory. *International Journal of Sports Marketing and Sponsoring, 22*(2), 293–311. https://doi.org/10.1108/IJSMS-08-2019-0086.

LeeAbcfg, K., & Johnson, J. A. (2020). Ambush marketing in sport Taekwondo and how to prevent it. *Ido Movement for Culture, 20*(4), 7–14. https://doi.org/10.14589/ido.20.4.2.

Leng, H. K., Wu, X., & Zhong, D. (2019). Effect of brand familiarity on sponsor recall: Evidence from swimming competitions. *International Journal of Asian Business and Information Management, 10*(3), 49–60. https://doi.org/10.4018/IJABIM.2019070103.

Liebl, J. (2021). Erfolgsfaktoren von Influencer Marketing mit Sportlern für eine positive Kundenwahrnehmung. Eine empirische Analyse. Hochschule Hof, Hof.

Limbach, M. (2020). Erfassung der Effektivität von Sportsponsoring als Marketingkommunikationsinstrument auf der impliziten und expliziten Verarbeitungsebene von Konsumenten als Handlungsgrundlage für operative und strategische Managemententscheidungen Hannover: Institutionelles Repositorium der Leibniz Universität Hannover.

Limbach, M., Schmidt, S., Wiedmann, K. P., Langner, S., & Schiessl, M. (2019). Communicating sponsor brands playfully in video games: Evaluating the impact of in-game advertising on dual brand knowledge. *Journal of Global Sport Management, 4*(3), 211–235. https://doi.org/10.1080/24704067.2018.1477520.

Limbach, M., Fessler, P., Schmidt, S., & Buckler, F. (2020). Die Wirksamkeit von Sportsponsoring in der Marketingkommunikation – Der Einfluss von Teamrivalität auf den impliziten und expliziten Markenwert. In B. Keller, H.-W. Klein, A. Wachenfeld-Schell, & T. Wirth (Hrsg.),

Marktforschung für die Smart Data World: Chancen, Herausforderungen und Grenzen (S. 229–251). Springer Fachmedien. https://doi.org/10.1007/978-3-658-28664-4_16.

Lin, H. C., & Bruning, P. F. (2020). Comparing consumers' in-group-favor and out-group-animosity processes within sports sponsoring. *European journal of marketing, 54*(4), 791–824. https://doi.org/10.1108/EJM-03-2018-0195.

Lopez-Gonzalez, H., & Griffiths, M. D. (2018). Understanding the convergence of markets in online sports betting. *International Review for the Sociology of Sport, 53*(7), 807–823. https://doi.org/10.1177/1012690216680602.

Lu, S., Zhu, W., & Wei, J. (2021). The relationships of communication intensity, CEO commitment, cause fit and media reputation: Evidence from Chinese marathon title sponsors. *International Journal of Sports Marketing and Sponsoring, 22*(2), 220–239. https://doi.org/10.1108/IJSMS-11-2019-0130.

Maanda, P. M., Abratt, R., & Mingione, M. (2020). The influence of sport sponsoring on brand equity in South Africa. *Journal of Promotion Management, 26*(6), 812–835. https://doi.org/10.1080/10496491.2020.1745984.

Madushani, G., & Gunawardane, N. (2020). Role of sports sponsorings in developing brand equity. *International Journal of Business and Management Invention (IJBMI), 9*(9), 26–34. https://doi.org/10.35629/8028-0909022634.

Mamo, Y., James, J. D., & Andrew, D. P. S. (2022). Consumer perceptions of sport sponsor's corporate social responsibility activities. *Journal of Global Sport Management, 7*(1), 135–157. https://doi.org/10.1080/24704067.2018.1561207.

Manoli, A. E. (2022). Strategic brand management in and through sport. *Journal of Strategic Marketing.* https://doi.org/10.1080/0965254X.2022.2059774.

McGee, D. (2020). On the normalisation of online sports gambling among young adult men in the UK: A public health perspective. *Public Health, 184*, 89–94. https://doi.org/10.1016/j.puhe.2020.04.018.

Melovic, B., Rogic, S., Smolovic, J. C., Dudic, B., & Gregus, M. (2019). The impact of sport sponsoring perceptions and attitudes on purchasing decision of fans as consumers-relevance for promotion of corporate social responsibility and sustainable practices. *Sustainability (Switzerland), 11*(22). https://doi.org/10.3390/su11226389.

Menn, A., & Putzing, F. (2019). Nachhaltigkeitssponsoring im Sport: Chancen, Risiken und Nutzen für Akteure und Stakeholder. In A. Hildebrandt (Hrsg.), *CSR und Sportmanagement: Jenseits von Sieg und Niederlage: Sport als gesellschaftliche Aufgabe verstehen und umsetzen* (S. 267–281). Springer. https://doi.org/10.1007/978-3-662-59651-7_22.

Morgan, A. (2019). An examination of women's sport sponsoring: A case study of female Australian Rules football. *Journal of marketing management, 35*(17–18), 1644–1666. https://doi.org/10.1080/0267257X.2019.1668463.

Murphy, P. E., Laczniak, G. R., & Harris, F. (2016). *Ethics in marketing: International cases and perspectives* (2. Aufl.). Taylor and Francis. https://doi.org/10.4324/9781315626642.

Næss, H. E. (2020). Corporate greenfluencing: A case study of sponsoring activation in Formula E motorsports. *International Journal of Sports Marketing and Sponsoring, 21*(4), 617–631. https://doi.org/10.1108/IJSMS-09-2019-0106.

Narayan, P. K., Rath, B. N., & Prabheesh, K. P. (2016). What is the value of corporate sponsoring in sports? *Emerging Markets Review, 26*, 20–33. https://doi.org/10.1016/j.ememar.2016.02.003.

Naseer, A., Javed, S., & Murtaza, G. (2021). A study of promotion of sports through sponsorings and institutional growth at club level. *International Review of Social Sciences, 9*(1), 1–7.

Naveed, H. M., Hongxing, Y., Haris, M., Hussain, K., Altaf, S., & Khalid, M. (2020). Impact of sports sponsoring on share prices of sponsoring firm: Evidence from Pakistan Supper League (PSL). *Social Sciences, 10*(6), 268–283. https://doi.org/10.6007/IJARBSS/v10-i6/7286.

Nguyen, T., & Galinski, L. (2020). Digital-Marketing, Sportsponsoring und E-Sports – Warum E-Sports ein Blue Ocean ist. In M. Terstiege (Hrsg.), *Digitales Marketing – Erfolgsmodelle aus der Praxis: Konzepte, Instrumente und Strategien im Kontext der Digitalisierung* (S. 259–277). Springer Fachmedien. https://doi.org/10.1007/978-3-658-26195-5_16.

Nufer, G. (2016). Ambush marketing in sports: An attack on sponsoring or innovative marketing? *Sport, Business and Management: An International Journal, 6*(4), 476–495. https://doi.org/10.1108/SBM-05-2013-0008.

Nuseir, M. T. (2020). The effects of sponsoring on the promotion of sports events. *International Journal of Business Innovation and Research, 22*(2), 191–207. https://doi.org/10.1504/IJBIR.2020.107838.

Nuss, T., Scully, M., Wakefield, M., & Dixon, H. (2019). Unhealthy sport sponsoring at the 2017 AFL Grand Final: A case study of its frequency, duration and nature. *Australian and New Zealand Journal of Public Health, 43*(4), 366–372. https://doi.org/10.1111/1753-6405.12920.

Oczki, J., & Pleskot, W. (2020). Financing a basketball club in Poland – The case of twarde pierniki S.A. *Journal of Physical Education and Sport, 20,* 1050–1054. https://doi.org/10.7752/jpes.2020.s2146.

Olson, E. L. (2018). Are rival team fans a curse for home team sponsors? The moderating effects of fit, oppositional loyalty, and league sponsoring. *Marketing Letters, 29*(1), 115–122. https://doi.org/10.1007/s11002-017-9441-6.

Otto, F., & Rumpf, C. (2018). Animation intensity of sponsoring signage: The impact on sport viewers' attention and viewer confusion. *Sport, Business and Management: An International Journal, 8*(2), 177–194. https://doi.org/10.1108/SBM-05-2017-0029.

Pan, P. L., & Phua, J. (2020). Connecting sponsor brands through sports competitions: An identity approach to brand trust and brand loyalty. *Sport, Business and Management: An International Journal, 11*(2), 164–184. https://doi.org/10.1108/SBM-01-2019-0003.

Park, Y., & Kwak, D. H. (2022). Exploring the empirical evidence of social desirability bias (SDB) in sport consumer research. *International Journal of Sports Marketing and Sponsoring, 23*(1), 173–189. https://doi.org/10.1108/IJSMS-03-2021-0055.

Parnell, D., & Krustrup, P. (2017). *Sport and health: Exploring the current state of play*. Taylor and Francis. https://doi.org/10.4324/9781315266459.

Paulauskas, J. L. (2018). *Der Sponsoring-Funnel: empirische Untersuchung eines modelltheoretischen Ansatzes zur Darstellung des Einflusses von Sportsponsering auf das Konsumverhalten in der Automobilindustrie*. Institutionelles Repositorium der Leibniz Universität Hannover.

Peluso, A. M., Rizzo, C., & Pino, G. (2019). Controversial sports sponsorings: Effects of sponsor moral appropriateness and self-team connection on sponsored teams and external benefit perceptions. *Journal of Business Research, 98,* 339–351. https://doi.org/10.1016/j.jbusres.2019.01.068.

Pena, B. G., Papadimitriou, D., & Costa, L. D. (2020). An exploration of the corporate objectives of the Rio 2016 Olympic sponsors. *Journal of Human Sport and Exercise, 15*(Proc1), 1–10. https://doi.org/10.14198/jhse.2020.15.Proc1.01.

Peris-Ortiz, M., Álvarez-García, J., & De la Cruz Del Río-Rama, M. (2017). *Sports management as an emerging economic activity: Trends and best practices*. Springer International Publishing. https://doi.org/10.1007/978-3-319-63907-9.

Piaggio, L. R. (2019). Sugar-sweetened beverages and sports sponsoring. The right to health of children and adolescents at stake. *Archivos Argentinos de Pediatria, 117*(1), E8–E13. https://doi.org/10.5546/aap.2019.eng.e8.

Piggin, J., Souza, D. L. D., Furtado, S., Milanez, M., Cunha, G., Louzada, B. H., Graeff, B., & Tlili, H. (2019). Do the Olympic games promote dietary health for spectators? An interdisciplinary study of health promotion through sport. *European Sport Management Quarterly, 19*(4), 481–501. https://doi.org/10.1080/16184742.2018.1562484.

Piland, M. B. (2020). Banks, sports sponsorings and COVID: Three ways to win. *American Bankers Association. ABA Banking Journal, 112*(6), 18–19.

Plewa, C., Carrillat, F. A., Mazodier, M., & Quester, P. G. (2016). Which sport sponsorings most impact sponsor CSR image? European journal of marketing, *50*(5–6), 796–815. https://doi.org/10.1108/EJM-02-2015-0078.

Popp, B., & Horbel, C. (2017). *Consumer-scepticism towards sponsoring and its impact on sport sponsoring*. University of Bern.

Popp, B., & Woratschek, H. (2016). Introducing branded communities in sport for building strong brand relations in social media. *Sport Management Review, 19*(2), 183–197. https://doi.org/10.1016/j.smr.2015.06.001.

Prowse, R., Storey, K., Olstad, D. L., Carson, V., & Raine, K. D. (2022). Choice, motives, and mixed messages: A qualitative photo-based inquiry of parents' perceptions of food and beverage marketing to children in sport and recreation facilities. *International Journal of Environmental Research and Public Health, 19*(5). https://doi.org/10.3390/ijerph19052592.

Pyun, D. Y., Cho, H., & Leng, H. K. (2020). Applicability of belief measures for advertising to sponsoring in sport. *International Journal of Sports Marketing and Sponsoring, 21*(2), 351–369. https://doi.org/10.1108/IJSMS-06-2019-0059.

Rai, J. S., Itani, M. N., Singh, A., & Singh, A. (2021). Delineating the outcomes of fans' psychological commitment to sport team: Product knowledge, attitude towards the sponsor, and purchase intentions. *Journal for Global Business Advancement, 14*(3), 357–382. https://doi.org/10.1504/JGBA.2021.116720.

Rajabi, A. G., Talebpour, M., Martinent, G., Bodet, G., & Kafashpor, A. (2020). A multidimensional conceptualization of the sponsor-sponsee fit in sport. *Managing Sport and Leisure, 25*(5), 321–343. https://doi.org/10.1080/23750472.2020.1723430.

Rehm, G. (2019). Aufstieg der Kleinen. In A. Hildebrandt (Hrsg.), *CSR und Sportmanagement: Jenseits von Sieg und Niederlage: Sport als gesellschaftliche Aufgabe verstehen und umsetzen* (S. 283–287). Springer. https://doi.org/10.1007/978-3-662-59651-7_23.

Renier, O., Dalakas, V., & Melancon, J. (2021). Does fandom influence marketing executives' valuations of sports sponsorings? Insight from the French Soccer League. *Services Marketing Quarterly, 42*(3–4), 194–207. https://doi.org/10.1080/15332969.2021.1976003.

Risch-Kerst, M. (2016). D. Bewertung der Erscheinungsformen des Ambush Marketing. In *Ambush Marketing und Markenschutz: Die Eventmarketingmarke als Abwehrmittel gegen Nicht-Sponsoren sportlicher Großereignisse* (S. 231–237). Springer Gabler. https://doi.org/10.1007/978-3-658-12175-4_4.

Risch-Kerst, M. (2018). Sportsponsoring und Ambush Marketing im Wettstreit um Recht und Moral. In A. Schneider, J. Köhler, & F. Schumann (Hrsg.), *Fairplay im Sport: Beiträge zur Wertedebatte und den ethischen Potenzialen* (S. 83–115). Springer Fachmedien. https://doi.org/10.1007/978-3-658-21342-8_6.

Rogic, S., Djurisic, V., Radonjic, M., & Vukovic, S. (2019). Importance of loyalty to a sport event for the level of sponsoring awareness. *Sport Mont, 17*(2), 63–68. https://doi.org/10.26773/smj.190611.

Rogic, S., Misnic, N., Radonjic, M., & Djurisic, V. (2020). Testing sponsoring recall and recognition after the games of the small states of Europe – Montenegro 2019. *Sport Mont, 18*(2), 33–39. https://doi.org/10.26773/smj.200619.

Rojas-Méndez, J. I., Davies, G., Jamsawang, J., Sandoval Duque, J. L., & Pipoli, G. M. (2019). Explaining the mixed outcomes from hosting major sporting events in promoting tourism. *Tourism Management, 74,* 300–309. https://doi.org/10.1016/j.tourman.2019.04.001.

Rose, M., Rose, G. M., Merchant, A., & Orth, U. R. (2021). Sports teams heritage: Measurement and application in sponsoring. *Journal of Business Research, 124*, 759–769. https://doi.org/10.1016/j.jbusres.2020.03.040.

Ruda, W. (2018). Sponsoring im Motorsport. In B. Reuter (Hrsg.), *Motorsport-Management* (S. 233–266). Springer Gabler. https://doi.org/10.1007/978-3-662-57703-5_10.

Rumpf, C., & Breuer, C. (2018). Focus on brand choice: Assessing the behavioral response to sponsoring-linked communication. *Journal of Sport Management, 32*(6), 531–540. https://doi.org/10.1123/jsm.2017-0294.

Sainsbury, E., Hendy, C., Magnusson, R., & Colagiuri, S. (2018). Public support for government regulatory interventions for overweight and obesity in Australia. *BMC Public Health, 18*(1). https://doi.org/10.1186/s12889-018-5455-0.

Sartori, A., Stoneham, M., & Edmunds, M. (2018). Unhealthy sponsoring in sport: A case study of the AFL. *Australian and New Zealand Journal of Public Health, 42*(5), 474–479. https://doi.org/10.1111/1753-6405.12820.

Schafraad, P., & Verhoeven, J. W. M. (2019). Headwinds in sports sponsoring. *International Journal of Sports Marketing and Sponsoring, 20*(3), 538–552. https://doi.org/10.1108/IJSMS-10-2018-0108.

Schmidt, S., Limbach, M., Langner, S., Wiedmann, K. P., Albertsen, L., & Reiter, P. (2018). Official sports sponsoring fortress vs ambush marketing attack: Investigating the impact on implicit and explicit brand knowledge. *International Journal of Sports Marketing and Sponsoring, 19*(1), 91–108. https://doi.org/10.1108/IJSMS-10-2016-0071.

Schönberner, J., Woratschek, H., & Ellert, G. (2021). Hidden agenda in sport sponsoring – The influence of managers' personal objectives on sport sponsoring decisions. *Sport Management Review, 24*(2), 204–225. https://doi.org/10.1016/j.smr.2020.07.001.

Schönberner, J., Woratschek, H., & Buser, M. (2022). Understanding sport sponsoring decision-making–an exploration of the roles and power bases in the sponsors' buying center. *European Sport Management Quarterly, 22*(3), 293–312. https://doi.org/10.1080/16184742.2020.1780459.

Schröer, C. (2019). Eye Tracking in der Sportsponsoring-Forschung. In C. S. E. M. Dinkel & S. Ronft (Hrsg.), *Eye Tracking in der Sport-und Veranstaltungsbranche* (1. Aufl., Bd. 2, S. 27–37). Fakultät Wirtschaft Duale Hochschule Baden-Württemberg Mannheim.

Schröer, C. (2021). Sportevents als emotionale Kommunikationsplattform. In S. Ronft (Hrsg.), *Eventpsychologie: Veranstaltungen wirksam optimieren: Grundlagen, Konzepte, Praxisbeispiele* (S. 891–905). Springer Fachmedien. https://doi.org/10.1007/978-3-658-28888-4_41.

Schwizer, D. (2021). Gestaltungsoptionen zur Aktivierung im Sportsponsoring. In *Aktivierung im Sportsponsoring: Gestaltung strategischer Partnerschaften aus Sponsorenperspektive* (S. 159–176). Springer Gabler. https://doi.org/10.1007/978-3-658-34215-9_6.

Scully, M., Brennan, E., Durkin, S., Dixon, H., Wakefield, M., Barry, C. L., & Niederdeppe, J. (2017). Competing with big business: A randomised experiment testing the effects of messages to promote alcohol and sugary drink control policy. *BMC Public Health, 17*(1). https://doi.org/10.1186/s12889-017-4972-6.

Scully, M., Wakefield, M., Pettigrew, S., Kelly, B., & Dixon, H. (2020). Parents' reactions to unhealthy food v. pro-health sponsoring options for children's sport: An experimental study. *Public Health Nutrition, 23*(4), 727–737. https://doi.org/10.1017/S1368980019003318.

Shah, P., & Shah, S. (2020). Company sponsorings in major sports events-a market study. *Pramana Research Journal, 10*(4), 203–221.

Shoffner, S., & Koo, G. Y. (2020). Examining the effects of unhealthy product sponsors and csr on sport sponsoring authenticity and the sporting event. *Journal of Global Sport Management*. https://doi.org/10.1080/24704067.2019.1702475.

Shoffner, S., Slavich, M., & Koo, G. Y. (2021). New jerseys: Exploring the influence of NBA team jersey sponsorings on teams and sponsors. *International Journal of Sports Marketing and Sponsoring, 22*(4), 633–651. https://doi.org/10.1108/IJSMS-10-2019-0111.

Silva, A. (2022). Team identification and sponsors' altruistic motives on the effectiveness of professional soccer sponsoring. *Managing Sport and Leisure*. https://doi.org/10.1080/23750472.2022.2084636.

Slåtten, T., Svensson, G., Connolley, S., Bexrud, C., & Lægreid, T. (2017). The Sponsoring Motive Matrix (SMM): A framework for categorising firms' motives for sponsoring sports events. *European Journal of Tourism Research, 15*, 143–166. https://doi.org/10.54055/ejtr.v15i.268.

Spindler, C. (2020). Sportsponsoring. Rechtliche Herausforderungen aus Unternehmenssicht. Integrität und Compliance im Sport| Internationale Bezüge des Sports und des Sportrechts|Schiedsrichter im Recht, Tagungsband der wfw-Sportrechtsseminare 2016–2018. *Schriften zum Sportrecht, 51*, 47–60. https://doi.org/10.5771/9783748909828.

Ströbel, T., Woratschek, H., & Winterstein, T. (2017). *Have you thought about the club's image? The role of sport club image for sponsoring goals*. 25th conference of the European Association for Sport Management (EASM), Bern.

Sudolska, A., & Łapińska, J. (2020). Implementation of the CSR concept through sport sponsoring: The case of the polish chemical capital group. *Journal of Physical Education and Sport, 20*, 1100–1105. https://doi.org/10.7752/jpes.2020.s2153.

Suenaga, Y., & Takeda, F. (2021). The impact of postponing the Olympics on stock markets. *International Advances in Economic Research, 27*(3), 219–232. https://doi.org/10.1007/s11294-021-09833-4.

Sung, H., Nam, C., Kim, M., & Han, S. H. (2016). Spillover effect of sport team performance on the value of corporate sponsors and affiliated firms. *International Journal of Sport Finance, 11*(1), 79–96. https://www.scopus.com/inward/record.uri?eid=2-s2.0-85019161633&partnerID=40&md5=138860532480f9c47b97e65324fe5b23.

Takeda, F. (2022). Do sport sponsoring announcements help or hurt rival sponsors' market values?: Comparing the stock returns of sponsors and their rivals in the United States and Japan. *Journal of advertising research, 62*(2), 167–175. https://doi.org/10.2501/JAR-2022-007.

Tan, S. Y., & Pyun, D. Y. (2018). The effectiveness of sponsoring of the f1 singapore grand prix: Recall and recognition. *International Journal of Asian Business and Information Management, 9*(1), 1–12. https://doi.org/10.4018/IJABIM.2018010101.

Thomas, O., Kucza, G., & Schuppisser, S. (2021). Can sports sponsoring affect consumers' motivation for sports consumption? *Journal of Promotion Management, 28*(7), 893–922. https://doi.org/10.1080/10496491.2021.2009611.

Toh, B., Leng, H. K., & Phua, Y. X. P. (2022). Effect of colours on sponsor recall. *Asia Pacific Journal of Marketing and Logistics*. https://doi.org/10.1108/APJML-12-2021-0905.

Toscani, G., & Prendergast, G. (2019). Arts sponsoring versus sports sponsoring: Which is better for marketing strategy? *Journal of Nonprofit and Public Sector Marketing, 31*(4), 428–450. https://doi.org/10.1080/10495142.2018.1526748.

Tsordia, C., Papadimitriou, D., & Apostolopoulou, A. (2018). Building a sponsor's equity through brand personality: Perceptions of fans and rivals. *Sport, Business and Management: An International Journal, 8*(5), 454–468. https://doi.org/10.1108/SBM-09-2017-0050.

Tsordia, C., Papadimitriou, D., & Parganas, P. (2018). The influence of sport sponsoring on brand equity and purchase behavior. *Journal of Strategic Marketing, 26*(1), 85–105. https://doi.org/10.1080/0965254X.2017.1374299.

Tsordia, C., Apostolopoulou, A., & Papadimitriou, D. (2021). Does team identification of satellite fans influence brand-related sponsoring outcomes? What we learned from Manchester United supporters in Malaysia. *Journal of Strategic Marketing.* https://doi.org/10.1080/0965254X.2021.2004208.

Tyler, B. D., Cobbs, J., Satinover Nichols, B., & Dalakas, V. (2021). Schadenfreude, rivalry antecedents, and the role of perceived sincerity in sponsoring of sport rivalries. *Journal of Business Research, 124*, 708–719. https://doi.org/10.1016/j.jbusres.2019.09.029.

Ullah, F., Ullah, H., & Mahreen, F. (2021). Sponsorings in sports events and stock price behavior: Evidence from Pakistan Super League. *City University Research Journal, 11*(2), 212–232.

Vance, L., Raciti, M. M., & Lawley, M. (2016). Beyond brand exposure: Measuring the sponsoring halo effect. *Measuring Business Excellence, 20*(3), 1–14. https://doi.org/10.1108/MBE-07-2015-0037.

Vance, L., Raciti, M. M., & Lawley, M. (2021). Moral judgements of junior sports sponsorings: An emerging mediator of sponsor goodwill. *Australasian Marketing Journal.* https://doi.org/10.1177/18393349211061614.

Vinberg, M., Durbeej, N., & Rosendahl, I. (2020). Gambling and gambling problem among elite athletes and their professional coaches: Findings from a Swedish total population survey of participants in four sports. *International Gambling Studies, 20*(2), 262–281. https://doi.org/10.1080/14459795.2020.1726990.

Wagner, U., Hansen, K. R., Kristensen, M. L., & Josty, M. (2019). Improving service-center employees' performance by means of a sport sponsoring. *International Journal of Sports Marketing and Sponsoring, 20*(1), 43–60. https://doi.org/10.1108/IJSMS-10-2017-0109.

Waguespack, B., & Ambrose, S. (2019). Airline sponsorings and sports: An exploratory review of major airline engagement. *Journal of Air Transport Studies, 10*(1), 110–124. https://doi.org/10.38008/jats.v10i1.19.

Wakefield, L., Wakefield, K., Keller, K. L., & Rivers, A. (2021). Are brands wasting money on sport sponsorings? A new look at brand personality, brand equity, and official sponsoring effects. *Journal of Advertising Research, 61*(2), 192–211. https://doi.org/10.2501/JAR-2020-029.

Walraven, M., Koning, R. H., Bijmolt, T. H. A., & Los, B. (2016). Benchmarking sports sponsoring performance: Efficiency assessment with data envelopment analysis. *Journal of Sport Management, 30*(4), 411–426. https://doi.org/10.1123/jsm.2015-0117.

Walzel, S. (2019a). Beziehungsmanagement im Sport (Sponsoring). In S. Walzel & V. Römisch (Hrsg.), *Teamsport Management: Eine umfassende und interdisziplinäre Betrachtung* (S. 249–267). Springer Fachmedien. https://doi.org/10.1007/978-3-658-23045-6_13.

Walzel, S. (2019b). Sportsponsoring – Kommunizieren und finanzieren. In G. Nowak (Hrsg.), *Angewandte Sportökonomie des 21. Jahrhunderts* (S. 135–155). Springer Gabler. https://doi.org/10.1007/978-3-658-26968-5_7.

Walzel, S., & Nowak, G. (2022). Clever or foolish? Playing with the rivalry in leveraging sports sponsorings of SMEs. *International Small Business Journal, 40*(1), 47–67. https://doi.org/10.1177/02662426211009081.

Walzel, S., & Nowak, G. (2022). Clever or foolish? Playing with the rivalry in leveraging sports sponsorings of SMEs. *International Small Business Journal: Researching Entrepreneurship, 40*(1), 47–67. https://doi.org/10.1177/02662426211009081.

Walzel, S., & Schubert, M. (2018d). *Sportsponsoring: Grundlagen, Konzeption und Wirkungen.* Springer Gabler. https://doi.org/10.1007/978-3-662-55246-9.

Wang, M. C. H. (2017). Investigating the different congruence effects on sports sponsor brand equity. *International Journal of Sports Marketing and Sponsoring, 18*(2), 196–211. https://doi.org/10.1108/IJSMS-05-2017-089.

Woratschek, H., & Schönberner, J. (2022). Entscheidungen im Sportsponsoring: Auswahlprozess, Ziele und Hidden–Agenda. *Zeitschrift für Kommunikation und Markenmanagement, 66*(3), 62–66.

Yazdanparast, A., & Bayar, O. (2020). Olympic sponsorings and brand value: An empirical analysis. *Journal of Advertising, 50*(2), 139–159. https://doi.org/10.1080/00913367.2020.1856737.

Yuan, S., & Gao, Y. (2022). When sports sponsoring incurs brand risk: The roles of team performance, brand familiarity and team identification. *International Journal of Sports Marketing and Sponsoring*. https://doi.org/10.1108/IJSMS-10-2021-0198.

Yuan, S., Huo, C., & Malik, T. H. (2019). The negative spillover effect in sports sponsoring: An experiment examining the impact of team performance on sponsor's brand trust. *International Journal of Sports Marketing and Sponsoring, 20*(3), 477–494. https://doi.org/10.1108/IJSMS-01-2018-0003.

Yun, L., Kim, K., & Cheong, Y. (2020). Sports sponsoring and the risks of ambush marketing: The moderating role of corporate reputation in the effects of disclosure of ambush marketers on attitudes and beliefs towards corporations. *International Journal of Advertising, 39*(7), 921–942. https://doi.org/10.1080/02650487.2019.1710971.

Yunos, M. N., Zanuddin, H., & Abdullah, J. C. P. G. (2019). The impacts of fans' attachment, sincerity and social media usage on attitude toward sports sponsoring. *International Journal of Recent Technology and Engineering, 8*(2, Special Issue), 334–339. https://www.scopus.com/inward/record.uri?eid=2-s2.0-85070670687&partnerID=40&md5=1838baa39dd0123c60ffcf210d1d3a95.

Zaharia, N., Biscaia, R., Gray, D., & Stotlar, D. (2016). No more „good" intentions: Purchase behaviors in sponsoring. Journal of Sport Management, 30(2), 162–175. https://doi.org/10.1123/jsm.2015-0347.

Zapata Agüera, S., & Martínez Caro, L. (2021). An explanatory model of the influence of consumer exposure to sport sponsoring event. *Sport in Society, 28*(7), 1–19. https://doi.org/10.1080/17430437.2021.1922389.

Zerhouni, O., Bègue, L., Duke, A. A., & Flaudias, V. (2016). Dynamic exposure to alcohol advertising in a sports context influences implicit attitudes. *Alcoholism: Clinical and Experimental Research, 40*(2), 422–428. https://doi.org/10.1111/acer.12966.

Zhu, C. W. (2020). Adjudicating sartorial elegance from the court – The sumptuary impulse in the law of modern sports sponsoring against ambush marketing. *Queen Mary Journal of Intellectual Property, 10*(1), 62–86. https://doi.org/10.4337/qmjip.2020.01.03.

Printed by Printforce, the Netherlands